STRATEGIC
MANAGEMENT
CASES

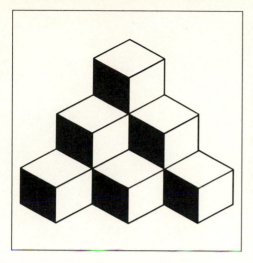

STRATEGIC MANAGEMENT CASES

Neil H. Snyder
McIntire School of Commerce—University of Virginia

Alan J. Rowe
School of Business Administration—
University of Southern California

Richard O. Mason
Edwin L. Cox School of Business—Southern Methodist University

Karl E. Dickel
The Boston Consulting Group—Dusseldorf, West Germany

▲▼▼ **ADDISON-WESLEY PUBLISHING COMPANY**

Reading, Massachusetts • Menlo Park, California • New York
Don Mills, Ontario • Wokingham, England • Amsterdam • Bonn
Sydney • Singapore • Tokyo • Madrid • San Juan

Library of Congress Cataloging-in-Publication Data
Strategic management cases / Neil H. Snyder . . . [et al.].
    p.   cm.
  ISBN 0-201-54616-7
  1. Strategic planning—Case studies. I. Snyder, Neil H.
HD30.28.S7295 1991
658.4′012—dc20   90-40468
                                                 CIP

ISBN 0-201-54616-7
1 2 3 4 5 6 7 8 9 10-MA-95 94 93 92 91

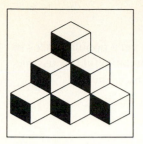

Preface

The world is changing so rapidly today that it is difficult to keep abreast of all that is happening. This is especially true in the strategic management course and in the writing of strategic management textbooks. Therefore, finding the right cases and making them accessible to professors in a timely manner is more important today than ever before. Our goal with this book is to do just that.

In this book, we have included a total of 38 cases, 19 of which did not appear in *Strategic Management: A Methodological Approach, 3rd Edition* by Rowe, Mason, Dickel, and Snyder. Twenty-four of the cases cover firms in seven industry groups. The industry focus gives professors the flexibility to contrast different approaches and strategies used by different companies and to involve students in deciding which approaches and strategies they think work best. Seven industry groups are included in this book:

Grocery

The grocery cases represent three of the best-known firms in the industry. Safeway is a very large retailer that is experiencing tremendous competition and a takeover threat. Food Lion is a very profitable, rapidly growing firm with a competitive advantage in pricing and margins. It has become one of the innovative leaders in the grocery business. Finally, A&P is an old firm with well-established traditions, strong unions, and poor performance. Together these cases cover the grocery industry from a variety of perspectives.

Broadcasting/Entrepreneurship

These cases cover the growth of Turner Broadcasting System and Ted Turner from the beginning of his attempt to build a network to 1990, when he is turning his attention toward politics and social causes.

Textiles

These cases focus on some of the most critical problems facing textile manufacturers in particular and manufacturing firms in general (i.e., labor problems, shrinking margins, government protection, foreign competition, and the need for modernization). They have proven to be very popular cases in some of our own classes, and they set the scene for meaningful discussions about the importance of the manufacturing sector in our society.

Brewing

This section has five cases in all. Three of them deal with the industry leader, Anheuser-Busch, and take that firm through 1986. The other two cases enhance this section by focusing on a foreign brewer (Molson) and a small brewer (Golden Gate).

Steel

These cases focus on the trials and tribulations of an older, more traditional U.S. steel manufacturer, Wheeling-Pittsburgh, and the vitality and strength of a newcomer to the U.S. industry, Nucor.

Airline

The three cases in this section (Delta, Eastern, and Texas Air) appeared in *Strategic Management: A Methodological Approach, 3rd Edition*. They represent a good sample of firms in the industry, and they have received favorable reviews from professors who have used them in class.

Banking

Both of the cases in this group appeared in *Strategic Management: A Methodological Approach, 3rd edition*. They address, from the perspectives of merging and acquiring, the growth issue, which all banks in the United States face today. The National Westminster Bank case deals specifically with the problems inherent in merging and acquiring.

In addition to the cases on firms in seven specific industries, this book includes eight excellent cases on small businesses, three of which focus on serious ethical issues, and three of which examine acquisitions and leveraged buyouts. Since most students in strategic management courses will eventually work for small firms, it is very useful for them to think about the strategic issues small firms encounter. The cases cover the following businesses:

- a marina
- an accounting firm
- a paint company

- an arts and crafts shop
- a movie theater company
- a welding and steel fabrication business
- a bookstore
- a petroleum jobber

To say that ethics is important in today's business environment is an understatement. It is absolutely essential for business students to consider firms that are facing ethical dilemmas. This book will enable you to bring these issues to your students in a powerful way. Cases in this area include:

- A.H. Robins and the Dalkon Shield
- Union Carbide and the Bhopal accident
- the Manville Corporation and their asbestos problem

Finally, the instructor's manual accompanying the book provides professors with a wealth of information and analysis that can be used effectively to generate class discussion and to provoke students to think beyond the cases themselves. We hope you enjoy using this text.

Charlottesville, Virginia   N.H.S.
Los Angeles, California   A.J.R.
Dallas, Texas   R.O.M.
Dusseldorf, Germany   K.E.D.

Contents

INDUSTRY

Airline   326

INDUSTRY

Banking   412

STRATEGIC ISSUE

Small Business   503

STRATEGIC ISSUE

Ethics   625

STRATEGIC ISSUE

Mergers, Acquisitions, and Leveraged Buyouts   693

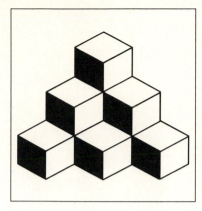

STRATEGIC MANAGEMENT CASES

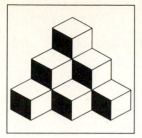

INTRODUCTION

HOW TO ANALYZE CASES

NEIL H. SNYDER

Because strategic management and business policy is the capstone course in the business curriculum, case analyses in the course focus on general management decisions, or decisions made at the executive level of the organization. This is the level where questions about strategy formulation and implementation are considered and ultimately decided. In addition, decisions regarding the mission of the organization, corporate philosophy, basic values and beliefs, and corporate policies are addressed at this level.

Of course, executives cannot make good decisions unless they have a wealth of analytical information to help them formulate opinions and make judgments. The information they need must come from every department in the firm including marketing, finance, accounting, production, and research and development. Furthermore, the information they receive will come from every management level in the organization. It may come through the management hierarchy, or it may be obtained directly from each level by the executives. In diversified firms, all this information is needed from each of the diversified pieces of the business before strategic decisions can be made.

The kinds of information gathered and analyzed and the way the information is presented to the executives are extremely important. Thus, this chapter is designed to help students think through, analyze, and present their recommendations for strategic management and business policy cases. The outline below is a good one to consider when making strategy formulation and implementation decisions.

DEVELOPING RELEVANT INFORMATION

History of the Firm

A case analysis is not complete unless it places the decision being made in historical context. Corporations do not exist in a vacuum. They are living organisms that change over time and are affected by their environments. Thus, to understand where a firm is headed in the future, you must first understand where it is today and how it got there. A firm's past will not dictate its future opportunities completely, but it will constrain the number and types of feasible alternatives it should consider. The first step in a case analysis is to study and understand the history of the firm.

The Key Executives

Executives are people, just like anybody else. They have personal and professional needs and expectations; they are prone to get angry from time to time; they have their biases; they like sports; and they like to spend time with their families. The difference between an executive and a lower-level manager is that the executive's needs, expectations, biases, etc., are far more likely to influence the direction of the firm than those of the lower-level manager. Thus, a comprehensive case analysis simply cannot overlook the top executives in the firm. To the contrary, it must take into account a vast array of personal and subjective issues, or the analysis will not, in fact cannot, be accurate.

The Competitors

A comprehensive case analysis should identify the firm's most important competitors. The following information should be obtained on each one of them:

- Their competitive advantages and weaknesses
- Their market share
- Their sales in dollars and units
- Their profitability
- Other relevant data

The Industry

Information on the industry as a whole should be obtained also. It is important to understand the types of change and the directions of change occurring in the industry. For example, if you were studying the Anheuser-Busch case, it would be crucial to understand the effects of the group Mothers Against Drunk Driving on beer sales. This is just one example, but many similar examples should be considered for each industry in which the business you are studying is involved.

The Functional Parts of the Business

Information on the firm's internal operations should be obtained, including information on performance in these, and other, areas:

- Production
- Research and development
- Marketing
- Finance (including a complete analysis of the firm's financial position)
- Personnel, especially managerial personnel
- All other relevant functional areas

DEVELOPING THE STRATEGIC PLAN

Once all the relevant information needed to develop a strategic plan has been obtained, it must be analyzed. Then strategic decisions must be made about the firm's future. A strategic analysis should be comprehensive and should include analyses of the following:

- The firm's mission
- The firm's objectives
- The firm's strengths and weaknesses
- Opportunities and threats confronting the firm

Upon completion of the analysis, the next step is to develop a list of feasible alternatives the firm might pursue in the future. Although there will be a rather long list of feasible alternatives available to any firm, only a few of them will be good enough to deserve in-depth analysis. Thus, it is important to develop a list of criteria to help determine which alternatives are best. For example, if a firm is very strong in the marketing area, alternatives that take advantage of its marketing strength would be better than those that do not. Similarly, if a firm is very weak in marketing but strong in production, it would lean toward alternatives that use its production advantage.

The bottom line in a strategic analysis is to match up a firm's strengths with the opportunities available to it. At the same time, executives in the firm must pay attention to the areas in which they are weak, because they are vulnerable at these points. Furthermore, they must keep a careful eye on the environment while it is changing in order to anticipate any threats that may be emerging.

Once the best of the feasible alternatives have been identified, the next step is to determine which of them to pursue. It is very likely that the firm's executives will want to pursue more than one alternative at a time if possible. Thus, it is important to keep in mind the limitations the firm has in each of its functional areas and in each of its industries. Deciding how aggressive to be is a very personal matter that will be affected significantly by the personalities of the executives themselves and their propensities to take risks.

The final step in a case analysis is to develop pro forma balance sheets and income statements for your selected strategy and to develop a timeline showing the years in which the changes you are proposing will be implemented. These documents are powerful tools for selling your strategic choices to others, including executives, professors, and other students.

Following is a short article on strategic planning that I wrote with William Glueck several years ago. It explains the strategic planning process in detail, and it should serve as a guide as you prepare your case analyses.

APPENDIX

 ## STRATEGIC PLANNING

NEIL H. SNYDER   •   WILLIAM F. GLUECK

Strategic planning is a process that includes a set of interactive and overlapping decisions leading to the development of an effective strategy for a firm. The process includes the following:

- The determination of the firm's mission
- The selection of goals or objectives the firm wishes to pursue
- The formulation of assumptions about changes occurring in the firm's external environment
- The identification of opportunities and threats emerging from the firm's external environment
- An assessment of the internal strengths and weaknesses of the firm
- The identification of feasible strategic alternatives available to the firm
- The choice of an alternative(s) the firm wishes to pursue
- The development of an implementation plan to facilitate achievement of the firm's objectives
- The design of a control or feedback system to monitor the firm's performance while the strategic plan is being implemented

Managers undertake strategic planning for a number of reasons. First, many managers believe that strategic planning will increase their firm's effectiveness, and there exists a substantial body of academic research to support this belief. Second, the strategic planning process itself promotes feelings of accomplishment and satisfaction. As managers and planners work

---

The material presented in this article is synthesized from *Readings in Business Policy and Strategy from Business Week*, 2d ed., by William F. Glueck and Neil H. Snyder, McGraw-Hill, New York, 1982.

From Bittle and Ramsey, eds., *Handbook for Professional Managers*. New York: McGraw-Hill, 1985. Reprinted with permission.

together to formulate strategy and implementation plans, they develop confidence in their ability to understand and manage their situation. This tends to be very gratifying and satisfying. Third, strategic planning facilitates adaptation to change. Fourth, strategic planning is a process through which the efforts of divisions, functions, and individuals can be coordinated. Fifth, when major reorganizations or changes in top management occur, strategic planning can help to educate the new top-management team about the internal and external opportunities and constraints the team members face. Finally, when an organization is not performing well, strategic planning may be undertaken to identify the problems and solutions.

STRATEGY MAKERS

Strategy makers are the people who formulate the firm's mission and the objectives the firm will seek to achieve. They also determine the way in which objectives will be pursued. Generally, the strategy-making group consists of the firm's top managers, selected members of the board of directors, and others who, because of particular skills or expertise, are asked to participate in the strategic planning process. Strategy makers do not have the freedom to choose a strategy arbitrarily without regard for internal and external constraints on the firm. The external environment offers both opportunities and threats. Strategy makers must avoid environmental threats while pursuing opportunities, but the firm's internal strengths and weaknesses will restrict the number of opportunities the firm can pursue. For example, if the strategy makers find an investment opportunity for which they need $10 million in capital and they can raise only $5 million, that investment opportunity is not a feasible alternative for the firm. Along a different vein, the values prevailing in the firm act as constraints on what the strategy makers can do.

ANALYZING THE FIRM'S ENVIRONMENT

Three sectors of the environment produce changes that strategy makers must monitor if their firms are to be successful in the long run: (1) the general environment, (2) the market, and (3) the supply sector.

The General Environment

The general environment includes the following forces affecting or potentially affecting the firm: the government, the economy, consumer pressures and attitudes, and population and wealth changes.

The Government. The government—federal, state, or local—can change its structure, pass laws, issue regulations, and become or cease to become a major customer or competitor of the firm. Government action or inaction is very important to business, and most knowledgeable people agree that the government sector will increase its influence on business over the next decade.

The Economy. The economy affects firms in many ways, including the following:

- Unemployment rates may affect the demand for the firm's products or services and the availability of labor.
- Inflation rates affect the pricing of the firm's products and services.
- The Federal Reserve's money supply policy can affect the availability of capital and the cost of capital.

The general status of the economy, which is a consequence of government policy, consumer decisions, and managerial decisions, affects different firms differently. Some products or services tend to hold up better in economic downturns than others.

Consumer Pressures and Attitudes. Consumer attitudes and values toward various products and services change over time. For example, some consumer attitudes toward cigarettes, liquor, drugs, gambling casinos, massage parlors, X-rated movies, bingo, and other products and services are frequently very strong. If the firm is involved in any of these businesses, it is likely to be affected by the changing values of its offerings to the public. These examples may be extreme, but consumer pressures and attitudes influence the demand for many other products as well. Consider the changes in consumer attitudes toward the following over the past few years:

- Oil companies before and after the energy crisis
- Oil company profits before and after deregulation
- Small cars before and after the energy crisis

Population and Wealth Changes. Changes in the characteristics of the population affect most firms. For example:

- Gerber Baby Food executives are quite concerned about the drop in the birthrate from 1957 to 1983.
- Coca-Cola Company executives are concerned about the population's getting older and drinking fewer soft drinks.
- Anheuser-Busch is concerned about the shift in adult drinking habits to wine from beer.
- Government executives are concerned about the population's getting older and not producing enough tax revenue to fund their programs.

The Market

The second factor most executives watch closely is the marketplace in which they compete to distribute their goods or provide their services. Some of the aspects of the market that the executives must analyze if they are to be effective strategists are these:

- Major new products and services introduced in the industry
- Major shifts in the pricing structure of the products or services
- Major shifts in the demand for the products and services
- Major shifts in consumer preferences affecting the firm's products and services
- Major competitors entering or leaving the industry

Most studies show that strategists examine the market environment very closely. In many industries, it is the primary factor. In others, governmental factors or shifts in the economy are most important.

The Supply Sector

The final environmental concern is the supply sector. This sector provides the raw materials, money, and equipment needed by the firm to offer its service or produce its product. Some components of the supply sector that strategists must monitor include:

- Changes in the availability of major raw materials, subassemblies, etc.
- Changes in the prices of raw materials, subassemblies, etc.
- Entry or exit of major suppliers, raw material producers, etc.
- Technological breakthroughs on the supply side

The gathering of supply-sector information usually involves the executives' phoning or talking with knowledgeable people such as subordinates, bankers, industry analysts, and other executives in the industry. How intensely they seek information and on what factors depends on the executives and the industry. For example:

- If the company is clearly the most powerful firm (say, General Motors, Xerox, IBM) in the industry, it may be somewhat less concerned with competitors' moves than if it were the smallest, weakest firm.
- If the firm has millions of customers (General Foods, Goodyear) rather than a very few (McDonnell Douglas), it may pay less attention to each customer.

• If the firm is dependent on a few suppliers (such as firms using copper), it may pay close attention to the supply factor.

Executives tend to focus their environmental analysis on forces to which they are must vulnerable in the short run.

ANALYZING THE FIRM'S STRENGTHS AND WEAKNESSES

The organizational units most frequently examined for strengths and weaknesses are marketing, operations, finance/accounting, and personnel/management. Below is a list of factors managers can evaluate within each unit.

1. Marketing
   a. Competitive structure and market share
   b. Marketing research systems
   c. Product mix
   d. Product-services line
   e. Channels of distribution and geographic coverage, including international efforts
   f. Pricing strategy for products and services
   g. Sales force effectiveness
   h. Advertising effectiveness
   i. Marketing promotion and packaging
   j. Service after the purchase
   k. Marketing policies

2. Operations
   a. Raw materials cost
   b. Raw materials availability
   c. Inventory control systems
   d. Capacity utilization
   e. Integration of operations
   f. Management information systems
   g. Equipment utilization
   h. Location of facilities and offices
   i. Operations procedures
   j. Costs of operations compared with those of competitors
   k. Research and development
   l. Patents and similar legal protection for products, processes, and similar trade secrets

3. Finance/Accounting
   a. Cost of capital relative to industry
   b. Capital structure
   c. Relations with managers and stockholders
   d. Tax conditions
   e. Barriers to new entry because of high entry costs
   f. Financial planning, working capital, and capital budgeting procedures
   g. Accounting systems for cost, budget and profit planning, and auditing procedures

4. Personnel/Management
   a. Quality of employees and managers
   b. Labor costs
   c. Relations with trade unions
   d. Personnel relations policies
   e. Corporate image and prestige
   f. Organizational structure and climate
   g. Company size relative to industry
   h. Strategic planning system
   i. The firm's record for reaching objectives
   j. Relations with regulatory and governmental bodies
   k. Functional experience and track record of top management

STRATEGIC CHOICE DECISIONS

The *strategic choice process* begins as strategy makers compare and contrast the data gathered during the internal and external analysis and identify feasible strategic alternatives for implementation. These alternatives should reflect a match between the firm's strengths and weaknesses and the opportunities and threats in its environment. Ultimately, one or more of these alternatives will be chosen and detailed implementation plans will be prepared.

If the environment offers major opportunities that match up with major internal strengths, the conditions are right for a *growth* strategy. If the environment offers threats that coincide with major internal weaknesses, the conditions are right for a retrenchment or *turnaround* strategy. If the environment and internal strengths signal growth in one part of the firm and weaknesses and threats produce strain in another part, the conditions are right for a *combination* strategy. If no major changes are indicated from the environmental and internal analyses, the firm will choose a *stability* strategy.

It is helpful to examine each of these strategies in greater depth.

Stability Strategy

A stability strategy is one a firm pursues

- when it continues to serve the same or very similar customers.
- when it continues to pursue the same or very similar objectives (adjusting the expected level of achievement about the same percentage each year).
- when its main strategic decisions focus on incremental improvement of functional performance.

Strategy makers might choose a stability strategy for one or more reasons. For example:

- The strategy makers believe the firm is doing well, and they perceive no need to change.
- The strategy makers are risk averse, and a stability strategy is less risky than other strategies.
- The firm has grown rapidly in the past, and the strategy makers believe the time has come to consolidate and to focus on creating a more efficient and manageable operation.
- The firm is experiencing pressure from the government not to grow, at least in certain areas, because of potential antitrust violations.

Growth Strategy

A growth strategy is one a firm pursues when its strategy makers formulate objectives that are significantly more ambitious than the firm's past achievement level. The most frequent change in objectives in a growth strategy is to raise the market share or sales objectives.

A firm might pursue a growth strategy for these reasons:

- The strategy makers equate growth with success.
- The industry or industries in which the firm does business is or are growing rapidly, and a choice not to grow is a choice to sacrifice market share.
- The strategy makers believe society benefits from growth.
- The strategy makers are achievement-oriented individuals.

There are many varieties of growth strategies. For example:

- Firms can grow by acquiring other firms (external growth).

- They can grow horizontally—that is, in the same type of business.
- They can grow vertically—that is, by moving forward and acquiring or developing firms in the market channel or by moving backward by acquiring or developing suppliers.
- Firms can grow internally by offering existing products to new markets or by creating new products for existing markets.

Retrenchment Strategy

A retrenchment strategy is pursued by a firm when its strategy makers decide to improve performance by:

- focusing on functional improvement, especially reduction of costs (also called a turnaround strategy).
- reducing the number of functions the firm performs by becoming a captive company.
- reducing the number of products it produces and/or markets it serves.
- liquidating part or all of the firm's assets (the ultimate retrenchment strategy).

Retrenchment strategies are used when strategy makers believe performance in a product line, division, or company in question is less than satisfactory and prospects for improvement are not good. By retrenching, the strategy makers free up some of their resources for more productive use elsewhere.

Combination Strategy

A firm pursues a combination strategy when its main strategic decisions focus on simultaneously using more than one of these strategies (stability, growth, and retrenchment) in one or more divisions of the company. Another form of the combination strategy uses several grand strategies over a period of time. For example, a firm's strategy makers may decide on a strategy which calls for rapid growth followed by stability.

Each of these strategies can be effective when the situation dictates its choice. The strategy makers select the strategy they believe represents the best match between their firm's strengths and weaknesses and opportunities and threats in the environment. Their choice is influenced by their past strategic choices, their willingness to take risks, and their power to make a choice.

IMPLEMENTATION AND EVALUATION

In the implementation phase, the strategy makers first make sure they have developed an appropriate organization structure. For example, in earlier stages of development, firms tend to organize functionally. That is, vice presidents reporting to the president have responsibility for particular business functions and have titles such as vice president–marketing. If the firm's strategy leads it to grow in product/service scope and/or geographically, it tends to shift to a decentralized divisional structure. In this stage, the staff members reporting to the president lead product/service, geographic, or similar units. The functional units then report to these executives.

The second implementation step is to place in key positions executives with the background and motivation to make the new strategy successful. Then functional policy decisions must be made to bring the strategic choice to fruition.

Policy Formulation

Policies are decision guides to action designed to make the strategy work. They connect strategic and implementation decisions by specifying how the strategic decisions will be implemented. In the policy formation process, it is crucial to explain the chosen strategy in terms of policies that are compatible and workable. It is not enough for managers merely to decide to change their firm's strategy. They must define precisely how they plan to get where they want to go, when they want to get there, and how efficiently they want to operate as they go. Managers do so by preparing policies to implement the strategy.

Policies must be developed for key functional decisions in the following areas:

- Operations/production
- Finance/accounting
- Personnel
- Marketing and logistics
- Research and development

Thus, if the strategic choice is to grow, policy decisions that are consistent with the growth strategy must be made. A sample list of policy questions in each of the functional areas follows:

Operations/Production

- Can we handle the added business with our present facilities and number of shifts?
- Must we add equipment, facilities, shifts? Where?
- Can we become more efficient by better scheduling?
- What is the firm's inventory safety level? How many suppliers does it need to obtain major supplies?
- What level of productivity and costs should the firm seek to realize?

- How much emphasis should there be on quality control?
- How far ahead should we schedule production? Should we guarantee delivery?
- Are we going to be operations or production leaders in the latest equipment and methods?

Finance/Accounting

- Where will we obtain additional funds for growth—internally or externally?
- If we wish to obtain additional funds externally, how should we obtain them? Where should we obtain them?
- What will growth do to our cash flow?
- What accounting systems and policies should we use (for example, LIFO or FIFO)?
- What capital structure policy (no debt or heavily leveraged) should we pursue? What policy should we pursue with regard to ownership?
- How much cash and other assets should we keep on hand?

Personnel

- Do we have an adequate work force?
- How much hiring and retraining are necessary?
- What types of individuals do we need to recruit college graduates? Minority groups? How should we recruit? By advertising? Personal contact?
- What should be the methods for selection? Informal interview? Very sophisticated testing?
- What should be the standards and methods for promotion? From within? By seniority?
- What incentive plans, benefits, labor relations policies, etc., should we have?

Marketing and Logistics

- Which specific products or services should be expanded? How?
- Which channels should be used to market these products or services? Should we use exclusive dealerships or multiple channels?
- How should we promote these products or services? Is it our policy to use large amounts of TV advertising? Heavy personal selling expenses? Price competition?
- Do we have an adequate sales force?
- What distribution policies do we want?

Research and Development

- What new projects are necessary to support our growth?

- Should we contract some of these functions out?
- How much should we spend on research and development?

There is also a time dimension in the policy formulation process. Some policy decisions can be made and implemented immediately (for example, changing from LIFO to FIFO, hiring unskilled workers). Others take long lead times to come to fruition (such as research and development, construction of new plants). In effect, managers create a cascade of policies. Long-range policy decisions guide and constrain them in the formulation of medium-range and short-range policies.

Evaluation of Strategic Planning

After the strategy is implemented, top managers must evaluate its effectiveness. Such evaluation is the phase of the strategic planning process during which top managers determine whether their strategic choice as implemented is meeting the objectives of the firm. Additionally, the evaluation can be qualitative or quantitative. For example, the quantitative criteria may include the following:

- Net profit
- Stock price
- Dividend rates
- Earnings per share
- Return on capital
- Return on equity
- Market share
- Growth in sales
- Days lost per employee as a result of strikes
- Production costs and efficiency
- Distribution costs and efficiency
- Employee turnover and absenteeism

If the top managers believe the strategy is working, they continue to implement it. If it is not, they shift to another strategy or adjust the current strategy to make it more effective.

CONCLUSION   Strategic planning is not a panacea, although it can be very helpful if it is implemented properly. Under certain conditions, however, strategic planning almost always fails to live up to the expectations of top managers. When this situation occurs, unnecessary frustration and anxiety set in. Why may strategic planning fail? Several reasons are suggested:

- Lack of top-management commitment
- Lack of critical skills in key areas
- Lack of coordination
- Inability to forecast accurately
- Overemphasis on short-run results
- Overemphasis on long-run results
- Failure to remain flexible to handle unanticipated contingencies
- Complexity of the situation
- Failure to be specific about expected outcomes
- Failure to organize properly
- Poor communications
- Failure to evaluate and modify the strategy as needed

INDUSTRY
GROCERY

CASE 1

Safeway Stores, Inc.

NEIL H. SNYDER · TAMMY CARTER · JOY HERBERT
ROBIN KENNARD · BRUCE MLOTT · AVRON STOLOFF

INTRODUCTION

On the morning of July 25, 1986, tension filled the air at the headquarters of Safeway Stores. Peter Magowan, chief executive officer of Safeway, waited for an afternoon meeting with the board of directors as he pondered the events of the last month and wondered what lay ahead for Safeway. From the beginning of June, Magowan had watched his dream of building Safeway Stores into a market leader grow dim after the Dart Group threatened to take control of the business.

HISTORY OF THE FIRM

Safeway was incorporated in 1926, and most of its business was concentrated in the western United States. Today Safeway stores are located primarily in the Washington, D.C., area, the West, the Southwest, and overseas. The firm owns 1,900 stores in the United States, 700 of which are superstores, and 600 stores in foreign countries such as Australia, the United Kingdom, Canada, and West Germany. In addition, the Company operates 2,170 free-standing specialty shops and 100 Liquor Barns. Currently, the Liquor Barns are the fastest growing segment of the business.

Safeway is a growing and profitable retailer of groceries and related consumer goods and services worldwide. It employs 162,000 people, and on a typical day 4 million customers visit Safeway stores. In addition to the obvious benefits of increased sales and earnings from foreign operations, Safeway uses its multinational presence to minimize the economic risk associated with operating in any one country.

Safeway is an innovative and aggressive competitor, but that was not always the case. According to Peter Magowan, "We are a very different company today. In the past we had a tendency not to experiment. We watched what someone else would do and then, cautiously, if it was a good idea, we would do it."[1] Since Magowan took control of the firm in 1980, he has closed marginal stores and consolidated activities whenever possible.

A few of Safeway's innovations include supermarkets with natural food centers, cheese shops, expanded wine selections, cosmetic centers, and full-line floral departments. Safeway has redesigned its strategy to become a leader in the modern superstore segment of the grocery business. This move away from more conventional grocery stores came about "from listening to our customers and employees," according to Magowan.[2]

The Magowan Family

Peter Magowan's family has a long history of contributions to Safeway Stores. Magowan's grandfather, Charles Merrill, of Merrill, Lynch, Pierce, Fenner and Smith, was a major force in Safeway when it was incorporated. Robert Magowan, Peter's father, was Safeway's CEO from 1959 to 1970. He is credited with developing Safeway into one of the world's leading food retailers. His most notable achievements included establishing a commitment to customer satisfaction, streamlining and decentralizing administrative staff functions, and introducing professional management methods. By the time he retired at the end of 1970, the firm's net earnings had quintupled and sales had increased by more than 150 percent.

When Peter Magowan was appointed CEO in January 1980, headquarters buzzed like a swarm of bees. Tempers flared because older senior executives had been passed over for promotion, and a 39-year-old man with family connections had been given the nod instead. Despite the accusations of appointment by nepotism, young Magowan "has brought to Safeway vigor and enthusiasm—intangible assets, which have resulted in very tangible advances in sales and earnings."[3]

Peter Magowan's educational credentials are quite impressive. His alma maters include Groton Preparatory School, Stanford University, Oxford University, and the Johns Hopkins School of Advanced International Studies. Since his appointment, Magowan has built 850 new stores and remodeled 680 more. According to Harry Sunderland, Safeway's executive vice-president and chief financial officer, "He [Magowan] redeveloped the store system and the merchandising program into a modern superstore structure, streamlined the management and strengthened the balance sheet."[4]

SAFEWAY'S ATTITUDE TOWARD SOCIAL RESPONSIBILITY

Safeway participates in a variety of charities and volunteer projects. According to Peter Magowan, "While we must maintain a well-run and profitable company to fulfill our financial obligation to our stockholders, we must also recognize our moral commitment to the society in which we do business."[5]

Safeway's support of the search for missing children is only one example of this commitment. To aid the search for missing children, Safeway includes photographs of these children on grocery bags and milk cartons. It also provides help following natural disasters, donates food and nonfood items to food banks, and sponsors the fingerprinting and photographing of children.

INDUSTRY

According to experts, the typical grocery shopper is motivated more by price than any other factor. Thus, grocery retailers battle each other routinely with half-price sales, double-coupon deals, and other low-price strategies. As a result of competitive pricing, most grocers have been experiencing significant difficulty maintaining profit margins. In addition, consumers are spending a smaller percentage of their disposable income on food. De-

EXHIBIT 1

Grocery Store Sales

YEAR	1980	1981	1982	1983	1984	1985
Sales ($ millions)	220.8	240.9	252.0	263.8	279.4	292.2
Percent change	10.5%	9.1%	4.6%	4.7%	5.9%	4.6%

SOURCE: *Progressive Grocer*, April 1986.

EXHIBIT 2

1985 Grocery Store Sales

	NUMBER OF STORES	PERCENT OF TOTAL	SALES ($ MILLIONS)	PERCENT OF TOTAL
All stores	154,000	100.0%	292,200	100.0%
Supermarkets	30,505	19.8	209,820	71.8
Convenience stores	45,400	29.5	20,410	7.0
Other small stores	78,095	50.7	61,970	21.2

SOURCE: *Progressive Grocer*, April 1986.

spite this trend, U.S. grocery sales increased by 4.6 percent to $292.2 billion in 1985.

In 1985, 71.8 percent of grocery sales occurred in supermarkets (independent and chain), 21.2 percent occurred in smaller grocery stores, and 7.0 percent in convenience stores. Although the total number of supermarkets in the United States increased by 330 units in 1985, the distribution of the increase reveals some interesting results. In 1985, the number of independent grocery stores increased by 610 units, and the number of chain grocery stores declined by 280 units.[6] (See Exhibits 1 and 2.)

CONCEPTS FOR DELIVERING GROCERIES TO CONSUMERS	Since the onslaught of the combination store, superstore, and recent introduction of the hypermarket, the format of the supermarket has changed dramatically from the conventional store it once was.

Combination Stores

Combination stores span from 19,000 to 35,000 square feet of floor space, and they devote 33 percent or more of that space to nonfood consumer products. They usually contain a pharmacy, a health and beauty aids section, a floral section, and a general merchandise area that includes items such as greeting cards and books. The combination store concept is experiencing increasing popularity at present, and there has been a trend toward expanding combination stores to include delicatessens, bakeries, and fresh fish markets as well as banking facilities. Margins in combination stores tend to be higher than the margins in conventional stores or warehouse stores (21.23 percent as compared with 20.74 percent and 12.21 percent, respectively).

Superstores

Superstores are larger cousins of the combination store. "Superstores are markets with 40,000 square feet or more, containing a much wider range of products than is found in conventional stores. They have been deemed the strongest format by chain managers and executives followed by superwarehouses and combination stores."[7] Their popularity is growing among some segments of consumers in many parts of the country.

The Hypermarket

The success of a French store named Carrefour has influenced the development of a new concept in retailing called the hypermarket. This oversized (135,000 square feet) combination of a supermarket and a discount store sells everything from produce to television sets and accounts for 12 percent of

EXHIBIT 3

Attributes Important to Consumers in Grocery Store Selection

RANK	CHARACTERISTIC
1	Cleanliness
2	All prices clearly marked
3	Low prices
4	Freshness date marked on products
5	Accurate, pleasant checkout clerks
6	Good produce department
7	Shelves usually kept well stocked
8	Convenient store location
9	Good parking facilities
10	Short wait for checkout

SOURCE: *Progressive Grocer*, April 1986.

the retail trade in France.[8] Legislation has been enacted in France to help small shopkeepers by barring construction of these hypermarkets without government approval. Consequently, French firms have opted to expand their operations in the United States. In 1984, a French company opened a hypermarket in Cincinnati called Bigg's Hyper Shoppe. It is reported that the company is currently losing money due to its location on the outskirts of the population center, although it sells about $100 million worth of goods a year. Plans are being developed now for opening other hypermarkets in Denver and Florida.

Good service, effective merchandising, quality employees, and optimal location are the keys to success for the leading supermarkets today. Most chains are expanding by using upscale stores with gourmet foods and ethnic departments with a variety of foods targeted at niche markets. To increase store loyalty, retailers are paying more attention to the customers' changing needs and wants (see Exhibit 3). Lower prices, fresh produce, convenient location, and customer service all influence where customers shop. In addition to these factors, the time constraints of the working woman have influenced shopping habits.

COMPETITION

Nationally

On the national level, Safeway is the industry leader followed by Kroger, American Stores, Lucky Stores, and Winn-Dixie, respectively. Safeway has stores in eighteen of the twenty-five fastest-growing cities in the

EXHIBIT 4

Sales (Dollar Amounts in Millions)

	1985	1984	1983	1982
Safeway	19,651	19,642	18,585	17,633
Kroger	17,124	15,923	15,236	14,472
American	13,890	12,119	7,984	7,508
Lucky	9,382	9,237	8,388	7,973
Winn-Dixie	7,774	7,302	7,019	6,764

SOURCE: Above companies' 1985 Annual Reports.

United States and in nine of the ten fastest-growing states.[9] (See Exhibits 4 and 5.)

Kroger has expanded its operation by focusing on grocery sales, drug sales, and convenience store sales. By focusing on the sale of nonfood items, it has effectively segmented its market to produce additional growth and new customers. Kroger is planning the construction of a minimall in Atlanta called Kroger CitiCenter. It will have 87,000 square feet of space, and it will help to move Kroger rapidly into a much broader market.

American Stores is currently the third-largest grocery retailer, but it is the largest operator of drugstores in the United States. American Stores has been a pioneer in the development of combination stores. They generate 50 percent of their sales in combination stores from nonfood items. The industry average is 20 percent.[10] In an industry where margins are typically very low, American Stores tends to be more conscious of the bottom line than most competitors.

Lucky Stores are located primarily in California, central Florida, and the Midwest. In the markets it serves, it has a reputation for being a price leader.

EXHIBIT 5

Number of Stores

	1985	1984	1983	1982
Safeway	2,365	2,571	2,507	2,454
Kroger	2,882	2,379	2,386	2,233
American	N/A	N/A	N/A	N/A
Lucky	1,465	1,395	1,629	1,590

SOURCE: Above companies' 1985 Annual Reports.

Sales are divided among food stores, Gemco stores (one-stop shopping), and specialty stores that sell automotive, fabric, and other products.

Winn-Dixie is the fifth-largest grocery retailer in the United States. It is a dominant force in the Southeast, and it has developed a new concept that it calls "Marketplace." These stores feature 45,000 square feet of space in which products of various kinds are sold (e.g., drugs, cheeses, and bath items). In addition, it has introduced a new superstore/warehouse format to complement its traditional supermarkets in smaller towns where there is less competition.

Regionally

Although national grocery store chains account for a large dollar volume of sales, the majority of grocery sales are made by independent or regional firms. Safeway faces stiff competition at the regional level where small firms, by national standards, dominate markets. For example, Giant holds 42 percent of the market in the Washington, D.C./Baltimore area compared with 33 percent for Safeway.[11] Giant is an innovative, vertically integrated firm. It owns a bakery division and a frozen dessert processing plant. In addition, its computerized patient profile makes its pharmacy section appealing to older customers.

There are many more examples of regional firms dominating markets. In the Houston, Texas, area, Randall's controls 16 percent of the market. Ukrop's controls the lion's share of the Richmond, Virginia market. Ralph's in Los Angeles, Farm Fresh in Virginia, and Publix in Florida are all major competitors in their areas. In addition, a relatively new competitor, Food Lion out of Salisbury, North Carolina, is growing rapidly in the Southeast and mid-Atlantic states and putting intense price pressure on all the grocery stores in the markets they enter.

Competitors outside the industry have put pressure on supermarkets as well. Fast-food restaurants, discount stores, drugstores, convenience stores, and specialty shops may compete with national grocery store chains for the consumer's grocery dollar.

Two troublesome issues, the trend toward industry consolidation and lower profit margins, are being monitored closely by industry executives today because these trends have the potential to alter the nature of competition in the industry. To combat these trends, it is believed that grocery executives will turn to increased vertical integration and expansion of the nonfood and service departments in their stores.[12]

MARKETING

In the 1970s, Safeway was timid. It was "in awe of government regulations, hesitant about advertising loss leaders for fear of running out of the advertised items, and reluctant to match prices with aggressive discounters."[13]

When Peter Magowan took charge, he changed Safeway's image. He began by implementing a plan for divesting operations with poor prospects for growth. This led to the closing of stores in several markets (Omaha, Nebraska; Memphis, Tennessee; and southwest Missouri). With funds from the divestiture, Safeway purchased forty-six Weingarten stores in Houston, Texas, from Grand Union and twenty-three stores from Thriftimart in southern California. This restructuring gave it a more powerful presence in these key markets.

Magowan also changed the firm's philosophy toward the sale of products carrying the Safeway brand name. Over time, it had developed an overreliance on the sale of these products, because the profit margins were higher.[14] However, customers were not attracted to them. Thus, it was difficult for Safeway to attract new customers who shopped at other stores to buy national brands. In 1985, Safeway's private label program included thirty brand names representing 2,100 items carried in a typical store. Under Magowan's leadership, the firm has focused on attracting new customers through national brand product support.[15]

Magowan expects the U.S. market and Safeway's new superstores to generate most of the company's future growth. After conducting thousands of customer surveys, Safeway learned that most of its shoppers preferred superstores. It now operates 700 of them, and it is replacing its smaller stores with the larger variety. The company's superstores are usually profitable within a year, and they are more profitable in the long run than conventional stores.[16]

Advertising

Safeway spends more than $47 million a year in major media advertising alone. At this level of spending, it ranks in the top 200 companies in the United States in this category.

In 1985, a major new advertising campaign was started with the theme, "You work an honest day, you get an honest deal at Safeway."[17] Safeway uses centralized advertising in magazines and on television to obtain greater exposure and a consistent image. Local Safeway divisions are allowed to develop their own advertising copy within the national theme guidelines.[18]

Specialization and Diversification

In 1985, Safeway opened 2,170 new bakeries, seafood counters, soup bars, and similar specialty departments.[19] In addition, it opened three gourmet stores called Bon Appetit. These changes reflect a significant adjustment in the firm's basic philosophy and a movement toward increased specialization and diversification. They also represent a shift in focus toward the 25- to 44-year-old grocery shopper who wants competitive prices, quality food, convenient locations, and one-stop shopping.[20]

RESEARCH AND DEVELOPMENT

Technological developments play an important role in marketing operations at Safeway. Recently, it installed a companywide Direct Product Profitability (DPP) system for 80 percent of the products it sells. DPP is designed to ensure consumer awareness of the most popular products sold by focusing on optimal shelf placement. In the grocery business, shelf-space allocation decisions and decisions that result in ensuring that popular products are always available are among the most important ones made. The DPP program works in conjunction with two other systems: Shelf Allocation Management (SAM) and Direct Store Delivery (DSD). These programs are intended to help maximize sales and profits by improving merchandising decisions made at the store level.[21]

OPERATIONS

Safeway opened 114 new stores worldwide during 1985. After disposing of 125 older, smaller stores in the beginning of 1986, it opened 90 more by year end. Although Safeway has widespread market coverage in general, Magowan's cost-cutting efforts and associated store closing moves have essentially removed the company from the intensely competitive Northeast and upper-Midwest.[22]

As of June 1986, Safeway operated over 1,900 stores in the United States. Internationally, it owned stores in Canada and the United Kingdom, the latter of which had sales of $4.26 billion in 1985. It also owned 49 percent of Casa Ley's Mexican operations and 20 percent of Woolworth's Ltd.'s Australian operations.[23]

Recently, Safeway sold its Australian stores to Woolworth's Ltd. of Australia in return for a 20 percent equity interest in that operation and two seats on its board of directors. Peter Magowan characterized this move as an expansion of the Safeway holdings in Australia, not a reduction in its foreign presence, saying that it was a good move because of Woolworth's intention to pursue "significant investment" in the Australian retail market.[24]

A subsidiary, Safeway Holdings, Inc., was formed in 1971 as a food-processing division with about 105 plants.[25]

In addition to its grocery operations, Safeway is the largest retail florist and the second-largest drugstore chain in the world. Safeway's operations are far reaching, and their influence extends well beyond groceries.

FINANCE

Safeway was experiencing financial difficulties prior to Magowan's appointment. From 1978 to 1981, net income had declined 32 percent and the company was burdened "with top-heavy management, deteriorating capital ratios, and an obsolete U.S. store system."[26] Under Magowan's leadership, Safeway's stock price more than doubled between 1982 and 1984.[27]

EXHIBIT 6

Comparative Income Analysis
(Dollar Amounts in Thousands Except Per Share Data)

12 WEEKS ENDED JUNE 15: 1984		12 WEEKS ENDED JUNE 15: 1985	
Sales	4,525,000	Sales	4,548,440
Net income	47,550	Net income	49,910
EPS	.81	EPS	.83

MID-YEAR 1984:		MID-YEAR 1985:	
Sales	8,928,340	Sales	9,100,400
Net income	69,560	Net income	75,580
Avg shares	58,929	Avg shares	60,046
EPS	1.18	EPS	1.26

12 WEEKS ENDED JUNE 15: 1986	
Sales	4,571,810
Net income	45,620
EPS	.75

MID-YEAR 1986:	
Sales	9,037,500
Net income	72,640
Avg shares	61,015
EPS	1.19

Although 1985 sales leveled off from 1984 figures, net income increased 25 percent over the period. Exhibit 6 provides comparative income analysis information. Much of the increase in net income in 1985 was due to a windfall of $40 million from the sale of the Australian division in the third quarter of 1985 and an accounting change to the LIFO method of inventory valuation that resulted in an increase in after-tax earnings of $2.8 million.[28]

Three-fourths of Safeway's 1986 sales were accounted for by the U.S. divisions, and Magowan plans to invest $650 million a year over the next several years to develop these divisions and add more stores. The company's sales in the first half of 1986 were $9.1 billion, and net income was $72.6 million. These figures represent a 0.07 percent drop in sales and a 3.9 percent drop in earnings from the first half of 1985. (See Exhibit 6.) Most of the decline in sales can be attributed to intense competition in the grocery industry and the closing of smaller stores at a faster pace than the opening of new stores. The strength of the U.S. economy over this period has done little to boost Safeway's sales except in the higher-priced product segments, where the new specialty stores appear to be doing well.[29]

SAFEWAY'S EXECUTIVE STRUCTURE

Exhibit 7 presents Safeway's executive structure as of July 1986.

According to one division manager in the company, Magowan is "obsessed with leaving a mark"[30] in the grocery business. This obsession may have resulted in some internal dissension among top executives in the firm. Within the past year, six of Magowan's top executives have resigned their positions.

EXHIBIT 7

Executive Structure as of July 1986

NAME	TITLE	AGE
Peter A. Magowan*	Chief Executive Officer; Chairman of the Board	44
Harry D. Sunderland*	Executive Vice-President; Chief Financial Officer	51
James A. Rowland*	President and Chief Operating Officer	62
Edward N. Henney*	Executive Vice-President, Supply Operations	61
E. Richard Jones	Executive Vice-President, Information Services and Planning	42

SOURCE: Safeway Stores Inc., 1985 Annual Report.

*Member of the Board of Directors

Note: Insiders control about 1 percent of total stock.

DEALING WITH A TAKEOVER THREAT

On July 9, 1986, the Dart Group, a company one-sixtieth the size of Safeway, announced its first bid of $58 a share in an attempt to take over Safeway Stores Incorporated. Since the middle of May, rumors about a takeover attempt had been heard on Wall Street, "causing severe disruption in the trading of Safeway stock following their [Dart's] purchase of three million shares."[31]

By the end of June, the Dart Group had acquired 5.9 percent of Safeway's 61 million shares. On Wall Street, it had a reputation for "chasing acquisitions only for the fun of being bought out" and making a profit.[32] Other companies it had pursued in a similar manner included May Department Stores, Beatrice Company, and Jack Eckerd Corporation. As an example, the Dart Group was unsuccessful in its bid to take over Jack Eckerd Corporation, but it made $9 million before the deal was over. To protect themselves from the unwanted takeover of their operations, these firms assumed a great deal of debt that affected their balance sheets in a negative way.

The initial offer by Dart to gain control of Safeway amounted to about $3.54 billion. If accepted, the purchase would be financed through debt and other securities. Wall Street did not react positively to the offer. *Standard & Poor's* placed both of the companies on its CreditWatch, saying that "if the takeover occurs, then Safeway's cash flow would be burdened substantially by the additional debt service obligations."[33] If the deal were to be finalized, the huge debt would almost force Dart to divest parts of Safeway.

In response to the takeover attempt, Safeway filed a lawsuit in federal court alleging that Dart "violated federal securities and racketeering laws."[34] The suit indicated that Dart "failed to disclose its intention in acquiring the company's stock" and that its only intention was to "coerce Safeway to repurchase the Safeway stock acquired by them in a greenmail transaction or to reap a quick profit for themselves."[35]

Dart responded by increasing its offer to $64 a share. This represents an increase of about $360 million and might indicate a desire for a friendly merger.

Dart requested a friendly merger after rumors circulated about Safeway's intention to talk with a group of New York investment bankers about taking the company private in a leveraged buyout. This move would save the company from Dart's control, but it raises questions about Safeway's ability to handle the interest expenses that would result. Safeway's profit margin was only 1.2 percent in 1985. Another alternative Safeway might have is to restructure the company and sell off its assets.

A decision must be made. Exhibits 8, 9, 10, and 11 present both Safeway's and Dart's financial data.

EXHIBIT 8   **Safeway Stores, Inc., Balance Sheet (Dollars in Thousands)**

	1985	1984	1983
ASSETS			
Current assets:			
Cash	$ 54,593	$ 49,179	$ 51,682
Short-term investments	170,021	25,263	23,892
Receivables	111,870	105,166	91,642
Merchandise inventories			
FIFO cost	1,878,281	1,881,525	1,722,260
Less LIFO reductions	312,715	318,281	289,006
	1,565,566	1,563,244	1,433,254
Prepaid expenses and other current assets	124,431	118,537	128,676
Total current assets	2,026,481	1,861,389	1,729,146
Property:			
Land	247,769	236,876	210,427
Buildings	431,410	345,001	305,006
Leasehold improvements	600,091	557,504	459,711
Fixtures and equipment	2,164,072	2,023,914	1,789,136
Transport equipment	186,831	186,485	173,576
Property under capital leases	1,010,277	1,144,409	1,155,493
	4,640,450	4,494,189	4,093,349
Less accumulated depreciation	2,003,752	1,894,333	1,731,138
Total property, net	2,636,698	2,599,856	2,362,211
Investments in affiliated companies	122,195	27,251	26,519
Other assets	55,237	48,733	56,487
Total assets	$4,840,611	$4,537,229	$4,174,363
LIABILITIES AND STOCKHOLDERS' EQUITY			
Current liabilities:			
Notes payable	$ 80,848	$ 44,913	$ 50,156
Current obligation under capital leases	43,396	45,427	45,841
Current maturities of notes and debentures	52,049	48,274	24,723
Accounts payable	1,151,426	1,038,268	1,017,094
Accrued salaries and wages	167,798	167,739	163,021
Other accrued expenses	201,357	170,905	154,373
Income tax payable	27,827	20,431	43,081
Total current liabilities	1,724,701	1,535,957	1,498,289

EXHIBIT 8	Continued		
	1985	**1984**	**1983**

LIABILITIES AND STOCKHOLDERS' EQUITY (continued)

	1985	1984	1983
Long-term debt:			
Obligations under capital leases	625,551	746,178	765,307
Notes and debentures	689,470	646,532	422,362
Total long-term debt	1,315,021	1,392,710	1,187,669
Accrued claims and other liabilities	178,275	139,539	98,051
Total liabilities	3,217,997	3,068,206	2,784,009
Stockholders' equity:			
Common stock—$1.66 2/3 par value			
Authorized 150,000, 150,000, and 75,000 shares			
Outstanding 60,846, 59,854, and 58,760 shares	101,411	99,756	97,933
Additional paid-in capital	273,776	246,964	222,851
Cumulative translation adjustments	(164,035)	(155,994)	(114,087)
Retained earnings	1,411,462	1,278,297	1,183,657
Total stockholders' equity	1,622,614	1,469,023	1,390,354
Total liabilities and stockholders' equity	$4,840,611	$4,537,229	$4,174,363

SOURCE: Safeway Stores, Inc., 1985 Annual Report.

EXHIBIT 9	Safeway's Notes and Debentures (Dollar Amounts in Thousands)		
	1985	**1984**	**1983**
Mortgage notes payable, secured	$416,379	$363,627	$263,250
Commercial paper and bank borrowings	90,000	100,000	49,000
Industrial development revenue bonds	68,245	57,680	33,132
7.40% sinking fund debentures, unsecured, due in installments through 1997	18,209	37,255	37,780
Other notes payable, unsecured	148,686	136,234	63,923
	741,519	694,806	447,085
Less current maturities	52,049	48,274	24,723
Long-term debt	$689,470	$646,532	$422,362

SOURCE: Safeway Stores, Inc., 1985 Annual Report.

EXHIBIT 10   Safeway's Income Statement
(Dollar Amounts in Thousands Except Per Share Data)

	1985	1984	1983
OPERATIONS			
Sales	$19,650,542	$19,642,201	$18,585,217
Cost of sales	14,872,247	15,004,547	14,249,843
Gross profit	4,778,295	4,637,654	4,335,374
Operating and administrative expenses	4,350,635	4,214,443	3,920,736
Operating profit	427,660	423,211	414,638
Gain on sale of foreign operations	49,046		
Other income, net	49,816	26,874	20,565
Income taxes	(122,316)	(113,811)	(117,630)
Net income	$231,300	185,011	183,303
Cash dividends per share	$ 1.625	$ 1.525	$ 1.425
Avg. shares of common stock outstanding	60,360	59,227	56,163
FINANCIAL STATISTICS			
Working capital	$ 301,780	$ 325,432	$ 230,857
Additions to property	621,758	701,678	541,238
Depreciation	333,398	295,290	264,553
Total assets	4,840,611	4,537,229	4,174,363
Long-term debt	1,315,021	1,392,710	1,187,669
Equity of common stockholders	1,622,614	1,469,023	1,390,354
Per share	26.67	24.54	23.66
Cash dividends on common stock	98,135	90,371	80,961
OTHER STATISTICS			
Employees at year end	164,385	168,590	162,088
Stores opened during year	114	195	145
Stores closed/sold during year	320	131	92
Total stores at year end	2,365	2,571	2,507
Total store area at year end (thous. sq. ft.)	70,292	73,284	69,818
Avg. annual sales per store	$ 7,687	$ 7,531	$ 7,395

SOURCE: Safeway Stores, Inc., 1985 Annual Report.

| EXHIBIT 11 | Dart Group Corporation and Subsidiaries, Consolidated Balance Sheets (Dollar Amounts in Thousands) | |

	JANUARY 31	
	1985	**1986**
ASSETS		
Current assets:		
Cash (including short-term investments of $43,136 in 1984)	$ 7,609	$ 44,544
Marketable securities	196,572	30,631
Net accounts receivable	5,178	874
Other	580	49
Net C/A of discontinued operations	—	17,622
	233,263	105,425
Property and equipment:		
Furniture, fixtures, and equipment	2,064	1,043
Leasehold improvements	2,415	1,152
Property under capital leases	7,177	—
	11,656	2,159
Accumulated depreciation and amortization	889	315
	10,767	1,180
Investment in Crown Books Corporation	6,641	4,215
Other assets	752	667
Long-term assets of discontinued operations	—	22,553
Deferred tax benefit	5,020	231
Total assets	$256,243	$134,971
LIABILITIES AND STOCKHOLDERS' EQUITY		
Current liabilities:		
Current portion of long-term debt	$ 400	$ 400
Trade accounts payable	11,185	903
Income taxes payable	9,063	617
Accrued salaries	11,473	1,741
Accrued taxes	593	277
Other accrued liabilities	2,918	3,119
Capital lease obligations	260	—
	35,892	7,057
Long-term debt	677	1,080
Obligation under capital leases	6,847	—
Share of deficit of Trac Auto West	7,191	2,936
Minority interest	18,060	16,967
L-T liabilities of discontinued operations	—	17,489
Total liabilities	68,667	45,529

EXHIBIT 11 Continued

	JANUARY 31	
	1985	1986
LIABILITIES AND STOCKHOLDERS' EQUITY (continued)		
Stockholders' equity:		
Class A common stock	1,603	1,584
Class B common stock	303	303
Paid-in-surplus	48,132	32,153
Retained earnings	139,287	57,151
Treasury stock	(1,749)	(1,749)
	187,576	89,442
Total liabilities and stockholders' equity	$256,243	$134,971

SOURCE: 10K Report filed with SEC.

NOTES

1. Del Marth, "Why Safeway Stopped Playing It Safe," *Nation's Business*, August 1984, p. 41.
2. *Ibid.*, p. 41.
3. *Ibid.*, p. 42.
4. *Ibid.*, p. 41.
5. Larry Schaeffer, "A Class Act of Giving," *Progressive Grocer*, October 1985, p. 94.
6. "53rd Annual Report," *Progressive Grocer*, April 1986.
7. *Ibid.*, p. 30.
8. "French Hypermarkets Form Carrefour," *The Wall Street Journal*, May 20, 1986, p. 32.
9. *Value Line Investment Survey*, 1986.
10. "Special Report," *Advertising Age*, April 28, 1986, p. 27.
11. Bill Saporito, "The Giant of the Regional Food Chains," *Fortune*, November 25, 1985, pp. 27–28.
12. "Outlook," *Progressive Grocer*, April 1986.
13. Del Marth, *op. cit.*, p. 42.
14. "A Stodgy Standpat Giant No More," *Progressive Grocer*, October 1984, p. 32.
15. Eric Nee, "Safeway Pares Down Private Label Brands," *Supermarket News*, p. 58.
16. Del Marth, *op. cit.*, p. 43.
17. "Second 100 Leading Advertising Chains," *Advertising Age*, March 1986, p. 51.
18. *Ibid.*, p. 52.
19. *Ibid.*
20. "A Stodgy Standpat Giant No More," *op. cit.*, p. 32.

21. Susan Sandler, "System Tied to Other Programs," *Supermarket News*, January 28, 1985, pp. 1–2.
22. "Second 100 Leading Advertising Chains," *op. cit.*, p. 51.
23. *Value Line Investment Survey*, 1986.
24. Marilyn Chase, "Safeway Unit, Australian Firm Set Merger Pact," *The Wall Street Journal*, August 15, 1985, p. 8.
25. *Value Line Investment Survey*, 1986.
26. "A Stodgy Standpat Giant No More," *op. cit.*, p. 32.
27. Del Marth, *op. cit.*, p. 43.
28. Marilyn Chase, *op. cit.*, p. 8.
29. *Value Line Investment Survey*, 1986.
30. Paula Dwyer, "Safeway's Chief Runs into Double Trouble," *Business Week*, June 30, 1986, p. 42.
31. "Dart Group Launches Offer for Safeway," *The Wall Street Journal*, July 9, 1986, p. 3.
32. Bill Saporito, "The Most Feared Family in Retailing," *Fortune*, June 22, 1987.
33. "Dart Group Plans Debt and Securities of Up to $3.9 Billion for Safeway Offer," *The Wall Street Journal*, July 10, 1986, p. 4.
34. "Dart Group Launches Offer for Safeway," *op. cit.*, p. 3.
35. Cathy Cohn, "Dart Challenges Safeway Lawsuit," *Supermarket News*, July 7, 1986, p. 1.

Food Lion, Inc.

NEIL H. SNYDER · JANET L. CASWELL

HISTORY OF THE FIRM

In 1957, three Winn-Dixie employees opened their first supermarket in Salisbury, North Carolina, under the name Food Town. Although cofounders Ralph Ketner, Brown Ketner, and Wilson Smith all had considerable retail experience in the grocery industry, Food Town struggled in its early years. Various marketing gimmicks were implemented (the company gave away trading stamps and even free automobiles), but the stores failed to win the loyalty of customers. In fact, Ralph Ketner had to close nine of the sixteen stores during the first ten years of operation. He blamed much of this failure on the underpricing techniques of Winn-Dixie. By 1966, only seven Food Town stores remained.

In response to the problem, Ketner adopted the idea of slashing prices on all items sold in the stores. He realized that a drastic increase in volume would be necessary to make this approach work and keep the company afloat. The company theme of LFPINC or "Lowest Food Prices in North Carolina" became popular as both customers and sales increased greatly. Sales rose 54 percent to $8.9 million, and profits rose 165 percent to $95,000 in the first year under the new policy.[1]

In 1970, the company went public. Établissements Delhaize Frères et Cie, a Belgium grocery chain, purchased 47.6 percent of the stock in 1974. Today, Delhaize controls 50.6 percent of the voting stock and has five of the ten seats on the board of directors.[2] The company changed its name to Food Lion in 1983, to avoid confusion with another similarly named chain. Also, the company began implementing its expansion program.

Today, Food Lion has expanded into eight states, from Delaware to Florida, and is considered to be one of the fastest-growing retail grocers in the country. Food Lion president and CEO Tom E. Smith explains, "Our goal is to bring extra low grocery prices to as many people in the Southeast as possible."[3]

Food Lion has 27,000 employees and continues to operate conventional size stores (21,000–29,000 square feet) and to offer discount prices. The company remains committed to expansion throughout the Southeast and has avoided moving into the sales of general merchandise in its stores. A food consultant's comments highlight the company's success in the aforemen-

---

This case was prepared by Janet L. Caswell under the direction of Neil H. Snyder at the University of Virginia. This case is designed to be used as a basis for discussion and is not intended to reflect positively or negatively on the administrative practices of Food Lion. Copyright 1988 by Neil H. Snyder. All rights reserved.

tioned areas. He states that Food Lion is "probably the best example of commitment to a format and operating style in the industry today. And although it is a conventional store operator, it also stands as an excellent practitioner of niche marketing. The stores aren't fancy, but beat everyone on price, and the company doesn't make many mistakes."[4]

Ralph Ketner

Since cofounding Food Lion, Ralph Ketner has continued to be a force behind its success. In 1968, it was his idea to adopt the strategy of discount pricing and his LFPINC theme that promoted the company. He acted as chief executive officer until 1986, when he passed the reins to President Tom Smith. Despite resigning as CEO, Mr. Ketner still exerts considerable influence over the operation of Food Lion. He remains chairman of the board of directors and plans to retain this position until 1991. In addition, Delhaize signed an agreement in 1974 to vote with Ketner for ten years. This agreement was later extended and will be in effect until 1989.[5]

Tom E. Smith

President and CEO Tom Smith is very much responsible for Food Lion's growth and success. This is largely attributed to his involvement with the company since his youth. At age seventeen, Smith began as a bag boy at Food Lion's first store. He attended night school at Catawba College and

EXHIBIT 1

Store Distribution

LOCATION	NUMBER OF STORES	PERCENT OF TOTAL
North Carolina	233	49.1%
Virginia	112	23.5
South Carolina	74	15.6
Tennessee	29	6.1
Georgia	19	4.0
Florida	6	1.3
Delaware	1	0.2
Maryland	1	0.2
Total	475	100.0%

SOURCE: *Standard & Poor's Stock Report*, p. 3905.

graduated in 1964 with an A.B. degree in business administration. After working for Del Monte the next six years, he was hired as Food Lion's sole buyer. Smith developed the successful strategy of stocking fewer brands and sizes than his competitors. He also took advantage of wholesaler specials by purchasing large volumes at discount prices. He was named vice president for distribution in 1974, and later became executive vice president in 1977. His continued success in these areas led to his promotion to president in 1981, at the age of 39. In 1986, he was named CEO.

Smith views himself as a planner who carefully molds the company's growth while keeping a close eye on the operations. This style has enabled him to react to and resolve any problems quickly and effectively. He has been a primary reason for Food Lion's constant commitment to its overall strategy of discount pricing and cost reduction. Smith has also become well known through his participation in over 50 percent of the Food Lion commercials. This media exposure has brought him recognition not only in the Southeast, but as far away as San Francisco and even Scotland, from visiting customers.[6] These commercials portray Smith as a hardworking and very trustworthy manager.

FOOD LION'S ATTITUDE TOWARD SOCIAL RESPONSIBILITY

Food Lion is recognized as a corporate neighbor, and it takes pride in performing charitable acts. In 1986, the company received the Martin Luther King Award in recognition of its humanitarian efforts. Food Lion received the award after completing a series of commendable projects. Most notable was the donation of trucks to aid the southeastern farmers during the drought in 1987. These trucks enabled the farmers to transport hay from Indiana. Also, the company was cited for providing equal opportunity employment and establishing express lanes for handicapped customers.[7]

INDUSTRY

Several trends in the supermarket industry may cause concern for many retail grocers. During 1987 there was a decline in the percentage of disposable income spent for food at home. After discounting inflation, real sales did not increase from 1986. As Exhibit 2 shows, food-at-home spending accounted for more retail sales than any other category in 1983. However, slow growth has caused a reduction in this percentage, leaving food stores in second place behind auto dealers. Another interesting trend has been the growth in sales of eating and drinking establishments during this same period.

The grocery industry is also experiencing competition from other types of stores. Discount department and drugstores are starting to sell more pack-

EXHIBIT 2

Division of U.S. Retail Sales

DIVISION OF SALES	1983	1984	1985	1986	1987*
Food stores	22.0%	21.1%	20.6%	20.4%	20.3%
Eating and drinking	9.9	9.6	9.7	10.0	10.1
Drug and proprietary	3.5	3.4	3.4	3.4	3.6
General merchandise	11.1	11.0	10.9	10.7	11.0
Furniture and appliances	4.6	4.8	5.0	5.4	5.5
Auto dealers	19.8	21.6	22.6	22.9	22.2
Hardware and lumber	4.4	4.7	4.8	5.2	4.7
Clothing	5.3	5.3	5.4	5.5	5.8
Gas stations	8.5	7.8	7.3	6.1	5.7
All others	10.9	10.7	10.4	10.4	11.2

SOURCE: Bureau of the Census (revised), 1987.
*First six months

aged foods. Many fast-food restaurants continue to sell a larger variety of prepared foods for takeout. Sales from specialty shops, which concentrate on one particular type of food, have increased as well. Wholesale clubs have also been of concern to retail grocers. These clubs have been effective at luring many customers away from conventional supermarkets. Supermarkets stressing discount prices have been hurt most by the emergence of the wholesale clubs.

In response to these trends, most grocery chains are stressing the idea of one-stop shopping. New store formats and product offerings are abundant. These ideas attempt to obtain a product mix that stresses higher margined items and services, as well as create an atmosphere that causes consumers to view the supermarket as more than a place to buy groceries. Items such as flowers, greeting cards, videocassettes, and drugs are appearing more frequently in many supermarkets. There has also been a greater emphasis on stocking perishables.

Clearly, the strongest trend in the industry is the use of bigger stores. Several experts believe that the increased size is necessary to provide the variety that many consumers desire. One chain president expressed this sentiment. "Customer satisfaction starts with the store design: one-stop shopping, complete service departments and integrating a drugstore and pharmacy into the store."[8] Much of this trend is a result of the massive increase in working women. The greater number of dual-income families, single parents, and singles living alone also contributes to the growth in one-stop shopping. Speed and convenience are two characteristics that these consumers often desire.

The one-stop shopping concept has resulted in several new store formats. Combination stores offer consumers a variety of nonfood items. These stores can be as large as 35,000 square feet, with 25 percent of the space devoted to nonfood and pharmacy items. Superstores are similar to the combination stores in that they offer a wide selection of general merchandise items. These stores are all larger than 40,000 square feet and are thought to be the strongest format for the near future. Exhibit 3 shows chain executives' views on the prospects for the various formats that exist today.

The newest and largest of the formats is the hypermarket. Currently, 55 of these stores exist in the United States. The typical hypermarket ranges in size from 125,000 to 330,000 square feet and requires $25 to $50 million in sales per year just to break even.[9] Normally, 40 percent of the floor space in hypermarkets is devoted to grocery items and the remaining 60 percent is used for general merchandise. Their success depends on a variety of factors. Freeway access, population density, and visibility are all key variables that contribute to a hypermarket's success. A majority of the stores are run by companies that are not U.S. food retailers. For example, Wal-Mart has opened several stores under the Hypermarket USA name. Also, Bruno's, a retail grocery chain, is teaming up with K mart to build a store in Atlanta.[10]

Because of the trend to expand store size, the number of stores declined for the first time in years. However, the larger store sizes resulted in an

---

EXHIBIT 3   **Chain Executives' Opinions on Prospects for New Formats**

	EXCELLENT	GOOD	FAIR/POOR
Superstores	56%	36%	8%
Combination	38	53	9
Convenience stores	26	39	35
Super warehouses	22	39	39
Hypermarkets	10	33	57
Specialty	8	37	55
Wholesale clubs	6	30	62
Conventional	4	35	59
Warehouse stores	1	17	79

SOURCE: *Progressive Grocer*, April 1988.

increase in actual square footage. Many small units have been closed due to the openings of larger stores. In many market areas, there continue to be too many stores and too few customers to support them. This is going to be an even bigger concern given the advent of the combination stores and hypermarkets, since they tend to attract customers from a wider area than the conventional stores.

Although the majority of retailers believe that the bigger stores are necessary to be successful in the future, there is a large group that believes the industry is going overboard in its attempt to provide one-stop shopping. Chain executive Carole Bitter believes that the emphasis on size is unfounded. "There has been an ego problem in the industry that has led to overbuilding and has driven up store sizes and has increased the number of formats."[11] Proponents of conventionals claim that the larger stores are too impersonal to be attractive to everyone. They also believe that many consumers desire the conventional type of store, and that this format will continue to be successful. Although many consumers claim that they want more service departments, studies have shown that the shoppers are not willing to pay enough for such departments in order to make them profitable. Exhibit 4 reveals what the average shopper desires. One-stop shopping capabilities rates only 26th on the list.

COMPETITION

In recent years, competition in the Southeast has become quite intense. Previously, this area was characterized by predominantly conventional stores. Combination and superstores were scarce. However, many retailers realized

EXHIBIT 4

Store Attributes Desired by Consumers

RANK	CHARACTERISTIC
1	Cleanliness
2	All prices labeled
3	Low prices
4	Good produce department
5	Accurate, pleasant clerks
6	Freshness date marked on products
7	Good meat department
8	Shelves kept well stocked
9	Short wait for checkout
10	Convenient store location

SOURCE: *Progressive Grocer,* April 1988.

EXHIBIT 5	Competitive Data				
	KROGER	**LUCKY**	**WINN-DIXIE**	**BRUNO'S**	**FOOD LION**
Number of stores	2,206	481	1,271	111	475
Employees	170,000	44,000	80,000	10,655	27,033
Sales ($ million)	$ 17,660	$ 6,925	$ 8,804	$ 1,143	$ 2,954
Sales/employee	103,881	157,386	110,049	107,265	109,267
Net profit ($ million)	$ 246.6	$ 151	$ 105.4	$ 31	$ 85.8
Net profit margin	1.4 %	2.2 %	1.2 %	2.7 %	2.9 %
Gross margin	22.4	25	22	20.8	19.2
Current ratio	1.1	0.83	1.65	1.63	1.41
Return on equity	24.5	46.3	15.2	15.4	25.3
Return on assets	5.5	11.8	7.9	10.33	10.6
Long-term debt/equity	0.69	0.38	0.03	0.04	0.26
Earnings per share	3.14	3.92	2.72	0.79	0.27
Average P/E ratio	15.1	10.2	13.9	23.1	35.3

that the Southeast was a prime location for the newer formats. (See Exhibit 5.) In 1984, Cub Foods opened three large, modern stores in the Atlanta area in an attempt to challenge Kroger's dominance in the Southeast. This move marked the beginning of several competitive shakeups in the South.

Kroger

Kroger operates 1,317 supermarkets and 889 convenience stores in the South and Midwest. In 1987, sales were nearly $18 billion. More than 95 percent of the floor space is either new or has been remodeled during the past ten years.[12] This is a result of the chain's move to larger combination and superstore formats. Kroger has not been as successful as it would like. The company realizes a net profit margin of approximately 1 percent. This is partly due to its new outlets cannibalizing its existing stores and has causes some store sales comparisons to be relatively flat.[13]

In response to the disappointing profit margins, Kroger is planning to decrease its capital spending plans by about $300 million. It is hoped that this will reduce interest costs as well as keep start-up expenses down. Also, the firm is cutting corporate overhead 20 percent. As for future store designs, Kroger is considering the curtailment of the new super-warehouse stores. These stores combine low grocery prices with high-priced service departments and have not appealed to a large segment of the market. Furthermore, the company is planning to reduce store remodeling in mature market areas.[14]

Winn-Dixie

Winn-Dixie is the fourth largest food retailer in the country with sales of nearly $9 billion. The chain operates 1,271 stores in the Sunbelt area, with the heaviest concentration of stores located in Florida, North Carolina, and Georgia. During the past few years, Winn-Dixie has been hurt by the influx of competition in the Southeast. As a result, profit margins have dipped to just over 1 percent. Net income also declined in 1987. Management points to a lack of investment in new stores and a rather slow response to competitors' underpricing methods as the main reasons for the decline in profits.[15]

Management has adopted several new strategies to combat the competition. Foremost is the move to larger store formats. In the past, the chain operated mostly conventional stores and depended on operating efficiencies to realize sizable profits. However, management believes that it is now necessary to alter the stores in response to changing consumer needs. At the end of 1987, the average supermarket was 27,700 square feet. There are approximately 250 new stores in the 35,000–45,000 square foot range, and they are expected to account for nearly half of all sales in the next five years.[16] The units in the 35,000-square-foot category are combination stores that are operated under the Winn-Dixie name. The 45,000-square-foot stores employ the superstore format and use the name Marketplace. Emphasis is being placed on service departments as well as price-sensitivity.

Other changes involve management. Last year, the company eliminated a layer of management, which resulted in 60 layoffs. The firm is also adopting a decentralized strategy which divides the company into twelve operating units. Each division is allowed to develop its own procedures and image. It is hoped that this will help the stores cater to the consumers in each market area more effectively.

Lucky Stores

Lucky operates nearly 500 supermarkets throughout the country. The majority of these are located in California; however, the chain does operate 90 stores in Florida. In 1986, Lucky began a major restructuring. This resulted in the sale of all the nonfood businesses. Also, the company has concentrated on increasing the store size to enable the sale of more service and nonfood items. The average size of the stores at the end of 1986 was 31,000 square feet.[17]

At the end of the year, there was much speculation that American Stores

Company would begin to pursue an unsolicited tender offer for all outstanding shares of Lucky common stock. American is a leading retailer in the country and operates mostly combination food and drug stores.

Bruno's

Bruno's operates approximately 100 supermarkets and combination food and drugstores in the Southeast. This chain pursues a strategy of high-volume sales at low prices. Another strategy involves the use of four different formats under various names. "Consumer Warehouse Foods" stores are relatively small warehouse-type stores that emphasize lower prices and reduced operating costs. "Food World" stores are large supermarkets that offer a variety of supermarket items at low prices. "Bruno's Food and Pharmacy" stores promote the idea of one-stop shopping through the combination store format. Finally, "FoodMax" stores are superwarehouses that offer generic and bulk foods in addition to the national labels.[18]

The company is also well known for its innovative forward-buying program. Bruno's is able to purchase goods at low prices because of its 900,000-square-foot distribution center that houses excess inventory. This strategy has been very successful as the company boasts one of the highest operating (4.8 percent) and net profit margins (2.7 percent).[19]

EXPANSION AT FOOD LION

Food Lion has continued to grow and expand in the Southeast. During 1987, the chain opened 95 new stores while closing only 8, bringing the total to 475. (See Exhibit 6.) With the exception of 4 supermarkets, Food Lion operates its stores under various leasing arrangements. The number of stores has grown at a ten-year compound rate of 24.1 percent.[20] With this expansion has come impressive growth in both sales and earnings over the same period. The firm has attained 29.7 percent sales and 30.9 percent earnings compounded over the past ten years.[21]

The existence and further development of distribution centers serve as the core for continued expansion. At the end of 1987, four such centers has been completed. These are located in Salisbury and Dunn, North Carolina, Orangeburg County, South Carolina, and Prince George County, Virginia. Two additional centers are planned for Tennessee and Jacksonville, Florida. These distribution centers enable Food Lion to pursue expansion using its "ink blot" formula. Using this strategy, new stores are added to an existing market area in order to saturate the market. "If anyone wants to go to a competitor, they'll have to drive by one of our stores," explains CFO Brian Woolf.[22] Despite the emergence of new stores, cannibalization has not been a problem. In fact, same-store sales increase approximately 8 percent annually. When Food Lion enters a new area, the strategy of underpricing the

EXHIBIT 6

Growth and Expansion (Dollars in Thousands)

YEAR	NUMBER OF STORES	SALES	NET INCOME
1987	475	$2,953,807	$85,802
1986	388	2,406,582	61,823
1985	317	1,865,632	47,585
1984	251	1,469,564	37,305
1983	226	1,172,459	27,718
1982	182	947,074	21,855
1981	141	666,848	19,317
1980	106	543,883	15,287
1979	85	415,974	13,171
1978	69	299,267	9,481

SOURCE: Food Lion Annual Reports.

competitors is employed. Such a strategy has caused average food prices to decline 10–20 percent in some parts of the country.[23] Every new store is constructed no farther than 200 miles from a distribution center. With continued expansion, new distribution centers whose radii overlap an existing distribution territory are erected in order to keep warehouse and transportation costs down.

Moreover, Food Lion continues to employ a "cookie-cutter" approach to its new stores. Rather than purchase existing stores, the firm much prefers to build new ones from scratch. All the stores fall into the conventional store category. The majority are 25,000 square feet and cost only $650,000 to complete. These stores emphasize the fruit and vegetable departments. Approximately 40 percent of the new stores are 29,000 square feet and contain a bakery/delicatessen. These are placed after careful consideration is given to the demographics and psychographics of the area. Normally, new stores turn a profit within the first six months of operation. In comparison, most competitors construct slightly larger stores that cost over $1 million to complete.[24]

The standard size of the stores has allowed the company to keep costs down while sticking to basics. Aside from the bakery departments, Food Lion has stayed away from service departments such as seafood counters and flower shops. Such departments are often costly due to the increase in required labor. Also, Food Lion has remained a retail grocery chain, shunning the idea of moving into the general merchandise area. This structure has prompted Food Lion to be compared to both Wal-Mart and McDonald's.

With the steady increase in stores over the past ten years comes an increase in the need for quality employees. In an interview last March, Smith expressed concern over the high dropout rate of high school students.[25] Food Lion relies heavily upon recent graduates, and the current trend may signal a decline in the quality of the average worker. Food Lion has responded to the labor problem by setting up an extensive training program for its 27,000 employees. These programs range from in-store training at the operational level to comprehensive training programs for potential managers. In addition, the firm continues to offer programs at headquarters in order to upgrade the work of the upper staff. Management is also attempting to increase the use of computers within the company. More specifically, Smith is hoping to utilize computer systems to handle much of the financial reporting aspects in the individual stores in an attempt to lessen the need for more employees.

ADVERTISING

Rather than employ costly advertising gimmicks, such as double coupon offers, Food Lion's advertising strategy combines cost-saving techniques with an awareness of consumer sentiment. Smith is the company's main spokesman, appearing in over half of the television commercials. Not only has this method kept advertising expenses down, but it has also made the public aware of both Smith and his discount pricing policy. By producing most of the ads in-house and using only a few paid actors, the cost of an average TV spot is only $6,000. Also, the company policy of keeping newspaper ads relatively small results in annual savings of $8 million. Food Lion's advertising costs are a mere 0.5 percent of sales, one-fourth of the industry average.[26]

The content of the ads is another reason for Food Lion's Success. Many of the TV spots feature some of the cost-cutting techniques used by the firm. One theme often mentioned at the end of an ad states, "When we save, you save." Another commonly used theme states "Food Lion is coming to town, and food prices will be coming down." Before moving into the Jacksonville, Florida, area, Food Lion launched a nine-month advertising campaign. Many of these ads focused on innovative management methods that permit lower prices to be offered in the stores. For example, one ad demonstrates how a central computer is used to help control freezer temperatures. Other ads attempt to characterize Food Lion as a responsible community member. One such spot describes the importance that management places on the preventive maintenance of its forklifts and tractor-trailers.

Smith has also used the media to react to potential problems. For instance, Winn-Dixie launched an advertising attack against Food Lion reminding customers how competitors have come and gone. The company countered with an ad featuring Tom Smith in his office reassuring customers. "Winn-Dixie would have you believe that Food Lion's low prices are going to crumble and blow away. Let me assure you that as long as you keep shopping at Food Lion, our lower prices are going to stay right where they belong—in Jacksonville."[27] Smith also reacted quickly to a possible conflict in eastern Tennessee in 1984. Several rumors circulated which linked the Food Lion logo to Satanic worship. In response, Smith hired Grand Ole Opry star Minnie Pearl to appear in the Tennessee advertisements until the stories disappeared.[28]

INNOVATIONS

The grocery industry is characterized by razor-thin margins. While most retail grocery chains have failed to introduce new innovations in the industry, Food Lion has employed several techniques that enable the firm to offer greater discounts on nearly all its products. These innovations help Food Lion to realize a profit margin of nearly 2.9 percent, twice the industry average. Many of the innovations are ingenious cost-cutting ideas. CFO Woolf explains the company credo of doing "1,000 things 1 percent better."[29] Such a philosophy has resulted in keeping expenses at 14 percent of sales. This represents only 66 percent of the industry average.

Examples of the ideas are abundant. Rather than purchase expensive plastic bins to store cosmetics, Food Lion recycles old banana crates. These banana boxes are also used for storing groceries in warehouses. These innovations save the company approximately $200,000 a year.[30] Furthermore, the firm utilizes waste heat from the refrigerator units to warm part of the stores. Also, motion sensors automatically turn off lights in unoccupied rooms. Costs are further reduced by Food Lion's practice of repairing old grocery carts rather than purchasing newer, more expensive models. Perhaps the greatest savings can be attributed to the carefully planned distribution system. This system allows management to take advantage of wholesalers' specials. The centralized buyout-and-distribution technique allows products for all stores to be purchased at one volume price.

Moreover, labor costs remain lower than those of many competitors. Smith is vehemently opposed to the use of unionized labor. Despite protests from the United Food and Commercial Workers International Union claiming that Food Lion's wages are well below union standards, management has continued to please its workers and avoid unionization. In fact, Smith believes its employee benefit package is unequaled in the industry. A profit-sharing plan linking an employee's efforts in making Food Lion profitable with wealth accumulation for the future is already in use. Plans to improve long-term disability insurance benefits are under way.[31] In contrast, several other chains have experienced problems solving labor union problems. For example, a month-long strike by Kroger's Denver-area employees resulted in concessions on wages, benefits, and work rules. Safeway employees were also given quick concessions after threatening to close down several stores.[32]

Other innovations are designed to increase sales. Food Lion often sells popular items such as pet food and cereal at cost in an attempt to draw more customers into the stores. The company makes $1 million a year selling fertilizer made up of discarded ground-up bones and fat. Lower prices are also feasible due to the policy of offering fewer brands and sizes than competitors. The company has increased its private label stock, which now includes at least one unit in every category. These two methods allow the company to price its national brand products below many competitors' private brands. As mentioned earlier the smaller store size and sale of mostly food items have contributed to the high profit margin realized by the company.

FINANCE

Food Lion's sound financial structure has enabled the company to continue expanding without becoming overextended or burdened with heavy debt repayments. The firm's capital structure consists of 26 percent long-term debt and 74 percent equity. The majority of growth has been financed through internally generated funds. (See Exhibit 7.) The company does not want to grow at the expense of profits. With careful planning, Food Lion has been very successful in this area, and has been able to maintain very impressive margins throughout the expansion period.

The growth in Food Lion's stock prices also reflects the sound financial position of the company. This growth illustrates the continued confidence of

EXHIBIT 7   **Financial Ratios**

YEAR	OPERATING MARGIN	NET PROFIT MARGIN	RETURN ON ASSETS	RETURN ON EQUITY	LONG-TERM DEBT AS PERCENT OF CAPITAL
1987	6.8%	2.9%	14.2%	32.4%	26.0%
1986	6.9	2.6	14.1	29.8	24.0
1985	6.3	2.6	14.4	29.1	20.5
1984	6.3	2.5	13.6	30.2	22.8
1983	5.9	2.4	13.0	28.3	25.9
1982	5.6	2.3	15.7	28.1	18.0
1981	6.7	2.9	18.1	32.3	12.4
1980	5.9	2.8	17.7	33.4	15.5
1979	6.7	3.2	20.0	39.0	19.0
1978	6.9	3.2	19.5	38.3	22.8

SOURCE: 1987 Food Lion Annual Report.

investors in the future productivity of the firm. In response to the rapid rise of stock prices, management has declared two stock splits since late 1983, when the two separate classes of stock were formed from the previous single class. These splits are designed to keep the price of the stock low enough to be attractive and affordable to all investors. Exhibit 8 shows the adjusted stock prices beginning in 1983, when the two classes were formed.

Furthermore, the per-share data reveals the success Food Lion has achieved over the past decade. (See Exhibit 9.) These figures also illustrate investors' desire for Food Lion stock. More specifically, the price/earnings ratio indicates how much investors are willing to pay for a dollar of the company's earnings. In 1987, Food Lion's P/E ratio was the 83d highest of all the companies listed in the *Value Line Investment Survey*.

EXHIBIT 8

Adjusted Stock Prices

	CLASS A		CLASS B	
	HIGH	**LOW**	**HIGH**	**LOW**
1983				
IV	2⅛	1⅝	2⅛	2
1984				
I	1⅝	1⅜	1¾	1⅜
II	1⅝	1⅜	1⅝	1½
III	1⅞	1⅜	1⅞	1½
IV	2¼	1⅞	2⅜	1⅞
1985				
I	2⅝	2⅛	2⅞	2¼
II	3⅛	2¼	3⅛	2¾
III	3	2¾	3	2⅞
IV	3¾	2¾	3¾	2⅞
1986				
I	4½	3⅜	4⅞	3⅜
II	6⅛	4⅛	7⅛	4⅝
III	7¼	5½	9	6⅞
IV	6⅛	5	7⅜	5⅞
1987				
I	7⅝	6⅛	8½	6⅜
II	8⅛	6⅞	8½	7
III	12¼	7¾	13	8¼
IV	13⅜	7¾	14¼	8

SOURCE: Food Lion Annual Reports.

EXHIBIT 9	**Per Share Data**				
	YEAR	EPS	P/E RANGE	DIVIDENDS	PAYOUT RATIO
	1987	.27	54–22	.04⅛	15%
	1986	.19	47–17	.01⅞	9
	1985	.15	25–15	.01¼	8
	1984	.12	20–12	.00¾	6
	1983	.09	28–19	.00¾	8
	1982	.07	32–12	.00¾	9
	1981	.06	17–10	.00⅝	9
	1980	.05	13–9	.00½	9
	1979	.05	17–8	.00½	9
	1978	.03	11–5	.00⅛	4

SOURCE: *1988 Standard & Poor's Stock Report*, p. 3906.

FUTURE

Next week, Tom Smith is meeting with the board of directors to discuss and present his ideas for the next few years. Given the recent troublesome trends in the grocery industry as well as the increasing competition in the Southeast, he is reviewing the future strategy of Food Lion. Foremost in his mind is the extent to which Food Lion should continue to expand operations of its conventional stores in this area. He is also pondering movement into other market areas. Smith wants to be sure that the company will be able to finance future growth without greatly changing its current capital structure. Although the current success of Food Lion is quite impressive, Mr. Smith realizes that other grocery chains have experienced problems by not responding to the changing environment. He wants to be certain that this does not happen to Food Lion.

EXHIBIT 10	**Food Lion, Inc. Balance Sheet**				
	1987	1986	1985	1984	1983
ASSETS					
Cash and equivalents	$ 15.5	$ 22.0	$ 2.7	$ 24.4	$ 5.2
Receivables	39.8	27.2	21.8	15.6	11.6
Inventories	385.3	258.9	193.9	136.7	118.3
Other current assets	3.3	3.3	2.4	1.4	0.9
Total current assets	$443.9	$311.4	$220.8	$178.0	$135.9

EXHIBIT 10   Continued

	1987	1986	1985	1984	1983
ASSETS (continued)					
Plant—gross	498.6	400.4	303.2	218.8	189.2
Less: Accumulated depreciation	136.7	106.9	84.3	65.7	50.9
Plant—net	$361.9	$293.5	$218.9	$153.1	$138.3
Construction in progress	0.7	6.4	13.1	0.0	0.1
Land	4.1	6.2	3.5	1.7	1.7
Buildings	85.5	58.6	34.8	32.2	20.2
Equip. and machines—net	207.4	159.5	122.1	81.6	73.4
Natural resources	0.0	0.0	0.0	0.0	0.0
Leases	64.1	62.7	45.4	37.7	32.9
Unconsolidated subsidiaries	0.0	0.0	0.0	0.0	0.0
Other investments	0.0	0.0	0.0	0.0	0.0
Intangibles	0.0	0.0	0.0	0.0	0.0
Other assets	0.0	0.0	0.0	0.0	0.0
Deferred charges	0.0	0.0	0.0	0.0	0.0
Total assets	$805.8	$604.9	$439.7	$331.2	$274.2
LIABILITIES AND NET WORTH					
Debt in current liabilities	$ 96.1	$ 54.4	$ 28.1	$ 2.0	$ 22.3
Income taxes payable	14.7	13.5	2.5	7.5	4.9
Accounts payable	144.3	106.4	79.3	57.4	44.3
Other current liabilities	60.7	48.6	45.0	37.7	23.4
Total current liabilities	$315.8	$222.9	$154.9	$104.7	$ 94.8
Debt structure:					
Convertible	0.0	0.0	0.0	0.0	0.0
Subordinated	0.0	0.0	0.0	0.0	0.0
Notes	60.0	0.0	0.0	0.0	0.0
Debentures	5.8	6.9	18.0	17.3	18.4
Other long-term debt	5.0	35.2	5.1	2.5	1.5
Capital lease obligation	53.6	52.6	37.8	33.5	28.7
Less: Debt (1 year)	3.3	3.3	2.9	2.0	2.4
Total long-term debt	$121.0	$ 91.4	$ 58.0	$ 51.3	$ 46.2
Other liabilities	1.4	1.2	1.1	1.2	0.8
Deferred taxes and ITC	28.3	24.5	18.2	10.6	8.7
Minority interest	0.0	0.0	0.0	0.0	0.0
Total liabilities	$466.6	$340.0	$232.3	$167.8	$150.6
Equity structure:					
Preferred stock	0.0	0.0	0.0	0.0	0.0
Redeemable preferred stock	0.0	0.0	0.0	0.0	0.0
Common stock	160.9	80.3	26.6	26.5	26.2
Capital surplus	0.1	0.5	6.1	5.3	0.0
Retained earnings	173.3	184.1	174.7	131.6	97.4
Common equity	339.2	264.9	207.4	163.4	123.6
Total stockholders' equity	$339.2	$264.9	$207.4	$163.4	$123.6
Total liabilities and net worth	$805.8	$604.9	$439.7	$331.2	$274.2

SOURCE: Lotus® One Source Databases Compustat Tapes.

EXHIBIT 11

Food Lion, Inc. Income Statement

	1987	1986	1985	1984	1983
Sales	$2,953.8	$2,406.6	$1,865.6	$1,469.6	$1,172.5
Cost of goods sold	2,385.3	1,948.8	1,521.3	1,206.9	968.9
Selling, gen. and admin.	366.6	296.1	226.6	169.5	134.4
Operating income	$ 201.9	$ 161.7	$ 117.8	$ 93.2	$ 69.1
Depreciation and amort.	(37.4)	(29.6)	(21.4)	(16.7)	(14.1)
Interest expense	(13.8)	(9.2)	(7.2)	(5.1)	(4.6)
Interest capitalized	0.0	0.0	0.0	0.0	0.0
Non-operating income (exp.)	0.0	0.0	0.0	0.0	0.0
Special items	0.0	0.0	0.0	0.0	0.0
Pre-tax income	$ 150.7	$ 122.9	$ 89.2	$ 71.4	$ 50.5
Income taxes:					
Income tax (fed.)	51.9	48.1	29.3	28.1	17.5
Income tax (st.)	9.2	6.7	4.7	4.1	2.7
Income tax (frn.)	0.0	0.0	0.0	0.0	0.0
Deferred taxes	3.8	6.3	7.6	1.9	2.5
Minority interest	0.0	0.0	0.0	0.0	0.0
Income before extra. items and disc. opns.	$ 85.8	$ 61.8	$ 47.6	$ 37.3	$ 27.7
Extraordinary items	0.0	0.0	0.0	0.0	0.0
Discontinued operations	0.0	0.0	0.0	0.0	0.0
Net income	$ 85.8	$ 61.8	$ 47.6	$ 37.3	$ 27.7
Preferred dividends	0.0	0.0	0.0	0.0	0.0
Available for common:					
Before adjustments	$ 85.8	$ 61.8	$ 47.6	$ 37.3	$ 27.7
After adjustments	$ 85.8	$ 61.8	$ 47.6	$ 37.3	$ 27.7
Per share:					
EPS (primary)					
Excluding extraord. and discontinued items	$ 0.27	$ 0.20	$ 0.15	$ 0.12	$ 0.09
Including extraord. and discontinued items	$ 0.27	$ 0.20	$ 0.15	$ 0.12	$ 0.09
EPS (fully diluted)					
Exluding extraord. and discontinued items	$ 0.27	$ 0.20	$ 0.15	$ 0.12	$ 0.09
Including extraord. and discontinued items	$ 0.27	$ 0.20	$ 0.15	$ 0.12	$ 0.09
Dividends per share	$ 0.05	$ 0.02	$ 0.01	$ 0.01	$ 0.01
Comm. shares out (primary)	321.4	320.2	318.8	315.5	314.2
Comm. shares out (diluted)	321.4	320.2	NA	NA	NA
Supplementary items:					
Advertising expend.	NA	NA	NA	NA	NA
Amortization of intang.	0.0	0.0	0.0	0.0	0.0
Capital expenditures	113.6	107.6	91.1	42.8	46.8
Depletion expenses	0.0	0.0	0.0	0.0	0.0
Depreciation expenses	37.4	29.6	21.4	16.7	14.1
Excise taxes	0.0	0.0	0.0	0.0	0.0
Foreign currency adj.	NA	NA	NA	NA	NA
Interest exp. on LT debt	NA	NA	NA	NA	NA
Interest income	0.0	0.0	0.0	0.0	0.0
Labor expense	NA	NA	NA	NA	NA
Pension and retirement exp.	NA	NA	NA	NA	NA
Research & development	0.0	0.0	0.0	0.0	0.0
Unconsol. subsids. (EQ)	0.0	0.0	0.0	0.0	0.0

SOURCE: Lotus® One Source Databases Compustat Tapes.

EXHIBIT 12 Food Lion, Inc., Ratio Report

	FISCAL YEAR END									
	1987	1986	1985	1984	1983	1982	1981	1980	1979	1978
Sales performance:										
Dollars of sales	2,953.8	2,406.6	1,865.6	1,469.6	1,172.5	947.1	666.9	543.9	416.0	299.3
$ change from prior year	547.2	540.9	396.1	297.1	225.4	280.2	123.0	127.9	116.7	80.8
% change from prior year	22.74%	29.00%	26.95%	25.34%	23.80%	42.02%	22.61%	30.75%	39.00%	38.66%
Sales per employee (thous.)	109.27	115.31	109.17	114.95	116.44	109.19	108.05	112.88	101.29	88.49
Profitability performance										
Income before extraordinary items and discount. opns.	85.8	61.8	47.6	37.3	27.7	21.9	19.3	15.3	13.2	9.5
$ change from prior year	24.0	14.2	10.3	9.6	5.9	2.5	4.0	2.1	3.7	3.0
% change from prior year	38.79%	29.92%	27.56%	34.59%	26.83%	13.14%	26.36%	16.07%	38.94%	60.04%
Return on sales %	2.90%	2.57%	2.55%	2.54%	2.36%	2.31%	2.90%	2.81%	3.17%	3.17%
Return on equity %	28.41%	26.18%	25.67%	25.99%	25.03%	24.89%	28.07%	28.96%	33.12%	32.18%
Interest expense after tax	7.83	4.64	3.86	2.65	2.53	1.27	0.85	0.98	0.83	0.70
Minority interest	0.00	0.00	0.00	0.00	0.00	0.00	0.00	0.00	0.00	0.00
Return on assets %	12.16%	11.84%	12.35%	12.32%	11.38%	12.41%	15.72%	15.85%	17.80%	17.87%
Return on invested capital %	21.02%	19.89%	19.82%	19.40%	19.08%	20.79%	23.98%	23.79%	26.00%	27.31%
Gross profit to sales %	19.25%	19.02%	18.46%	17.88%	17.36%	16.92%	17.20%	16.87%	17.36%	17.13%
SG and A expense to sales %	12.41%	12.30%	12.14%	11.53%	11.47%	11.34%	10.47%	10.95%	10.69%	10.27%
Asset management:										
Sales to assets	3.67	3.98	4.24	4.44	4.28	4.45	4.78	5.11	4.81	4.55
Sales to current assets	6.65	7.73	8.45	8.25	8.63	8.99	10.13	12.30	11.08	10.55
Sales to net plant	8.16	8.20	8.52	9.60	8.48	8.80	9.07	8.74	8.50	7.99
Inventory turnover—COGS	6.19	7.53	7.85	8.83	8.19	8.77	10.30	12.25	11.69	11.43
Inventory turnover—Sales	7.67	9.30	9.62	10.75	9.91	10.56	12.44	14.74	14.15	13.79
Days COGS in inventory	58.95	48.48	46.52	41.33	44.55	41.60	35.44	29.79	31.22	31.94
Sales to accounts rec.	74.22	88.56	85.62	94.40	100.92	93.92	89.85	112.82	135.10	129.11
Average collection period	4.92	4.12	4.26	3.87	3.62	3.89	4.06	3.24	2.70	2.83
Financial management:										
Total liab. to equity	1.38	1.28	1.12	1.03	1.22	1.18	0.79	0.78	0.89	0.95
Total assets to equity	2.38	2.28	2.12	2.03	2.22	2.18	1.79	1.78	1.89	1.95
Current liabilities to equity	0.93	0.84	0.75	0.64	0.77	0.88	0.57	0.52	0.59	0.59
Long-term debt to equity	0.36	0.35	0.28	0.31	0.37	0.23	0.15	0.19	0.25	0.31
Sales to equity	8.71	9.09	9.00	8.99	9.48	9.68	8.57	9.10	9.09	8.86
Net plant to equity	1.07	1.11	1.06	0.94	1.12	1.10	0.94	1.04	1.07	1.11
Interest expense to sales %	0.47%	0.38%	0.39%	0.35%	0.39%	0.24%	0.23%	0.32%	0.36%	0.43%
Times interest earned	11.95	14.33	13.32	15.06	11.96	18.23	23.81	16.52	16.94	14.59
Liquidity management:										
Current ratio	1.41	1.40	1.43	1.70	1.43	1.22	1.48	1.41	1.40	1.42
Quick ratio	0.19	0.24	0.17	0.40	0.19	0.18	0.28	0.23	0.30	0.33
Sales to cash	190.15	109.27	694.58	60.14	227.57	196.90	155.30	294.79	91.14	NA
Capital expenditures $	105.84	104.20	68.16	41.56	55.50	45.67	19.02	19.50	16.03	12.11
Advertising expense to sales %	NA	NA	NA	NA	NA	NA	NA	NA	NA	NA
R&D cost to sales %	0.00	0.00	0.00	0.00	0.00	0.00	0.00	NA	NA	NA
Rental expense to sales %	1.31	1.18	1.02	0.92	0.90	0.90	0.86	0.69	0.64	NA

SOURCE: Lotus® One Source Databases Compustat Tapes.

NOTES

1. Richard Anderson, "That Roar You Hear Is Food Lion," *Business Week,* August 24, 1987, p. 66.

2. *Ibid.,* p. 66.

3. 1987 Food Lion, Inc., Annual Report, p. 1.

4. Richard DeSanta, "Formats: Growing Apart, Coming Together," *Progressive Grocer,* January 1987, p. 37.

5. Ketner Gives up Food Lion Reins," *Supermarket News,* January 6, 1987, p. 18.

6. Anderson, "That Roar You Hear Is Food Lion," p. 65.

7. 1986 Food Lion, Inc., Annual Report, p. 4.

8. "Retail Operations: The New Basics," *Progressive Grocer,* September 1987, p. 56.

9. David Rogers, "Hypermarkets Need Something Special to Succeed," *Supermarket Business.* May 1988, p. 26.

10. *Ibid.*

11. "Retail Operations," p. 62.

12. *Standard & Poor's Standard Stock Reports,* p. 1318.

13. *Value Line Investment Survey,* 1987, p. 1511.

14. *Ibid.,* p. 1511.

15. *Standard & Poor's,* p. 2491.

16. Winn-Dixie Strategy," *Supermarket News,* March 3, 1987, p. 12.

17. *Standard & Poor's,* p. 1387.

18. *Ibid.,* p. 3358M.

19. John Liscio, "Beefing up Profits," *Barron's,* May 25, 1987, p. 18.

20. 1987 Food Lion, Inc., Annual Report, p. 9.

21. *Ibid.,* p. 9.

22. "Beefing up Profits," p. 19.

23. "Food Lion's Roar Changes Marketplace," *Tampa Tribune,* April 5, 1988, p. 1.

24. "That Roar Your Hear Is Food Lion," p. 65.

25. "Food Lion, Inc.," *The Wall Street Transcript,* March 28, 1988, p. 88890.

26. "That Roar You Hear Is Food Lion," p. 65.

27. "Food Lion, Winn-Dixie in Animated Squabble," *Supermarket News,* September 14, 1987, p. 9.

28. "That Roar You Hear Is Food Lion," p. 66.

29. *Ibid.,* p. 65.

30. "Ad Series Heralds First Florida Food Lion," *Supermarket News.* March 2, 1987, p. 12.

31. 1986 Food Lion, Inc., Annual Report.

32. *Value Line Investment Survey,* August 28, 1987, p. 1501.

The Great Atlantic and Pacific Tea Company, Inc.

NEIL H. SNYDER • TINA ARNDT

HISTORY OF THE FIRM

The hundred-year war by unhappy competitors against the Great Atlantic and Pacific Tea Company's policy of "high quality and low price" began in 1869.[1] In the 1870s, A & P quickened their pace of opening retail stores by concentrating in the states least damaged by the Civil War. Their strategy was to use quality, price, and premiums to promote sales volume. The 1880s followed with continued rapid growth. This growth included product-line expansion and private-label enlargement.

The build-up of the A & P grocery chain began when the "Merchant Prince," John Hartford, decided to change the shape of the grocery industry by developing a network of small neighborhood stores that belonged to one corporation. To make the strategy attractive to consumers, he reduced prices, eliminated every unnecessary selling expense, including credit selling, home deliveries, telephone orders, stamps, premiums, and advertising, and he moved quickly to open new stores.[2] In the process, he encountered a problem that he had not fully appreciated when he undertook the growth strategy: finding enough well-qualified people to manage the new stores. To solve the problem, he adopted a policy of hiring outgoing and personable applicants and indoctrinating them with the A & P philosophy. To maintain a high degree of consistency among the new stores, he wrote a store managers' manual that detailed the importance of such things as cleanliness, correctly pricing each commodity display, and cash control procedure.

In addition, he offered career opportunities to immigrants and many first-generation Americans. Hartford believed that the success of the business rested on employee loyalty. To instill loyalty in his workers, he paid above-average wages to his people, and he offered generous pension benefits to retired employees.

In 1925, the strategy of achieving volume through low prices began to lose its effect, and it became increasingly difficult to maintain control over the rapidly growing grocery store chain.[3] Hartford's solution to this problem was to decentralize the operation into six operating divisions, but the solution was only temporary. The real problem, and the one that was not addressed, was that the "American consumer never fully believed the depth of the sincerity and urgency . . . attached to the A & P sales policy."[4] A & P entered the Great Depression without having solved this big problem, but the economic difficulties associated with the Depression gave rise to the concept of the modern supermarket, and low prices again became a competitive advantage.

The rapid growth of the supermarket concept in the United States increased concern about concentrated market power, and legislative restraints on chain store expansion became a distinct possibility. A & P moved quickly to respond to these issues and to head off the threat of litigation.

After World War II, antitrust legislation threatened the dissolution of the company, but by the end of 1950, the conversion from small service stores to supermarkets was virtually complete.[5] At this time, A & P's sales volume exceeded the combined sales of Safeway and Kroger, its two largest competitors.[6] However, the corporation was experiencing difficulties. "In a period of explosive national growth, A & P's development was severely curtailed by management policy that siphoned profits into dividends, had an obsessive passion against borrowing, and looked only to depreciation as the source of funds for capital development. Thus, in the four years ending in 1962, A & P development was limited to replacing an average of 205 obsolete stores per year and opening approximately 55 additional new stores per year. In a 4500 store chain, this amounted to 5 percent annual obsolescence replenishment and 1 percent new store increase."[7]

The firm's new strategy focused on "the abandonment of central corporate policy, (which) was the major contributor to A & P's failure in the 1960s."[8] A & P's market share continued to decline as competitors continued to open new, bigger, and better stores. The chain was forced to lay off employees. Customers complained that they were not finding adequate displays of fresh products, and A & P was losing money.

A PROGRESSION OF CEOs

In 1968, Mel Alldredge became chairman of the board. Along with his new management team he decentralized the corporation into 33 autonomous retail divisions. His strategy was to efficiently provide America with wholesome and nutritious foods at affordable prices. He attempted to do this with modernization, growth, and expansion. However, his plan did not work because it failed to keep up with what the competition was doing.

In 1971, William Kane became chairman of the board. Just two years later, in 1973, Gulf + Western approached A & P with a tender offer for 15 percent of the company's stock.[9] Although the management of A & P opposed the offer, it had an injurious effect on management morale, and as a result, A & P began to lose its sense of direction. In 1973, the board demanded that management bring in an outside consultant. However, the problems with management were not solved, and management's morale continued to be low. To make matters worse, the firm's ability to compete for market share deteriorated further as its competitors built more modern and efficient stores.

A & P's real problem can be attributed to its CEOs. The CEO's primary functions are to formulate strategies and policies, to communicate them in terms that are simple and easy to understand, and to establish priorities for implementing policies.[10] While A & P stood firmly by its low price strategy, consumers were demanding much more of them. They wanted a combination of service, quality, and selection in addition to reasonable prices.

To help them address these problems, the company brought in a consulting firm. The consultants outlined A & P's strengths, which included

- a well-established consumer franchise for the company and its private label,
- a strong balance sheet,
- an experienced and loyal corps of field and middle managers, and
- well-developed manufacturing and distribution capability.

The consultants also identified the firm's weaknesses, which included the following:

- The location of the company's market strength was in an unattractive market.
- The company's facilities, specifically its stores and warehouses, were undersized and poorly utilized.
- Personnel development and training had been neglected.
- A large proportion of the company's assets were committed to unprofitable areas in the heart of the chain's geography.[11]

In 1975, A & P brought in its first outside CEO on the recommendation of consultants to change the face of the company. Jonathan Scott, the new CEO, initiated a rebuilding program that included the establishment of a corporate real estate department that was to stake out choice locations for stores. In addition, he abandoned A & P's traditional policy of contracting mostly short-term leases.[12] Furthermore, Scott closed all of the firm's marginal and unprofitable stores, and he began a construction and refurbishing program that resulted in the opening of 91 new stores. During this time, the "Price and Pride" advertising campaign was introduced, the company changed its logo, and stores started staying open 24 hours.

This new rebuilding program resulted in dramatic changes. In 1976, A & P experienced record sales of $7.2 billion. This 10.7 percent increase was a strong rebound and morale booster. The changes that contributed to these results included

- decentralization of buying,
- an increase in the average size of A & P stores,

- the doubling of nonfood sales, and
- the new executive management team.[13]

But there were problems, too. The company's operations were not as steady as they should have been. A couple of strategy options were outlined in an attempt to keep A & P on track. These options included

- an attempt to resurrect the strategy upon which A & P was founded with a goal of having the lowest prices in the industry, and
- an effort to create a new and clearly defined corporate strategy by prioritizing the various elements that contribute to A & P's success (product selection, quality, price, store ambience, service, and special departments).[14]

Management did not have much opportunity to act on these options, because in 1978 the company's stock plunged. The Hartford Foundation, named for the original owners and the holders of the majority of A & P's stock, decided to sell their interest in the company that same year.[15] A & P started negotiations with Erivan Haub of the West German Tengelmann Group to buy shares. After he analyzed the firm's condition, Haub bought 42 percent of the stock for $79 million. Many knowledgeable people wondered about the soundness of this decision when in the first quarter, sales dropped 8 percent. Haub quickly invited A & P corporate officers to Germany for an orientation by Tengelmann, and he increased his ownership interest to 45 percent of the company.[16] In 1979, A & P lost $3.8 million on sales of $6.7 billion.[17]

A & P's problems were summed up nicely by William I. Walsh:

> Historically, the financial community has attributed A & P's decline to prolonged sales deterioration stemming from the failure of management to follow population movements out of the big cities and into the suburbs and the sunbelt area of America. In truth, A & P's deterioration can also be traced to management's failure to maintain effective cost controls. The higher cost resulting from this failure mandated the forfeiture of the noticeable "lower retail prices" which, over the years, had brought customers into A & P's smaller stores. Further, these higher costs, and resulting higher retails, were the primary cause of the general dismal performance of those new, larger stores which A & P did open in the suburbs, and this dismal record of performance, in turn, discouraged more widespread, aggressive development, and thus further aggravated the company's decline.[18]

JAMES WOOD TAKES OVER AS CEO

On April 29, 1980, A & P announced Scott's resignation, and James Wood, who was formerly the chairman and CEO of Grand Union, was elected by A & P's board of directors to replace Scott in both positions of chairman and CEO. Wood was acquired at a substantial cost to A & P. His five-year contract called for a yearly base salary of $400,000, plus a $300,000 bonus and an option on 200,000 shares, as well as 10 percent ownership if he chose to stay until 1985.[19]

Wood, a 51-year-old British national, had been described as a very likeable man who "exudes a high level of confidence."[20] After four consecutive poor quarters in 1980, the company, under Wood's plan of reorganization, was divided into ten geographic operating entities "directed toward achieving closer co-ordination and control."[21] His strategy was

1. to modernize stores in areas where it was known that A & P would be profitable and to spend heavily on the profitable Canadian subsidiary,

2. to fix up badly deteriorated stores in New York City and Chicago that previous management had written off,

3. to replace old stores with new ones in major markets within two years, and

4. to test a warehouse-type store in Chicago.[22]

However, the plan had problems because

- Wood had not made sufficient improvements in the firm's distribution system,
- few of the day-to-day operations people had been replaced, and
- a new store concept that was successful in Germany flopped in the U.S.[23]

All the while, Haub continued to buy more A & P shares and by February 1981, Tengelmann owned 50.3 percent of the firm's stock. This ownership interest now gave Haub the voting power he needed to do what he wanted with A & P.[24]

Between April 1981 and September 1982 A & P closed nearly 500 stores, eliminated all of the in-house manufacturing except coffee and baked goods, reduced the number of employees by 25 percent, obtained wage concessions from labor unions in contract negotiations, and cut overhead costs by 0.3 percent. In September 1982, new incentive programs were introduced for store managers, new store formats were tried, and there was a proposal to inject $200 million into the company by terminating its pension plan and recapturing the plan's surplus assets.[25]

This retirement plan proposal was passed by the board of directors, and, in response, the employees filed a class action lawsuit to prevent the diversion of plan assets.

A & P also obtained new wage contracts at lower rates in return for a complex set of allowances that essentially gave employees an opportunity to earn a percentage of sales, a participatory role in management, and an option to buy and operate Super Fresh (an A & P subsidiary) stores.[26]

A & P encountered another problem in 1982. The ratio of its debt to total capitalization rose to 74 percent. This highly leveraged position meant big risks, and the firm's total long-term debt was $128.4 million.[27]

In June 1983, Wood described the company's situation in the following way:

> We are today a company on the threshold of a new era. Our reduced size, lower cost structure and substantially improved financial condition now provide the opportunity for significant growth. Now that the turnaround has been accomplished, A & P is firmly committed to our most important goal, permanent profitability and a pattern of consistent growth, and progress toward these goals can be measured quantitatively by the basic yardsticks of earnings per share, and a share of the market.[28]

Wood went on to say that the corporate goals would be achieved "through close attention to the fundamentals of effective cost controls and dedication to development of retail operations that provide 'maximum customer service.'"[29]

Wood's statement indicated that once again there were significant changes in the company's corporate strategy. A & P was moving toward a policy of "cost control" and "maximum service" to achieve profitability and growth. Thus, it seemed that "quality," "low price," and "selection" were given lower priorities.[30]

In 1983, due to the substantial cuts introduced by Wood, A & P experienced its best year in net income since 1970. Placing greater emphasis on the sale of brand name merchandise along with the elimination of most of A & P's private labels brought about marked improvements in the firm's gross margin.[31]

Not only were operating costs cut across the board, but improvements were made in relations between A & P and its unions. The primary problem between labor and management was the high cost of labor, and A & P's labor costs were out of line with those of neighboring nonunion operations. Thus, A & P found that it was impossible to compete on a price/value basis.[32] The industry average of labor costs to total was between 9 percent and 10 percent. A & P's labor cost to total cost ratio rose to a high of 13 percent. Given the very narrow margins in the grocery industry, this difference was not acceptable and could not be allowed to continue.

The following information is from A & P's 1983 annual report.

EXHIBIT 1   Statement of Consolidated Operations
(Dollars in Thousands Except Per Share Figures)

	FISCAL 1983	FISCAL 1982	FISCAL 1981
Sales	$5,222,013	$4,607,817	$6,226,755
Cost of merchandise sold	4,041,033	3,575,901	4,903,227
Gross margin	1,180,980	1,031,916	1,323,528
Store operating, general, and administrative expense	1,038,476	914,404	1,251,584
Depreciation and amortization	54,205	49,870	67,411
Income from operations	88,299	67,642	4,533
Interest (expense) income:			
Interest expense	(30,809)	(30,132)	(35,596)
Interest income	6,461	7,551	6,430
Interest expense—net	(24,348)	(22,581)	(29,166)
Income (loss) before income taxes, revitalization program, and			
extraordinary credit	63,951	45,061	(24,633)
Anticipated cost of revitalization program	—	—	(200,000)
Income (loss) before income taxes and extraordinary credits	63,951	45,061	(224,633)
Provision for income taxes	(32,550)	(23,700)	(7,000)
Income (loss) before extraordinary credits	31,401	21,361	(231,633)
Extraordinary credit—tax loss carry-forward utilization	16,150	9,850	—
Extraordinary credit—pension	—	—	130,000
Net income (loss)	$ 47,551	$ 31,211	$ (101,633)
Per common share:			
Income (loss) before extraordinary credits	$ .84	$ .57	$ 6.19)
Extraordinary credit—tax loss carry-forward utilization	.43	.26	—
Extraordinary credit—pension	—	—	3.47
Net income (loss)	$ 1.27	$ .83	(2.72)

EXHIBIT 2   Statement of Consolidated Stockholders' Equity
(Dollars in Thousands)

	FISCAL 1983	FISCAL 1982	FISCAL 1981
Common stock:			
Balance forward	$ 37,405	$ 37,393	$ 37,393
Exercise of options	104	12	—
	$ 37,509	$ 37,405	$ 37,393

EXHIBIT 2	Continued	FISCAL **1983**	FISCAL 1982	FISCAL 1981
Capital surplus:				
Balance forward		$ **421,109**	$ 421,052	$ 421,052
Exercise of options		**606**	57	—
		$ **421,715**	$ 421,109	$ 421,052
Cumulative translation adjustment:				
Balance beginning of year		$ **(4,061)**	$ (4,218)	$ —
Exchange adjustment		**(1,844)**	157	—
		$ **(5,905)**	$ (4,061)	$ —
Retained earnings (deficit):				
Balance forward		$ **(125,081)**	$ (156,292)	$ (54,659)
Net income (loss)		**47,551**	31,211	(101,633)
		$ **(77,530)**	$ (125,081)	$ (156,292)

EXHIBIT 3	Consolidated Balance Sheet (Dollars in Thousands)	FEBRUARY 25, 1984	FEBRUARY 25, 1983
ASSETS			
Current assets:			
Cash and short-term investments		$ **65,195**	$ 98,449
Accounts receivable		**49,929**	58,094
Inventories		**494,034**	414,650
Properties held for sale		**38,153**	17,809
Prepaid expenses		**6,955**	3,799
Total current assets		**654,266**	592,801
Property:			
Land		**10,673**	10,443
Buildings		**41,087**	45,026
Equipment		**282,616**	244,850
Store fixtures and leasehold improvements		**181,314**	144,956
Total—at cost		**515,690**	445,275
Less accumulated depreciation and amortization		**(221,108)**	(199,940)
		294,582	245,335
Real property leased under capital leases		**110,955**	104,083
Property—net		**405,537**	349,418
Other assets (includes $130 million prepaid pension)		**140,125**	145,176
		$1,199,928	$1,087,395

EXHIBIT 3   Continued

	FEBRUARY 25, 1984	FEBRUARY 25, 1983

LIABILITIES AND STOCKHOLDERS' EQUITY

Current liabilities:

Current portion of long-term debt	$ 19,007	$ 11,859
Current portion of obligations under capital leases	12,562	10,679
Accounts payable	291,180	232,410
Accrued salaries, wages, and benefits	70,434	61,381
Accrued taxes	29,518	30,872
Current portion of closing reserves and other accruals	65,184	60,531
Total current liabilities	487,885	407,732
Long-term debt	106,152	116,557
Obligations under capital leases	153,031	143,160
Deferred income taxes	12,214	8,811
Closing reserves and other liabilities	64,857	81,763

Stockholders' equity:

Preferred stock—no par value; authorized—3,000,000 shares; issued—none

Common stock—$1 par value; authorized—80,000,000 shares; issued and outstanding 37,508,556 and 37,404,784 shares respectively

....	37,509	37,405
Capital surplus	421,715	421,109
Cumulative translation adjustment	(5,905)	(4,061)
Retained earnings (deficit)	(77,530)	(125,081)
Total stockholders' equity	375,789	329,372
	$1,199,928	$1,087,395

EXHIBIT 4   Statement of Changes in Consolidated Financial Position (Dollars in Thousands)

	FISCAL 1983	FISCAL 1982	FISCAL 1981

SOURCE OF FUNDS

From operations:

Income (loss) before extraordinary credit	$ 31,401	$ 21,361	$(231,633)
Expenses (income) not requiring (providing) working capital:			
Depreciation and amortization	45,579	41,642	56,599
Amortization of real property leased under capital leases	8,626	8,228	10,812
Charge in lieu of current U.S. income tax	16,150	9,850	—
Anticipated cost of revitalization program—net (non-current portion)	—	—	106,600
Deferred income taxes	3,403	4,394	489
Deferred investment tax credits	—	—	(143)
Working capital provided from operations before extraordinary credit	105,159	85,475	(57,276)
Extraordinary credit	16,150	9,850	130,000
Extraordinary credit not providing working capital	(16,150)	(9,850)	(130,000)
Total working capital provided from operations	105,159	85,475	(57,276)

EXHIBIT 4	Continued			
		FISCAL 1983	FISCAL 1982	FISCAL 1981

SOURCE OF FUNDS (Continued)

	FISCAL 1983	FISCAL 1982	FISCAL 1981
Disposition of property	2,243	5,875	17,496
Transfer of property to current portion of closing reserves	2,196	15,900	49,001
Obligations under capital leases	3,185	(4,508)	(9,812)
Decrease in property leased under capital leases due to store closings and terminations	3,497	964	29,204
Decrease in property due to foreign currency translation	756	3,980	—
Proceeds from borrowings	—	—	14,144
Decrease in non-current notes receivable	2,225	(2,908)	(959)
Other	8,328	7,578	2,420
Total	127,589	112,356	44,218

DISPOSITION OF FUNDS

	FISCAL 1983	FISCAL 1982	FISCAL 1981
Acquisition of Kohl's (excludes working capital acquired)	21,019	—	—
Expenditures for property	72,564	33,128	68,406
Property leased under capital leases	10,007	5,787	654
Decrease in obligations under capital leases due to store closings and terminations	5,616	6,307	38,830
Decrease in cumulative translation adjustment	1,844	4,061	—
Current maturities and repayment of long-term debt	11,741	11,859	15,760
Transfer of non-current reserves to current liabilities	23,486	41,907	4,598
Total	146,277	103,049	128,248
Increase (decrease) in working capital	(18,688)	9,307	(84,030)
Working capital—beginning of year	185,069	175,762	259,792
Working capital—end of year	$166,381	$185,069	$ 175,762

INCREASE (DECREASE) IN COMPONENTS OF WORKING CAPITAL

	FISCAL 1983	FISCAL 1982	FISCAL 1981
Cash and short-term investments	$(33,254)	$ 42,811	$ (52,050)
Accounts receivable	(8,165)	9,028	3,711
Inventories	79,384	(63,453)	(109,388)
Properties held for sale	20,344	(180)	(16,096)
Prepaid expenses	3,156	(3,532)	(100)
	61,465	(15,326)	(173,923)
Accounts payable	58,770	(36,077)	(62,896)
Current portion of long-term debt	7,148	10,042	80
Current portion of obligations under capital leases	1,883	(483)	(1,689)
Accrued expenses	7,699	(117)	(23,059)
Current portion of closing reserves and other accruals	4,653	2,002	(2,329)
	80,153	(24,633)	(89,893)
INCREASE (DECREASE) IN WORKING CAPITAL	$(18,688)	$ 9,307	$ (84,030)

Notes to Consolidated Financial Statements

SUMMARY OF SIGNIFICANT ACCOUNTING POLICIES

Fiscal Year—The Company's fiscal year ends on the last Saturday in February. Fiscal 1983 ended February 25, 1984, fiscal 1982 ended February 26, 1983, and fiscal 1981 ended February 27, 1982, each comprising 52 weeks.

Common Stock—As of February 25, 1984, the principal stockholder of the Company, Tengelmann Warenhandelsgesellschaft ("Tengelmann") owned 50.7% of the Company's common stock.

Principles of Consolidation—The consolidated financial statements include the accounts of the Company and its subsidiaries, all of which are wholly-owned.

Foreign Operations—In fiscal 1982, the Company elected to adopt the principles of Financial Accounting Standards Board Statement No. 52, "Foreign Currency Translation." Assets and liabilities of foreign subsidiaries as of February 25, 1984 and February 26, 1983 have been translated at year-end rates. Fiscal 1983 and 1982 income and expense accounts have been translated at average rates prevailing during the year.

Inventories—Inventories are valued at the lower of cost or market, with cost being determined on the following bases: inventories in stores—average cost under the retail method; other inventories, primarily in warehouses and food processing facilities—cost on a first-in, first-out basis.

Properties—The Company leases a substantial portion of its facilities and a majority of store leases are considered to be operating leases.

Owned land and buildings generally consist of stores, food processing facilities, and warehouses. Equipment, store fixtures, and leasehold improvements, generally, are owned, although the Company has equipment leasing programs for store equipment and trucks, most of which are accounted for as capital leases. Properties designated for sale and leaseback have been classified as current assets.

For financial reporting purposes, depreciation and amortization are provided, generally on the straight line method, over the estimated useful lives of the respective assets. Buildings are depreciated based on lives varying from twenty to fifty years and equipment based on lives varying from three to twelve years. Equipment and real property leased under capital leases are amortized over the lives of the respective leases.

Pre-opening Costs—Costs incurred in the opening of new stores are expensed in the quarter in which the store is opened.

Closed Facilities—The Company provides for the estimated loss on the disposition of leased or owned facilities in the period in which the decision to close the facility is made. For significant closing programs, provisions are established for estimated closing and other related costs. The sales for those stores included in such significant closing programs are excluded from the statement of consolidated operations from the effective dates of inclusion in the programs.

Income Taxes—The Company's policy is to provide deferred taxes in recognition of timing differences between income for financial reporting and income tax purposes. However, due to the Company's U.S. tax loss carry-forward position, no deferred U.S. taxes have been provided on the differences between financial and taxable income.

Retirement Plans—Annual costs of the Companies' pension plans consist of normal cost, amortization over 40 years of unfunded prior service cost as of January 1, 1976, amortization over 30 years of changes in the unfunded actuarial liability resulting from plan amendments and changes in actuarial assumptions and amortization over 15 years of annual actuarial gains or losses. Annual costs under union/management administered plans are expensed as provided for in the respective collective bargaining agreements.

Compensated Absences—The Company accrues for vested and non-vested vacation pay. Liabilities for compensated absences of $35.7 million and $30.9 million for 1983 and 1982, respectively, are included in the balance sheet caption "Accrued salaries, wages and benefits."

Earnings Per Share—Net income (loss) per share is based on the weighted average number of common shares outstanding during the respective fiscal years. Stock options outstanding (common stock equivalents) had no material effect and, therefore, were excluded from the computation of net income (loss) per share.

OPERATIONS IN GEOGRAPHIC AREAS

The Company has been engaged in the retail food business since 1859 and currently does business under the names A&P, Super Fresh Food Markets, Family Mart, Super Plus, Kohl's, and Compass Foods. Sales and revenues in the table below reflect sales to unaffiliated customers in the United States and foreign countries (principally Canada).

(DOLLARS IN THOUSANDS)	FISCAL 1983	FISCAL 1982	FISCAL 1981
Sales			
Domestic	$4,328,059	$3,841,218	$5,558,384
Foreign	893,954	766,599	668,371
Total	$5,222,013	$4,607,817	$6,226,755
Income (loss) from operations			
Domestic	$ 63,536	$ 47,063	$ (11,057)
Foreign	24,763	20,579	15,590
Total	$ 88,299	$ 67,642	$ 4,533
Assets			
Domestic	$1,008,604	$ 938,813	$1,023,971
Foreign	191,324	148,582	117,708
Total	$1,199,928	$1,087,395	$1,141,679

INDEBTEDNESS

During fiscal 1983, the Company entered into a $100 million seven-year Credit Agreement with various banks. The Agreement allows the Company to borrow amounts up to $100 million on a revolving basis, until September 1, 1986. At the end of that period, the Company has the right to convert any amount up to $100 million into a four-year term loan which amortizes equally in semi-annual installments. There were no borrowings under this Credit Agreement during fiscal 1983. The Company has an additional $47 million in formal lines of credit with banks. There were no borrowings made under these lines during fiscal 1983, 1982, or 1981.

Long-term debt (exclusive of current maturities) consists of:

(DOLLARS IN THOUSANDS)	FEBRUARY 25, 1984	FEBRUARY 26, 1983
9½% Senior Notes, due in annual installments of $10,000 through October 1, 1992	$ 80,000	$ 90,000
9⅞% Mortgage Notes, due in monthly installments of $83 through September 29, 1997	12,667	13,667
Other notes, interest rates of ⅞% to 15¾% due 1985 to 2002	13,485	12,890
	$106,152	$116,557

The Company's loan agreements contain, among other things, certain restrictive provisions including restrictions on the payment of cash dividends, the maintenance of working capital and limitations on the incurrence of additional indebtedness and lease commitments. Under one agreement, the Company is prohibited from declaring or paying dividends (other than stock dividends) on its common stock. Under that agreement, as of February 25, 1984, the Company would have had to have additional Consolidated Net Earnings (as defined) in excess of $105 million in order to declare any dividends on its outstanding common stock, in which event, the payment would be limited to 75% of such excess.

Maturities of long-term debt during each of the next five fiscal years are 1984–$19,007,000; 1985–$11,856,000; 1986–$11,658,000; 1987–$11,679,000; 1988–$11,727,000.

The maturities of long-term debt in 1984 and the current portion of long-term debt in the accompanying balance sheet include $6.7 million of mortgage debt due after 1984 which related to properties held for sale which are expected to be sold during the current fiscal year.

CLOSING FACILITIES

During 1981, the Board of Directors approved the development and implementation of a comprehensive revitalization program involving the sale or disposition of a significant number of unprofitable and marginal stores, certain food processing plants, and related support facilities. In the fourth quarter of fiscal 1981, the Company provided $200 million for the current and estimated future expenses related to this program. The provision included losses from operations from the decision date to date of closings, estimated loss on the disposal of equipment and leases, employee severance payments, and other related costs. The revitalization program has been substantially completed and the total of the costs incurred with the estimated remaining costs approximates the amount initially provided.

Included in accounts receivable are notes receivable to $1.6 million at February 25, 1984 and $12.7 million at February 26, 1983 at interest rates ranging from 5% to 17%, principally relating to the sale of closed facilities.

Activity related to reserves provided for closing of facilities including prior programs is shown below.

(DOLLARS IN THOUSANDS)	FISCAL 1983	FISCAL 1982	FISCAL 1981
Balance forward	$44,248	$85,123	$15,453
Anticipated cost of revitalization program	—	—	200,000
Charges—Net	(23,486)	(40,875)	(130,330)
	$20,762	$44,248	$85,123

Included in the above tables are fixed assets which have been transferred to current and non-current liabilities for balance sheet presentation in 1983 and 1982. "Closing reserves and other liabilities" include $16.2 million and $39.7 million at February 25, 1984 and February 26, 1983, respectively, which represents the non-current portion of closing reserves.

ACQUISITION

On October 1, 1983, the Company acquired the net assets of Kohl's Food Stores ("Kohl's"), a Division of Brown and Williamson Tobacco Corporation, from BATUS Inc. for $31.2 million in cash. Kohl's is a Milwaukee based supermarket chain operating 75 stores. The acquisition has been accounted for as a purchase and, accordingly, the results of operations of Kohl's are included in the Statement of Consolidated Operations from the date of acquisition. The excess of the fair value of net assets acquired over the purchase price has been applied as a reduction of the value of property acquired. Pro forma information has been omitted as such information would not be materially affected by the results of Kohl's prior to the date of acquisition.

LITIGATION

In the 1974 Annual Report, the Company reported on an antitrust judgment entered in favor of a Mr. Bray and five other cattle producers or feeders in the amount of $35.8 million plus interest. The Company settled this action in 1975 (for payments ending in 1980 having a present value of about $7 million, which was charged to operations in fiscal 1975) and the judgment was vacated and the action dismissed.

During 1975, 1976, 1977 and 1981, seventeen similar antitrust actions alleging violations of sections of the Sherman Act were filed in several states, and all of these were considered for pretrial purposes in the Dallas Federal Court. One of the actions was purportedly brought on behalf of a class consisting of all persons who are engaged in the business of raising fat cattle who have not otherwise filed claims and who sold more than 100 head of cattle per year. Each of these suits names the Company and other retail food chains as defendants and asks damages and other relief, which may include an injunction.

On June 14, 1982, the District Judge hearing the federal court actions entered a judgment dismissing the substantial damage claims of the complaints on the ground that plaintiffs had not sold directly to the retail food chain defendants, following Illinois Brick Co. v. the State of Illinois, 431 US 720 (1977). The District Judge's decision was affirmed on appeal by the Fifth Circuit Court of Appeals on July 25, 1983. The U.S. Supreme Court denied review of the Fifth Circuit Court's decision on February 21, 1984. Requests for an injunction and other relief remain pending in these actions.

The Company denies all allegations of wrongdoing in the above-mentioned actions. No provision for possible liability has been made in the accompanying financial statements.

On October 30, 1981, as a result of the Company's announced intention to terminate its existing retirement plan ("Plan") and substitute a new plan therefor, suit was brought in Newark, New Jersey Federal Court by a former executive, on behalf of himself and on behalf of a class of Plan participants, against the Company, its directors, its principal shareholders, and others. The complaint alleged that the proposed recapture by the Company of approximately $200 million in surplus Plan assets was improper under applicable law and sought both to prevent distribution of the assets to the Company and to require distribution to the Plan participants. An agreement in principle to settle such suit was reached in April 1982, pursuant to which Plan benefits to participants will be increased at a cost of $50 million. A judgment approving the settlement was entered by the Court on March 18, 1983, and the judgment was affirmed by the Third Circuit Court of Appeals on December 29, 1983.

In December 1981, as the result of a charge filed on October 18, 1974, the Equal Employment Opportunity Commission ("Commission") filed suit in Philadelphia Federal Court alleging that the Company, several international unions, and certain of their locals have violated the Civil Rights Act of 1964, as amended, by engaging in patterns and practices of employment discrimination. In such suit the Commission seeks to enjoin the defendants from the alleged discrimination in hiring, promotion, and other employment practices and require remedial measures, detailed implemental procedures, and payments to alleged victims of discrimination. On May 16, 1983, the district court granted summary judgment in the Company's favor. The decision is on appeal to the Third Circuit Court of Appeals.

The Company is also involved in various other claims, administrative agency proceedings, and other lawsuits arising out of the normal conduct of its business.

Although the ultimate outcome of the legal proceedings cannot be predicted, the Company's present opinion is that any resulting liability will not have a material effect upon the Company's financial position.

LEASE OBLIGATIONS

The Company operates primarily in leased facilities. Lease terms generally range up to twenty-five years for store leases and thirty years for other leased facilities, with options to renew for additional periods. The majority of the leases contain escalation clauses relating to real estate tax increases, and certain of the store leases provide for increases in rentals when sales exceed specified levels. In addition, the Company leases some store equipment and trucks because of financial and tax considerations.

The Company accounts for leases in accordance with Statement No. 13 of the Financial Accounting Standards Board. Accordingly, the consolidated balance sheet includes:

(DOLLARS IN THOUSANDS)	FEBRUARY 25, 1984	FEBRUARY 26, 1983
Real property leased under capital leases	$186,976	$170,756
Equipment leased under capital leases	40,960	36,742
....	227,936	207,498
Accumulated amortization	99,136	85,890
....	$128,800	$121,608

The value of equipment leased under capital leases is included with owned equipment in the accompanying balance sheet.

The assets and obligations for stores leased under capital leases which are closed prior to lease expiration are eliminated from the accounts as of the date of the decision to close and an accrual is provided for anticipated costs to be incurred upon the ultimate disposition of the facility.

Rent expense for operating leases consists of:

(DOLLARS IN THOUSANDS)	1983	1982	1981
Minimum rentals	$43,440	$39,528	$64,651
Contingent rentals	4,629	2,694	4,046
....	$48,069	$42,222	$68,697

The minimum annual rentals for leases in effect at February 25, 1984 are shown in the table below. All amounts are exclusive of lease obligations and sublease rentals applicable to facilities provided for in the Company's revitalization program and other closing programs.

Minimum Annual Rentals

(DOLLARS IN THOUSANDS) FISCAL	EQUIPMENT	CAPITAL LEASES REAL PROPERTY	OPERATING LEASES
1984	$ 7,709	$ 23,213	$ 45,674
1985	6,784	22,809	42,558
1986	4,346	22,275	38,348
1987	2,993	21,720	34,383
1988	2,722	21,444	31,326
1989 and thereafter	510	191,783	211,435
	25,064	303,244	$403,724
Less executory costs	—	(9,587)	
Net minimum rentals	25,064	293,657	
Less interest portion	(6,283)	(146,845)	
Present value of net minimum rentals	$18,781	$146,812	

STOCK OPTIONS

The Company has a stock option plan, approved by the stockholders in June 1975, and since amended under which officers and key employees may be granted statutory incentive stock options (pursuant to section 422A of the Internal Revenue Code) and non-statutory options to purchase not more than 1,500,000 shares of common stock at not less than the fair market value at grant dates. At February 25, 1984, there were 394,650 shares available for future option grants and 398,400 were available at February 26, 1983. Of the stock options outstanding at February 25, 1984, 225,923 shares were exercisable at the date of grant and 762,055 at cumulative 25% increments after each of the first through fourth anniversaries of the grants. A summary of option transactions is shown in the table below.

	INCENTIVE OPTIONS	NON-QUALIFIED OPTIONS	OPTION PRICE PER SHARE	TOTAL OPTION PRICE
Outstanding, February 27, 1982	—	848,000	$ 4.94 to $12.44	$5,982,000
Fiscal 1982:				
Transfers	304,004	(304,004)	—	—
Granted	394,540	20,460	5.50 to 8.94	2,400,000
Canceled or expired	—	(163,000)	5.75 to 12.44	(1,530,000)
Exercised	—	(12,000)	4.94 to 5.88	(69,000)
Outstanding, February 26, 1983	698,544	389,456	4.94 to 12.06	6,783,000

	INCENTIVE OPTIONS	NON-QUALIFIED OPTIONS	OPTION PRICE PER SHARE	TOTAL OPTION PRICE
Fiscal 1983				
Granted	76,803	23,197	11.44 to 12.88	1,223,000
Canceled or expired	(67,803)	(28,447)	5.50 to 12,96	(692,000)
Exercised	(79,272)	(24,500)	5.19 to 11.69	(710,000)
Outstanding, February 25, 1984	628,272	359,706	$ 4.94 to $12.88	$6,604,000
Shares becoming exercisable in:				
Fiscal 1982	56,169	17,706	$ 5.63 to $ 8.19	$ 436,000
Fiscal 1983	161,290	11,834	$ 5.50 to $ 8.94	$ 999,000
Shares exercisable:				
February 26, 1983	102,125	349,875		
February 25, 1984	187,018	307,709		

In September 1983, the Board of Directors amended the 1975 Stock Option Plan, subject to shareholders' approval, to provide for granting of stock appreciation rights ("SAR's"). SAR's may be granted with respect to some or all of the shares granted under a new non-statutory or statutory incentive stock option (pursuant to section 422A of the Internal Revenue Code) or an existing non-statutory stock option. A SAR allows the optionee, in lieu of exercising his option, to receive at the discretion of the stock option committee, shares of common stock, cash, or a combination of shares and cash having a fair market value on the date of exercise equal to the excess of the fair market value on the date of exercise of one share of common stock over the option price per share under the related option. Recipients and terms of individual grants are determined by a committee selected by the Board of Directors. As of April 10, 1984 SAR's have been granted for 286,847 shares at $4.94–$12.57 per share (market value of stock options at grant date).

INCOME TAXES

The provision for income taxes consists of the following:

(DOLLARS IN THOUSANDS)	FISCAL 1983	FISCAL 1982	FISCAL 1981
Current:			
Federal	$16,150	$ 9,850	$ —
Canadian..................................	11,895	8,197	6,111
State and local	1,102	1,259	543
Amortization of investment tax credits	—	—	(143)
	29,147	19,306	6,511
Deferred—Canadian.........................	3,403	4,394	489
	$32,550	$23,700	$7,000

The anticipated cost of the closing programs is deductible for income tax purposes only as costs actually are incurred. The realization of the entire potential tax benefit of such costs is not considered assured beyond a reasonable doubt because of the Company's existing tax loss carry-forward.

The deferred Canadian provisions result from the excess of depreciation deductions of a Canadian subsidiary for tax purposes over amounts recorded for financial statement purposes, and a provision for tax on current undistributed earnings of Canadian subsidiaries. Approximately $7 million of deferred income taxes have not been provided on undistributed earnings of foreign subsidiaries considered to be permanently invested. Approximately $49.5 million of retained earnings of the Company's Canadian subsidiaries can be remitted without an additional tax provision.

Investment tax credits, previously utilized for tax purposes, were deferred and amortized over the estimated useful lives of the related assets ending in fiscal 1981.

At February 25, 1984, the Company had a U.S. operating loss carry-forward, for financial statement purposes, of approximately $260 million, which arose principally from provisions for closing of facilities made in fiscal 1974, 1978, and 1981.

For tax purposes, the Company's operating loss carry-forward as of February 25, 1984 is approximately $292 million which expires starting in fiscal 1990 through fiscal 1998. The principal differences between the carry-forward for financial statement and tax purposes is due to timing differences, particularly costs relating to closed facilities and the 1981 extraordinary credit—pension. In addition, the Company has unused investment tax credits of approximately $40 million. These unused credits, which have not been recognized for financial statement purposes, will expire during fiscal years 1988 through 1998.

During fiscal 1981, the Company entered into an agreement, the substance of which was solely to sell the tax benefits—investment tax credits and accelerated depreciation associated with $11.9 million of certain machinery and equipment placed in service after January 1, 1981, under the Safe Harbor Clause of the Economic Recovery Tax Act of 1981. An amount proportionate to the benefits derived from continuing operations has been recognized as income in the consolidated statement of operations in fiscal 1982 and 1981.

The difference between the Company's effective tax rate and the U.S. and Canadian statutory rate is attributable to the fact that no U.S. tax provision was required for fiscal 1981 due to the U.S. operating losses, a lower statutory rate for a Canadian non-resident subsidiary, the effective rates of state and local income taxes and unrealized foreign exchange translation gains and losses.

RETIREMENT PLANS

The Company provides retirement benefits for substantially all non-union and some union employees under the Company Retirement Plans. Most other full-time and certain part-time employees are covered by industry plans administered jointly by management and union representatives. The cost of all retirement plans amounted to $18.2, $17.5, and $25.8 million in fiscal 1983, 1982 and 1981, respectively.

A comparison of accumulated plan benefits and plan net assets for the Company's plans is as follows:

(DOLLARS IN THOUSANDS)	DECEMBER 31, 1983	1982
Actuarial present value of accumulated plan benefits:		
Vested	$ 21,235	$ 9,153
Non-vested	7,303	5,035
	$ 28,538	$ 14,188
Net assets available for benefits	$380,029	$329,912

The weighted average rate of return used in determining the actuarial present value of accumulated plan benefits was 9.5 and 10.0 percent in fiscal 1983 and 1982 respectively. The assumed rate of return used was that published by the Pension Benefit Guaranty Corporation, an agency of the U.S. Government, for the applicable valuation date.

During 1981, the Company announced, as part of a comprehensive revitalization program, that it intended to terminate the Company Employees' Retirement Plan and to establish a new, more flexible and attractive plan. The termination would enable the Company to utilize a surplus that has developed in the Plan as a result of overfunding. On October 30, 1981, a former executive of the Company filed a class action suit to prevent distribution to the Company of the surplus. On April 5, 1982, a preliminary settlement agreement allowing the Company to terminate the Plan was reached. The agreement was upheld in Federal Court and entered as a final judgment on March 18, 1983 and affirmed by the Third Circuit Court of Appeals on December 29, 1983. Based on no further appeal and the appropriate regulatory approvals, the Company anticipates the termination of the Plan to occur in fiscal 1984 at which time a new plan will be implemented.

An extraordinary credit of $130 million was recorded in fiscal 1981 which represents the present value of the future economic benefit attributable to the purchase of annuities for pension plan participants in anticipation of the termination of the Plan.

The Company's Canadian pension plans are not required to report to U.S. governmental agencies pursuant to ERISA and do not otherwise determine the actuarial value of accumulated benefits or net assets available for benefits as calculated and disclosed above. For those plans, the actuarially computed value of vested benefits as of December 31, 1983 and 1982 was exceeded by the total of those plans' assets and balance sheet accruals.

The Company could, under certain circumstances, be liable for substantial unfunded vested benefits or other costs of jointly administered union/management plans.

THE EFFECTS OF CHANGING PRICES (UNAUDITED)

Basis of Preparation

The supplementary financial data presented in the tables below disclose estimated effects of inflation on certain historical financial data as required by Statement No. 33 of the Financial Accounting Standards Board (FASB No. 33), Financial Reporting and Changing Prices. The Company's primary financial statements are presented on an historical cost basis, that is, on a basis of the prices in effect when the transactions occurred. The data that follow attempt to adjust the historical amounts for the effects of inflation. The required disclosures are experimental in nature and two separate approaches to presenting the data are mandated, as follows:

The Constant Dollar basis presents historical cost information adjusted for changes in the general purchasing power of the dollar. The Consumer Price Index for All Urban Consumers (CPI-U), prepared by the U.S. Department of Labor, is used to measure the effects of general inflation. These constant dollar basis disclosures do not purport to represent appraisal values, replacement costs, or any other measures of current values.

The Current Cost basis reflects historical cost information adjusted to show the estimated current costs of inventory and property, plant and equipment which have generally increased over time at a rate different from that of the Consumer Price Index. Because of the rapid turnover of inventories, the carrying value of inventories is assumed to approximate current cost; therefore, cost of merchandise sold reflects approximate current cost at time of sale.

The current cost calculations for acquiring the same service potential as the Company's owned assets involve a number of judgments as well as the use of estimating techniques employed to limit the cost of accumulating the data. The data reported should not be thought of as precise measurements of the assets and expenses involved, but instead approximations of the price changes that have occurred in the Company's operating environment.

The current cost of stores operating under capital leases and store equipment was estimated using the unit pricing method. The current costs of all other fixed assets were estimated using the indexing method. Current cost depreciation is based on the average current cost of property and equipment during the year. Depreciation expense was computed by applying the ratio of historical cost depreciation expense to the current cost of these assets.

FASB No. 33 requires that income taxes not be adjusted for the effects of general inflation and specific prices and also requires adjustment of inventories but not the related accounts payable amounts in determining cost of merchandise sold in the constant dollar calculations.

EXHIBIT 5   **Statement of Income (Loss) Continuing Operations Adjusted for Changing Prices**

AT FEBRUARY 25, 1984 (DOLLARS IN THOUSANDS)	HISTORICAL FINANCIAL STATEMENTS	ADJUSTED FOR GENERAL INFLATION (CONSTANT $)	ADJUSTED FOR SPECIFIC PRICES (CURRENT COST)
Statement of Consolidated Operations			
Sales	$5,222,013	$5,222,013	$5,222,013
Cost and expenses:			
Cost of merchandise sold	4,041,033	4,061,186	4,041,033
Depreciation and amortization......................	54,205	90,535	94,435
Other costs...	1,062,824	1,062,824	1,062,824
Total cost and expenses	5,158,062	5,214,545	5,198,292
Income before income taxes	63,951	7,468	23,721
Net income (loss)	47,551	(8,932)	7,321
Changes in carrying values			
Gain (loss) from decline in the purchasing power of net amounts owed		20,756	20,756
Increase in current cost of inventories and property, plant, and equipment...........................			51,406
Less effect of increase in general price level			28,244
Excess of increases in specific prices over increase in the general price level.........................			23,162

EXHIBIT 6   **Property, Plant and Equipment—Adjusted for Changes in Specific Prices**

AT FEBRUARY 25, 1984 (DOLLARS IN THOUSANDS)	AS REPORTED	AS ADJUSTED
Property, plant, and equipment—net	$405,537	$665,176

EXHIBIT 7	**Five-Year Comparison of Selected Supplementary Financial Data Adjusted for Effects of Changing Prices**

	(DOLLARS IN THOUSANDS, EXCEPT PER SHARE FIGURES—IN AVERAGE 1983 CONSTANT DOLLARS)				
FOR THE FISCAL YEAR	**1983**	1982	1981	1980	1979
Sales...................................	**$5,222,013**	$4,759,875	$6,780,936	$8,359,477	$9,037,010
Historical cost information adjusted for general inflation:					
Net income (loss)....................	**(8,932)**	(13,474)	(187,602)	(170,041)	(143,708)
Net income (loss) per common share	**(.24)**	(.36)	(5.02)	(5.34)	(5.77)
Net assets at year end	**593,901**	569,992	583,377	838,610	872,597
Historical cost information adjusted for specific prices:					
Net income (loss)....................	**7,321**	(32,923)	(203,218)	(120,051)	(62,894)
Net income (loss) per common share	**.20**	(.88)	(5.43)	(3.77)	(2.53)
Excess of increases in specific prices over increases in the general price level	**23,162**	4,298	13,517	57,395	(96,362)
Net assets at year end	**622,786**	597,142	654,091	955,339	1,058,025
Other information:					
Purchasing power gain on net amounts owed	**20,756**	18,129	54,416	85,484	116,634
Market price per common share at year end	**$11.76**	$10.51	$5.04	$6.87	$9.71
Average consumer price index.......	**300.5**	290.8	275.9	251.3	222.2

Management Overview

The effect of inflation on the Company's financial results is significant as it relates to inventory, the historical cost of property, plant and equipment (including real property and equipment leased under capital leases), and the related depreciation and amortization expense. Because property, plant, and equipment are purchased over an extended period of time, ongoing replacement of existing facilities would be at a much greater cost than that reflected on the balance sheet in historical dollars. Also, depreciation and amortization expense, as reflected in the Company's primary financial statements, includes a ratable portion of those historical dollar costs of property, plant, and equipment against sales, which are stated in current dollars. The difference between the Statement of Income (Loss) from Continuing Operations Adjusted for Changing Prices and the primary financial statements is due to the effect of adjusting inventory balances and related cost of merchandise sold and the increase in depreciation and amortization expense to reflect average fiscal 1983 dollars and specific prices.

The management of the Company cautions that the data presented reflect the effects of the overall inflation rate as measured by the CPI-U and specific prices. Such data are not necessarily indicative of the impact of inflation on the Company's operations. No attempt has been made to calculate the benefit derived from potential price increases to offset higher depreciation and amortization costs, nor does such data reflect economies, such as sales and labor productivity and more efficient use of energy, which normally accompany the investment in new productive capacity or the fact that certain square footage may not be replaced. Also, the effect of inflation on accounts payable in the constant dollar calculation is not considered. Additionally, no attempt has been made to determine the effect of inflation on the Company's operating leases.

EXHIBIT 8

Five-Year Summary of Selected Financial Data
(Dollars in Thousands Except Per Share Figures)

FOR THE FISCAL YEAR	1983	1982	1981	1980	1979
Operating results					
Sales	$5,222,013	$4,607,817	$6,226,755	$6,989,529	$6,684,179
Income (loss) before extraordinary					
credit...........................	31,401	21,361	(231,633)	(43,049)	(3,807)
Net income (loss)	47,551	31,211	(101,633)	(43,049)	(3,807)
Per share results (a)					
Income (loss) before extraordinary					
credit...........................	.84	.57	(6.19)	(1.35)	(.15)
Net income (loss)	1.27	.83	(2.72)	(1.35)	(.15)
Financial position					
Current assets	654,266	592,801	608,127	782,050	696,057
Current liabilities	487,885	407,732	432,365	522,258	465,571
Working capital	166,381	185,069	175,762	259,792	230,486
Current ratio.....................	1.34	1.45	1.41	1.50	1.50
Total assets	1,199,928	1,087,395	1,141,679	1,308,983	1,230,522
Loss-term debt—less current					
maturities	106,152	116,557	128,416	130,032	130,681
Capital lease obligations—long-					
term...........................	153,031	143,160	153,975	202,617	202,200
Equity					
Stockholders' equity	375,789	329,372	302,153	403,786	390,584
Dividends per share..............	—	—	—	—	—
Book value per share (a)	10.03	8.81	8.08	12.68	15.69
Weighted average shares					
outstanding....................	37,455,944	37,398,884	37,392,784	31,833,356	24,892,137
Number of stockholders	27,289	29,312	31,311	33,404	34,704
Other					
Number of employees.............	53,000	40,000	45,000	60,000	63,000
Number of stores at year end	1,022	1,016	1,055	1,543	1,542
Total store area (square feet)	23,276,000	22,601,000	23,742,000	33,052,000	33,057,000

(a) Based on the weighted average number of common shares outstanding each year.
(b) 53 weeks; all other years contained 52 weeks.

NOTES

1. From *The Rise and Decline of The Great Atlantic and Pacific Tea Company* by William I. Walsh. Copyright © 1986 by William I. Walsh. Reprinted by arrangement with Carol Publishing Group. A Lyle Stuart Book.

2. *Ibid.*, p. 26.

3. *Ibid.*, p. 34.

4. *Ibid.*, p. 38.

5. *Ibid.*, p. 67.

6. *Ibid.*, p. 69.

7. *Ibid.*, p. 90.

8. *Ibid.*, p. 114.

9. *Ibid.*, p. 150.

10. *Ibid.*, p. 161.

11. *Ibid.*, p. 168.

12. *Ibid.*, p. 172.

13. *Ibid.*, p. 179.

14. *Ibid.*, p. 189.

15. *Ibid.*, p. 192.

16. *Ibid.*, p. 196.

17. Holly Hokis, "A & P's Wood: Still Intrigued by the Challenge," *Chain Store Age Executive* 63, June 1987, p. 19.

18. Walsh, p. 202.

19. Jeff Blyskal, "Auf Wiedersehen, A & P?," *Forbes*, August 3, 1981, p. 48. Reprinted with permission.

20. Hokis, p. 19.

21. Walsh, p. 206.

22. Blyskal, p. 48.

23. Blyskal, p. 48.

24. Walsh, p. 208.

25. Charles Paiker, "A & P Awaits the Results of Major Surgery," *The Progressive* 46, October 1982, p. 26.

26. Paiker, p. 26.

27. Paiker, p. 26.

28. Walsh, p. 234.

29. Walsh, p. 234.

30. Walsh, p. 234.

31. "A & P: Story of a Turnaround," *Chain Store Age Executive* 59, September 1983, p. 49.

32. "Story," p. 49.

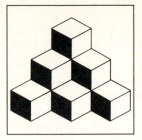

INDUSTRY

BROADCASTING/
ENTREPRENEURSHIP

CASE 4

Turner Broadcasting System, Inc. (A)

NEIL H. SNYDER • MELANIE D. SHEIP

TED TURNER: ENTREPRENEUR

In 1962, at age 24, Ted Turner faced some very difficult decisions—more difficult than most people ever face. His father committed suicide and left an outdoor (billboard) advertising business that was $6 million in debt and short of cash. Rejecting the advice of the company's bankers, who believed he was too inexperienced to run the company, Turner chose not to sell the firm, but instead, to build it. He immediately sold some of the company's assets to improve its cash position, refinanced its debt, renegotiated contracts with customers, hired new salespeople, and literally turned the company around. The company's debt was paid off by 1969, and in 1970, having secured the future of Turner Advertising, Ted Turner purchased Channel 17, an Atlanta independent UHF television station. Although Channel 17 is widely recognized today as a profitable business, in 1970 it was only two years old, losing $50,000 per month, and competing in a market dominated by three firmly rooted network stations in Atlanta.

Recently, because of Ted Turner's phenomenal financial success, jour-

---

nalists have begun to explore Ted Turner, the man. Below are excerpts from a *Wall Street Journal* article:

Associates of broadcaster Ted Turner like to retell the story of his victory in a 1979 yachting race because they think it says it all about the man.

Mr. Turner's boat, *Tenacious,* battled 40-foot waves whipped by 65-knot winds in the Irish Sea to win the Fastnet race. Of the 306 boats that started the race, only 87 finished, and in one of ocean racing's greatest tragedies, 19 sailors drowned.

After his extraordinary display of skill and courage, Mr. Turner at dockside callously reminded his somber British hosts that in the 16th century the Spanish Armada ran into similar trouble. "You ought to be thankful there are storms like that," he said, "or you'd all be speaking Spanish." . . .

The flamboyant Southerner, called a visionary by some and a buffoon by others, seems a bit of both. Widely referred to as "Terrible Ted" and "The Mouth of the South," he has been charged with hypocrisy for preaching family values and then appearing drunk in public, and for criticizing the networks' TV "garbage" while boasting to *Playboy* magazine that he has photographed nude women. . . .

Friends and colleagues attribute both Mr. Turner's successes and his excesses to a personality riddled with contradictions. "Ted is a brilliant person," says Irwin Mazo, a former Turner accountant, "but he also borders on egomania." Although he often talks hard-line conservatism, Mr. Turner seems genuinely concerned about pet liberal issues like overpopulation, world hunger, and nuclear proliferation. He presides over a major news organization but says he limits his newspaper reading to glances at *USA Today* and the Atlanta papers' sports sections. He professes to admire the courtly values of the Old South yet often treats his senior executives like servants.

The conflicting sides are cemented by an overwhelming tenacity. "He competes in everything he does," says Jim Roddey, a former Turner executive and sailing buddy who has known him for twenty-five years. "He sails like he conducts business—it's all or nothing." Indeed, when he saw an Atlanta Braves game-night promotion threatened by lack of participants, he jumped into the contest: He rolled a baseball around the infield with his nose and emerged with blood streaming from forehead to chin.

That incident, his friends say, demonstrates both Mr. Turner's love of publicity and his willingness to sacrifice his dignity in his drive to win. . . .

Mr. Turner was thrust into the business world more than twenty years ago, when his father committed suicide immediately after selling most of the family billboard business. Then 24 years old, Mr. Turner challenged the would-be buyers and regained control of the company. "He could have lost it all," recalls Mr. Mazo, the accountant. But then as apparently now, says Mr. Mazo, "Ted is willing to put all his chips on the table and roll the dice."

In 1970, with the billboard business reestablished, Mr. Turner gambled next on buying a floundering Atlanta UHF television station. In 1976, he transformed it into one of the nation's most profitable stations by having its signal bounced off a satellite and into the nation's cable-TV systems. He channeled Turner Broadcasting's profits from the superstation into a round-the-clock news service dubbed Cable News Network. Five years later, as CNN approaches profitability, Mr. Turner is looking for a new challenge.

Throughout, Mr. Turner's revolutionary moves have been scoffed at by the broadcasting establishment, just as brokers now are scoffing at his CBS take-over bid. Even Turner confidants have been skeptical about his moves. "He's made about $500 million and at least $400 million of that was on deals I told him not to do," chuckles Mr. Roddey, the former Turner executive who admits to advising the company to stick with billboards. . . .

Mr. Turner's management technique isn't any more conventional. "He's not a manager," says Mr. Roddey. "He's not hands-on. He always used to tell me I was getting bogged down in the details, like making the payroll."

But the volatile executive is "a very tough guy to work for," says Reese Schonfeld, the first president of CNN, who left after a dispute with Mr. Turner over hiring and firing. "I've seen him abuse a lot of people. Once you let him humiliate you, he'll walk all over you." Mr. Schonfeld says Mr. Turner has a habit of ordering his senior executives to fetch drinks for him.

Not all Turner employees have such gripes. Lower-level workers at CNN, housed in the basement of Turner Broadcasting's Atlanta headquarters, say their encounters with Mr. Turner are infrequent and nonconfrontational. But life in Turner's executive suite looks stressful: In June 1983, for example, when Mr. Bevins was 36, he was struck by a heart attack while in Mr. Turner's office. Mr. Bevins declines to discuss the incident. . . .

In recent years, however, both Mr. Turner and his company have toned down. Aides say the change began when Mr. Turner began to realize that obtaining control of a network might someday be within his grasp. He began to position himself for an eventual combination, they say.

For Mr. Turner, that meant dropping off the interview trail and scaling down his public excesses. He repeatedly declined to be interviewed for this story, for instance. While hardly prim these days, "he's become more discreet," says one longtime Turner employee. And with age, his friends say, has come a dose of maturity. "Lately he talks a lot about world peace, nuclear war, improving the environment," says Gary Jobson, tactician aboard many of Mr. Turner's winning yachts.[1]

Turner's perspective on business is interesting to say the least. He is quoted as saying

I don't think winning is everything. It's a big mistake when you say that I think trying to win is what counts. Be kind and fair and make the world a better place to live, that's what's important. . . . I think the saddest people I've ever met were people with a lot of wealth. If you polled 90 percent of the people and asked them what they want most, most would want to be millionaires. I'll tell you, you've got to be one to know how unimportant it is. . . . I'm blessed with some talents. I've made a lot of money, more than I ever thought I would. . . . But if I continue to be successful, I would like to serve my fellow man in some way other than doing flips at third base. . . . People want leadership, somebody to rally around, and I want to be a leader.[2]

CREATING A NETWORK: WTBS, THE SUPERSTATION

WTBS is the pioneer of the superstation concept. Owned and operated in Atlanta, Georgia by the Turner Broadcasting System, Inc., Channel 17 is an independent UHF television station whose signal is beamed via satellite to television households nationwide. Ted Turner, TBS president and chairman of the Board, purchased Channel 17 in January 1970. By merging the then Turner Communications Corporation with Rice Broadcasting, he gained control of the television outlet, which became WTCG, flagship station of the Turner Communications Group.

Realizing that WTCG's programming could be made available by satellite to millions of television viewers throughout the country, Turner originated the *superstation* concept. In short, the superstation is a reworking of the traditional television network concept, in which one station acts as original programming supplier for a multiplicity of distant cable markets. On December 16, 1976, WTCG made history, as its signal was beamed to cable systems nationwide via a transponder on RCA's Satcom I satellite. Satcom I was replaced by Satcom II–R in January 1982, and by Galaxy I in January 1985.

In 1979, the Turner Communications Group was renamed Turner Broadcasting System, Inc., and to reflect this change the WTCG call letters became WTBS. The company estimates that as of February 29, 1984, WTBS was beamed into approximately 75 percent of U.S. cable homes and 35 percent of U.S. television homes.

WTBS broadcasts 24 hours a day, acquiring its programming primarily from film companies, syndicators of programs that have run successfully on television networks, and its sports affiliates. WTBS currently has available 4,100 film titles for its programming needs, the majority of which are available for multiple runs. In addition, approximately 500 titles are under contract and will become available for programming purposes in the future. Approximately 23 percent of the purchased programming has been obtained from Viacom International, Inc., and 17 percent from MCA. WTBS has not obtained more than 10 percent of its purchased programming needs from any other single supplier, and approximately 1,900 hours of programming broadcast on WTBS during 1983 were produced internally, or under contract. WTBS plans to produce more programs internally in the future.

WTBS derives revenue from the sale of advertising time, and advertising prices depend on the size of WTBS's viewing audience and the amount of available time sold. Since February 1981, the A. C. Nielsen Company has been measuring the audience level of WTBS for use by the company and its advertisers. The demand for advertising time on cable television is significantly lower than that for advertising time on the three major networks because of the relatively small size of the cable network audiences and the fact that cable has not penetrated significantly in many of the major urban markets. The board of directors of TBS anticipates that the continued growth of the cable television (CATV) industry, particularly in the major urban markets, will result in increased demand on the part of advertisers.

The revenues of WTBS also include amounts obtained from direct-response advertising, which represent fees received by the company for the sale of products it promotes by advertisement. The company broadcasts advertisements for the products during unsold advertising time, and the products are ordered directly by viewers through the company by mail or telephone. WTBS collects a fee for each order. In 1983, these fees amounted to 6.6 percent of total advertising revenues for WTBS.

Advertising time for WTBS as well as the company's cable news services are marketed and sold by the company's own advertising sales force consisting of approximately 101 persons located in sales offices in New York, Chicago, Detroit, Los Angeles, and Atlanta.

According to the *Wall Street Journal*

> It's hard to laugh at Mr. Turner's operations now, or at least the WTBS operation. His superstation, one of the nation's most popular cable services, now beams a steady diet of sports, movies and reruns into almost 34 million U.S. households, or about 84 percent of all homes equipped for cable.
>
> It has revolutionized the cable-television business, says Ira Tumpowsky, a Young & Rubicam Inc. senior vice president who oversees the agency's cable-TV buying. "He's the person who moved cable from a reception industry to a marketing industry," the advertising executive says.[3]

TBS Sports

In January 1976, TBS acquired the Atlanta Braves professional baseball club, and on December 29, 1976, the Atlanta Hawks professional basketball club was acquired. Although both teams have consistently lost money, they have provided TBS with excellent sports programming, and the Atlanta Braves have a national following. TBS aired 150 Braves games and 41 Hawks games in 1984.

Along with a full schedule of Atlanta Braves baseball and Atlanta Hawks basketball, TBS Sports offers NCAA basketball, NBA basketball, NCAA football, Southeastern Conference football, and a variety of special sports presentations. For example, TBS Sports telecast the NASCAR circuit's Richmond 400, college football's Hall of Fame Bowl, and World Championship Wrestling during 1984.

Recently, baseball Commissioner Peter Ueberroth persuaded Ted Turner to make annual payments to other major-league teams if he continued to broadcast Braves games across the nation over his cable station. Turner has agreed to make these payments, totaling more than $25 million according to the *Wall Street Journal*, into a central fund for five years.[4] This agreement is a compromise. Ueberroth had wanted to end nationwide cable broadcasts of baseball games, because they were hurting the profits of teams in other cities. Ueberroth is reported to have said that superstations are the most serious problem facing professional baseball today.[5]

Ted Turner is said to be as creative with his sports franchises as he is with TBS. For example, the *Wall Street Journal* concluded that

Even in the stodgy game of baseball, Mr. Turner has displayed some business acumen. The Atlanta Braves franchise that he bought in 1976 was mired in mediocrity. Mr. Turner beefed up its farm system, paid top dollar to lure stars from elsewhere, and transmitted across the nation practically every game the team played. Average attendance at Braves' home games last year was 21,834, triple the figure for 1975. The Braves are widely considered pennant contenders this season.

In baseball, as in his other businesses, Mr. Turner has managed to outrage both his employees and his peers. Mr. Turner once tried to demote a slumping star to the minor leagues. At another point, he named himself manager of the team. Such antics led to a collision with the then-Commissioner of baseball, Bowie Kuhn, and to Mr. Turner's temporary suspension from the game. According to one biography, Mr. Turner pleaded with Mr. Kuhn: "I am very contrite. I would bend over and let you paddle my behind, hit me over the head with a Fresca bottle."[6]

CNN

Through its subsidiary Cable News Network, Inc. (CNN), which began broadcasting on June 1, 1980, TBS provides a 24-hour news programming service that is available to CATV systems throughout the United States and in some foreign countries. The programming includes comprehensive reporting of domestic and international news, sports, business, and weather, plus analysis, commentary, and reports by its staff of experts and investigative reporters. CNN obtains news reports from its bureaus in various U.S. and foreign cities. Each of these bureaus is equipped to provide live reports to CNN's transmission facility in Atlanta, thereby providing the capability for live coverage of news events around the world. In addition, news is obtained through wire services, television news services by agreement with television stations in various locations worldwide, and from freelance reporters and camera crews.

CNN employs over 160 journalists, executives, and technicians. The news channel was initially received by 193 CATV systems serving approximately 1.7 million subscribers. As of December 31, 1983, 4,278 CATV systems serving approximately 25.1 million subscribers received CNN's programming.

According to the *Wall Street Journal*

During its five years of losses, CNN has grown to become the nation's most popular cable service, available in some 32 million homes. And this year, the company indicates, CNN should move into the black. Though still not an equal of the high-powered network news operations, CNN is nipping at their heels, and doing it on a bargain-basement budget.

CNN is weak on features says Jim Snyder, News vice-president of Post-Newsweek Stations Inc., the broadcasting division of the Washington Post Co., but it covers breaking news "as well as anybody." A recent Washington Journalism Review assessment of the channel carried the headline "CNN Takes Its Place Beside the Networks."[7]

CNN Headline News

CNN offered another 24-hour news service to cable operators effective December 31, 1981. Referred to as CNN Headline News (CNN HN), this service utilizes a concise, fast-paced format, programming in half-hour cycles throughout the day. CNN HN employs approximately 225 people, and its start-up required the construction and furnishing of a studio facility and additional transmitting facilities. The resources and expertise of CNN are utilized by CNN HN for accumulation of news material. Its revenues are derived from the sale of advertising on CNN HN and from fees charged for the syndication of CNN HN directly to over-the-air television and radio stations.

The number of cable homes receiving the CNN HN signal increased from approximately 5.4 million in October 1983 to approximately 9.1 million as a direct result of TBS's agreement to acquire CNN HN's major cable news competitor (The Satellite News Channel). Despite this increase in cable homes, TBS executives do not expect CNN HN to be profitable in 1984.

Cable Music Channel

On October 26, 1984, TBS launched its own brand of music video programming to compete with MTV. The Cable Music Channel started with 2.5 million households, about half the expected subscriber count company executives had predicted. However, by November 30, 1984, the Cable Music Channel's title and affiliate list was sold to MTV Networks, Inc., for $1.5 million in cash and advertising commitments at a loss of $2.2 million. Cable Music Channel President/TBS Executive Vice President Robert Wussler acknowledges that operator resistance was largely responsible. "We didn't get the homes and we weren't about to get 3 or 5 million homes. We surveyed the field, felt we had a good product, but the industry obviously embraced MTV. The future in terms of acquiring subs was bleak and we felt strongly that this was our best course of action."[8]

| KEY EXECUTIVES AND OWNERSHIP | Ted Turner is aided by highly qualified, experienced men. Robert J. Wussler, executive vice president, had twenty-one years experience with CBS, including his appointment as president of the CBS Sports Division, before joining TBS in August 1981. |

William C. Bevins, Jr., is vice president of finance, secretary, and treasurer as well as a director of the company. Previously, he was affiliated with Price Waterhouse for ten years, most recently as senior manager.

Henry L. (Hank) Aaron has been vice president, director of player development for the Atlanta Braves since 1976, and the vice president of community relations and a director of the company since 1980. He was previously a professional baseball player with a total of twenty-eight years of experience in professional sports, and he holds the world's record for the most home runs hit by a professional baseball player.

Burt Reinhardt became president of CNN in 1982 and a director of CNN in 1983. He was employed by the company in 1979 and was instrumental in organizing CNN. Previously, he served as executive vice president of UPI Television News and executive vice president of the Non-Theatrical and Educational Division of Paramount Pictures.

Gerald Hogan joined the company in 1971 and served as general sales manager of WTBS from 1979 until 1981. He became senior vice president of Turner Broadcasting Sales, Inc., in 1982.

Henry Gillespie joined TBS in 1982 as chairman of the board of Turner Program Services, Inc. Prior to that, he served as president of Columbia Pictures Television Distribution and president of Viacom Enterprises.

J. Michael Gearon has been a director of the Company, president of Hawks Management Company, and general partner of Atlanta Hawks, Ltd., operator of the Atlanta Hawks professional basketball team, since 1979. He previously owned a real estate brokerage and development firm in Atlanta, Georgia.

OWNERSHIP PHILOSOPHY

Currently, Ted Turner owns 86 percent of the common shares outstanding. Exhibit 1 presents TBS common stock ownership of selected individuals. Most of the stockholders besides Turner and his family are either directors or executive officers of TBS.

FINANCIAL ISSUES

Debt Philosophy

TBS is a highly leveraged company that emphasizes the building of asset values. At present, the company has a $190 million revolving credit agreement extending until 1987, and $133 million of this credit line has been borrowed. Concerning long-term debt, the company has incurred debt restructuring fees that it expenses as interest based on the weighted average of the principal balance outstanding throughout the term of the agreement. The company paid restructuring fees of $3.65 million during 1983, and the balance due at year end is classified as current and long-term in accordance with the payment terms of the agreements.

EXHIBIT 1   **TBS Common Stock Ownership**

NAME OF BENEFICIAL OWNER	AMOUNT	PERCENT OF CLASS
R. E. Turner	17,579,922	86.2%
William C. Bevins, Jr.	20,000	0.1
Peter A. Dames	98,910	0.5
Karl Eller	1,000	—
Tench C. Coxe	128,285	0.6
J. Michael Gearon	31,500	0.2
Martin B. Seretean	20,800	0.1
William C. Bartholomay	210,700	1.0
Allison Thornwell, Jr.	215,912	1.1
All directors and officers as a group (27 persons)	18,421,489	90.4%

SOURCE: Turner Broadcasting System 1984 Annual 10-K Report

Under terms of its 1983 debt agreement, the company is limited with regard to additional borrowings, cash dividends, and acquisition of the company's common stock. TBS is also required, among other things, to maintain minimum levels of working capital and to meet specified current ratio requirements. It is important to note that the company was not in compliance with certain restrictive covenants of its loan agreement on December 31, 1983. TBS received waivers of these restrictions from lenders; accordingly, the amounts due have been classified in accordance with the original terms of the agreement.

Owner's Equity

Characteristic of firms in the growth stage of the business life cycle, TBS has experienced mostly negative earnings since its inception (see Exhibit 2). Most of its losses have resulted from the high start-up costs associated with the divisions that have been created in the past ten years. Exhibit 3 shows balance sheet information for the years 1977 to 1983.

Working Capital

During 1983, the company was unable to generate sufficient cash flow from operations to meet its needs. Working capital deficits were primarily funded through short-term credit lines and financing agreements with vendors,

EXHIBIT 2   **TBS Historical Common Size Income Statement**
(Dollar Amounts in Thousands)

	1977		1978		1979	
REVENUE						
Broadcasting	$19573	51.9%	$23434	62.1%	$27789	73.7%
Cable production	0	0.0	0	0.0	0	0.0
Sports	6706	17.8	8181	21.7	7395	19.6
Management fees	1782	4.7	2094	5.6	2285	6.1
Other	738	2.0	134	0.4	252	0.7
Total revenue	$28799	76.3%	$33843	89.7%	$37721	100.0%
COST OF EXPENSES						
Cost of operation	$12767	33.8%	$13219	35.0%	$16997	45.1%
S, G, & Administration	10729	28.4	12736	33.8	14460	38.3
Amortization film contracts	1178	3.1	1571	4.2	2290	6.1
Amortization player/other contracts	1556	4.1	1599	4.2	1508	4.0
Depreciation of P, P, and E	934	2.5	1037	2.7	1222	3.2
Interest expense/amortization debt	1291	3.4	1323	3.5	2098	5.6
Other	1251	3.3	0	0.0	0	0.0
Total costs and expenses	$29706	78.8%	$31485	83.5%	$38575	102.3%
Income (loss) from operation	$−907	−2.4%	$2358	6.3%	$−854	−2.3%
Equity loss—limited partners	−1053	−2.8	−1225	−3.2	−2014	−5.3
Income before gains or dispositions	−1960	−5.2	1133	3.0	−2868	−7.6
Gain on disposition of property	0	0.0	395	1.0	312	0.8
Income before tax and extra. items	−1960	−5.2	1528	4.1	−2556	−6.8
Provision (benefit) for taxes	−728	−1.9	669	1.8	−1060	−2.8
Income before extra. items	−1232	−3.3	860	2.3	−1496	−4.0
Gain on prepayment of debt	0	0.0	343	0.9	0	0.0
NET INCOME (LOSS)	$−1232	−3.3%	$1203	3.2%	$−1496	−4.0%

1980		1981		1982		1983	
$35495	65.0%	$55329	58.2%	$96647	58.3%	$136217	60.7%
7201	13.2	27738	29.2	49708	30.0	65169	29.0
9211	16.9	8840	9.3	16263	9.8	21401	9.5
2473	4.5	2835	3.0	2717	1.6	1462	0.7
230	0.4	305	0.3	306	0.2	283	0.1
$54610	100.0%	$95047	100.0%	$165641	100.0%	$224532	100.0%

EXHIBIT 2 — Continued

1980		1981		1982		1983	
$35124	64.3%	$49036	51.6%	$81187	49.0%	$105695	47.1%
25218	46.2	37067	39.0	60343	36.4	80722	36.0
2803	5.1	4010	4.2	7497	4.5	8674	3.9
1210	2.2	0	0.0		0.0		0.0
2172	4.0	3469	3.6	4182	2.5	4706	2.1
4437	8.1	9673	10.2	13084	7.9	14383	6.4
0	0.0	0	0.0	0	0.0	0	0.0
$70964	129.9%	$103255	108.6%	$166293	100.4%	$214170	95.4%
$ − 16354	− 29.9%	$ − 8208	− 8.6%	$ − 652	− 0.4%	$10362	4.6%
− 2905	− 5.3	− 5215	− 5.5	− 2698	− 1.6	− 3350	− 1.5
− 19259	− 35.3	− 13423	− 14.1	− 3350	− 2.0	7012	3.1
15694	28.7	0	0.0		0.0		0.0
− 3575	− 6.5	− 13423	− 14.1	− 3350	− 2.0	7012	3.1
200	0.4	0	0.0		0.0		0.0
− 3775	− 6.9	− 13423	− 14.1	− 3350	− 2.0	7012	3.1
0	0.0	0	0.0		0.0		0.0
$ − 3775	− 6.9%	$ − 13423	− 14.1%	$ − 3350	− 2.0%	$7012	3.1%

EXHIBIT 3 — TBS Historical Common Size Balance Sheet
(Dollar Amounts in Thousands)

	1977		1978		1979	
CURRENT ASSETS						
Cash	$1351	3.6%	$154	0.4%	$342	0.9%
Accounts receivable	3537	9.4	4951	13.1	6322	16.8
Less: allow. for doubt. accts.	431	1.1	547	1.5	415	1.1
Net accounts receivable	3106	8.2	4404	11.7	5907	15.7
Prepaid expenses	1250	3.3	563	1.5	585	1.6
Notes payable—S–T	0	0.0	0	0.0	0	0.0
Curr. port. def. prog. prod. cost		0.0		0.0		0.0
Film contract rights—current	1128	3.0	2055	5.4	2570	6.8
Other current asssets	1359	3.6	528	1.4	644	1.7
Total current assets	$8194	21.7%	$7704	20.4%	$10048	26.6%

EXHIBIT 3   **Continued**

	1977		1978		1979	
CURRENT ASSETS						
Film contract rights	$3193	8.5%	$5632	14.9%	$7537	20.0%
Inv. in limited partnerships	1000	2.7	2578	6.8	2480	6.6
Net prop., plant, and equipment	6543	17.3	7784	20.6	13381	35.5
Notes receivable—L–T	1146	3.0	404	1.1	514	1.4
Deferred program prod. costs		0.0		0.0		0.0
Deferred charges	0	0.0	0	0.0	0	0.0
Net contract rights	6165	16.3	4947	13.1	3628	9.6
Intangible assets	0	0.0	0	0.0	0	0.0
Other assets	1624	4.3	1349	3.6	1696	4.5
Total assets	$27865	73.9%	$30398	80.6%	$39284	104.1%
CURRENT LIABILITIES						
Accounts payable	$2043	5.4%	$2615	6.9%	$1351	3.6%
Accrued expenses	0	0.0	0	0.0	1752	4.6
Deferred income	0	0.0	0	0.0	216	0.6
Short-term borrowings	0	0.0	0	0.0	6642	17.6
Long-term debt—current	5411	14.3	4910	13.0	2704	7.2
Obligation—film RTS (current)	0	0.0	0	0.0	3344	8.9
Debt restructure fees (current)	0	0.0	0	0.0	0	0.0
Income taxes payable	0	0.0	0	0.0	0	0.0
Total current liabilities	$7454	19.8%	$7525	19.9%	$16009	42.4%
Long-term debt	$15968	42.3%	$16329	43.3%	$14158	37.5%
Unfunded pension cost	283	0.8	283	0.8	283	0.8
Deferred income taxes	1076	2.9	1980	5.2	918	2.4
Deferred income	0	0.0	0	0.0	0	0.0
Debt restructure fees payable	0	0.0	0	0.0	0	0.0
Obligations—emp. contracts	0	0.0	0	0.0	1410	3.7
Obligations—film rights	0	0.0	0	0.0	3631	9.6
Other liabilities		0.0		0.0		0.0
Total liabilities	$24781	65.7%	$26117	69.2%	$36409	96.5%
Common stock, par .125	1024	2.7%	1024	2.7%	2663	7.1%
Capital in excess	1541	4.1	1572	4.2	291	0.8
Retained earnings (deficit)	1095	2.9	2298	6.1	802	2.1
	$3660	9.7%	$4894	13.0%	$3756	10.0%

EXHIBIT 3   Continued

	1977		1978		1979	
CURRENT LIABILITIES						
Less shares of stock—treasury		0.0%		0.0%		0.0%
Notes rec.—sales of CS-treasury		0.0		0.0		0.0
Treasury stock	−576	−1.5%	−613	−1.6%	−881	−2.3%
Total stockholders' equity	$6744	17.9%	$9175	24.3%	$6631	17.6%
Total liabilities and stockholders' equity	$31525	83.6%	$35292	93.6%	$43040	114.1%

1980		1981		1982		1983	
$489	0.9%	$504	0.5%	$538	0.3%	$594	0.3%
10662	19.5	18868	19.9	25728	15.5	34186	15.2
793	1.5	1164	1.2	1997	1.2	2418	1.1
9869	18.1	17704	18.6	23731	14.3	31768	14.1
552	1.0	1086	1.1	1378	0.8	2177	1.0
0	0.0	0	0.0	0	0.0	0	0.0
	0.0		0.0	2490	1.5	2660	1.2
2521	4.6	3495	3.7	4516	2.7	12163	5.4
1591	2.9	1433	1.5	2585	1.6	2305	1.0
$15022	27.5%	$24222	25.5%	$35238	21.3%	$51667	23.0%
$5660	10.4%	$9464	10.0%	$15633	9.4%	$26057	11.6%
2027	3.7	900	0.9	1900	1.1	1633	0.7
26647	48.8	28698	30.2	67555	40.8	71505	31.8
920	1.7	0	0.0	0	0.0	0	0.0
	0.0		0.0	4460	2.7	11432	5.1
0	0.0	9623	10.1	6585	4.0	13926	6.2
2784	5.1	2084	2.2	1583	1.0	1246	0.6
0	0.0	0	0.0	0	0.0	25567	11.4
958	1.8	1970	2.1	2232	1.3	2805	1.2
$54018	98.9%	$76961	81.0%	$135186	81.6%	$205838	91.7%

EXHIBIT 3 **Continued**

1980		1981		1982		1983	
$2079	3.8%	$3926	4.1%	$7548	4.6%	$6954	3.1%
7196	13.2	11152	11.7	16750	10.1	22551	10.0
700	1.3	2226	2.3	7220	4.4	7083	3.2
17907	32.8	42783	45.0	49924	30.1	0	0.0
8430	15.4	3005	3.2	4266	2.6	14473	6.4
2456	4.5	3465	3.6	5613	3.4	11317	5.0
0	0.0	2253	2.4	3000	1.8	3650	1.6
163	0.3	0	0.0	0	0.0	0	0.0
$38931	71.3%	$68810	72.4%	$94321	56.9%	$66028	29.4%
$9825	18.0%	$7165	7.5%	$42802	25.8%	$122404	54.5%
283	0.5	283	0.3		0.0		0.0
918	1.7	2834	3.0		0.0		0.0
0	0.0	1313	1.4	646	0.4	562	0.3
0	0.0	4207	4.4	3000	1.8	650	0.3
2221	4.1	2560	2.7	3442	2.1	5201	2.3
2662	4.9	3943	4.1	7379	4.5	13959	6.2
	0.0		0.0	1097	0.7	7507	3.3
$54840	100.4%	$91115	95.9%	$152687	92.2%	$216311	96.3%
$2663	4.9%	$2663	2.8%	$2663	1.6%	$2663	1.2%
602	1.1	1508	1.6	1508	0.9	1508	0.7
− 2973	− 5.4	− 16396	− 17.3	− 19746	− 11.9	− 12734	− 5.7
292	0.5%	− 12225	− 12.9%	− 15575	− 9.4%	− 8563	− 3.8%
	0.0%		0.0%	− 474	− 0.3%	− 754	− 0.3%
	0.0		0.0	− 1452	0.9	− 1156	− 0.5
− 1114	− 2.0%	− 1929	− 2.0%	− 1926	− 1.2%	− 1910	− 0.9%
$ − 530	− 1.0%	$ − 26379	− 27.8%	$ − 17501	− 10.6%	$ − 10473	− 4.7%
$54310	99.5%	$64736	68.1%	$135186	81.6%	$205838	91.7%

program suppliers, and others during the first three quarters of the year. A large percentage of cash outflow resulted from the debt restructuring fees.

TBS faces several uncertainties that could arise out of normal operations that might require additional cash. However, management feels that the current financing program will be adequate to meet the company's anticipated needs. In the unlikely event that these uncertainties do materialize and require cash in excess of the anticipated amounts, because of limitations in existing loan agreements there is no assurance that the company can obtain additional borrowings that might be needed to meet these excess needs.

Dividend Policy

TBS has not paid a cash dividend since 1975. In view of the unavailability of funds to the company and restrictions in its loan agreements against any dividend payments, it is not anticipated that dividends will be paid to holders of its common stock in the foreseeable future.

Capital Structure

At present, 97 percent of TBS's capital structure consists of long-term debt. In the fourth quarter of 1984, TBS was considering a public offering to raise $125 million to pay off its bank debt. The company planned to use a combination of ten-year notes, stocks, and warrants to raise the capital. Based on preliminary plans, the offering would boost the number of shares outstanding from the current 20.3 million to 22.2 million, reducing the percentage of shares held by Turner from 87 percent to 79 percent.

INDUSTRY AND COMPETITION

The dramatic increase in the number of alternative sources of television broadcasting has led to a measurable drop in the audience shares of the three major networks. Consequently, there is a great deal of pressure for change in the television industry. Pay and ad-supported cable, independent broadcast stations, and videocassettes are all seen as contributing to the decline. In the next decade, it is believed that television entertainment may shift toward a broader range of outlets including ad hoc and regional networks, pay-per-view networks, and more reasonably priced videocassette recorders.

Networks

Although television audience viewing is growing, the big three networks are concerned about the decline in their audience shares and about when the decline will stop. The availability of syndicated programs is becoming scarce

EXHIBIT 4   Decline in Network TV Audience

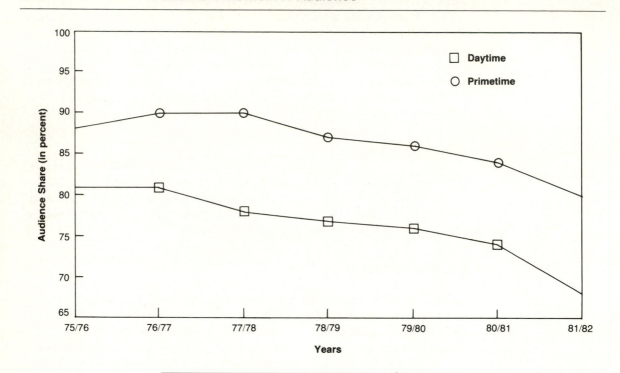

SOURCE: DDB Needham Worldwide Media Research, based on data from Nielsen Media Research.

as new broadcasters race to buy up existing shows. However, networks have an advantage in this competition because of their programming expertise and facilities. Exhibit 4 shows how precipitous the decline in network television audience share was between 1975–1976 and 1981–1982.

Independents

Independent television stations have experienced phenomenal growth in the past fifteen years. In 1971, there were 65 independent broadcasters with losses of $24 million serving 30 markets in the United States. In 1980, 179 independent stations with profits of $158 million served 86 markets. This growth can be largely attributed to the FCC's financial interest rule that prohibits the big three networks from syndicating programs that they originally aired and from owning any financial interest in programming produced by others. The independents thus have been able to compete against the networks by airing former network hit shows at key times during the day, including prime time.

Cable

The cable industry is in the midst of a gigantic building boom that can be attributed to two advances. First, there was an increase, from 12 to 54, in the number of channels picked up by cable operators. Second, in 1975, Home Box Office (HBO) started sending its signal via satellite; other stations, including WTBS, followed and were able to easily attain national distribution for their cable programming.

The Fall 1984 Cable Study Report, conducted by Mediamark Research, Inc., found that the median age of pay television subscribers was 35.2 years, with an average yearly income of $29,879. *Cablevision,* the trade magazine of the cable industry, projects that the percentage of pay television subscribers will jump from 23 percent of the population in 1984 to 27 percent in 1986. Most of the cable industry's profits will be invested in the wiring of additional homes, particularly those in major urban areas. The high costs associated with wiring these areas had previously kept cable operators out. Now, cities represent more than four-fifths of the potential market.

Ad-Supported Cable

With the emergence of cable television as a national delivery system, many media people became excited about a concept called *narrowcasting*. Narrowcasting consists of the programming of one particular type of entertainment (e.g., ESPN—a sports channel) that enables a programmer to target his audience and thus attract specific advertisers at higher rates. Although several narrowcasting networks exist, their success has been very limited because of the lack of quality programming. Dave Martin, vice president for broadcasting at Campbell-Ewall said, "Narrowcasting allows an advertiser to take advantage of a specific opportunity. . . . If it works, though, there is nothing on the mass level that will parallel the opportunity of true narrowcasting to a target audience."[9] Another good example of successful narrowcasting is Music Television (MTV). Narrowcasting is not the only form of ad-supported cable. Stations such as WTBS in Atlanta, WGN in Chicago, and WOR in New York have been successful with their broad-based programming.

Pay Television

Pay television has been the leader in the cable industry, and it is currently experiencing significant change. Most of the change is being introduced by motion picture companies that are trying to become more directly involved in pay television. For example, Columbia Pictures teamed up with Time, Inc., parent of HBO, and CBS in an attempt to grab a large share of the pay-television market and to become involved in pay-per-view (PPV) television. PPV requires a subscriber to pay an additional fee to view certain major programs. Thus far, most PPV has not been profitable because of the high prices viewers must pay for the programs.

A major threat to large pay-television systems comes from smaller private delivery systems. For example, SMATV is a private system that picks up cable signals using a satellite dish and sends the signal via cable to a group of apartment houses, hotels, or clusters of private homes. SMATV has been extremely effective in urban areas previously ignored by other cable systems. This system does not offer the potential, however, of other systems such as multipoint distribution system (MDS) or direct broadcast satellite (DBS).

FCC Rulings

Television broadcasting is subject to the jurisdiction of the Federal Communications Commission (FCC) under the Communications Act of 1934, as amended. Among other things, FCC regulations govern the issuance, term, renewal, and transfer of licenses that must be obtained by persons to operate any television station. The FCC's recent proposal to repeal its network syndication and financial interest rules is strongly supported by the three major networks. Currently, the networks cannot syndicate their own programs, nor can they have a financial interest in programs produced by others. This rule prevents the networks from making money from their shows in syndication. Independent television stations, on the other hand, have grown substantially under this rule because of their ability to air former hit shows.

Independent broadcasters argue that repeal of the financial interest rule will increase the possibility of the networks' monopolizing and withholding off-network, syndicated, prime-time entertainment programming. However, CBS, NBC, and ABC contend that this possibility would not materialize, because the networks have neither the incentive nor the opportunity to discriminate against the independents.

To make the television industry more competitive, the FCC is preparing to adopt a plan to expand the 7–7–7 rule to the 12–12–12 rule. Currently, television station owners are allowed to own only seven AM and seven FM radio stations in addition to seven television stations. This limitation was adopted in the 1950s to encourage program diversity in the marketplace. Under the new plan, media companies would be allowed to own as many as twelve television stations only if the audience reach of the stations does not exceed 25 percent of the national viewing audience. This plan would eventually result in an increase in the number of television station owners capable of competing with the three major broadcast networks.

Another important issue facing the FCC concerns the reexamination of the fairness doctrine, the 35-year-old requirement that broadcasters cover "controversial issues" and air contrasting views. FCC Chairman Mark S. Fowler says that "the government shouldn't be the one to decide what's fair and what isn't."[10] However, defenders of the fairness doctrine counter that the airwaves are a scarce public resource that must be protected from abuse. Under Fowler's administration, the FCC has continued to expand its deregulatory efforts by abolishing regulations and relaxing rules that restrict regional concentration and multiple ownership of broadcast stations. "These are the areas where the agency must regulate, but in the choice between competition and regulation, competition is far better for the consumer," says Fowler.[11]

The Changing Landscape of Competition

Clearly, competition in the home entertainment industry in general and television in particular is changing. VCRs are the hottest items going. Exhibit 5 shows how rapidly factory sales of VCRs have risen since 1982. Exhibit 6 shows that firms competing in the cable industry have made significant progress over the last twenty years wiring homes in the United States. Finally, Exhibit 7 shows how rapidly sales of videocassette tapes have increased. There can be no doubt that the landscape of competition is changing.

OUTLOOK FOR THE FUTURE

The future of the cable industry is still bright. According to Robert J. Wussler, executive vice president of TBS, "I don't think the momentum is out of the game, although I certainly think the bloom is off the rose. But all you have to do is come to a couple of cable conventions and see that there's still enough money around and there are still enough young people around to execute all the ideas people can dream up. No, there's still a lot of momentum around, even if it's not the gold rush."[12] Wussler believes broadcasting in general has hit a plateau or is shrinking. Due to the rise of independents, cable, direct broadcast satellites, videocassette recorders, and our various lifestyles, he does not believe broadcasting is becoming more powerful. According to Wussler, broadcasters do not need to worry about getting bigger again, but instead they must worry about getting smaller and about how they are going to manage being smaller. As for cable industry growth, Wussler does not see many limitations. Although it is a tough business to get into today because it requires a lot of capital and there are channel capacity problems, the cable industry has a bright future.

If the cable industry continues to grow and superstations proliferate, TBS will face more competition. According to the *Wall Street Journal*, some industry observers have questioned whether Turner Broadcasting could hold up if superstation imitators proliferated beyond the handful now operating.[13]

EXHIBIT 5   **Factory Sales of VCRs**

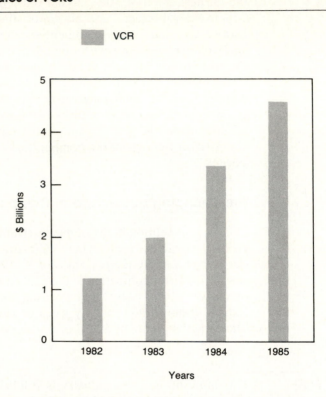

Figures for 1985 are projected

SOURCE: Electronic Industries Association, *Richmond Times-Dispatch*, July 5, 1985. Reprinted with permission.

But Bonnie Cook, an analyst for J. C. Bradford & Co. in Nashville, dismisses that notion. She believes that anybody can transform a television station into a superstation, but cable systems can carry only a limited number of channels. Thus, it is unlikely that the number of superstations will increase dramatically.

Television broadcasting is changing. In early 1985, Capital Cities Communications, Inc., purchased ABC, and in April 1985 Ted Turner made a move to acquire CBS for $5.4 billion including no cash. This acquisition attempt attracted praise, criticism, and ridicule. According to the *Wall Street Journal*

Mr. Turner has long broadcast his drive to run a network. Some associates contend that this desire became almost an obsession after Capital Cities Com-

EXHIBIT 6

Homes with Cable

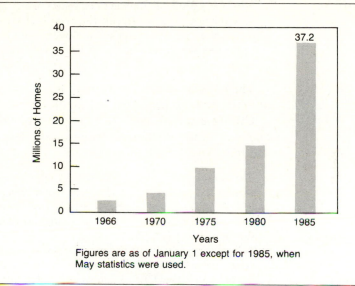

Figures are as of January 1 except for 1985, when
May statistics were used.

SOURCE: National Cable Television Association using Arbitron estimates for 1985, *Richmond Times-Dispatch*, July 4, 1985. Reprinted with permission.

EXHIBIT 7

Tape Sales to Dealers

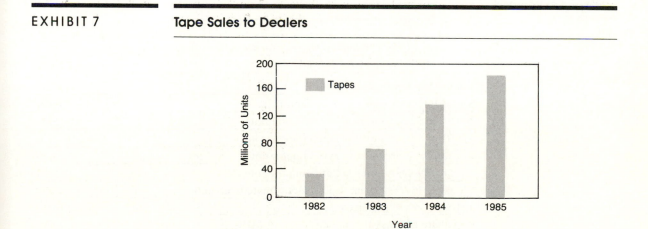

Figures for 1985 are projected

SOURCE: Electronic Industries Association, *Richmond Times-Dispatch*, July 5, 1985. Reprinted with permission.

munications Inc. last month agreed to acquire American Broadcasting Co. CBS thus was seen as Mr. Turner's last chance, because RCA, the parent of NBC, was probably too big to be taken over.

William C. Bevins, Jr., the financial vice-president of Turner Broadcasting, denies that the ABC acquisition move forced Mr. Turner's hand. But he concedes that the transaction "certainly crystallized where the various regulatory agencies stood and that the timing was propitious."[14]

The package offered by Turner, which is reputed to be made up primarily of junk bonds, is presented in Exhibit 8.

CBS rejected Turner's offer as inadequate and took steps to prevent a takeover. Andy Rooney, a regular on the television program "60 Minutes," had this to say about Turner's offer:

Ted Turner, the Atlanta, Ga., money operator, yachtsman and baseball team owner, has applied to the Federal Communications Commission for its approval of his scheme to take CBS away from its present owners. He has offered CBS stockholders a grabbag of what are known on Wall Street as "junk bonds" for their shares in CBS. . . .

I offer my services in trying to locate a new anchorman for the CBS Evening News and someone else to do pieces at the end of "60 Minutes" because if Ted Turner takes over CBS, I doubt very much that Dan Rather will want his job and I know darn well I won't.[15]

On May 7, 1985, TBS announced a first quarter loss of $741,000, compared with a $5.3 million loss a year earlier.

EXHIBIT 8   **Turner Broadcasting System Inc.'s Package for CBS**

For each of CBS's 30 million shares, Turner offers the following package:

TYPE OF SECURITY	FACE VALUE
$46 of 15% 7-year senior note	$ 46.00
$46 of 15½% 15-year senior debenture	46.00
$10.31 of 5-year Series A Zero coupon note	5.00
$11.91 of 6-year Series B Zero coupon note	5.00
$15.90 of 8-year Series C Zero coupon note	5.00
$18.38 of 9-year Series D Zero coupon note	5.00
$30.00 of 16¼% 20-year senior subordinated debenture	30.00
1 share of $2.80 preferred	16.50
0.75 share of Class B common	16.50
Total	$175.00*

SOURCE: Wall Street Journal, April 19, 1985. Reprinted by permission of the *Wall Street Journal*, © Dow Jones & Company, Inc., 1985. All Rights Reserved Worldwide.

*This is the face value of the offer for each CBS share. Analysts say there isn't any way of currently evaluating the market value of the package because the issues don't yet exist.

NOTES

1. *Wall Street Journal*, April 19, 1985, pp. 1, 6. Reprinted by permission of *The Wall Street Journal*, © Dow Jones & Company, Inc. 1985. All Rights Reserved Worldwide.

2. *Atlanta Constitution*, January 8, 1977.

3. *Wall Street Journal, op. cit.*

4. *Ibid.*

5. *Richmond Times-Dispatch*, January 28, 1985.

6. *Wall Street Journal, op. cit.*

7. *Ibid.*

8. *CableVision*, December 10, 1984.

9. *Business Week*, May 7, 1984.

10. *Ibid.*

11. *Ibid.*

12. *Broadcasting*, December 12, 1983.

13. *Wall Street Journal, op. cit.*

14. *Ibid.*

15. *Richmond Times-Dispatch, op. cit.* Reprinted with permission.

Turner Broadcasting System, Inc. (B)

NEIL H. SNYDER • DONNA BIEMILLER • KERRIE MORRISON
DIANE REIFF • LAURA WEISS

AN ABORTED TAKEOVER ATTEMPT

For many years, Ted Turner's interest in acquiring a major television network was widely known. Finally in late April 1985, Ted Turner made his move and announced his intention to purchase CBS, a goal that seemed unattainable because CBS is seventeen times bigger than TBS. In preparation for this action, CNN had been offered for sale to the three major networks in 1981. CBS offered $250 million and NBC $200 million. One of Turner's stipulations about the sale of CNN was that he was to be paid in stock. When the networks realized that this deal would make Turner the largest single stockholder of the company acquiring CNN, they promptly withdrew their offers. As recently as March 1985, Turner was still trying to entice CBS into a deal that would enable Turner to gain control of CBS in a friendly manner, but his attempts failed. Undaunted, Ted Turner, with the aid of E. F. Hutton & Co., made an offer to the shareholders of CBS to gain control of the network by exchanging debt for stock in a hostile takeover attempt.

To acquire CBS, TBS would have had to borrow heavily and offer a variety of high-risk debt securities in exchange for the CBS stock. At the time of the offer, CBS's net worth was estimated at $7.6 billion, or $254 a share. The face value of Turner's offer was for $175 a share in securities, but estimates of the market value of the offer ranged from $155 to $130 a share.

Besides TBS stock, the other securities offered to CBS shareholders were low-quality, high-risk junk bonds paying 15 percent interest or higher and zero-coupon bonds that require the payment of the principal and interest in a lump sum at maturity. Zero coupons would have allowed Turner to borrow $600 million and pay nothing until 1990. In addition, each share of TBS offered to CBS shareholders would have had only 1/10 of a vote. Thus, Turner would have maintained control of 73 percent of the voting rights in TBS stock.

If Turner's offer had been accepted, he would have acquired the broadcast network and four of the five CBS-owned and -operated television stations. Turner had planned to sell one station, the CBS Records group, the CBS publishing group, radio stations, and various other holdings for $3.1 billion and to apply the proceeds from these sales to the debt. Selling off these pieces of CBS would have reduced the total cost of the deal from $7.6

EXHIBIT 1

A Summary of the Offer Made by Ted Turner to Acquire CBS

	FACE VALUE	ESTIMATED MARKET VALUE
Interest-bearing "junk bonds"*	$122.00	$105.00
Zero coupon notes**	20.00	19.00
TBS stock***	16.50	15.00
1 share preferred		
¾ share class B		
common		
Total	$175.90	$150.00

Estimated total market value
of offer—$4.5 billion

*15% senior notes due 1992
  15.5% senior debenture due 2000
  16.25% senior subordinated debenture due 2005
**Four series with maturity range 1990–1994 with effective interest rate of 15%
***One share preferred $2.64

billion to $4.5 billion. Exhibit 1 presents a financial summary of the offer to CBS.

From the perspective of CBS stockholders, the proposed offer would result in the exchange of a $3 per year CBS dividend for $21.71 in interest and preferred stock dividends from TBS. Although the offer sounds very appealing, Wall Street analysts expressed concern about the security of the TBS assets.

THE CBS RESPONSE

To ward off the hostile takeover attempt, CBS had several alternatives. One option was to find a "white knight," a more suitable and friendly merger partner. Another possibility, and the one preferred by CBS directors, was to increase their debt and buy back their own stock. By raising additional debt, CBS would make their acquisition by Turner even riskier, because the combined debt of CBS and TBS after the merger would virtually guarantee failure. Additionally, the stock repurchase would leave fewer shares available for purchase by Turner.

Subsequently, CBS purchased 6.4 million shares of their stock, roughly 21 percent of the shares outstanding, at a cost of $960 million. The price paid by CBS for the stock was $40 per share in cash, plus $110 per share in senior notes at 10⅞ percent interest due to mature in 1995. A "poison pill," a maneuver designed to make CBS an unattractive takeover target in the future, was added by the placing of limits on the amount of debt CBS can carry.

The plan also included the sale of $123 million in new convertible preferred shares to institutional investors.

To prevent the repurchase plan, Turner filed a suit against CBS accusing its directors of a breach of fiduciary duty. The complaint alleged that the board was motivated by self interest and that it was attempting to insulate the CBS shareholders from Turner's offer. On July 30, both the FCC and a federal judge in Atlanta ruled that the board had acted in a fair and reasonable manner and in the best interest of the company. Since he was lacking sufficient cash to compete with the CBS stock repurchase offer and lacking the ability to wage a proxy battle, these rulings ended any hope Ted Turner had of gaining control of CBS at that time.

REPERCUSSIONS

TBS reported that it lost $6.7 million on revenues of $99.3 million in the second quarter of 1985. In total, the takeover attempt cost TBS $18.2 million. According to *Newsweek*, it may have been worth it to Turner just to be in the spotlight for a few weeks (*Newsweek,* April 29, 1985).

The cost of the failed merger attempt to CBS was very high. They purchased approximately 21 percent of their stock at a cost of $960 million. Since the takeover attempt ended, CBS has had serious financial difficulties and several members of its top management group have been dismissed.

Turner Broadcasting System, Inc. (C)

NEIL H. SNYDER · DONNA BIEMILLER · KERRIE MORRISON
DIANE REIFF · LAURA WEISS

INTRODUCTION

"On March 25, 1986, Ted Turner completed the $1.5 billion acquisition of MGM/UA and immediately sold UA to Kirk Kerkorian for $480 million. MGM/UA shareholders received "$20 in cash and one share of new TBS preferred stock. . . ." for each MGM/UA share they owned (*The Atlanta Constitution,* March 26, 1986). The cash portion of the acquisition was financed with junk bonds yielding returns to investors ranging from 12.5 percent to 14.5 percent.

TURNER DEVELOPS AN INTEREST IN MGM

Turner became interested in acquiring MGM in the early 1980s when the cost of leasing movies for WTBS began to increase rapidly. According to the *New York Times* (March 30, 1986):

> Mr. Turner had begun to have problems buying movies for the Atlanta Superstation. . . . In many cases, he was still paying the low rates for films that he had been charged in the 70's, when WTBS was just beginning to develop a national audience. That irritated Hollywood, and MGM even refused to lease films to WTBS. By 1985, Mr. Turner was worried that profit margins were beginning to erode as ad revenues failed to keep pace with costs at the Superstation, which accounts for 80 percent of the operating profits of Turner Broadcasting's core businesses. "There was no question that movie fees were rising," Mr. Turner said. "I mean every time we signed a new contract, it was more, more, more." So when he read last summer that MGM/UA was for sale, Mr. Turner jumped.*

But there are at least two other reasons why Turner wanted to make a deal to increase his stake in the entertainment industry, and they help explain why he moved so quickly to acquire MGM after his earlier attempt to acquire CBS failed. First, according to William Bevins, "The way the [entertainment] business was consolidating, to be a factor long-term, we either had to increase the distribution base—that would have been the CBS transaction—or acquire some software. That was the MGM deal."*

Second, "Mr. Turner was also betting on 'one factor that nobody considers' . . . what he calls 'colorization,' a technical process that he believes will

---

*Copyright © 1986 by *The New York Times* Company. Reprinted by permission.

enhance the value of old black-and-white movies. When a color version of *Miracle on 34th Street* was shown on WTBS, its ratings tripled."*

Mr. Turner's ego played a part as well. According to Turner, "Without MGM, there was a question mark with advertisers about our long-term viability. They used to throw that up at me. Early on, there was a certain group of people in the New York establishment: the same sort of thinking that gave me such a hard time at one time in the New York Yacht Club. You know: 'He's from Georgia, we don't need him around here. Here is a quarter, go shine my shoes.' You know: Stepin Fetchit."*

In Turner's opinion, buying MGM was the natural thing to do after the CBS deal fell through. But the risk involved in this acquisition was great, and the outcome of the decision will not be known for several years.

THE EFFECTS OF THE MGM DEAL ON TBS

TBS is now more leveraged than most analysts think is reasonable. "Many industry observers say the enormous debt leaves Turner with a house of cards that could collapse with the slightest downturn in the economy."†

But Turner is accustomed to having his ideas criticized, and he seems to thrive on proving the experts wrong. In fact, some experts suggest that "Turner has fortified his cable empire for an inevitable battle with the major broadcasting networks. . . . When the dust settles in a few months, it will be clear to more people that Turner, sooner than anyone else, is capable of taking on the TV networks he has tried to buy or beat."†

Competing with the networks will not be easy, because the operating costs are very high. John Malone, president of Denver-based Tele-Communications, Inc., said, "It will take a program budget of about $500 million annually to make TBS competitive with the networks in prime time. . . . TBS currently spends about $100 million on programming."†

Turner believes the acquisition of MGM will not affect the operation of TBS. "Our ongoing operations have not been and will not be affected in any way, shape or form," he claimed. "In the financing package we obtained to complete the deal, we got $200 million in overfunding that is earmarked for operations. It allows us to go ahead with a full slate of motion pictures in Los Angeles, and we have the capital to go ahead with all of the other projects at WTBS and CNN."†

In response to comments by industry analysts that Turner paid too much for MGM, Turner had this to say:

> We'll just have to wait and see. . . . Those are the same people who said that WTBS wouldn't work on a satellite, and that CNN wouldn't work and that we

---

*Copyright © 1986 by *The New York Times* Company. Reprinted by permission.
†© 1986, *The Atlanta Journal and Constitution,* March 30, 1986.

paid too much for the Braves, etc., etc. . . . Only we know what we plan to do, and they don't have a basis to comment."*

It was reported that Turner considered selling stock in TBS to reduce the firm's debt. Since he owns 81 percent of the company, he could sell 31 percent and raise about $120 million without giving up control. However, industry experts say that the overall company is not worth as much as the individual parts because the firm is so heavily in debt. They doubt Turner will choose this course of action.

Another option being actively explored is selling TBS assets to help reduce the debt. In late October 1985, TBS announced its intention to put 20 percent to 50 percent of CNN on the market to raise cash. CNN is valued at $600 million. As one would expect, before any deal can be finalized the proposed buyer's goals must be consistent with those of CNN and Turner must remain in control. An offer from NBC was rejected earlier because Turner refused to relinquish editorial control to a rival.

WHAT DID TURNER BUY WHEN HE ACQUIRED MGM?

Turner's deal with MGM/UA puts him at the helm of a large, vertically integrated motion picture and television business. Turner acquired the MGM film library, which contains 3,650 films including such classics as *Singing in the Rain, Gone with the Wind, Ben Hur,* and *The Wizard of Oz.* Along with this library, Turner acquired the rights to a broad variety of television shows. Shows produced under the MGM/UA banner will be the property of both Turner's TBS and Kerkorian's new United Artists. Each will have half-ownership in the newly formed MGM/UA Distribution Co., which will continue to distribute the shows to major networks as well as to other broadcasters. The MGM package also includes a 44-acre studio complex in Culver City, California, with 24 soundstages and a film processing laboratory that handled 532 million feet of film in fiscal year 1984.

MGM AND MOVIE PRODUCTION

Despite its successful history, MGM/UA has been struggling with financial difficulties for the past few years. As with any major studio, the company's fortunes depend on its ability to release successful motion pictures. Lately, the box office results of MGM movies have not been good. For the fiscal year ending August 1985, MGM/UA lost $116 million.

It is no secret that Turner wants MGM to continue its movie production operation. "Of course, I want MGM to stay involved in the production of motion pictures if we can figure out a way to raise the money and do it. We would have to have a partner or a joint venture of some sort. So we've got

*© 1986, *The Atlanta Journal and Constitution,* March 30, 1986.

to find someone that thinks the way we do in order to do that. But we're not ruling out new movie projects by any means."* According to Alan Ladd, Jr., chairman and chief executive officer of MGM, it is Turner's "desire to provide MGM with every available resource to sustain the studio's growth as a leading supplier of worldwide entertainment product." †

MGM AND TELEVISION PRODUCTION

MGM/UA Entertainment Co., the division in charge of television broadcast material, released only one television series in 1985—"Lady Blue" on ABC. In 1984, two MGM/UA series were canceled not long after introduction—"Jessie" and "Paper Dolls," both on ABC. In contrast, other major studios such as Universal Television, Columbia, Paramount, Warner Brothers, and 20th-Century Fox produced twelve, seven, five, three, and four television series, respectively.

NEW OPTIONS FOR TURNER AND TBS

Before the MGM acquisition was completed, there was a great deal of speculation about what Ted Turner might do with the people and assets of his new firm. Frank Rothman, chairman and chief executive officer of MGM/UA at the time of the acquisition, agreed to stay on until the deal was completed, and he characterized negotiations with Turner as "harmonious and pleasant." ‡

But MGM has not performed well lately, and some movie industry insiders say that changes must be made if the firm is going to be turned around. One unidentified MGM studio executive believes that Turner may have difficulty engineering the needed changes. "Turner may know television," he said, "but he's just another amateur when it comes to making films. His best hope is to put together a good team of seasoned people and let them have their head." [1]

The MGM acquisition gives Turner options he has not had in the past. He can differentiate his superstation from the major networks and from independent television stations by offering "the best of both worlds"—old movies and television programs as well as new releases. Reruns shown on the superstation have gained new popularity, especially with baby boomers. Broadcast industry executives say these shows embody traditional values. "The formerly hokey and corny is now heartwarming and refreshing," says Dan Greenblatt, president of distribution at LBS Communications, Inc., a distributor of television programs. [2]

---

*© 1986, *The Atlanta Journal and Constitution,* March 30, 1986.
†© 1986, *The Atlanta Journal and Constitution,* March 26, 1986.
‡© 1985, *The Atlanta Journal and Constitution,* August 11, 1985.

Turner can now produce his own movies to compete with major network programming. In addition, it has been suggested that Turner is considering launching a new pay-cable movie service that utilizes the MGM library to compete with HBO, Showtime, and The Movie Channel.[3]

There has been further speculation that Turner might attempt to turn Atlanta into the "Hollywood of the East." Filmmakers say that low labor and production costs and beautiful scenery make Georgia an ideal location for shooting pictures. Georgia has already been the site for a wide variety of major motion pictures that have turned out to be box-office bonanzas.

There is also speculation that Turner has aspirations beyond building a media empire. "Hollywood hands [are] welcoming the wild man of Dixie as a kindred spirit. . . . Those who know him say Ted Turner desperately wants to be the next William Paley, the founder of CBS, and ultimately President of the United States."[4]

NOTES

1. *Dun's Business Month,* September 1985.
2. *Wall Street Journal,* August 20, 1985.
3. *The Atlanta Journal and Constitution,* October 10, 1985.
4. *Newsweek,* April 29, 1985.

Turner Broadcasting System, Inc. (D)

NEIL H. SNYDER

THE DEAL OF A LIFETIME MAY HAVE TURNED SOUR

According to the *Wall Street Journal* (June 5, 1987), Ted Turner ". . . in effect, gave up control of his life's work. In exchange for the money to stabilize his debt problems, he granted a group of cable-television operators, including Time, Inc., broad authority to oversee—and if necessary to veto— the management decisions of Turner Broadcasting System, Inc. . . ."

The article went on to say that the MGM/UA deal was like

a bomb, with a slow-burning fuse. The bomb was the preferred stock that was to pay dividends in common shares beginning this month; unless redeemed, it could eventually have reduced Mr. Turner's common-stock holdings from 80 percent currently to a minority. To prevent that, Turner Broadcasting on Wednesday sold two new classes of preferred shares, amounting to 37 percent of the company's voting stock, to the cable companies for $562.5 million. The company will use the money to redeem the original preferred shares. . . .

Mr. Turner still owns 51 percent of his company's voting stock, and he remains chairman. But the board has been expanded to 15 members, and the cable operators have elected seven of them. A supermajority of 12 directors will be required to approve each item of the annual budget. The supermajority will also be required to approve acquisitions, asset sales, borrowings, refinancings, amendments to bylaws, dividends, top-level executive changes and anything that isn't in the budget and costs more than $2 million.

Furthermore, if Turner Broadcasting doesn't bring its remaining debt problems under control within a year, the cable companies get an outright majority of the board. And if Mr. Turner decides to sell his stake, they have the right of first refusal to buy it. . . .

"It's clear from the transaction as it's structured—and I think it's an economic fact of life—that Ted no longer owns the company," says William Bevins, Turner Broadcasting's chief financial officer.*

WHAT NEXT FOR TED TURNER?

This turn of events raises some obvious questions. First among them is whether Ted Turner will be satisfied with his new, much less powerful role. Can he serve as leader of TBS now that he can be prevented from pursuing his goals if he cannot persuade twelve of fifteen TBS directors that what he wants to do is also what is best for the company? The key word to consider is persuade. Ted Turner has not had to concern himself with persuading people in his company. In the past when he decided what he wanted to do, he simply did it.

Those who know him best suggest that Turner will not want to play this role. If they are correct, then what is next for Ted Turner? He is a very wealthy man who is about fifty years old and who has an enormous amount of talent and energy. Will he be a politician? Will he be a manager? Will he be a humanitarian who is willing to devote the rest of his life to pursuing world peace? Will he be an empire builder?

Exhibit 1 presents summary data about TBS as of May 1987.

EXHIBIT 1   **Turner Broadcasting System, Inc.**

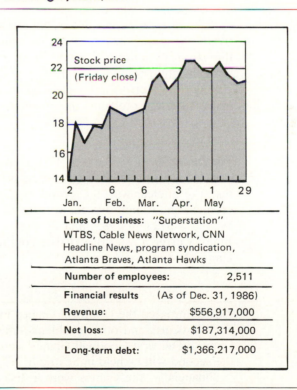

Lines of business: "Superstation"
WTBS, Cable News Network, CNN
Headline News, program syndication,
Atlanta Braves, Atlanta Hawks

Number of employees:	2,511
Financial results (As of Dec. 31, 1986)	
Revenue:	$556,917,000
Net loss:	$187,314,000
Long-term debt:	$1,366,217,000

SOURCE: *Wall Street Journal*, June 5, 1987. Reprinted by permission of the *Wall Street Journal*, © Dow Jones & Company, Inc. 1987. All Rights Reserved Worldwide.

Turner Broadcasting System, Inc. (E)

NEIL H. SNYDER · SUSAN SUMMERS

Ted Turner: Clergyman, Politician, Statesman or Businessman?

As Ted Turner's wealth and influence have grown, his interests have changed dramatically as well. Once an outsider looking in and desperately desiring acceptance as a business leader, he is now regarded as a broadcasting guru. That is not to say that all his ideas have worked, but rather that he has had several important ideas that have the potential to revolutionize, or are revolutionizing, the way we see the world. What next for Ted Turner? Having achieved his business goals, what is on his agenda? From his actions it is difficult to tell.

According to Turner, his push to be a force in broadcasting was not motivated by money or power. He sees himself as a crusader instead. "I think that strong actions need to take place. I'm not doing it for myself. I'm doing it for the children and their children and for the people in the world who are getting ripped off—the people who want to live in peace and harmony and want to see our problems solved before we destroy the planet." [1]

BETTER WORLD SOCIETY

The Better World Society (BWS) is a nonprofit organization whose primary purpose is to produce programming aimed at easing world tension and the threat of nuclear war. Its secondary purpose is to solve the overpopulation problem and to improve environmental conditions. [2] The BWS was founded by Ted Turner in 1985, and its board members include former president Jimmy Carter, Lester Brown (head of the Audubon Society), and others with United Nations backgrounds. [3]

GOODWILL GAMES

Turner initiated the Goodwill Games in partnership with the Soviet Union after boycotts and other problems emerged as a standard of the Olympic Games. The first Goodwill Games were held in Moscow in July 1986, and the second will be held in Seattle in July 1990.

Financially, the Games were a disaster for Turner. He lost millions of dollars. In addition, viewer ratings were low, the broadcasts were criticized as lacking "substance and human drama," and its announcers were inadequate.[4] Other problems with the event included accusations by Carl Lewis and two other U.S. athletes that the Soviets cheated by scheduling preliminary track heats to tire the Americans and by giving performance-improving drugs to Seige Bubka, who won the pole vault event and set a new world record.[5]

In addition, the U.S. Defense Department refused to allow twelve servicemen, including nine U.S. boxers, to participate in the Games. The Defense Department justified their decision by claiming that the Games were for commercial purposes. Turner, on the other hand, said the U.S. government was trying to "harm the games."[6] Turner was also criticized for "hiring athletes."[7] He donated over $6 million to U.S. athletic programs, the participants in the Games were given $3000 each, and he decided which sports would be played.[8]

Despite these and other problems, Turner remained confident about the potential of the Goodwill Games to bring the United States and the Soviet Union together. He said he was more concerned about this aspect of the Games than anything else.[9]

CABLE NEWS NETWORK (CNN)

Turner has turned a fledgling, high-risk venture into what has become one of the best, if not the best, broadcast news operations in the world. It is seen in every major city in the world, and it is required viewing for all the leaders of the world. CNN is distancing itself from the network news operations by breaking important stories and by offering more on the scene coverage. To date, CBS, NBC, and ABC have not responded effectively to CNN, and CNN's popularity is growing.

DISARMAMENT

"Let's call it a tie and call it off."[10] That is Ted Turner's opinion on the arms race. He believes the Soviets fear a nuclear war as much as we do. Thus, according to Turner, we should slash the military budget to $75 billion and cut the waste (e.g., bombers, etc.).[11]

THE ENVIRONMENT

In Turner's opinion, the money not spent on the military should be spent on global education, the environment, acid rain, etc.[12] To the best of the authors' knowledge, Mr. Turner has not offered a solution to the towering twin deficits faced by the United States (budget and trade). Turner owns movie production and distribution facilities that he uses to address these issues. For example, Turner produced *Nightbreaker,* an anti-nuclear drama starring Martin Sheen, *Incident at Dark River,* starring Mike Farrell as a man whose daughter was killed by toxic waste dumped into a river by a local factory, and *Captain Planet,* a cartoon show with a superhero who fights environmental villains.

In addition, Turner developed "Ten Voluntary Initiatives" that he believes will help solve our environmental problems. For example:

- We should promise to treat all people with dignity, respect, and friendliness.
- We should help the unfortunate to enjoy the benefits of a decent life, including clean air.
- We should avoid using toxic chemicals or other pollutants whenever possible and wherever practical.
- We should promise not to have more than two children per family.
- We should support the United Nations in its effort to improve the condition of the planet.[13]

ABORTION

In the summer of 1989, TBS broadcast a pro-abortion documentary titled *Abortion: For Survival.* The biased portrayal of the abortion issue and the fact that the program never addressed many critical and, at this time, unresolved issues (e.g., murder of a living fetus, harvesting fetal tissue as a cash crop for medical research and human transplants, etc.) led many anti-abortion sympathizers to denounce the program. Turner responded by calling them a bunch of "Bozos."[14] Later he said that he regretted having made that statement, because that was his personal view and not the view of Ted Turner, president of TBS. He went on to say, "These people (anti-abortionists) talk about adoption as an alternative. That is a bunch of bull. The biggest problem we have in the world is the population explosion. There are 100 million kids in the world that are up for adoption [an unsubstantiated number] right now. Adopt them."[15]

NOTES

1. "To Russia with Hype: Ted Turner Tackles Cold War with TV," *Broadcasting,* November 25, 1985, p. 81.

2. *Ibid.,* p. 81.

3. Daniel Seligman, "The Junk Man," *Fortune,* July 8, 1985, p. 137.

4. William Taaffe, 'Goodwill, But Not a Very Good Show," *Sports Illustrated,* July 21, 1986, p. 55.

5. "Turner Taking a Bath in Moscow," *Broadcasting,* July 14, 1986, pp. 33–35.

6. *Ibid.,* p. 34.

7. "Let These New Games Begin," *Sports Illustrated,* July 7, 1986, p. 9.

8. *Ibid.,* p. 9.

9. "Games to Begin Saturday," *Seattle Times,* July 3, 1986.

10. David C. Kotok, "Turner Pushes for New Uses of Arms Money," *Omaha World Herald,* May 23, 1985.

11. Richard Zoglin, "The Greening of Ted Turner," *Time,* January 22, 1990, pp. 58–60.

12. Kotok. *op. cit.*

13. "Hear, O Israel," *The Economist,* November 4, 1989, p. 36.

14. Zoglin, *op. cit.,* p. 60.

15. Zoglin, *op. cit.,* p. 60.

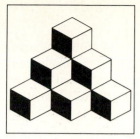

INDUSTRY
TEXTILES

C A S E 9

Watson, Inc.

NEIL H. SNYDER • RANDY BRYAN

HISTORY OF THE FIRM

Watson, Inc., was founded in Pineville, South Carolina, in May 1866. Originally the firm's name was Watson Weaving, but the name was changed in 1975 to reflect changes taking place in the textile industry. The firm began by weaving the abundant supply of cotton grown in the South into cloth used in the manufacture of men's shirts. The first plant contained four looms and employed twenty people. The firm's founder, Robert Watson, Sr., managed all of the plant's operations. By the turn of the century, the firm owned three plants and employed four hundred people. Watson, Sr., retired in 1910 and his son took over. Watson, Jr., stepped down in April 1950, and Watson III became the president and chief executive officer of the firm his grandfather had begun.

WATSON'S PRODUCTS

Watson, Inc.'s primary products include fabrics used in the manufacture of men's shirts, sheets, and towels. The shirt material is primarily oxford cloth. The material hasn't changed much in the last forty years and is still produced the way it was years ago (i.e., using long production runs and labor-intensive techniques). Customers for this fabric are some of the largest apparel manufacturers in the country, and include companies such as Arrow, Eagle shirtmakers, and Huntington Clothiers. Buyers for these firms tend to be very price sensitive.

THE BOARD OF DIRECTORS

The board is composed of fifteen members and is chaired by Robert Watson III. Robert Watson IV is vice chair and is considered to be the likely candidate to succeed his father. Other family members on the board include Robert IV's three brothers, his brother-in-law, and two nephews. The other board members include John Langhorn of First Pineville Bank and Trust; William Callis, inventor of the revolutionary Series Three Looms introduced in the company's plants in the mid-1960s; State Senator Lucius Freeman; Thomas Barnes, president of the Pineville Chamber of Commerce; and two long-time family friends.

FINANCIAL INFORMATION

Watson's 1989 sales volume was $200 million, but sales have been declining since the mid-1980s.

Sales (dollars in millions)

1977	1978	1979	1980	1981	1982	1983	1984	1985	1986	1987	1988	1989
177	182	188	194	201	206	210	214	213	209	207	203	200

Watson's margins have come under increasing pressure and are currently among the lowest in the industry. Expenditures on new equipment have been minimal and have remained for the past several years at levels that are only sufficient to cover replacement of worn-out machines. The board recently reviewed a proposal from Zwiegtach, a German weaving-machine manufacturer, to install new, fully automated equipment in eight of the Watson facilities. The capacity of the eight refitted plants would surpass that of the current twelve. The plan would have cost Watson $75 million over two years and was deemed to be too expensive.

Due to the firm's strong equity base and lack of expansion, Watson has been able to avoid any long-term debt. Short-term funding is used to cover seasonal fluctuations in working capital requirements.

STOCK

Watson's stock was first traded on the American Stock Exchange in 1959. Today, trading in Watson's stock remains light and prices have fallen dramatically over the last eighteen months. The board has maintained an 83 percent dividend payout ratio over the last nine years and feels that these payments have been the basis for the market's valuation of the firm's stock. Fifty-two percent of the outstanding common shares are controlled by members of the Watson family.

SALES

Watson's sales have shown negative growth since the mid-1980s. The firm's top managers and its board have assumed that this problem was due to increasing pressure from imports. Products from less-developed countries and the Pacific Rim are cheaper than those produced in America largely because of their lower labor costs.

LABOR SUPPLY

Watson's twelve production facilities are located in rural areas. Textile workers in the United States are among the lowest paid of all manufacturing employees. Since Watson is located in areas with generally depressed economies, it is able to employ large numbers of hard-working individuals for relatively little pay. The average Watson employee earns $6.88 per hour. Watson has maintained good relations with its employees over the years and has been an active participant in community affairs. The firm is also the single largest employer in all of the communities in which it operates. Due to these factors, the firm has been able to withstand attempts by the Amalgamated Textile Workers of America to organize unions in all of its plants.

CONSOLIDATION

The textile industry is very different today than it was ten years ago. There are fewer firms. Many small, independent producers have been taken over by huge conglomerates. Others have simply closed their doors and liquidated assets. The effect has been a more efficient industry with more productive plants, better customer relations, improved distribution systems, and higher profits. The consolidation has not been without costs, both human and financial. Thousands of loyal employees have been replaced by new high-tech or "World Class" technology imported from Japan and West Germany. This new equipment is not cheap and has been financed largely through long-term debt. The average debt-to-equity ratio for the industry has climbed from 1.1 in 1982 to 2.0 in 1989.

WATSON REMAINS INDEPENDENT

Robert Watson III has been in the textile business all of his life. He has watched most of his competitors close their doors or merge with other firms. He is proud that his family has been able to retain control of the firm. It is important to him that the firm remain independent. After all, the company bears his name.

Large textile firms have made several attempts to buy Watson, Inc. Although each of the offers would have yielded a substantial gain for the Watson family, Mr. Watson has maintained that the family will not relinquish control, and that the firm's slumping sales can be reversed.

THE ANNUAL VISIT

At 10 A.M. Robert Watson III began his annual inspection of his Greenville, North Carolina, weaving operation. It struck him that this was the 39th time he had conducted this tour in his current capacity. He was pleased with his decision to spend so heavily on the Series Three equipment in the mid-1960s. These machines had served him well, and with the excellent maintenance program developed over the years, he had no reason to doubt their continued good service to the company.

Fred Dextor is the plant manager, and he has been with the company for 35 years. Fred likes to remind Robert that his employees serve the firm well, and that many of them have been working in the plant their entire adult lives. With respect to the Series Three equipment, Fred commented, "With our people operating these machines and their great service record, these babies are turning out products of better quality than the day we installed 'em."

Robert left the plant pleased with its operation. He had built an organization that could take advantage of large economies of scale and produce huge fabric lot sizes with reduced costs.

BACK IN THE OFFICE

When Robert returned to his office in Pineville, he began to wonder how, with his operations so efficient, his margins could be disappearing. He was selling fewer pounds of fabric. He was getting less money per pound for fabric sold. Raw material costs had undergone some wild swings over the past decade, but prices had increased enough to cover the increase in cost. Insurance had gone up a great deal, and Robert was looking at the possibility of self-insuring. Other costs had increased at a rate comparable with increases in the CPI. Mr. Watson concluded that very little could be done internally to reduce costs without undertaking an expensive modernization program, reducing the number of employees, and providing better training for the employees he kept.

THE WASHINGTON EFFORT

Watson called many of his friends who were in the textile industry together for a week-long meeting at the Willard Hotel in Washington, D.C. It was apparent that everyone was feeling the margin squeeze.

Eli Spencer of Goldenit Industries said, "There's no way for us to make current operations any more efficient. I've had production specialists working on my floors for seventeen years. They tell me now that they're through; there's not another ounce of productivity that we can squeeze out of these plants."

Tom Bates of Bates Mills said, "I asked for and received all of the wage concessions I can morally and realistically hope to receive. My people really understand the problems we're having, and they want to help."

Mr. Watson, desiring to move the group into action, made this statement: "It's obvious that we are at a tremendous disadvantage. We can't compete against these poor countries that pay nothing to their workers. We can't compete against countries that have uninhibited access to the world's cotton markets when we're forced to buy U.S. cotton at an inflated price. We've got to have help from the boys up on that hill. We won't make it otherwise. I think we should lobby for protection. I hope the rest of you agree and that you will join me in my effort to get protection."

THE ANNUAL BOARD MEETING	As Robert Watson IV prepared himself for the meeting, he began to wonder whether or not his father's course of action was the best for the firm in the long run. He knew that they were under attack from foreign producers, but he was uncertain about what to do. Should they expand by buying more plants? Add more Series Three technology? Change product lines? Close plants? Modernize equipment? Move operations? He was unsure about the answers to these questions, but he believed they should be asked at the annual board meeting. He doubted whether the board could answer the questions, because his uncles always seemed anxious to finish things and get out of the meeting. Additionally, his father did not like to have his decisions questioned, and his style was to tell the board what the problems were and what they should do to solve them. The meetings rarely exceeded ninety minutes in length.

At 1:30, after a long lunch in the executive dining room, the chairman called the meeting to order. Mr. Watson then presented his views on the firm's position. He expressed concern about margins and sales erosion, and he offered his plan to combat it by lobbying for protection in Washington as *the* solution.

A brief discussion of the firm's financial condition followed. Then came the vote on dividend policy. As in years past, the recommendation from Watson III was to maintain current payout levels. The vote moved around the table to his left. There were fourteen yeas when it was Watson IV's turn to vote. He voted no. It was obvious from Watson III's reaction that he was surprised. Below is the exchange that followed:

WATSON III: "Do you want to increase the payout?"

WATSON IV: "No. Decrease it, substantially."

WATSON III: "What would you suggest that we do with the cash?"

WATSON IV: "Invest in a modernization strategy."

WATSON III: "Why?"

WATSON IV: "Because what you're proposing will lead to the slow and painful death of the firm, and I don't want any part of it."

Acquisition of Northrop by Winslow

NEIL H. SNYDER • STOREY CHARBONNET

It was late on Friday afternoon as Gary Cross left the Winslow Textile plant in Charleston, South Carolina. It had been a very long day, and the next week would be one of the most difficult Gary had faced at Winslow. On Monday morning, Gary was expected to make a presentation to the board of directors to address the problems at Winslow and what could be done to solve them.

He could list a number of problems. Yet there was no single culprit that he could pinpoint as the root cause of them, and finding a solution was not going to be easy. As Gary drove home, he thought about the changes that had taken place in his job over the past decade and about the changes that would have to take place at Winslow during the next several years in order for Winslow to survive and prosper in the 1990s.

GARY CROSS'S BACKGROUND

Gary had grown up in a large family. He had four brothers and three sisters, so he learned at a very young age what it was like to get along with others. In addition, he knew what it was like to work hard and to share, and he understood how important it was for everyone in the family to feel a part of the group. Although his family was not wealthy, they had the necessities of life, and Gary's father always tried to involve every member of the family in important decisions. Gary appreciated the opportunity to voice his opinions, and he carried this tradition forward into his work life by encouraging his employees to share their views with him.

Gary graduated from North Carolina State University with honors in 1965. Upon graduation, he looked for a job in a small firm because he did not want to work for a large company. He had always been skeptical of large firms because he thought people did not matter very much to their managers. Furthermore, he believed that individual participation would not be appreciated or rewarded in a large firm. The people he knew who worked for large firms always seemed to be unhappy, and he attributed their problems to the way the firms were managed. Gary believed that life was too short to waste time in a place where he would be unhappy.

It was no surprise when, in the fall in 1965, Gary accepted a job with Northrop Textiles. Northrop was a small, nonunion textile firm that enjoyed success because of the dedication and hard work of its employees and because of their good relations with management. Northrop's incentive programs were designed to reward all of its employees according to their performance, and Northrop's average productivity per employee far surpassed that of the industry.

Gary started out with Northrop as a management trainee, and he performed well. In 1968, he became a department manager, and he enjoyed this job immensely. The working environment within the firm was especially enjoyable for Gary because it reminded him of his family. In 1971, only three years after becoming department manager, Gary was promoted to plant manager.

INCENTIVE PROGRAMS AT NORTHROP

Northrop was expanding cautiously, but its profits were growing rapidly. In 1973, 10 percent of the company's profits were distributed to the firm's employees. In the early years of the incentive program, individual employees were rewarded according to their personal accomplishments, but it had evolved into a program that rewarded the entire workforce equally. If a 10 percent bonus was in order, then every employee got a 10 percent bonus. The logic of the program centered on the belief that all members of the plant contribute to the final product and, therefore, they should be rewarded equally, not according to their individual production. Peer pressure to perform was strong at Northrop, and it was uncommon for anyone who was not willing to work hard to last longer than six months with the firm.

John Lassiter, the sole owner of Northrop, had decided when he first opened the plant that his employees ultimately determined whether his firm would succeed. Therefore, he decided to reward them well for their hard work, loyalty, and dedication. However, it was understood by every employee that during bad times there would be no bonuses. Only twice in its history had the company experienced losses. Both times, the employees had been willing to take pay cuts to help the company.

CONSOLIDATION IN THE INDUSTRY

The textile industry was undergoing consolidation through merger and acquisition. Sales were dropping as imports increased, margins were falling as equipment and technology became outdated, and debt within the industry was increasing at a rapid rate. Most textile company owners saw increasing debt to modernize as a fact of life, and the owners of firms that wanted to survive adjusted their thinking to accommodate the new realities in the industry.

A DECISION FOR NORTHROP

In 1977, Mr. Lassiter was approached by Winslow Textile, a larger firm, with an offer to buy Northrop. The purchase would have meant substantial capital gains for Mr. Lassiter and the other members of the board, who together owned 52 percent of the common shares outstanding. The board had discussed this possibility before, but they thought Northrop was better off going it alone. Thus, the idea of Northrop being acquired by Winslow was rejected.

NICHE STRATEGY

As foreign competitors began to dominate the labor-intensive commodity markets within the textile industry, domestic firms began to look elsewhere for market share to avoid competition. Thus the niche strategy evolved. Domestic firms attempted to create demand for specialty products just as the Italians had created a demand for silk ties in the 1970s. Mr. Lassiter and the board at Northrop wondered if this strategy would work over the long run. But it was being presented to them as the wave of the future, so they accepted it. Over the years, several members of the board had lingering doubts about the decision to reject Winslow's offer.

PROBLEMS AT NORTHROP

Northrop's sales and margins continued to increase in 1978. Thus, John Lassiter and the board saw no reason to change the formula that had led to their success. Unfortunately, in 1979, sales fell short of expectations for the first time in eight years. In 1980, sales declined again, and the problem was attributed to rapidly increasing import growth. It was becoming quite obvious that increasing textile imports into the United States were beginning to take their toll on domestic firms and that U.S. firms were paying much more for labor than their foreign competitors.

WINSLOW ACQUIRES NORTHROP

Over the years conditions worsened, and John Lassiter was forced to consider the possibility of the firm's merging or being acquired. In 1985, Winslow again approached Northrop with an offer to buy the company. Northrop's board believed that any attempt to avoid the acquisition would be foolish. They saw no other alternative. Northrop simply did not have the cash, nor could they raise the necessary capital, to purchase the technologically advanced equipment needed to survive and prosper in the rapidly changing textile industry.

In late 1985, Winslow acquired Northrop for about half what it had offered for the company in 1977. At the time of the purchase, Winslow's sales were seven times greater than Northrop's, and they believed that acquiring Northrop would help them to compete in the competitive global market of the 1990s. With their larger size and Northrop's first-rate management team and workforce, Winslow thought it was prepared to do battle in the global market.

TRANSITION PERIOD

On the strong recommendation of John Lassiter, Gary Cross was asked to manage a large division of Winslow. The management style at Winslow was not at all like Northrop's. Thus, there was an adjustment period for everyone, including the Northrop and Winslow employees. In addition, the Winslow workforce was unionized and had gone on strike three times in the past nine years.

It was no surprise to anyone when the Northrop employees saw a substantial increase in their base pay after the acquisition, but there was no bonus or incentive program. The Northrop group quickly learned that they could do quite well financially without putting out a great deal of effort, and they knew that if they put out extra effort it did not pay. In fact, they received the same salary no matter how hard they worked. The Winslow environment was not at all like what the Northrop environment had been.

Most of the Northrop group of employees showed no outward signs that they disliked the new system. But the most loyal, hard working, and devoted members of the group seemed to resent it. In fact, turnover was beginning to be a problem in the latter group. Even Gary wondered about the fairness of some employees' working hard and earning no more than those who did only what they had to do to get by. More important, there did not seem to be any real unity among the workers.

WINSLOW'S WORKFORCE

Profits soared for the first three years after the acquisition. Then sales began to decline. Declining sales led to declining profits, and in 1989 Winslow asked their employees to take a pay cut. Instead of accepting the cut as a necessity, the Winslow employees threatened to strike.

In mid-1989, work at Winslow ceased temporarily as its employees initiated the first of two strikes that year. The union believed the problems at Winslow were due to poor management and that they had nothing to do with labor costs. They acknowledged that labor costs were higher at Winslow than in most foreign countries, but they also knew that Winslow had the latest technology available. The union contended that management could operate the firm profitably, thus they were unwilling to make any wage concessions.

CONCLUSION

Gary could not resist the temptation to compare Winslow and Northrop. Since the acquisition, he had not enjoyed his work very much, and he was thinking about finding another job. He particularly disliked the lack of trust and the selfishness that seemed to pervade the organization. As Gary drove home from work that night, he wondered what he might tell the board on Monday.

INDUSTRY
BREWING

CASE 11

Anheuser-Busch Companies, Inc. (A)

NEIL H. SNYDER • DOUGLAS J. WORKMAN • RICH BONAVENTURA
JOHN CARY • SCOTT McMASTERS • KAREN COOK

BACKGROUND OF THE FIRM

In 1852, Georg Schneider opened the Bavarian Brewery on the south side of St. Louis, Missouri. Five years later the brewery faced insolvency. In 1857, it was sold to competitors who renamed it Hammer and Urban. The new owners launched an expansion program with the help of a loan from Eberhard Anheuser, a successful soap manufacturer at the time. By 1860, the brewery had faltered once again and Anheuser assumed control. Four years later, his son-in-law, Adolphus Busch, joined the brewery as a salesman. Later Adolphus became a partner and finally president of the company. Busch was the driving force behind the company's success and, in 1879, the company name was changed to Anheuser-Busch Brewing Association.

An important reason for the brewery's success was Adolphus Busch's innovative attempt to establish and maintain a national beer market. In 1877, he launched the industry's first fleet of refrigerated freight cars. He also pioneered the application of a new pasteurization process. Busch's talents were not limited to technology alone; he concurrently developed merchandising techniques to complement his technological innovations. By 1901, annual sales had surpassed the million-barrel mark for the first time.

August A. Busch succeeded his father as president of Anheuser-Busch in 1913. With the advent of Prohibition, he was forced to harness the company's expertise and energies into new directions (i.e., corn products, baker's

---

This case was prepared by Douglas J. Workman, Neil H. Snyder, Rich Bonaventura, John Cary, Scott McMasters, and Karen Cook of the McIntire School of Commerce, University of Virginia. Reprinted with permission.

yeast, ice cream, commercial refrigeration units, truck bodies, and nonalcoholic beverages). These efforts kept the company from collapsing during the dry era. With the passage of the Twenty-first Amendment, Anheuser-Busch was back in the beer business. To celebrate, a team of Clydesdale horses was acquired in 1933—the Budweiser Clydesdales.

In 1946, August A. Busch, Jr., became president and chief executive officer. During his tenure, the company's beer operation flourished. Eight breweries were constructed and annual sales increased from 3 million barrels in 1946 to more than 34 million in 1974. The corporation also diversified extensively, adding family entertainment centers, real estate, can manufacturing, transportation, and a major league baseball franchise.

August A. Busch III was elected president in 1974 and chief executive the following year, making him the fifth Busch to serve in that capacity. Thus far under his direction, Anheuser-Busch has accomplished the following: opened its tenth brewery; introduced Michelob Light, Anheuser-Busch Natural Light, and Würzburger Hofbräu; opened a new Busch Gardens theme park; launched the largest brewery expansion projects in the company's history; vertically integrated into new can manufacturing and malt production facilities; and diversified into container recovery, soft drinks, and snack foods.

THE INDUSTRY AND COMPETITION

Ninety percent of Anheuser-Busch's sales come from its beer products. (Generically, the term *beer* refers to any beverage brewed from a farinaceous grain.) The type of beer consumed in America today originated in the 1840s with the introduction of lager beer. Lager beer is bottom fermented (meaning yeast settles to the bottom during fermentation). The beer is then aged (or lagered) to mellow, resulting in a lighter, more effervescent potation. Prior to 1840, Americans' tastes closely resembled British tastes (i.e., leaning toward ale, porter, and stout). The influx of German immigrants in the 1840s initially increased the importance of lager beer because of the influence of German tastes and brewing skills.

By 1850, there were 430 brewers in the United States producing a total of 750,000 barrels per year, and by the end of the decade, there were 1,269 brewers producing over 1 million barrels per year. At that time, brewers served relatively small local areas. In the latter half of the nineteenth century, several significant technological advances were adapted to the beer industry including refrigeration, mechanized bottling equipment, and pasteurization. The latter innovation enabled brewers to ship warm beer and store it for a longer period of time without refrigeration. With developments in transportation technology, the twentieth century saw the rise of the national brewer. The combined impact of these technological advances resulted in greater emphasis on marketing as the primary instrument of competition.

EXHIBIT 1   **Number of Breweries and Brewery Firms: 1946–1976**

YEAR	PLANTS	FIRMS
1946	471	
1947	465	404
1948	466	
1949	440	
1950	407	
1951	386	
1952	357	
1953	329	
1954	310	263
1955	292	
1956	281	
1957	264	
1958	252	211
1959	244	
1960	229	
1961	229	
1962	220	
1963	211	171
1964	190	
1965	179	
1966	170	
1967	154	125
1968	149	
1969	146	
1970	137	
1971	134	
1972	131	108
1973	114	
1974 (June)	108	
1976	94	49

SOURCE: For the years 1946–1974: *Brewing Industry Survey* (New York: Research Company of America, 1973, 1974); 1947–1972 (for number of firms): U.S. Bureau of the Census, *Census of Manufacturers;* and 1976: *Brewers Digest Brewery Directory,* 1977.

The modern era of the brewing industry began with the end of World War II. Prior to that time, only a few brewers sold beer nationally, and they primarily operated out of a single plant. To offset additional transportation costs not incurred by local or even regional brewers, the national firms advertised their beers as being of premium quality and charged a premium price. This structural change in the industry (from predominantly local or regional to national producers) in the post–World War II time period has resulted in a steady decline in the number of brewers and plants and an increase in the market concentration of the large national brewers. Exhibit 1 shows the number of breweries and brewery firms for 1946–1976. Exhibit 2 shows concentration ratios for 1935–1977.

In the period following World War II, annual beer sales hit a record high in 1947 and then declined and stagnated until 1959. Exhibit 3 shows per capita demand trends in total beer, packaged beer, and draft beer for this time period.

Many analysts blamed the lack of growth in demand upon demographic factors. According to *Brewers Almanac 1976* (p. 82), past industry surveys have shown that persons in the 21 to 44 age group account for about 69

EXHIBIT 2

National Beer Sales Concentration Ratios: 1935–1977 (Percent)

YEAR	FOUR FIRM	EIGHT FIRM
1935	11	17
1947	21	30
1954	27	41
1958	28	44
1963	34	52
1966	39	56
1967	40	59
1970	46	64
1972	52	70
1973	54	70
1974	58	74
1975	59	78
1976	59	80
1977	63	83

SOURCE: For the years 1935–1972: U.S. Bureau of the Census, *Census of Manufacturers* (based on value of shipments, establishment basis); 1973: based on share of total sales of U.S. brewers in *Brewing Industry Survey* (1974); 1974–1975: based on sales data in *Advertising Age,* November 3, 1975, and December 27, 1976; and 1976–1977: based on sales data in *Modern Brewery Age,* February 14, 1977, and February 13, 1978, by permission.

EXHIBIT 3

Analysis of Per Capita Beer Demand in the United States, 1935–1963

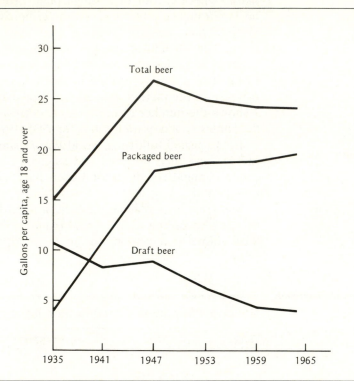

SOURCE: John G. Keane (Ph.D., University of Pittsburgh).

percent of beer consumption. Since this age group exhibited little growth during 1948–1959, population demographics offer a good explanation for stagnated demand during this period. However, other factors must be introduced to account for post-1959 growth because beer sales grew more than twice as fast as the number of people in that age group.

ECONOMIES OF SCALE

A major reason for the growth of national firms is the economies of scale obtained in their plant operations. Economies of scale in plant size enable brewers to obtain the lowest possible unit cost. According to Dr. Kenneth G. Elzinga of the University of Virginia (an authority on the brewing industry), the minimum efficient size (MES) plant capacity for the brewing industry is 1.25 million barrels per year. Cost savings accrue from water-processing equipment, sewage facilities, refrigeration equipment, management, laboratories, and custodial cost reductions. Scale economies from most of these sources continue to plant capacities of 10 million barrels per year, but beyond the size of 4.5 million barrels, cost savings are negligible. Exhibit 4 shows one method used to estimate the extent of economies of scale: the survivor test.

Economies of scale played a central role in the restructuring of the brewing industry, which led to the demise of hundreds of breweries between 1945 and 1970. Moreover, according to Charles F. Keithahn of the Bureau of Economics of the Federal Trade Commission, an analysis based solely on economies of scale would indicate a decline in firm concentration over the 1970s (in a world in which all plants are of minimum efficient size but no larger). Exhibit 5 shows the minimum market share a firm with a MES plant would need for survival.

THE EFFECTS OF MERGERS ON INDUSTRY CONCENTRATION

Leonard Weiss of the University of Wisconsin at Madison developed a means of delineating the impact of mergers on an industry's structure. Using Weiss's methodology, Dr. Elzinga found that mergers accounted for a negligible amount of the concentration occurring in the brewing industry. In fact, concentration trends in the brewing industry are rather unique in that

EXHIBIT 4

Surviving Breweries by Capacity: 1959–1973

LISTED CAPACITY BARRELS (000)	1959	1961	1963	1965	1967	1969	1971	1973
0–25	11	9	8	7	3	3	2	2
26–100	57	51	46	44	33	23	19	11
101–250	51	44	39	30	26	23	19	11
251–500	40	37	33	24	18	14	14	10
501–750	14	15	13	12	13	15	12	5
751–1,000	16	19	20	20	22	20	20	15
1,001–1,500	14	14	12	13	15	13	13	13
1,501–2,000	4	5	5	3	3	8	8	7
2,001–3,000	5	6	6	7	5	6	9	9
3,001–4,000	3	3	4	5	5	3	3	3
4,001 +	2	2	3	3	4	7	7	11

SOURCE: Compiled from plant capacity figures listed in the *Modern Brewery Age Book* (Stamford, Conn.: Modern Brewery Age Publishing Co., various years); and industry trade sources. These figures do not include plants listed only on a company-consolidated basis (in the case of multiplant firms) or single-plant firms not reporting capacity in the *Blue Book*. Most plants list their capacity.

EXHIBIT 5

Economies of Plant Scale Expressed as a Percentage of Total Industry Production for 1970, 1975, 1980

	PRODUCTION (MILLIONS OF BARRELS)	MES PLANT AS A PERCENTAGE OF PRODUCTION
1970	134.7	.9%
1975	150.3	.8
1980 (estimated)	176.8	.7

SOURCE: Dr. Willard Mueller, from testimony before the Subcommittee on Antitrust and Monopoly of the Committee of the Judiciary, United States Senate, 95th Congress, 2d sess. (1978).

most of the increased concentration was brought about by internal expansion rather than by merger or acquisition. Strict enforcement of the antitrust laws by the Justice Department (DOJ) is the reason that mergers have accounted for such a small share of the increase in concentration. But the DOJ, through its rigid enforcement of the antitrust laws, may have promoted the end result it was seeking to prevent—increased national concentration. With the elimination of the merger route, the national brewers were forced to expand internally. They built large new breweries, which were more efficient than the older, smaller ones. If mergers had been permitted, the national firms might have acquired old, small breweries and might have grown more slowly than they actually did.

THE EFFECT OF ADVERTISING

Forced to expand internally in a capital-intensive industry (it costs between $25 and $45 for each additional barrel of capacity), the national firms sought to ensure a steady demand for their products. The need for larger markets resulting from increased capacity coincided with the development of television, which led to an increase in the firms' desired level of product identification. Advertising, particularly television spots, became the key to product differentiation in an industry where studies have shown that under test conditions beer drinkers cannot distinguish between brands. Exhibit 6 shows comparative advertising expenditures for ten brewers. Exhibit 7 shows relative advertising effectiveness.

In the last decade, a new rivalry has developed among major national brewers (this time at the instigation of Miller Brewing Company). In 1970, Philip Morris completed an acquisition of Miller and, according to Dr. Willard F. Mueller of the University of Wisconsin, Philip Morris's multiproduct and multinational operations in highly concentrated industries enabled it to

EXHIBIT 6

Barrelage Sold, Measured Media Advertising Expenditures, and Advertising Expenditures, Per Barrel, Ten Leading Brewers, 1972–1977

	PHILIP MORRIS–MILLER				ANHEUSER-BUSCH		
YEAR	BARRELS (000)	ADVERTISING* ($000)	A/B†		BARRELS (000)	ADVERTISING* ($000)	A/B†
1977	24,410	$42,473	$1.74		36,640	$44,984	$1.23
1976	18,232	29,117	1.60		29,051	25,772	0.89
1975	12,862	20,894	1.62		35,200	19,237	0.55
1974	9,066	12,140	1.34		34,100	12,359	0.36
1973	6,919	10,002	1.45		29,887	12,936	0.43
1972	5,353	8,400	1.57		26,522	14,808	0.56

	SCHLITZ				PABST		
YEAR	BARRELS (000)	ADVERTISING* ($000)	A/B†		BARRELS (000)	ADVERTISING* ($000)	A/B†
1977	22,130	$40,830	$1.85		16,300	$10,843	$0.62
1976	24,162	33,756	1.40		17,037	9,112	0.53
1975	23,279	23,173	1.00		15,700	9,007	0.57
1974	22,661	17,977	0.79		14,297	7,711	0.54
1973	21,343	16,615	0.78		13,128	6,422	0.49
1972	18,906	17,782	0.94		12,600	6,142	0.49

	COORS				OLYMPIA (HAMM 1975)		
YEAR	BARRELS (000)	ADVERTISING* ($000)	A/B†		BARRELS (000)	ADVERTISING* ($000)	A/B†
1977	12,824	$ 3,966	$0.25		6,831	$ 8,470	$1.24
1976	13,665	1,626	0.12		6,370	5,430	0.85
1975	11,950	1,093	0.09		5,770	5,555	0.96
1974	12,400	801	0.06		4,300	2,764	0.64
1973	10,950	699	0.06		3,636	2,323	0.64
1972	9,785	1,332	0.14		3,330	2,491	0.75

EXHIBIT 6 **Continued**

	HEILEMAN (GRAIN BELT 1975)			STROH		
YEAR	BARRELS (000)	ADVERTISING* ($000)	A/B†	BARRELS (000)	ADVERTISING* ($000)	A/B†
1977	6,245	$ 4,636	$0.74	6,114	$ 7,212	$1.18
1976	5,210	3,616	0.69	5,765	5,017	0.87
1975	4,535	2,864	0.63	5,133	3,950	0.77
1974	4,300	2,329	0.54	4,364	3,477	0.80
1973	4,420	2,243	0.51	4,645	3,145	0.68
1972	3,675	2,260	0.61	4,231	3,567	0.84

	SCHAEFER			C. SCHMIDT		
YEAR	BARRELS (000)	ADVERTISING* ($000)	A/B†	BARRELS (000)	ADVERTISING* ($000)	A/B†
1977	4,700	$ 4,219	$0.90	3,571	$ 3,912	$1.10
1976	5,300	2,516	0.47	3,450	2,703	0.78
1975	5,881	2,637	0.45	3,330	2,269	0.68
1974	5,712	2,308	0.40	3,490	3,035	0.87
1973	5,500	2,438	0.44	3,520	2,916	0.83
1972	5,530	2,994	0.54	3,194	2,104	0.66

SOURCE: Company sales for 1970–1976 from *Advertising Age,* various issues; 1977 sales, table 1.

*Advertising expenditures in six measured media as reported in *Leading National Advertisers,* various issues.
†Advertising per barrel.

engage in cross-subsidization of its brewing subsidiary. This capacity, coupled with the relatedness of the marketing function between Philip Morris and Miller, provided a powerful vehicle for industry restructuring. Miller adopted aggressive market segmentation and expansion strategies, thus increasing their capacity five-fold between 1970 and 1977. According to Dr. Mueller, a doubling of 1977 capacity was planned by 1981. Exhibit 8 shows comparative financial data on Philip Morris and the rest of the leading brewers.

In 1975, Miller found a successful method for promoting a low-calorie beer, Lite, which they had purchased from Meister Brau, Inc., of Chicago, in 1972. They spent heavily, around $6.00 per barrel, to introduce it nationwide. However, Lite's success was not wholly attributable to heavy adver-

EXHIBIT 7   Relative Media Advertising Effectiveness by Beer Brand,
1975–1978

	MEDIA ADVERTISING EXPENSE ($ MILLION)	TOTAL BARRELS (MILLION)	ADVERTISING EXPENSE PER BARREL	BARREL CHANGE 1978 VERSUS 1974	ADVERTISING EXPENSE PER INCREMENTAL MILLION BARRELS
Premium category					
Budweiser	$71.5	100.2	$ .71	1.1	$65.00
Miller High Life	60.5	61.3	.99	13.5	4.48
Schlitz	70.4	59.3	1.18	(5.2)	n.a.
Light category					
Lite	63.8	22.9	2.79	8.4	7.60
Anheuser-Busch					
Natural Light	24.0	3.8	6.32	2.3	10.43
Michelob Light	6.5	0.9	7.22	0.9	7.22
Schlitz Light	30.3	3.6	8.42	0.7	43.29
Super premium category					
Michelob	35.9	23.0	1.56	4.3	8.35
Lowenbrau	29.4	1.7	17.29	1.2	24.50

SOURCE: C. James Walker III. *Competition in the U.S. Brewing Industry: A Basic Analysis* (New York: Shearson Hayden Stone, September 26, 1979).

n.a. = Not available.

EXHIBIT 8   Assets, Sales, Net Profit, Net Income on Stockholders' Investment, and Total Advertising Expenditures, 1977 (Dollar Amounts in Millions)

COMPANY	ASSETS	SALES	NET PROFIT	TOTAL PROFIT ON EQUITY	TOTAL ADVERTISING
Philip Morris (Miller)	$4,048	$3,849*	$335	19.8%	$277
Anheuser-Busch	1,404	1,838	92	13.5	79
Joseph Schlitz	727	937	20	5.5	55
Pabst Brewing	396	583	22	8.1	27
Adolph Coors	692	593	68	12.2	15‡
Total 2d to 5th	3,219	3,951	202	9.8†	176
Philip Morris as a percent of 2d to 5th	126%	97%	166%	202%	157%

SOURCE: "500 Largest Industrials." *Fortune,* May 1977: advertising data reported in individual company Security and Exchange Commission's form 10-K reports for 1977.

*Excludes U.S. and foreign excise taxes.
†Unweighted average.
‡Estimate.

tising. Low-calorie beers were promoted in the past with a notable lack of success. Through marketing research, Miller discovered that a significant portion of the beer market is composed of young and middle-aged men who are sports fans with dreams of athletic prowess. In advertising Lite, Miller relied predominantly on retired athletes renowned for their speed and agility. The message was that one could drink a lot of Lite and still be fast, not that one could drink Lite to keep from getting fat.

By 1975, Schlitz and, to some extent, Anheuser-Busch began to increase their own advertising expenditures and made plans to enter the low-calorie beer market. This was done not only as a response to Miller's aggressiveness, but also because of a general lack of growth in demand in the face of increasing industry capacity. By 1978, nine of the ten largest brewers had light brands on the market. Exhibits 9–11 show brand shipment breakdowns for the three major brewers.

Currently the only company with the financial resources to battle Miller and its multinational conglomerate backer is Anheuser-Busch, the industry leader. Anheuser-Busch responded aggressively to Miller's program. In 1977, Anheuser-Busch surpassed Miller and Schlitz in advertising expenditures by spending over $44 million.

Exhibit 12 shows market share performance for the top five brewers and all others in the 1974–1978 period.

Clearly, Anheuser-Busch's and Miller's growth has been at the expense of the regional brewers and the faltering national brewers (Schlitz and Pabst). C. James Walker III, an industry analyst for Shearson Hayden Stone, Inc., estimates only 2.7 percent per year industry growth for the early 1980s. The capital-intensive nature of the industry, coupled with huge advertising outlays, makes it very unlikely that any firm will be able to challenge the two leaders. To quote August Busch III, "This business is now a two-horse race."

ORGANIZATION OF ANHEUSER-BUSCH

Effective October 1, 1979, Anheuser-Busch, Inc., became a wholly owned subsidiary of a new holding company, Anheuser-Busch Companies, Inc., and the outstanding shares of Anheuser-Busch, Inc., were exchanged for an equal number of shares of the holding company. Concerning this change, August A. Busch III said,

> The holding company's name and address will more clearly communicate the increasingly diversified nature of our business, thereby reflecting not only our position of leadership in the brewing industry, but also our substantial activities in yeast and specialty corn products, family entertainment, transportation, can manufacturing, real estate, and other businesses. The new structure will also provide management with increased organizational and operational flexibility.

EXHIBIT 9

Estimated Anheuser-Busch Brand Breakdown: 1974–1978; Shipments in Barrels (Millions)

	1978	1977	1976	1975	1974
Budweiser	27.5	25.4	21.1	26.2	26.4
Michelob	7.4	6.4	5.0	4.2	3.1
Michelob Light	0.9	—	—	—	—
Busch	3.5	3.3	3.0	4.8	4.6
Natural	2.3	1.5	—	—	—
Total	41.6	36.6	29.1	35.2	34.1

SOURCE: C. James Walker III. *Competition in the U.S. Brewing Industry: A Basic Analysis* (New York: Shearson Hayden Stone, September 26, 1979).

EXHIBIT 10

Estimated Miller Brewing Brand Breakdown: 1974–1978; Shipments in Barrels (Millions)

	1978	1977	1976	1975	1974
High Life	21.3	17.3	13.5	9.2	7.8
Lite	8.8	6.4	4.6	3.1	0.4
Lowenbrau	1.2	0.5	0.1	0.0	—
Other	0.0	0.0	0.2	0.5	0.9
Total	31.3	24.2	18.4	12.8	9.1

SOURCE: C. James Walker III. *Competition in the U.S. Brewing Industry: A Basic Analysis* (New York: Shearson Hayden Stone, September 26, 1979).

EXHIBIT 11

Estimated Schlitz Brewing Brand Breakdown: 1974–1978; Shipments in Barrels (Millions)

	1978	1977	1976	1975	1974
Schlitz	12.7	14.3	15.9	16.8	17.9
Old Milwaukee	4.3	4.9	5.5	5.2	3.9
Schlitz Light	0.7	1.3	1.4	0.2	—
Malt Liquor	1.7	1.4	1.3	1.0	0.8
Primo	0.2	0.2	0.1	0.1	0.1
Total	19.6	22.1	24.2	23.3	22.7

SOURCE: C. James Walker III. *Competition in the U.S. Brewing Industry: A Basic Analysis* (New York: Shearson Hayden Stone. September 26, 1979).

EXHIBIT 12 — Market Share Performance

1978 / 1977

	BARREL SHIPMENTS (MILLION)	MARKET SHARE	BARREL INCREMENT (MILLION)	PERCENT INCREASE (DECREASE)	BARREL SHIPMENTS (MILLION)	MARKET SHARE	BARREL INCREMENT (MILLION)	PERCENT INCREASE (DECREASE)
	1978				1977			
Anheuser	41.6	25.1%	5.0	13.7%	36.6	22.9%	7.5	25.8%
Miller	31.3	18.9	7.1	29.3	24.2	15.2	5.8	31.5
Schlitz	19.6	11.8	(2.5)	(11.3)	22.1	13.9	(2.1)	(8.7)
Pabst	15.4	9.3	(0.6)	(3.8)	16.0	10.0	(1.0)	(5.9)
Coors	12.6	7.6	(0.2)	(1.6)	12.8	8.0	(0.7)	(5.2)
Top 5	120.5	72.7	8.8	7.9	111.7	70.0	9.5	9.3
All others	41.7	25.2	(3.5)	(7.7)	45.2	28.3	(3.0)	(6.2)
U.S. industry	162.2	97.9	5.3	3.4	156.9	98.4	6.5	4.4
Imports	3.45	2.1	0.8	30.8	2.6	1.6	0.2	8.3
All beer	165.6	100.0	6.1	3.8	159.5	100.0	6.7	4.5

1976 / 1975

	BARREL SHIPMENTS (MILLION)	MARKET SHARE	BARREL INCREMENT (MILLION)	PERCENT INCREASE (DECREASE)	BARREL SHIPMENTS (MILLION)	MARKET SHARE	BARREL INCREMENT (MILLION)	PERCENT INCREASE (DECREASE)
	1976				1975			
Anheuser	29.1	19.0%	(6.1)	(17.3)%	35.2	23.4%	1.1	3.2%
Miller	18.4	12.0	5.6	43.8	12.8	8.5	3.7	40.7
Schlitz	24.2	15.8	0.9	3.9	23.3	15.5	0.6	2.6
Pabst	17.0	11.1	1.3	8.3	15.7	10.4	1.4	9.8
Coors	13.5	8.8	1.6	13.4	11.9	7.9	(0.4)	(3.3)
Top 5	102.2	66.9	3.3	3.3	98.9	65.8	6.4	6.9
All others	48.2	31.5	(1.5)	(3.0)	49.7	33.1	(3.3)	(6.2)
U.S. industry	150.4	98.4	1.8	1.2	148.6	98.9	3.1	2.1
Imports	2.4	1.6	0.7	41.2	1.7	1.1	0.3	21.4
All beer	152.8	100.0	2.5	1.7	150.3	100.0	3.4	2.3

EXHIBIT 12   Continued

	1974		INCREASED BARREL SHIPMENTS (MILLION)	1974–1978	
	BARREL SHIPMENTS (MILLION)	MARKET SHARE		MARKET SHARE POINT CHANGE	COMPOUNDED ANNUAL SHIPMENT GROWTH
Anheuser	34.1	23.2%	7.5	+ 1.9	5.1%
Miller	9.1	6.2	22.2	+12.7	36.2
Schlitz	22.7	15.4	(3.1)	– 3.6	(3.3)
Pabst	14.3	9.7	1.1	– 0.4	1.9
Coors	12.3	8.4	0.3	– 0.8	0.4
Top 5	92.5	63.0	28.0	+ 9.7	6.8
All others	53.0	36.0	11.3	–10.8	(4.9)
U.S. industry	145.5	99.0	16.7	– 1.1	2.7
Imports	1.4	1.0	2.0	+ 1.1	24.9
All beer	146.9	100.0	18.7	0.0	3.1

SOURCE: C. James Walker III. *Competition in the U.S. Brewing Industry: A Basic Analysis* (New York: Shearson Hayden Stone, September 26, 1979).

Each of our businesses can eventually be operated as separate companies under Anheuser-Busch Companies, Inc., with responsibilities divided among management personnel.

This reorganization will help facilitate our long-range plan to not only continue to grow in production and sales of beer but also to continue to expand and diversify into other areas which offer significant opportunities for growth.

Additionally, Busch announced that Fred L. Kuhlmann, executive vice president, had been elected vice chairman of the board of Anheuser-Busch Companies, Inc., and that Dennis P. Long had been elected president and chief operating officer of Anheuser-Busch, Inc., a subsidiary of the holding company. Long has overall responsibility for the conduct of the company's beer business, and he reports to Busch. (Busch is chairman and chief executive officer of Anheuser-Busch, Inc.)

Also, Long was elected a member of the corporate office of Anheuser-Busch Companies, Inc. Three individuals comprise the corporate office. They are Busch, Kuhlmann, and Long. Kuhlmann and Long consult with Busch on major corporate matters and they assist him in implementing corporate policy.

Busch announced that the operating executives of two other divisions and subsidiaries had been named presidents of their respective operating units. W. Robert Harrington was named president of industrial products, and W. Randolph Baker was named president of Busch Gardens.

KEY EXECUTIVES[1] August A. Busch III was born June 16, 1937, attended public and private schools in St. Louis, the University of Arizona, and the Siebel Institute of Technology, a school for brewers in Chicago. He is chairman of the board and president of Anheuser-Busch Companies, Inc., and he began his career with the company in 1957 in the St. Louis malt house. Since that time, he has worked in practically every department of both the brewing and operations divisions. In 1962 he moved into marketing, working in the field with wholesalers, as well as company-owned branches in all areas of the country. Returning to St. Louis, he was promoted to assistant sales manager, regional brands, and later was named sales manager for regional brands where he was responsible for the marketing of Busch throughout the product's marketing area.

Busch was named a member of the company's board of directors and appointed vice president, marketing operations, in 1963. He became general manager in July 1965; executive vice president and general manager in April 1971; president in February 1974; chief executive officer in May 1975; and chairman of the board in April 1977.

Fred L. Kuhlmann, a native of St. Louis, is vice chairman of the board of directors and executive vice president of Anheuser-Busch Companies, Inc. He joined Anheuser-Busch, Inc., in August 1967 as general counsel and was elected a vice president in January 1971; senior vice president, administration and services, and a member of the board of directors in February 1974; executive vice president, administration, in June 1977; and was elected to his present position in October 1979.

Kuhlmann received his A.B. degree from Washington University in St. Louis and his LL.B. from that institution's school of law. He also has an LL.M. degree from Columbia University School of Law in New York. He has been active in several business and civic groups and serves as a director of the St. Louis National Baseball Club, Inc., and Manufacturers Railway Company. He is also a director of Boatmen's National Bank of St. Louis, Civic Center Redevelopment Corporation, and St. Louis Regional Commerce and Growth Association.

Dennis P. Long, 44, president of Anheuser-Busch, Inc., has extensive experience spanning more than 25 years at Anheuser-Busch both in brewing and nonbrewing areas, and he attended Washington University in St. Louis, Missouri. After serving as national price administrator in beer marketing from 1960 to 1964, he was promoted to assistant to the vice president of beer marketing operations and worked in the field with the nationwide beer wholesaler network as well as with the company-owned branch distribution centers. He was promoted to assistant to the vice president and general manager in 1965.

In 1972, Long was elected group vice president responsible for the Busch Gardens and industrial products division and Busch Properties, Inc. Under Long's leadership, the industrial products division became the nation's leading producer of baker's yeast; the division's sales of both yeast and corn products and its profitability increased to record proportions. He also headed the transition of Busch Gardens from beer promotional facilities to a separate profit center. Since then, a new Busch Gardens has been opened in Williamsburg, Virginia, and that division also operates profitably. Since taking charge of Busch Properties, Inc., the real estate subsidiary has embarked further into residential and resort development in addition to the commercial-industrial field, and the performance of Busch Properties has improved markedly.

In June 1977, Long became vice president and general manager of the beer division, and since that time has embarked upon a strong effort to increase beer sales volume and profitability. His efforts include new and expanded marketing efforts, increased productivity in brewing and packaging, and a strong cost control and cost reduction effort.

PRODUCTS OFFERED BY ANHEUSER-BUSCH

Over the past five years, Anheuser-Busch's beer division has accounted for approximately 90 percent of consolidated net sales. The beer division of Anheuser-Busch produces Budweiser, Michelob, Busch, Michelob Light, Classic Dark, and Anheuser-Busch Natural Light. The remaining 10 percent of the consolidated net sales comes from family entertainment (Busch Gardens division), can manufacturing, container recycling, transportation services (St. Louis Refrigerator Car Company and Manufacturers Railway Company), major league baseball (St. Louis Cardinals), real estate development (Busch Properties, Inc.), and the manufacture and sale of corn products, brewer's yeast, and baker's yeast (industrial products division). Anheuser-Busch is the nation's leading producer of baker's yeast with a market share well over 40 percent. Exhibit 13 presents data by product line.

During 1978, Anheuser-Busch made significant progress in redefining its diversification objectives as a means of building for the future. A corporate policy was established to concentrate initially on developing new food and beverage products that are compatible with the existing capabilities and, where possible, on distributing these products through the company's existing wholesaler network. The company is at present working on developing a line of snack foods, reportedly called Eagle Snacks, which would also be compatible with existing production and distribution facilities.

The company began test marketing Würzburger Hofbräu beer in the United States early in 1979. This full-bodied, premium German beer will be brewed in Würzburg, West Germany, and shipped in large insulated barrels to the United States, where it will be bottled by Anheuser-Busch and distributed through the company's wholesaler network.

Anheuser-Busch has a new installation in St. Louis, Missouri, that annually produces 1.8 million pounds of autolyzed yeast extract, a flavoring agent for processed foods. As the only producer of the extract in the United States with its own captive supply of brewer's yeast, Anheuser-Busch entered this new venture with a decided competitive advantage.

EXHIBIT 13   **Revenue Generated by Product Class**
(Dollar Amounts in Thousands)

	1978	1977	1976	1975	1974
Consolidated sales	$2,701,611	$2,231,230	$1,752,998	$2,036,687	$1,791,863
Federal and state beer taxes	441,978	393,182	311,852	391,708	378,772
Consolidated net sales	$2,259,633	$1,838,048	$1,441,146	$1,644,979	$1,413,091
Beer division	2,056,754	1,691,004	1,282,620	1,480,481	1,271,782
Percent of consolidated net sales	91%	92%	89%	90%	90%
Other divisions*	$ 202,879	$ 147,044	$ 158,526	$ 164,498	$ 141,309
Percent of consolidated net sales	9%	8%	11%	10%	10%

SOURCE: Anheuser-Busch Company, Inc., annual reports, 1974–1978.

*All other divisions include: industrial products division; Busch Gardens division; Busch Properties, Inc.; transportation; and the St. Louis Cardinals.

Anheuser-Busch's well-known family of quality beers includes products in every market segment. Budweiser has been brewed and sold for more than 100 years. Premium Bud, available in bottles, cans, and on draft nationwide, is the company's principal product and the largest selling beer in the world. Michelob was developed in 1896 as a "draught beer for connoisseurs." Super-premium Michelob is sold nationally in bottles, cans, and on draft.

With a greater percentage of the population entering the weight-conscious 25- to 39-year-old range, Anheuser-Busch has introduced Michelob Light. It has 20 percent fewer calories than regular Michelob. When introduced in 1978, it was the first super-premium light beer. In order to capitalize on this by transferring the consumer appeal for Michelob to Michelob Light, Anheuser-Busch communicates "the heritage of Michelob and the taste of Michelob Light" in its advertising. Michelob Light is available nationwide in cans, bottles, and on draft. Anheuser-Busch also offers Natural Light for weight-conscious beer drinkers.

Busch Bavarian beer was introduced in 1955 as a low-priced beer in direct competition with sub-premium regional beers. In April 1978, a smoother, sweeter, and lighter Busch beer was successfully test marketed in New England as a premium-priced brand to capitalize on anticipated growth of the premium segment of the market in future years. In 1979, with new package graphics and advertising, premium Busch was introduced in areas where the company previously marketed Busch Bavarian.

Anheuser-Busch's expanding corporate programs of vertical integration into can manufacturing and barley malting play an important role in overall beer division activities and profitability. The company's various vertically integrated enterprises provide an added advantage in controlling the cost and supply of containers and ingredients. Vertical integration helps to reduce cost pressures in brewing operations and to ensure continuity and quality of supply.

Metal Container Corporation, a wholly owned subsidiary of Anheuser-Busch Companies, produces two-piece aluminum beer cans at facilities in Florida, Ohio, and Missouri. Container Recovery Corporation, another wholly owned subsidiary of Anheuser-Busch Companies, operates container recovery facilities in Ohio and New Hampshire that are actively involved in collecting and recycling aluminum cans.

The company's materials acquisition division is responsible for purchasing all agricultural commodities, packaging materials, supplies, and fuel. Its objective is to increase stability and flexibility in the procurement of commodities and materials. This division investigates alternative methods of supply, analyzes vertical integration opportunities available to the company, and monitors the supply and cost of all commodities purchased by Anheuser-Busch.

Anheuser-Busch processes barley into brewer's malt at plants in Manitowoc, Wisconsin (total capacity of 8.5 million bushels annually) and Moorhead, Minnesota (annual capacity of 6.4 million bushels). These two malt production facilities provide the company with the capability to self-manufacture approximately one-third of its malt requirements.

The industrial products division produces corn syrup and starch for numerous food applications, including the processing of canned frozen foods and the manufacture of ice cream and candy. Additionally, the division markets starch and resin products used in the manufacture of paper, corrugated containers, and textiles. The company's corn processing plant in Lafayette, Indiana, currently has a grind capacity of 11 billion bushels of corn yearly.

The company's brewer's yeast food plant in Jacksonville, Florida, has a yearly capacity of 3 million pounds. The debitterized brewer's food yeast is sold to health food manufacturers for use in a variety of nutritional supplements. Busch Entertainment Corporation, the company's family entertainment subsidiary, operates theme parks in Florida and Virginia. Unique blends of natural beauty and family entertainment activities and attractions are featured in both locations. Busch Properties, Inc., is the company's real estate development subsidiary. It is currently involved in the development of both residential and commercial properties at sites in Virginia and Ohio. St. Louis Refrigerator Car Company, Manufacturers Railway Company, and five other companies comprise Anheuser-Busch's transportation subsidiaries. They provide commercial repair, rebuilding, maintenance and inspection of railroad cars, terminal railroad switching services, and truck cartage and warehousing services.

MARKETING

Anheuser-Busch has a coast-to-coast network of eleven breweries that are selectively situated in major population and beer consumption regions. Once the beers leave the breweries, distribution to the consumer becomes the responsibility of 959 wholesale distribution operations and eleven company-owned beer branches that provide the company with its own profit centers within the distribution system. The beer branches perform sales, merchandising, and delivery services in their respective areas of primary responsibility. The company's beer branches are located in Sylmar and Riverside, California; Denver, Colorado; Chicago, Illinois; Louisville, Kentucky; New Orleans, Louisiana; Cambridge, Massachusetts; Kansas City, Missouri; Newark, New Jersey; Tulsa, Oklahoma; and Washington, D.C.

The beer industry has always been a highly competitive industry. Success depends on volume, and sales by the nation's top five brewers account for an estimated 70 percent of the total market. There is intense competition among the industry leaders. According to *Value Line,* it is expected that, by 1980, the top five brewers will account for approximately 80 percent of the market.

Competitive pressures have led Anheuser-Busch to take an aggressive stance in its marketing strategy. Anheuser-Busch is the country's largest brewer in terms of barrel sales per year and the 34th largest national advertiser. The 1978 annual report of Anheuser-Busch said their marketing efforts were "the most extensive and aggressive in company history," stressing product and packaging innovations, brand identity, and off-premise merchandising. The company is entering the 1980s with new packaging innovations and new marketing programs. The aggressive packaging is aimed at further market segmentation and penetration. At present the company sells more than eighty basic packages.

Anheuser-Busch's advertisements have traditionally been aimed at communicating the quality of the company's beer products that appeal to virtually every taste and price range. Television advertisements and sports sponsorships continue to be the major focal point for marketing the company's beer brands. Television advertisements focus on prime-time programming and sports. To increase its presence on college campuses, Anheuser-Busch utilizes a unique marketing team of 400 student representatives at major colleges and universities across the country.

Anheuser-Busch has enlarged its marketing staff in the beer division. A field sales task force has been established to provide immediate and concentrated assistance in markets needing a sales boost. The national accounts sales department was created to provide better marketing coordination and communication between the company's sales staff and large national chain accounts such as grocery stores, convenience stores, fast-food outlets, hotels, motels, liquor chains, and athletic stadiums. The marketing services department coordinates and expands activities in the areas of sales promotion, merchandising, special markets, point-of-sale, and incentive programs.

PRODUCTION FACILITIES

Reviewing the production facilities utilized by Anheuser-Busch provides insight into the growth pattern of the organization. Devotion to investment in plant capacity has been extensive in the past decade, and the future capital expenditure program allows for further expansion and modernization of facilities (annual report, 1978).

The largest subsidiary of Anheuser-Busch Companies is the beer production sector. Exhibit 14 is a listing of the geographically dispersed breweries with their corresponding annual capacity in millions of barrels and dates of first shipments.

As can be seen from this exhibit, many of the beer production facilities are quite new. Plants in St. Louis and Newark have undergone extensive modernization programs to upgrade older facilities and equipment and ensure consistent quality regardless of brewery location. In 1980, Anheuser-Busch purchased a brewery formerly owned and operated by Schlitz. The seller was forced to close the plant as a result of declining sales due to competitive pressures.

Commitments to plant expansion have been extensive in the past few years. For example, capital expenditures will approach $2 billion for the five

EXHIBIT 14

Production Facility Locations and Capacities

	MILLIONS OF BARRELS	BEGINNING OF SHIPMENT
St. Louis, Missouri	11.6	1880
Los Angeles, California	10.0	1954
Newark, New Jersey	4.7	1951
Tampa, Florida	2.2	1959
Houston, Texas	2.6	1966
Columbus, Ohio	6.2	1968
Jacksonville, Florida	6.5	1969
Merrimack, New Hampshire	2.8	1970
Williamsburg, Virginia	7.5	1972
Fairfield, California	3.5	1976
Baldwinsville, New York	6.0	1982

SOURCE: Anheuser-Busch annual reports.

years ending 1983, with 93 percent for beer-related activities, according to industry analyst Robert S. Weinberg. Expansion is currently being undertaken at several of the eleven breweries. At the Los Angeles plant, the largest expansion project, capacity is being increased by more than 6 million barrels. Capacity in Williamsburg, Virginia, is being increased threefold.

Plant expansion in the areas of can manufacturing and industrial products manufacturing is being conducted at rapid rates. Vertical integration into can manufacturing and malt production is requiring substantial increases in plant investment. Can production facilities were completed in Jacksonville, Florida, in 1974, Columbus, Ohio, in 1977, and a new plant will be completed in 1980 in Arnold, Missouri. Nearly 40 percent of cans used will be provided internally by 1980. In addition, two can recycling facilities are currently in operation.

MONEY MATTERS AT ANHEUSER-BUSCH

Exhibits 15, 16, 17, and 18 contain relevant financial data on Anheuser-Busch. The data cover the years from 1969 to 1978.

RESEARCH AND DEVELOPMENT

According to the 1978 Securities and Exchange Commission's form 10-K report, Anheuser-Busch "does not consider to be material the dollar amounts expended by it during the last two fiscal years on research activities

EXHIBIT 15 Per Share Data (Dollars)

YEAR END DECEMBER 31	1978	1977	1976	1975	1974	1973	1972	1971	1970	1969
Book value	16.71	15.07	13.72	13.17	11.93	11.11	10.25	9.20	8.02	7.03
Earnings*	2.46	2.04	1.23	1.88	1.42	1.46	1.70	1.60	1.40	1.01
Dividends	0.82	0.71	0.68	0.64	0.06	0.60	0.58	0.53	0.42¼	0.40
Payout ratio	33%	35%	55%	34%	42%	41%	34%	33%	30%	39%
Prices—High	27¾	25¼	38⅝	39⅝	38	55	69	57½	39⅝	36¼
Low	17½	18¾	20¾	24½	21	28⅝	51	37	27⅙	28¼
Price-earnings ratio	11–7	12–9	31–17	21–13	27–15	38–20	41–30	36–23	28–19	36–29

SOURCE: *Standard OTC Stock Reports*, 46, no. 125, sec. 5, (October 31, 1979). Copyright © 1990 Standard & Poor's Corporation. All rights reserved.

Data as originally reported. Adjusted for stock dividends of 100 percent April 1971.
*Before results of discontinued operations of −0.09 in 1972.

EXHIBIT 16 — Income Data (Dollar Amounts in Millions)

YEAR ENDED DECEMBER 31	REVENUES	OPERATING INCOME	PERCENT OPERATING INCOME OF REVENUES	CAPITAL EXPEN-DITURES	DEPRECI-ATION	INTEREST EXPENSE	NET BEFORE TAXES*	EFFECTIVE TAX RATE	NET INCOME*	PERCENT NET INCOME OF REVENUES
1978	2,260	288	12.8%	229	66.0	28.9	206	46.0%	111	4.9%
1977	1,838	246	13.4	157	61.2	26.7	170	45.9	92	5.0
1976	1,441	181	12.6	199	53.1	26.9	103	46.4	55	3.8
1975	1,645	226	13.8	155	51.1*	22.6	16.5	48.7	85	5.2
1974	1,413	164	11.6	126	45.0	11.9	122	47.3	64	4.5
1973	1,110	162	14.6	92	41.1	5.3	126	48.1	66	5.9
1972*	978	184	18.8	84	39.0	6.0	147	48.0	76	7.8
1971	902	170	18.9	73	35.0	6.6	136	47.3	72	7.9
1970	793	155	19.5	65	33.8	7.1	121	48.2	63	7.9
1969	667	122	18.2	71	30.1	7.4	93	51.2	45	6.8

*Before results of discontinued operations of −0.09 in 1972.

EXHIBIT 17   Balance Sheet Data (Dollar Amounts in Millions)

DECEMBER 31	CURRENT			TOTAL ASSETS	RETURN ON ASSETS	LONG-TERM DEBT	COMMON EQUITY	TOTAL CAPITAL	PERCENT LONG-TERM DEBT OF CAPITAL	RETURN ON EQUITY
	CASH	ASSETS	LIABILITIES	RATIO						
1978	196	492	255	1.9	1,648	7.3%	427	754	1,393	30.7%	15.5%
1977	154	400	212	1.9	1,404	6.9	337	680	1,191	28.3	14.0
1976	135	347	167	2.1	1,268	4.5	341	618	1,101	30.9	9.1
1975	224	420	161	2.6	1,202	7.9	342	594	1,041	32.9	15.0
1974	89	252	113	2.2	931	7.5	193	538	818	23.6	12.3
1973	60	176	100	1.8	765	9.0	93	501	666	14.0	13.6
1972*	69	166	81	2.0	698	11.3	99	462	617	16.1	17.4
1971	69	163	75	2.2	654	11.3	117	414	579	20.1	18.5
1970	61	158	78	2.0	605	10.8	128	358	527	24.3	18.6
1969	45	142	65	2.2	550	8.4	135	314	485	27.8	15.1

SOURCE: *Standard OTC Stock Reports*, 46, no. 125, sec. 5 (October 31, 1979). Copyright © 1990 Standard & Poor's Corporation. All rights reserved.

*Before results of discontinued operations of −0.09 in 1972.

EXHIBIT 18

Ten-Year Financial Summary (Dollar Amounts in Thousands, Except Per Share and Statistical Data)

	1978	1977	1976	1975	1974
CONSOLIDATED SUMMARY OF OPERATIONS					
Barrels sold	41,610	36,640	29,051	35,196	34,097
Sales	$2,701,611	$2,231,230	$1,752,998	$2,036,687	$1,791,863
Less federal and state beer taxes	441,978	393,182	311,852	391,708	378,772
Net sales	2,259,633	1,838,048	1,441,146	1,644,979	1,413,091
Cost of products sold	1,762,410	1,462,801	1,175,055	1,343,784	1,187,816
Gross profit	497,223	375,247	266,091	301,195	225,275
Less marketing, administrative, and research expenses	274,961	190,470	137,797	126,053	106,653
Operating income	222,262	184,777	128,294	175,142	118,622
Interest income	11,693	7,724	10,304	10,944	9,925
Interest expense	(28,894)	(26,708)	(26,941)	(22,602)	(11,851)
Other income net	751	4,193	1,748	1,816	4,840
Loss on partial closing of Los Angeles Busch Gardens (1)			10,020		
Income before income taxes	205,812	169,986	103,385	165,300	121,536
Income taxes	94,772	78,041	47,952	80,577	57,517
Income before extraordinary item	111,040	91,945	55,433	84,723	64,019
Extraordinary item (2)					
Net income	$ 111,040	91,945	$ 55,433	$ 84,723	$ 64,019
Per share (3)					
Income before extraordinary item	2.46	2.04	1.23	1.88	1.42
Net income	2.46	2.04	1.23	1.88	1.42
Cash dividends paid	37,013	32,036	30,646	28,843	27,041
Per share (3)	.82	.71	.68	.64	.60
Dividend payout ratio	33.3%	34.8%	55.3%	34.0%	42.3%
Average number of shares outstanding (3)	45,138	45,115	45,068	45,068	45,068
Book value per share	16.71	15.07	13.72	13.17	11.93
Balance sheet information:					
Working capital	236,396	188,069	194,814	268,099	145,107
Current ratio	1.9	1.9	2.2	2.7	2.3
Plant and equipment, net	1,109,243	951,965	857,073	724,914	622,876
Long-term debt	427,250	337,492	346,737	342,167	193,240
Debt to debt plus total equity	34.5%	31.7%	34.0%	35.6%	25.7%
Deferred income taxes	153,080	125,221	99,119	80,748	66,264
Deferred investment tax credit	58,053	48,371	43,074	24,293	21,157
Shareholders' equity	754,423	680,396	618,429	593,642	537,762
Return on shareholders' equity	15.1%	14.2%	9.2%	15.0%	12.3%
Other information:					
Capital expenditures	228,727	156,745	198,735	155,436	126,463
Depreciation	66,032	61,163	53,105	51,089	45,042
Total payroll cost	421,806	338,933	271,403	268,306	244,437
Effective tax rate	46.0%	45.9%	46.4%	48.7%	47.3%

SOURCE: Anheuser-Busch Companies Inc., annual reports, 1969–1978.

Notes to 10-year financial summary:

(1) In December 1976, the company decided to close a portion of the Los Angeles Busch Gardens and convert the remainder to a sales promotion facility. Closing a portion of the Gardens resulted in a nonoperating charge of $10,020,000 (before reduction for income tax benefits of approximately $5 million). This nonoperating charge, which reduced

EXHIBIT 18   **Continued**

	1973	1972	1971	1970	1969
CONSOLIDATED SUMMARY OF OPERATIONS					
Barrels sold	29,887	26,522	24,309	22,202	18,712
Sales	$1,442,720	$1,273,093	$1,173,476	$1,036,272	$871,904
Less federal and state beer taxes	333,013	295,593	271,023	243,495	205,295
Net sales	1,109,707	977,500	902,453	792,777	666,609
Cost of products sold	875,361	724,718	658,886	579,372	490,932
Gross profit	234,346	252,782	243,567	213,405	175,677
Less marketing, administrative, and research expenses	112,928	108,008	108,087	92,660	84,113
Operating income	121,418	144,774	135,480	120,745	91,564
Interest income	4,818	3,299	3,102	3,715	3,604
Interest expense	(5,288)	(6,041)	(6,597)	(7,104)	(7,401)
Other income net	5,287	4,855	4,065	3,420	5,171
Loss on partial closing of Los Angeles Busch Gardens (1)					
Income before income taxes	126,235	146,887	136,050	120,776	92,938
Income taxes	60,658	70,487	64,412	58,227	47,627
Income before extraordinary item	65,577	76,400	71,638	62,549	45,311
Extraordinary item (2)		4,093			
Net income	$ 65,577	$ 72,307	$ 71,638	$ 62,549	$ 45,311
Per share (3)					
Income before extraordinary item	1.46	1.70	1.60	1.40	1.02
Net income	1.46	1.70	1.60	1.40	1.02
Cash dividends paid	27,037	26,109	23,784	18,991	17,843
Per share (3)	.60	.58	.53	.425	.40
Dividend payout ratio	41.1%	36.0%	33.1%	30.4%	39.2%
Average number of shares outstanding (3)	45,063	45,020	44,887	44,686	44,616
Book value per share	11.11	10.25	9.20	8.02	7.03
Balance sheet information:					
Working capital	82,352	88,711	92,447	85,102	80,963
Current ratio	1.8	2.1	2.2	2.1	2.3
Plant and equipment, net	541,236	491,671	453,647	416,660	387,422
Long-term debt	93,414	99,107	116,571	128,080	134,925
Debt to debt plus total equity	15.3%	17.2%	21.4%	25.6%	29.2%
Deferred income taxes	54,281	41,456	34,103	27,274	23,212
Deferred investment tax credit	17,225	14,370	14,276	13,563	12,577
Shareholders' equity	500,784	461,980	413,974	358,476	314,121
Return on shareholders' equity	13.6%	16.5%	18.6%	18.6%	15.1%
Other information:					
Capital expenditures	91,801	84,217	73,214	65,069	66,396
Depreciation	41,059	38,970	34,948	33,795	30,063
Total payroll cost	221,049	190,517	176,196	156,576	133,872
Effective tax rate	48.1%	48.0%	47.3%	48.2%	51.2%

earnings per share by 11 cents, has been reported in accordance with *Accounting Principles Board Opinion No. 39,* which was effective September 30, 1973.

(2) In December 1972, the company decided to close a portion of the Houston Busch Gardens and convert the remainder to a sales promotion facility. Closing a portion of the Gardens resulted in an extraordinary after-tax charge against 1972 earnings of $4,093,000, or 9 cents per share, net of applicable income tax benefits of $4,006,000.

(3) Per share statistics have been adjusted to give effect to the two-for-one stock split in 1971.

relating to the development of new products or services or the improvement of existing products or services. In addition, the company does not consider the number of employees engaged full time in such research activities to be material." The company is, however, extensively involved in research and development.

R & D funds are currently being used to develop new food and beverage products that are consistent with the company's production and distribution capabilities. The organization has a corn products research group that recently developed several new and very profitable modified food starches. In addition to these, Anheuser-Busch's research on possible new beer products helped to place Michelob Light and Anheuser-Busch Natural Light beers on the market.

Along with research on new and profitable products, the company is striving to cut packaging costs by doing research in the production of aluminum. Anheuser-Busch paid $6 million in 1978 to a major international aluminum company, Swiss Aluminum Ltd., for access and participation rights in this company's ongoing research in the development of certain new technologies in aluminum casting. This area should greatly reduce costs in the future.

Besides product and container research, Anheuser-Busch's R & D departments are studying matters of social concern. The reasons for this type of research are to enable the company to remain active in its social responsibility as a public corporation, and to strengthen its influence in reducing government regulations and thus avoid possible costly restrictions to its operations. Research to determine the causes of alcoholism and develop effective treatment and prevention programs, in cooperation with the United States Brewers Association, is one example of the company's effort here. Other examples relate to environmental matters. In an independent effort toward developing and utilizing alternative energy systems, other than scarce natural gas and oil, Anheuser-Busch is researching solar energy. In 1978, the company installed a new pilot project at its Jacksonville, Florida, brewery. At this plant, solar energy is being tested in pasteurizing bottled beers. In addition to this, the company is developing new land application programs aimed at soil enrichment and energy conservation. Under these programs, rich soil nutrients are taken from the breweries' liquid wastes and used to grow various crops, primarily sod, grass, and grains.

FUTURE

In his letter to the shareholders in the 1978 annual report, August A. Busch III discusses Anheuser-Busch's expansion and diversification plans. He writes:

We continue to commit substantial resources to provide the capacity necessary to support our planned sales growth and to maintain our industry leadership. Future growth and profitability also depend, however, on our willingness to commit funds and energies to the development of new products and new areas of business activity.

For a number of years, we have been investing considerable sums of money and a great deal of effort in the area of vertical integration of our beer business . . . new can and malt plants and, more recently, in exploring the possibility of producing our own aluminum sheet used in the manufacture of cans. These activities have proved to be successful in controlling costs and we will continue to pay close attention to vertical integration.

We are also exploring opportunities to diversify into other business ventures which are not beer related. We can do this either through acquisitions or through internal development of new products. At the present time we are emphasizing a program aimed at maximizing use of existing capabilities. We are in the process of developing internally a line of soft drinks and other consumer products which can be distributed through our wholesale network. We recognize from the outset that we may not achieve success in every one of these new ventures. However, the financial risks are relatively small and the potential rewards are considerable.

C. James Walker III, an industry analyst, believes that Anheuser-Busch expects a 1981 shipment level of 55 million barrels indicating 9.2 million barrel growth in 1979–1981. This is comparable to what should be achieved in 1977–1979. However, without the presence of a visible new major category similar to Miller Lite, Walker doubts that growth in the 1980s can match the expansion of the late 1970s; new brands such as Würzburger and Busch Premium seem unlikely to garner the growth that Natural Light and Michelob Light may attain. Exhibit 19 shows Walker's estimates for 1981, which would make Anheuser-Busch fall 6 percent shy of its goal of 98 percent capacity utilization.

Busch, on the other hand, is more optimistic. He writes:

In anticipation of what we can expect to encounter in the marketplace we have developed strong and aggressive marketing and promotion programs to enhance our position as industry leader. We will be introducing more new products and new packages to keep Anheuser-Busch in the forefront of market segmentation. And, we will be intensifying our emphasis on the quality of our products.

Competitive pressures will demand the most dedicated and creative efforts that we can muster, but we are confident that with: our strong sales momentum, our quality products, our great wholesaler family, and the team effort of our employees, we will have another successful year and will continue to build a solid corporate foundation for future growth and profits.

EXHIBIT 19   Estimated Volume by Brewer, 1978 and 1981

	1978		1981*		1978–1981	
	BARREL SHIPMENTS (MILLIONS)	MARKET SHARE	BARREL SHIPMENTS (MILLIONS)	MARKET SHARE	BARREL INCREMENT (MILLIONS)	COMPOUNDED ANNUAL RATE OF GROWTH
Anheuser-Busch	41.6	25.1%	51.5	28.7%	+ 9.9	7.4%
Miller	31.3	18.9	44.9	25.0	+13.6	12.6
Schlitz	19.6	11.8	17.2	9.6	− 2.4	(3.8)
Pabst	15.4	9.3	14.7	8.2	− 0.7	(1.2)
Coors†	12.6	7.6	17.2	9.6	+ 4.6	11.1
Top 5	120.5	72.8	145.5	81.1	+25.0	6.6
All others‡	41.7	25.2	28.4	15.8	− 13.3	(9.7)
U.S. industry	162.2	97.9	173.9	97.0	+11.7	2.3%
Imports	3.4	2.1	5.4	3.0	+ 2.0	16.5
All beer	165.6	100.0%	179.3	100.0%	+ 13.7	2.7%

SOURCE: C. James Walker III. *Competition in the U.S. Brewing Industry: A Basic Analysis* (New York: Shearson Hayden Stone, September 26, 1979).

*Estimated.

†Coors was in a 16-state market in 1978 and an estimated 19-state market in 1981 (additions: Arkansas, Louisiana, and Minnesota).

‡In 1981, the operations of Blitz-Weinhard are included with Pabst; in 1978, about 600,000 barrels of Blitz are in the all-others group.

NOTES

1. The information presented in this section was obtained from the corporate headquarters of Anheuser-Busch Companies, Inc.

Anheuser-Busch Companies, Inc. (B)

NEIL H. SNYDER • KATHERINE CART • GARY McDAVID
LESLIE ST. LOUIS • MICHELLE THOMAS • KEN TREMAIN

INTRODUCTION

Originating in the United States during the 1840s, lager beer, a light beer with a mellow taste, did not take long to gain popularity; and the American beer industry grew as consumers' tastes shifted away from heavy German beers to lager. As the ability of beer manufacturers to produce beer in large quantities increased, a structural change took place in the beer industry that eventually led to the establishment of national as opposed to regional firms. Over the past 125 years, the realization of economies of scale by large producers has caused consolidation in the beer industry. Between 1860 and 1985, the number of breweries in the United States declined from 1,269 to 85. As industry sales volume has grown and the number of firms in the industry has declined, advertising has become the primary tool used to differentiate between beers and to expand and maintain market share. Blind taste tests have shown that beer drinkers cannot consistently distinguish between brands.

Currently, the brewing industry faces two significant challenges that have the potential to reduce even further the number of producers in the industry: saturation and changing consumer attitudes.

Saturation

Between 1975 and 1980, the beer industry expanded at an annual rate of approximately 4 percent, but in 1982 the growth rate was less than 1 percent. Nineteen eighty-two may have been the turning point for industry sales volume increases, and it was the first year in 25 years that domestic beer producers as a group experienced a profit decline.[1] In 1984, beer industry sales declined 0.3 percent while other beverages were experiencing significant gains. For example, wine sales in 1984 were up 3.5 percent, and soft drink sales increased by 7.5 percent. To make matters worse, the industry had excess beer production capacity in 1983 estimated at 40 million barrels. Exhibit 1 shows total capacity and capacity utilization for six leading U.S. brewers.

The saturation problem has led many brewers to diversify. Anheuser-Busch has entered markets such as food products, industrial products, and

EXHIBIT 1

Brewing Capacity and Usage, 1983 (Millions of Barrels)

BREWER	CAPACITY	PERCENT UTILIZATION
Anheuser-Busch	66.5	91.0
Miller	54.0	69.4
Stroh	32.6	74.5
Heileman	26.5	66.0
Coors	15.5	88.4
Pabst	15.0	85.3

entertainment. Additionally, large brewers are becoming more vertically and horizontally integrated. According to Wall Street analysts, the beer industry's sales volume has been and will remain flat. Anheuser-Busch is the only firm in the industry that has been able to maintain annual growth while industry sales have been stagnant.

Changing Consumer Attitudes

"Domestic brewers are up against the campaign against drunk driving, a national trend toward health and fitness, and the presence of a small but growing foreign-beer segment."[2]

The beer industry felt the first legislative blow in 1984 when Congress moved to establish a national minimum drinking age. Although this attempt failed, the federal government "blackmailed" most states into raising their drinking ages to 21 by threatening to cut off highway funds if they did not. The problems with teenage drinking have been made clear by powerful lobbying groups such as Mothers Against Drunk Drivers (MADD). The industry responded to the threat of even more restrictive legislation by developing low-alcohol beers, but sales of these products have been disappointing. Although the pressure on Congress to regulate the producers of alcoholic beverages has lately declined somewhat, it has been proposed that television commercials displaying the consumption of alcohol should be banned.

Most industry analysts agree that the fitness fad has leveled off and that the introduction of light beers satisfied the demands of consumers concerned about fitness. However, imported beers remain a significant threat to domestic beer producers. Imports have achieved a 4 percent share of the U.S. market, and it is expected that future growth in import beer sales will be 10 to 12 percent per year. Anheuser-Busch is vulnerable to these and other threats to the consumption of beer, because it produces most of its revenue from the sale of beer (see Exhibit 2).

EXHIBIT 2   **Anheuser-Busch: 1984 Revenues**

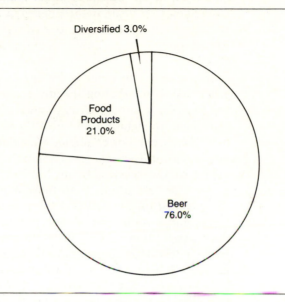

**ANHEUSER-
BUSCH'S POSITION
WITHIN THE
BREWING
INDUSTRY**

Anheuser-Busch's 1984 beer sales were up 5.8 percent over 1983 sales levels. The combined market share of Anheuser-Busch's products was 34.6 percent in 1984, up from 32.6 percent in 1983. Meanwhile, Miller Brewing reported no increase in sales for 1984 and a market share of only 20 percent. Utilizing segmentation strategies, international marketing, and new product development, Anheuser-Busch plans to continue its growth in the beer industry despite analysts' predictions of no aggregate domestic industry growth.

Anheuser-Busch believes that the international market can help it sustain its record of continuing sales growth. According to *Business Week*, it is nearly three times the size of the U.S. market.[3] John H. Purnell, chairman of Anheuser-Busch International, Inc., explains that "while we aren't out to conquer the world overnight, this [foreign beer sales] has the potential to become a significant profit contributor to the parent company."[4] Emanuel Goldman, a securities analyst, agrees with Purnell. He suggests that Anheuser-Busch's earnings from foreign markets could go to 15 percent of sales and 10 percent of earnings in ten years.

Success in the foreign market has come steadily for Anheuser-Busch, but it has had setbacks, too. Budweiser is by far the best selling non-Japanese beer in the Japanese market with sales increasing from 500,000 cases in 1981 to an estimated 2 million cases in 1984, and Budweiser captured 6 percent of the Israeli market in only six months. However, attempts to enter the two largest beer markets in the world have not been successful. Anheuser-Busch pulled out of the German market after being there only six months, and it worked for four years in the English market before joining forces with Allied Breweries, Ltd. According to *Business Week,* "If you are serious about the beer business, then you are going to have to participate in non-U.S. markets."[5]

Segmenting the country by age, population, location, and even ethnic group and then targeting specific groups has enabled Anheuser-Busch to attract more consumers to its products in the domestic market. As products gain name recognition and identity within a specific niche, product sales have increased. For example, Michelob has been marketed successfully to young, upwardly mobile professionals, and Natural Light is targeted toward people who want a less-filling beer but would rather drink beer at home than at a bar or restaurant. With these marketing techniques, Anheuser-Busch has matched its competitors' sales efforts product for product.

Careful introduction of new products sets Anheuser-Busch apart from their competitors. One industry analyst compared the speed of Anheuser-Busch's test-marketing efforts with the steady plodding of the Clydesdale horses—slow but steady.[6] When Anheuser-Busch enters a market, it utilizes its enormous advertising strength. For example, after waiting four years before entering the light beer market, Anheuser-Busch now has three successful light beers: Natural Light, Michelob Light, and Bud Light. Recently, Anheuser-Busch introduced a beer with less alcohol, LA, and it has provided significant advertising support to establish the product in the marketplace. The company spends $47.40 per barrel to promote LA, but only $1.69 per barrel to promote Budweiser. One area in which Anheuser-Busch sees great potential for growth is the wine cooler market. Currently, it is developing a wine cooler through its new subsidiary, Anheuser-Busch Wines, Inc., and it plans to introduce wine for sale in stainless steel returnable kegs. Exhibit 3 shows Anheuser-Busch beer production by brand.

EXHIBIT 3	**1984 Anheuser-Busch Production by Brand (Millions of Barrels)**

Budweiser	44.3
Michelob	6.7
Busch	4.3
Bud Light	0.4
Michelob Light	2.8
Natural Light	1.2
LA	0.4
Other	0.1

THE COMPETITION
Because of the shrinking domestic beer market, brewers must now take market share from competitors in each of the segmented categories. Thus, the industry is experiencing a proliferation of new products supported by enormous marketing budgets. It is reported that industry advertising spending was up 9 percent in the first half of 1984.[7] In addition to new brands, beers once sold regionally are now being marketed in broader distribution networks. For example, Anheuser-Busch has begun to market Busch on the national level and Adolph Coors has expanded its market for its beers, including Coors and Coors Light. The trend toward increased industry concentration seems destined to continue, and Anheuser-Busch and Miller are expected to hold 70 percent of the beer market by 1990. Additionally, increased competition from imports has intensified the problem, and many brewers are seeking new products (e.g., wine coolers and nonalcoholic beers) and diversification into other areas.

Miller

Miller has been Anheuser-Busch's primary competitor since Philip Morris acquired it in 1970. During the 1970s, Miller moved from seventh to second place in the brewing industry and surprised industry leaders with its successful introduction of Lite beer. Anheuser-Busch responded by increasing its advertising budget and taking Miller on in a head-to-head battle. In addition, Anheuser-Busch implemented a new strategic plan. The plan was to flank each Miller product in each category with two Anheuser-Busch products. For example, Budweiser and Busch flank Miller High Life in the premium category.[8]

Anheuser-Busch won the battle with Miller, and its lead continues to increase. Despite the fact that Anheuser-Busch and Miller were the only two brewers to increase their volume in 1984, Miller's premium brands (Miller High Life and Lowenbrau) are not competing well, and the growth in sales for Lite is declining. To offset these declines, Miller has been rapidly introducing new products. In the past two and a half years Miller has introduced at least eight new brands. Among these are two popularly priced beers, Meisterbrau and Milwaukee's Best, that were introduced to help support the faltering Miller High Life. It is also test marketing two bottled draft beers, Miller High Life Genuine Draft and Plank Road. Both are premium beers that will compete with Budweiser and Miller High Life.

Three prominent Wall Street beverage analysts have suggested that Miller's difficulties have arisen because of the decline of its flagship brand, Miller High Life.[9] They have speculated that, if Miller High Life sales do not stop eroding, it might be downgraded to a popularly priced product, which could hurt Anheuser-Busch. According to the analysts, "Anheuser should be rooting for a mitigation of the erosion, something in that in-between land. What happens to High Life is very important to Anheuser."[10]

Miller has recently changed ad agencies for its High Life account, indicating that it plans to turn that brand's sales around. Additionally, Miller has excess capacity. This problem is exemplified by Miller's $450 million brewery recently constructed in Trenton, Ohio, which is not being used.

Heileman

In regional markets, Heileman sales have been very effective against Anheuser-Busch by using a strategy that entails acquiring struggling local brewers at low costs and then reintroducing their brands with aggressive marketing. Anheuser-Busch has responded with "heavy price competition from its Busch brand," and Heileman has halted its planned expansion in the Southeast.[11]

Coors

Currently, Coors is expanding outside of its western markets, and its expansion drive has constrained its efforts to introduce new products. Additionally, Coors has met stiff opposition in the north where Stroh's and Heileman are very strong. Some analysts have suggested that unless Coors can stop the erosion of its premium brands in its primary states of Texas, California, and Florida, it may become a candidate for a corporate takeover.[12]

Stroh's

Stroh's, on the other hand, has the economies of scale and size (24 million barrels of capacity per year) to be an efficient national brewer. It has obtained modern brewing facilities nationwide through its acquisition of Schaefer and Schlitz. Its only weaknesses in comparison with Anheuser-Busch and Miller are its financial position and its distribution network. Stroh's is expected to play a major role in the future of the industry.[13]

Imported Beers

Imported beers are becoming more competitive in the United States, and they are experiencing a growth rate of approximately 12 percent in the domestic market. Their growth is attributed to five factors: (1) they are perceived to be of higher quality; (2) because of the high value of the dollar, they are affordable; (3) they have "snob appeal"; (4) Americans are traveling abroad more and developing a taste for imported beers; and (5) American consumers are becoming more selective in their buying habits.[14] Topping the list of imports is Heineken, with a 34 percent share followed by Molson, with a 13.4 percent share. Beck's and Amstel Light are expected to show particularly good growth, especially Amstel Light.[15]

EXHIBIT 4

1984 Production—Top Six Brands (Millions of Barrels)

		MARKET SHARE
Budweiser	44.3	24.2
Miller Lite	18.0	9.9
Miller High Life	14.5	7.9
Coors	8.7	4.8
Old Milwaukee	7.1	3.9
Michelob	6.7	3.7

Exhibit 4 shows production and market share statistics for the top six beer brands in the United States. Exhibit 5 shows beer consumption in the United States between 1975 and 1983 by type of beer. Exhibit 6 shows the 1984 sales of the six leading producers of beer in the United States.

MARKETING AND ADVERTISING

Over the past decade, Anheuser-Busch has, by means of massive marketing and ad campaigns, managed to transform Budweiser into one of the most familiar trademarks in the world. This is evidenced by the fact that Budweiser commercials have the best recall of beer ads nationally among consumers. Its aggressive marketing has already left the number two beer

EXHIBIT 5

Beer Consumption by Type (Millions of Barrels)

TYPE	1975	1980	1981	1982	1983	PERCENTAGE CHANGE 1982–83
Popular	65.4	30	30.1	29.5	30.5	3.4
Premium	71.6	102.3	101.4	95.7	94.6	−1.1
Super-premium	0.5	11.5	11.2	10.6	10.1	−4.7
Light	2.8	22.1	26.2	32.5	34.1	4.9
Imported	1.7	4.6	5.2	5.8	6.3	8.6
Malt liquor	3.8	5.5	0.6	6.4	6.4	0.0
Ale	N.A.	1.9	1.8	1.8	1.7	−5.6
Total	150.3	177.9	181.9	182.3	183.7	0.8

EXHIBIT 6

1984 Sales of Six Leading U.S. Beer Producers

RANK	COMPANY	1984 SALES (DOLLAR AMOUNTS IN MILLIONS)
1	Anheuser-Busch	5,490,000
2	Miller	2,928,000
3	Stroh's	1,600,000
4	Heileman	1,207,394
5	Coors	937,876
6	Pabst	752,365

producer, Miller Brewing Company, far behind even though the two were close competitors just five years ago. Anheuser-Busch's growth is particularly dramatic when measured against the backdrop of a domestic beer market that has been stagnant for four years. August Busch III gave much of the credit for Anheuser-Busch's strong showing to "aggressive advertising and merchandising surrounding the Anheuser-Busch sponsorship of the Olympic Games."[16] Last year, Anheuser-Busch spent $245 million for advertising, $122 million on network sports events advertising alone.

VERTICAL INTEGRATION AT ANHEUSER-BUSCH

Anheuser-Busch is a highly vertically integrated firm. The following is a list of Anheuser-Busch's vertically integrated components:

- *Metal Container Corporation:* This subsidiary is a can and lid manufacturer with three metal container can plants.
- *Busch Agricultural Resources, Inc.:* This subsidiary processes barley into brewer's malt. In 1984, this subsidiary supplied Anheuser-Busch with 32 percent of its malt requirements.
- *Container Recovery Corporation:* This can recycling subsidiary functions in two ways—by collecting aluminum cans from consumers for recycling, and by operating three container recycling process plants.
- *St. Louis Refrigerator Car Company:* This transportation subsidiary has been in existence since 1878 and is involved in the maintenance of railroad cars as well as in the operation of 650 specially insulated railroad cars for the transportation of Anheuser-Busch's beer products.
- *Manufacturers Railway Company:* This transportation subsidiary provides terminal rail switching services to St. Louis industries and operates a fleet of hopper cars and boxcars.
- *International Label Company:* This company is a joint venture between

Anheuser-Busch and Illochroma International, S.A., of Brussels, Belgium. The main function of this company is the production of metalized labels.

DIVERSIFICATION AT ANHEUSER-BUSCH	In addition to the brewing side of Anheuser-Busch's business, the firm has diversified into a number of related and unrelated businesses. Below is a list of Anheuser-Busch's diversified operations:

- *Busch Industrial Products:* In 1984 this subsidiary was the leading producer and marketer of compressed baker's yeast in the United States. This subsidiary also produces autolyzed yeast, which is used for processed meats.

- *Busch Entertainment:* This family entertainment subsidiary operates two Busch Garden theme parks in Florida and Virginia. A water park called *Adventure Island* is adjacent to Busch Gardens in Florida. In addition, Anheuser-Busch owns Sesame Place in Pennsylvania, a twenty-first century play park oriented toward education and entertainment.

- *Anheuser-Busch International:* This international licensing and marketing subsidiary formed in 1980 brews Budweiser in Canada, Japan, Israel, and the U.K. Anheuser-Busch also exports to Hong Kong, Singapore, Guam, New Zealand, Panama, and Sweden.

- *Eagle Snacks, Inc.:* In January 1982 the Eagle Snacks Division was incorporated as Eagle Snacks, Inc., a wholly owned subsidiary of Anheuser-Busch. "In 1984, Eagle Snacks, Inc., began self-manufacturing virtually all of its snack products through the expansion of its Robersonville, N.C., plant and through the start-up of additional lines at the Campbell-Taggart (C-T) Fort Payne, Alabama, plant."[17] Eagle Snacks are distributed through Anheuser-Busch wholesaler and C-T distribution systems in approximately 200 markets in the United States. They are available in restaurants, bars, hotels, supermarkets, convenience stores, airport lounges, and airlines.

- *Busch Properties, Inc.:* This real estate subsidiary was established in 1970. It is currently involved in the development of a residential project in Virginia and the development of commercial properties in Virginia, Ohio, and California.

- *Busch Corporate Centers:* Anheuser-Busch owns several business centers (Columbus, Williamsburg, Fairfield).

- *Civic Center Corporation:* This corporation was acquired in 1981. It has redeveloped 43 blocks of downtown St. Louis. This subsidiary also owns Busch Stadium, St. Louis Sports Hall of Fame Museum and Gift Shop, Stadium Club, and four parking garages.

- *St. Louis National Baseball Club:* This subsidiary owns the St. Louis Cardinals baseball team.

- *Busch Creative Services Corporation:* This communications subsidiary was formed in 1980. It offers a variety of multimedia, print, film, and other corporate and marketing communications material. In 1985 this subsidiary acquired Innervision Productions, Inc., a producer of TV commercials and industrial training films.

• *Campbell-Taggart:* In 1982 Anheuser-Busch purchased Campbell-Taggart for $560 million. Campbell-Taggart is currently the nation's second-largest bakery. Campbell-Taggart's subsidiaries are involved in the production and distribution of baked goods (mainly bread), refrigerated dough and salad products, frozen Mexican food, and packaged goods to food service companies. In addition to these operations, Campbell-Taggart also has manufacturing operations in Spain, France, and Brazil. The Spanish subsidiary is the largest baker in Spain.

FINANCES AT ANHEUSER-BUSCH

Anheuser-Busch's financial statements are shown in Exhibit 7, consolidated balance sheet; Exhibit 8, statement of income; Exhibit 9, statement of changes in shareholders' equity and convertible redeemable preferred stock; and Exhibit 10, statement of changes in financial position.

EXHIBIT 7
Consolidated Balance Sheet for Anheuser-Busch Companies, Inc., and Subsidiaries (Dollar Amounts in Millions)

ASSETS YEAR ENDED DECEMBER 31,	1984	1983
CURRENT ASSETS		
Cash and marketable securities (marketable securities of $69.3 in 1984 and $185.8 in 1983 at cost, which approximates market)	$ 78.6	$ 218.4
Accounts and notes receivable, less allowance for doubtful accounts of $2.8 in 1984 and $2.9 in 1983	275.6	283.6
Inventories		
Raw materials and supplies	212.7	196.5
Work in process	65.7	61.1
Finished goods	37.5	41.2
Total inventories	315.9	298.8
Other current assets	106.2	96.8
Total current assets	776.3	897.6
INVESTMENTS AND OTHER ASSETS		
Investments in and advances to unconsolidated subsidiaries	42.9	57.7
Investment properties	18.1	9.1
Deferred charges and other non-current assets	87.1	73.7
Excess of cost over net assets of acquired business, net	85.3	87.9
	233.4	228.4

The accompanying statements should be read in conjunction with the Notes to Consolidated Financial Statements [Appendix A].

EXHIBIT 7   Continued

ASSETS YEAR ENDED DECEMBER 31,	1984	1983
PLANT AND EQUIPMENT		
Land	80.0	70.1
Buildings	1,398.1	1,303.6
Machinery and equipment	2,920.5	2,622.8
Construction in progress	395.3	311.6
Other real estate	6.7	5.8
	4,800.6	4,313.9
Less accumulated depreciation	1,285.6	1,109.7
	3,515.0	3,204.2
	$4,524.7	$4,330.2

LIABILITIES AND SHAREHOLDERS' EQUITY YEAR ENDED DECEMBER 31,	1984	1983
CURRENT LIABILITIES		
Accounts payable	$ 338.2	$ 327.8
Accrued salaries, wages, and benefits	150.3	142.5
Accrued interest payable	26.8	29.9
Due to customers for returnable containers	31.8	31.1
Accrued taxes, other than income taxes	43.6	64.3
Estimated income taxes	39.0	48.4
Other current liabilities	66.3	78.5
Total current liabilities	696.0	722.5
Long-term debt	835.8	961.4
Deferred income taxes	755.0	573.2
Minority shareholders' interest in consolidated subsidiaries	—	20.6
Convertible redeemable preferred stock (liquidation value $300.0)	286.9	286.0

COMMON STOCK AND OTHER SHAREHOLDERS' EQUITY

	1984	1983
Preferred stock, $1.00 par value, authorized 32,498,000 shares in 1984 and 1983; none issued	—	—
Common stock, $1.00 par value, authorized 200,000,000 shares in 1984 and 1983; issued 48,641,869 and 48,514,214 shares, respectively	48.6	48.5
Capital in excess of par value	173.2	167.2
Retained earnings	1,829.3	1,555.4
Foreign currency translation adjustment	(6.6)	(3.7)
	2,044.5	1,767.4
Less cost of treasury stock (1,564,152 shares in 1984 and 119,552 shares in 1983)	93.5	0.9
	1,951.0	1,766.5
Commitments and contingencies	—	—
	$4,524.7	$4,330.2

EXHIBIT 8   Consolidated Statement of Income for Anheuser-Busch Companies, Inc., and Subsidiaries (Dollar Amounts in Millions Except Per Share Data)

YEAR ENDED DECEMBER 31,	1984	1983	1982
Sales	$7,158.2	$6,658.5	$5,185.7
Less federal and state beer taxes	657.0	624.3	609.1
Net sales	6,501.2	6,034.2	4,576.6
Cost of products sold	4,414.2	4,113.2	3,331.7
Gross profit	2,087.0	1,921.0	1,244.9
Marketing, administrative, and research expenses	1,332.3	1,220.2	752.0
Operating income	754.7	700.8	492.9
Other income and expenses:			
Interest expense	(102.7)	(111.4)	(89.2)
Interest capitalized	46.8	32.9	41.2
Interest income	22.8	12.5	17.0
Other expense, net	(31.8)	(18.8)	(8.1)
Gain on sale of Lafayette plant	—	—	20.4
Income before income taxes	689.8	616.0	474.2
Provision for income taxes:			
Current	118.4	133.7	92.4
Deferred	179.9	134.3	94.5
	298.3	268.0	186.9
Net income	$ 391.5	$ 348.0	$ 287.3
Earnings per share:			
Primary	$ 7.40	$ 6.50	$ 5.97
Full diluted	7.40	6.50	5.88

The accompanying statements should be read in conjunction with the Notes to Consolidated Financial Statements [Appendix A].

EXHIBIT 9

Consolidated Statement of Changes in Shareholders' Equity and Convertible Redeemable Preferred Stock for Anheuser-Busch Companies, Inc., and Subsidiaries (Dollar Amounts in Millions Except Per Share Data)

	SHAREHOLDERS' EQUITY					CONVERTIBLE REDEEMABLE PREFERRED STOCK
	COMMON STOCK	CAPITAL IN EXCESS OF PAR VALUE	RETAINED EARNINGS	TREASURY STOCK	FOREIGN CURRENCY TRANSLATION ADJUSTMENT	
Balance at December 31, 1981	$45.6	$ 67.2	$1,094.9	$ (0.9)		
Net income			287.3			
Cash dividends ($1.38 per share)			(65.8)			
Shares issued under stock option plans		1.0				
Shares issued in the acquisition of a company						$285.0
Shares issued upon conversion of the 9.00% convertible debentures	2.8	94.5				
Balance at December 31, 1982	48.4	162.7	1,316.4	(0.9)		285.0
Net income			348.0			
Cash dividends:						
Common ($1.62 per share)			(78.3)			
Preferred ($3.60 per share)			(29.7)			
Shares issued under stock option plans	0.1	4.5				
Accretion of preferred stock			(1.0)			1.0
Foreign currency translation adjustment					$(3.7)	
Balance at December 31, 1983	48.5	167.2	1,555.4	(0.9)	(3.7)	286.0
Net income			391.5			
Cash dividends:						
Common ($1.88 per share)			(89.7)			
Preferred ($3.60 per share)			(27.0)			
Shares issued under stock option plans	0.1	6.0				
Accretion of preferred stock			(0.9)			0.9
Shares acquired as treasury stock				(92.6)		
Foreign currency translation adjustment					(2.9)	
Balance at December 31, 1984	$48.6	$173.2	$1,829.3	$(93.5)	$(6.6)	$286.9

The accompanying statements should be read in conjunction with the Notes to Consolidated Financial Statements [Appendix A].

163

EXHIBIT 10

Consolidated Statement of Changes in Financial Position for Anheuser-Busch Companies, Inc., and Subsidiaries (Dollar Amounts in Millions)

YEAR ENDED DECEMBER 31,	1984	1983	1982
SOURCE OF FUNDS			
Net income	$ 391.5	$ 348.0	$ 287.3
Depreciation and amortization	203.4	187.3	133.6
Deferred income taxes	181.8	118.1	97.4
Total funds provided by current operations	776.7	653.4	518.3
Issuance of convertible redeemable preferred stock	—	—	285.0
Increase in long-term debt	7.8	32.7	259.8
Issuance of common stock on conversion of 9.00% debentures	—	—	97.3
Investment in unconsolidated subsidiaries	14.8	1.2	(12.1)
Disposition of Lafayette plant	—	—	20.6
Other, net	(2.6)	18.3	(79.4)
Total	796.7	705.6	1,089.5
USE OF FUNDS			
Capital expenditures	519.2	428.0	355.8
Dividends paid to stockholders	116.7	108.0	65.8
Decrease in long-term debt	133.4	40.3	108.1
Decrease in short-term debt	—	25.0	4.5
Installment purchase obligation	—	—	40.0
Acquisition of subsidiary	—	—	560.0
Acquisition of minority interests	20.6	—	—
Acquisition of treasury stock	92.6	—	—
Increase in investment properties	9.0	—	—
Increase (decrease) in non-cash working capital	45.0	(92.6)	27.4
Total	936.5	508.7	1,161.6
Increase (decrease) in cash and marketable securities	$(139.8)	$ 196.9	$ (72.1)
NON-CASH WORKING CAPITAL			
Increase (decrease) in non-cash current assets:			
Accounts and notes receivable	$ (8.0)	$ 40.1	$ 95.8
Inventories	17.1	(9.0)	79.4
Other current assets	9.4	(22.2)	49.4

EXHIBIT 10   **Continued**

YEAR ENDED DECEMBER 31,	1984	1983	1982
NON-CASH WORKING CAPITAL			
Decrease (increase) in current liabilities:			
Accounts payable	(10.4)	(21.6)	(96.4)
Accrued salaries, wages, and benefits	(7.8)	(11.4)	(49.7)
Accrued interest payable	3.1	(0.1)	(2.5)
Due to customers for returnable containers	(0.7)	(3.9)	(0.9)
Accrued taxes, other than income taxes	20.7	(1.6)	(2.6)
Estimated income taxes	9.4	(22.0)	(21.2)
Other current liabilities	12.2	(40.9)	(23.9)
Increase (decrease) in non-cash working capital	$ 45.0	$ (92.6)	$ 27.4

The accompanying statements should be read in conjunction with the Notes to Consolidated Financial Statements [Appendix A].

APPENDIX A

NOTES TO CONSOLIDATED FINANCIAL STATEMENTS

1. SUMMARY OF SIGNIFICANT ACCOUNTING PRINCIPLES AND POLICIES

This summary of significant accounting principles and policies of Anheuser-Busch Companies, Inc., and its subsidiaries is presented to assist the reader in evaluating the company's financial statements included in this report. These principles and policies conform to generally accepted accounting principles and have been consistently followed by the company. The format of the Consolidated Statement of Changes in Financial Position at December 31, 1984 has been revised from a "working capital" format to a "cash flow" format. Accordingly, the format revision has been applied retroactively to all prior periods presented in the statement.

Principles of Consolidation

The consolidated financial statements include the company and all its subsidiaries. Certain subsidiaries which are not an integral part of the company's primary operations are included on an equity basis. The Consolidated Statement of Income includes the operations of Campbell Taggart since November 2, 1982.

Foreign Currency Translation

Effective January 1, 1983 the company adopted Financial Accounting Standard No. 52, "Foreign Currency Translation." In the application of this statement, exchange adjustments resulting from foreign currency transactions generally are recognized in income, whereas adjustments resulting from translations of financial statements are reflected as a separate component of shareholders' equity. The Consolidated Statement of Changes in Shareholders Equity and Convertible Redeemable Preferred Stock includes the foreign currency translation adjustment.

Inventories and Production Costs

Inventories are valued at the lower of cost or market. Cost is determined under the last-in, first-out method for substantially all brewing inventories and under the first-in, first-out method for substantially all food product inventories.

Plant and Equipment

Plant and equipment is carried at cost and includes expenditures for new facilities and those which substantially increase the useful lives of existing plant and equipment. Maintenance, repairs and minor renewals are expensed as incurred. When properties are retired or otherwise disposed of, the related cost and accumulated depreciation are removed from the respective accounts and any profit or loss on disposition is credited or charged to income.

Depreciation is provided principally on the straight-line method over the estimated useful lives of the assets (buildings 2 percent to 10 percent and machinery and equipment 4 percent to 25 percent).

Capitalization of Interest

Interest relating to the cost of acquiring certain fixed assets is capitalized. This interest is included as part of the cost of the related asset and is amortized over its estimated useful life.

Income Taxes

The provision for income taxes is based on elements of income and expense as reported in the Consolidated Statement of Income. The company has elected to utilize certain provisions of federal income tax laws and regulations to reduce current taxes payable.

Deferred income taxes are recognized for the effect of differences between financial and tax reporting. Investment tax credit is included in income when assets are placed in service or when the credit can be claimed under federal income tax laws relating to qualified progress expenditures.

Expenditures Which Provide Possible Future Benefits

Research and development, advertising, promotional costs and initial plant costs are charged against income in the year in which these costs are incurred.

Net Income per Share of Common Stock

Primary earnings per share of common stock are based on the average number of shares of common stock outstanding during the respective years (52.9 million in 1984, 53.5 million in 1983 and 48.1 million in 1982). The convertible redeemable preferred shares are common stock equivalents; accordingly, these shares are assumed to have been converted into common stock at the date of their issuance and are included in the weighted average shares outstanding in computing primary earnings per share.

The company's 9.00 percent convertible subordinated debentures (issued in 1980) were called for redemption and converted into 2.8 million shares of common stock on April 29, 1982. Fully diluted earnings per share are computed on the assumption that these convertible securities and all outstanding stock options were converted into common stock as appropriate. Interest expense on the convertible subordinated debentures, net of income taxes, is added back to net income in the fully diluted earnings per share calculation.

2. ACQUISITION AND DISPOSITION

On November 2, 1982, the company acquired all of the outstanding common stock of Campbell Taggart, Inc. (Campbell Taggart). Campbell Taggart, through its operating subsidiaries, is engaged in the production and sale of food and food-related products. The cost of the acquisition was $560.0 million, consisting of $275.0 million paid in cash for approximately 50 percent of Campbell Taggart's outstanding common stock and 7.5 million shares of Anheuser-Busch convertible redeemable preferred stock with an estimated fair value of $285.0 million issued in exchange for the remaining Campbell Taggart common stock.

The acquisition has been accounted for using the purchase method of accounting. Campbell Taggart's assets and liabilities have been recorded in the company's financial statements at their estimated fair values at the acquisition date. The excess cost of acquisition over the estimated fair value of the net assets is being amortized on a straight-line basis over forty years.

Assuming the acquisition of Campbell Taggart had occurred on January 1, 1982, the pro forma combined net sales would have been $5.6 billion for

1982. The pro forma combined net income and net income per share for 1982 would not have been materially different than that reported in the Consolidated Statement of Income.

In March 1982, the company sold its corn refining plant in Lafayette, Indiana, resulting in a nonrecurring, after-tax gain of $13.3 million or $.28 per share (fully diluted). Sales and income from operations of this plant for the year ended December 31, 1982 were not material.

3. INVENTORY VALUATION

Approximately 75 percent of total inventories at December 31, 1984 and 1983 are stated on the last-in, first-out (LIFO) inventory valuation method. Had the average-cost method been used with respect to such items at December 31, 1984 and 1983, total inventories would have been $105.8 million and $94.9 million higher, respectively.

4. CREDIT AGREEMENTS

In August 1982, the company entered into a ten-year revolving credit agreement with a group of eleven domestic banks. In December 1983, the agreement was amended to provide for a maximum borrowing of $400.0 million. Interest on the loans will be based, at the option of the company, on the prime rate, the domestic CD rate plus ½ percent, or the Euro-Dollar rate plus ⅜ percent for the first five years, and at scheduled rate increases for periods thereafter. In addition, a negotiated sub-prime borrowing feature is available for the entire term of the agreement. At December 31, 1984 and 1983, the company had no outstanding borrowings under this agreement.

In June 1981, the company entered into a multicurrency revolving credit agreement aggregating $100.0 million or the equivalent amount in alternative currencies. This commitment extends through March 27, 1986. Interest on borrowings in Euro-Dollars and alternative currencies will be ⅜ percent over the Euro Basic Rate, as defined, and on United States currency borrowings, at the company's option, at either a floating rate equal to the prevailing Domestic Floating Base Rate, as defined, plus ¾ percent or at a fixed rate equal to the Domestic Fixed Base Rate, as defined, plus ½ percent. At December 31, 1984 and 1983, the company had no outstanding borrowings under this agreement.

Fees under these agreements and prior agreements amounted to $1.1, $3.3, and $3.7 million in 1984, 1983, and 1982, respectively.

5. LONG-TERM DEBT

The only long-term debt issued by the company during 1984 was industrial revenue bonds. During November 1984, the company redeemed all of its $100 million 16½ percent Guaranteed Notes due 1988. Pursuant to the early call provision of the notes, the redemption price was 101.5 percent of the principal amount, or $101.5 million. In October 1982, the company filed a shelf registration with the Securities and Exchange Commission covering up to $200.0 million of debt securities. On October 12, 1982, $100.0 million of 11⅞ percent sinking fund debentures due 2012 were issued under this shelf registration. The company has the option to issue the remaining $100.0 million of debt securities at such time as it considers appropriate.

Long-term debt at December 31 consists of the following:

	1984	1983
	(In millions)	
9.90% Notes due 1986	$100.0	$100.0
15.375% Notes due 1991	50.0	50.0
16.50% Guaranteed notes due 1988	—	100.0
11.25% Guaranteed bonds due 1990	100.0	100.0
Sinking fund debentures	449.6	472.3
Industrial revenue bonds	73.5	74.3
Other long-term debt	62.7	64.8
	$835.8	$961.4

The company's sinking fund debentures at December 31 are as follows:

	1984	1983
	(In millions)	
5.45% debentures maturing 1984 to 1991, less $11.8 in treasury in 1984 and $2.5 in 1983	$ 2.4	$ 13.9
6.00% debentures maturing 1984 to 1992, less $2.1 in treasury in 1984 and $3.4 in 1983	18.2	19.6
7.95% debentures maturing 1985 to 1999, less $10.0 in treasury in 1984 and $11.2 in 1983	83.5	88.8
9.20% debentures maturing 1986 to 2005, less $4.5 in treasury in 1984	145.5	150.0
8.55% debentures maturing 1989 to 2008	100.0	100.0
11.875% debentures maturing 1993 to 2012	100.0	100.0
	$449.6	$472.3

The aggregate maturities on all long-term debt are $15.9, $120.8, $20.2, $19.7, and $24.2 million, respectively, for each of the years ending December 31, 1985 through 1989.

6. STOCK OPTION PLANS

In December 1981, the company adopted an Incentive Stock Option Plan and a Non-Qualified Stock Option Plan for certain officers and key employees. These plans were approved by the shareholders in April 1982. Under the terms of the plans, options may be granted at not less than the fair market value of the shares at the date of grant. The Non-Qualified Stock Option Plan provides that optionees may be granted Stock Appreciation Rights (SARs) in tandem with stock options. The exercise of a SAR cancels the related option and the exercise of an option cancels the related SAR. The Stock Option Committee of the Board of Directors granted SARs under the 1981 Non-Qualified Stock Option Plan with respect to options for 48,880 and 81,800 shares in 1984 and 1983, respectively. At December 31, 1984 and 1983, 2,223,916 and 2,371,313 shares, respectively, were reserved for possible issuance under the 1981 plans.

Presented below is a summary of changes in stock options under the incentive Stock Option Plan and the Non-Qualified Stock Option Plan for the year ended December 31:

	1984	1983
Outstanding at beginning of year	1,543,864	1,279,739
Options granted	375,120	435,540
Options/SARs exercised	(189,825)	(139,937)
Options cancelled	(24,091)	(31,478)
Options outstanding at end of year	1,705,068	1,543,864
Options exercisable at end of year	1,099,264	765,055
Option price range per share	$40.81–$73.69	$40.81–$73.44

7. PENSION PLANS

The company has pension plans covering substantially all of its employees and follows the policy of funding all pension costs accrued. Total pension expense was $71.9, $74.0, and $52.7 million in 1984, 1983, and 1982, respectively. In 1984, the company changed the actuarial investment rate of return assumption for funding purposes from 5½% to 6½% on several of the company's salaried and hourly pension plans. The effect of this change on net income was not material. A comparison of the actuarial present value of accumulated plan benefits and plan net assets, as of the most recent actuarial date, generally January 1, for the company's salaried and hourly paid pension plans combined, is presented below:

	1984	1983
	(In millions)	
Actuarial present value of accumulated plan benefits:		
Vested	$293.2	$265.6
Nonvested	34.4	34.2
	$327.6	$299.8
Net assets available for benefits	$497.7	$418.7

The weighted average assumed rate of return used in determining the actuarial present value of accumulated plan benefits was 8.5% in 1984 and 1983.

---

8. INCOME TAXES

The provision for income taxes includes the following for each of the three years ended December 31:

	1984	1983	1982
	(In millions)		
Current tax provision			
Federal:			
Provision	$136.2	$156.4	$123.2
Charge in lieu of taxes	—	—	11.9
Investment tax credit:			
Normal	(35.1)	(32.5)	(35.0)
TRASOP	—	(6.8)	(7.6)
Safe harbor leases	—	—	(11.9)
	101.1	117.1	80.6
State and foreign	17.3	16.6	11.8
	118.4	133.7	92.4
Deferred tax provision:			
Federal	171.0	126.4	88.2
State and foreign	8.9	7.9	6.3
	179.9	134.3	94.5
	$298.3	$268.0	$186.9

In 1982 the company purchased tax benefits in the form of accelerated cost recovery allowances and investment tax credits under "safe harbor" leases as defined in the Economic Recovery Tax Act of 1981. The purchase price of these benefits is recorded as an asset which is amortized through a charge to the current tax provision during the initial years of the lease. That portion of the amortization related to the investment tax credit is recorded as a charge in lieu of taxes. In subsequent years of the lease, deferred income taxes are provided for the difference between the tax and the financial aspects of the lease. The effect of these leases on net income is not material.

The deferred tax provision results from timing differences in the recognition of income and expense for tax and financial reporting purposes. The primary differences are the calculation of depreciation for tax purposes using accelerated methods and shorter lives and expensing for tax purposes interest cost capitalized for book purposes. These timing differences had a tax effect of $178.5 million in 1984, $155.2 million in 1983, and $113.0 million in 1982.

The Tax Equity and Fiscal Responsibility Act of 1982 required the company to reduce the tax basis of depreciable property by one-half of the investment tax credit claimed on the tax return. The effect of the basis reduction is to reduce the financial impact of the normal investment tax credit to $31.1 and $26.4 million in 1984 and 1983, respectively.

The company's effective tax rate was 43.2 percent, 43.5 percent, and 39.4 percent in 1984, 1983, and 1982, respectively. A reconciliation between the statutory rate and the effective rate is presented below:

	1984	1983	1982
Statutory rate	*46.0%*	46.0%	46.0%
Charge in lieu of taxes	—	—	2.5
Investment tax credit:			
Normal	*(5.1)*	(5.3)	(7.4)
TRASOP	—	(1.1)	(1.6)
Safe harbor leases	—	—	(2.5)
State income taxes, net of federal benefit	*1.9*	1.9	1.9
Other	*.4*	2.0	.5
Effective tax rate	*43.2%*	43.5%	39.4%

9. COMMON AND PREFERRED STOCK

In March 1984, the Board of Directors amended a 1982 resolution to authorize the company to purchase up to 4.8 million shares of its common stock. The shares will be used for the conversion to common stock of preferred stock issued in connection with the acquisition of Campbell Taggart. In 1984, 1,444,600 shares were purchased for $92.6 million.

In connection with the acquisition of Campbell Taggart, the company issued 7,500,766 shares of convertible redeemable preferred stock, par value $1. The convertible redeemable preferred stock has a redemption value of $40, requires dividend payments at a rate of $3.60 per year, is non-callable for five years and subject to mandatory redemption at the end of fifteen years. The preferred shares are also convertible into .645 of a share of the company's common stock and have voting rights in this ratio. The difference between the redemption value and the carrying value is being amortized over fifteen years.

10. COMMITMENTS AND CONTINGENCIES

In connection with the plant expansion and improvement program, the company has commitments for capital expenditures of approximately $489.5 million at December 31, 1984.

Obligations under capital leases are not material.

The company and certain of its subsidiaries are involved in claims and legal proceedings in which monetary damages and other relief are sought. The company is contesting these claims and proceedings. However, their resolution is not expected to occur quickly and their ultimate outcome cannot presently be predicted. In any event, it is the opinion of management that any liability of the company or its subsidiaries for such claims or proceedings will not materially affect its financial position.

11. BUSINESS SEGMENTS

The company has identified its principal business segments as beer and beer-related, food products, and diversified operations. The beer and beer-related segment produces and sells the company's beer products. Included in this segment are the company's raw material acquisition, malting, can manufacturing and recycling operations.

The food products segment consists of the company's food and food-related operations which include the operations of Campbell Taggart since November 2, 1982. In addition, this segment includes the company's yeast and snack food subsidiaries.

Diversified operations consist of the company's entertainment, communications, transportation, and real estate operations.

Sales between segments, export sales, and sales by geographic area are not material. The company's equity in earnings of unconsolidated subsidiaries has been included in other income and expense. No single customer accounted for more than 10 percent of sales.

The following summarizes the company's business segment information for 1984, 1983, and 1982 (in millions).

1984	Beer and beer-related	Food products	Diversified operations	Eliminations	Consolidated
Net sales	$5,390.1	$1,353.5	$170.4	$(412.8)	$6,501.2
Operating income*	728.2	16.5	10.0		754.7
Depreciation and amortization expense	141.1	42.3	20.0		203.4
Capital expenditures	393.1	106.7	19.4		519.2
Identifiable assets	3,214.7	811.8	128.0		4,154.5
Corporate assets†					370.2
Total assets					4,524.7

1983	Beer and beer-related	Food products	Diversified operations	Eliminations	Consolidated
Net sales	$4,907.7	$1,320.4	$150.2	$(344.1)	$6,034.2
Operating income*	649.9	47.3	3.6		700.8
Depreciation and amortization expense	129.5	40.3	17.5		187.3
Capital expenditures	348.1	54.8	25.1		428.0
Identifiable assets	2,994.1	768.6	143.7		3,906.4
Corporate assets†					423.8
Total assets					4,330.2

1982	Beer and beer-related	Food products	Diversified operations	Eliminations	Consolidated
Net sales	$4,488.1	$282.8	$145.1	$(339.4)	$4,576.6
Operating income*	464.1	23.5	5.3		492.9
Depreciation and amortization expense	110.8	8.8	14.0		133.6
Capital expenditures	310.1	23.4	22.3		355.8
Identifiable assets	2,758.1	779.3	148.9		3,686.3
Corporate assets†					216.5
Total assets					3,902.8

*Operating income excludes other expense, net, which is not allocated among segments. For 1984, 1983, and 1982 other expense, net of $64.9, $84.8, and $18.7 million, respectively, includes net interest expense, minority interests, other income and expense, equity in earnings of unconsolidated subsidiaries and a nonrecurring gain of $20.4 million on the sale of the Lafayette corn refining plant in 1982.
†Corporate assets principally include cash, marketable securities, investment in equity subsidiaries, goodwill, and certain fixed assets.

12. ADDITIONAL INCOME STATEMENT INFORMATION

The following amounts were charged to costs and expenses:

	1984	1983	1982
		(In millions)	
Maintenance	$253.5	$261.4	$216.8
Depreciation and amortization	$203.4	$187.3	$133.6
Taxes, other than income taxes:			
Payroll	$ 90.3	$ 82.3	$ 44.7
Real and personal property ..	37.6	36.1	30.1
Franchise and other	16.2	14.2	7.8
Total	$144.1	$132.6	$ 82.6
Advertising costs	$480.2	$403.9	$322.3

13. QUARTERLY FINANCIAL DATA (UNAUDITED)

Summarized quarterly financial data for 1984 and 1983 (in millions, except per share data) appear below:

	Net sales		Gross profit		Net income		Primary net income per share	
	1984	1983	1984	1983	1984	1983	1984	1983
First quarter	$1,468.8	$1,390.8	$ 459.1	$ 432.9	$ 77.7	$ 68.7	$ 1.45	$ 1.28
Second quarter	1,691.4	1,559.4	557.4	512.8	113.4	98.5	2.13	1.84
Third quarter	1,761.8	1,585.1	578.9	516.4	128.5	113.8	2.44	2.13
Fourth quarter	1,579.2	1,498.9	491.6	458.9	71.9	67.0	1.38	1.25
Total year	$6,501.2	$6,034.2	$2,087.0	$1,921.0	$391.5	$348.0	$7.40	$6.50

REPORT OF INDEPENDENT ACCOUNTANTS

One Centerre Plaza
St. Louis, Missouri 63101
314/425-0500

February 6, 1985

To the Shareholders and Board of Directors of Anheuser-Busch Companies, Inc.

In our opinion, the accompanying Consolidated Balance Sheet and the related Consolidated Statements of Income, Changes in Shareholders Equity and Convertible Redeemable Preferred Stock, and of Changes in Financial Position present fairly the financial position of Anheuser-Busch Companies, Inc. and its subsidiaries at December 31, 1984 and 1983, and the results of their operations and the changes in their financial position for each of the three years in the period ended December 31, 1984, in conformity with generally accepted accounting principles consistently applied. Our examinations of these statements were made in accordance with generally accepted auditing standards and accordingly included such tests of the accounting records and such other auditing procedures as we considered necessary in the circumstances.

/s/ Price Waterhouse

NOTES

1. Pierce and Robinson, *Strategic Management* (Homewood, Ill.: Irwin, 1985), p. 511.

2. Stevenson, "How Anheuser-Busch Brews Its Winners," *New York Times*, August 4, 1985.

3. "Overseas Beer Market," *Business Week*, October 22, 1984.

4. *Ibid*.

5. *Ibid*.

6. "Betting on Beer without Buzz," *Fortune*, June 25, 1984.

7. *Industry Surveys*, April 11, 1985.

8. *The New York Times*, August 2, 1985.

9. "Is the Beer Industry Drying Up?" *Beverage World*, February 1985.

10. *Ibid*.

11. *Ibid*.

12. "Brewers Fight for Share in a Declining Market," *Beverage Industry*, January 1985.

13. "Is the Beer Industry Drying Up?" *Beverage World*, February 1985.

14. "Why Import Sales Are Booming," *Beverage Industry*, July 1985.

15. *Industry Surveys*, April 11, 1985.

16. "Anheuser-Busch Companies," *Advertising Age*, September 26, 1985.

17. Anheuser-Busch's 1983 Annual Report.

Anheuser-Busch Companies, Inc (C)

NEIL H. SNYDER · KELLAM WHITE

INTRODUCTION

In 1986, Anheuser-Busch Companies, Inc., experienced yet another record year. All divisions were profitable. The brewing subsidiary, Anheuser-Busch, Inc., achieved record sales of 72.3 million barrels of beer (38 percent of market share). Expansion into international markets increased with the signing of two licensed-brewing agreements for A-B to be brewed, starting in 1987, by Guinness Ireland, Ltd., in Ireland and by United Breweries, Ltd., in Denmark. Internal diversification continued with the development of new non-beer beverage products through the Anheuser-Busch beverage group.

At the close of 1986, all appeared well at A-B. However, in early 1987, scandals threatened the powerful industry leader. Key executives were accused of accepting kickbacks, A-B President Dennis Long resigned, and the Brooklyn-based bottler of Soho Natural Soda sued the beverage group for allegedly copying Soho's flavors and logo in its development of the newest Anheuser product, Zeltzer Seltzer.

KICKBACK CHARGES AND RESIGNATIONS

Since Philip Morris acquired Miller Brewing Company in the early 1970s, A-B has implemented an aggressive marketing strategy. Refusing to let go of its market leadership, Anheuser has adopted many innovative marketing campaigns over the last decade. As a result of its aggressive advertising efforts, the company has become the nation's top events sponsor, concentrating on professional sports.

In early 1987, Anheuser faced allegations that key marketing executives had accepted kickbacks. A-B's director of promotions was accused of having accepted funds that were ultimately used to purchase a new sports car. In addition, two vice presidents were said to have received kickbacks totaling $150,000. As a result of these allegations, all three executives have left the company.

One further consequence of the above allegations was to force the retirement of the president of A-B, Inc., Dennis P. Long. Though not charged with any misconduct, Long took responsibility for the scandal. A well-respected administrator within the brewing industry, Long had been with A-B for 35 years. He was second only to A. A. Busch III and was a key player in helping A-B attain marketplace dominance.

ZELTZER SELTZER

The Anheuser-Busch beverage group recently entered the expanding bottled-water industry with its natural soda, Zeltzer Seltzer. Though initially the product will be in limited distribution, officials at A-B feel confident that existing financial and distribution resources will ensure the success of Zeltzer. Furthermore, the beverage group recently acquired a strategically located, high-quality production and packaging facility.

To market Zeltzer Seltzer, Anheuser will once again adopt an innovative marketing strategy. The company is relying on two uncharacteristic marketing tools: animation and word-of-mouth advertising. The initial advertising campaign, which will cost only an estimated $5 million, will include three animated TV commercials which will air only on Music Television. During the past year, the natural soda industry went from sales of 0 to $260 million by relying largely on word-of-mouth advertising, and Anheuser expects this trend to continue. Since the seltzer segment of the bottled-water industry is believed to have few potential new competitors and very vulnerable existing brands, a more heavily advertised newcomer could easily attain market dominance.

Shortly following Anheuser's introduction of Zeltzer Seltzer, American Natural Beverage Company, producer of Soho Natural Soda, filed suit against the beverage group in New York. Soho contends that the Zeltzer Seltzer label displays the same checkerboard pattern and uses the same script lettering as its own soda. Soho claims that A-B is in violation of a New York trade law that prohibits new products from using trademarks and packaging similar to that of existing products.

In the past decade, Anheuser-Busch has been largely unsuccessful in its attempts to diversify into other beverages. LA, the heavily advertised low-alcohol beer, has not fared well. Baybry's, a champagne-based cooler, and Dewey Stevens, a low-calorie wine cooler, have both done poorly in the cooler industry. A-B hopes that the superior quality and unique taste of Zeltzer Seltzer, combined with a modest advertising campaign, will result in a successful attempt at diversification into non-beer beverages.

Exhibits 1 to 4 show selected financial information for A-B.

EXHIBIT 1	Consolidated Balance Sheet, Anheuser-Busch Companies, Inc., and Subsidiaries (in Millions)

DECEMBER 31,	1986	1985
ASSETS		
Current assets:		
Cash and marketable securities (marketable securities of $13.2 in 1986 and $119.9 at 1985 at cost, which approximates market)	$ 69.4	$ 169.6
Accounts and notes receivable, less allowance for doubtful accounts of $3.4 in 1986 and $3.1 in 1985	373.0	301.7
Inventories		
Raw materials and supplies	294.2	225.4
Work in process	84.6	73.5
Finished goods	49.0	38.8
Total inventories	427.8	337.7
Other current assets	150.4	156.5
Total current assets	1,020.6	965.5
Investments and other assets:		
Investments in and advances to unconsolidated subsidiaries	99.7	56.7
Investment properties	16.5	16.5
Deferred charges and other non-current assets	131.6	97.5
Excess of cost over net assets of acquired business, net	137.8	99.3
	385.6	270.0
Plant and equipment:		
Land	102.3	91.8
Buildings	1,725.9	1,578.7
Machinery and equipment	3,804.2	3,381.4
Construction in progress	466.9	288.9
	6,099.3	5,340.8
Less accumulated depreciation	1,671.7	1,454.9
	4,427.6	3,885.9
	$5,833.8	$5,121.4

SOURCE: Anheuser-Busch Companies, Inc., annual report.

EXHIBIT 1   **Continued**

DECEMBER 31,	1986	1985
LIABILITIES AND SHAREHOLDERS' EQUITY		
Current liabilities:		
Short-term debt	$ 34.7	$ —
Accounts payable	491.7	425.3
Accrued salaries, wages, and benefits	180.0	177.1
Accrued interest payable	31.0	30.1
Due to customers for returnable containers	34.0	33.1
Accrued taxes, other than income taxes	63.7	56.9
Estimated income taxes	71.8	31.3
Other current liabilities	108.7	84.0
Total current liabilities	1,015.6	837.8
Long-term debt	1,126.8	861.3
Deferred income taxes	1,090.8	961.7
Convertible redeemable preferred stock (liquidation value $297.9)	286.9	287.6
Common stock and other shareholders' equity:		
Preferred stocks		—
Common stock, $1.00 par value, authorized 400,000,000 shares in 1986 and 200,000,000 shares in 1985 and 1984; issued 295,264,924, 146,633,977, and 48,641,869 shares respectively	295.3	146.6
Capital in excess of par value	6.1	90.4
Retained earnings	2,472.2	2,142.3
Foreign currency translation adjustment	.9	(4.4)
	2,774.5	2,374.9
Less cost of treasury stock (26,399,740, 8,114,453 and 1,584,152 shares in 1986, 1985 and 1984, respectively)	460.8	201.9
	2,313.7	2,173.0
Commitments and contingencies	—	—
	$5,833.8	$5,121.4

| EXHIBIT 2 | Consolidated Statement of Income, Anheuser-Busch Companies, Inc., and Subsidiaries (in Millions, Except Per-Share Data) |

YEAR ENDED DECEMBER 31,	1986	1985	1984
Sales	$8,401.7	$7,683.3	$7,158.2
Less federal and state excise taxes	724.5	683.0	657.0
Net sales	7,677.2	7,000.3	6,601.2
Cost of products sold	4,969.2	4,676.1	4,414.2
Gross profit	2,708.0	2,324.2	2,087.0
Marketing, administrative, and research expenses	2,702.9	1,491.9	1,332.3
Operating income	1,005.1	832.3	754.7
Other income and expenses:			
Interest expense	(96.9)	(93.4)	(102.7)
Interest capitalized	33.2	37.2	46.8
Interest income	9.6	21.3	22.8
Other expense, net	(9.8)	(16.9)	(31.8)
Income before income taxes	941.2	780.5	689.8
Provision for income taxes:			
Current	291.2	130.1	118.4
Deferred	132.0	206.7	179.9
Net income	$ 518.0	$ 443.7	$ 391.5
Earnings per share	$ 1.69	$ 1.42	$ 1.23

SOURCE: Anheuser-Busch Companies, Inc., annual report.

EXHIBIT 3 — Financial Information by Business Segment

1986:	BEER BEER-RELATED	FOOD PRODUCTS	DIVERSIFIED OPERATIONS	ELIMINATIONS	CONSOLIDATED
Net sales	$5,898.2	$1,552.7	$247.3	$(21.0)	$7,677.2
Operating income*	945.8	56.6	2.7		1,005.1
Depreciation and amortization expense	192.3	60.5	24.7		277.5
Capital expenditures	544.8	164.3	68.2		777.3
Identifiable assets	4,083.8	1,114.1	178.0		5,375.9
Corporate assets**					457.9
Total assets					5,833.8

1985:	BEER BEER-RELATED	FOOD PRODUCTS	DIVERSIFIED OPERATIONS	ELIMINATIONS	CONSOLIDATED
Net sales	$5,412.6	$1,416.4	$189.6	$(18.3)	$7,000.3
Operating income*	797.0	28.5	6.8		832.3
Depreciation and amortization expense	161.7	53.2	21.2		236.1
Capital expenditures	461.2	103.7	36.1		601.0
Identifiable assets	3,515.6	935.9	174.6		4,626.1
Corporate assets**					495.3
Total assets					5,121.4

1984:	BEER BEER-RELATED	FOOD PRODUCTS	DIVERSIFIED OPERATIONS	ELIMINATIONS	CONSOLIDATED
Net sales	$5,001.7	$1,343.9	$169.5	$(13.9)	$6,501.2
Operating income*	728.2	16.5	10.0		754.7
Depreciation and amortization expense	141.1	42.3	20.0		203.4
Capital expenditures	393.1	106.7	19.4		519.2
Identifiable assets	3,214.7	811.8	128.0		4,154.5
Corporate assets**					370.2
Total assets					4,524.7

SOURCE: Anheuser-Busch Companies, Inc., annual report.

*Operating income excludes other expense, net, which is not allocated among segments. For 1986, 1985, and 1984 other expense, net of $63.9, $51.8, and $64.9 million, respectively, includes net interest expense, minority interests, other income, and expense and equity in earnings of unconsolidated subsidiaries.

**Corporate assets principally include cash, marketable securities, investment in equity subsidiaries, excess of cost over net assets of acquired business and certain fixed assets.

EXHIBIT 4

1986 Financial Highlights (in Millions, except Per Share, Employee, Shareholder, and Statistical Data)

YEAR ENDED DECEMBER 31,	1986	1985	PERCENT
Barrels of beer sold	72.3	68.0	6.3
Sales	$8,401.7	$7,683.3	9.3
Excise taxes	724.5	683.0	6.1
Net sales	7,677.2	7,000.3	9.7
Net income	518.0	443.7	16.7
Earnings per share	1.69	1.42	19.0
Cash dividends:			
Common stock	120.2	102.7	17.0
Per share	.44	.36⅔	20.0
Preferred stock	26.9	27.0	(.4)
Per share	3.60	3.60	—
All taxes	1,323.6	1,174.4	12.7
Capital expenditures	777.3	601.0	29.3
Depreciation and amortization ...	277.5	236.1	17.5
Effective tax rate	45.0%	43.2%	1.8%
Return on shareholders' equity ..	20.5%	18.9%	1.6%

FINANCIAL CONDITION AT DECEMBER 31

	1986	1985	PERCENT
Working capital	$ 5.0	$ 127.7	(96.1)
Plant and equipment, net	4,427.6	3,885.9	13.9
Long-term debt	1,126.8	861.3	30.8
Convertible redeemable preferred stock	286.9	287.6	(.2)
Common stock and other share- holders' equity	2,313.7	2,173.0	6.5
Per common share	8.61	7.84	9.8
Number of employees	41,805	39,313	6.3
Number of common shareholders	53,225	39,338	35.3

SOURCE: Anheuser-Busch Companies, Inc., annual report.

Note: All per-share information reflects the September 12, 1986, two-for-one stock split. 1986 net income and earnings per share reflect the adoption in 1986 of Financial Accounting Standards No. 87 (FAS 87), Employers' Accounting for Pensions. The financial effect of FAS 87's adoption was to increase 1986 net income $23 million and earnings per share $.08.

Molson Breweries of Canada

PETER KILLING · ANDREW INKPEN

Mickey Cohen, the chief executive officer of The Molson Companies Limited (TMCL) was preparing for a board meeting that would take place on January 12, 1989. The main item on the agenda was a proposed merger between TMCL's Molson Brewing Group (Molson) and Carling O'Keefe Breweries of Canada Limited (Carling), owned by Elders IXL Limited (Elders). The new company would be established as a separate, self-financing entity with both TMCL and Elders having equal ownership. The company would be the largest brewer in Canada with more than 50 percent of the market.

Cohen thought that the Carling merger offered the best prospects for Molson's future success in the brewing industry, both inside and outside Canada. He was convinced that without the merger, Molson would be vulnerable in an industry that was becoming increasingly international, competitive, concentrated, and efficiency driven. Although Cohen was confident that the business synergies created by a Molson–Carling merger would be attractive to the TMCL board, he was less sure that the board would be willing to accept the equal ownership arrangement, an issue that had been at the forefront of the negotiations over the past nine months.

THE CANADIAN BREWING INDUSTRY

The Canadian brewing industry was characterized by comprehensive regulation and declining beer consumption. From 1975 to 1988, the Canadian adult population grew by 25 percent while beer sales increased by only 10 percent, resulting in per capita consumption erosion of 11 percent. The shift in consumer demand away from beer was prompted by several factors: increased health and safety consciousness, changing age demographics, and greater-taxation-based price escalation for beer relative to other beverages and consumer products. In 1989, there were no indications of any significant reversal in the no-growth trend; volume was expected to remain static or to decline slightly over the next five years.

This case was prepared by Andrew Inkpen under the direction of Peter Killing, associate professor, for the sole purpose of providing material for class discussion. Copyright 1989, The University of Western Ontario. Reprinted with special permission from The University of Western Ontario.

Government Regulation

Canada's framework of liquor laws and policies had its genesis in the period 1900–1935. Under pressure from the temperance movement, provincial governments across Canada introduced legislation to restrict the production, distribution, and sales of alcoholic beverages of all types. The aim of the movement was to discourage, if not eliminate, the consumption of alcohol.

Interprovincial trade barriers that restricted the shipment of beer between provinces were a key element in the brewing regulatory structure. Except for the Maritime provinces, beer had to be brewed in the province in which it was sold. In the Maritime provinces, out-of-province beer was sold but subject to higher taxes and markups. The brewed-in-province requirements were the primary cause for the fragmented production across many small and inefficient plants with the brewers unable to allocate production between plants. As a comparison, the average plant size in Canada was 1.1 million hectolitres (hL) versus 6.3 million hL in the United States. The size of an efficient plant in the United States was estimated to have risen to more than 10 million hL by the late 1980s.

Taxation of beer was also an important regulatory device and was used as both a major government funding source and as a social "sin tax," which suited the anti-alcohol movement. The provincial taxes added to beer were the single largest cost component in the price of beer. The federal government also had an impact on the cost of production through both federal commodity taxes and control over malting barley, the most important ingredient in the brewing process. Malting barley could only be purchased from the Canadian Wheat Board, which charged brewers a price 2.5 times that paid by U.S. brewers. The combination of commodity and sales taxes accounted for more than 50 percent of the average beer retail price, ranking Canadian beer taxes the third highest among beer-consuming nations. In the United States, taxes averaged 16 percent, ranking the United States nineteenth.

Additional areas under the jurisdiction of provincial governments included the distribution, advertising, sale, and pricing of beer. Except for Quebec and Newfoundland, beer was sold in government-owned or -controlled outlets. In Ontario, the Brewer's Retail company distributed 95 percent of Ontario-brewed products; the other 5 percent was sold through government liquor stores. The Brewer's Retail was owned by Ontario brewers and sold only Ontario-brewed beer. Imported beer was sold in the government liquor stores.

Beer advertising was slowly being deregulated. For example, in Ontario, billboard advertising of beer became legal in 1987. All provincial legislation provided, either directly or indirectly, that provincial authorities could control beer pricing. About 93 percent of the beer sold in Canada was in the same price segment, the regular segment. The remainder was accounted for by premium priced beer (2 percent) and lower priced beer (5 percent). In the western provinces and especially Alberta and British Columbia, price competition had developed as provincial governments moved toward open pricing. In Ontario, price competition was allowable above a price floor but other than a few premium priced brands, all the beer sold in the Brewer's Retail had the same price. Beer pricing in Quebec was quite competitive because beer was sold through independent grocers and "depanneurs." In Atlantic Canada, beer pricing was tightly controlled.

Over the past two decades, the laws governing the beer industry had been substantially liberalized, resulting in more open pricing, reductions in drinking age limits, easing of advertising restrictions, and reduced product introduction and packaging controls. However, the broad regulatory framework involving different provincial standards for production, promotion, distribution, packaging, sales, and interprovincial shipments continued to influence industry structure. This regulation made it necessary for the three national brewers to shape their operations to ten relatively distinct and small marketing areas.

The Canadian regulatory framework had been good for both the government and the brewers. Until recently, Ontario, for example, was one of the most lucrative beer markets in the world with some of the highest margins and one of the most cost-efficient distribution systems. The Ontario government generated huge tax revenues from beer sales and was able to control price, distribution, and advertising. The large U.S. brewers were prevented from capitalizing on their cost efficiencies because there was no price competition and more important, interprovincial barriers largely kept the U.S. beer off the shelves.

However, by the late 1980s, the brewing industry, especially in Ontario, was coming under increasing Canadian and international pressures for deregulation and a removal of barriers to entry for foreign competition.

National and International Pressures for Deregulation

The national pressures for deregulation heightened when the Annual Conference of First Ministers, held in Toronto in 1987, endorsed in principle a general reduction or elimination of interprovincial trade barriers, including those relating to beer. An Interprovincial Negotiating Panel on liquor board marketing practices was appointed. As of early 1989, the Panel had not reached a consensus on action to be taken.

The international pressures were coming from two sources. First, in 1987, a General Agreement on Tariffs and Trade (GATT) panel sided with the European Community (EC) ruling that Canada's pricing, listing, and marketing practices for alcoholic beverages violated its obligations as a GATT member. The ruling was subsequently confirmed by GATT Council. Intensive negotiations began between the Canadian government and the EC over the alleged Canadian discrimination against imported beer, wine, and spirits. Eventually, an agreement was reached that required Canada to open its market to beer imported from EC member states and to remove discriminatory pricing practices. To date, no action had been taken by the Canadian government for two reasons: one, the government claimed that the interprovincial trade situation had to be settled before the market could be opened to imports, and two, the implications of the Canada–U.S. Free Trade Agreement had yet to be resolved.

The Canada–U.S. Free Trade Agreement

When free trade talks between Canada and the United States began in the mid-1980s, the Canadian brewers argued for an exemption. They insisted that their inefficiencies relative to U.S. brewers were a direct result of provincial barriers imposed by the government. In October 1987, the brewers' lobbying efforts paid off. Beer and malt beverages were almost entirely exempt from free trade because both Canadian and U.S. negotiators recognized that the industry needed time to adjust. The exemption was agreed to by the U.S. negotiators because of the Canadian government's expressed commitment to support industry adjustment. The exemption allowed Canada to continue to limit access of U.S. brands to distribution channels and to impose higher taxes on U.S. beer. The only change passed was the removal of tariffs imposed on cross-border shipments.

The exclusion from the free trade agreement and the Canadian government's willingness to agree to industry adjustment was seen by industry analysts as a window of opportunity for Canadian brewers to accomplish three things:

> Satisfy GATT that our beer market will become an open market; provide Canadians with more competitive and possibly lower priced beer products; and give the industry time to gear up for the inevitable competition with U.S. firms five to ten years down the road.[1]

THE UNITED STATES BREWING INDUSTRY

The U.S. brewing industry was dominated by a small number of firms. However, compared to Canada, a very different competitive environment existed in the United States, primarily because of less regulation and a much larger market (see Exhibit 1 for comparative information on the Canadian and U.S. industries). For the major brewers, the entire country represented one market with only minor regulatory differences between the states. Therefore, these brewers concentrated on establishing a limited number of national brands that generated substantial production and marketing efficiencies. Beer was distributed to wholesalers who were then free to distribute to retail selling points, which in most states tended to be grocery stores, convenience stores, and drug stores. Prices were controlled only to the extent of taxation.

The two largest firms were Anheuser-Busch, Inc., the U.S. industry leader since 1957, with a 1987 market share of 42.0 percent, and Miller Brewing Company with a share of 21.7 percent. The next three firms in the

EXHIBIT 1

The Canadian and U.S. Brewing Industries

1987 DATA	CANADA	U.S.
Per capita beer consumption (liters)	81.9	89.7
Domestic production, including exports (000,000 hL)	23.1	213.0
Total exports (000,000 hL)	2.6	3.9
Total imports (000,000 hL)	0.42	11.1
Canadian exports to the U.S. (000,000 hL)	2.3	
U.S. exports to Canada (000,000 hL)		0.26
Average labor cost per hL (Canadian figure is for Ontario and Quebec) (CDN$)	$12.00	$6.80
Brewery worker production per hour (hL)	1.30	4.37
Estimated production and marketing costs per hL using a representative mix of cans, bottles, and draft (CDN$)	$85.18–102.21[1]	$68.14

SOURCE: *ERC Statistics 1988, Beverage Industry Annual Manual, Modern Brewery Age,* TMCL.

[1]Canadian production costs vary considerably by province depending on plant size and capacity utilization. The U.S. costs are for a representative Anheuser-Busch brewery and do not vary significantly in different regions because plant locations are a function of the market and not government regulation.

top five were The Stroh Brewery Company with a share of 11.9 percent; G. Heileman Brewing Company with 9.0 percent; and Adolph Coors Company with 8.6 percent.[2] (see Exhibit 2 for information on the five largest brewers). These five firms competed on a national basis in an industry in which all brewers (both national and regional) except for Anheuser-Busch, Coors, and Miller were losing market share.

Until the late 1960s, competition in the U.S. brewing industry was largely on the basis of price; there was little product differentiation and virtually no market segmentation on the basis of quality. However, with the acquisition of Miller by Philip Morris, Inc., in 1969, the brewing industry entered a period of transition that transformed beer into a differentiated consumer packaged good and shifted the focus of competition from product price to product image.

Prior to the Philip Morris acquisition, Miller's national market share was about 4 percent. Philip Morris, a large cigarette manufacturer, used its cigarette marketing techniques of brand segmentation, package variation, and market segmentation along with massive advertising expenditures to move Miller from seventh place in 1970 to second place by 1977. The other brewers were forced to respond to Miller's marketing strategy with their own retar-

EXHIBIT 2　　　　**1987 U.S. Brewers Information**

	ANHEUSER-BUSCH	MILLER[1]	STROH[2]	HEILEMAN[3]	COORS
Net sales	8,258	3,105		1,174	1,351
Operating profit	1,129	170		88	89
Total assets	6,492	1,779[4]		706	1,457
Debt equity	33:67			32:68	3:97
Brewing return on equity	27%	9%		26%	8%
Number of plants	12	6[5]	7	11	1
Annual capacity (000,000 Hls)	100	65	30	20	30
Estimated utilization rate	96%	82%	84%	62%	90%
Maximum plant capacity	13.0	8.5	24.2	10.0	N/A
Minimum plant capacity	1.9	4.5	2.9	0.1	N/A

SOURCE: Annual reports, *1987 Modern Brewery Age Blue Book,* Wood Gundy Investment Research, *1988 Beer Industry Update*.

[1]Complete financial data is not available because Miller is owned by Philip Morris.
[2]The Stroh Brewing Company is privately owned and financial information is not available.
[3]1986 data
[4]Identifiable assets.
[5]Does not include a 9.4 million hL plant in Ohio that was built and not used.

geted marketing programs. Media spending on national brands was substantially increased. In 1987, media advertising expenditures in U.S. dollars by the major brewers were: $304 million by Anheuser-Busch; $171 million by Miller; $46 million by Stroh; $16 million by Heileman; and $85 million by Coors.[3]

By the late 1980s, the top ten brands (four brewed by Anheuser-Busch, three by Miller, two by Coors, and one by Stroh) accounted for over 70 percent of the market. The leader, Budweiser, had a market share of 27.6 percent, while the second place brand, Miller Lite, had a share of 10.7 percent.[4] In place of the flagship brands of the 1960s and '70s such as Schlitz and Pabst Blue Ribbon, new products including Miller Lite, Budweiser Light, and Coors Light had become dominant. Of the major national brands of the 1970s, Budweiser was an exception with its continued share growth.

Canadian Penetration of the U.S. Market

Canadian penetration in the U.S. had been mainly in the import market, the only segment showing sustained growth. The import segment grew from 2.6 percent of total consumption in 1980 to 5.0 percent in 1987 (see Exhibit 3).

EXHIBIT 3

U.S. Beer Imports (Millions of Barrels)

	1980	1981	1982	1983	1984	1985	1986	1987
Total imports	4.6	5.2	5.8	6.3	7.2	7.9	8.8	9.4
Percentage increase	2.2	15.2	11.5	8.6	14.3	9.7	11.4	7.0
Percentage of consumption	2.6	2.9	3.2	3.4	3.9	4.3	4.7	5.0

SOURCE: *Beverage Industry/Annual Manual 1989* and *Modern Brewery Age*.

In the overall import market, Canadian brands had a 21 percent share, which was third behind the Netherlands (27 percent) and Mexico (26 percent) (see Exhibit 4 for the import market share of the leading brands). The leading Canadian exporter was Molson with over 15 percent of its total sales going to the U.S. market. Of the other national Canadian brewers, Labatt Breweries of Canada's exports totaled 5 percent of sales and Carling's were 3.5 percent.

EXHIBIT 4

Leading U.S. Imported Beer Brands (Millions of Gallons)

BRAND	1984	PERCENTAGE OF MARKET	1985	PERCENTAGE OF MARKET	1986	PERCENTAGE OF MARKET	1987	PERCENTAGE OF MARKET
Heineken	74.0	33.1	77.5	31.6	81.5	29.9	66.0	22.4
Corona	1.7	0.9	10.0	4.1	30.0	11.0	55.0	18.7
Molson	29.7	13.3	31.0	12.7	31.5	11.5	31.9	10.8
Becks	20.0	8.9	22.5	9.2	23.5	8.6	24.0	8.1
Moosehead	14.5	6.5	12.5	5.1	13.1	4.8	14.0	4.8
Labatt	10.0	4.4	11.0	4.5	11.9	4.4	13.7	4.7
Amstel*	4.0	1.8	6.0	2.4	7.5	2.7	8.0	2.7
Tecate	3.5	1.5	4.5	1.8	7.0	2.5	8.0	2.7
Dos Equis	5.5	2.4	6.0	2.4	6.5	2.4	8.0	2.7
Foster	3.0	1.3	3.3	1.4	4.5	1.6	7.3	2.5
St. Pauli Girl	8.3	3.7	10.0	4.1	10.0	3.7	6.5	2.2
Carling O'Keefe	5.0	2.2	5.2	2.1	5.4	2.0	4.6	1.6
Others	45.1	20.2	45.6	18.6	40.6	14.9	47.4	16.1
Total volume	223.2		244.9		272.8		294.5	

SOURCE: *Beverage Industry/Annual Manual*.
*Distributed by Heineken

The United States ran a beer trade deficit with Canada of more than 2 million hL in 1987. Over 10 percent of Canada's beer production was exported to the United States while the United States exported only 1 percent of its production. However, the U.S. export figures did not include the U.S. beer brewed under license in Canada that capitalized on spillover advertising. These licensed brands comprised about 14 percent of Canadian consumption.

THE MAJOR CANADIAN BREWERS

The Canadian brewing industry was dominated by three firms: Labatt Breweries of Canada (Labatt) with a share of 41.9 percent; Molson with 31.6 percent; and Carling O'Keefe Breweries of Canada Limited (Carling) with 19.6 percent (see Exhibit 5 for market share trends and Exhibit 6 for provincial market share data).

Labatt Breweries of Canada

Labatt's brewing operation was part of John Labatt Ltd., a diversified food and beverage company with businesses in three main sectors: brewing, agricultural products, and packaged foods. Labatt was controlled by Brascan Ltd., a large Canadian holding company (see Exhibit 7 for Labatt financial information).

Labatt's market share leadership can be traced back to several events that occurred over the past decade. By 1979, Labatt and Molson had about equal shares of a stagnating beer market. Realizing that profitability could only be sustained through share improvement and not overall market growth, Labatt made the first move in the so-called brand and packaging "wars" of the 1980s. In 1980, Labatt introduced Budweiser under license, the first Canadian brewer to license a major U.S. brand, and quickly gained a 3–5 percent share. The other brewers were forced to follow Labatt's lead with their own "Canam" brands—Carling licensed Miller products and Molson licensed Coors brands.

Labatt's next move was in response to a Carling initiative. Prior to 1983, all bottled Canadian beer produced for the domestic market was packaged in a standard brown compact (stubby) returnable bottle that required a bottle opener (bottles accounted for about 78 percent of the market). This standard facilitated a very simple return system because each brewer used the same bottles. In 1983, Carling broke with tradition and introduced Miller High Life and Miller Lite packaged in tall bottles. Both Labatt and Molson, hoping that the bottles would not be a success, held off introducing the new containers. However, the tall bottles were a tremendous success with Miller brands estimated to have captured up to 9 percent of the total market four

EXHIBIT 5   **Canadian Market Shares**

	72	73	74	75	76	77	78	79	80	81	82	83	84	85	86	87	88
Labatt	33.9	36.9	35.9	36.6	37.6	38.4	38.6	36.6	36.5	34.9	36.7	36.3	34.6	38.0	39.1	40.3	41.9
MBC	29.9	30.5	31.6	33.5	33.6	33.9	34.1	36.2	35.9	35.1	35.8	34.7	31.5	30.6	29.8	31.5	31.6
Carling	30.6	28.3	26.1	25.3	24.9	24.1	23.2	22.7	23.2	22.8	23.1	24.3	28.2	25.0	22.8	22.0	19.6
Other	5.3	4.0	6.1	4.2	3.3	2.9	3.2	3.5	3.5	3.8	2.9	3.6	4.2	4.8	4.5	4.7	4.7
Imports	0.3	0.3	0.3	0.4	0.6	0.7	0.9	1.0	0.9	3.4	1.5	1.1	1.5	1.6	3.8	1.5	2.2
Total	100.0	100.0	100.0	100.0	100.0	100.0	100.0	100.0	100.0	100.0	100.0	100.0	100.0	100.0	100.0	100.0	100.0

SOURCE: TMCL, Brewers Association of Canada, and Statistics Canada.

EXHIBIT 6

Provincial Market Share Data at November 30, 1988

| | PERCENTAGE SHARE | | | PERCENTAGE OF CANADIAN SALES |
	MOLSON	CARLING	LABATT	
Newfoundland	19	28	53	2.3%
Nova Scotia	—	—	82	3.0
Prince Edward Island	2	—	53	0.4
New Brunswick	—	—	43	2.3
Quebec	33	31	36	26.1
Ontario	40	15	41	39.6
Manitoba	14	29	57	3.9
Saskatchewan	40	23	37	2.9
Alberta	42	20	29	8.2
British Columbia	26	22	44	10.9
NWT/Yukon	—	—	—	0.3
				100.0%

SOURCE: Molson, Labatt breweries.

Note: Neither Molson nor Carling had breweries in the Maritime provinces. These markets were dominated by Labatt and Moosehead Breweries, a privately owned brewer with plants in Dartmouth, N.S. and Saint John, N.B.

EXHIBIT 7

John Labatt Financial Information Year Ended June 30 (in Millions)

| | TOTAL | | BREWING GROUP | |
	1987	1988	1987	1988
Net sales	3,802.2	4,611.0	1,016.3	1,136.6
Net profit	266.9	294.6	120.9	140.1
Assets employed	1,673.1	1,835.7	428.8	527.3
Capital expenditures	157.1	209.0	56.1	76.5
Average growth in sales 1984–88		20.3%		13.5%
Average growth in earnings before interest and taxes		14.6%		14.5%

SOURCE: John Labatt, Ltd., annual report.

months after introduction. In 1984, Carling's market share was at its highest level in ten years.

Labatt responded to Carling's initiative in 1984 by introducing a tall bottle with a twist-off cap, a new packaging device common in the United States. Labatt's early leadership in twist-off caps was estimated to have added about 1.5–3.0 percent to its total market share. The twist-off cap also helped Labatt launch its Blue brand as the first real national brand in a Canadian market that had traditionally been dominated by regional brands. In 1984, Molson converted several of its major brands to tall bottles.

By 1989, bottled beer was packaged in a myriad of returnable tall bottles, most with twist-off caps. The industry standard bottle was part of history. Because of the sorting required for recycling, distribution costs had increased substantially, without a corresponding increase in overall market revenue. In addition, the brewers were forced to make sizable write-offs for their compact bottles on-hand in the mid-1980s.

Labatt in 1989

In 1989, Labatt produced 31 different brands and operated twelve breweries in 9 provinces. Labatt's leading brand, Blue, was sold in all provinces and had an estimated 18 percent national share. The closest brands in market share were Molson Export, which was not sold in western Canada, with a 9 percent share; Molson Canadian with 8 percent and sold nationally; and Labatt's 50 Ale with 8 percent and sold in all provinces except B.C. Carling's strongest brand was O'Keefe Ale with a 6 percent share and sold only in Ontario and Quebec. Carling's Miller High Life was sold nationally but had a relatively low share.

Labatt had a capacity utilization rate of 95 percent, compared with 78 percent for Molson and 61 percent for Carling. Labatt's profitability, return on equity, and brewing operating income from assets deployed were the highest in the Canadian industry, comparing favorably with major U.S. brewers. Labatt favored the maintenance of the regulatory status quo and was fundamentally opposed to the liberalization of interprovincial and international trade barriers.

In 1987, Labatt's estimated advertising expenditure was $36 million while Molson's was $28 million and Carling's $26 million. Labatt had close ties with Anheuser-Busch, and like the American firm, focused its brand development through sports and community events; for example, Labatt's owned 45 percent of the Toronto Blue Jays, a major league baseball team. Labatt's import sales in the United States were increasing at a greater rate than either Molson or Carling with 1987 shipments up by 16 percent. In 1987, Labatt acquired the U.S. regional brewer, Latrobe Brewing Company. Labatt also had associations with regional brewers in the United Kingdom and had targeted European operations from this U.K. base.

Carling O'Keefe Breweries of Canada Limited

Carling, in operation since 1843, was the third largest brewer in Canada and operated seven breweries (see Exhibits 8 and 9 for Carling financial information). In April 1987, Elders IXL Limited (Elders) acquired Carling from Rothmans of Pall Mall Canada for $450 million. Carling was Elders' first brewing acquisition in North America and was seen by many observers as Elders' beachhead for an assault on the U.S. beer market.

Elders, based in Melbourne, Australia, was one of Australia's leading international companies with 1988 consolidated revenues of $15.35 billion (Australian)[5] and 32,000 employees worldwide (see Exhibit 10 for Elders financial information). Elders consisted of over 400 subsidiary companies with core businesses in brewing, finance, international trading (wool, meat, brewing materials, and grain), and agricultural activities.

Since 1981, Elders had grown rapidly through acquisition. In 1983, Elders acquired Carlton and United Breweries Limited, Australia's largest brewer, and in 1986, purchased Courage Limited, Britain's sixth largest brewer. By 1988, Elders' Brewing Group was the world's seventh largest brewer with a reputation for both high-quality beer and efficient manufacturing. With a

EXHIBIT 8

Carling O'Keefe Breweries of Canada, Ltd., Income Statements (in Millions)

	1984[1]	1985	1986	1987[2]	1988
Revenue	869.3	833.4	832.9	888.4	953.4
Operating expenses				862.9	876.2
Interest on long-term debt				9.1	38.9
Other interest				2.8	1.6
Earnings before unusual items and income taxes				15.5	36.7
Unusual item					5.0
Earnings before income taxes				15.5	41.7
Net earnings	73.0	8.1	6.6	10.8	21.8

SOURCE: Carling annual reports.

[1]Because the brewing group was one of several Carling operating groups prior to 1987, complete brewing financial data is not available.
[2]The year-end for 1984–1987 was March 31. Elders IXL acquired Carling O'Keefe Limited and its subsidiary companies with effect from April 23, 1987. During the 1987 fiscal year, the Carling's non-brewing businesses, which had accounted for about 8–9% of total revenue, were sold. On July 1, 1987, IXL Holdings Canada, Inc., and the Carling companies were amalgamated to form Carling O'Keefe Breweries of Canada, Ltd. The year-end was changed to June 30. The 1988 figures are for the year ended June 30, 1988.

EXHIBIT 9

Carling O'Keefe Breweries of Canada, Ltd., Consolidated Balance Sheet (in Millions)

	JUNE 30, 1988	JULY 1, 1987
ASSETS		
Current assets		
Cash	—	0.4
Accounts receivable	70.0	59.5
Inventories	79.3	85.6
Prepaid expenses	13.7	14.5
Deferred income taxes	6.8	17.6
Total current assets	169.9	177.6
Property, plant, and equipment	545.0	523.1
Less accumulated depreciation	25.7	3.8
	519.2	528.3
Other assets (Note 1)	31.9	30.8
	721.0	736.7
LIABILITIES AND SHAREHOLDERS' EQUITY		
Current liabilities		
Bank indebtedness	7.4	13.6
Accounts payable and accrued liabilities	130.0	158.5
Due to customers for returnable containers	19.3	19.9
Excise and sales taxes	34.1	31.8
Dividends payable	0.5	0.5
Total current liabilities	191.3	224.4
Long-term liabilities (Note 2)	403.7	417.8
Deferred income taxes	66.3	53.1
Shareholders' equity		
Capital stock	40.6	41.0
Retained earnings	20.6	0.7
Cumulative translation adjustments	(1.6)	(0.3)
Total shareholders' equity	59.7	41.4
	721.0	736.7

SOURCE: Carling annual reports.

Note 1: Other assets include investments and receivables, sports franchises, and deferred charges and other assets.

Note 2: The effect of the amalgamation between IXL Holdings Canada, Inc., and the Carling O'Keefe companies was that the debt of approximately $396 million, being the purchase price paid by IXL Holdings Canada, Inc., for the common shares of Carling O'Keefe, Limited, and the principal business operations were in the same company.

EXHIBIT 10   **Elders IXL Financial Information Year Ended June 30 (in Millions (AU$))[1]**

	1985	1986	1987	1988
INCOME STATEMENT				
Revenue	6,995	7,659	10,560	15,350
Profit before interest, tax, and abnormal items	301.5	347.5	758.5	1,133.7
Net interest expense	163.3	113.0	282.1	315.1
Income tax expense	24.9	27.6	127.7	294.0
Minority interest and preference dividends	1.7	27.9	85.3	75.9
Abnormal items			133.8	236.3
Net profit	111.7	179.0	263.4	448.6
BALANCE SHEET				
Shareholders' equity	588	761	2,094	3,312
Total assets	2,147	4,795	9,795	9,298
Return on equity	19.0%	23.5%	19.0%	20.7%
Debt-equity ratio	0.70:1	0.63:1	0.68:1	0.32:1
BREWING GROUP				
Revenue	1,631	1,586	3,424	4,705
Profit	65	81	353	657
Average capital employed	N/A	N/A	2,395	3,954
Return (earnings before interest and taxes) on average capital employed	N/A	N/A	14.8%	16.6%

SOURCE: Elders annual reports.

[1]On June 30 1988, 1 Australian dollar was worth CDN$ 0.96.

focus on its Foster's Lager brand, Elders marketed its products in more than 80 countries.

Elders' organizational structure was decentralized with each of the core businesses established as a separate operating group. Each group was headed by a managing director responsible for developing the group's operating activities and reporting directly to the chairman and chief executive, John Elliott. As the orchestrator of Elders' major acquisitions, Elliott had a reputation as an intense and aggressive negotiator, a style that was often attributed to his days as an amateur football player. Elliott was described as follows:[6]

Elliott looks like, and is, a tough customer. A former player and now chairman of a local Melbourne "Aussie rules" [football] club, he has a nose that looks as if it has been comprehensively remodelled by flying knees and elbows.

Elliott was determined to make Foster's Lager a truly global brand. He developed a clever marketing strategy, putting the Australian flag on the beer can and creating an award-winning series of commercials with Australian actor and comedian, Paul Hogan, promoting Foster's as the "golden throat-charmer." Elliott was effusive when asked to comment on the quality of Foster's Lager and liked to compare it to "an angel crying on your tongue."

Foster's was established as Elders' flagship brand and became Australia's leading beer in both domestic and export markets. Prominent neon signs were created for Picadilly Circus, London; Times Square, New York; and the Hong Kong harbor. In Britain, Foster's was able to displace the Danish lager, Carlsberg, and take over third place in the draft lager competition.

In the year subsequent to the takeover of Carling, Elders' reduced Carling's production costs significantly and completed a $200 million expansion and modernization program started by the previous owners. Carling produced 23 brands of beer in Canada and owned the promotion rights for the Toronto Argonauts football club and the Quebec Nordiques hockey club. Carling exported several Canadian brands to the United States through a wholly owned subsidiary that distributed Carling beer to sixteen states.

In 1988, Carling suffered a setback when it lost the license to brew Carlsberg, the most successful non-U.S. licensed brand in Canada with a share of 2–3 percent. The brewers of Carlsberg, unhappy that their competitors (Elders) in the U.K. were the Canadian licensees of Carlsberg, transferred the license to Labatt in July 1988. With the loss of Carlsberg and the failure of Foster's (brewed by Carling) to make up the loss, Carling's downward trend continued in 1988 with share dropping to less than 20 percent by late 1988.

Molson Breweries of Canada

Molson Breweries of Canada was part of TMCL, a diversified Canadian multinational corporation with more than 11,000 employees and revenues of $2.4 billion for the year ended March 31, 1988 (see Exhibit 11 for TMCL financial information). Besides the Molson Brewing Group, TMCL had major operations in three other business groups: chemical specialties, retail merchandising, and sports and entertainment. The chemical specialties group operated through Diversey Corporation, one of the four largest companies in the specialty chemical industry worldwide. The core of the retail merchandising group was Beaver Lumber Company, Canada's largest supplier of lumber, building materials, and related hard goods. Exhibit 12 presents TMCL business group financial information.

EXHIBIT 11 **TMCL Financial Information Year Ended March 31 (in Millions)**

	1984	1985	1986	1987	1988
INCOME STATEMENT					
Revenue	1,800.2	1,871.8	2,011.5	2,250.4	2,434.9
Interest expense	21.2	24.0	23.2	17.7	12.6
Earnings before income taxes	108.0	66.0	66.0	86.9	132.9
Income taxes	38.4	19.9	24.6	33.7	53.2
Minority interest				0.8	1.0
Net earnings	51.3	45.2	35.9	52.3	78.7
Cash provided from operations	109.6	100.5	94.3	106.5	138.0
BALANCE SHEET					
Working capital	188.0	184.8	199.2	195.8	210.1
Total assets	986.7	1,033.9	1,137.7	1,236.8	1,365.4
Long-term debt	238.0	238.8	251.8	176.6	184.7
Shareholders' equity	382.8	402.2	427.9	533.6	591.2
Return on shareholders' equity	13.9%	11.5%	8.7%	10.9%	14.0%
Net debt-equity ratio	0.52:1	0.61:1	0.56:1	0.25:1	0.23:1
BREWING GROUP					
Sales before excise taxes	1,024.7	1,062.8	1,128.2	1,275.0	1,383.4
Net sales	726.5	746.6	794.7	882.8	965.3
Operating profit	88.1	30.0	30.0	50.1	77.8
Total assets	423.2	467.4	480.9	489.8	525.2
Capital expenditures	42.6	49.5	31.7	36.3	53.3
Depreciation	19.7	23.0	25.3	29.0	32.6
Return on assets	20.8%	6.4%	6.2%	10.2%	14.8%

SOURCE: TMCL annual reports.

EXHIBIT 12 **TMCL Business Groups, Year Ended March 31, 1988 (in Millions)**

	BREWING	CHEMICAL SPECIALITIES	RETAIL MERCH.	SPORTS ENTER.
Revenues	965.3	685.4	362.5	50.4
Profit before interest and taxes	77.8	44.0	25.4	3.0
Total assets	525.2	396.5	277.6	N/A
Average annual growth in revenue 1984–88	6.9%	11.2%	5.3%	N/A

Molson Breweries was founded by John Molson in 1786 and in 1989 was North America's oldest continuing brewer. For two centuries the Molson family played a significant role in shaping the firm's strategy. In 1989, the family controlled more than 50 percent of the voting stock and owned about 20 percent of the equity. The current chairman of TMCL was Eric Molson, the great-great-great grandson of John Molson. The brewing operation and its 200-year heritage was an important part of the corporate culture of TMCL. The 1986 Annual Report, commemorating the 200th anniversary of TMCL, described the heritage as follows:

> Inheriting the legacy of a giant is a privilege, of course, but also a challenge. In every age, there are those whose achievements live beyond them and become integral parts of society as a whole. Such a man was John Molson. . . . A common thread links this extraordinary array of interests and achievement. It has two strands. One is an unswerving commitment to quality; John Molson insisted on doing things well. The other is an open-minded, open-hearted welcoming of challenge as opportunity. John Molson didn't wait for someone else to take the initiative, when he saw opportunities he seized them. This is the heritage that has been passed across two centuries to the Molson Companies today.

Until 1955, Molson was primarily a regional brewer serving the Quebec market. By the early 1960s, the company had expanded its brewing business and had plants in most Canadian provinces. In 1967, Molson made its first major diversification move with the acquisition of Vilas Industries Limited, a furniture manufacturer, and a year later acquired Anthes Imperial Limited, an industrial conglomerate producing such products such as business forms, gasoline pumps, metal office furniture, and hot water heaters. Over the next ten years, the company, now called The Molson Companies Limited, sold the Vilas and Anthes operations and acquired Diversey Corporation and Beaver Lumber. In 1988, TMCL's non-brewing operations accounted for 45 percent of revenue and 49 percent of operating profit and the various operating groups were largely decentralized and managed as independent entities.

Declining Share and Rebuilding

By the late 1970s, Molson had outdistanced Carling as the number two brewer in Canada and had a steadily increasing market share. The strength of the Canadian operation, along with a thriving U.S. export business accounting for 15 percent of production, contributed to an "aura of invincibility" in the organization. Molson looked to the U.S. market for acquisition targets. The first serious consideration was the Pabst Brewing Company, a company faced with substantial excess capacity after several years of declining market share. In 1980, Molson entered into with negotiations with Pabst and went so far as making an offer, which Pabst rejected. In retrospect, senior management conceded, "we were fortunate not to acquire Pabst—we were likely naive in thinking that we would be able to rejuvenate the ailing firm."

Following the Pabst negotiations, Molson had a series of discussions with other U.S. brewers, including Heileman and a smaller brewer, Olympia Brewing Co., but none yielded any concrete results. Then, before any further U.S. developments could occur, the "wars" of the 1980s erupted in the Canadian market, which forced Molson to put its U.S. expansion strategy on hold. The result of the wars was a substantial drop in Molson's share and earnings. Market share, over 36 percent in 1979, dropped below 30 percent by 1986. Earnings peaked in 1983 at $126.6 million and then fell to $30 million in both 1985 and 1986. Molson's management realized that before resources could be utilized for international expansion, the Canadian position would have to be strengthened.

Launching a Canam brand was the first step in the rebuilding effort. Coors and Coors Light were introduced in November 1985. By 1989, Coors Light was the most successful Canam brand. In 1985, Molson formed the Master's Brewing Company, a short-lived partnership with the Coors Brewing Company and a German brewer. In 1988, a deal was signed with the Kirin Brewery Company of Japan, the world's fourth largest brewer, to brew Kirin beer under license for export to the United States.

Projects Columbus and Caesar

Molson argued for the exclusion of beer from the Free Trade Agreement until interprovincial trade barriers were dismantled and the brewers were given time to restructure. The company thought it unlikely that beer would remain an exception from free trade for very long. Suspecting that free trade and the elimination of interprovincial trade barriers would become reality within ten years, Molson was again prompted to look outside Canada for expansion opportunities. In August 1987, Projects Columbus and Caesar were launched with the objective of developing a strategy and action plan for the survival of the Molson brewing "institution" by

1. retaining a profitable base of operations in Canada,

2. becoming a major factor in the North American brewing industry, and

3. expanding beyond North America, initially in the United Kingdom and Japan.

Project Columbus focused on options for entering the U.S. domestic market. Investment in or a partnership with a U.S. brewer were considered the only feasible entry strategies. The smaller national brewers, Heileman, Stroh, and Pabst, were not considered attractive long-term partners, and Anheuser-Busch and Miller had existing license agreements with Labatt and Carling. Although Project Columbus did not achieve its objectives, the project was important in that TMCL and Molson gained some understanding of the reality of doing a major deal with a U.S. brewer.

The second strategic initiative, Project Caesar, sought to expand Molson's international market beyond Canada and the United States. This was not the first time Molson had looked outside North America. In the 1970s, the company attempted to purchase a French brewer. However, because the board did not have a deep conviction toward European investment, the deal was never concluded. This experience raised a critical question for the board and one that remained in 1989:

> Should TMCL invest its 200-year-old brewing heritage and expertise in the brewing industry outside Canada or should the firm invest in industries outside brewing that are located in Canada?

Project Caesar was driven by a conviction that the brewing industry was going global. According to senior management:

> We are all watching the same television with the same videos and listening to the same hit parade. Everybody is using the same vocabulary and wants to use the same brands. In Europe, people want to drink the same brands of beer as people in North America.[7]

Project Caesar identified the United Kingdom and Japan as prime international markets. Japan was seen as a huge potential market with per capita beer consumption about half that of Canada and still growing. To date, Molson beer had been sold in Japan primarily "in gift packs as a funny beer from a funny place." A decision was made to nurture and develop the Molson brand to the point that a licensing deal could be done with a Japanese brewer.

The U.K. beer market was the second largest in Europe. Foreign brands were playing an increasingly important role as drinking habits changed from traditional ales to lagers. Imports had captured over 6 percent of the U.K. market and 25 percent of all beer sales were continental brands, most brewed in the U.K. under license. To establish a long-term share in the U.K. market, management believed that Molson had three options: (1) ship more beer and charge premium prices; (2) brew on the continent; (3) establish a licensing relationship with a major U.K. brewer. Before making a commitment to one of the options, Molson decided to invest significant amounts in the U.K. market to build up its brands.

Molson in 1989 produced and marketed 22 brands across Canada and had a share of 31.9 percent. Molson also had a cross-licensing agreement with Moosehead Breweries of New Brunswick to brew and sell Moosehead beer under license outside Atlantic Canada and for Moosehead to brew and sell Molson products in the Maritime provinces, where Molson had no breweries. Molson was actively involved in sponsorships and promotions, including the Montreal Canadiens hockey club (owned by TMCL); Hockey Night in Canada; the Molson Indy car race; and various other sport, concert, and community events. Molson's importing agency in the United States, Martlet, was a wholly owned company and carried out a full range of business activities including marketing, advertising, brand positioning, distribution, credit, and related activities. Martlet distributed Molson products in all 50 states.

MOLSON AND CARLING

Almost immediately after Elders' acquisition of Carling, senior management of TMCL met with John Elliott and Peter Bartels, the chief executive of Elders Brewing Group. The meetings were initially nothing more than "getting-to-know-you meetings" and were described as follows:

> The initial meetings with Elders were very positive; Elders brewed good beer and ran a very tight operation. The Elders people showed both openness and a willingness for action. Our perception was that both companies understood the business internationally but Elders had done something about it. . . . Elders saw our strategy in the U.K. as very positive and a potential companion with Foster's which had been there for eighteen years.

Several possible deals between the two companies were discussed. Molson suggested combining the two firms' Western Canadian operations because with deregulation and U.S. competition both brewers were finding it very difficult to operate in the West. However, Carling and Elders management were not interested in a deal that involved only part of their organization.

In April 1988, Elders approached TMCL about a possible merger of their respective Canadian brewing operations. Elders' approach coincided with Molson's realization that nothing was happening with Project Columbus and also that the most important factor in a North American strategy would be a strong and efficient domestic infrastructure. Elders' proposal, subsequently called Project 40 by Molson, called for both TMCL and Elders to have equal ownership in the new organization.

Project 40

From the start, TMCL and Molson saw that the business synergies in Project 40 made sense given the changing nature of the global brewing industry. In the short term, the merger would provide a base for the operational efficiencies needed to combat and survive the threat from partial or total Canadian deregulation. In the longer term, Project 40 would establish a strategic alliance with Elders, a committed and significant player in the international brewing industry. The alliance would improve the potential to build the Molson name in the U.K. and other markets by drawing on Elders' distribution system. The alliance would also enhance the likelihood of making a successful move in the U.S. market either by acquisition or alliance, particularly because of Elders' brewing links and financial capability.

TMCL and Molson senior management viewed Elders as the right partner for several reasons:

1. Carling's brewing operations offered synergy for the Canadian market and both Elders and Molson had similar U.S. development interests.

2. Elders was viewed as an aggressive, results-oriented organization with a proven track record as brewers and a commitment to a significant global presence.

3. Elders had the management and financial capacity needed for success in the international brewing industry of the future.

In addition, Molson had come to the conclusion that there were few, if any, desirable acquisition or partnership candidates in the United States. In Canada, a Molson/Labatt merger was considered impossible because of Canadian combines legislation.

As the discussions continued over the summer, the specific business elements of the merger began to emerge. On August 22, these elements were presented to the TMCL Board. The merger called for a rationalization of sixteen plants to nine, leaving one plant in each province and increasing utilization to 90 percent (see Exhibit 13 for the size and locations of Molson and Carling plants). The estimated savings in operating costs[8] would be $25 million in 1990, $95 million in 1991, and $120 million in 1992. The market share of the new company would be over 50 percent and marketing emphasis would be on the key Molson brands and Carling's O'Keefe, Foster's, and

---

EXHIBIT 13 **Brewing Facilities of MBC and Carling**

MBC	CAPACITY (000s of hLs)	CARLING	CAPACITY (000s of hLs)
St. John's, Nfld.	260	St. John's, Nfld.	220
Montreal, Que.	2,700	Montreal, Que.	2,336
Toronto, Ont.	2,800	Etobikoke, Ont.	3,097
Barrie, Ont.	1,750	Winnipeg, Man.	397
Winnipeg, Man.	275	Saskatoon, Sask,	262
Edmonton, Alta.	400	Calgary, Alta.	772
Regina, Sask.	325	Vancouver, B.C.	882
Lethbridge, Alta.	400		
Vancouver, B.C.	950		

SOURCE: TMCL and Carling, industry experts.

Miller brands. In the United States, Carling's import operation would be combined with Molson's importer, Martlet.

Molson anticipated that the merger impact on the marketplace would be substantial, increasing competitive intensity and potentially accelerating deregulation. Labatt was expected to continue its aggressive spending to combat the new share leader and a Labatt/Anheuser-Busch alliance was considered possible. A price-based reaction from Labatt was also considered very likely, although in most provinces it would have to wait until further deregulation.

Stalled Negotiations

By November, the TMCL/Elders negotiations had been under way for over six months and although both sides agreed on the potential synergies in the alliance, no real progress was being made on the structure of the deal. A key reason for the lack of progress was that TMCL and Molson management had serious reservations about 50/50 ownership. In particular, there were concerns about which party would control the following: the governance of the new entity; brand marketing support; CEO appointment; financing of the deal; and selection of board members. Perhaps the most serious reservation about equal ownership was the loss of control over the Molson name and its associated heritage. According to a TMCL executive, "We were hanging tough because we wanted to retain control." The Molson people involved in the discussions also argued that a 50/50 deal did not make sense given that Molson was almost twice the size of Carling.

The idea of giving up control over the Molson heritage was a particularly contentious issue and one that prompted a search for other options besides the Carling merger. Late in the summer, Molson's North American options were reviewed in the hope that another alternative could at least be considered. Only one option from Project Columbus seemed realistic enough to re-evaluate. This option involved "doing a Kirin" (brew a beer for export to the U.S.) with a major U.S. import brand such as Beck's of Germany or Heineken of the Netherlands. Heineken, the world's third largest brewer and the brewer of the most popular import in the United States, was thought to be a possibility. Heineken, however, proved not to be interested.

At this point, TMCL began to believe that the Carling merger was the only deal possible. However, the two sides were still not close to an agreement. By November, the Elders people were getting very frustrated to the extent that some TMCL executives thought they might walk away from the deal. If they did, TMCL had identified a possible outcome that was not particularly in TMCL's favor: Carling might be broken up and its assets sold, with the Ontario and Quebec operations possibly going to Labatt. It was this situation in early November that faced the new CEO and president of TMCL, Mickey Cohen.

Mickey Cohen

Marshall (Mickey) Cohen, 53, graduated from law school in 1960 and joined a prominent Toronto law firm as a tax and securities lawyer, becoming a partner in 1965. In 1970, he was a member of an advisory group to the House of Commons committee that was looking at the government's 1969 paper on tax reform. This position led Cohen to an advisory position in the Department of Finance, and by 1971 he was assistant deputy minister. In 1978, he was promoted to deputy minister of Energy Mines and Resources, following by a year as deputy minister of Industry Trade and Commerce and then another stint at Energy. In 1982, Cohen was appointed as deputy minister of Finance where he remained until 1985. He then left the government to take a position as president and chief operating officer of Toronto-based Olympia and York Enterprises Ltd.

While practicing law and working in the government, Cohen developed skills as a masterful bargainer and dealmaker. His management style relied heavily on delegation and he was well known as an able and unflappable negotiator. Cohen started as president and chief executive officer of TMCL on November 7, 1988, only the third president in the company's history who was not a brewer. He characterized his role at Molson as an "overseer of their diverse operations." He further added:

> Clearly, I am not a brewmaster. I am not a chemical engineer. I am certainly not an entertainer. I am not there to run the individual businesses. . . . What I see are four good businesses, a very strong balance sheet, a company that is coming off a very good year and therefore, an enormous opportunity. . . . We have a new economic world coming at us in the next decade. The game is getting tougher, more competitive. One thing I see is to really take Molson into the next century. . . . I think that what I bring are some people skills, some strategic insights, and a sense of how to get shareholder values.[9]

Cohen and the Alliance

Cohen described the situation he found when he arrived at TMCL:

> The alliance deal was not materializing because the three constituents, the Molson family, the board, and senior management, had been unable to resolve their uncertainty about several factors: one, the future of the Molson name and tradition; two, the implications of entering a partnership with a much larger and more international partner; and three, the reality of a deal of that magnitude. Everyone agreed that a deal had to be done but there was no champion. The focus was on the structural issues instead of the alliance business synergies.

Cohen was convinced of the advantages of the alliance and the vulnerabilities associated with remaining a central Canadian regional brewer in a global industry. Cohen immediately set about resurrecting the negotiations. Within 48 hours of joining TMCL, he sent a message to Elliott (whom he knew from discussions held while he was with Olympia and York) indicating that TMCL was still interested in the alliance. A meeting was scheduled for November 24 in London, England.

The November 24 Meeting

Cohen met with both Elliott and Peter Bartels. Elliott indicated that he still wanted to do the deal but did not want majority ownership. However, it soon became clear that Elliott wanted a very attractive "exit option" for Elders to sell its shares to TMCL if TMCL insisted on controlling the alliance. As a result, 50/50 ownership seemed like the only realistic option. Both parties agreed that it would be preferable if Molson and Carling could work together without the partners having the option to exit the partnership in the event of a conflict. Cohen indicated that he would start working on the numbers and talk to his board. A tentative meeting was planned for January 1989.

The November 28 TMCL Board Meeting

Following the London meeting, Cohen realized that TMCL did not have the luxury of time; he described the deal as "like a courtship—it would not wait." The deal had been on the table for nine months and Cohen was fairly certain Elliott would not wait much longer. More important, Elliott wanted to do the deal and as far as Elders' North America strategy was concerned, needed the alliance more than Molson.

At the TMCL board meeting on November 28, Cohen reported, "I think the deal can and should be done." He challenged the TMCL conventional wisdom about partnerships and argued that the merger was not a way of selling the brewery but a vehicle for staying in the business and making the Molson name international. He explained to the board why he favored 50/50 ownership:

> Elders wants too high a price if they give up control and besides, 51/49 deals are "the seeds of trouble" because they eliminate the opportunity for forced reconciliation. And, if TMCL is in control, we are really only becoming a larger Canadian brewer, as opposed to becoming an equal partner with a major international firm. A 50/50 deal will allow us to retain a discrete investment in brewing and should generate cash which we can use elsewhere.

The next board meeting was planned for January 12, 1989, when the progress of the deal would be reviewed.

The Deal

Cohen immediately got started with the preliminary legal and financial groundwork necessary to make the deal a reality. He also set up a meeting with Elliott and Bartels for January 15, three days after the next TMCL board meeting. Cohen had John Carroll, the president of Molson, spend a week with Ted Kunkel, Carling's president, to see if they were compatible and to see if they could rough out an organization chart for the new company. Carroll reported back that he thought Molson and Carling could work well together.

The specific deal that Cohen hoped to sell to the TMCL board, and one that he thought would be acceptable to Elders, incorporated the following elements:

1. The Canadian and U.S. operations of Molson and Carling would be managed as a single entity and ownership and control would be on a 50/50 basis.
2. The entity management would report to a jointly controlled supervisory board. Both partners would have veto rights over substantive matters at board level.
3. No exit from the partnership would be permitted for the first five years except by mutual consent.
4. The merged entity would be called Molson Breweries with the stronger Molson products as the core brands, therefore ensuring the preservation of the Molson name.

The plant rationalization would take place over a period of three years. Plants in Newfoundland, Manitoba, Saskatchewan, and Alberta would be closed in year one; plants in British Columbia and Ontario in year two; and a Quebec plant in year three. The remaining facilities would be upgraded and capacity expanded by about 3 to 4 million hL. The projected cost of the rationalization was $220 million, requiring cash outlays of $92 million in year one, $83 million in year two, and $45 million in year three. Of the 7,500 employees in the new company, about 1,400 would be made redundant by the rationalization. Cohen knew that industrial relations issues associated with the redundancies would be a high risk. Therefore, a first-class plan for severance, retirement, and termination would have to be a major priority.

A final consideration was the financial structure of the alliance. Cohen proposed a financial structure that would make Molson Breweries a free-standing self-financing entity and allow TMCL, over time, to withdraw capital from the brewing business for investment in other segments, providing downside protection in the event of any adverse developments in the future. The amount of cash available for withdrawal would be based on the relative valuations of the partners' asset contributions.

Although the two partners would have equal ownership, TMCL's asset contribution would be substantially greater than Carling's. It was agreed that Molson's brewing assets were worth about $1 billion and Carling's about $600 million. To even out the $400 million difference, Cohen proposed that the new company borrow $400 million, which would be distributed to TMCL. He also proposed borrowing a further $400 million to be distributed equally to the two partners, giving TMCL access to a total of $600 million in cash. The debt financing of Molson Breweries would be non-recourse to the partners and would be based on a target debt-equity ratio of 1:1 based on written-up asset values. Carling's long-term debt of about $400 million would remain an obligation of Elders.

This financing arrangement laid the groundwork for a 50/50 partnership, because both partners would be "worth" the same, and provided TMCL with its sought-after downside protection.

NOTES

1. *The Globe and Mail,* November 12, 1987.
2. *Modern Brewery Age,* Annual Statistical Study, 1988.
3. *Leading National Advertisers,* New York.
4. *Beverage Industry Annual Meeting 1989.*
5. In early January 1989, one Australian dollar was worth CDN$ 1.02.
6. *Financial Post,* July 6, 1987, p. 16.

7. As an example of the global trend, Anheuser-Busch had recently licensed Carlsberg A/S of Denmark to produce Budweiser in Denmark to coincide with the introduction of Danish satellite television.
8. Author's estimates.
9. *Globe and Mail,* October 19, 1988, p. B5. Reprinted with permission.

The Golden Gate Brewing Company

RICHARD I. LEVIN · BRENT CALLINICOS

At a booth in Harry's, a local bar overlooking the San Francisco Bay, James Cook poured a fresh glass of amber-colored Golden Gate Lager and dropped a bottle cap onto the beer's head. The cap floated like a lily pad on the foam. "That's what you get from using all malt, no rices or corn—a very firm head," he said. "It looks like whipped cream and acts like egg whites, as my father used to say." When Cook's glass was finished, the inside was coated with strips of foam, "Belgian lace" in brewer's jargon, and a sign of a beer's purity. "People usually think of a local beer as crummy, cheap beer. I plan to change the way they think," Cook said.

James Cook, age 36, was president of the fledgling Golden Gate Brewing Company, the brewer of Golden Gate Lager, and sixth consecutive eldest son in the Cook family to become a brewer. Cook was a former high-paid, high-powered management consultant with the Boston Consulting Group. He held a Harvard B.A., M.B.A., and J.D. The Golden Gate Brewing Company was incorporated in 1984 and Golden Gate Lager was introduced in San Francisco on July 4, an appropriate day, but accidental timing according to Cook. Cook's goal was to establish Golden Gate Lager as a superpremium beer with a distinctive taste:

> I intend to go head-to-head against imported beers. Nowhere in the world but America do they drink so much imported beer. Here, imported beer is popular because our domestic beer is so bad. My work is to give Americans an alternative to drinking foreign beers. I want to start a revolution in the way people think about American beer. There is nothing wrong with standard domestic beers, for what they are. They are clean, consistent, and cheap. But they are also bland and mediocre. They are mass market products. People can recall, off the top of their heads, the advertising, the slogans, and the music for most beers, but they can't remember the taste.

THE SITUATION

For years, small local breweries had either closed down or been acquired by one of the industry leaders. The advent of small boutique breweries, in California, Colorado, and New York, making limited quantities of quality beer, had opposed this trend. Cook acknowledged the odds and history were against small regional breweries. But Cook was betting on a combination of

This case was written by Dick Levin and Brent Callinicos under support provided by the Business Foundation of North Carolina.

his family's brewing background, management training, and a limited target market to create long-term Golden Gate Lager drinkers.

Golden Gate Lager is currently sold in two locations, San Francisco and Munich. As of November 1985, the current sales volume of 6,000 cases per month represents less than one minute of production for Anheuser-Busch, the longstanding industry leader. Cook reports that he has sold as much beer in the past six months as Anheuser-Busch makes in about six minutes. "They spill more beer every hour than I make in a month." In six months, the Golden Gate Brewing Company has sold 25,000 cases in California. His more than 200 accounts range from liquor stores to exclusive hotels to neighborhood bars, such as Harry's. Exhibits 1 through 3 provide industry background, population demographics of the San Francisco/Oakland area, and general demographics of U.S. beer drinkers.

EXHIBIT 1

Beer Industry Facts and Terms

Dimensions of the Industry

The annual wholesale value of the brewing industry's products in 1985 was $13.7 billion.

Total employment in the industry was close to 40,000 people.

The average hourly earnings of a brewing industry employee was $18.27 in 1985, a 3.2 percent increase over 1984.

In a recent typical year, the industry's gross assets amounted to $6,639,979,000. Its net worth, computed from income tax returns, was $3,377,780,000.

What the Industry Buys

Agricultural commodities, the output of more than 4 million acres of farm land, worth $700 million plus, are used annually by the brewing industry. These include:

- 4.9 billion pounds of 143.8 million bushels of choice malt—worth $380 million
- Other select grains, chiefly corn and rice—worth $221 million
- Hops—value to the grower of $80 million

Some 86.9 percent of all beer sold is packaged in cans or bottles. In one year, the brewing industry uses more than

- 33.1 billion steel and aluminum cans,
- 19.2 billion bottles in returnable and nonreturnable form, and
- $525 million for interest, rentals, repairs, and maintenance.

The industry's annual bill for containers—cans, bottles, kegs, and related packaging materials purchased from other American industries, is close to $4.5 billion. Supplies and services of numerous kinds are also required in brewing and distributing malt beverages. Annual average outlays for these include:

- Fuel, power, and water—$420 million
- Wholesale payroll—$1.8 billion
- Brewery equipment and improvements—$550 million

EXHIBIT 1   **Continued**

The Industry's Products and Terminology
Beers fall into two broad categories—those that are top-fermented and those that are bottom-fermented.

Bottom-fermented

Pilsner/Pilsener. The world's most famous beer style, it was named after the excellent beer brewed in Pilsen, Czechoslovakia, for the past 700 years. It is a pale, golden-colored, distinctly hoppy beer.

Lager. All bottom-fermented beers are lagers. This is a generic term, though it is sometimes applied to the most basic bottom-fermented brew produced by a brewery. In Britain and the United States, the majority of lagers are very loose, local interpretations of the Pilsner style.

Top-fermented

Ale. Generic term for English-style top-fermented beers. Usually copper-colored, but sometimes darker. It is usually paler in color and differs in flavor from lager beer.

Stout. Darker in color and sweeter or maltier than ale. The darkest, richest, maltiest of all regularly produced beers.

"Malt Liquor." This is a term conjured up to describe beers that exceed a country's legal alcohol levels—5 percent in the United States. They are most often made as lagers, but the American version can be sweetish or more bitter than the traditional lagers.

Barrel. This refers to a full barrel, which has a volume of 31 gallons.

EXHIBIT 2   **Population Characteristics of the San Francisco/Oakland Area, 1980**

| | | | AGE COMPOSITION | | |
YEAR	POPULATION	PERCENTAGE CHANGE	AGE	POPULATION	PERCENTAGE OF TOTAL
1960	2,649,000	N/A	Under 18	1,296,000	25.02%
1970	3,109,000	17.37%	18–24	666,000	12.86
1980	3,251,000	4.5	25–34	989,000	19.10
			35–44	668,000	12.90
			45–54	536,000	10.35
			55–64	491,000	9.48
			65–Over	533,000	10.29
			Under 21	1,571,000	30.33

EXHIBIT 2   Continued

ETHNIC COMPOSITION

RACE	PERCENTAGE OF TOTAL
White	62.37%
Black	10.71
Spanish	9.64
Indian	10.93
Eskimo	0.47
Other*	5.88

EDUCATION (PERSONS 25 YEARS OLD AND OVER)

YEARS OF EDUCATION	PERCENTAGE OF TOTAL
Less than five	3%
High school only	71
Four years college or more	26
Median school years completed	13

OCCUPATIONAL PROFILE

GROUP	PERCENTAGE OF TOTAL
Managerial and professional	28.28%
Technical and sales-related	35.43
Service occupations	11.84
Farming/forestry/fishing	1.15
Craft/repair group	11.12
Operators/laborers	12.18

INCOME BREAKDOWN

INCOME	HOUSEHOLDS	PERCENTAGE OF TOTAL
Under $5,000	199,763	10.12%
$5,000–$9,999	243,278	12.32
$10,000–$19,999	511,225	25.90
$20,000–$34,999	611,279	30.97
$35,000–$49,999	258,758	13.11
$50,000–Over	149,577	7.58
Total households	1,973,880	
Median income	$20,607	

SOURCE: U.S. Bureau of the Census, *Census of Population*, 1980.

*Includes Japanese, Chinese, Filipino, Korean, Asian Indian, Vietnamese, Hawaiian, and Samoan.

EXHIBIT 3   1983 U.S. Beer Drinker Demographics

	PERCENTAGE OF THE POPULATION DRINKING					
	DOMESTIC	LIGHT	IMPORTED	MALT	ALE	DRAFT
All adults	39.6%	24.4%	15.8%	8.3%	8.6%	26.2%
Males	54.0	28.6	22.0	11.0	12.0	35.6
Females	26.6	20.6	10.3	5.9	5.5	17.7
Age						
18–24	51.2	29.1	26.6	14.8	14.0	36.5
25–34	49.0	30.8	20.8	10.9	10.9	36.1
35–44	39.3	27.8	15.8	7.3	7.8	26.8
45–54	35.5	23.5	13.5	5.6	7.0	22.8
55–64	30.9	16.7	8.5	4.1	5.6	16.9
65 or older	23.4	13.0	4.6	4.3	3.8	9.8

EXHIBIT 3 **Continued**

	PERCENTAGE OF THE POPULATION DRINKING					
	DOMESTIC	LIGHT	IMPORTED	MALT	ALE	DRAFT
College graduate	47.5	32.2	28.0	6.0	12.4	36.3
Attended college	45.3	30.0	22.0	8.9	11.9	33.5
High school graduate	38.4	23.9	13.6	8.4	7.8	25.8
Not high school graduate	23.6	17.4	8.5	9.2	5.6	16.7
Employed full time	46.2	30.2	20.4	9.0	10.5	33.2
Part time	36.7	24.9	17.7	8.0	9.0	26.5
Not employed	32.1	17.3	10.1	7.6	6.2	17.7
Professional	48.2	32.8	27.1	7.4	12.8	37.0
Clerical/sales	38.6	29.8	17.6	7.3	9.2	29.2
Craftsperson/supervisor	52.9	30.7	17.7	9.1	8.4	36.3
Other employed	44.3	25.5	16.2	11.5	9.6	28.9
Single	50.8	28.5	29.0	14.9	14.5	36.5
Married	38.3	24.1	12.9	6.1	7.1	24.6
Divorced	30.7	20.2	11.0	8.7	6.7	19.6
Parents	41.0	26.5	14.5	8.8	7.7	27.9
White	39.8	24.9	15.8	6.1	8.4	27.4
Black	36.8	19.3	14.4	25.4	9.8	16.4
Other	42.0	27.6	25.6	12.7	7.5	27.6
Geographic location						
Northeast	42.9	22.0	22.3	7.2	13.5	27.7
East Central	39.1	24.2	11.6	7.5	9.3	27.2
West Central	42.3	29.0	13.1	7.4	5.6	30.3
South	32.7	22.8	11.1	9.6	6.4	21.0
Pacific	45.1	26.1	22.3	9.5	7.8	28.4
Household income						
$40,000+	45.6	29.7	24.1	6.0	11.8	32.7
$30,000+	44.2	28.8	22.5	6.0	10.7	32.0
$25,000+	44.1	28.4	21.3	6.4	10.3	31.4
$20–24,999	38.1	26.0	14.0	6.8	7.7	27.5
$15–19,999	42.5	26.7	14.5	10.9	8.7	28.8
$10–14,999	36.0	20.9	11.2	9.1	7.1	21.7
under $10,000	32.3	16.5	9.5	11.3	6.5	16.6

"By my standards I have been very successful," said Cook. While demand has been strong, he wondered if it would last. "People who drink imports will try it because it's new, but will Golden Gate Lager be just a flash?" Cook is hoping there are enough beer aficionados in San Francisco, but he is wondering if he should try to expand in Europe, or if he should concentrate on the West Cost, the East Coast, or selected cities throughout the country. How fast should he expand? With several comparable local brews being sold in the area, will his marketing strategy have to change? What are the risks involved? Cook realized he needed to make some strategic decisions.

INDUSTRY OVERVIEW

Historically, the U.S. beer industry had many small local producers, but now it is dominated by the six largest brewers (see Exhibits 5 and 6). In 1876 there were 2,685 breweries; in 1952 there were only 350; and in 1982 there were 79 (Exhibit 4). Major firms were more willing to purchase struggling regional producers or construct new facilities in the South and West so as to establish nationwide distribution of their brands.

Following several years of flat or nearly flat sales, beer consumption declined about 0.7 percent in 1984 (Exhibit 7), the first decline in 27 years; production declined approximately 1.2 percent (Exhibit 8). Per capita consumption of beer also declined (Exhibit 9), and for 1985, per capita consumption is estimated to remain at the 1985 level of 24 gallons. The long-term outlook for the industry is less encouraging. Chris Lole of the Stroh Brewery Company believes beer sales will remain flat for the next ten, possibly twenty, years.

However, there is one segment of growth in this troubled industry—imports. Imported brands have grown from 0.7 percent of total consumption in 1970 to 3.4 percent in 1983 (aided somewhat over the years by a strong U.S. dollar). Imports occupy the high ground in terms of quality in consumers' perception, and trading up continues to benefit imports. As import volume has grown, an increasing number of brands have appeared, and many more are now being advertised. The continued growth in this segment, coupled with the decline in domestic sales, meant an increase in imports' share to almost 4 percent in 1984.

For regional and smaller brewers, it is becoming increasingly difficult to

EXHIBIT 4   **Operating Breweries by Census Region**

REGION	1952	1960	1970	1982	PERCENTAGE OF TOTAL 1952	1982
Northeast	100	62	45	18	28.0%	22.8%
North Central	164	99	61	25	45.9	31.6
South	42	33	26	20	11.8	25.3
West	51	35	22	16	14.3	20.3
Total United States	357	229	154	79	100.0%	100.0%

EXHIBIT 5

Leading U.S. Brewers' Domestic Beer Market Share

BREWER	1970	1975	1980	1982	1983	1984
Anheuser-Busch	18.2%	23.7%	28.9%	33.5%	34.1%	34.6%
Miller	4.2	8.7	21.5	22.3	21.1	22.1
Stroh	2.7	3.5	3.6	13.0	13.7	13.5
G. Heileman	2.5	3.1	7.7	8.2	9.9	9.3
Adolph Coors	6.0	8.0	8.0	6.8	7.7	7.2
Pabst	8.6	10.5	8.7	6.8	7.2	6.8
Genesee	1.2	1.5	2.1	1.9	1.8	1.9
C. Schmidt	2.5	2.2	2.1	1.8	1.8	1.7
Falstaff	5.4	5.0	2.3	1.8	1.5	1.8
Pittsburgh			0.6	0.6	0.6	0.5
Other	48.7	33.8	14.5	3.3	0.6	0.6
Total	100.0%	100.0%	100.0%	100.0%	100.0%	100.0%

EXHIBIT 6

Barrelage of Top Ten Brewers—1984 Compared to 1983

	1983	1984	GAIN/LOSS BARRELS*	GAIN/LOSS PERCENT
Anheuser-Busch	60,500,000	64,000,000	3,500,000	5.8%
Miller	37,470,000	37,520,000	50,000	0.1
Stroh	24,300,000	23,900,000	(400,000)	−1.6
G. Heileman	17,549,000	16,760,000	(789,000)	−4.5
Adolph Coors	13,719,000	13,187,000	(532,000)	−3.9
Pabst	12,804,000	11,562,000	(1,242,000)	−9.7
Genesee	3,200,000	3,000,000	(200,000)	−6.3
C. Schmidt	2,800,000	2,500,000	(300,000)	−10.7
Falstaff	2,705,000	2,338,000	(367,000)	−13.6
Pittsburgh	1,000,000	950,000	(50,000)	−5.0
All others	3,597,000	2,134,000	(1,463,000)	−40.7
Total	179,644,000	177,851,000	(1,793,000)	−1.0%

*In 31-gallon barrels.

EXHIBIT 7

U.S. Beer Sales—Domestic Brands and Imported Brands

	31-GALLON BARRELS (MILLIONS)		PERCENT OF TOTAL		PERCENT CHANGE
	1983	1984	1983	1984	
Domestic beer	177.5	175.3	96.6%	96.1%	−1.2%
Imported beer	6.3	7.2	3.4	3.9	14.3
Total sales	183.8	182.5	100.0	100.0	−0.7

EXHIBIT 8

Production of Malt Beverages in the United States for Selected Years (Thousands)

YEAR	BARRELS	YEAR	BARRELS
1904	48,265	1977	172,229
1914	66,189	1978	171,639
1924	4,891	1979	183,515
1934	37,679	1980	188,374
1944	81,726	1981	194,542
1954	92,561	1982	193,984
1964	103,018	1983	195,664
1974	153,053	1984	193,416

EXHIBIT 9

Per Capita U.S. Consumption of Malt Beverages, 1974–1984

YEAR	GALLONS	YEAR	GALLONS
1974	20.9	1980	24.3
1975	21.3	1981	24.6
1976	21.5	1982	24.4
1977	22.4	1983	24.2
1978	23.1	1984	24.0
1979	23.8		

move a product that is falling in demand and cannot be backed by the advertising revenues of the large national breweries. Interestingly, the microbrewer/brew pub trend continues. More and more entrepreneurs are allured by the prospects of concocting their own distinctive beer and operating their own business.

EXTERNAL THREATS

Several external threats were affecting the beer industry: First, the U.S. population is more concerned about healthier lifestyles, which potentially reduces beer consumption. Consumption and the purchase-pattern preference of 25- to 40-year-olds have changed dramatically in recent years. This group, because of interests in appearance, exercise, and career advancement, exhibits a preference for drinks with fewer calories and lower alcohol content. Over-40 drinkers are also increasingly health- and diet-conscious.

An important negative factor for future beer sales is demographics. Growth of the 18-to-34 age group is winding down. Beer sales have closely tracked the baby boom age bulge in the population. The teenage population (the source of most new drinkers) has been decreasing and is forecast to continue its decline. Brewers, therefore, confront a decline in potential new users. In addition, the young adult population (20 to 29 years) is also declining. The beer industry relies on this segment to replace sales lost due to attrition in the drinking population. Finally, people between the ages of 30 and 49 will increase substantially and by 1990 will constitute 30 percent of the population. Historically, this group has been an important beer-drinking group. However, industry analysts say this group is the one most concerned about alcohol abuse and drunk driving.

The beer industry faces another demographic change that will create problems. Blue-collar workers have traditionally been the heaviest consumers of beer. Today, the economy is shifting toward the service sector and the blue-collar work force is declining.

The emergence of wine coolers is also taking a toll on the beer industry. Wine coolers appeal to beer drinkers and to nonbeer drinkers. Coolers are, to some extent, a beer substitute. Introduced five years ago, there are about 50 cooler brands now available that contain 6 percent alcohol. Retail sales in 1984 were $360 million and in 1985 approached $700 million. However, cooler sales for 1986 are projected at 35 million cases, versus the 2.5 billion cases of the beer market. Some analysts believe that wine coolers are firmly established, while others contend that coolers are just a fad.

The market will shrink further due to stiffer penalties for drunk driving and the rise of the national legal drinking age to 21. The growing awareness of the need for responsible drinking habits has been fostered by groups such as Mothers Against Drunk Drivers (MADD). According to MADD, about 55 percent of all highway fatalities in 1983 were alcohol related; 1984 figures indicated a small decline to 54 percent.

In July 1984, President Ronald Reagan signed into law the National Minimum Drinking Age Act, which grants the federal government the authority to withhold federal highway funds from states that fail to raise their legal drinking age to 21 by 1987. When the law was enacted there were 27 states and the District of Columbia with a minimum age below 21, but many have introduced legislation to raise the age, or are expected to. Some 360 new laws regarding drunk driving have been passed nationwide since 1981. Many states and municipalities have banned "happy hours," which encourage increased alcohol consumption through discount prices. Also, there are 37 states with statutes holding the establishments and hosts liable for the subsequent behavior of intoxicated patrons or guests. These could also serve to reduce beer consumption.

INDUSTRY REACTION

Faced with these problems, many other industries would retrench, concentrate on keeping primary profit-making brands afloat, and try to ride out the storm. The brewery industry's response has been almost the opposite. New brands and extensions have appeared on retailers' shelves at a record pace. Beers that had been available only regionally are being moved into broader distribution. New light beers, low-alcohol beers, low-priced beers, super-premium beers, and malt liquors have emerged. Exhibit 10 lists the brands introduced in 1984 by both national and regional brewers.

The major U.S. brewers introduced 26 new products or line extensions in 1984. Two-thirds of these new product introductions were low-alcohol or low-calorie products. Anheuser-Busch (A-B) was the first major brewer to unveil its low-alcohol entry, LA; and regional brewers soon got into the act. To date, however, the low- and no-alcohol products have not worked out well. They are viewed as weak with no zing. They seem to appeal to the drinker who does not drink very much beer to begin with, in contrast to light beers, which appeal to the heavy beer drinker.

While new product introductions slowed in 1985, the beer industry is doing everything possible to attract new customers. A shrinking market means brewers must steal share from competitors. Lower-priced brands have been introduced and major firms, particularly Anheuser-Busch and Miller, have expanded their advertising budgets.

TAXES

The brewing industry confronts another problem, the ever-present threat of increased taxation. Beer is one of the most highly taxed consumer products. Taxes constitute the largest individual item in the price of beer. The federal excise tax is $9 a barrel, and state taxes average approximately $5.41 a barrel. Combined annual federal, state, and local taxes equal almost $3 billion. While the government earns over $14 for each barrel of beer sold, the brew-

EXHIBIT 10

Domestic Beer Brands Introduced in 1984

BRAND	BREWER
Black Label 11-11 Malt Liquor	Heileman
Black Label LA*	Heileman
Blatz LA*	Heileman
Big Man Malt Liquor	Eastern Brewing
Choice*	F. X. Matt
Golden Hawk	Schmidt
Ice Man Malt Liquor	Pabst
I. C. Golden Lager	Pittsburgh
King Cobra Malt Liquor	Anheuser-Busch
LA†	Anheuser-Busch
Light-N-Lo*	Latrobe
Little Kings Premium	Schoenling
Lone Star LA*	Heileman
Low Alcohol Gold*†	Pabst
Low Alcohol Pabst Extra Light*†	Pabst
Meister Brau Light	Miller
Milwaukee's Best	Miller
Old Style LA*	Heileman
Oscar Wildes's	Pearl
Plank Road Original Draft	Miller
Rainier LA*	Heileman
Schaefer Low Alcohol*	Stroh
Schmidt LA*	Heileman
Select Special 50 Low Alcohol*	Pearl
Sharpe's LA*	Miller
Silver Thunder Malt Liquor	Stroh

*Low in alcohol.
†Repositioned brand.

ing industry's average profit rate per barrel after taxes is estimated between $2 and $3. The federal government was debating the merits of increased excise taxes on beer as part of a plan to reduce the federal deficit. It was common for state and local governments to raise taxes on beer periodically. In California, where Golden Gate was headquartered, brewers paid taxes equal to $1.24 per barrel.

INTERNAL/ INDUSTRY FACTORS

The major causes of consolidation in the beer industry were economies of scale and product differentiation. Economies of scale, which occur when large plants produce at lower unit costs than smaller ones, existed in both the brewing and bottling processes. The increased capacity attained by many individual breweries over the past twenty years has forced the closing or sale of numerous regional producers. Industry experts contend that the wave of consolidation has not ended. Currently there is excess capacity and certain plants are inefficient (Exhibit 11). Except for A-B, the industry is operating between 75 percent and 85 percent of capacity.

Even though the U.S. beer industry is suffering from overcapacity, two brewers announced expansion plans during 1985. Adolph Coors Company intends to build a $70 million beer packaging plant in Virginia, and, if sales justify it, the facility will be expanded to include full brewing facilities. G. Heileman Brewing Company plans to construct a new brewery in Milwaukee. The facility will specialize in more costly imported-style beers. The industry's overcapacity was accentuated by Miller Brewing's decision to write-down $140 million of its $450 million new plant and Stroh Brewery Company's decision to close its older, underutilized Detroit plant.

Successful product differentiation occurs when a firm convinces customers that real or imagined differences in its beer render it preferable to that of the competitors. Larger brewers, with national sales and multiplant operations, can often more easily attain this high-quality image than local or

EXHIBIT 11

U.S. Brewing Industry Capacity and Usage—1983

BREWER	PLANTS	TOTAL CAPACITY (MILLION)	SHIPMENTS	PERCENT OF CAPACITY
Anheuser-Busch	11	66.5	60.5	91.0%
Miller	7	54.0	37.5	69.4
Stroh	7	32.6	24.3	74.5
G. Heileman	12	25.5	17.5	68.6
Adolph Coors	1	15.5	13.7	88.4
Pabst	4	15.0	12.8	85.3
Genesee	1	4.0	3.2	80.0
C. Schmidt	2	5.0	3.2	64.0
Falstaff	5	5.0	2.7	54.0
Pittsburgh	1	1.2	1.0	83.3
All others	34	7.4	3.7	50.0
Domestic total	85	231.7	180.1	77.7%

regional brewers. There also appear to be economies of scale in brand proliferation and product extensions. Large brewers can more easily (and cost-effectively) segment all price and product categories. The high fixed costs associated with advertising new brands can be spread over a large sales volume that smaller brewers do not have. Large firms can realize lower advertising costs on each barrel than small firms.

Advertising has grown considerably in importance and in expense. In 1984 brewers spent an estimated $780 million. Advertising expenditures in 1983 averaged $2.74 per barrel. The evidence that high advertising expenditures and high profit levels are positively correlated is, however, somewhat mixed. At Schlitz, for example, advertising expenditures on each barrel rose dramatically at a time when sales and operating profit per barrel both fell. Similarly, Coors had higher profit figures when advertising expenditure levels were extremely low and lower profits when advertising outlays accelerated. However, A-B and Miller have increased both profit on each barrel and market share, at a time when advertising expenditures increased.

IMPORTS

Imports are expected to perform well throughout the remainder of the 1980s. Between 1980 and 1984, the quantity of beer imported increased about 12 percent annually. Five countries, the Netherlands, Canada, West Germany, Mexico, and the United Kingdom, account for about 90 percent of all U.S. imports, but over 40 other countries ship beer to the United States. The imports' share of the U.S. beer market has grown from 1.1 percent in 1975 to 3.9 percent in 1984. Many beer wholesalers felt imports would capture at least 10 percent of the total U.S. beer market by 1990.

Ten years ago, imported beers were esoteric products consumed by a small elite, in a handful of markets. Since then, the industry has exploded with beer drinkers' desire, taste, and imagery fueling this growth. According to industry analyst Emanuel Goldman, "The imports have image. We live in a self-indulgent age that's getting more and more self-indulgent, and people want something different. They can get something different, upscale, and feel good about it with imports. There is a tremendous selection, too. The consumer seems to feel that imports are superior beers."

The top ten imported brands dominate about 87 percent of the sales (Exhibit 12). Heineken maintains the lead with an estimated 34 percent of the market, while Molson holds second place with 13.4 percent. Fortifying the Canadian segment is Moosehead in the number four spot and Labatt in the fifth place with 6 percent and 4.5 percent of the market, respectively. Beck's is in third place with 8.9 percent of the market and its closest German competitor, St. Pauli Girl, ranks sixth.

Favorable demographics and an improving economy have aided this segment. The rise of the Hispanic population and the popularity of Mexican cuisine has fared well for Mexican beers, while the growing Asian population

EXHIBIT 12   **Top Imported Beer Brands**

TOP TEN	SECOND TEN (ALPHABETICALLY)
1. Heineken (Netherlands)	11. Carta Blanca (Mexico)
2. Molson (Canada)	12. Dinkelacker (Germany)
3. Beck's (Germany)	13. Dortmunder (Germany)
4. Moosehead (Canada)	14. Grolsch (Netherlands)
5. Labatt (Canada)	15. Guinness (United Kingdom)
6. St. Pauli Girl (Germany)	16. Kirin (Japan)
7. Dos Equis (Mexico)	17. Kronenbourg (France)
8. Foster's Lager (Australia)	18. O'Keefe (Canada)
9. Amstel Light (Netherlands)	19. San Miquel (Philippines)
10. Corona (Mexico)	20. Tecate (Mexico)

has given rise to a host of Chinese and Japanese brews. Most significant has been the appeal of imported beer to status-conscious consumers. A prime market eager for imported beers has been the young urban professionals, with a desire for unusual and different products, especially those of a foreign bent.

An estimated ten new imported beers entered the United States every month in 1984. Exhibit 13 provides a partial list of the imported brands introduced in 1984.

There are two major obstacles in trying to capture American market share. The first is Van Munching & Company, which distributes Heineken. Heineken, with its commanding market share, essentially sets the benchmark pricing level for much of the import category. Many feel you cannot enter the U.S. market if you are above Heineken in price. The second major problem is a paradox created by the very success of the category, namely brand proliferation and the resulting market dilution.

Success hinges on the ability to come up with a unique selling proposition to cut through the multitude of brands competing for available market share. One technique used by imports is a unique packaging profile. The theory behind this is that the consumer knows none of the beers, but will try the one that looks a little different. This is supported by the number of American beer drinkers who first bought Grolsch, if for no other reason than to see what sort of brew was in its distinctive bottle with the old-fashioned wire closure and ceramic stopper. More imports are also moving to green bottles for their products. Consumer research shows that Americans feel green glass is more appealing for a light-colored beer.

EXHIBIT 13   Imported Beer Brands Introduced in 1984

BRAND	COUNTRY	BRAND	COUNTRY
ABC Stout	Singapore	Hombre	Mexico
Affligem	Belgium	John Peel Export	Britain
Alfa Beer	Holland	Jever Pilsner	West Germany
Anchor Pilsener	Singapore	Kaiser	Germany
Bamburger Hofbrau	Germany	Koff Stout	Finland
Brador	Canada	Kronenhaler*	Austria
Broken Hill	Australia	Lindener	West Germany
Catillio Beer	Italy	Lorimer	Britain
Castle St.	Britain	Maes Pils	Belgium
China Beer	Taiwan	Oktober Beer	West Germany
China Clipper	China	Orangebloom	Holland
Danish Light	Denmark	Pacifico	Mexico
De Koninck	Belgium	Rolland Light	Germany
Dempseys	Ireland	Scandia Gold	Denmark
Elan*	Switzerland	Tientan	China
Feingold Pils	Austria	Vaux	Britain
Felinfoel	Britain	Vienna Lager	Austria
Festive Ale	Britain	Warteck*	Switzerland
Glacier*	Sweden	Wolfbrau	Germany
Golden Ox	Germany	Yuchan Beer	China
Grizzly Beer	Canada	Zero*	Germany

*Denotes low or nonalcoholic brand.

Even though beer tasting and tavern promotion nights are the most cost-effective ways to promote public awareness, reliance on heavy advertising is increasing. In 1985 Van Munching spent an estimated $22 million advertising and promoting Heineken. For Molson $15 million was spent. St. Pauli Girl had a $14 million budget, and Mexican Tecate plans regional advertising at $4 million in 1986. Although imports account for less than 4 percent of the beer market, the category held 10 percent of all beer advertising in 1984. About five imported beers represent 78.9 percent of all imported beer advertising. Heineken leads the list of import advertisers with 33.9 percent, Molson has 20.5 percent, Amstel Light follows with 15.8 percent, Moosehead and St. Pauli Girl trail with 4.5 percent and 4.2 percent, respectively.

However, some importers are not marketing at all and some import companies have ten to twenty restaurants and delicatessens to whom they sell beer.

EXPORTS

Confronted with a static-to-declining domestic market, beer producers are being forced to seek new markets abroad. A-B sees the international market, which is more than twice as large as the U.S. market, as critical to U.S. brewers' long-term success. Miller Vice President Alan Easton echoes this view, "Anybody who is really serious about being in the beer industry is going to have to consider participating in non-U.S. markets." Because substantial foreign opposition exists, brewers are seeking to expand government efforts to negotiate for trade barrier reductions.

Currently, the United States is Canada's major export customer for beer. In contrast, the United States is a residual supplier of beer to Canada. Canadian provinces protect local producers by severely limiting beer imports. But some provinces, particularly in western Canada, are insisting that foreign beers be imported freely. The new Liberal government in Ontario (37 percent of Canada's beer drinkers reside in Ontario) is promising to break up the Ontario brewers' retail monopoly.

Anheuser-Busch is relying on licensees to brew regular Budweiser for its overseas production, marketing, and distribution. To meet A-B standards, the licensees import ingredients from the United States and their production must be approved by Anheuser's four international brewmasters, as well as Chairman August A. Busch III. Licensees are brewing Bud in Britain, Japan, and Israel. Negotiations are being conducted in Australia, Korea, and the Philippines. Anheuser is also considering the purchase of foreign breweries and exports to about ten other countries. Budweiser has failed, however, to crack the West German market, and Bud sales in France have been a disappointment.

NATIONAL BREWERS

Anheuser-Busch, Inc.

The St. Louis-based "King of Beers" has the most profitable product mix in the industry and is least in need of price increases. The key to its growth has been the world's best-selling beer, Budweiser. Bud has taken a big part of the youth market from Miller High Life and now commands a 24 percent market share (Exhibits 14 and 15). A good product reputation and a powerful distribution network of virtually exclusive distributors contributes to A-B's success. A-B has marketing muscle; its average wholesaler does a 50 percent greater volume than a Miller counterpart. A-B also has exposure; advertising expenditures in 1985 were $440 million. A-B has created the ability to

EXHIBIT 14

Top Five National Brewers

1984 RANK	COMPANY NAME	PRINCIPAL BRANDS
1.	Anheuser-Busch, Inc. St. Louis, Missouri	Budweiser, Bud Light, Michelob, Michelob Light, Busch, Natural Light, LA, King Cobra Malt Liquor
2.	Miller Brewing Co. Milwaukee, Wisconsin	Miller High Life, Miller Lite, Plank Road, Milwaukee's Best, Meister Brau, Sharpe's LA, Lowenbrau, Genuine Draft
3.	The Stroh Brewery Co. Detroit, Michigan	Stroh's, Stroh's Light, Old Milwaukee, Piels, Schlitz, Signature, Schaefer, Goebel, Silver Thunder Malt Liquor
4.	G. Heileman Brewing Co. La Crosse, Wisconsin	Old Style, Old Style LA, Special Export, Blatz, Rainier, Black Label, Lone Star, 11-11 Malt Liquor
5.	Adolph Coors Company Golden, Colorado	Coors, Coors Light, Herman Josephs, George Killian's Irish Red

EXHIBIT 15

Top Ten Brands for 1984

RANK	BRAND	MARKET SHARE	BRAND GROWTH
1	Budweiser	24.0%	5.0%
2	Miller Lite	10.0	2.0
3	Miller High Life	7.8	−18.0
4	Coors	5.0	−5.0
5	Old Milwaukee	3.8	1.5
6	Michelob	3.8	−3.5
7	Pabst	3.4	−20.0
8	Stroh	3.2	2.0
9	Old Style	2.9	−5.0
10	Bud Light	2.3	10.5
Top 10		66.2%	−30.5%

outspend its competitors because its gross margin and gross profits are growing while others' are not. Moreover, A-B is in the driver's seat as far as pricing goes.

Miller Brewing Company

Acquired in 1970 by Philip Morris, Inc., Miller surged during the '70s and continues to be in the number two position. The premium-priced High Life brand has been losing momentum and its luster as sales erode. However, the Lite brand is doing well, but faces more competition. Miller's strategy of introducing two low-priced, low-profit beers, Meister Brau and Milwaukee's Best, is questioned by analysts. They believe this maneuver, coupled with a large advertising budget, cannot succeed. Miller is innovating at the higher segment with Plank Road and Miller High Life Genuine Draft. It is trying to reposition Lowenbrau as a brand with worldwide image. Since the Lowenbrau that Miller sells in the United States is brewed in Milwaukee, not Munich, this campaign has failed in the past. Miller remains hopeful about its future.

The Stroh Brewery Company

Until 1981 this family-owned brewery, founded in 1849, was primarily a regional brewer. Since acquiring F&M Schaefer Brewing Company in 1981 and Jos. Schlitz Brewing Company in 1982, Stroh has carved a comfortable lead over its nearest competitor, G. Heileman. The acquisition of Schlitz gave Stroh a strong national wholesalers' network to distribute the rest of its products. Stroh's national rollout had some bad introductions in the Northeast, but it has a solid product line—Stroh's, Old Milwaukee, Schaefer, and superpremium Signature. A company with good management, Stroh will be a difficult force to contend with because it has minimized unit costs and is operating at full capacity. Moreover, because it is a private company, it does not have to show good quarterly returns; it just has to generate enough cash flow to cover the family's needs.

G. Heileman Brewing Company

The G. Heileman Brewing Company entered 1984 leading the industry in five-year profitability and growth. Its return on equity averaged 31.7 percent. It has eleven breweries—five in the Midwest and two each in the South, Southwest, and Northwest. Heileman's growth is a result of acquisition, and it has expanded its own distribution network by acquiring companies with well-established distribution systems. Despite excellent, street fighting management and good marketing, Heileman lacks a national image for its 50-plus brands. This makes competing with A-B difficult. Heileman is, however, competing with the imports by building a new small plant exclusively for the production of a specialty beer. It does not want to mix the new beer with its domestic brands.

Adolph Coors Company

Famous for using Rocky Mountain spring water in its flagship Coors brands, Coors is expanding its distribution eastward. The rollout has worked very well, especially in New England, where it ran ads at the rate of one TV commercial per second to introduce its brands. Also, Coors seems to have stemmed the market share erosion in its core territories out West and hopes to regain the lost ground. Coors Light is doing very well and in 1985 accounted for 40 percent of Coors' total barrelage. The success of Coors Light is helping to elevate the confidence that both the consumers and the wholesalers have in the Coors brand name. The imported superpremium George Killian's Irish Red is also making strong headway.

THE REGIONAL/ SMALL BREWERS

In an industry increasingly dominated by a few firms, several regional brewers have endured and continue to flourish. Some have 150-year histories and others have only recently emerged. All stand as evidence that hometown loyalties and the strength of the regional market can be cornerstones of success.

Some of the strategies for survival being used include: (1) the specialty brewer serving the moderate beer drinker and catering to the growing market of image-enhanced goods in select markets; (2) the dual-purpose brewer who wants to serve his loyal home market while developing more prestigious and distinctive beers for select markets; and (3) the more traditional regional brewer whose markets are blue collar and whose customers are more loyal than those in the more transient metropolitan areas.

The Genesee Brewing Company, Rochester, New York

Founded just after Prohibition's demise, Genesee is now the seventh largest brewery in America. Genesee's territory has been expanding and now includes all of the East Coast, Ohio, Indiana, Kentucky, West Virginia, and the province of Ontario. Genesee has implemented major advertising campaigns and had an impressive growth rate throughout the 1970s, with sales increasing at an average annual rate of 10.3 percent.

The F. X. Matt Brewing Company, Utica, New York

The F. X. Matt Brewing Company reflects the tradition of family involvement that characterizes the industry. Besides a strategy of capital improvements, three other factors have been keys to success: consistent quality, loyal personnel, and a hands-on management philosophy. The extensive product line includes: Utica Club; Utica Club Light; Utica Club Cream Ale; Matt's Premium; Matt's Premium Light Choice, a low-alcohol beer; Maximus Super Beer, with a 6.5 percent alcohol content; and Saranac 1888, the newest product. Approximately 125 distributors carry Matt products throughout New York, Pennsylvania, parts of New England, and north-central Colorado. Distributors must have a good game plan, ability to cover the market, competence, and a certain way of doing business.

Anchor Brewing Company, San Francisco, California

In 1965 Fritz Maytag, heir to part of the Maytag appliance fortune, bought this bankrupt brewery. Using his personal finances, he embarked on an extensive capital investment plan to renovate and replace equipment. Anchor, operating at a loss for ten years, went into the black in 1975. Anchor's initial annual capacity of 600 barrels has been expanded to 50,000 barrels. In 1984 Anchor produced over 37,000 barrels. The brewery's flagship, Anchor Steam Beer, accounts for 80 percent of sales and Anchor Porter and Anchor Liberty constitute 7 percent of total sales. The remaining sales volume is made up by a barley ale, wheat beer, and its Christmas ale.

While the brewery initially self-distributed its products, it now uses two distributors on the West Coast. With over 100 total distributors, Anchor is available on the West Coast; in parts of Maryland; Delaware; Virginia; Washington, D.C.; New Jersey; Connecticut; and Massachusetts. The company has done almost no advertising, but relies instead on distinctive packaging.

A quasi-market research study provided the following buyer profile: The buyers are young adults, upscale, predominately college-educated, and very knowledgeable about beer. Many drink a variety of beers and consider themselves aficionados. They drink primarily imported brands and enjoy a rich, distinctive taste in the beer they consume.

Maytag explains Anchor's success as follows: "We start with a respect for the brewing tradition and a reputation for integrity. It's a concept that starts with the product. Our brew is low key, high quality, and nonestablishment. We actually try to make a beer that most people don't like—heavy, hoppy, and flavorful. It's traditional and distinctive, not designed for high volume, but for rapid growth, with relatively high margins, on a small scale."

THE MICROBREWERS

The American brewing industry has one small, dedicated group of mavericks. These are the microbrewers, defined as brewers with annual production under 15,000 barrels. Microbreweries are as individual as the personalities of their owners, yet all share an attitude of respect and enthusiasm for the brewer's art.

Jack McAuliffe, an unemployed sailor who started the first microbrewery in 1976 in Sonoma, California, reintroduced top-fermented English-type ale in the United States. His New Albion Brewery survived only a few years, but others have followed. Today there are about 25 micros and another 30 are set to begin production in 1986. Exhibit 16 provides a comprehensive list of American microbreweries.

Real ale is not the only style produced by microbreweries. A new American-style nouveau lager has emerged on the market. This bottom-fermented beer is decidedly more hoppy and brewed in the German Reinheitsgebot tradition.

Reinheitsgebot dates from 1516, when the Bavarian ruler of that day, Wilhelm IV, limited the ingredients in beer to water, malted barley, hops, and yeast. In West Germany, Norway, and a few other countries, all beer produced for local consumption must be Reinheitsgebot pure, with only those four ingredients, no cereals, no additives, and no enzymes. The new wave of micro-beers in the United States are nearly all made to these specifications.

The West Coast is a hotbed of microbrewery activity. The area is an ideal geographic market for these niche beers, because of the generally high personal incomes, coupled with a widespread awareness and appreciation of small wineries. The classic flavor and quality these breweries achieve, combined with their antiestablishment stance, has resulted in attractive alternatives for the price-inelastic, high-end beer drinker.

Microbrewing, however, is a risky business, even on the West Coast. In 1982 in the San Francisco Bay area, there were five micros in business. Only two are still brewing. With a failure rate of more than 40 percent, this business is not for amateurs. Micro success is often unattainable, because of competition from imported labels and a high-cost production set-up that requires super-premium pricing to eke out a profit margin. Microbreweries are faced with the dilemma of needing to increase production to build market share and trim unit costs, yet having to contend with a mature and oversaturated market that simply does not justify scaling up.

Because of their low volume sales, it is also difficult to find distributors willing to carry the brands of microbrewers. The few that are receptive are normally attracted by label graphics and by superlative quality. Most distributors cannot, or will not, distribute a label that sells in such small numbers. Therefore, most microbrewers rely on personalized preselling of their brew to retailers, supplemented with point-of-purchase displays to generate buyer interest.

EXHIBIT 16   **American Microbreweries and Brew Pubs**

NAME	LOCATION
Riley-Lyon Brewing Company	Little Rock, Arkansas
Palo Alto Brewing Company	Mountain View, California
Sierra Nevada Brewing Company	Chico, California
Stanislaus Brewing Company	Modesto, California
Thousand Oaks Brewing Company	Berkeley, California
Golden Gate Brewing Company	Berkeley, California
Boulder Brewing Company	Boulder, Colorado
Snake River Brewing Company	Caldwell, Idaho
Millstream Brewing Company	Amana, Iowa
Boston Beer Company	Boston, Massachusetts
Montana Beverage Company	Helena, Montana
The Manhattan Brewing Company	New York, New York
Old New York Brewing Company	New York, New York
Wm. S. Newman Brewing Company	Albany, New York
Columbia River Brewing Company	Portland, Oregon
Widmer Brewing Company	Portland, Oregon
Reinheitsgebot Brewing Company	Plano, Texas
Chesapeake Bay Brewing Company	Virginia Beach, Virginia
Hart Brewing Company	Kalama, Washington
Hales Ales Ltd.	Coleville, Washington
Independent Ale Brewing, Inc.	Seattle, Washington
Kemper Brewing Company	Rolling Bay, Washington
Kuefner Brewing Company	Monroe, Washington
Yakima Brewing and Malt Company	Yakima, Washington
Brew Pubs:	
Buffalo Bill's Microbrewery & Pub	Hayward, California
Mendocino Brewing Co.	Hopeland, California
Hopeland Brewing	Hopeland, California

The strategy of the micros involves charging a little more, maintaining a rigorous quality-conscious image, and providing more and more beer drinkers with the joys of fresh, wholesome, handmade brews. Their market goal is to make premium an adjective that means something in the beer business.

Sierra Nevada Brewing Company, Chico, California

Located in a farming and college town near Sacramento, this ale brewery has a current sales volume of 3,000 barrels. Started in 1979, the first brew was sold in 1981. Sierra Nevada produces pale ale, porter, and stout, which all retail for about $18 a case. The firm also sells full and half kegs of draft ale and a Christmas ale. Operating efficiency and a steadily growing reputation among serious beer lovers have proven to be keys for survival. But owner/brewer Camusi predicts a shakeout among microbrewers, a direct result of an overcrowded specialty market.

The critical areas of size and capacity may be the deciding factors in its long-term success. Sierra Nevada has added to its capacity every year and now approaches an annual capacity of 7,500 barrels. Its draft beer, accounting for a large percentage of its volume, enables the brewery to avoid the crowded single bottle market. Camusi believes growth is essential for survival. According to Camusi, "The really small brewery is just not a viable business anymore."

Mendocino Brewing Company, Hopeland, California

Situated 100 miles north of San Francisco, this brewery was formed from the equipment and staff of the defunct New Albion Brewery. Mendocino has overcome many of the economic viability issues of distribution and scale by operating a "brew pub." Approximately 660 barrels a year of ale, porter, and stout are sold through the pub under the name of the Hopeland Brewery. Mendocino produces a wide variety of products, with Red Tail Ale its mainstay.

This amber, heavy-bodied, English-style brew sells in a one-and-a-half-liter magnum bottle for $6. Its Black Hawk Stout, pale ale, and Christmas, summer, and spring ales sell on draft at the pub. The owners describe Mendocino as a domestic alternative that provides a small group of beer drinkers with a fresh, premium product. By selling exclusively to a local market, Mendocino has overcome the problem of finding distributors.

Boulder Brewing Company, Boulder, Colorado

Founded in 1979 by a small group of home brewers, this brewery sold its first beer on July 3, 1980. Boulder's products are unpasteurized, English-type brews. The two products, Boulder Extra Pale Ale and Boulder Stout, are sold in 12-ounce nonreturnable bottles. No draft is produced. Accounts are served by wholesale distributors who approached the company. Distribution is confined to the state of Colorado, with a network of twelve outlets currently handling the brewery's products. Although the company enjoys considerable free publicity, word-of-mouth advertising serves as its primary source of demand. Marketing resources are focused on upgrading packaging graphics. A public stock offering in September 1983 financed the company's capitalization and construction of its recently completed $1.1 million brewery. Forty million common shares were issued at five cents a share, raising a total of $2 million. The new facility covers about 14,000 square feet and annual capacity now stands at 15,000 barrels.

The Old New York Beer Company, New York, New York

The first of the nouveau lagers came from New York in 1982, when Matthew Reich introduced New Amsterdam Amber, a rich, hoppy, full-bodied, all malt lager beer. Reich invested his life's savings, $10,000, and hired Dr. Joseph Owades, an international brewing consultant and director for the Center for Brewing Studies in San Francisco, to design a lager beer similar to Anchor Steam.

Reich had always dreamed of being a brewer. While working as the director of operations at Hearst Magazine, he often wished he was out creating his own beer. He believed there was room for a connoisseur's beer, the kind poured from kegs, without rice or corn—a pure beer. For two years Reich and Owades slaved over the beer's body, color, and taste, during which time Reich still worked at Hearst.

Based on a fifteen-page business plan, 22 private investors invested $255,000 to form a limited partnership. In the summer of 1982 Reich left Hearst, and that August he began buying brewing time at F. X. Matt Brewing Company in Utica, New York. New Amsterdam Amber ferments for one week and ages for 26 days before being bottled or kegged and shipped to Manhattan.

In 1983, Old New York Beer Company sold 44,000 cases for $600,000. Sales doubled to $1.2 million in 1984, with earnings of $50,000 (after taxes). Reich expects to reach a sales level of $1.8 million in 1985 on 100,000 cases. The average retail price for a six-pack is $6.

Like other micros, Reich personally sold his brew, first approaching trendy restaurants and bars in Manhattan. While he originally intended to target only New York, his beer is now available in 21 states, including the West Coast. Reich's initial success has enabled him to raise an additional $2.2 million from two venture capital firms. He is using the money to construct a new brewery in Manhattan that will also have a restaurant, a tap room, and a visitors' center. Although this action dilutes Reich's holding in the company to 25 percent, it improved Old New York's image and increased its annual production capacity to 30,000 barrels. When the brewery is completed late in 1986, he will be able to triple 1985's expected production.

THE GOLDEN GATE BREWING COMPANY

James Cook, christened Charles James, attended Harvard College, where he majored in government and graduated with honors in 1971. For the next three years, he was a mountaineering instructor with Outward Bound. In 1974 he returned to Harvard to study law and business administration. In 1977 Cook climbed to the snow-covered peak of Alaska's 20,320-foot Mount McKinley. "After traveling for weeks and seeing nothing but white," he recalls, "I wondered what magic sight awaited me at the summit. And when I got to the top, there it was, glowing in the light, an empty beer can, planted like somebody's flag. Ah," he exclaims, "the power of beer is transcendent!"

With a J.D. and M.B.A., Cook joined the Boston Consulting Group (BCG). He spent seven years honing his management skills and advising industrial, primarily international, managers. After six years he got tired of telling other people how to run their companies and decided to start his own. "I wanted to create something, I wanted to make something of my own," said Cook. Cook's choices boiled down to either brewing beer or building a chain of for-profit medical clinics in Seattle. The consultant in Cook voted for the doc-in-the-box setup. But as the eldest son of a fifth-generation brewer, he figured he really did not have a choice.

Cook vividly remembers the smell of fermenting beer on days he visited his father at work. "I liked it. I never liked hard liquor and never understood wine. Even now I drink two–three beers a day, rarely less, rarely more. Breweries are neat places and the brewmaster has the best job. He walks around, tastes beer and makes changes. It's almost like playing God," notes Cook. Cook believes he was put on earth for one thing—"to make the greatest beer in the United States." He recalled:

> On the surface it was an insane thing to do, but I was convinced there was a small emerging market for what I wanted to do. It was the time for microbreweries and hand-crafted beers, and it seemed tragic that I was ending a line of five generations of brewers. I realized Americans had begun to appreciate premium beers in recent years, especially on the West Coast, but I felt they relied too heavily on imported beers, which are inherently inferior. I think that the American appreciation of beer is very much in its infancy. We're in the Blue Nun stage of beer drinking. There was a time when people thought that Blue Nun was a great wine, just as now there are people who think Heineken and Beck's are great beers. In fact, they're the Schlitz of Europe. They have a certain mystique, but it's a phony mystique. These beers aren't fresh. Beer has a shelf life that's not a whole lot longer than orange juice. And you'd never think of buying orange juice from Germany.

In Germany, they don't drink Beck's. They drink the local beer. Americans have this notion that the further away a beer is made, the better it is. But the imports we get in America not only have preservatives, which are illegal in Germany, but by the time they arrive here, they are almost always spoiled, stale and/or skunked. Beer must be fresh. It deteriorates the instant you put it in a bottle. The day it leaves the brewery, it goes downhill. The travel time in importing beer and use of green bottles that expose beer to damaging light can often mean the expensive imported beer is not what it claims to be.

The Start-Up

Although Cook had no formal education in brewing, he studied notes and material his father had saved from the Siebel Institute of Brewing in Chicago where he learned to be a brewmaster. Although American tastes in mass-marketed beers favor light, paler versions, Cook decided to buck the tide, go with family tradition, and brew a full-bodied lager. He wanted a connoisseur's beer, brewed in an old-world tradition.

His father suggested he revive the old family formula. After searching his father's attic in Cincinnati, Cook found his great-great-grandfather's original recipe, first developed by his ancestor in the 1870s. With his family's formula, Cook hired biochemist and brewery consultant Joseph L. Owades to aid in devising the final formula. In the summer of 1984, Cook traveled to the fermentation lab at the University of California at Davis and worked with Owades on translating Louis Cook's Midwestern American lager into a 1980s West Coat superpremium beer.

The formula is water, malt, hops, and a special yeast strain developed by Owades. The hops is the best in the world, Tettnang and Hallertau Mittelfreuh hops, imported from Bavaria at a cost of $4.50 a pound. A pound of ordinary hops costs 55 cents. The hops, according to Cook, is key as it gives the beer its flavor. Two-row summer malted barley and some caramel malt are used for color and body. While many people think water is the most important ingredient that goes into beer, it is, in fact, the least important. The quality of the yeast strain is much more important, but seldom talked about as it lacks advertising appeal. Cook points out, "When you listen to what people advertise about their beers, it's things that have real macho appeal—fire brewing, beechwood aging, mountain spring water. What matters are things like hops, malt, and yeast. Unfortunately, they don't have the advertising appeal of cool mountain streams."

To make this beer formula a reality Cook needed to raise capital. He tossed in all his personal savings, $100,000, and raised an additional $300,000 from friends, business associates, clients, and even his father. "While you can start a small boutique brewery with $400,000, a good lager is difficult to produce in a microbrewery. A lager requires more sophisticated brewing equipment and more careful handling than the ale produced by most micros. I was forced to find an existing brewery, and luckily, I was able to find a brewery in Berkeley that was perfect for my purposes," relates Cook.

The Brewing Process

Golden Gate's hundred-year-old recipe requires a craft brewing process not used by American brewers in this century. The sweetness is drawn from the malt through a process traditional in Germany, but rarely used anymore by American brewers. Fresh hops are added in six stages during the brewing process to give the beer its complex hop character. (The usual process is to add hops only during the cooking stage of production, when boiling extracts the greatest amount of bitterness and, therefore, is more economical.) Cook's beer then goes through a second fermentation that carbonates the beer and also removes some of its impurities for a smoother taste. A final addition of fresh hops is made to the beer as it ages to impart the striking aroma. This is a labor-intensive technique. Golden Gate takes 40–45 days to make—one day to cook, seven days to ferment, and about two weeks to ferment the second time. The rest of the time is lagering, or aging. These efforts in the brewing process create the full-bodied flavor, rich with coppery color.

The beer is produced in batches, between 250–300 barrels a batch. Cook currently travels to the brewery every one to two weeks to oversee the brewing of a new batch. He follows the process step-by-step to ensure his recipe is followed precisely.

Packaging

Golden Gate is currently only bottled; no draft beer is produced. The classic American beer bottle, the twelve-ounce longneck, or bar bottle, that requires an opener is used. This shape and the cap offer the most protection from light and oxidation. The bottle is also a dark brown, because a dark bottle protects beer from light, a deadly enemy of beer. Beer left in light for more than ten minutes begins to spoil.

After being bottled in Berkeley, the beer arrives in San Francisco four hours later. Cook has hired two truck drivers and leases trucks. Each trip to San Francisco costs about $800 per truck. Initially, 500 cases per week were delivered, but this has grown to about 1,500 cases per week. (Each truck has a maximum capacity of 2,500 cases.) The beer is delivered to an old San Francisco brewery, where Cook rents office and warehouse space, prior to distribution.

Organization

The employment roster of the Golden Gate Brewing Company numbers five people including James Cook—the brewer and chief salesman. In addition to two truck drivers, there is a part-time bookkeeper and an accounts manager, Rhonda Kallman, who was Cook's secretary at BCG. Her numerous and varied duties include selling and even delivering when necessary. To keep overhead as low as possible, the business has no secretary, no typewriter, and no computer. Cook also took a 75 percent pay cut from his BCG salary.

Financial Information

According to Cook, the Golden Gate Brewing Company, "is still in the red, but we're getting back toward recovering our losses. The business after six months is doing remarkably well." Exhibit 17 shows the Golden Gate Brewing Company's income statement for the first six months of operations. Golden Gate sells for about 25 cents more per bottle than Heineken, between $1.75 and $3.50 per bottle retail.

A six-pack retails for about $6.50 and a case varies from $20 to $24. Asked if he thought the high price might limit sales, Cook said, "I don't drink wine, but I understand a good bottle of wine costs about $30. Well, for the price of a mediocre bottle of wine, you can go out and buy a six-pack of the best beer in America." Golden Gate wholesales for about $16 a case.

Golden Gate Lager costs two to three times what it costs to brew imported beers. The delivered cost into San Francisco was initially listed at $12 a case, but, because of increased volume, it is now down to $10.50 a case. Other expenses include salaries, office/warehouse rent, truck leasing, marketing and promotion, public relations, general administrative expenses, and taxes.

Advertising and Marketing

Golden Gate Lager spends no money advertising its beer. The main marketing element is quality and freshness, and the main marketing tool is personal selling and word-of-mouth. Tabletop display cards are also placed in bars and restaurants in and around San Francisco. In addition, a little blue miniature booklet, each hand-applied, dangles from each long-stem bottle. The booklet is entitled "Why Is This Special Beer Different?" and describes the beer, brewing process, and flavor. The first booklet order alone cost $35,000.

During the summer of 1985 Cook experimented with advertising. Placards were placed on the sides of San Francisco's tour buses. While it was relatively cheap advertising at $5,000 per month, Cook is not sure it was worth

EXHIBIT 17   **1985 Income Statement for Golden State Brewing Co.**

	1985
Sales	$408,000[1]
Cost of goods sold	273,000[2]
Gross margin	135,000
Less:	
Shipping	840[3]
Salaries and wages	101,003[4]
Office/warehouse rent	4,800[5]
Truck leasing	20,800[6]
Marketing and promotion	55,000[7]
Repairs	1,000[8]
Depreciation	7,500[9]
General selling, administrative, and other expenses	9,057[10]
Net income (loss) before taxes	($65,000)

[1]Includes 25,000 cases sold in California and 500 in Munich.
[2]The first 3,500 cases cost $12/case, the rest cost $10.50/case.
[3]Includes shipping costs of $0.07/bottle for 500 cases shipped. (Larger shipments would decrease the per bottle cost.)
[4]Includes Cook's salary of $25,000 for July–December and average hourly earnings of his four employees of $18.27/hr. (Another 4 percent increase is expected in 1986.)
[5]Office and warehouse rent total $800 per month.
[6]Twenty-six truck trips were made into San Francisco in the first six months.
[7]Includes $35,000 for booklet and $10,000 for placards used in July and August.
[8]Cost of incidental repairs, including labor and supplies, which do not add materially to the value of the property.
[9]Depreciation is on the straight-line basis, assuming a 20-year useful life, no salvage value, one half year's depreciation taken in the first year and $300,000 of assets acquired.
[10]Included are salaries and wages not deducted elsewhere, amounts not otherwise reported, such as administrative, general and office expenses, bonuses and commissions, delivery charges, research expenses, sales discounts, and travel expenses.

it. "I don't think we generated enough sales to pay for it." This experience confirmed his gut feeling that small, specialized companies do better relying on word-of-mouth advertising and publicity. "The first thing you must have in business is a solid, substantial advantage over the alternatives. Somehow you've got to have a reason for people to buy your product, and it's got to be more solid than anything advertising can create. There are very few products that have really lasted long-term on marketing alone," says Cook. "However, nothing is so good that it automatically sells itself. You have to go out and hustle."

While he links the logistics of introducing this beer to those of a fine wine, with the best advertising being word-of-mouth, Cook was fortunate to gain a credible third-party endorsement. Less than two months after the introduction of Golden Gate Lager, it was crowned the Best Beer in America at the annual Great American Beer Festival in Denver. The 4,000-plus attendees selected one beer as best from over 102 entries. The resulting publicity played a major role in boosting sales. Cook, thrilled by the victory, said, "For a family that has been making beer for 150 years to suddenly get recognized as making the best beer in the country—that is the ultimate accolade."

James Cook also conducts his own market research and studies. Three nights a week he visits local pubs and restaurants. He questions patrons as to why they drink imports when they can have Golden Gate. He asks what they like about imported brands. He asks beer drinkers for their opinion of Golden Gate. If they have not tasted Golden Gate, he describes the flavor and suggests they try it. After a short conversation, he identifies himself as the brewer. Aside from polling patrons, Cook chats with bartenders and questions waitresses and waiters about sales. According to Cook, "The neatest thing is to come into a bar and see people drinking my beer. The second neatest thing is to take the empty cases out."

Distribution

"Getting the beer on the market boils down to a door-to-door campaign with restaurants, bar managers, and liquor store owners," says Cook. Cook wins new accounts by asking potential carriers to taste the beer. "The response is incredible," boasts Cook. "Bar managers and owners like the personal attention. It shows them how much you believe in your product."

Since Golden Gate requires an amount of personal attention and credibility that the normal beer sales and distribution channels cannot give, Cook has set up his own distribution company. He even goes as far as making deliveries, pinstriped suit and all, out of his station wagon when regular drivers can't get to a particular account on time. Cook realizes all this costs money, probably twice what traditional distributors pay. Cook is currently negotiating with a major regional beer distributor. Affiliation with a large distributor provides access to numerous, established accounts that Cook would otherwise have to pursue one by one. He wonders if this is a sound strategy.

Target Market

The Golden Gate Co.'s target is the beer drinker who know how to distinguish a well-made beer from an average to below-average one and cares more about quality and taste than advertising appeal. Cook believes the typical Golden Gate drinker could be anyone, from gourmets to yuppies to construction workers, who likes a good beer. The current diverse cross section of drinkers cuts across traditional demographics.

Export Plunge

In October 1985, Cook shipped 12,000 bottles (500 cases) of Golden Gate Lager to Munich, West Germany, a city with the most finicky beer drinkers in the world, becoming the first U.S. brewed beer to be sold in West Germany outside U.S. military bases. It took four weeks before the Wiehenstathan, or beer institute, gave Cook's beer its seal of approval. Obtaining an import license was the next task.

The 500 cases were sent to George Thaler, a business consultant friend and now part-time beer distributor, who attempts to get Germans to try, and then order, Golden Gate. Thaler explains his sales techniques as follows, "I bring three cold bottles with me, then I tell them what has happened to beer in America and then discuss the brewing process. Then we taste." Thaler says Germans like the beer, which helps both sales of Golden Gate and the image American products have. "It's a quality image for a U.S. product."

The Munich market is not without problems. In Munich, six breweries own 90 percent of all pubs and they will only serve their brand of beer. Therefore, Golden Gate is locked out of all but a few of Munich's restaurants, delicatessens, and hotels (the so-called free bars). In addition, while shipping costs add only 7 cents to the price of a bottle of Golden Gate, the beer costs 30–50 percent more than German draft beefs, or about 5½ marks more per beer. But Thaler explains that this is consistent with the product positioning. "We don't want student beer drinkers to get drunk on Golden Gate. We want the beer connoisseur to drink Golden Gate." Thaler presently has five accounts taking 70 cases per week which he delivers in the trunk of his Mercedes-Benz. The accounts range from a high-class delicatessen to a New York-style bar.

While Cook's plunge into West Germany is primarily to demonstrate his product's quality, he is now considering expansion. Thaler hopes to soon expand to Düsseldorf and Austria. Cook wonders what other markets he should pursue, how fast he should expand, and how much time he should devote to export possibilities. He is confident that his time-consuming brewing process and choice ingredients make Golden Gate competitive with the best of European brews.

Capital Needs

The Golden Gate Brewing Co. currently rents office and warehouse space at an old San Francisco brewery. This brewery with three-foot thick walls was abandoned in 1965. It was cheaper to abandon than to tear down. It is now owned by the nonprofit Neighborhood Development Corporation, but Cook has an option on about one-fourth of the building's 170,000 square feet. He hopes to be able to buy the building, renovate it, and brew Golden Gate in 40,000 square feet following funding completion. Cook estimates his needs at $3.75 million, with $1.1 million going for renovations and $2.1 million for new tanks and bottling gear. His goal is an annual capacity of 30,000 barrels. Initially, the project is expected to create 12 to 15 new jobs and potentially 55 to 60. Actual renovation and equipment installation is estimated to take 4 to 10 months.

Cook says it would be cheaper to build a brewery in the suburbs, but "romance" led him to the old San Francisco brewery. "I could save $800,000 if I moved to a suburban industrial park, but I don't want to make California, or West Coast Lager Beer. I want to make Golden Gate Lager."

Cook has explored several financing possibilities—industrial revenue financing, Urban Development Action Grants, and market rate financing.

INDUSTRIAL REVENUE FINANCING Industrial Revenue Bonds (IRB) are vehicles that developers and corporations use to raise low-interest financing for construction projects. They are issued by a municipality only to achieve tax-exempt status, and are not guaranteed by the full faith and credit of the government. IRBs are backed by the future revenue of the project. IRBs were originally designed to attract industry into communities for employment and economic benefits through the use of tax-exempt financing. IRB loans in San Francisco generally carry interest rates of 70 percent of prime with a 15-year balloon and a 30-year amortization.

The San Francisco Industrial Development Financing Authority (SFIDFA) must give initial approval to an application by Cook's Golden Gate Brewing Company. The revenue bonds must then gain City Council and mayoral approval. Cook is confident that the mayor will bestow enthusiastic support, since he campaigned on revitalizing San Francisco neighborhoods. Once the IRBs are approved, a bank must agree to loan the funds. Most banks require IRB loans to be secured by the personal guarantees of the principals.

URBAN DEVELOPMENT ACTION GRANTS The Urban Development Action Grant (UDAG) is another possibility. The UDAG is a flexible program that offers a source of cheap money. The maturity and interest rate are negotiated between the city and the borrower. The collateral is normally limited to the assets being financed (and personal guarantees). The UDAG can be used for fixed assets whose life expectancy exceeds seven years. The terms and conditions negotiated between the city and the borrower must be approved by the City Council and the U.S. Department of Housing and Urban Development. The UDAG process averages three to four months. Another important advantage of this subsidy is that the UDAG can be mixed with IRBs and other federal programs.

The UDAG subsidy does have one drawback. To raise money for future projects, the local program shares in the profits of the subsidized projects. This can restrict profit potential. Cook was not excited about sharing profits and/or giving up control or ownership.

MARKET RATE FINANCING   Another option for capital, explored by Cook, is market rate financing from local commercial banks. San Francisco has five major banks, one of which, the Bank of San Francisco, has already solicited the Golden Gate Brewing Co. Cook has yet to supply necessary financial statements or projections, however. The loan would be a mortgage, used to cover all the expenses associated with the completed property. The interest rate would be based on the prime rate. Cook feels that the rate on a commercial mortgage would be prime plus 1 percent for a 15-year balloon with a 30-year amortization.

Expansion/Growth Strategy

Winning the America's Best Beer Award, and the resulting publicity, caused many distributors from other states to solicit the Golden Gate Brewing Company and Golden Gate Lager. Cook has put several possible new accounts temporarily on hold and has turned down requests from distributors in Washington, Colorado, Kentucky, and Alaska. Cook's current agreement with the Berkeley Brewery to brew Golden Gate Lager limits production and Cook felt it was important to penetrate and service San Francisco first. Renovating the old San Francisco brewery, however, would provide a much higher production capacity level. Cook also realized that beer is regulated in 50 different ways in the United States. The bureaucratic red tape is complicated and time-consuming. Cook sometimes thinks it is easier to sell Golden Gate in Munich than in the United States. Germany requires only that the beer be pure.

Regardless, Cook wonders if he should expand, how quickly he should expand and where he should expand. Cook concedes that he will never slay the major domestic giants. "I don't compete with them. I make a different product and sell it for a different price. I compete with foreign beers." But he is uncertain of the strategy he should use.

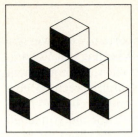

INDUSTRY

STEEL

Wheeling-Pittsburgh Steel Company (A)

NEIL H. SNYDER · JAYE GAMBLE
NADINE GREENSAID · GEORGE CONNOLLY

Wheeling-Pittsburgh Steel Company (W-P), the eighth largest domestic steelmaker, produced 3,895,000 tons of raw steel (2.9 percent of the industry total) and shipped 2,889,000 tons of finished products in 1978. The remainder of their output was sold in raw form to other producers of finished products.

W-P is a vertically integrated firm with annual raw steel capacity of about 4,400,000 net tons. Their production operations are geared primarily toward producing flat-rolled steel—steel that is made by rolling up long, thin bands of steel like a roll of paper towels. Rolled steel, which is adaptable to most processes, is used extensively for products in the auto, home appliance, farm construction, container, and pipe markets. Due to the combined influence of economic and business cycle trends, W-P has experienced especially sharp cyclical swings in earnings for the past several years.

HISTORY OF THE FIRM

In 1968, two small companies (Wheeling Steel and Pittsburgh Steel) agreed to a merger that they believed would improve their position in an industry that is dominated by big producers. When the two companies merged to become Wheeling-Pittsburgh Steel Company, Pittsburgh was an old-line, low-profit, limited-product-mix producer. Similarly, Wheeling was an unprofitable company because they possessed more steelmaking capacity than their finishing operations could handle. For Wheeling Steel (the eleventh largest domestic steel producer), a merger with Pittsburgh Steel (the fourteenth largest domestic steel producer) offered the opportunity to reverse a dangerous trend in earnings (between 1964 and 1967, Wheeling lost $29 million). Both companies produced flat-rolled steel, and each had equipment that would dovetail. In the merger agreement, Pittsburgh agreed to give Wheeling technical assistance on production and sales and to relieve Wheeling's financial pressures so that money could be raised for much needed facilities. Outside observers, however, were not enthusiastic about the marriage. One industry analyst stated that "the only thing synergistic about this merger will be its problems."

For the next several years, W-P's performance supported this skepticism. Saddled with debt, top-heavy with management, and scarred by a reputation as an unreliable supplier, W-P did little more than survive. But in 1974, everything came together. Net income increased to $73.4 million and sales jumped to $1 billion (up 36 percent over 1973) (see Exhibit 14.) The company's profit surge in 1974 reflected a worldwide increase in demand for steel that began in late 1973. But the surge was also due to the corporate revamping engineered by Robert E. Lauterbach, who, in 1974, became chairman and chief executive officer. Lauterbach made the following changes:

- He reduced the number of top executives from sixteen to six—all of whom had more than 25 years of experience in the steel industry.
- Bucking an industry trend toward increased diversification, he concentrated on shrinking the company to its essential core—the making of flat-rolled steel products.

Lauterbach's rationale for focusing on the essential core was quite simple. He said, "We're not going to remain in any business where our competitors can beat us to death with small plants, low labor costs, and low capital costs." Instead, he looked for markets with growth potential. According to Lauterbach, in the strong markets "we'll compete head on with the big guys."

But the 1974–1975 recession dealt W-P a stunning blow. Due to continuing cost pressures without adequate price increases in major product lines and weak demand for products such as automobiles, appliances, and containers, W-P's earnings were depressed in 1975. In 1976 this trend continued, and in 1977 W-P sustained a $25.6 million loss.

In 1978, Dennis J. Carney became chairman of the board of W-P. He had served as president and chief operating officer since 1976. Immediately after assuming the chairman position, Carney began to make changes. He renegotiated debt contracts, restaffed executive positions, and eliminated unprofitable finished steel items from W-P's product line. Additionally, Carney launched an offensive against W-P's big competitors by accusing them of perpetrating a "coldly calculated campaign" of underpricing flat-rolled steel products at W-P's expense.

In March 1979, W-P won approval for a loan package in excess of $150 million substantially guaranteed by state and federal agencies. These funds were earmarked for two major projects—building a railroad rail plant and purchasing pollution control equipment to comply with Environmental Protection Agency (EPA) pollution standards. The rail plant portion of the loan package produced substantial controversy in the United States steel industry.

INCREASED DEMAND FOR RAILROAD RAILS

While imports account for only 15–20 percent of the railroad rails sold in the United States, they are of higher quality than domestically produced rails. Due to the energy situation in the United States and the resulting increase in demand for mass transportation of people and freight, railroad usage has increased significantly. While the increase in demand for railroad transportation represented a significant opportunity for the depressed railroad industry, firms in the industry had allowed their roadbeds to deteriorate. Furthermore, railroad trains today are much faster and heavier than they once were. Thus, the opportunity afforded by increased demand resulted in the need for railroad firms to improve their roadbeds.

Faster and heavier trains require straighter and stronger rails. Because of the loan guarantees, W-P was prepared to become the domestic industry leader in railroad rail protection at a time when demand was increasing rapidly. Major steel producers such as U.S. Steel objected to government interference in a potentially lucrative market segment. Thus, steel producers became embroiled in a controversy that pitted domestic producers against one another and the government.

THE STEEL INDUSTRY

Overview

In June 1979, prospects for the steel industry looked good. The industry was producing at 90 percent of capacity, and products such as flat-rolled steel were experiencing generally strong demand despite the softness of the domestic auto industry. Demand for steel in capital goods industries was quite strong because important users of steel such as farm equipment manufacturers, machinery manufacturers, and the heavy construction industry were experiencing brisk demand. Thus, the demand for steel did not decline dramatically.

By the second half of 1979, however, a weakening of demand for steel could be detected. The softening of the consumer goods market finally materialized in a very pronounced way, and orders from the users of flat-rolled steel products declined across every market. Many steel producers feared that declines in orders might spread to the industrial markets. Thus, companies such as Wheeling-Pittsburgh and Jones and Laughlin, whose major product is flat-rolled steel, began to schedule maintenance on their heavy equipment. (Maintenance on heavy equipment used in steel production is delayed frequently until demand slackens to avoid costly delays in production.)

In the first half of 1980, the bottom fell out of the steel industry as the nation settled into a recession. High interest rates finally crushed the demand for steel products in industrial markets, and by June 1980, the steel industry was mired in its worst slump in ten years. The industry as a whole was producing at only 60 percent of capacity. Cost-cutting measures, such as layoffs, shorter work weeks, and plant closings were scheduled as the industry braced itself for an onslaught of red ink. To make matters worse, steel imports continued to increase at an alarming rate.

STEEL INDUSTRY PROBLEMS

Imports

Steel imports have accentuated the downside of the domestic steel industry's business cycle and deprived it of shipments and sales revenue needed to purchase new plant and equipment and modernize existing facilities. According to William A. Delancey, chairman of Republic Steel Corporation and president of the American Iron and Steel Institute, "I don't imply that imports alone are the root of the steel industry's problems, but imports have taken all of the growth in the domestic market in the past ten years and have substantially depressed the domestic industry's profitability."

The steel import problem is exacerbated because many foreign governments own or subsidize their steel industries. Thus, foreign steel producers can sell their products in the U.S. market at prices below their costs of production. The following references indicate how important this problem is:

IN CANADA

A report calling for a $350-million infusion to nudge Sydney Steel Corp. (Sysco) along a 10-year road to recovery has been released by Nova Scotia Premier John Buchanan, who said federal-provincial negotiations for the money are just starting.

With the release of the business plan, Buchanan said Ottawa would release the initial $7.5 million rehabilitation grant. The previous federal government of Joe Clark had promised the grant, but the present liberal government had held back until it saw the plan.

The business plan says the ailing, turn-of-the-century steel mill needs $350 million over 10 years for modernization, and then a further $175 million if a decision is made to introduce an oxygen steelmaking process.

A spokesman in Ottawa said it is expected that most of the money would come through normal federal-provincial financing agreements, such as those worked out with the department of regional economic expansion.*

American Metal Market
November 20, 1980

IN MEXICO

When the first slab of steel rolled out at Mexico's huge new mill here (Las Truchas) four years ago, President Luis Echeverria and other government dignitaries at the ribbon-cutting ceremonies were ecstatic. The government's decades-old dream of building a "pacific Pittsburgh" here in a west-coast jungle was finally coming true. President Echeverria saw an era of self-sufficiency in steel.

Today, as the government prepares to sink billions more into Las Truchas and other steel-expansion projects, a basic question is being raised: Can Mexico really achieve its planned threefold increase in steel output over the next decade? Plagued by poor planning, low productivity, labor strife, management corruption and myriad other problems, the struggling state-dominated steel industry clearly faces an enormous challenge.

So the government moves ahead with plans to invest more than $17.2 billion over the next decade to raise state steel production to 20.3 million metric tons annually, up from 4.5 million now. The Las Truchas plant alone is scheduled to produce 10 million tons a year in 1990, up from less than one million today, making it the largest steel mill in Latin America.†

Wall Street Journal
January 27, 1981

IN WEST GERMANY

Even though the West German steel industry could compete with the world's most cost-effective producers, it "cannot compete with the combined forces of Europe's taxpayers who subsidize their steelmakers to the tune of up to $60 a ton," Willy Korf, president of the newly formed European Independent Steelworkers Association, said here last week.

"Roughly 70 percent of all European steel enterprises, particularly those in Great Britain, France, Belgium, Luxembourg and Italy are either nationalized or financially dependent on the state," he said.‡

American Metal Market
March 25, 1981

---

*Reprinted with permission of American Metal Market, copyright 1980, Capital Cities/ABC, Inc.
†Reprinted by permission of the *Wall Street Journal,* © Dow Jones & Company, Inc. 1981. All Rights Reserved Worldwide.
‡Reprinted with permission of American Metal Market, copyright 1981, Capital Cities/ABC, Inc.

West German government officials will take up the matter of public steel subsidies with other European heads of state at a summit meeting in Maastricht, the Netherlands, on March 23–24.

A document published by the West German Iron and Steel Federation showed that steelmakers in other countries had been granted or promised aid totalling 60 billion German marks ($28.3 billion) in the 1975–83 period, or an average of about $47 for each metric ton of crude steel production. The average financial assistance worked down to 55 marks ($26) a ton for the French government, 64 marks ($30) for the Italian, 102 marks ($41) for the Belgian, and 185 marks ($87) for the British.*

American Metal Market
March 18, 1981

The generous state aid promised to Hoesch to build a new steel plant in Dortmund has irritated its hard-pressed competitors. Hoesch is to invest some DM550m ($314m) in the project in the next four years and it is getting more than $137m of this in cheap loans—half of each from the West German government and the government of North Rhine-Westphalia.

The terms are indeed favourable. The interest rate on the loans is a mere 4%, instead of the customary 8%. And after three years without having to make repayments Hoesch has been given 15 years in which to pay the money back—at its own pace.†

The Economist
March 1, 1980

IN FRANCE
Agreement has been reached on one of the two stages of the French government's plan for restructuring the special steel industry and an accord on the second stage is likely before the presidential elections in late April, officials at the Industry Ministry said.

In all, the restructuring program is expected to cost the equivalent of $325 million. The French taxpayer will pick up half the tab in the form of state aid to help four steel companies trim excess production capacity and improve productivity.‡

Wall Street Journal
March 18, 1981

Dumping

Dumping is a term used to describe the selling of steel products in the United States by foreign competitors at prices below production costs. This practice is prohibited by U.S. trade laws and is viewed as unfair competition by the

Commerce Department and the U.S. steel industry because many foreign governments own or subsidize their steel industries.

The Trigger Price Mechanism (TPM) was set up by the Commerce Department in 1978 to protect the U.S. steel industry from unfairly priced imports. Trigger prices were based upon the Japanese cost of production because Japan is considered the world's most efficient producer of steel. In effect, the trigger price was the minimum price at which foreign producers could sell their products in this country. Any attempt by foreign producers to sell their products below the floor price automatically resulted in dumping investigations. In January 1982, the Reagan administration discontinued the trigger price system.

According to the American Iron and Steel Institute report entitled *Steel at the Crossroads: One Year Later* (June 1981):

> The American Steel industry supports an open world trade system. Foreign steel should have an opportunity to compete in the American steel market so long as it is fairly traded. The industry has been a supporter of the Tokyo Round Trade Agreement involving more than 100 countries, which reduced tariffs and prompted efforts to remove nontariff barriers.
>
> Domestic steelmakers believe they are the principal low cost producers in the American market. But the U.S., the only major open steel market in the world, cannot ignore the penetration of unfairly traded imports. Heavy flows of such imports cripple the domestic industry and undermine its capability to continue as the principal supplier of steel for this market.
>
> There are no import restrictions on steel traded in the U.S. market in accordance with U.S. trade statutes and with internationally agreed upon trade rules. The Trigger Price Mechanism (TPM) is not a restriction, but rather an administrative procedure for identifying potential violations of U.S. trade law.
>
> U.S. trade law is consistent with international rules established in the Tokyo Round Agreements. These rules have become the international legal basis for expansion of world trade.
>
> The need for the TPM is accentuated by the currently depressed state of the world steel industry, in which more than one-half of the steel produced comes from government-controlled or government-subsidized steel companies. In a depressed world steel market, these producers sell their products at prices below average costs, in order to maintain home employment and obtain foreign exchange.
>
> Unfair steel imports transfer to American steel producers and workers the unemployment and adjustment problems that foreign producers and their governments are seeking to avoid.
>
> Enforcement of U.S. trade law through the TPM is the most effective answer to the problem and is essential to the industry's revitalization program.
>
> Accurate, up-to-date calculations of Japanese costs of steel production—the basis for the TPM—are integral to the success of the entire program. Expeditious use of the import surge provision is also a vital component of the TPM program. Removing products from coverage, failure to audit related party transactions which result in evasion of the system, and granting unjustified preclearances which weaken the TPM should be avoided. If imports take a signif-

icant share of the U.S. market by means of dumping or subsidization, American steel producers will not be able to accomplish their modernization goal.*

Dumping continues to be a problem with which U.S. steelmakers must come to grips. For example, according to the *Wall Street Journal* (October 2, 1981):

> Steel demand is slipping faster now than many in the industry had expected just a month or so ago. But the big worry among domestic producers isn't so much the extent of the decline as it is the share of this sagging market that they will be able to keep.
>
> Increasing their concern is this week's news that imported steel took a record 25% of the U.S. market in August. Although imported steel's market share since April has been above the 15% level tacitly conceded to the foreign mills since April, the magnitude and makeup of the August imports surprised most observers.
>
> August's imports of steel sheet products, for instance, jumped 62% from July levels. Yet domestic demand for these products, used to turn out cars and appliances, has been slack for months. Imports of structural steel shapes, destined for currently lackluster construction markets, rose 49% over the two-month period.
>
> Those figures "suggest that the U.S. steel market is under assault," says Robert R. D. Nickels, a steel economist at Chase Econometrics. Given already sluggish demand, he explains, "every incremental ton of imports just subtracts a ton from U.S. producers."
>
> In past weeks, domestic producers have been scaling back production, bringing the industry's operating rate into the low 70% range, where operating profits are hard to come by. The most recent casualty: Today U.S. Steel Corp. will close down one of two remaining blast furnaces and two openhearth steelmaking furnaces at its Fairless, Pa., works, idling 850 workers.†

European steel manufacturers are not unaware of the problems created when dumping occurs. According to the *Wall Street Journal* (October 13, 1981):

> European steel producers are planning to cut steel exports to the U.S. to avoid a trade battle with the American steel industry.
>
> The move is an apparent response to threats by U.S. steel producers to take legal actions against foreign steelmakers in view of the recent surge in steel imports. American steel producers charge that foreign producers are selling steel at unfairly low prices in the U.S., and that some of them are selling steel products heavily subsidized by their governments.
>
> Here at the annual conference of the International Iron and Steel Institute, U.S. producers aren't losing any opportunity to hand out warnings. Frederick G. Jaicks, chairman of Inland Steel Co. and the new chairman of the institute,

said in his inaugural address yesterday that if foreign steelmakers don't resolve the import problem on their own, U.S. companies will seek remedies under U.S. trade laws "sooner rather than later." On a more threatening note, David M. Roderick, chairman of U.S. Steel Corp., apparently told foreign steel-makers at a closed-door meeting that his company had little choice but to proceed with legal actions, according to some who attended the meeting.*

In November 1981, the Reagan administration announced that it intends to take legal action against steel producers in five foreign countries in an apparent attempt to prevent major U.S. steel firms from instigating massive resistance to steel imports. According to the *Wall Street Journal* (November 6, 1981):

> Commerce Secretary Malcolm Baldrige told the congressional steel caucus that he will file suits against the foreign steelmakers next week, as a signal to foreign producers that the government won't tolerate unfair use of subsidies or price discrimination.
>
> He also indicated that the administration may file a second group of actions later this month, after the department completes its investigation of last summer's "surge" in steel imports. The inquiry was to have been finished by now, but has taken longer than expected.
>
> The administration's move would mark the first time that the government has initiated action against "dumping" of products by foreign concerns, without waiting for U.S. concerns to bring suit. It is apparently designed to blunt, at least temporarily, threatened moves by U.S. steel producers.
>
> Major U.S. steelmakers have been warning they may file massive numbers of cases against leading foreign producers, actions the administration fears could set off a serious dispute between the United States and the European Common Market.*

Poor Financial Performance

Many domestic steel companies are experiencing a vicious cycle of inadequate returns on investment, resulting in an inability to raise capital for modernizing existing facilities or building new facilities, which results in inefficiency, which causes poor profit performance, further reducing return on investment. Furthermore, industry depreciation expenses understate inflation-impacted replacement costs of plant and equipment, which results in overstated earnings and high taxes. Additionally, steel industry cash flow trails industry in general, and government demands for anti-pollution devices to protect the environment have greatly increased operating costs and intensified the problem of low returns on investment because such expenditures do not produce any dollar return.

Thus, many producers in the domestic steel industry are permanently

*Reprinted by permission of the *Wall Street Journal*, © Dow Jones & Company, Inc. 1981. All Rights Reserved Worldwide.

liquidating millions of tons of steel capacity. Rather than investing in new facilities or modernizing existing facilities, many domestic steel producers are investing in non-steel-related products in an attempt to protect themselves through diversification. Ironically, liquidation could result in a shortage of domestic steel capacity by 1985.

Exhibits 1, 2, 3, 4, and 5 present data pertaining to steel imports and apparent steel supply, production and shipments, cash flow, corporate profit rates, and estimated capital expenditures for environmental control facilities, respectively.

Labor and Productivity Issues

Labor costs in the steel industry are higher than labor costs in any other manufacturing industry. This fact exacerbates steel's poor return on investment. Companies in the steel industry must take a large share of the credit for this situation. In order to protect themselves from the disrupting effects of strikes, the ten largest steel producers signed an experimental negotiating agreement that prohibits steel unions from striking in case of bargaining deadlocks and substitutes binding arbitration as the remedy for resolving such deadlocks.

Steel's collective bargaining agreement has produced an unparalleled record of peaceful negotiations—twenty years without a nationwide strike. But the cost of peace in terms of wages has been high. Even though profitability and productivity have been declining for years, the 1980 labor negotiations did not reverse the steel industry trend of paying extremely high wages. Adjusted for inflation, the labor agreement of June 1980 called for a 2.3 percent increase in hourly earnings and a 3.0 percent increase in hourly earnings, benefits, and social security combined. As wages have increased, however, industry employment has declined. In 1970, there were 531,000 employees in the steel industry, but by 1980 there were only 399,000.

Exhibit 6 presents data on hourly employment costs and average hourly earnings for the steel industry. Additionally, it shows increases in both statistics in relation to the Bureau of Labor Statistics' Consumer Price Index (Base Year 1961). Exhibit 7 presents statistical highlights for the U.S. Iron and Steel Industry from 1970 to 1980.

The United States Government

The government until recently has been unsympathetic about steel industry complaints of excessive pollution regulation and unfair imports. However, the government has had to change its position because the industry's plight

EXHIBIT 1

Imports and Apparent Steel Supply (Million Net Tons)

YEAR	TOTAL IMPORTS	APPARENT STEEL SUPPLY*	IMPORTS AS PERCENTAGE OF APPARENT STEEL SUPPLY
1970	13.4	97.1	13.8%
1971	18.3	102.5	17.9
1972	17.7	106.6	16.6
1973	15.1	122.5	12.4
1974	16.0	119.6	13.4
1975	12.0	89.0	13.5
1976	14.3	101.1	14.1
1977	19.3	108.5	17.8
1978	21.1	116.6	18.1
1979	17.5	115.0	15.2
1980	15.5	95.2	16.3

SOURCE: American Iron and Steel Institute. Reprinted with permission.
*Shipments from domestic mills plus imports minus exports.

EXHIBIT 2

Production and Shipments (Million Net Tons)

YEAR	RAW STEEL		STEEL SHIPMENTS
	PRODUCTION	PERCENT OF CAPABILITY*	
1970	131.5	N/A	90.8
1971	120.4	N/A	87.0
1972	133.2	N/A	91.8
1973	150.8	N/A	111.4
1974	145.7	N/A	109.5
1975	116.6	76.2%	80.0
1976	128.0	80.9	89.4
1977	125.3	78.4	91.1
1978	137.0	86.8	97.9
1979	136.3	87.8	100.3
1980	111.8	72.8	83.9

SOURCE: American Iron and Steel Institute. Reprinted with permission.
*Raw steel output as a percent of tonnage capability to produce raw steel for a sustained full order book. Not published prior to 1975.

EXHIBIT 3   Cash Flow Data (Millions of Dollars)

	PROFITS AFTER TAXES	DEPRECIATION, DEPLETION, ETC.*	GROSS CASH FLOW	CASH DIVIDENDS	NET INTERNAL SOURCES	CAPITAL EXPENDITURES	EXCESS (+) OR DEFICIT (−) NET INTERNAL SOURCES OVER CAPITAL EXPEND.	CHANGE IN LONG-TERM DEBT	CAPITAL EXPENDITURES AS A PERCENT OF NET INTERNAL SOURCES
1964	$ 992	$1,046	$2,038	$462	$1,576	$1,600	− $ 24	+ $ 179	101.5%
1965	1,069	1,117	2,186	468	1,718	1,823	− 105	+ 245	106.1
1966	1,075	1,199	2,274	483	1,791	1,953	− 162	+ 659	109.0
1967	830	1,444	2,274	481	1,793	2,146	− 353	+ 423	119.7
1968	992	1,316	2,308	452	1,856	2,307	− 451	+ 396	124.3
1969	879	1,173	2,052	489	1,563	2,047	− 484	+ 7	131.0
1970	532	1,128	1,660	488	1,172	1,736	− 564	+ 526	148.1
1971	563	1,123	1,686	390	1,296	1,425	− 129	+ 10	110.0
1972	775	1,216	1,991	402	1,589	1,174	+ 415	+ 85	73.9
1973	1,272	1,329	2,601	443	2,158	1,400	+ 758	+ 267	64.9
1974	2,475	1,553	4,028	674	3,354	2,115	+ 1,239	− 312	63.1
1975	1,595	1,591	3,186	658	2,528	3,179	− 651	− 1,054	125.8
1976	1,337	1,614	2,951	637	2,314	3,253	− 939	+ 1,262	140.6
1977	22	1,888	1,910	555	1,355	2,850	− 1,495	+ 992	210.3
1978	1,277	1,968	3,245	536	2,709	2,595	+ 114	+ 804	95.8
1979	1,154	2,453	3,607	593	3,014	3,312	− 298	− 46	109.9
1980	1,632	2,235	3,867	602	3,265	3,319	− 54	+ 659	101.7

SOURCE: American Iron and Steel Institute (for those companies reporting financial information). Reprinted with permission.

*Includes changes in reserves.

EXHIBIT 4   **Corporate Profit Rates: Steel Versus All Manufacturing Average**

| | STEEL COMPANY PROFITS AFTER TAXES (MILLIONS OF DOLLARS) | STEEL COMPANY PROFITS AFTER TAXES AS A PERCENT OF REVENUES | PROFITS AFTER TAXES AS A PERCENT OF STOCKHOLDERS' EQUITY* | |
			STEEL COMPANIES	ALL MANUFACTURING
1964	992	6.1%	9.0%	12.6%
1965	1,069	5.9	9.4	13.9
1966	1,075	5.9	8.9	14.2
1967	830	4.9	6.9	12.6
1968	992	5.3	8.2	13.3
1969	879	4.6	7.0	12.4
1970	532	2.8	4.1	10.1
1971	563	2.8	4.3	10.8
1972	775	3.4	5.8	12.1
1973	1,272	4.4	9.3	14.9
1974	2,475	6.5	17.1	15.2
1975	1,595	4.7	9.8	12.6
1976	1,337	3.7	7.8	15.0
1977	22	0.1	0.1	14.9
1978	1,277	2.6	7.3	15.9
1979	1,154	2.1	6.7	18.4
1980	1,632	3.0	9.0	16.6

SOURCES: American Iron and Steel Institute. Reprinted with permission.

*Based on equity at beginning of year.

has become so acute. William J. DeLancey of Republic Steel characterized the change in the following way:

> We can now be confident of moving into the eighties with the assurance of receiving a congressional audience which will give sympathetic attention to proposals aimed at strengthening the steel industry and making it healthy for the years ahead . . . It would be unrealistic to fail to recognize that in the area which has been the ultimate source of most of our problems, namely the federal establishment, there has been a positive change from apathy at best toward better understanding and, in some areas, support.

The two best examples of the improved relationship with the government are the Carter administration's expressed desire to establish a policy which addresses the problems of the industry and the establishment of a Steel Tri-

EXHIBIT 5   **Estimated Capital Expenditures for Environmental Control Facilities* (Millions of Dollars)**

YEAR FACILITIES BEGAN OPERATIONS	FOR WATER IMPROVEMENT	FOR AIR IMPROVEMENT	TOTAL
1951–1965	$ 209.6	$ 238.8	$ 448.4
1966	18.8	37.7	56.5
1967	54.7	39.4	94.1
1968	61.5	40.2	101.7
1969	71.0	67.1	138.1
1970	110.0	72.6	182.6
1971	73.4	88.2	161.6
1972	57.0	144.8	201.8
1973	34.7	65.4	100.1
1974	79.4	119.4	198.8
1975	131.8	321.3	453.1
1976	158.7	330.5	489.2
1977	205.7	329.1	534.8
1978	180.8	277.2	458.0
1979	201.2	449.6	650.8
1980	168.2	342.3	510.5
Total 1951–1980**	1,879.6	3,015.0	4,894.6
Authorized for 1981 and later	219.7	641.1	860.8

SOURCE: American Iron and Steel Institute. Reprinted with permission.

*Between 1951 and 1974 capital expenditures were for facilities placed in operation. Effective 1975, the data represents actual capital expenditures made during the year.

**Includes capital expenditures in years prior to 1975 for facilities not placed in operation as of January 1, 1975: $63.1 million for water, $51.4 million for air, $114.5 million in total.

partite Committee with labor, steel, and government representatives, dedicated to the formulation of a National Steel Policy.

According to *Steel at the Crossroads: One Year Later* (June, 1981):

> Numerous studies have since supported the steel industry's position and have made policy recommendations virtually identical with those of the industry. For example, the study of the OTA concluded, "A well-defined and vigorously implemented government policy has nurtured the Japanese steel industry's expansion and adoption of new technology. The U.S. steel industry, on the other hand, has been hurt by a long series of federal government policies that have frequently been uncoordinated, contradictory, and inattentive to critical issues."

EXHIBIT 6   Hourly Employment Costs and Average Hourly Earnings in the
Iron and Steel Industry

YEAR	CONSUMER PRICE INDEX ON 1961 100	AVERAGE HOURLY EARNINGS PER HOUR— INDEX 1961		EMPLOYMENT COSTS PER HOUR—INDEX 1961	
		ACTUAL	100	ACTUAL	100
1961	100.0	$ 3.20	100.0	$ 3.989	100.0
1962	101.1	3.29	102.8	4.155	104.2
1963	102.3	3.36	105.0	4.247	106.5
1964	103.7	3.41	106.6	4.355	109.2
1965	105.5	3.46	108.1	4.475	112.2
1966	108.5	3.58	111.9	4.633	116.1
1967	111.6	3.62	113.1	4.758	119.3
1968	116.3	3.82	119.4	5.032	126.1
1969	122.5	4.09	127.8	5.375	134.7
1970	129.8	4.22	131.9	5.677	142.3
1971	135.4	4.57	142.8	6.261	157.0
1972	139.8	5.15	160.9	7.075	177.4
1973	148.5	5.56	173.8	7.681	192.6
1974	164.8	6.38	199.4	9.078	227.6
1975	179.9	7.11	222.2	10.590	265.5
1976	190.3	7.86	245.6	11.744	294.4
1977	202.6	8.67	270.9	13.036	326.8
1978	218.0	9.70	303.1	14.303	358.6
1979	243.0	10.77	336.6	15.921	399.1
1980	275.7	11.84	370.0	18.451	462.5

Similarly, the GAO report said, "On the whole, both general and specific Government policy has not been consistently responsive to requirements for modernization. At times, it worked directly against modernization, as through the application of environmental regulations making it needlessly difficult for the industry to replace polluting old plant with cleaner, new plant. Each of the Federal policy decisions affecting the industry was framed with its own purpose in mind; no effort was made to assess their total impact on the industry's health."

Further, the Steel Tripartite Committee prepared a detailed examination of policy combinations which could cover the industry's capital short-fall (faster capital recovery and refundability, faster capital recovery and reduced capital expenditures, etc.) and then argued, "A piecemeal approach to the steel

EXHIBIT 7   Statistical Highlights—U.S. Iron and Steel Industry

	1980	1979	1978	1977	1976	1975	1974	1973	1972	1971	1970
PRODUCTION (MILLIONS OF NET TONS)											
Total U.S. pig iron	68.7	87.0	87.7	81.3	86.9	79.9	95.9	100.8	88.9	81.3	91.4
Total U.S. raw steel	111.8	136.3	137.0	125.3	128.0	116.6	145.7	150.8	133.2	120.4	131.5
Open hearth	13.0	19.2	21.3	20.0	23.5	22.1	35.5	39.8	34.9	35.6	48.0
Basic oxygen	67.6	83.2	83.5	77.4	79.9	71.8	81.6	83.3	74.6	63.9	63.3
Electric	31.2	33.9	32.2	27.9	24.6	22.7	28.7	27.7	23.7	20.9	20.2
Total Canadian raw steel	17.5	17.7	16.4	15.0	14.6	14.4	15.0	14.8	13.1	12.0	12.3
Total world raw steel	792.1	824.5	790.6	741.8	745.6	712.0	782.8	768.6	694.5	639.9	654.2
SHIPMENTS (MILLIONS OF NET TONS)											
Total steel mill products	83.9	100.3	97.9	91.1	89.4	80.0	109.5	111.4	91.8	87.0	90.8
Carbon	73.4	87.9	86.2	81.2	80.3	70.8	98.0	100.9	83.2	79.3	83.2
Alloy	9.4	11.0	10.5	8.8	8.1	8.4	10.2	9.4	7.8	7.0	6.9
Stainless	1.1	1.4	1.2	1.1	1.0	.8	1.3	1.1	.8	.7	.7
SHIPMENTS, MAJOR PRODUCTS, ALL GRADES (MILLIONS OF NET TONS)											
Shapes, plates, and piling	13.3	14.6	13.6	11.9	11.3	13.9	18.1	16.8	13.2	13.6	14.1
Bars and tool steel	13.3	17.6	16.9	15.4	14.2	13.4	18.5	18.2	15.5	14.2	14.6
Pipe and tubing	9.1	8.2	8.4	7.5	6.3	8.2	9.8	9.1	7.6	7.6	7.8
Wire and wire products	1.8	2.4	2.5	2.4	2.5	2.2	3.2	3.2	3.0	2.8	3.0
Tin mill products	5.7	6.3	6.1	6.4	6.4	5.7	7.5	7.3	6.1	6.8	7.2
Sheets and strip	33.6	43.5	43.6	41.7	42.3	30.8	45.0	49.4	39.9	35.6	35.1
SHIPMENTS, MAJOR MARKETS (MILLIONS OF NET TONS)											
Automotive	12.1	18.6	21.3	21.5	21.4	15.2	18.9	23.2	18.2	17.5	14.5
Steel service centers	16.2	18.2	17.3	15.3	14.6	12.7	20.4	20.4	16.8	14.4	16.0
Construction and contractor's products	11.9	13.7	13.1	12.1	12.0	12.0	17.6	17.2	13.6	13.6	13.4
Containers and packaging	5.6	6.8	6.6	6.7	6.9	6.1	8.2	7.8	6.6	7.2	7.8
Industrial and electrical machinery and equipment	7.0	8.8	8.8	8.2	7.9	7.3	9.7	9.7	8.2	7.5	7.9
EMPLOYMENT											
Average number of employees (thousands)	399	453	449	452	454	457	512	509	478	487	531

Annual wages and salaries (billions)	$10.9	$11.5	$10.3	$9.2	$8.3	$7.9	$7.9	$6.8	$5.8	$5.2	$5.2
Total employment cost/hr. worked (hrly. employees)	$18.45	$15.92	$14.30	$13.04	$11.74	$10.59	$9.08	$7.68	$7.08	$6.26	$5.68
FINANCIAL											
Net assets (billions)	$33.0	$31.0*	$30.1	$28.7	$27.4	$25.1	$22.8	$21.2	$20.5	$20.0	$19.7
Total revenue (billions)	$55.0	$55.7*	$49.5	$39.7	$36.5	$33.7	$38.2	$28.9	$22.6	$20.4	$19.3
Net income (millions)	$1,632	$1,154*	$1,277	$22**	$1,337	$1,595	$2,475	$1,272	$775	$562	$531
Long-term debt (billions)	$9.4	$8.7*	$8.8	$8.0	$7.0	$5.7	$4.7	$5.0	$5.2	5.1	5.1
Capital expenditures (billions)	$3.3	$3.3*	$2.6	$2.9	$3.3	$3.2	$2.1	$1.4	$1.2	$1.4	$1.7
Total dividends paid (millions)	$602	$593*	$536	$555	$637	$658	$674	$443	$402	$390	$487
Profit per dollar of sales	3.0¢	2.1¢	2.6¢	0.06¢**	3.7¢	4.8¢	6.6¢	4.5¢	3.5¢	2.8¢	2.8¢
Percent return on stockholders' equity†	9.0%	6.7%*	7.3%	0.1%**	7.8%	9.8%	17.1%	9.3%	5.8%	4.3%	4.1%
Debt/equity ratio	49.0	48.3*	49.5	45.5	38.9	33.1	29.0	34.5	38.0	38.3	39.2
CAPITAL EXPENDITURES FOR AIR AND WATER QUALITY CONTROL											
Capital expenditures (millions)	$510.5	$650.8	$458.0	$534.8	$489.2	$453.1	$267.2	$100.1	$201.8	$161.6	$182.6
Water (millions)	$168.2	$201.2	$180.8	$205.7	$158.7	$131.8	$106.9	$34.7	$57.0	$73.4	$110.0
Air (millions)	$342.3	$449.6	$277.2	$329.1	$330.5	$321.3	$160.3	$65.4	$144.8	$88.2	$72.6
FOREIGN TRADE (MILLIONS OF NET TONS)											
Imports, all steel mill products	15.5	17.5	21.1	19.3	14.3	12.0	16.0	15.1	17.7	18.3	13.4
Carbon	14.8	16.6	20.2	18.5	13.6	11.4	15.4	14.6	17.1	17.7	12.9
Alloy	.559	.728	.753	.580	.483	.448	.413	.434	.448	.415	.349
Stainless	.153	.169	.200	.178	.175	.167	.176	.128	.149	.192	.177
Dollar value (billions)	$6.9	$7.0	$6.9	$5.5	$4.0	$4.1	$5.1	$2.8	$2.8	$2.6	$2.0
Market penetration *(percentage)*	16.3	15.2	18.1	17.8	14.1	13.5	13.4	12.4	16.6	17.9	13.8
Exports, all steel mill products	4.1	2.8	2.4	2.0	2.7	3.0	5.8	4.1	2.9	2.8	7.1
Dollar value (millions)	$2,557	$1,878	$1,329	$1,037	$1,255	$1,862	$2,118	$1,004	$604	$576	$1,019

SOURCE: American Iron and Steel Institute. Reprinted with permission.

*Revised figure.

**Reflects substantial impact of permanent plant closings.

†As of January 1 of each year.

industry will accomplish little. The problems of the industry cover a number of areas including capital formation, trade, environmental regulation, technology, and the adjustment of workers and communities to changes in industry conditions. Progress in any one of these areas depends upon progress in others. With or without Government assistance, measures directed only at one of these areas cannot set the industry on a new path. A coordinated and integrated set of initiatives, maintained for a three to five year period, or longer, is required to remedy the industry's situation."

Finally, the GAO report summing up OTA's, the Tripartite Committee's, and its own views, said, "Our overall conclusions parallel those of both the Office of Technology Assessment (*Technology and Steel Industry Competitiveness:* 1980) and the Steel Tripartite Committee, which served as the basis for the Administration's latest program proposals. We also agree on priority policy action areas for industry revitalization. These include: assistance with capital formation to promote modernization investment; an effective trade policy to insure reasonable control of steel imports; and, increased flexibility in administering environmental laws."*

KEY EXECUTIVES AT WHEELING-PITTSBURGH

Dennis J. Carney, Chairman and Chief Officer

Carney, 60, was elected chairman of the board on January 25, 1978. He had served as president and chief operating officer of Wheeling-Pittsburgh since March 1, 1976.

Following his retirement from U.S. Steel after 32 years, where he was elected vice-president, long-range planning in 1965 and vice president, research in 1972, he joined Wheeling-Pittsburgh as vice president, operations.

Educated at the University of Pennsylvania, Harvard, and MIT, Carney became widely known for his many technical papers on metallurgy and iron and steel manufacturing.

In March 1978, Carney was awarded the Benjamin F. Fairless Award for distinguished achievement in iron and steel production and ferrous metallurgy by the American Institute of Mining, Metallurgical and Petroleum Engineers. In 1979, Carney was awarded a Distinguished Life Membership by the American Society for Metals for outstanding contributions to the advancement of the metal industry.

Robert F. Good, Vice President, Commercial

Good is responsible for Wheeling-Pittsburgh Steel's sales and marketing activities and coordination of commercial policies of subsidiary divisions.

Good served four years with the U.S. Air Force during World War II.

*American Iron and Steel Institute. *Steel at the Crossroads: One Year Later* (June 1981). Reprinted with permission.

Following his discharge with the rank of captain, he attended the University of Pittsburgh, graduating in 1949 to join Jones and Laughlin Steel.

In 30 years of service with Jones and Laughlin Steel Corporation, Good advanced through various sales positions to become vice president, sales in 1973. He retired in 1979 at which time he became engaged as a management consultant.

John C. Frueh, Senior Vice President and Chief Financial Officer

Frueh, 46, has eighteen years of executive experience in corporate finance and served since 1979 as executive vice president of CENTEX Corporation in Dallas.

He began his career in 1962 as manager, systems and procedures for PPG Industries in Milwaukee. Subsequently, he held positions as treasurer-controller, international for the A. O. Smith Corporation in Milwaukee; vice president-corporate controller of Avis Industrial Corporation in Detroit; and assistant corporate controller of Monsanto Company in St. Louis. In 1974, he was elected vice president-chief financial officer and director of Globe-Union, Inc., in Milwaukee, and in 1979, he was elected executive vice president of CENTEX Corporation.

Frueh is a graduate of Kalamazoo College and holds an M.B.A. awarded in 1958 by the University of Michigan. From 1958 until 1962 he served with the U.S. Army in Europe.

Thomas D. Moore, Executive Vice President

Moore, with 29 years of experience in steelmaking and finishing operations, last served as general manager of quality control for Jones and Laughlin Steel Corporation.

He began his career in 1951 at the Gary (Ind.) Works of U.S. Steel Corp., where he was a metallurgical observer. On graduation from Purdue University in 1957 with a degree in metallurgical engineering, he joined Armco Steel Corp. at Middletown, Ohio, where he served as a practice engineer, special assignments in the open hearth department.

He joined Inland Steel Co. in 1962 in the open hearth department, and in 1965 became assistant superintendent of Inland's No. 4 basic oxygen furnace and later he was appointed superintendent of No. 4 BOF and slab caster.

Moore joined Youngstown Sheet and Tube Co. in 1973 as assistant district manager, Indiana Harbor Works. In 1979 he was appointed general manager, flat roll, Western Division of Jones and Laughlin, with responsibility for flat roll steel operations at both the Indiana Harbor and the Hennepin, Ill., Works. A year later he became general manager of quality control.

In addition to his metallurgical degree, Moore holds an M.B.A. from Miami University, Oxford, Ohio. He was the recipient in 1961 of the

McKune Award of the American Institute of Metallurgical Engineers (AIME) for a research paper on open hearth furnace control.

INTERNAL OPERATIONS AT WHEELING-PITTSBURGH

Raw Materials

Wheeling-Pittsburgh owns or has a significant ownership interest in six large iron-ore-producing operations. These operations, located in Minnesota, Michigan, and Canada supplied 93 percent of W-P's iron-ore needs of 3,796,000 tons in 1979.

The corporation also owns or has a signficant ownership interest in four coal-mining operations in Pennsylvania, West Virginia, and Kentucky. Approximately 75 percent of Wheeling-Pittsburgh's coal requirements in 1979 were supplied by companies in which it has a significant ownership interest.

Coal and iron-ore needs not met by company interests are satisfied by open market purchases. The corporation's requirements of zinc, manganese, pig tin, limestone, and other raw materials needed to produce steel are purchased from other companies.

Exhibit 8 lists W-P's subsidiaries.

PRODUCTS AND MARKETS

W-P has two major steel-producing plants: the Steubenville plant headquartered in Steubenville, Ohio, and the Monessen plant headquartered in Monessen, Pennsylvania. Both plants produce raw steel ingots that are processed into "hot rolled" steel bands. The steel bands are either processed into rolled sheet steel for sale to steel users or they are processed into finished steel products by W-P.

Exhibit 9 presents the contributions to W-P's sales revenues by classes of similar products; Exhibit 10 shows W-P's shipments (net tons) by product class; Exhibit 11 shows W-P's shipments (net tons) by major market classification; and Exhibit 12 shows W-P's principal markets and the major market classification to which respective classes of products were sold, based upon shipments (net tons).

FINANCIAL MATTERS AT WHEELING-PITTSBURGH

Exhibits 13, 14, and 15 show W-P's per-share data, income data, and balance sheet data, respectively.

EXHIBIT 8   ## Wheeling-Pittsburgh's Subsidiaries

W-P does not have a parent. The subsidiaries of the corporation, all included in the consolidated financial statements, and the percentage of their voting securities owned by the corporation are as follows:

NAME	STATE OF INCORPORATION	PERCENTAGE OF VOTING SECURITIES OWNED BY W-P AT DECEMBER 31, 1979
Consumers Mining Company (2)	Pennsylvania	100%
Ft. Duquesne Coal Company	Kentucky	100
W-P Coal Company (2)	West Virginia	100
Daly Gas Company (1)	Pennsylvania	100
Harmar Coal Company	Pennsylvania	75
Mingo Oxygen Company	Ohio	100
Monessen Southwestern Railway Company	Pennsylvania	100
National Steel Fabric Company (1)	Pennsylvania	100
Pittsburgh-Canfield Corporation	Pennsylvania	100
Pittsburgh Steel Sales Company (1)	Pennsylvania	100
Standard Land and Improvement Company (1)	Pennsylvania	100
Three Rivers Coal Company (2)	West Virginia	100
Wheeling-Pittsburgh Trading Company	Delaware	100
Wheeling-Itasca Co.	Delaware	100

(1) Inactive.
(2) Consumers Mining Company owns 100% of the outstanding stock of W-P Coal Company and Three Rivers Coal Company.

The corporation also owns a substantial percentage, but in each case no more than 40 percent, of voting stock of each of eight other corporations or partnerships engaged in the mining or beneficiation of iron ore or the holding of iron ore reserve properties, and owns various percentages, but in each case not more than 40 percent, of the voting stocks of certain other corporations. These corporations have been omitted because, considered in the aggregate as a single subsidiary, they have not been considered to constitute a significant subsidiary.

EXHIBIT 9

Contributions to Sales Revenues

PRODUCTS	1979	1978	1977	1976	1975
Hot and cold rolled sheet and strip	43.3%	42.8%	45.0%	44.1%	35.6%
Tin mill	13.2	13.4	12.2	13.4	13.2
Coated sheet	12.4	10.8	11.1	11.2	9.9
Fabricated	13.3	12.2	13.1	11.8	12.2
Seamless tubular	8.1	10.8	9.6	8.6	15.1
Welded tubular	5.8	7.0	6.5	5.5	7.8
Other	3.9	3.0	2.5	5.4	6.2
	100.0%	100.0%	100.0%	100.0%	100.0%

EXHIBIT 10

Shipments (Net Tons) by Product Class

PRODUCTS	1979	1978	1977	1976	1975
Hot and cold rolled sheet and strip	56.4%	56.1%	59.0%	58.6%	51.7%
Tin mill	11.5	12.0	10.8	11.6	12.2
Coated sheet	11.5	9.8	9.9	10.3	9.6
Fabricated	9.2	8.5	8.9	7.9	8.3
Seamless tubular	4.2	5.6	5.1	4.4	7.8
Welded tubular	4.9	5.5	5.1	4.2	6.2
Other	2.3	2.5	1.2	3.0	4.2
	100.0%	100.0%	100.0%	100.0%	100.0%

EXHIBIT 11

Shipments (Net Tons) by Major Market Classification

MARKET CLASSIFICATION	1979	1978	1977	1976	1975
Automotive	16%	19%	23%	24%	20%
Service center	19	19	21	21	19
Construction	16	15	15	12	12
Converting and processing	12	14	12	13	16
Containers	12	11	9	11	11
Appliances	8	8	8	9	8
Oil and gas	4	6	5	3	5
Miscellaneous	13	8	7	7	9
	100%	100%	100%	100%	100%

EXHIBIT 12   **Principal Markets and Major Market Classifications to Which Respective Classes of Products Were Sold, Based upon Shipments (Net Tons)**

PRODUCTS	AUTOMOTIVE		CONSTRUCTION		CONTAINERS		APPLIANCES		OIL AND GAS		MISC.	
	1979	1978	1979	1978	1979	1978	1979	1978	1979	1978	1979	1978
Hot and cold rolled sheet and strip	23%	26%	7%	6%	7%	5%	12%	10%	—%	%	10%	8%
Tin mill	7	7	3	5	64	62	7	6	—	—	5	2
Coated sheet	20	15	23	16	1	—	7	4	—	—	11	7
Fabricated	—	—	93	93	—	—	3	3	—	—	—	—
Seamless tubular	3	7	3	4	—	—	—	—	70	77	11	3
Welded tubular	—	—	22	15	—	—	2	1	6	6	25	26
Other	7	3	—	—	—	—	—	—	—	—	80	79
Total products	16	19	16	15	12	11	8	8	4	6	13	8

EXHIBIT 13   **Per Share Data (Dollars)**

YEAR ENDED DEC. 31	1980	1979	1978	1977	1976	1975	1974	1973	1972	1971
Book value	90.75	88.80	79.00	75.12	83.56	84.06	85.68	79.38	74.96	71.46
Earnings	2.85	12.16	4.23	d7.70	0.05	d0.68	19.23	4.10	2.78	0.42
Dividends	Nil	1.00	Nil	Nil	Nil	1.05	0.35	Nil	Nil	Nil
Payout ratio	Nil	8%	Nil	Nil	Nil	NM	4%	Nil	Nil	Nil
Prices—High	24	24¾	14¼	20	23⅞	31⅞	23¼	21⅝	24¼	20½
Low	15	10⅝	8	8½	16	14⅛	13¼	10¼	15⅝	11½
P/E Ratio—	8–5	2–1	3–2	NM	NM	NM	1–1	5–3	9–6	49–27

SOURCE: *Standard & Poor's Stock Reports*, 1981. Copyright 1990 Standard & Poor's Corporation.

NEW PRODUCT DEVELOPMENT

Wheeling-Pittsburgh has completed construction of the world's most modern railroad rail mill at their Monessen location. It cost Wheeling-Pittsburgh approximately $105 million. Rail production will diversify the Wheeling-Pittsburgh product mix, and the company predicts that 12 percent of their total yearly shipments will come from rail production once the new plant is fully on line. Furthermore, W-P officials state that the production from the rail mill will relieve the critical shortage of quality railroad tracks in the United States today.

Currently C. F. & I. Steel's rail facility in Pueblo, Colorado, is the most modern rail mill in the United States. But aside from that plant, which supplies western rail needs, the eastern railmaking operations of Bethlehem and U.S. Steel were built in the early 1900s. Rail products of the older mills were suitable when trains carried lighter loads and traveled at slower speeds, but they cannot stand up under the constant pressure they get from faster and heavier trains. Domestic railroad companies have for years been demanding longer and stronger rails that stand up better, but they have been forced to rely on foreign railmakers to obtain quality rails.

Prior to entering the rail market, W-P conducted in-depth studies and held discussions with major domestic railroads. Based on their research, it was concluded that domestic demand was sufficient to justify building a new rail mill. The new mill is an ultramodern design using the latest in French and Japanese technology.

In December 1978, one year after President Carter announced his Inter-Agency Task Force on Steel, W-P took advantage of one of the task force's recommendations. They announced that they had obtained tentative federal loan guarantees and an EPA consent decree that included agreements with

EXHIBIT 14   Income Data (Millions of Dollars)

YEAR ENDED DEC. 31	REVS.	OPER. INC.	% OPER. INC. OF REVS.	CAP. EXP.	DEPR.	INT. EXP.	NET BEF. TAXES	EFF. TAX RATE	NET INC.	% NET INC. OF REVS.
1980	1,054	14	1.4%	147	39.1	22.9	9	NM	14.7	1.4%
1979	1,242	100	8.0%	54	35.7	18.4	60	16.7%	49.7	4.0%
1978	1,155	67	5.8%	32	34.5	15.5	23	18.8%	19.0	1.6%
1977	966	9	0.9%	45	34.7	14.5	d33	NM	d25.6	NM
1976	931	41	4.4%	51	31.8	12.3	1	NM	3.2	0.3%
1975	827	34	4.1%	61	30.3	12.8	Nil	NM	0.6	0.1%
1974	1,037	138	13.3%	54	28.5	10.4	105	30.4%	73.4	7.1%
1973	761	64	8.4%	28	30.1	10.2	26	30.8%	18.1	2.4%
1972	608	58	9.5%	22	29.9	9.7	20	35.0%	13.2	2.2%
1971	528	41	7.7%	18	29.4	9.7	6	19.2%	4.6	0.9%

SOURCE: *Standard & Poor's Stock Report*, 1981. Copyright 1990 Standard & Poor's Corporation.

EXHIBIT 15   **Balance Sheet Data (Millions of Dollars)**

| DEC. 31 | CASH | CURRENT | | | TOTAL ASSETS | RET. ON ASSETS | LONG-TERM DEBT | COMMON EQUITY | TOTAL CAP. | % LT DEBT OF CAP. | RET. ON EQUITY |
		ASSETS	LIAB.	RATIO							
1980	101	395	238	1.7	983	1.6%	280	353	717	39.0%	3.2%
1979	74	374	235	1.6	847	6.0%	170	341	593	28.6%	14.3%
1978	51	345	211	1.6	793	2.4%	189	298	561	33.7%	5.5%
1977	39	309	184	1.7	766	NM	209	282	562	37.2%	NM
1976	37	277	146	1.9	728	0.5%	183	310	561	32.6%	0.1%
1975	49	258	116	2.2	676	0.1%	160	309	536	29.8%	NM
1974	81	347	199	1.7	722	10.6%	113	314	495	22.8%	23.3%
1973	31	313	134	2.3	661	2.7%	140	290	498	28.2%	5.3%
1972	23	315	139	2.3	666	2.1%	155	274	495	31.2%	3.8%
1971	23	258	113	2.3	611	0.7%	138	260	465	29.7%	0.6%

SOURCE: *Standard & Poor's Stock Report*, 1981. Copyright 1990 Standard & Poor's Corporation.

state environmental agencies in West Virginia, Pennsylvania, and Ohio. In March 1979, the Pennsylvania Industrial Development Authority approved a $10 million loan to Wheeling-Pittsburgh. The loan is to be repaid over twenty years and the interest rate is 4 percent. The company also signed an EPA consent decree setting up a timetable for instituting environmental controls. The state loan and the consent decree cleared the way for loan guarantees by the Economic Development Administration (EDA) and the Farmers Home Administration of $100 million and 90 percent of $50 million, respectively. The loan guaranteed by the EDA is to be repaid over twenty years, and the loan guaranteed by the FHA is to be repaid over fifteen years. The interest rate on both loans is 11 percent. In the same month, Wheeling-Pittsburgh signed agreements for the purchase of up-to-date rail mill technology and equipment from Japanese and French producers.

W-P's government guaranteed loans have caused much controversy and anger within the U.S. steel industry. Bethlehem Steel, U.S. Steel, and C. F. & I. Steel Corporation have argued that the use of guarantees in this way was improper. The three companies claimed that the program is not intended for and should not be used to finance new product development and plant expansion.

In August 1979, the loan agreement with the federal agencies was signed. C. F. & I. Steel Corporation immediately filed suit in federal court to stop the loan agreement. C. F. & I., which had just started an expansion of rail capacity using private funds, argued that the government should not finance a large company's move into a new product line. T. J. Slater, president of C. F. & I., stated:

> . . . the decision to support Wheeling-Pittsburgh's entry into the rail business is "totally illogical" and is apt to create excess capacity in a presently healthy segment of the steel industry. Such decisions only serve to dry up sources of private risk capital available.

While C. F. & I. is concerned about the impact this action will have on future financing alternatives available to steel producers, they and other steel companies purport to perceive it as the first step toward nationalization of the steel industry. Bethlehem Steel's chairman, Lewis W. Fry, had this to say:

> We are distressed by the government's decision to use tax dollars to permit Wheeling-Pittsburgh to diversify its product lines. We believe the decision by two federal agencies to help a private company finance a new steel facility in the Greater Pittsburgh area violates the basic principles of our free enterprise system.

Wheeling-Pittsburgh does not agree with their competitors. They have said that the loan guarantees are just that—guarantees. W-P's management believes there is no question that they can and will be able to repay the loans when they are due. Additionally, they believe the controversy represents an attempt by the companies who currently produce railroad tracks to protect their market position. Wheeling-Pittsburgh's chairman, Dennis J. Carney, has stated:

> Three major producers have had a corner of the market for rails in this country for over 50 years. No new rail mills have been built in this country since the early 1900s . . . the real fact is that they don't want competition in rails, either domestic or foreign.

In May 1980, with legal proceedings still pending in federal court, Wheeling-Pittsburgh reached agreement with nine institutional lenders on a loan structure with the above-mentioned federal guarantees. The package furnished $160 million in funds. These loans along with $38 million raised privately were slated (1) to cover $86.5 million worth of pollution control equipment under the EPA consent decree and (2) to finance the nation's newest rail mill, worth $105 million.

THE FUTURE

The future of the steel industry in the United States is uncertain at present. Besides the problems mentioned in this case, some economists believe that steel production will shift from developed, industrial nations to less developed, Third World nations. For example John Kenneth Galbraith has said:

> What will be the major anxieties ten years hence? Some kind of rapport will have been established on incomes and prices and the regulation of public and private expenditure so that inflation will not be the primary problem. In Europe there will be much concern over regularizing the role of the mass of foreign workers. No one should imagine that they can be kept forever as a special subproletariat. All the older countries will be reconciled to the departure of the simple, tedious industries to the more competent countries of the Third World. Steel, heavy chemicals, tires, ordinary textiles, shipbuilding, will be gone. (Steel is aready in deep trouble in the United States, France, Britain, and the old districts of Belgium.) The older industrial countries will still have computers, aircraft, missiles, and other advanced weapons of mass destruction. And, if they survive their excellence in latter, they will have anything else requiring good or original design.[1]

NOTES

1. J. K. Galbraith, *Annals of an Abiding Liberal* (Boston: Houghton Mifflin Company), as quoted in G. Starling, *The Changing Environment of Business* (Boston: Kent Publishing Company, 1980), p. 297.

CASE 17

Wheeling-Pittsburgh Steel Company (B)

NEIL H. SNYDER · DEBORAH ALBRO · EILEEN GORDON
CONNIE LETT · MARTHA PARKER · SUSAN PENDERGAST

INTRODUCTION

On December 5, 1968, Wheeling Steel Corporation merged with Pittsburgh Steel Company to form Wheeling-Pittsburgh Steel Company (W-P). W-P is engaged in the manufacturing, processing, and fabricating of steel and steel products. Exhibits 1 through 4 contain pertinent information about W-P's products. The firm is currently the seventh largest integrated steel company in the United States. W-P has eleven operating plants and fourteen subsidiaries. Exhibits 5 and 6 show the location of W-P's plants and its subsidiary companies, respectively.

HEADING FOR A CRISIS

In 1978, Dennis J. Carney became chairman of W-P, and he faced several major problems including the company's low market share, poor reputation with its customers, erratic earnings, and old equipment. To deal with these problems, Carney embarked on a campaign to upgrade the company's facilities with funds obtained from a multitude of sources (see Exhibit 7). By increasing W-P's debt to modernize, a very heavy burden was placed on an already struggling organization. In 1983, W-P's bank credit lines expired and the company ended 1984 with its tenth loss in eleven quarters. Exhibits 8 through 10 show selected financial data, stock price information, and financial ratios, respectively.

Twice in two years Carney had persuaded the United Steelworkers Union (USW) to help W-P by granting wage concessions in excess of $150 million. However, these concessions were not necessarily a sign of good relations between labor and management. In fact, the USW and Chairman Carney were constantly at odds. Carney was viewed by the union as a highly controversial, autocratic, and abrasive leader. In the four years Carney was chairman, five top-level W-P executives resigned, and he is reported to have alienated a W-P director, and the company's largest stockholder, Allen Paulson, with his management style.

EXHIBIT 1

Percentage Contributions to Sales Revenues

PRODUCTS	1984	1983	1982
Hot and cold rolled sheet and strip	41.9%	35.8%	25.5%
Coated sheet	16.6	19.6	16.6
Fabricated	14.9	15.3	15.7
Tin mill	11.1	18.0	17.0
Rail products	8.9	5.3	4.2
Seamless tubular	1.2	0.2	8.4
Welded tubular	0.3	1.5	4.8
Other	5.1	4.3	7.8
	100.0%	100.0%	100.0%

EXHIBIT 2

Shipments by Product Class (Net Tons)

PRODUCTS	1984	1983	1982
Hot and cold rolled sheet and strip	53.6%	47.1%	37.3%
Coated sheet	13.2	16.7	17.1
Fabricated	10.5	10.9	12.1
Rail products	10.4	7.1	6.0
Tin mill	8.7	14.9	16.8
Seamless tubular	0.7	0.1	4.0
Welded tubular	0.4	1.3	4.3
Other	2.5	1.9	2.3
	100.0%	100.0%	100.0%

EXHIBIT 3

Shipments by Major Market Classification (Net Tons)

MARKET CLASS	1984	1983	1982
Automotive	11%	15%	15%
Intermediate markets	45	38	27
Construction	13	15	17
Containers	10	13	14
Appliances	5	7	8
Oil and gas	1	1	7
Rail transportation	10	7	5
Other	5	4	7
	100%	100%	100%

EXHIBIT 4   Principal Markets and Major Market Classifications to Which Respective Classes of Products Were Sold, Based Upon Shipments (Net Tons)

PRODUCTS	AUTOMOTIVE			CONSTRUCTION			CONTAINERS			APPLIANCES			OIL AND GAS			INTERMEDIATE		
	1982	1983	1984	1982	1983	1984	1982	1983	1984	1982	1983	1984	1982	1983	1984	1982	1983	1984
Hot and cold rolled sheet and strip	25%	17%	11%	7%	6%	4%	9%	8%	8%	14%	11%	7%	—%	—%	—%	36%	53%	65%
Tin mill	6	6	7	2	—	—	69	62	60	9	8	10	—	—	—	22	22	21
Coated sheet	28	38	38	16	15	10	—	—	—	6	5	6	—	—	—	44	38	43
Fabricated	—	—	—	88	82	79	—	—	—	2	—	—	—	—	—	10	18	20
Seamless tubular	1	—	—	1	1	—	—	—	—	—	—	—	97	99	96	1	—	4
Welded tubular	—	1	—	21	32	23	—	—	—	—	—	—	23	31	23	46	33	77

EXHIBIT 5

Wheeling-Pittsburgh Steel Corporation's plants

Canfield, Ohio
Martins Ferry, Ohio
Mingo Junction, Ohio
Steubenville, Ohio
Yorkville, Ohio
Allenport, Pennsylvania
Monessen, Pennsylvania
Benwood, West Virginia
Follansbee, West Virginia
Beech Bottom, West Virginia
Wheeling, West Virgina

EXHIBIT 6

Wheeling-Pittsburgh Subsidiary Companies

Consumers Mining Company*
W-P Coal Company*
Ft. Duquesne Coal Company*
Gateway Coal Company
Harmar Coal Company
Mingo Oxygen Company*
Monessen Southwestern Railway Company*
Pittsburgh-Canfield Corporation*
Three Rivers Coal Company*
Wheeling-Empire Company
Wheeling Gateway Coal Company
Wheeling-Itasca Company
Wheeling-Pittsburgh Trading Company
WMI, Inc.

*These wholly owned subsidiaries filed petitions for relief under Chapter 11 of the federal bankruptcy laws in the U.S. Bankruptcy Court for the Western District of Pennsylvania.

EXHIBIT 7   **Wheeling-Pittsburgh Debt**

SECURED LONG-TERM DEBT HOLDERS (DOLLAR AMOUNTS IN MILLIONS)

Mitsubishi Corporation*	$177.4
Prudential	51.7
Metropolitan Life	51.7
Aetna	20.7
Connecticut General	18.0
New York Life	15.1
Mutual of New York	13.2
Northwestern Mutual	13.2
Teachers	10.3
Pennsylvania IDA	9.0
Equitable	6.7
Massachusetts Mutual	4.2
John Hancock	3.4
Total	$394.6

REVOLVING WORKING CAPITAL LOANS (DOLLAR AMOUNTS IN MILLIONS)

Manufacturers Hanover	$24.8
Royal Bank of Canada	20.7
Security Pacific	16.5
Pittsburgh National Bank	8.3
Manufacturers National-Detroit	8.3
Continental Illinois	8.3
Canadian Imperial Bank	8.3
National Bank of Canada	8.3
Bank of Nova Scotia	8.3
First Pennsylvania Bank	4.1
North Carolina National	4.1
Total	$120.0

*Guaranteed in event of default by eleven bank lenders.

W-P's losses during 1982, 1983, and 1984 totaled more than $172 million. In addition, the company's long-term debt increased to more than $500 million in 1983, and its interest expense approached $60 million per year. To avoid bankruptcy, Carney turned to the USW and W-P's creditors for help in meeting the company's principal and interest payments. Exhibit 11 shows W-P's debt repayment schedule.

EXHIBIT 8

Wheeling-Pittsburgh's Financial Situation
(Dollar Amounts in Thousands)

	1981	1982	1983	1984
Net sales	$ 1,151,112	$ 755,083	$ 772,320	$ 1,049,215
Net income	60,059,000	(58,769,000)	(54,080,000)	(59,376,000)
Ni/Sh common stock	14.28	(15.98)	(15.74)	(14.12)
Pref div declared	3,763,000	4,976,000	8,373,000	8,308,000
Depreciation	42,989,000	38,219,000	40,361,000	48,729,000
Plant improvements	110,177,000	160,211,000	91,905,000	26,878,000
Working capital	195,477,000	230,026,000	101,216,000	124,968,000
Long-term debt	358,733,000	495,915,000	513,928,000	527,291,000
Raw steel production	2,944,000	1,818,000	2,222,000	2,804,000
Shipments (tons)	2,146,000	1,368,000	1,642,000	2,320,000

EXHIBIT 9

Wheeling-Pittsburgh's Stock Prices

	6% PRIOR PREFERRED		$5 CUMULATIVE PREFERRED		COMMON SHARES	
	HIGH	LOW	HIGH	LOW	HIGH	LOW
1978	58.75	45.00	49.50	40.50	14.00	9.00
1979	48.00	42.75	38.875	34.125	20.00	15.625
1980	42.75	38.25	38.75	31.50	23.375	17.625
1981	40.00	38.00	34.00	30.00	32.50	25.625
1982	38.50	34.00	33.00	28.00	17.00	13.0
1983	42.50	38.25	34.00	31.00	28.00	22.25
1984	38.00	32.00	36.00	25.00	22.50	13.625

The USW stated that it was the creditors' turn to help the company, but the creditors were unwilling to do so unless the USW agreed to help as well. Eventually, the USW relented. However, this time it presented a list of demands that included a complete restructuring of the company's long-term debt, two union seats on the company's board of directors, and a large share of W-P's common stock. W-P's creditors agreed to defer $90 million of debt due in 1985 and in 1986 in exchange for a lien on the company's $300 million in current assets. The USW found the creditors' offer unacceptable because

EXHIBIT 10

Wheeling-Pittsburgh's Financial Ratios

	1981	1982	1983	1984
Current	1.86	2.57	1.42	1.61
Debt	.58	.63	.69	.71
Debt-equity	.77	1.15	1.39	1.56
Times interest earned	2.93	(1.93)	(.92)	(.03)
Inventory turnover	6.74	4.73	5.09	6.30
Total assets turnover	1.03	.63	.62	.86
Gross profit margin	.09	(.01)	(.01)	.08
Profit margin on sales	.05	(.08)	(.07)	(.06)
Return on total assets	.07	(.02)	(.01)	(.00)
Return on equity	.13	(.14)	(.15)	(.18)

it provided too little help and because it would have given them a major claim on W-P's assets. The impasse in negotiations continued until April 16, 1985, when Wheeling-Pittsburgh filed for Chapter 11 bankruptcy.

The repercussions of W-P's bankruptcy and the implications for the steel industry, as a whole, are far reaching. Foremost is the issue of wage renegotiation. After declaring bankruptcy, W-P made it clear that it would not continue to honor previous labor agreements, and the company entered into negotiations with the union that culminated in the union's rejection of W-P's proposed 30 percent wage and benefit cuts. Finally, the bankruptcy court was asked to rule on the wage issue. If the court ruled in W-P's favor, the company's lower wage rates, coupled with court protection from its creditors, would place W-P in an excellent competitive position when it emerged from Chapter 11. Moreover, the ruling might set a downward trend in steel industry wage rates, thus making the domestic steel industry more competitive with foreign producers. Ultimately, the court ruled in W-P's favor.

After the ruling, W-P proposed to cut labor costs by 18 percent, or to about $17.50 an hour on the average. Previously, the USW had stated that if the average hourly wage were set lower than $18.50, the union would strike. Additionally, W-P indicated that it would not be able to make a $5 million pension fund payment due at the end of July 1985. For all practical purposes, this would end the health and life insurance benefits of W-P workers and place those pensioned in a precarious position. On July 21, 1985, the steel industry experienced its first major strike in twenty-six years. Eight thousand three hundred W-P employees walked off their jobs.[1]

EXHIBIT 11 **Wheeling-Pittsburgh's Debt Repayment for the Next Five Years (Dollar Amounts in Thousands)***

	1985	1986	1987	1988	1989
First mortgage bonds:					
5.45% series A due 1985	$ 12,600	$ —	$ —	$ —	$ —
9.50% series D due 1994	3,187	3,187	3,187	3,187	3,187
4% mortgage due 2001	376	391	407	423	447
Senior secured notes:					
11% series A due 2001	3,493	3,493	3,493	3,493	3,493
11% series B due 2001	2,007	2,007	2,007	2,007	2,007
11% series C due 1994	2,590	2,710	3,250	3,250	3,250
Notes payable to banks	—	40,000	40,000	40,000	—
8% supplier loan due 1985	2,412	—	—	—	—
8.5% supply contract, 1987	14,000	14,000	14,001	—	—
Loan agreement:					
A Tranche 12.875%, 1991	—	7,300	14,600	14,600	14,600
B Tranche 13% due 1991	—	—	—	10,000	20,000
Long-term leases:					
Revenue bond lease obligations at 6.75% to 9.25% due 2005	1,470	505	535	570	610
Other lease obligations due 1991	497	563	349	312	310
11% notes of W-P Coal Company due 1993	1,864	1,864	1,864	1,864	1,864
14% notes of Ft. Duquesne Coal Company due 1992	697	798	914	1,046	1,198
Amount reclassified due to filing a petition for reorganization under Chapter 11	(39,495)	—	—	—	—
Total	5,698	76,818	84,607	80,752	50,960

*Represents debt scheduled for payment in the indicated years prior to the corporation's filing a petition for reorganization under Chapter 11 of the bankruptcy laws except for the amount reclassified for 1985.

THE STEEL INDUSTRY

The steel industry is confronted with a host of problems that have caused several companies in the industry to contemplate bankruptcy. Included in this list are high labor costs, weak prices, and increasing foreign competition. Part of the problem is the product. Demand for steel is *derived demand,* meaning that its demand is contingent upon the demand for products in which it is used. Manufacturers of cars, bridges, ships, machine tools, and appliances are end-use buyers of steel. Because they are durable goods, these products can have their purchase postponed by consumers during economic downturns. Thus, steel demand is highly sensitive to inventory cycles, business cycle changes, the long-term investment outlook, and the rate of overall economic growth.[2]

Price Elasticity

The cost of steel usually represents only a small percentage of the cost of the end-use products in which it is used. However, steel producers are faced with an extremely price-elastic demand because of the homogeneity of the product and the lack of brand name differences. Thus far, steel producers have not differentiated their products effectively. To maintain market share and compete, steel producers must discount their prices when the demand for steel declines or competition intensifies. This practice has caused a steady decrease in steel prices over the past several years (see Exhibit 12). The problem is worsened by foreign steel producers who engage in "dumping," or selling steel products in the United States at prices below production costs.

EXHIBIT 12   **Composite Real Prices Received by U.S. Producers**

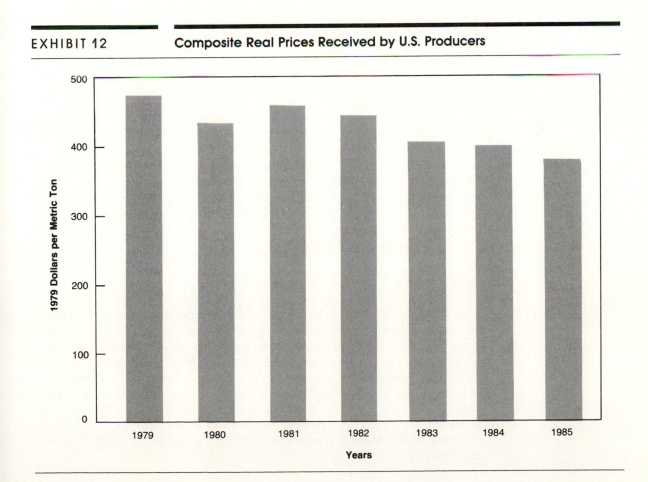

Imports

Recently, the steel industry has experienced a surge in imports that, in 1984, claimed 26.4 percent of the U.S. domestic steel market (see Exhibits 13 and 14). Government-imposed restrictions have attempted to help the domestic industry. For example, during 1964–1974 Voluntary Restraint Agreements between the United States and foreign steel-producing nations were in force. It was hoped that U.S. steel companies would use this period of protection to modernize their facilities. Yet, the industry's capital outlays fell below the 1968 level for each of the following six years, whereas wages and dividend payments rose considerably.[3]

In 1983 and 1984, when steel imports were approaching their highest levels of U.S. market share, many U.S. firms reacted by filing lawsuits charging foreign producers with dumping. President Reagan responded by announcing a new voluntary agreement in October 1984, which was designed to hold steel imports to a little over 20 percent of U.S. market share until 1989. As of October 1985, Voluntary Restraint Agreements had been reached with fourteen nations. The result of President Reagan's actions became visible in July 1985, when imports declined sharply. From June to July, steel imports fell from 2.3 million tons to 1.5 million tons.[4]

Capacity

Domestic steel production capacity experienced almost no growth between 1960 and 1980. Furthermore, the capacity of U.S. steel producers has been cut drastically since 1980 in an effort to bring it in line with demand. In 1980, domestic steel production capacity was 154 million tons; it was 134 million tons in 1984; and it is expected to fall to 120 million tons by 1987. Even though U.S. producers have reduced their capacity, they continue to use only a portion of that capacity. Exhibit 15 shows that the capacity utilization problem is one that is becoming more severe.

Cost Control

Cost control is another major concern of domestic steel producers. Labor and energy costs represent a large portion of total costs, and they have become the target of manufacturers' cost reduction efforts. Since a large part of their labor force is unionized, steel producers must bargain with the USW to set wage and benefit rates for labor contracts. Labor costs in the steel industry exceeded the manufacturing sector average by more than 90 percent in 1982. Additionally, although energy consumption per ton of steel produced decreased by 2 percent between 1973 and 1981 for U.S. firms, Japanese firms cut their energy consumption per ton by 11 percent during this time.[5]

EXHIBIT 13

U.S. Steel Industry: Imports

	IMPORTS, ALL STEEL MILL PRODUCTS (THOUSANDS OF NET TONS)	MARKET PENETRATION (PERCENTAGE OF TOTAL MARKET)	IMPORTS, SEMIFINISHED STEEL* (THOUSANDS OF NET TONS)
IMPORT LEVELS			
1984	26,163	26.4%	1,516
1983	17,070	20.5	822
1982	16,662	21.8	717
1981	19,898	18.9	790
1980	15,495	16.3	155
1979	17,518	15.2	345
1978	21,135	18.1	414
1977	19,307	17.8	298
1976	14,285	14.1	240
1975	12,012	13.5	243

	IMPORTS, ALL STEEL MILL PRODUCTS	IMPORTS, SEMIFINISHED STEEL
PERCENT INCREASE (DECREASE)		
1983–84	53.3%	84.4%
1982–83	2.4	14.6
1981–82	(16.3)	(9.2)
1980–81	28.4	409.7
1979–80	(11.5)	(55.1)
1978–79	(17.1)	(16.7)
1977–78	9.5	38.9
1976–77	35.2	24.2
1975–76	18.9	(1.2)

SOURCE: American Iron and Steel Institute (AISI) 1984 Annual Statistical Report.

*Examples of semifinished steel are ingots, billets, and slabs.

EXHIBIT 14

U.S. Steel Industry: Imports by Countries of Origin

	1984	1983	1982	1981	1980
IMPORT VOLUME (THOUSANDS OF NET TONS)					
Canada	3,167	2,379	1,844	2,899	2,370
Latin America	3,132	2,415	974	782	630
Europe	9,963	5,310	6,775	8,077	4,744
Asia and Africa	9,685	6,761	6,939	8,011	7,620
Australia and Oceania	216	206	130	129	132
Total imports of steel mill products	26,163	17,070	16,662	19,898	15,495
PERCENTAGE OF TOTAL IMPORTS					
Canada	12.1%	13.9%	11.1%	14.6%	15.3%
Latin America	12.0	14.2	5.8	3.9	4.1
Europe	38.1	31.1	40.7	40.6	30.6
Asia and Africa	37.0	39.6	41.6	40.3	49.2
Australia and Oceania	0.8	1.2	0.8	0.6	0.8
Total imports of steel mill products	100.0%	100.0%	100.0%	100.0%	100.0%
U.S. MARKET PENETRATION					
Canada	3.2%	2.9%	2.4%	2.7%	2.5%
Latin America	3.2	2.9	1.3	0.8	0.7
Europe	10.1	6.4	8.9	7.7	5.0
Asia and Africa	9.8	8.1	9.1	7.6	8.0
Australia and Oceania	0.2	0.2	0.2	0.1	0.1
Total imports of steel mill products	26.4%	20.5%	21.8%	18.9%	16.3%

SOURCE: AISI 1984 Annual Statistical Report.

In 1982, the aggregate net loss of the six largest domestic steel producers reached over $3 billion, and only slight improvements have been made since 1982 (Exhibit 16). These firms experienced losses in the first quarter of 1985 that amounted to an average of $17.00 per ton. In 1984, their average loss was $6.00 per ton. Exhibits 17 through 20 provide additional information about the global steel industry.

EXHIBIT 15   **Raw Steel Capacity Versus Production**

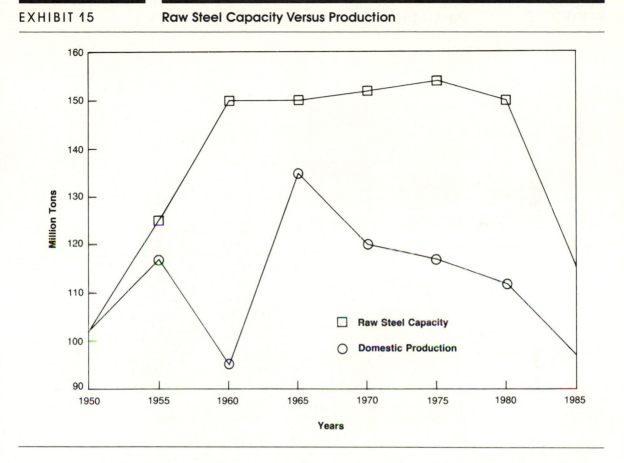

Due to the depressed condition of the steel industry, some companies are selling their most profitable units to improve their financial position. Other firms are seeking mergers with foreign steel producers. In April 1984, an agreement was reached between Nippon KoKan (NKK), Japan's second largest steel producer, and National Steel, the United States' fourth largest producer. NKK bought 50 percent of National, and it plans to spend $1 billion to modernize National's facilities. The improvement project is expected to cut National's operating costs by about $44 million per year. Mergers and joint ventures are two of the most attractive alternatives for domestic steel producers to acquire badly needed capital for improvements, as many of them are highly leveraged. Additionally, mergers and joint ventures give foreign firms easier access to the U.S. market.

EXHIBIT 16   **Aggregate Net Profits of the Six Largest U.S. Producers**

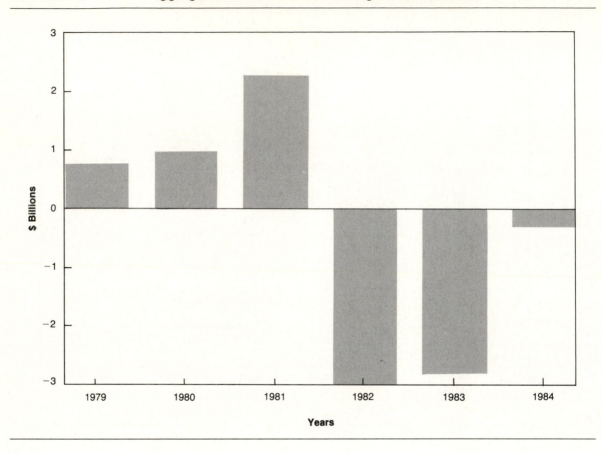

A Joint Venture

After two unsuccessful attempts to form joint ventures, in February 1984 W-P and Nisshin Steel Corporation of Japan reached an agreement. W-P registered to offer 1 million shares of common stock at $35.00 per share, and Nisshin Steel agreed to purchase 500,000 shares under the preemptive rights offering. Allen E. Paulson, chairman and president of Gulfstream Aerospace Corporation, and a member of W-P's board, agreed to purchase the remaining 500,000 shares. This transaction increased Paulson's holdings in W-P from 31.7 percent to 35.3 percent and gave Nisshin a 10 percent interest in the company. As part of the joint venture agreement, W-P invested approx-

EXHIBIT 17   Market Share by Firm

		1950			1960		
		MILLIONS OF NET TONS	PERCENTAGE OF DOMESTIC SHIPMENTS	PERCENTAGE OF DOMESTIC AND IMPORTED SHIPMENTS	MILLIONS OF NET TONS	PERCENTAGE OF DOMESTIC SHIPMENTS	PERCENTAGE OF DOMESTIC AND IMPORTED SHIPMENTS
U.S. Steel		22.6	28.4	28.0	18.7	26.3	25.2
Bethlehem		10.9	13.7	13.5	11.4	16.0	15.3
Republic		6.4	8.0	7.9	5.4	7.6	7.3
J&L							
Youngstown	merged 1978	6.8	8.5	8.4	7.0	9.8	9.4
National							
Granite City	merged 1971	4.0	5.0	5.0	5.3	7.5	7.1
Armco		3.0	3.8	3.7	5.0	7.0	6.7
Inland		3.3	4.1	4.1	5.1	7.2	6.9
Wheeling							
Pittsburgh	merged 1968	3.3	2.9	2.9	2.6	3.7	3.5
Total of above		60.3	74.5	73.5	60.5	85.1	81.4
Other domestic		20.3	25.5	25.2	10.6	14.9	14.3

		1970			1981		
		MILLIONS OF NET TONS	PERCENTAGE OF DOMESTIC SHIPMENTS	PERCENTAGE OF DOMESTIC AND IMPORTED SHIPMENTS	MILLIONS OF NET TONS	PERCENTAGE OF DOMESTIC SHIPMENTS	PERCENTAGE OF DOMESTIC AND IMPORTED SHIPMENTS
U.S. Steel		21.0	23.1	20.2	16.6	19.1	15.5
Bethlehem		13.8	15.2	13.2	11.6	13.3	10.9
Republic		6.7	7.4	6.4	6.5	7.5	6.1
J&L							
Youngstown	merged 1978	8.4	9.3	8.1	7.6	8.7	7.1
National							
Granite City	merged 1971	7.3	8.0	7.0	6.6	7.6	6.2
Armco		5.4	5.9	5.2	5.8	6.7	5.4
Inland		4.7	5.2	4.5	5.8	6.7	5.4
Wheeling							
Pittsburgh	merged 1968	2.9	3.2	2.8	2.1	2.4	2.0
Total of above		70.2	77.3	67.4	67.6	72.0	58.6
Other domestic		20.6	22.7	19.8	24.4	28.0	22.8

SOURCE: Barnett and Schorsch. *Steel: Upheaval in a Basic Industry*, (Cambridge, Mass.: Ballinger, 1983).

EXHIBIT 18

**U.S. Steel Industry: International Comparative Cost Structure
(Costs Per Metric Ton Shipped at Actual Operating Rates)**

	1980				
	U.S.	JAPAN	W. GERMANY	U.K.*	FRANCE
Revenue	$507.24	$426.66	$506.96	$ 514.23	$501.61
Labor	$175.11	$ 93.88	$164.56	$ 452.81	$172.87
Raw materials	292.12	259.61	289.68	456.63	299.96
Financial costs	39.93	82.85	63.04	159.57	105.53
Total costs/ton	$507.16	$436.33	$517.28	$1,069.02	$578.36
Exogenous cost factor				− 342.70	
				$ 726.32	
Pretax profit/ton	$ 0.08	$ 26.32	($10.33)	($212.09)	($76.74)

	1981				
	U.S.	JAPAN	W. GERMANY	U.K.	FRANCE
Revenue	$574.28	$496.52	$440.60	$456.59	$433.64
Labor	$185.19	$108.11	$145.10	$144.76	$143.14
Raw materials	320.58	287.85	284.26	384.86	296.39
Financial costs	39.76	93.32	57.28	77.06	90.60
Total costs/ton	$545.52	$489.28	$486.63	$606.68	$530.13
Pretax profit/ton	$ 28.75	$ 7.24	($46.03)	($150.10)	($96.49)

	1982				
	U.S.	JAPAN	W. GERMANY	U.K.	FRANCE
Revenue	$581.17	$453.79	$463.15	$453.11	$447.73
Labor	$214.54	$ 96.99	$162.08	$134.94	$146.08
Raw materials	359.18	279.30	289.84	342.07	293.42
Financial costs	65.34	84.04	66.03	76.32	94.33
Total costs/ton	$639.06	$460.33	$517.95	$553.32	$533.83
Pretax profit/ton	($57.89)	($6.54)	($54.80)	($100.21)	($86.10)

EXHIBIT 18   **Continued**

	1983				
	U.S.	**JAPAN**	**W. GERMANY**	**U.K.**	**FRANCE**
Revenue	$533.37	$467.43	$436.64	$413.48	$419.49
Labor	$173.08	$101.27	$152.94	$ 93.96	$156.80
Raw materials	345.44	274.54	268.17	290.01	257.52
Financial costs	64.62	96.08	60.86	53.40	91.47
Total costs/ton	$583.14	$471.89	$481.97	$437.36	$505.78
Pretax profit/ton	($49.77)	($4.47)	($45.33)	($23.89)	($86.29)

	1984				
	U.S.	**JAPAN**	**W. GERMANY**	**U.K.**	**FRANCE**
Revenue	$542.56	$450.30	$405.02	$378.95	$387.79
Labor	$149.10	$ 91.73	$117.18	$ 81.43	$128.20
Raw materials	347.00	256.84	245.17	262.86	235.42
Financial costs	66.85	88.71	46.63	46.21	72.77
Total costs/ton	$562.95	$437.28	$408.98	$390.51	$436.39
Pretax profit/ton	($20.39)	$ 13.02	($3.95)	($11.56)	($48.61)

	1985 (JAN.–JUNE AVERAGE)				
	U.S.	**JAPAN**	**W. GERMANY**	**U.K.**	**FRANCE**
Revenue	$523.90	$425.43	$387.11	$359.20	$368.03
Labor	$139.10	$ 83.05	$ 95.33	$ 64.66	$105.44
Raw materials	329.98	242.50	231.57	252.08	224.59
Financial costs	64.85	82.34	39.17	36.33	57.25
Total costs/ton	$533.93	$407.89	$366.07	$353.07	$387.38
Pretax profit/ton	($10.03)	$ 17.54	$ 21.04	$ 6.14	($19.36)

SOURCE: World Steel Dynamics (WSD) Price/Cost Monitor Report #7.
*Strike year in the U.K.

EXHIBIT 19

U.S. Steel Industry: International Comparative Unit Labor Costs (at Actual Operating Rates) 1980–1985

	U.S.				
	MAN HOURS PER TON SHIPPED		LABOR COST PER HOUR		UNIT LABOR COST (LABOR COST PER TON SHIPPED)
1980	9.17	×	$19.06	=	$174.78
1981	8.90	×	$20.78	=	$184.94
1982	8.65	×	$24.67	=	$213.40
1983	7.28	×	$23.70	=	$172.54
1984	6.67	×	$22.36	=	$149.14
1985 (Jan.–June)	6.02	×	$23.10	=	$139.06

	JAPAN				
	MAN HOURS PER TON SHIPPED		LABOR COST PER HOUR		UNIT LABOR COST (LABOR COST PER TON SHIPPED)
1980	9.15	×	$10.25	=	$93.79
1981	9.36	×	$11.55	=	$108.11
1982	8.90	×	$10.90	=	$97.01
1983	8.47	×	$11.96	=	$101.30
1984	7.71	×	$11.89	=	$91.67
1985 (Jan.–June)	7.51	×	$11.06	=	$83.06

	U.K.				
	MAN HOURS PER TON SHIPPED		LABOR COST PER HOUR		UNIT LABOR COST (LABOR COST PER TON SHIPPED)
1980	46.02	×	$9.96	=	$458.36
1981	15.06	×	$9.57	=	$144.12
1982	14.86	×	$9.14	=	$135.82
1983	11.87	×	$7.92	=	$94.01
1984	11.68	×	$6.98	=	$81.53
1985 (Jan.–June)	10.49	×	$6.18	=	$64.83

EXHIBIT 19   Continued

W. GERMANY		
	MAN HOURS PER TON SHIPPED	LABOR COST PER HOUR	UNIT LABOR COST (LABOR COST PER TON SHIPPED)
1980	11.04 ×	$14.93 =	$164.83
1981	11.00 ×	$13.19 =	$145.09
1982	12.26 ×	$13.28 =	$162.81
1983	12.05 ×	$12.71 =	$153.16
1984	10.21 ×	$11.49 =	$117.31
1985 (Jan.–June)	9.25 ×	$10.30 =	$95.28

FRANCE		
	MAN HOURS PER TON SHIPPED	LABOR COST PER HOUR	UNIT LABOR COST (LABOR COST PER TON SHIPPED)
1980	11.22 ×	$15.39 =	$172.68
1981	11.31 ×	$12.66 =	$143.19
1982	12.04 ×	$12.15 =	$146.29
1983	12.14 ×	$12.87 =	$156.24
1984	11.59 ×	$11.01 =	$127.61
1985 (Jan.–June)	10.86 ×	$9.71 =	$105.45

SOURCE: WSD Price/Cost Monitor Report #7.

imately $10 million in the Japanese steelmaker's stock. As a result of this agreement, a $40 million production line will be constructed at one of W-P's existing plants in the Ohio River Valley. The line is expected to be operating by 1986 and will produce rust-resistant galvanized steel for the auto industry. The production of rust-resistant steel is one of the few markets that is growing in the industry.[6]

MODERNIZATION PROGRAM

Over the last six years, W-P has been heavily involved in a modernization program that will enable the firm to satisfy its customers' demands for better quality and service, while remaining competitive with foreign and domestic

EXHIBIT 20

U.S. Steel Industry: World Production and Capacity Utilization (Percent)

	U.S.	JAPAN	EEC	DEVELOPING WORLD	COMMUNIST WORLD
1973	97.0%	88.4%	85.8%	65.7%	89.7%
1974	94.4	84.9	87.4	68.0	88.0
1975	76.8	73.1	63.5	68.4	88.5
1976	80.7	73.0	68.4	71.8	88.3
1977	79.0	64.9	62.1	70.2	87.2
1978	86.9	65.0	65.6	73.9	90.2
1979	87.9	71.5	69.2	78.1	87.4
1980	72.8	70.1	64.1	79.1	85.3
1981	77.5	63.9	63.7	72.5	81.1
1982	48.5	63.0	56.8	70.1	80.0
1983	55.3	61.6	59.0	67.6	83.1
FORECAST					
1984*	70.0%	66.3%	66.3%	67.1%	83.9%
1985*	80.8	70.8	73.2	68.5	85.3
1986*	91.3	79.7	81.8	68.2	92.2
1987*	71.8	78.7	76.9	64.9	89.2
1990*	78.3	86.0	75.5	70.5	90.0

SOURCE: World Steel Dynamics, *The Steel Strategist #10*, Paine Webber, Inc., December, 1984.

*Estimate

steel producers. Between 1979 and 1983, W-P spent approximately $536 million modernizing its facilities. During this time, the company's spending to enhance production facilities grew more than five times faster than the domestic industry average and more than four times faster than the average for Japanese firms. The construction of a new railroad rail mill utilizing the most advanced technology available in the world at a cost of $105 million consumed the lion's share of the firm's investment capital. Another component of the modernization plan was the construction of a new two-strand continuous slab caster and a new five-strand continuous bloom caster at a cost of $175 million.

These two casters employ the most advanced technology for quality control available in the world. The technology was obtained from Japan and Germany, and it utilizes automated and computerized equipment that will enable W-P to increase quality, expand production, conserve energy, and decrease operating costs. Mitsubishi financed the project, and the equipment was supplied by Hitachi Corporation of Japan and Mannesmann Demag AG of West Germany. Technical assistance and engineering for the slab caster was provided by the Nippon Steel Corporation. Technical assistance for the bloom caster was provided by August Thyssen-Hutte AG of West Germany.[7]

Additionally, as a part of its modernization program, W-P spent $15.7 million upgrading its 80-inch hot strip mill at its Steubenville plant. This expenditure was necessary for W-P to comply with Environmental Protection Agency (EPA) requirements. Since 1979, W-P has invested over $100 million to comply with other EPA regulations dealing with air and water quality control measures, and the company anticipates the promulgation of additional environmental regulations that will result in significant increases in its overall capital and operating expenditures.

THE FUTURE

On September 19, 1985, the *Wall Street Journal* reported that Dennis Carney was expected to resign on September 20 to pave the way for a strike settlement. Although it was suggested that Carney might change his mind, the newspaper said it "is extremely unlikely, chiefly because of the severance guarantee. The United Steel Workers union, whose protests in part contributed to Mr. Carney's anticipated resignation, have informally agreed to resume bargaining in earnest if Mr. Carney departs."[8]

According to Jerry Flint, the steel industry could be on the verge of an amazing recovery:

> It's easy to be negative about steel. Turnarounds that never came. Write-offs of $4.4 billion in assets and $7 billion in losses in four years. The six largest companies lost $325 million in the fourth quarter alone and this is in a strong economy. For the price of a couple TV stations, you could buy the great Bethlehem Steel Co. with its $5 billion in sales and 45,000 employees. . . .
>
> Drop steel imports 3 million tons to 4 million tons. Let the capital goods business improve, not a boom, just a normal upswing, enough to add another couple million tons to steel sales. Let the United Steelworkers union cooperate to cut labor costs in the bargaining this spring. You know what happens? The bloodletting in the steel industry ends, and the profits begin to flow, this year. . . .
>
> First, ask about productivity. This may be the untold miracle of American industry. "We're producing steel at fewer man-hours per ton in America than anybody else in the world now," says Lynn Williams, president of the United Steelworkers of America. "We have 4.6 man-hours in a ton, and by the end of this year it will be 4," says David Roderick, chairman of U.S. Steel. At Bethlehem productivity last year improved 5 percent from 1984, which was improved 12 percent from 1983, which was improved 15 percent from 1982. . . .
>
> Quality is another major plus. It's no secret that U.S. steel wasn't matching up. A few years ago the reject rate on Japanese steel was 1 percent to 1.5 percent, while American-made metal was running 5 percent to 10 percent, says

George Ferris, who once headed Ford Motor Co.'s steel operations and now runs Wheeling-Pittsburgh Steel. In an auto plant example, a bad coil means taking down the press for half an hour to change it, and losing production of 300 to 450 stampings. Today the American steelmakers say they are as good as anybody. "We're all [U.S. and Japan] around a 2 percent reject rate," says Ferris. "Yes, we've seen the quality of steel improve," says Roger Smith, chairman of General Motors. But he asks for even better quality, plus better steels, lighter, rustproof, more dent-resistant. . . .

Right now the biggest "if" in the turnaround is the union question. While U.S. productivity is high, wages and benefits are even higher—$17.18 an hour pay and $24.84 with benefits at Bethlehem. One product study on hot-rolled band, for example, showed 3.6 man-hours per ton in the United States to 3.4 in Japan, 6.9 in Brazil, 4.6 in Britain, and 5.5 in Korea. But the $20-plus labor cost meant $84 per ton for that hot-rolled against $16 for Korea and $37 for Japan.[9]

NOTES

1. *Wall Street Journal,* February 5, 1985–July 21, 1985.

2. Robert Bossong, "Industry Perspective: The Steel Industry—Stagnation, Decay, or Recovery," *Business Economics,* July 1985.

3. A. J. Kawahito, "Relative Profitability of the U.S. and Japanese Steel Industries," *Columbia Journal of World Business,* Fall 1984.

4. *Iron Age,* October 4, 1985.

5. Kawahito, *op. cit.*

6. Wheeling-Pittsburgh Steel Company's 1984 10K Report.

7. Wheeling-Pittsburgh Steel Company's 1983 10K Report.

8. *Wall Street Journal,* September 19, 1985.

9. *Forbes,* March 10, 1986. Reprinted by permission of *Forbes* magazine, March 10, 1986. © Forbes, Inc. 1986.

Nucor Corporation

CHARLES I. STUBBART · DEAN SCHROEDER

"It's the closest thing to a perfect company in the steel industry."

DANIEL ROLING, ANALYST FOR MERRILL LYNCH

With earnings growth over the past decade averaging better than 23 percent per year, Nucor prospered in the steel industry while giant companies barely survived. Few high-tech companies could match Nucor's record (see Exhibit 1). But in 1986, Nucor was moving into an era where the easy pickings were over. One securities analyst believed that Nucor would not be able to find alluring new opportunities, stating: "Their rapid growth of the last 10 years is simply not repeatable."

BACKGROUND

NUCLEAR CORPORATION   Nuclear Corporation of America was formed in 1955 by a merger of Nuclear Consultants, Inc., and parts of REO Motors. Between 1955 and 1964 various managements tried unsuccessfully to make a profit by way of acquisitions and divestitures. One of the acquisitions was Vulcraft, a steel joist manufacturer. By 1965 Nuclear Corporation was losing $2 million on sales of $22 million. A new group got control of the company in 1965 and installed Vulcraft general manager Ken Iverson (who headed the only profitable division) as president. "I got the job by default," Iverson said.

ENTRY INTO THE STEEL INDUSTRY   Iverson decided that Vulcraft—a manufacturer of steel joists for buildings—ought to make its own steel. His goal was to achieve a low-cost position so as to match or beat the low prices of imported steel: "We had some vision that if we were successful, we could expand and create another business by selling steel in the general marketplace." In 1968 Nucor built its first steel mill in Darlington, South Carolina. By 1985 Nucor operated four steel mills, six joist plants, two cold finishing plants, three steel deck plants, and a grinding ball plant throughout the South, Southwest, and West. About 65 percent of Nucor's steel was sold in open markets, while 35 percent went to Vulcraft and other Nucor products. Until the recession of 1982–83 sales and earnings grew at an astonishing clip.

Prepared by Professors Charles I. Stubbart and Dean Schroeder, the University of Massachusetts, Amherst, Mass.

293

EXHIBIT 1   Six-Year Financial Review, Nucor Corporation, 1980–1985

	1980	1981	1982	1983	1984	1985
Net sales	$482,420,363	$544,820,621	$486,018,162	$542,531,431	$660,259,922	$758,495,374
Costs and expenses:						
Cost of products sold	369,415,571	456,210,289	408,606,641	461,727,688	539,731,252	600,797,865
Marketing and administrative expenses	38,164,559	33,524,820	31,720,315	33,988,054	45,939,311	59,079,802
Interest expense (income)	(1,219,965)	10,256,546	7,899,110	(748,619)	(3,959,092)	(7,560,645)
	406,360,165	499,991,655	448,226,128	494,967,123	581,711,471	652,317,022
Earnings before taxes	76,060,198	44,828,966	37,792,034	47,564,308	78,548,451	106,178,352
Federal income taxes	31,000,000	10,100,000	15,600,000	19,700,000	34,000,000	47,700,000
Net earnings	$ 45,060,198	$ 34,728,966	$ 22,192,034	$ 27,864,308	$ 44,548,451	$ 58,478,352
Net earnings per share	$3.31	$2.51	$1.59	$1.98	$3.16	$4.11
Dividends declared per share	$.22	$.24	$.26	$.30	$.36	$.40
Percentage of earnings to sales	9.3%	6.4%	4.6%	5.1%	6.7%	7.7%
Return on average equity	29.0%	17.8%	10.0%	11.4%	16.0%	17.8%
Return on average assets	16.9%	10.3%	5.9%	7.0%	9.8%	11.2%
Capital expenditures	$ 62,440,354	$101,519,282	$ 14,788,707	$ 19,617,147	$ 26,074,653	$ 29,066,398
Depreciation	13,296,218	21,599,951	26,286,671	27,109,582	28,899,421	31,105,788
Sales per employee	150,756	155,663	133,156	148,639	176,069	197,011
Current assets	$115,365,727	$131,382,292	$132,542,648	$193,889,162	$253,453,373	$334,769,147
Current liabilities	66,493,445	73,032,313	66,102,706	88,486,795	100,533,684	121,255,828
Working capital	$ 48,872,282	$ 58,349,979	$ 66,439,942	$105,402,367	$152,919,689	$213,513,319
Property, plant, and equipment	$173,074,273	$252,616,074	$239,071,390	$213,304,817	$228,102,790	$225,274,674
Total assets	$291,221,867	$384,782,127	$371,632,941	$425,567,052	$482,188,465	$560,311,188
Long-term debt	$ 39,605,169	$ 83,754,231	$ 48,229,615	$ 45,731,000	$ 43,232,384	$ 40,233,769
Percentage of debt to capital	18.2%	28.3%	17.2%	15.0%	12.6%	10.1%
Shareholders' equity	$177,603,690	$212,376,020	$232,281,057	$258,129,694	$299,602,834	$357,502,028
Per share	$12.96	$15.25	$16.60	$18.32	$21.16	$24.97
Shares outstanding	13,699,994	13,927,014	13,991,882	14,090,181	14,161,079	14,315,005
Stockholders	22,000	22,000	22,000	21,000	22,000	22,000
Employees	3,300	3,700	3,600	3,700	3,800	3,900

Even during the recession Nucor managed to eke out a profit while other integrated steel companies lost billions.

STEEL INDUSTRY CONDITIONS, 1985

Companies competing in the U.S. steel industry in 1985 were of four distinct types: integrated U.S. companies, foreign manufacturers, minimills, and specialty steel producers. The large integrated domestic companies (see Exhibit 2) got their start at the turn of the century. Integrated companies held about 45 to 55 percent of the market. Specialty steel producers manufactured relatively low volumes of steel with varying degrees of hardness, purity, and strength. Imports of steel into the United States accounted for about 20 to 25 percent of domestic sales. (Imports probably held a larger share, taking into account the steel in imported automobiles and other products.) Minimills, which transformed scrap metal into steel using electric furnaces, had a market share of about 20 to 25 percent of the domestic market.

EXHIBIT 2

Production Capacity of Largest U.S. Integrated Steel Companies, 1984

FIRM	RAW STEEL CAPACITY (MILLIONS OF TONS PER YEAR)
1. U.S. Steel	26.2
2. LTV	19.1
3. Bethlehem	18.0
4. Inland	9.4
5. Armco	6.8
6. National	5.6
7. Wheeling-Pittsburgh	4.5
8. Weirton	4.0
9. Ford Motor Co. (Rouge Steel)	3.6
10. McLouth	2.0
11. CF&I	2.0 (partially closed)
12. Interlake	1.4
13. Sharon	1.0
14. California	2.1 (closed)
Total	105.7

SOURCE: Company reports; Oppenheimer & Co., *Metal Bulletin; Iron and Steel Works of the World*, 8th edition.

RECENT HISTORY Since the early 1970s integrated steel producers had suffered a painful decline. During 1965–74 steel demand was strong, and industry officials expected major growth after 1974. But they were wrong. Steel production in the United States had fallen from its 1974 level, and many analysts believed that the 1974 levels would never be reached again (Exhibit 3). Much of this decline was traceable to the long-term trends toward smaller, lighter cars, the inroads of competing materials (such as aluminum and plastics), a shift in emphasis away from smokestack industries to service industries, and greater use of imported steel in U.S. products.

Between 1960 and 1985 foreign competitors and domestic minimills invested heavily in building all-new facilities with the latest technology. Major integrated companies spent their investment capital on trying to spruce up existing plants and correct gross inefficiencies. Facing weak demand, having

---

EXHIBIT 3   **U.S. Raw Steel Production, Finished Steel Shipments, and Steel Imports, 1956–1984**

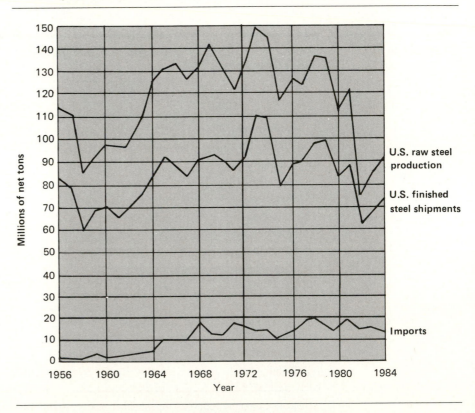

SOURCE: American Iron and Steel Institute, *Annual Statistical Reports.*

EXHIBIT 4   **Profitability of U.S. Domestic Steel Industry Relative to all Other Manufacturing Industries, 1972–1984**

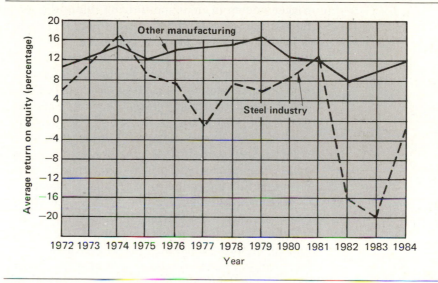

SOURCE: *Forbes*, May 1986. Reprinted by permission of *Forbes magazine*, © Forbes, Inc. 1986.

less efficient facilities, and with an appreciating U.S. dollar making the price of foreign-made steel cheaper and cheaper, the biggest domestic integrated companies suffered huge losses in the late 1970s and early 1980s (Exhibit 4).

Other problems also contributed to the rapid slide. The steelworkers union was able to negotiate large wage increases in 1968 and 1971, and union work rules hampered steel company efforts to increase productivity in their plants. Only in 1983 did the steelworkers union reluctantly agree to wage concessions and work rule modifications under the pressure of plant closings.

POOR INVESTMENTS   Expecting major increases in demand for 1975–85, integrated companies made large investments in ore mines and iron pelletizing facilities. An important share of their investment dollars went into meeting environmental regulations. Integrated companies' financial calculations persuaded them to stick with modifications of existing plants instead of building new "greenfield" plants. As a result, not one all-new integrated steel plant had been built for over twenty years in the United States. Given the high cost of capital, the complex environmental constraints, weak demand, and intense foreign/domestic competition, it was unlikely that any new integrated plants would be built in the United States in the foreseeable future.

IMPORTS AND PROTECTION   The steel strike of 1959 provided the first opportunity for foreign steel firms to make inroads into the U.S. market. By the 1980s—despite several attempts to limit imports via voluntary restraints and trigger pricing (a minimum pricing rule)—the integrated companies found themselves with 140 million tons of excess capacity, much of it in old, inefficient plants. They had no choice but to face the music, close many plants, and sell unproductive assets—a protracted and painful process for the companies, the steelworkers, and many local communities. Within one four-year period steelmakers wrote off $4.4 billion in assets and took $7 billion in losses. Steel companies, steelworkers, and endangered communities struggled mightily to persuade the Reagan administration and the Congress to limit steel imports. A reluctant Reagan administration agreed to negotiate voluntary restraints in 1985. Even so, to the integrated companies, the rust bowl communities, and to over 200,000 permanently laid-off steelworkers, it seemed that too little had been done too late.

Foreign steel imports in 1985 accounted for about 25 percent of the U.S. market in spite of the Reagan administration's negotiation bilateral voluntary restraints with foreign governments. These restraint agreements aimed at limiting imports to about 21 percent of the market. Sentiment was growing in Congress to stem the tidal wave of foreign imports in the face of a $130 billion trade deficit during 1985. Ken Iverson, Nucor's CEO, steadfastly argued against protecting the domestic steel industry:

> We've had this "temporary" relief for a long time. We had a voluntary quota system in the early 1970s. We had trigger prices in the late 1970s. And what happened during these periods? As soon as prices began to rise so that steel companies would begin to be profitable, they stopped modernizing. It's only under intense competitive pressure—both internally from minimills and externally from the Japanese and the Koreans—that the big steel companies have been forced to modernize. . . . In 1980 the industry still had rolling mills dating from the Civil War. . . . Out of all this turmoil will come a lot of things which are beneficial: more of an orientation toward technology, greater productivity, certainly a lot of changes in management structure.

FUTURE PROSPECTS   Speculating about 1986, steel producers expected another year like 1985: declining tonnage, stable prices, slightly declining import shares, and overall profitability near zero for the industry. Their forecasts hinged on a GNP growth of approximately 3 percent. Industry analysts foresaw that a reduction in imports (traced to the falling value of the U.S. dollar) would offset an expected decline in steel consumption. Demand for steel in machinery, railroad equipment, farm equipment, and other capital items was falling. Analysts were also uncertain about the 1986 demand for autos. Some estimates placed 1986 domestic steel shipments in the range of 70 to 75 million tons (not counting imports). The prospect of labor negotiations beginning in the second half of 1986 represented a major uncertainty for steel producers and customers.

EXHIBIT 5

Utilization Rates of U.S. Steelmaking Capacity, 1975–1985

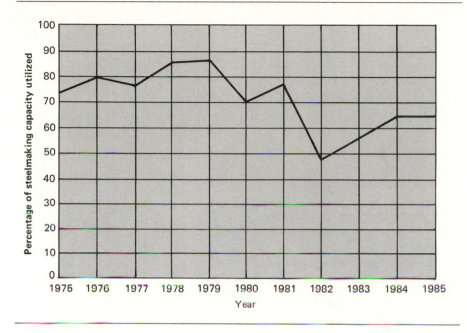

SOURCE: AISI statistics.

But there was a bright side too. Steel companies entered the year determined to extract concessions from the United Steelworkers Union. Companies had eliminated most of their grossly inefficient facilities. Prices were edging up. Capacity utilization approached 70 percent, compared to a low of 48 percent in 1982 (Exhibit 5). A weakening dollar made imports less attractive.

Analysts estimated that worldwide demand had stabilized. From 1979 to 1985 steel output in the industrial nations dropped precipitously from 442 million tons to 331 million tons. Capacity had been cut back 28 million tons in Europe, 23 million tons in the United States, and 17 million tons in Japan. One U.S. steel producer predicted that an additional 20 million tons in U.S. capacity would have to go. Exhibit 6 offers some industry projections for steel.

STEEL MINIMILLS: AN INDUSTRY WITHIN AN INDUSTRY

The United States had about 50 minimills. As U.S. Steel, Bethlehem, Republic, National, and LTV surrendered market share and lost billions, new entrants into the domestic market such as North Star, Nucor, Co-Steel,

EXHIBIT 6   **Steel Industry Projections for 1985, 1990, and 2000**

	1980 ACTUAL	1985 (PROJECTED)	PROJECTED RANGES			
			1990		2000	
			LOW	HIGH	LOW	HIGH
Import share of U.S. market (percent)	17.0%	24.0%	28.0	28.0%	32.0%	32.0%
Domestic shipments (millions of tons)	83.9	76.0	73.1	75.6	71.4	78.2
Imports (millions of tons)	17.2	24.0	28.4	29.4	33.6	36.8
Total shipments (millions of tons)	86.7	77.0	74.1	76.6	72.4	79.2
Minimill shipments (millions of tons)	12.0	14.4	20.5	20.5	29.0	29.0
Minimill capacity (millions of tons)	16.0	22.0	27.0	27.0	35.0	35.0
Minimill productivity (work hours per ton)	4.0	2.8	2.2	2.2	1.5	1.5
Integrated shipments (millions of tons)	74.7	62.6	53.6	56.1	43.4	50.2
Integrated raw steel production (millions of tons)	102.3	82.3	67.8	71.0	49.9	57.7
Integrated capacity (millions of tons)	138.4	108.3	80.0	81.6	55.4	64.1
Integrated productivity (work hours per ton)	9.5	7.2	6.0	6.0	4.5	4.5
Capacity utilization rate (percent)	75.3%	76.0%	85.0%	87.0%	90.0%	90.0%
Total employment (in thousands)	401.6	247.9	195.0	201.6	129.6	141.7

SOURCE: Barnett, *Minimills*.

Florida Steel, and others prospered—and even displaced imports. Contrary to typical relationships between scale and efficiency, minimills manufactured high-quality steel inexpensively, with plants of 200,000 to 1 million tons of annual electric-furnace capacity; integrated plants producing 2 million to 10 million tons using open-hearth and basic oxygen furnace equipment were the high-cost producers.

TECHNOLOGY   The electric-furnace technology of minimills was first developed by Northwestern Steel and Wire in the 1930s. Exhibit 7 shows a comparison of the two processes, integrated versus minimill; the comparative simplicity of minimills is apparent. First, minimills use electric arc furnaces compared to integrated plants that use open-hearth (about 10 percent) or basic oxygen furnaces (about 90 percent), as shown in Exhibit 8. Minimills simply charge scrap into an electric arc furnace to produce molten steel, then continuously cast the molten metal into semifinished shapes. Continuous casters eliminated reheating and increased the yield from molten

EXHIBIT 7   **Comparative Steelmaking Methods**

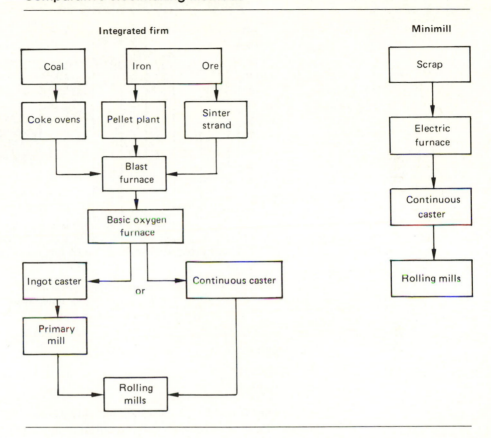

metal to finished product. Unlike integrated mills, minimills were expressly designed for rebuilding and technical updating. Many integrated plants used obsolete ingot-casting technologies.

   PRODUCT SPECIALIZATION   Early on, minimills fashioned small specialized steel products like reinforcing rods for use in concrete work, rather than making huge beams, slabs, or sheets. Product specialization increased their efficiency. Steel slabs were still predominantly the private preserve of the integrated companies. But, as time passed, minimill companies expanded their product lines. Exhibit 9 compares minimill product lines to integrated mill product lines. Nucor in 1985 produced cold-finished bars and was devoting a major innovative effort to the challenge of adapting minimill technology to sheet steel production. If Nucor could perfect this new technology,

EXHIBIT 8

U.S. Steel Production by Process, 1975–1985

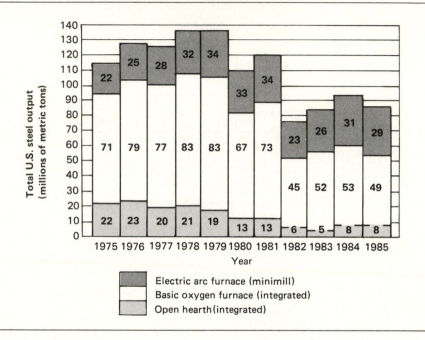

SOURCE: AISI statistics.

the company would be able to challenge integrated companies on their home ground—the flat-rolled steel used in automobiles, appliances, and roofing.

LOCATION   Only by the 1960s did minimills become a force within the industry. Their strategy was to utilize only electric furnaces and to locate their plants in regions near customer markets and scrap supplies but more distant from integrated plants (steel was expensive to ship). During the 1970s minimills grew explosively, capturing significant market shares (Exhibit 8).

INPUT COSTS   Scrap steel was the principal raw material input for minimill production. While the cost of iron ore had constantly risen (as rich, high-quality sources in the United States ran out), scrap remained plentiful. Over the last ten years scrap prices had declined relative to iron ore prices.

WORK FORCE FLEXIBILITY   Another important advantage of minimills was their work force flexibility. Most minimills employed nonunion workers. Union attempts to organize minimills had met with little success. Although nonunion minimill wages were not always lower than union wages, their

EXHIBIT 9	**Product Categories of Integrated Mills and Minimills**

PRODUCTS OF INTEGRATED MILLS	CAPABLE OF BEING MADE WITH PRESENT MINIMILL PRODUCTION TECHNOLOGY?
Slabs:	
Hot-rolled sheets	No
Cold-rolled sheets	No
Coated sheets	No
Plates	Yes
Welded pipe and tubs	Limited
Blooms and Billets:	
Wire rods	Yes
Bars	Yes
Reinforcing bars	Yes
Small structural shapes	Yes
Large structural shapes	Limited
Rails	No
Seamless tube	Yes
Axles	No

worker productivity was always much higher, primarily because of the flexibility and latitude management had in organizing work. Without union work rule restrictions, management could introduce labor-saving technology and link earnings to productivity.

PRODUCTIVITY   Electric furnace technology, work force flexibility, and constant efforts to operate facilities more efficiently added up to a significant cost advantage (that translated into a price advantage) for minimills. The advantage in 1985 was about $100 per ton ($375 for integrated firms versus $275 for minimills). Much of the advantage stemmed from the fact that output per worker at minimills ran about double the 350 tons per employee at integrated companies. Because minimill wages were comparable (some lower but not much) to workers' earnings in the unionized plants of bigger, integrated producers, minimills had about half the labor costs per ton of integrated companies.

DEVELOPMENTAL SEQUENCE   Minimills did not win their market niche overnight. Some minimills failed. While minimills had advantages in low-cost labor and low-cost scrap, they faced scale disadvantages and began with an untested technology and no customer base. The initial market penetration successes came in low-grade steel products. Then, as they learned and made operating improvements, they moved gradually and selectively to challenge

EXHIBIT 10		Leading Minimill Companies in United States, 1985	
FIRM	**PLANTS**	**CAPACITY (TONS)**	**PRODUCTS**
Nucor	4	2,100,000	Bars, small structurals
North Star	4	2,050,000	Bars, rods, small structural steel
Northwestern	1	1,800,000	Bars, rods, small and large structural steel
Co-Steel	2	1,750,000	Bars, rods, small and large structural steel
Florida Steel	5	1,560,000	Bars, small structurals

Note: The minimill segment consisted of 50 firms and 65 plants. Of total minimill production, 55 percent came from plants with less than 600,000 tons of annual capacity.

integrated mills and imports in an ever-broadening array of products but always where their relative cost position was strongest. The largest, and generally most successful, minimill companies in 1985 are shown in Exhibit 10.

INTENSIFIED COMPETITION Contrary to popular impressions about imported steel, minimills' production accounted for more of the displacement of integrated companies' share than had imports. The relationship between the minimills and the integrated companies resembled a successful guerrilla war. In 1985, however, the competitive scene was changing. Having used their lower costs to force integrated companies and imports out of many markets, minimills were beginning to compete against each other. An official at an integrated company noted: "Minimills have passed the stage of taking tonnage from integrated producers. We are concentrating on more sophisticated products where they can't compete. Let them have the inefficient products." Iverson observed: "We are now head to head against much tougher competition. It was no contest when we were up against the integrated companies. Now we are facing minimills who have the same scrap prices, the same electrical costs, and who use the same technologies.

Minimills coveted the bigger market for flat-rolled steel where profit margins were higher. But they were shut out of this segment by technological limitations. In technological capabilities, productivity, work force practices, and expanding products, Nucor was viewed as the leader among minimill producers. Nucor operated steel minimills in South Carolina, Nebraska, Texas, and Utah with a total capacity of about 2 million tons; this made Nucor about the tenth largest steel company in the United States.

VULCRAFT: THE OTHER HALF OF NUCOR

Ken Iverson said:

Most people think of us as a steel company, but we are a lot more than a steel company. The business is really composed of two different factors. One is manufacturing steel and the other is steel products. We like it if in an average year each factor contributes about 50 percent of our sales and 50 percent of our earnings. It is important for the company in the long run that we keep this balance. If one of them began to dominate the company it would cause problems we wouldn't like to see.

PRODUCTS   Vulcraft was the nation' largest producer of steel joists and joist girders. Steel joists and girders serve as support systems in industrial buildings, shopping centers, warehouses, high rise buildings, and to a lesser extent in small office buildings, apartments, and single-family dwellings. Vulcraft had six joist plants and four deck plants. Steel deck was used for floor and roof systems. In 1985 Vulcraft produced 471,000 tons of joists and girders and 169,000 tons of steel deck (Exhibits 11 and 12).

EXHIBIT 11   **Nucor's Steel Joist and Steel Production, 1975–1985**

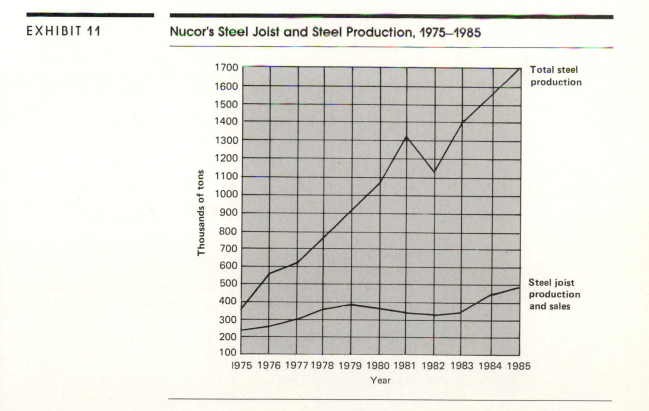

EXHIBIT 12   **Nucor's Steel Deck and Cold Finished Steel Sales, 1977–1985**

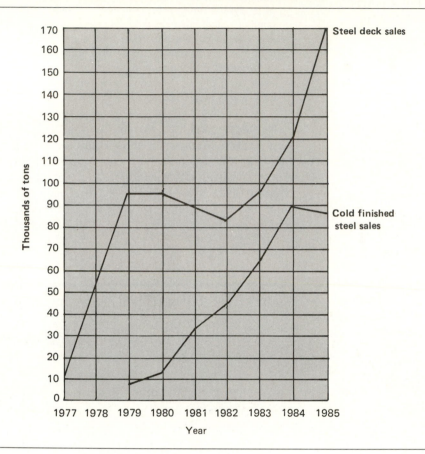

MANUFACTURING PROCESS   Joists were manufactured on assembly lines. The steel moved on rolling conveyors from station to station. Teams of workers at each station cut and bent the steel to shape, welded joists together and drilled holes in them, and painted the completed product.

COMPETITION   Many competitors participated in the joist segment, and a large number and variety of customers bought joists. Competition centered around timely delivery and price. Joist manufacturing was not capital intensive like basic steel-making, but was more of an engineering business. Vulcraft bid on a very high percentage of all new buildings that needed joists.

Sophisticated computer software was used to design the joists needed on a job and to develop bid estimates. Success also depended on marketing and advertising. Vulcraft had a 40 percent national market share in joists in 1985, making it the largest joist manufacturer in the United States. In 1985 Vulcraft manufactured joists for about 15,000 buildings. Vulcraft management pursued a strategy of being the low-cost supplier of joists.

ORGANIZATION   Each Vulcraft plant was managed by a general manager who reported directly to Dave Aycock, president of Nucor. Each Vulcraft general manager had spent many years in the joist business. In general, the Vulcraft division's relationships with corporate headquarters paralleled those of the steel division.

OTHER NUCOR BUSINESSES

In addition to steel and joists, Nucor operated three cold finish plants that produced steel bars used in shafting and machining precision parts; a plant that produced grinding balls used by the mining industry; and a research chemicals unit that produced rare earth oxides, metals, and salts. Exhibits 11 and 12 show Nucor's sales by business.

KEN IVERSON AND THE NUCOR CULTURE

Iverson had consciously modeled Nucor on certain bedrock values: productivity, simplicity, thrift, and innovation.

PRODUCTIVITY   Iverson liked to contrast Nucor to integrated companies. He recounted a field trip he took to an integrated steel plant when he was a student at Purdue: "This was the late afternoon. We were touring through the plant, and we actually had to step over workers who were sleeping there. I decided right then that I didn't ever want to work for a big steel plant." The average Nucor worker produced 700 to 800 tons of steel per year versus 350 tons per employee at integrated companies; total labor costs at Nucor averaged less than half that at integrated producers. At the production level, people were arranged into groups of 25 to 35 people. Each group had a production standard to meet and a steep bonus schedule for exceeding its standard. Nucor production workers could earn $30,000 or more in a good year. Producing steel and joists entailed hard, hot, dirty, and occasionally dangerous jobs. Performance at all levels of the company was rigidly tied to efficiency and profitability criteria.

SIMPLICITY AND THRIFT   Iverson and other managers at Nucor had developed practices and symbols that conveyed simplicity. One of their notable achievements was a streamlined organizational structure. Only four levels separated the official hierarchy: workers, department managers, division managers, corporate. Iverson said:

> You can tell a lot about a company by looking at its organization charts. . . . If you see a lot of staff, you can bet that it is not a very efficient organization. . . . Secondly, don't have assistants. We do not have that title and prohibit it in our company. . . . And one of the most important things is to restrict as much as possible the number of management layers. . . . It is probably the most important single factor in business.

Iverson's pioneering approach in steel was beginning to be copied by the bigger companies:

> I spent two days as a lecturer at a business school not long ago. One of the students heard me talk about getting rid of management layers. He spoke up and said that when he visited U.S. Steel's new pipe mill near Birmingham, Alabama, the thing they were most proud of wasn't the technology but that they had only 4 management layers instead of the usual 10.

Nucor's spartan values were most evident at its corporate headquarters. Instead of having a handsome, expensive showcase building sited on landscaped grounds, Nucor rented a few thousand square feet of the fourth floor of a nondescript office building with an insurance company's name on it. The only cue that Nucor was there was its name (listed in ordinary size letters) in the building directory. The office decor was spartan, simple, and functional. Only sixteen people worked in the headquarters—no financial analysts, no engineering staff, no marketing staff, no research staff. The company assiduously avoided the normal paraphernalia of bureaucracy. No one had a formal job description. The company had no written mission statement, no strategic plan, and no MBO system. There was little paperwork, few regular reports, and fewer meetings. Iverson commented on his staff and how it functioned.

> They are all very sharp people. We don't centralize anything. We have a financial vice president, a president, a manager of personnel, a planner, internal auditing, and accounting. . . . With such a small staff there are opportunities you miss and things you don't do well because you don't have time . . . but the advantages so far outweigh the disadvantages. . . . We focus on what can really benefit the business. . . . We don't have job descriptions, we just kind of divide up the work.

INNOVATION   Nucor was a leading innovator among steel minimills and in the joist business as well. Plant designs, organizational structure, incentives, and work force allocations synchronized with cultural pressure for constant innovative advancements. Iverson projected that minimills could eventually capture as much as 35 to 40 percent of the steel business if they succeeded in developing technological advances that enabled them to produce a wider variety of steel products very economically. The breakthroughs hinged on revamping continuous casting technology. Currently, a minimill couldn't produce certain shapes. Iverson thought the key to unlock the door was the "thin-slab caster":

> We are trying to develop a thin slab. Then we could produce plate and other flat-rolled products. Right now the thinnest slab that can be produced is 6 inches thick. If we can get down to 1½ inches with the thin slab caster, then we can map out the growth for another 10 years. We could build those all over the country. We're trying to develop this new technology in our Darlington mill. The investment will probably run $10 to $20 million. Now, if we could do it, the new mills would probably cost about $150 million.

Many analysts doubted that such a breakthrough was really in the offing, but Iverson believed it would come within three years and was monitoring seven experimental programs.

KEN IVERSON: PUBLIC FIGURE   Nucor's success had made Iverson a public figure. He had been interviewed by newspapers, magazines, radio, and TV; he spoke to industry groups and business schools; and he had been called to testify before Congress. He explained why he was willing to devote his time to these extracurricular activities.

> Generally, our policy is to stay as far away as we can from government . . . except that I felt so strongly about protectionism that I thought I should make my views known—especially because our view is so different from the other steel mills. . . . Talking to investors is an important part of the company's relationship with the marketplace . . . the company gets a direct benefit and it makes good sense. . . . I do some talks at business schools just from the stand-point that I get pleasure out of that. . . . We do occasionally hire MBAs, but we haven't had much success with them.

Iverson had a casual, informal, and unaffected style. His office was nei-ther large nor furnished with expensive decorations. For lunch he took vis-itors across the street to a delicatessen—their "executive dining room"—for a quick sandwich. Nucor had no executive parking spaces, no executive restrooms, no company cars. Everyone, including Iverson, flew coach class. When Iverson went to New York he rode the subway instead of taking a limousine or taxi. Other Nucor managers followed Iverson's example, shun-ning ostentation, luxury, and status symbols common among other success-ful companies.

Managers at Nucor described Iverson's management style:

> Ken is straightforward. If he says something you can pretty well count on it. He sets the tone and the direction and everybody pitches in. That's the way he acts and approaches things—directly.
>
> Ken is one of the greatest leaders the steel industry has ever had.
>
> Ken is liberal with people and conservative with money.

ORGANIZATION

ORGANIZATION STRUCTURE Following Iverson's lean-management philosophy, only four levels of management separated Iverson from the hourly employees. At corporate headquarters they joked that with four promotions, a janitor could become CEO! Exhibit 13 depicts Nucor's organization chart. Below the corporate level the company was organized into divisions. These divisions roughly correspond to plant locations.

Recently, under the pressure of the growing size of the company and Iverson's busy public role, the jobs of president and CEO were separated. By

EXHIBIT 13　　　**Nucor's Organization Structure, 1985**

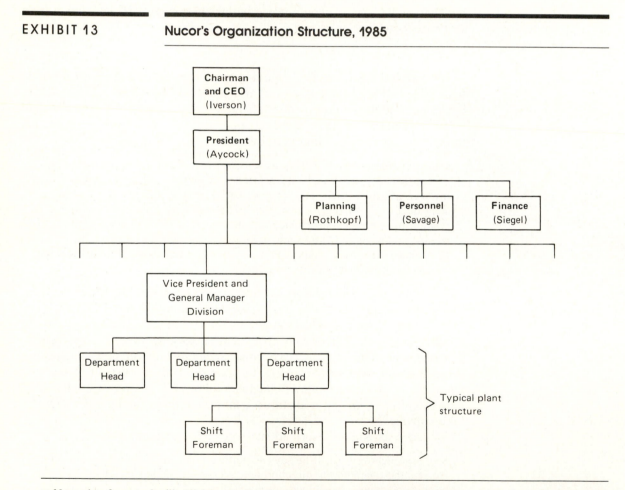

e: Nucor has four steel mills (divisions), six joist plants, three cold-finished steel plants, a grinding ball plant, and a arch chemicals division—each is headed by a vice president and general manager.

trying to be "everything to everyone," Iverson was spreading himself a little thin. Dave Aycock was promoted from a plant manager's job to president, responsible for day-to-day operations of Nucor; Aycock talked about his new role:

> I worked at Vulcraft when it was acquired by Nucor in 1955. . . . I've been in this new job for about a year. . . . It's very exciting. . . . If I had actually known roughly half of what I thought I knew, I would probably have been more valuable. . . . Most of my time has been spent learning the personalities, the reactions, and philosophies of the operating personnel. . . . Many of them were glad to see the change because they thought Ken was overworked.

DIVISION MANAGEMENT   Because Nucor had no headquarters staff and because of top management's great confidence in operating personnel, division managers played a key role in decision making. Iverson said of the division managers: "They are all vice presidents, and they are behind our success. They make the policies of this company. Most of them have been with Nucor at least ten years. But a vice president's pay is based on how this company does—not on how well the vice president's division does—it's the group concept again."

CORPORATE–DIVISION INTERACTION   Contact between divisions and corporate headquarters was limited to a report of production volume, costs, sales, and margin—the Monthly Operations Analysis. Each month every division received the "smiling face" report, comparing all the divisions across about a dozen categories of efficiency and performance. One division manager described how Iverson delegated and supervised:

> Mr. Iverson's style of management is to allow the manager all the latitude in the world. His involvement with managers is quite limited. As we have grown, he no longer has the time to visit with division managers more than once or twice a year. . . . In a way I feel like I run my own company because I don't get marching orders from Mr. Iverson. He lets you run the division the way you see fit, and the only way he will step in is if he sees something he doesn't like, particularly bad profits, high costs, or whatever. But in the four years I've worked with him I don't recall a single instance where he issued an instruction to me to do something differently.

The casewriters asked a division manager how the corporate officers would handle a division which wasn't performing as it should:

> I imagine he (Aycock) would call first and come out later, but it would be appropriate to the situation. Ken and Dave are great psychologists. Right now, for instance, the steel business is showing a very poor return on assets, but I don't feel any pressure on me because the market is not there. I do feel pressure to keep my costs down, and that is appropriate. If something went wrong Dave would know.

How does Nucor respond to problems in management performance?

> We had a situation where we were concerned about the performance of a particular employee . . . a department manager. Ken, Dave, and I sat down with the general manager to let him know where we were coming from. So now the ball is in his court. We will offer support and help that the general manager wants. Later I spent a long evening with the general manager and the department manager. Now the department manager understands the corporate concern. Ken will allow the general manager to resolve this issue. To do otherwise would take the trust out of the system. . . . We are not going to just call someone in and say "We're not satisfied. You're gone." . . . But, eventually, the string may run out. Ken will terminate people. He takes a long time to do it. I respect that. Ken would rather give people too much time than too little.

Important issues merited a phone call or perhaps a visit from a corporate officer. A division manager told the casewriters that he talked to headquarters about once a week. Divisions made their own decisions about hiring, purchasing, processes, and equipment. There was no formal limit on a division manager's spending authority. Sales policy and personnel policy were set at the corporate level. Divisions didn't produce a plan, but: "People in this company have real firm ideas about what is going on and what will be happening . . . mostly by word of mouth."

Relationships between the divisions were close. They shared ideas and information, and sold each other significant amounts of product.

DECISION MAKING Division managers met formally in a group with corporate management three times a year at the "Roundtable." Sessions began at 7 A.M. and ended at 8 P.M. At these meetings, budgets, capital expenditures, and changes in wages or benefits were agreed on, and department managers were reviewed. Iverson waited for a consensus to emerge about an alternative before going ahead with a decision. He did not impose decisions. Corporate officers described Nucor's decision-making processes:

> Over a long period of time, decisions in this company have been made at the lowest level that they can—subject to staying within the philosophy of the company. We get a lot of work done without too many managers. Ken has the business courage to stay out of the small things. It takes a lot of courage for general managers to resist the temptation to control every event.
>
> I can walk into Ken's office anytime and talk about anything I want to talk about. Agree or disagree with anything he has done. I don't agree with every decision that is made. I have the right to disagree. Sometimes I disagree strongly. Ken hears me out. Ken listens to other people. He does not feel that he is always right. Sometimes he will change his mind.
>
> I remember when I first started to work for Nucor and I was sitting down with Ken Iverson. He told me, "John, you are going to make at least three mistakes with this company in the first few years that you are with us. Each one of these mistakes will cost us $50,000. I want you to be aggressive, and I

want you to make decisions. One word of caution. We don't mind you making the mistakes, but please don't make them all in one year."

Ken defers a decision when the executives are strongly divided to give people a chance to consider it more. Ken is a superb negotiator. He might look at the various positions and say "I have a compromise," and lay that out. Many times he can see a compromise that everyone is comfortable with.

FINANCIAL POSITION	The theme of simplicity also extended to financial matters. Sam Siegel, Nucor's vice president of finance, did not use a computer. He told the casewriters: "When you make too many calculations they get in the way of business. Each of the divisions uses computers for many purposes, including financial analysis. You could make an economic case for centralizing some of that here at corporate headquarters. We could save money and create all kinds of information, but then we would have to hire more people to study that information."

INVESTMENTS   No financial analysts worked at corporate headquarters. Nucor did not use sophisticated models of discounted cash flow or complicated formulas to govern capital expenditures, preferring an eclectic capital investment policy. Iverson commented: "Priority? No. We don't even do that with capital expenditures. Sometimes we'll say . . . we won't put up any buildings this year. . . . But in recent years we've been able to fund anything we felt we needed. We don't do it by priorities." Responding to a query about whether the company used an internal hurdle rate of return, Iverson said:

> We look at it from the standpoint of whether it's replacement and if it's modernization, what the payback period is, or if it is a new facility. In many cases the payback on a new steel mill is longer than you would like, but you can't afford not to do it. I think maybe that is where other manufacturing companies go wrong—where they have these rigid ideas about investments. If you don't put some of these investments in, after four or five years you are behind. . . . You can't afford to fall behind, even if you don't get the payback. That's why the integrated steel companies didn't put in continuous casters, because they couldn't get the payback they wanted. . . . Now they have got to do it. . . . From an economic point of view they didn't do anything wrong, they didn't make a mistake.

FINANCIAL REPORTING   Each division had a controller who reported directly to the division manager and indirectly to Siegel. Siegel saw the role of his controllers as being broad: "Controllers who merely do financial work are not doing a good job. A controller should become involved with key plant operations . . . should learn the whole operation." Siegel spent only about one-half of his own time on strictly financial matters, contributing the other half toward "problems, issues, and projects" of importance to the company.

FINANCIAL CONDITION   According to Siegel, the company was in good financial condition except for having too much invested in short-term assets (Exhibits 14 and 15). Wall Street analysts had speculated about what Nucor might decide to do with its excess short-term assets.

HUMAN RESOURCES

Besides being known for its stunning success in joists and steel, Nucor was also known for its remarkable human resources practices. The casewriters visited a Vulcraft plant and talked with a department manager who had worked at Vulcraft for sixteen years about what made Nucor different:

> Our plants are located strategically. The company puts them in rural areas, where we can find a good supply of quality labor—people who believe in hard work. We have beaten back three unionizing campaigns in the last 10 years. These employees are very loyal. In fact, we had to hire a guard to protect the union organizers from some of our workers. We see about 3 percent turnover and very little absenteeism. They are proud of working with us. It's fun when they come to you and ask for work.

Why did Nucor do so well with employees?

> Most companies want to take their profits out of their employees. We treat employees right. They are the ones who make the profits. Other companies aren't willing to offer what is needed to allow people to work. They can't see the dollar down the road for the nickel in their hand. Nucor's people make it strong.

Nucor's incentive systems had been a subject of much discussion and comment. *Fortune* estimated in 1981 that Nucor's workers earned an average of $5,000 more than union steelworkers. Moreover, Nucor workers were the highest paid manufacturing, blue-collar workforce in the United States.

> **Casewriter:** But doesn't that prove the point—that American steelworkers earning $30,000 per year have priced the industry out of business?
> **Iverson:** They earn every bit of it! Sure, it's generous. . . . There's a reason for it. It's hot, hard, dirty, dangerous, skilled work. We have melters who earn more than $40,000, and I'm glad they earn it. It's not what a person earns in an absolute sense, it's what he earns in relation to what he produces that matters.

The incentive system at Nucor had several key elements. John Savage, manager of personnel services, explained the company's personnel philosophy:

> Our employee relations philosophy has four primary components. . . . Management's first and foremost obligation to employees is to provide them the

EXHIBIT 14 Balance Sheets, Nucor Corp., 1984 and 1985

	1984	1985
Assets		
Current assets:		
Cash	$ 2,863,680	$ 8,028,519
Short-term investments	109,846,810	177,115,854
Accounts receivable	58,408,244	60,390,448
Contracts in process	8,462,815	10,478,296
Inventories	73,797,302	78,641,805
Other current assets	74,522	114,125
Total current assets	253,453,373	334,769,147
Property, plant, and equipment	228,102,790	225,274,674
Other assets	632,302	267,367
Total assets	$483,188,465	$560,311,188
Liabilities and Stockholders' Equity		
Current liabilities:		
Long-term debt due within one year	$ 2,402,462	$ 2,402,462
Accounts payable	32,691,249	35,473,011
Federal income taxes	23,705,195	27,597,464
Accrued expenses and other current liabilities	41,734,778	55,782,891
Total current liabilities	100,533,684	121,255,828
Other liabilities:		
Long-term debt due after one year	43,232,384	40,233,769
Deferred federal income taxes	38,819,563	41,319,563
	82,051,947	81,553,332
Stockholders' equity:		
Common stock	5,669,757	5,732,382
Additional paid-in capital	18,991,334	24,299,195
Retailed earnings	275,035,788	327,816,850
	299,696,879	357,848,427
Treasury stock	(94,045)	(346,399)
Total stockholders' equity	299,602,834	357,502,028
Total liabilities and stockholders' equity	$482,188,465	$560,311,188

EXHIBIT 15   **Statement of Changes in Financial Position, Nucor Corp., 1983–1985**

	1983	1984	1985
Funds provided:			
Operations:			
Net earnings	$27,864,308	$44,548,451	$58,478,352
Depreciation of plant and equipment	27,109,582	28,899,421	31,105,788
Deferred federal income taxes	8,200,000	5,600,000	2,500,000
Total funds provided by operations	63,173,890	79,047,872	92,084,140
Disposition of plant and equipment	274,138	377,259	788,726
Decrease in other assets	—	—	364,935
Issuance of common stock	2,201,183	2,006,460	5,387,182
Total funds provided	$65,649,211	$81,431,591	$98,624,983
Funds applied:			
Purchase of property, plant, and equipment	$19,617,147	$26,074,653	$29,066,398
Increase in other assets	354,170	259,229	—
Reduction in long-term debt	2,498,615	2,498,616	2,998,615
Cash dividends	4,216,854	5,081,771	5,697,290
Acquisition of treasury stock	—	—	269,050
Increase in working capital	38,962,425	47,517,322	60,593,630
Total funds applied	$65,649,211	$81,431,591	$98,624,983
Analysis of change in working capital:			
Increase (decrease) in current assets:			
Cash	$ (4,283,370)	$ (3,521,115)	$ 5,164,839
Short-term investments	38,445,234	37,177,195	67,269,144
Accounts receivable	16,424,874	7,297,872	1,982,204
Contracts in process	8,402,160	1,404,012	2,015,481
Inventories	7,723,168	17,242,200	4,844,503
Other current assets	(366,052)	(35,593)	39,603
Net increase (decrease)	61,346,514	59,564,211	81,315,774
Increase (decrease) in current liabilities:			
Long-term debt due within one year	799,000	—	—
Accounts payable	14,186,217	(4,443,835)	2,781,762
Federal income taxes	2,278,813	8,891,286	3,892,269
Accrued expenses and other current liabilities	5,120,059	7,599,438	14,048,113
Net increase (decrease)	22,384,089	12,046,889	20,722,144
Increase in working capital	$38,962,425	$47,517,322	$60,593,630

opportunity to earn according to their productivity. . . . Next, we are obligated to manage the company in such a way that employees can feel that if they are doing their job properly, they will have a job tomorrow. . . . Third, employees must believe that they are treated fairly. . . . Lastly, employees must have an avenue of appeal if they believe they are being treated unfairly, to Mr. Iverson himself if necessary.

Everyone at Nucor participated in incentive plans. These incentives took several different forms depending on the type of work involved.

PRODUCTION INCENTIVES Production groups of 25 to 30 employees were given clearly measurable production tasks. About 3,000 Nucor employees made joists and steel under production incentives based on historical time standards. If, for example, a group produced a joist in 50 percent less than standard time, they got a 50 percent bonus. Bonuses were paid at the end of the following week. When equipment sat idle, no bonus accrued. If an employee was absent for a day, he or she lost a week's bonus—a difference amounting to as much as $7 per hour. The system was very tough:

> If you work real hard and you get performance, the payment is there next week. . . . You worked like a dog and here is the money. . . . There are lots of people who don't like to work that hard, and they don't last for long. We have had groups get so mad at a guy who wasn't carrying his weight that they chased him around a joist plant with a piece of angle iron and were gonna kill him. . . . Don't get the idea that we're paternalistic. If you are late even five minutes you lose your bonus for the day. If you are late by more than 30 minutes because of sickness or anything else, you lose your bonus for the week. We do grant four "forgiveness" days a year. We have a melter, Phil Johnson, down in Darlington. One day a worker arrived at the plant and said that Phil had been in an auto accident and was sitting by his car on Route 52 holding his head. The foreman asked, "Why didn't you stop to help him?" The guy said, "And lose my bonus?"

Many Nucor workers earned between $30,000 and $40,000 per year. Nucor's monetary incentives made the company attractive to jobseekers (see Exhibit 14). Iverson told a story about hiring new workers:

> We needed a couple new employees for Darlington, so we put out a sign and put a small ad in the local paper. The ads told people to show up Saturday morning at the employment office at the plant. When Saturday rolled around, the first person to arrive at the personnel office was greeted by 1,200 anxious jobseekers. There were so many of them that the size of the crowd began to interfere with access into and out of the plant. So the plant manager called the state police to send some officers over to control the crowd. But, the sergeant at the state police barracks told the plant manager that he couldn't spare any officers. You see, he was short-handed himself because three of his officers were at the plant applying for jobs!

MANAGERIAL COMPENSATION   Department managers received a bonus based on a percentage of their division's contribution to corporate earnings. In an operating division such bonuses could run as high as 50 percent of a person's base pay. In the corporate office the bonus could reach 30 percent of base pay. Employees such as accountants, secretaries, clerks, and others who didn't work in production got a bonus based on either their division's profit contribution or corporate return on assets.

Senior officers had no employment contracts or pension plan. More than half of their compensation was based on company earnings. Their base salaries were set at about 70 percent of market rates for similar jobs. Ten percent of pretax earnings were set aside and allocated to senior officers according to their base salary. The base level was tied to a 12 percent return on shareholder's equity. Half the bonus was paid in cash, and half was deferred in the form of Nucor stock. In a profitable year officers could earn as much as 190 percent of their base salary as bonus and 115 percent on top of that in stock.

OTHER COMPENSATION INCENTIVES   Nucor also operated a profit sharing trust. The plan called for 10 percent of pretax earnings to be assigned to profit sharing each year. Of that amount, 20 percent was paid to employees in the following year, and the remainder was held to fund the worker retirement program. Vesting in the trust was 20 percent after one year and 10 percent each following year. The arrangement had the effect of making the retirement income of Nucor employees depend on the company's success. Additionally, Nucor paid 10 percent of whatever amount an employee was willing to invest in Nucor stock, gave employees five shares of stock for each five years of employment, and occasionally paid extraordinary bonuses.

Lastly, Nucor ran a scholarship program for children of full-time employees. In 1985 over 300 were enrolled in universities, colleges, and vocational schools. Since the program's inception over 900 students had participated. One family had educated eight children on Nucor's plan.

NO LAYOFFS   Nucor had never laid off or fired an employee for lack of work. Iverson explained how the company handled the need to make production cutbacks:

> When we have a difficult period, we don't lay anybody off. . . . We operate the plants four days a week or even three days. We call it our "share the pain program." . . . The bonus system remains in place, but it's based on four days' production instead of five. The production workers' compensation drops about 25 percent, the department managers' drops 35 to 40 percent, and the division manager's can drop as much as 60 to 80 percent. Nobody complains. They understand. And they still push to get that bonus on the days they work.

THE DOWNSIDE   Nucor's flat structure and steep incentives also had certain negative side effects. First, the incentive system was strictly oriented toward the short term. If a general manager was thinking about a major capital investment project, he was also thinking about reducing his short-term income. Iverson described how the ups and downs of the incentive plans affected officers: "If the company can hit about 24 percent return on equity, the officers' salary can reach 300 percent of the base amount. It maxed out in 1979 and 1980. In 1980 and 1981 total officers' compensation dropped off. In 1980 I earned about $400,000, but in 1981 I earned $108,000. So officers have to watch their lifestyle!" Iverson's 1981 pay made him, according to *Fortune,* the lowest paid CEO in the *Fortune 500* industrial ranking. Iverson commented that it was "Something I was really a little proud of."

Second, promotions came very slowly. Many managers had occupied their current jobs for a very long time. Additionally, Nucor experienced problems in developing the skills of its first-line supervisors.

Many other companies studied Nucor's compensation plans. The casewriters asked John Savage about the visits other companies made to study Nucor's system:

> Many companies visit us. We had managers and union people from General Motors' Saturn project come in and spend a couple of days. They were oriented toward a bureaucratic style. . . . You could tell it from their questions. I was more impressed with the union people than with the management people. The union people wanted to talk dirty, nitty-gritty issues. But the management people thought it was too simple, they didn't think it would work. Maybe their business is too complex for our system. . . . We never hear from these visitors after they leave. . . . I believe it would take five to seven years of working at this system before you could detect a measurable change.

High wages and employment stability got Nucor listed in the book *The 100 Best Companies to Work for in America.* A division manager summed up the Nucor human relations philosophy this way: "It's amazing what people can do if you let them. Nucor gives people responsibility and then stands behind them." Exhibit 16 presents selected excerpts from interviews with hourly employees about their jobs at Nucor.

STRATEGIC PLANNING

Nucor followed no written strategic plan, had no written objectives (except those stated in the incentive programs), and had no mission statement. Divisions promulgated no strategic plans. We asked Sam Siegel about long-range strategic planning. He confided: "You can't predict the future. . . . No matter how great you may think your decisions are, the future is unknown. You don't know what will happen. . . . Nucor concentrates on the here-and-now. We do make five-year projections, and they are good for about three months. Five to ten years out is philosophy." We also asked Bob Rothkopf (planning director) about planning at Nucor:

> I work on the strategic plan with Ken twice a year. It's formulated out of the projects we are looking at. He and I talk about the direction we feel the com-

EXHIBIT 16   **Excerpts of Interviews with Hourly Employees at Nucor**

Jim

Jim is 32 years old, did not finish high school, and has worked at Vulcraft for ten years. He works at a job that requires heavy lifting. Last year he earned about $38,500.

> This is hard physical work. Getting used to it is tough, too. After I started as a spliceman my upper body was sore for about a month. . . . Before I came to work here I worked as a farmer and cut timber. . . . I got this job through a friend who was already working here. . . . I reckon I was very nervous when I started here but people showed me how to work. . . . The bonuses and the benefits are mighty good here . . . and I have never been laid off. . . . I enjoy this work. . . . This company is good to you. They might let employees go if they had problems, but first they'd give him a chance to straighten out. . . . In 1981 things were slow and we only worked three or four days a week. Sometimes we would spend a day doing maintenance, painting, sweeping. . . . and there wasn't no incentive. I was glad I was working . . . I was against the union.

Kerry

Kerry is 31 years old, married, and about to become a parent. He has worked on the production line for about three years.

> I was laid off from my last job after working there five years. I went without work for three months. I got this job through a friend. My brother works as a supervisor for Nucor in Texas. . . . This is good, hard work. You get dirty, too hot in the summer and too cold in the winter. They should air-condition the entire plant (laughs). On this joist line we have to work fast. Right now I'm working 8½ hours a day, six days a week. . . .I get good pay and benefits. Vulcraft is one of the better companies in Florence (South Carolina). . . . Everyone does not always get along, but we work as a team. Our supervisor has his off days. . . I want to get ahead in life, but I don't see openings for promotion here. Most of the foreman have had their jobs for a long time, and most people are senior to me in line. . . . This place is very efficient. If I see a way to improve the work, I tell somebody. They will listen to you.

Other comments from hourly workers

I am running all day long. It gets hot and you get tired. My wife doesn't like it because sometimes I come home and fall asleep right away.

When something goes down, people ask how they can help. Nobody sits around. Every minute you are down it's like dollars out of your pocket. So everybody really hustles.

pany is going. . . . The elements of the most recent plan are that we take the basic level of the company today and project it out for five years. We look at net sales, net income, under different likely scenarios. In this last plan I looked at the potential effects of a mild recession in 1986. . . . We add new products or projects to that baseline.

Rothkopf had responsibility for generating most of the information he used in his forecasts. He often used consultants or other companies to get the information he needed. None of the other senior executives or division managers got deeply involved in this planning process.

Nucor didn't rely on its strategic planning system to make strategic decisions. Rothkopf described how strategic decisions were reached:

> Projects come from all over. Some come from our general managers, or from our suppliers, our customers . . . or come walking in the door here. Iverson is like a magnet for ideas, because of who he is and what Nucor is. . . . We evaluate each project on its own, as it comes up. As each opportunity arises, we go in and investigate it. Some investigations are short; we throw out quite a few of them. We don't make any systematic search for these ideas.

Rothkopf compared Nucor's planning to formal strategic planning done by other companies:

> I think there might be some advantages for us to do that sort of thing. However, our business has been pretty simple. Our businesses are all related and easy to keep track of. When a big decision comes up we discuss it. That's easy because of the simple structure of the company. . . . Planning has disadvantages . . . time-consuming . . . expensive . . . hard to get the information for it . . . tends to get bureaucratic.

Although Nucor had no formal planning system, important strategic decisions loomed on the company horizon. Exhibit 17 provides information on Nucor's strategic options.

NUCOR'S FUTURE: WHAT NEXT?

In spite of Nucor's remarkable successes, Iverson stated a modest, cautious view of the company's capabilities:

> We are not great marketers or financial manipulators. . . . We do two things well. We build plants economically and we run them efficiently. We stick to those two things. . . . Basically, that's all we do. We are getting better at marketing, but I wouldn't say we are strong marketers . . . that is not the base of the company. . . . We're certainly not financial manipulators. We recognized a long time ago how important it was for us to hold down overhead and management layers.

Iverson talked about the future of Nucor:

> The company's position is much different than it was in past years. In the 60s we nearly went bankrupt. It was a miniconglomerate, so I got rid of half the

EXHIBIT 17   A Summary Review of Nucor's Strategic Options

STRATEGIC CONSIDERATIONS	OPTION 1 BUILD A SEAMLESS TUBE MILL	OPTION 2 GET INTO PREENGINEERED BUILDINGS
Market	About $2.5 billion Oilfield equipment companies Commodity Mature, competitive, low growth Integrated companies sell here	$350 million Small growth Numerous competitors, all sizes Regional, fragmented Not a commodity
Investment	$150–180 million	$5–7 million generates $15–20 million in four years. Want about 20 percent market share in five to six years
Time period needed	About two years	8–12 months
Fit to present activities	Could sell some product to joist division Increase efficiency	Already manufacturing parts for such buildings
Revenues/profits	Sales $240–270 million 20–25 percent profit before taxes	About same as present earning power
Support among executives	Some active support Analyses in process	Joist division favors it Corporate execs divided
Skills and resources	Know market Have most skills, others not too hard to learn	Selling to whole new market Manufacturing skills help
Downside risk	Risky, uncertain market	New market to understand Can do gradually Not very risky

STRATEGIC CONSIDERATIONS	OPTION 3 BUILD BAR MINIMILL	OPTION 4 ACQUIRE BAR MINIMILLS
Market	Same as current	Same as current
Investment	$50–70 million for a 250,000 ton mill	A six- to seven-year-old, 175,000-ton mill costs $50 million to build Earns $10–15/ton before tax
Time period needed	18 months	± 1989, 1987 earliest
Fit to present activities	Perfect fit	Obvious, yes
Revenues/profits	$65–75 million sales. Lose money years one and two. Over long term make $4–10 million before taxes.	$45 million sales, earns ± $1 million Under Nucor, such a mill can see sales of $60 million, earn ± $5 million
Support among executives	Quite a bit	Unknown
Skills and resources	In place, no problems	OK, in place
Downside risk	No growth in market. Must take business from entrenched competitors	Antitrust? Company culture might not fit; exposure to union problems

EXHIBIT 17	Continued

STRATEGIC CONSIDERATIONS	OPTION 5 INNOVATIVE FLAT-ROLLED MINIMILL	OPTION 6 BUILD BOLT PLANT
Market	25–30 million tons Stable, a commodity Integrated mills dominant	$800 million Mature, stable Commodity dominated by four companies
Investment	$125–$175 million for 400,000 to 600,000 ton mill	$25 million/plant
Time period needed	Could build four plants in 5–10 years	
Fit to present activities	Extends product range Sales to joist division Keeps steel/joist "balance"	Steel currently produced goes into product
Revenues/profits	Must project 25 percent profit before tax to justify Lower cost $100/ton?	$28–32 million sales per plant
Support among executives	High company support; spending $10 million to develop process at Darlington	Agreed to build one plant
Skills and resources	Don't know marketing of flat-rolled products Must learn flat-rolling of steel	Need marketing skills
Downside risk	Must invest $10–15 million in any case Hard to invest new technology Competitors leap-frog with new processes Estimate 50–75 percent chance it will work	If foreign steel is barred in United States, bolts get "dumped" here. International prices of bolts unstable.

STRATEGIC CONSIDERATIONS	OPTION 7 INCREASE DIVIDENDS	OPTION 8 PURCHASE NUCOR STOCK FOR TREASURY
Market	Stockholder reaction uncertain Number of shares × increase	14,000,000 shares at $5 currently Number of shares × price
Time period needed	Anytime	One to two years
Fit to present activities	Change in philosophy	Underlines management confidence
Revenues/profits	N/A	Sell shares for profit? Enrich remaining stockholders?
Support among executives	Iverson thinking about it	At the right price/earnings ratio
Skills and resources	N/A	N/A
Downside risk	If earnings slip, could pressure ability to invest	Price of stock could decline

EXHIBIT 17   Continued

	OPTION 9
STRATEGIC CONSIDERATIONS	**DIVERSIFICATION OUTSIDE STEEL PRODUCTS OR JOISTS**
Market	Faster growing markets open
Investment	Nucor has $100–150 million Could borrow more
Time period needed	One to two years
Fits to present activities	Depends on business
Revenues/profits	Greater profitability?
Support among executives	Very little
Skills and resources	Nucor understands heavy manufacturing Nucor has skills in streamlined management Employee-relations philosophy
Downside risk	Company has to learn new things? Might require different organizational set-up.

company. We started all over again. We built steel mills. From the late 60s to the 80s our constraints were financial. We decided that we wanted debt to be less than 30 percent of capital. That restricted the number of mills we could finance. But then in the 1980s things changed. Our restraints are not financial now. We no longer see the opportunities in minimills which we saw in the 60s and 70s. So, what direction should the company go? We have about $120 million in cash and short-term securities.

Since we don't see much opportunity for building additional minimills, we have been looking at various alternatives . . . merger or acquisition, internal growth . . . buying back our own stock . . . and other things. It goes forward by project. We looked at buying another steel company that had problems. Dave visited their plant. Bob (the planner) did some projections on what it would cost us to put that mill in shape. We also have an outside consultant working on it. That is what we have done so far (Iverson points to a report). . . . We are looking at the bolt business too. About 95 percent of bolts used in the United States are made outside of the United States. We are studying whether we should spend $25 million to build a plant. . . . Maybe we ought to buy our own stock. It reduces the number of shares and increases the per share earnings. I feel comfortable with that, given the price/earnings ratio we are at.

We are thinking about a seamless tube mill. That business seems to meet many of our requirements. Also, the Vulcraft people believe that we could easily enter the business of preengineered buildings. Although that is a new market for us, it's not very risky, and it is a logical extension of the joist business.

We are also talking to the Japanese about a joint venture to produce large and medium structural steel shapes. That's a 6 million ton market worth about $2 billion per year. It's cyclical because it's tied to the construction industry. Imports have about 32 percent of that. We might invest $200 million. We know this market, but we lack some technology which the Japanese can supply. We would be 51 percent partners and run the plant.

Was he worried about a takeover?

I really don't expect someone to try to take us over. We have a staggered board. So if someone tries to do it they will have to wait for quite a while to control enough directors. We have other provisions in the bylaws which would make a takeover difficult. Besides, we're in a lousy business—steel.

What about an acquisition by Nucor?

We have some problems with going that route. We don't have any experience with acquisitions; all our growth has been internally generated. The second thing, we would never acquire outside our business, which is the manufacture of steel and steel products. We might be able to go into some nonferrous metals. But if we went into, say, textiles or something else like that . . . it's not . . . If stockholders want to invest in those businesses, let them do it themselves. Conglomeration is a lot of nonsense.

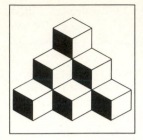

INDUSTRY
AIRLINE

CASE 19

Texas Air Corporation (1985)

TIMOTHY M. SINGLETON · ROBERT McGLASHAN

Texas Air Corporation (TAC) is the holding company for Continental Air, New York Air, and several other airline-related operations. Its chairman and CEO, Frank Lorenzo, has become one of the most interesting business personalities in the United States. In 1985, at the age of 44, he seemed to be on the verge of completing a deal for the acquisition of TWA, which, combined with Continental, would create the second largest domestic air carrier and have international operations that virtually covered the globe. At the time of airline deregulation in 1978, Lorenzo was reported to have said, "By 1990 there will be only six major airlines in the United States. Our goal is to emerge as one of them." Observers speculated that the TWA acquisition attempt by Lorenzo and TAC, if successful, would accomplish that goal and, as one airline analyst put it, "give Lorenzo a license to print money."

AIRLINE INDUSTRY BACKGROUND

The airline industry has had a glorious rise in importance since Orville and Wilbur Wright's experiment at Kitty Hawk. The obvious uses of the flying machine received serious attention during the two world wars that followed.

The research and written case information were presented at the Case Research Symposium and were evaluated by the Case Research Association's Editorial Board. This case was prepared by Timothy Singleton, North Georgia College, and Robert McGlashan of the University of Houston–Clear Lake as a basis for class discussion.

Distributed by the Case Research Association. All rights reserved to the authors and the Case Research Association. Permission to use the case should be obtained from the Case Research Association and Timothy Singleton.

Initial research was performed by Lonnie Nesrsta, Ken Hunter, Gerald Scott, Godwin Okoro, Robert Buck, Gene Magee, Terry Miller, Bill Parrish, and Gail Lewis of the University of Houston–Clear Lake.

Since the government wanted to ensure the full development of its potential, policies were set to achieve this end.

The modern executor of this policy was the Civil Aeronautics Board (CAB). For many years the CAB nurtured and protected the airline industry to achieve the use of high-quality equipment and provide service to all corners of the country. This semisubsidization has recently been seen as a stone around the neck of free enterprise because high prices, high wages, and inefficiencies have run rampant in the airlines.

In 1978 the spirit of deregulation swept through the airline industry. The structured concepts of major trunk carriers that operated heavily traveled long-distance routes and intrastate feeders that collected passengers from more remote regions began to wither. Frank Lorenzo was prepared as airline CEOs tried to change the strategic direction of their lumbering organizations.

LORENZO'S BACKGROUND

Born to a beauty shop owner in Queens, New York, in 1940, Frank Lorenzo is a good example of a self-made man. He was interested in flying, like many young men at that time, and he was determined enough to actually become a licensed pilot. Educated in business as an undergraduate at Columbia University and a graduate of Harvard, Frank gained business savvy and a friend and future business associate, Robert Carney.

In 1966, after working for three years in the financial departments of Eastern and TWA, Lorenzo and Carney launched Lorenzo, Carney, and Co., an airline financial advisory firm, which later spawned Jet Capital Inc., with plans for the leasing of aircraft to smaller airlines. Their desire to own an airline became apparent when they tried to acquire Mohawk Airlines. This move was thwarted when Allegheny Airlines came to Mohawk's rescue. Lorenzo and Carney's efforts then turned to consulting because they found a need for their airline and business skills among New York banks.

TEXAS INTERNATIONAL AIRLINES

By 1971 a Sunbelt operation named Texas International Airlines (TI) was in desperate financial trouble. This intrastate feeder was profitable under the name of Trans Texas Airways until its 1966 buyout by a group of Minnesota investors. One of the nervous creditors of TI, Chase Manhattan Bank, was looking for some assurance that its loans would be maintained. By luck, fate, or clever maneuvers the Lorenzo–Carney team was conveniently ready to offer its consulting services.

Within a year, Lorenzo and Carney had gained control of TI by investing their consulting fees and restructuring TI's debt. They controlled this company of "good ol' boys" in 1971 with 59 percent of the voting stock. Lorenzo effected a quick turnaround; losses were $7.4 million in 1971 and $1.7 million in 1972. By 1973, profit was $121,000, and it rose to $257,000 in 1974. He consolidated the company by spinning off subsidiaries and instituted more cost-efficient operations.

In December 1974, TI found itself fighting a strike. Labor mistrusted management's tactics, and Lorenzo believed the company could not survive as a union company that competed with nonunion firms unless it gained some concessions. The strike ended four months later, essentially on Lorenzo's terms. Southwest Airlines made certain advances during that time, and TI posted about a $4 million loss for 1975. Ironically, in later years, TI was found guilty of conspiracy and antitrust violations against Southwest in what was called "The Great Texas Air War."

Lorenzo and his team developed a low-fare concept called "Fly for Peanuts" that they hoped would bring the company out of the doldrums. It did just that. By 1976, TI was gaining profitably with increased load factors on planes. The Civil Aeronautics Board, under pressure from proponents of deregulation, began to experiment with low fares by allowing TI to expand into more markets.

Spurred on by a now-healthy organization, Lorenzo once again set his sights on takeover targets. After securing substantial backing, he began to implement a hostile takeover of National Airlines in the spring of 1978. Managing to acquire 24.5 percent of the outstanding National stock, at an average of $25 per share, he realized that TI could not complete the takeover. A sell-out to a "white knight," Pan Am, at $50 per share netted TI about $46 million in after-tax profits. It is interesting to note that this happened just after Lorenzo publicly announced that National's stock was really worth $76 per share. In the fall of 1979 he began another attempt, this time aimed at TWA. After accumulating 4 percent of outstanding shares, Lorenzo settled for about a $6 million profit after several meetings with TWA management.

In June 1980, part of Lorenzo's management team abruptly left TI to try running their own airline, People Express. They hoped to make a profit by applying the low-fare idea to a short-distance commuter. Frank answered his former associates by creating New York Air.

In March 1980, TI was transformed into a subsidiary of the Texas Air Corporation (TAC) as Frank Lorenzo consolidated some operations and expanded others. New York Air was formed by using jets that were newly acquired from Swissair and by hiring nonunion labor. The unionized pilots of TI strongly complained about the new carrier.

THE CONTINENTAL ACQUISITION

The combination of deregulation, recession, overcapacity, and fare discounting had financially ravaged many of the major airlines. And Continental had its share of the industry's problems. In 1981, Continental Airlines amassed losses of approximately $60 million, the third consecutive year that the airline operated at a loss. The passenger load factor for the year declined to an average of 57.6 percent from 58.1 percent for 1980.

At a private meeting with Continental's chairman, Robert F. Six, Lorenzo tried to negotiate a friendly takeover and was turned down. Thus began Lorenzo's hostile bid for Continental. In early 1981, Lorenzo announced that Texas International had acquired 9.4 percent of Continental's stock and intended a takeover. Alvin Feldman, then head of Continental, was pursuing a merger with Western Airlines, another carrier with significant financial problems. When Texas International made its tender offer of $13 per share for Continental on February 9, 1981, Western dropped out of the picture. It appeared that Continental's only hope of evading Lorenzo's clutches lay in the proposed employee stock ownership plan.

Texas International had spent a borrowed $93 million to purchase half of Continental's stock. Industry sources questioned why Lorenzo wanted the airline, which had lost $20.7 million on revenue of $992 million in 1980 and had dropped $34.7 million in the first half of 1981. However, Lorenzo felt that a merger with Continental was needed to instantly obtain hubs at Denver, Houston, and Los Angeles. This complemented TI's spokelike route system and provided larger planes to broaden its fleet of shorter-range DC-9s. "The deregulated environment," said Lorenzo, "requires a strong, integrated carrier with a substantial hub facility. As we merge, we are also going to be able to combine our market strength, taking advantage of our flight concentration in Houston and Denver and our ability to advertise and promote much more aggressively."[1] He planned to operate both airlines (Texas International and Continental) as a single entity, Continental Airlines Corp., which in turn would be a subsidiary of Texas Air Corporation.

Even as the threat of an unfriendly takeover by TI became more real, Continental management sought to improve its financial position by cutting costs. In August 1981, Continental announced a program that included employee layoffs and a 10 percent salary cut for the company's management. In October the company's pilots agreed to a 10 percent wage reduction, and the company continued to negotiate unsuccessfully for concessions with the unions representing other groups of employees.[2]

The battle between Continental and Texas International was bitter, drawn out, and expensive. Both sides enlisted the help of legal and political heavyweights. TI used the law firm of the Democratic National Chairman, Charles Manatt, one of whose partners was a former Democratic congressman. Continental, for its part, persuaded Senator Dennis DeConcini of Arizona to cosponsor legislation that would have reversed a California court decision that had discredited the proposed employee buy-out. The legislation was intended as a rider to President Reagan's all-important tax bill. Incidentally, Senator DeConcini's brother was a Continental pilot.

Lorenzo had tough times with Continental from the beginning. The carrier had always treated its employees well and was considered to be "the proud bird with the golden tail." On the other hand, Texas International was known for its "peanut fare," and Lorenzo's style was deeply resented.[3]

Animosity toward Lorenzo was widely shared at Continental and throughout the airline industry. It had its roots largely in TI's labor relations reputation and the establishment of New York Air, the nonunion sister company. Paul Eckel, a Continental pilot, led the crusade by Continental employees to stop the merger, saying, "We are willing to make any sacrifice to keep Frank Lorenzo from coming on our property."[4] With the aid of lawyers, bankers, and other consultants paid by Continental, the newly formed Continental Employees' Association, headed by Eckel, developed an Employees Stock Ownership Plan (ESOP). It proposed borrowing $185 million, which would enable the employees to buy the airline, giving the ESOP 51 percent of the total stock outstanding. The loan, to be guaranteed by the company, would be repaid from employees' future earnings.

Lorenzo was outraged and challenged the ESOP in the California courts. In the hopes of heading off the plan at Continental's annual meeting on May 6, 1981, he petitioned the CAB for approval to exercise voting control over Texas International's Continental shares.[5] To ensure that TI's position got a good hearing in the California courts and regulatory agencies, Lorenzo secured the services of a political heavyweight in the Los Angeles office of the Manatt law firm. He also went to Sacramento to meet with key legislators and was introduced to strong lobbyists by two of his own people who were well connected politically.[6]

With the eventual pullout of financing for the employee buy-out plan, and after CAB approval, the last barrier to completion of the acquisition was White House approval. That came on October 12, 1981, when President Reagan sanctioned the acquisition, thereby allowing Texas International to take full control of the 50.3 percent of Continental's shares that had been held in trust pending approval (see Exhibits 1 and 2). The cost of the shares was $96.6 million.[7]

CONTINENTAL–TEXAS INTERNATIONAL: AFTER THE MERGER

The cutbacks begun in 1981 continued at a quickened pace with the takeover of Continental by the cost-conscious TI. In early 1982 the existing route structure was examined, and several unprofitable routes were eliminated. Additional employee layoffs were implemented, and the company management was restructured. A new round of negotiations with the unions was begun in an attempt to gain productivity improvements and more efficient work rules. One company executive said that the carrier "could not continue to exist on temporary solutions, and must get more productivity out of its unionized personnel on a permanent basis, not just for a year or two."[8] The goal of the actions was to achieve at least a break-even operation by the end of 1982.

On October 31, 1982, Texas International and Continental were integrated into a single operation. The resulting Continental Airlines Corporation became a wholly owned subsidiary of Texas Air Corporation, employing a total of 13,500 persons (see Exhibits 3 and 4). Lorenzo, who was given credit by

EXHIBIT 1   Routes of Texas International and Continental Airlines

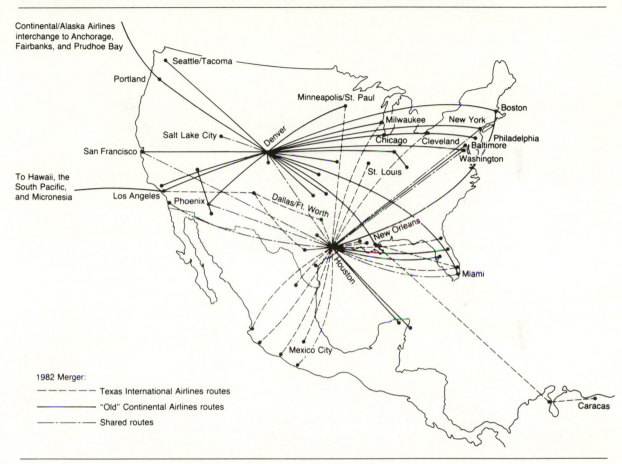

Continental/Alaska Airlines
interchange to Anchorage,
Fairbanks, and Prudhoe Bay

Seattle/Tacoma

Portland

Minneapolis/St. Paul

Boston

Milwaukee   New York

Salt Lake City   Denver   Chicago   Cleveland   Philadelphia
Baltimore
San Francisco   Washington

St. Louis

To Hawaii, the
South Pacific,
and Micronesia

Los Angeles   Phoenix   Dallas/Ft. Worth

New Orleans

Houston   Miami

Mexico City

1982 Merger:

– – – – – – – Texas International Airlines routes

——————— "Old" Continental Airlines routes

–·–·–·–·– Shared routes

Caracas

many for the salvation of Texas International from bankruptcy eleven years earlier, said that "Texas International's high productivity and low fares will continue to be an important element of our strategy for the new Continental."[9]

The merger of the two airlines was accompanied by a realignment of long-term debt. Securing loan agreements was made possible in part by several cost-reduction and revenue-improvement programs, including an agreement with Continental's pilots that was to reduce costs in 1983 by an estimated $45 million. This agreement, signed in August 1982, involved changes in the work rules including, among other things, provisions allowing Continental

EXHIBIT 2

Texas Air Corporation Airline Route System

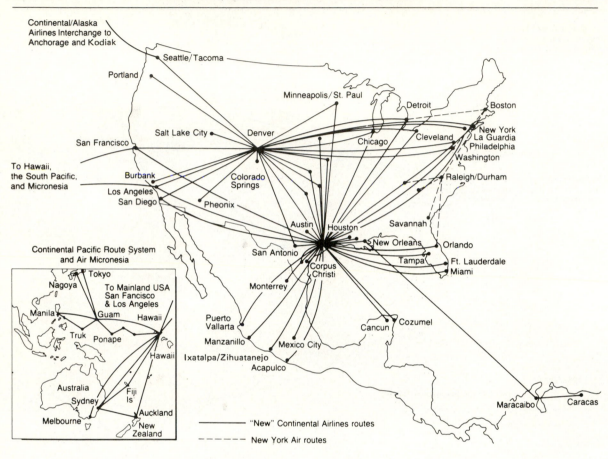

to increase the number of flying hours for pilots. The agreement did not involve a major change of pay for the pilots.[10]

The consolidation of the two airlines continued in the early part of 1983. In January the top management positions were merged, and in February a relocation of the corporate offices from Los Angeles to Houston, the home of Texas Air Corporation, was announced. In March 1983, Continental was authorized to issue a public stock offering of 2 million units worth an estimated $40 million.[11] Also in March 1983 it was announced that American General Corporation would invest $40 million in Continental in the form of notes accompanied by five-year warrants providing for the purchase of ap-

EXHIBIT 3   Texas Air Stock Ownership

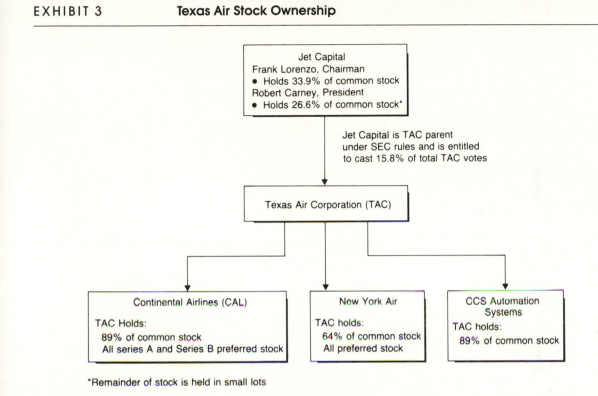

*Remainder of stock is held in small lots

SOURCES: Texas Air Corporation, 1983 Annual Report; 1981 TAC Proxy.

proximately 20 percent interest in Continental for $42.5 million. Mr. Lorenzo said the investment would be useful in providing financial assistance in further expansion of Continental.[12] The total new financing lined up by Continental between November 1982 and March 1983 was almost $200 million (see Exhibits 5 through 8).[13]

However, financial difficulties continued to plague Continental and many other major airlines. Despite concessions involving changes in work rules, reduction in personnel, and wage cuts by various unions, the cost of labor continued its dramatic rise in 1983. The average annual pay per employee was $41,811 in the first quarter of 1983. Labor costs represented 37 percent of the total expenses of the major and national carriers, and wages continued to increase at rates that were much higher than those for the manufacturing sector. In comparison, the average annual pay per employee for the new entrant airlines, such as New York Air, a wholly owned subsidiary of Texas

EXHIBIT 4   Texas International/Texas Air Corporation: Board of Directors

	TI									TAC				
	1971	1972	1973	1974	1975	1976	1977	1978	1979	1980	1981	1982	1983	1984
Francisco A. Lorenzo	X	X	X	X	X	X	X	X	X	X	X	X	X	X
I. H. Handmaker	X	X	X	X	X	X	X	X	X	X	X	X	X	X
Carl R. Pohlad	X	X		X	X	X	X	X	X	X	X	X	X	X
P. B. Brooks	X	X	X	X										
P. R. Christen	X	X	X	X	X	X								
D. E. Benson	X	X	X	X	X									
Howard Wolf	X	X	X	X	X	X								
M. J. Levitt	X	X												
M. M. Meyers	X	X												
W. L. Lane	X													
R. L. Sicard	X													
S. A. Caria	X													
I. H. Feidt	X													
Robert J. Carney			X	X	X	X	X	X	X	X	X	X	X	X
Robert Garrett			X	X	X				X	X	X	X	X	X
A. Thomas Hickey			X	X	X	X	X	X	X	X	X	X	X	
Howard P. Swanson			X	X	X	X	X	X	X					
R. D. Gallaway			X	X	X									
W. W. Parrish					X	X								
Donald C. Burr					X	X	X	X	X					
Ben Barnes					X	X								
James W. Wilson							X	X	X	X	X	X	X	X
Harry T. Chandis										X				
Sanford E. McCormick											X	X	X	X
Robert D. Snedeker												X	X	X
Robert F. Six												X	X	
Stephen M. Wolf													X	

SOURCE: *Moody's Transportation Index*, 1971–1984.

EXHIBIT 5	Texas Air Corporation: Financial and Operating Data, 1971–1980 (Dollar Amounts in Thousands Except Per Share Data)		

	1980	1979	1978
SUMMARY OF OPERATIONS			
Passenger revenues	$ 266,837	$ 213,218	$ 158,185
Other revenues	24,659	20,943	22,007
Total operating revenues	$ 291,496	$ 234,161	$ 180,192
Total operating expenses	284,949	218,825	164,118
Operating income (loss)	$ 6,547	$ 15,336	$ 16,074
Interest and debt expense—net	$ 19,650	$ 15,092	$ 6,656
Other (income) expense—net	(20,402)	(48,051)	(3,733)
Provision for income taxes	2,630	6,900	5,174
	$ 1,878	$ (26,059)	$ 8,097
Income (loss) from continuing operations	$ 4,669	$ 41,395	$ 7,977
Income (loss) from Tropicana Hotel	—	—	—
Extraordinary items	—	—	5,174
	$ 4,669	$ 41,395	$ 13,151
Earnings (loss) per common and common equivalent share	$ 0.64	$ 5.88	$ 2.17
Earnings (loss) per common share assuming full dilution	0.64	4.84	2.05
FINANCIAL INFORMATION (AT YEAR END)			
Current assets	$ 196,169	$ 156,927	$ 39,785
Current liabilities	82,871	68,452	44,578
Working capital (deficit)	113,298	88,475	(4,793)
Net investment in flight equipment	158,062	143,824	83,592
Total assets	386,428	319,201	194,955
Total long-term debt	217,790	175,295	113,213
Net worth (deficit)	89,903	81,218	40,784
Common stock price range	14¾–6⅜	13⅝–7½	16⅜–7⅛
GENERAL STATISTICS[1]			
Employees at year end	3,500	3,400	3,000
In scheduled service for the year:			
Passengers boarded	3,970,197	4,073,019	3,699,079
Revenue passenger miles (000s)	2,241,586	2,186,297	1,560,553
Available seat miles (000s)	3,898,422	3,523,128	2,601,677
Passenger load factor	57.5%	62.1%	60.0%
Break-even load factor	55.8%	57.6%	55.0%
Average fare	$ 67.10	$ 52.35	$ 42.76
Yield per revenue passenger–mile	$ .1189	$ 0.0975	$ 0.1014

[1]Texas International only.

EXHIBIT 5   Continued

1977	1976	1975	1974	1973	1972	1971
$ 122,038	$ 102,051	$ 60,594	$ 74,431	$ 62,758	$ 58,181	$ 56,203
22,749	18,342	18,529	17,345	14,547	14,907	13,788
$ 144,787	$ 120,383	$ 79,123	$ 91,776	$ 77,305	73,088	$ 69,991
132,623	114,375	79,833	87,711	73,618	70,348	71,591
$ 12,164	$ 6,018	$ (710)	$ 4,065	$ 3,687	$ 2,740	$ (1,600)
$ 4,305	$ 3,496	$ 3,510	$ 4,267	$ 4,128	$ 4,324	$ 4,821
(379)	(957)	29	(459)	(562)	(63)	156
1,034	822	—	43	13	—	—
$ 4,960	$ 3,361	$ 3,539	$ 3,851	$ 3,579	$ 4,261	$ 4,977
$ 7,204	$ 2,657	$ (4,249)	$ 214	$ 108	$ (1,521)	$ (6,577)
—	—	—	—	—	$ 199	$ (839)
1,034	822	—	43	13	(305)	—
$ 8,238	$ 3,479	$ (4,249)	$ 257	$ 121	$ (1,707)	$ (7,416)
$ 1.52	$ 0.70	$ (3.48)	$ 0.02	$ (0.03)	$ (1.42)	$ (6.19)
1.52	0.70	(3.48)	0.02	(0.03)	(1.42)	(6.19)
$ 37,266	$ 27,287	$ 21,457	$ 18,846	$ 19,127	$ 18,793	$ 16,216
44,433	33,401	30,301	26,160	23,698	21,748	36,726
(7,167)	(6,114)	(8,844)	(7,314)	(4,571)	(2,955)	(20,510)
55,661	43,723	46,856	47,790	46,262	52,152	56,604
108,796	78,868	73,575	73,998	80,076	75,307	78,946
61,610	49,966	50,302	51,739	56,548	55,476	64,621
11,749	4,267	760	4,932	4,573	5,214	(7,527)
8–2⅛	3⅝–1⅝	2¾–1¼	3⅞–1	4¾–1⅞	7–4	8–3½
2,600	2,300	2,150	2,000	2,153	2,019	2,089
3,002,913	2,397,256	1,515,196	2,116,605	2,045,933	2,160,928	2,220,515
1,167,059	946,756	580,269	758,949	681,904	686,353	705,853
2,022,907	1,767,488	1,167,349	1,506,193	1,484,787	1,374,167	1,494,642
57.7%	53.6%	49.7%	50.4%	45.9%	49.9%	47.2%
53.9%	51.9%	53.3%	50.1%	45.5%	51.5%	52.7%
$ 40.64	$ 42.57	$ 39.99	$ 35.17	$ 30.67	$ 26.92	$ 25.31
$ 0.1046	$ 0.1078	$ 0.1044	$ 0.0981	$ 0.0920	$ 0.0848	$ 0.0796

EXHIBIT 6

Continental Airlines: Selected Financial and Statistical Data
(Dollar Amounts in Thousands)

	1983	1982	1981	1980	1979
OPERATING REVENUES					
Passenger	$ 995,994	$1,261,642	$1,245,215	$ 879,593	$807,694
Other	116,991	165,373	154,435	112,426	120,288
Total operating revenues	$1,112,985	$1,427,015	$1,399,650	$ 992,019	$927,982
OPERATING EXPENSES					
Wages, salaries, and related costs	$ 420,600	$ 492,053	$ 532,866	$ 401,481	$380,089
Aircraft fuel	321,509	437,560	432,425	295,255	227,614
Depreciation and amortization	75,991	86,950	84,002	59,262	56,353
Other	445,206	445,045	398,823	282,229	271,847
Total operating expenses	$1,263,306	$1,461,608	$1,448,116	$1,038,227	$935,903
NONOPERATING EXPENSE (INCOME)					
Interest expense	$ 69,304	$ 89,152	$ 100,526	$ 42,099	$ 30,182
Capital interest	(181)	(1,348)	(4,521)	(4,974)	(1,673)
Other	(996)	(77,460)	(60,724)	(47,500)	(4,645)
Total nonoperating expenses, net	$ 68,127	$ 10,344	$ 35,291	(10,375)	$ 23,864
EARNINGS (LOSS) BEFORE INCOME TAXES	(218,448)	(44,937)	(83,757)	(35,833)	(31,785)
Income taxes (credits)	—	(3,133)	(3,859)	(15,129)	(18,600)
Net earnings (loss)	$ (218,448)	$ (41,804)	$ (79,898)	$ (20,704)	$ (13,185)
ASSETS, LIABILITIES AND STOCKHOLDERS' EQUITY					
Current assets:					
Cash and temporary investments	$ 64,686	$ 37,123	$ 76,082	$ 31,717	$ 34,670
Accounts receivable—net	84,449	152,495	155,306	106,381	118,629
Spare parts and supplies—net	27,728	33,422	42,729	36,938	23,497
Prepayment and other	21,946	26,828	15,661	5,816	5,007
Total current assets	$ 198,809	$ 249,868	$ 289,778	$ 180,852	$181,803
PROPERTY AND EQUIPMENT					
Owned property and equipment (net)	$ 546,040	$ 619,758	$ 706,847	$ 482,715	$545,590
Capital leases	124,958	134,868	145,365	115,544	—
Total property and equipment	$ 670,998	$ 754,626	$ 852,212	$ 598,259	$545,590
Total other assets	38,336	48,575	41,051	5,038	11,314
Total assets	$ 908,143	$1,053,069	$1,183,041	$ 784,149	$738,707

EXHIBIT 6   Continued

	1983	1982	1981	1980	1979
CURRENT LIABILITIES					
Current portion of long-term debt	17,087	68,780	66,943	38,305	53,484
Current portion of capital leases	3,452	5,116	4,169	1,631	—
Accounts payable	16,812	119,314	111,595	64,549	82,131
Other	63,387	198,857	205,641	141,950	116,061
Total current liabilities	$ 100,738	$ 392,067	$ 388,348	$ 246,435	$251,676
ESTIMATED LIABILITIES SUBJECT TO CHAPTER 11 REORGANIZATION PROCEEDINGS	$ 737,610	$ —	$ —	$ —	$ —
Long-term obligations	172,178	583,948	679,629	328,797	243,979
Other (deferred credits)	6,812	27,185	23,391	18,043	30,195
Stockholders' equity:					
Stock and paid-in capital	182,420	121,704	121,704	88,953	88,698
Retained (deficit) earnings	(291,615)	(71,835)	(30,031)	101,921	124,159
Total stockholders' equity	$ (109,195)	$ 49,869	$ 91,673	$ 190,874	$212,857
Total liabilities and stockholders' equity	$ 908,143	$1,053,069	$1,183,041	$ 784,149	$738,707

SOURCE: Continental Airlines Company records.

Note: 1979–1980 Continental Airlines only: 1981—Pro Forma CAL and TXI combined; 1982–1983—CAC.

Air Corporation, was $22,000. Labor costs represented only 18 percent of the total expenses of these airlines. A report issued by the CAB in December 1982 stated:

> A significant disequilibrium exists between the labor costs of the smaller new airlines and the labor costs of the large established airlines. Nevertheless, the major airlines have generally not yet significantly increased worker productivity. Over time, market forces will tend to eliminate this disequilibrium either by raising costs of the low-cost airlines or by reducing costs of the high-cost airlines.

The market forces in 1983 tended primarily to the latter of these equalizing forces—that of reducing costs of the high-cost airlines. For example, Pan Am showed an operating profit of $46.5 million in the second quarter of 1983 in part because it reduced its labor cost early in the year through major wage

EXHIBIT 7	Texas Air Corporation: Five-year Summary of Selected Financial and Statistical Data (Dollar Amounts in Thousands Except Per Share Data)				
	1983	**1982**	**1981**	**1980**	**1979**
SUMMARY OF OPERATIONS					
Operating revenues					
Passenger	$ 1,124,189	$ 1,356,122	$ 649,491	$ 266,837	$ 213,218
Other	122,026	160,198	69,909	24,659	20,943
Total operating revenues	1,246,215	1,516,320	719,400	291,496	234,161
Operating expenses	1,382,087	1,562,289	760,246	284,949	218,825
Operating income (loss)	(135,872)	(45,969)	(40,846)	6,547	15,336
Other income (expense)					
Interest and debt expense—net	(67,785)	(87,107)	(40,964)	(4,238)	(11,067)
Minority interest in subsidiaries	—	20,861	12,077	27	—
Other—net	25,793	60,107	17,755	4,284	44,026
Total other income (expense)	(41,992)	(6,139)	(11,132)	73	32,959
Income (loss) before income taxes	(177,864)	(52,108)	(51,978)	6,620	48,295
Income tax (credit) provision	2,076	(3,133)	(4,793)	2,630	6,900
Extraordinary items	—	—	—	—	—
Net income (loss)	$ (177,864)	$ (48,975)	$ (47,185)	$3,990	$ 41,395
Net income (loss) per share					
Primary	$ (14.58)	$ (7.27)	$ (8.11)	$ (0.55)	$ (5.88)
Fully diluted	$ (14.58)	$ (7.27)	$ (8.11)	$ (0.55)	$ (4.84)
FINANCIAL SUMMARY					
Current assets	$ 304,455	$ 326,391	$ 352,549	$ 195,490	$ 156,927
Current liabilities	134,547	415,956	405,002	82,871	68,452
Property and equipment—net	839,525	839,332	928,358	177,968	158,307
Total assets	1,177,959	1,191,978	1,301,316	385,749	319,201
Long-term debt—net	259,212	515,948	605,001	196,236	154,491
Obligations under capital leases—net	55,656	144,808	156,213	11,347	13,940
Redeemable preferred stock	23,219	24,464	4,400	4,899	5,548
Stockholders' equity	(49,649)	63,477	40,453	84,325	75,670
Common stock price range	11¾–4¾	13⅞–4	15⅛–5⅛	14¾–6⅜	13⅝–7½

EXHIBIT 7	Continued				
	1983	**1982**	**1981**	**1980**	**1979**
STATISTICAL SUMMARY					
Continental Airlines*					
Available seat miles (000)	15,396,477	19,270,121	17,474,238	17,865,646	19,175,563
Revenue passenger–miles (000)	9,274,257	11,157,365	10,069,734	10,359,077	11,674,282
Load factor	60.2%	57.9%	57.6%	58.0%	60.9%
Revenue passengers	10,236,004	11,355,711	10,285,713	11,404,046	13,192,855
Average fare per passenger	$97.30	$111.30	$121.06	$100.49	$77.38
Average yield per revenue passenger–mile	10.74¢	11.31¢	12.37¢	11.06¢	8.74¢
Average length of passenger trip (miles)	906	872	850	828	885
Revenue aircraft–miles (000)	110,703	137,678	127,393	135,480	146,097
Average length of aircraft flight (miles)	662	638	620	585	590
Average daily utilization of aircraft (block hours)	7:19	9:02	9:08	9:51	10:46
New York Air†					
Available seat miles (000)	1,146,584	1,110,478	735,494		
Revenue passenger–miles (000)	656,601	606,654	460,832		
Load factor	57.3%	54.6%	67.2%		
Revenue passengers	2,103,681	1,738,095	1,562,017		
Average fare per passenger	$60.94	$54.36	$40.89		
Average yield per revenue passenger–mile	19.5¢	15.57¢	13.86¢		
Average length of passenger trip (miles)	312	349	295		
Revenue aircraft–miles (000)	10,307	9,878	6,238		
Average length of aircraft flight (miles)	300	330	287		
Average daily utilization of aircraft (block hours)	8:08	8:45	8:90		

SOURCE: Texas Air Corporation 1982, 1983 Annual Reports.

*Reflects the combined operations of Continental and Texas International.
†New York Air began service in December 1980.

and production concessions by its principal unions. The Air Lines Pilots Association at Northwest Airlines accepted a plan to fly more hours and increase productivity as part of their new labor contract. Other airlines were also able to convince employees, including pilots, to accept changes that would reduce labor costs and improve profitability.

At Continental, however, the labor situation seemed only to get worse. Losses since 1979 had been a staggering $500 million. The airline management blamed these losses, in part, on the "intolerable and well-above-

EXHIBIT 8   TI/TAC Yearly Stock Prices, 1971–1985

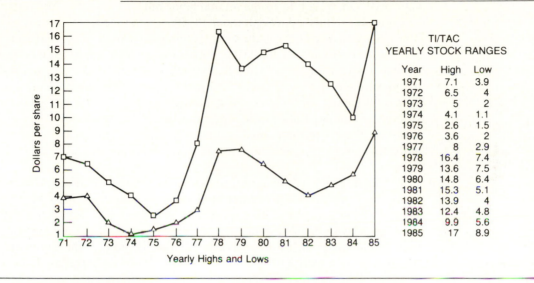

TI/TAC YEARLY STOCK RANGES		
Year	High	Low
1971	7.1	3.9
1972	6.5	4
1973	5	2
1974	4.1	1.1
1975	2.6	1.5
1976	3.6	2
1977	8	2.9
1978	16.4	7.4
1979	13.6	7.5
1980	14.8	6.4
1981	15.3	5.1
1982	13.9	4
1983	12.4	4.8
1984	9.9	5.6
1985	17	8.9

market labor costs structure" that had evolved before deregulation.[14] Efforts to further reduce labor costs were largely unfruitful. In August 1983, following eighteen months of contract negotiations, Continental Airlines and 2,100 employees belonging to the International Association of Machinists and Aerospace Workers entered a 30-day impasse period at the direction of a federal mediator. Continental had offered the employees a 19 percent pay raise but was also asking for changes in the work rules to allow improvements in productivity and did not provide any additional wage increases before 1985.[15] A strike followed, but Continental's operations continued when many of the strikers crossed the picket lines and others were replaced.[16]

Lorenzo also demanded deep concessions from the airline's other unions. His offer was to exchange a 35 percent share of nonvoting stock in the company for wage concessions estimated at $150 million, including changes proposed to the striking unions and management pay cuts. These concessions, Lorenzo claimed, were necessary for the airline to survive. His plan, according to the company's estimate, would make its employees the largest single stockholder in the airline industry. The offer included a bonus of 4 million shares of Continental stock to the 12,000 employees. In addition, there were stock options that could be exercised through March 1985: 8 million shares at 85 percent of market price, purchased over a two-year period through payroll deduction. There was also a profit-sharing provision in the plan. Management expected the $150 million estimated annual cost saving to reverse the company's operating losses. Replacement of the striking machinists with lower-paid workers and contract employees had already cut an estimated $20 million from the annual labor bill.

Lorenzo established a September 19, 1983, deadline for acceptance of the offer. After that date, he indicated, Continental would take whatever measures were necessary to cut costs. This convinced the union leaders that the company was trying to provoke them into joining the striking machinists on the picket lines. Lorenzo could then replace them as he had the machinists, thereby breaking the unions. This, union leaders felt, had been Lorenzo's strategy all along. Labor contended that there was no cash crisis and no imminent danger to the company and that claims to the contrary were little more than weak excuses that would allow Lorenzo to bring labor to its knees.[17]

The flight agent, clerical, and reservations groups voted overwhelmingly for the cost restructuring plan. However, members of the Flight Attendants Union and the Air Lines Pilots Association rejected the offer. Stephen Wolf, president of Continental, and Lorenzo sought to reach an accommodation with the unions. With union accommodations unlikely, the company fast running out of cash, and Chapter 11 at the door, Wolf resigned. Lorenzo assumed Wolf's former duties as president of Continental as well as his own as chairman of Texas Air.

CHAPTER 11 FOR CONTINENTAL

On September 24, 1983, four days after expiration of the contract deadline, Continental filed for Chapter 11 bankruptcy. The company claimed that burdensome labor contracts threatened to force it into liquidation. At the time of filing, Continental had over $58 million in cash and marketable securities and over $230 million in accounts receivable.[18] However, most of the cash was apparently in restricted accounts. The company later said that its working cash had dropped to the $25 to $30 million level.

Two days later, on September 26, Continental Airlines filed an emergency motion asking the bankruptcy court to reject its union contracts in connection with its Chapter 11 filing. Continental then proceeded to change the work rules and wage rates for its employees. This action touched off a series of suits and allegations by the unions regarding the activities and events leading up to the reorganization.

The first of the suits came three weeks after Continental's filing of Chapter 11. The three unions that represented the majority of Continental's workers—the Air Lines Pilots Association, the International Association of Machinists and Aerospace Workers, and the Union of Flight Attendants—filed a motion in federal bankruptcy court asking that Continental's petition for protection under Chapter 11 be thrown out. The unions contended that Continental's bankruptcy filing was made to "abrogate existing contractual obligations, not to improve the ability to pay the existing debt."[19] The following week, the Air Lines Pilots Association (ALPA) filed a $100 million lawsuit charging that Continental refused to bargain in good faith, that it exhibited coercion in dealings with individual pilots, and that it filed for Chapter 11 to abrogate its contract with ALPA.

ALPA had traditionally taken a conservative position on labor disputes. However, on October 18, 1983, ALPA President Henry Duffy accompanied AFL-CIO President Lane Kirkland to Washington to lobby for legislation that would prohibit the use of bankruptcy to void union contracts. In addition, ALPA requested that the lawmakers consider a "limited form" of regulation for the airline industry preventing carriers from charging fares that are too low to allow a profit. To encourage the striking Continental pilots, ALPA authorized strike payments of up to $43,000 per year.[20]

During bankruptcy proceedings, Continental's employee unions took the position that the bankruptcy filing followed a conspiracy by the airline to transfer assets to Texas Air Corporation at less than their market value for the purpose of degrading Continental's financial position. This conspiracy, the unions contended, was undertaken to set the stage for the bankruptcy filing. The unions presented evidence at the hearing that was collected from financial records obtained from Continental. Examples of these transactions included the following:

- Landing rights at three gates at National Airport, Washington, D.C., were purchased by New York Air, a wholly owned subsidiary of Texas Air Corporation. The purchase price, agreed upon as $757,000, was never transferred to Continental Airlines. Continental claimed that this was an embarrassing oversight.

- A group of paintings was purchased from Continental by Texas Air Corporation for a price of $600,000, the appraised value. The unions claimed that another appraisal placed the value of the paintings at about $1 million.

- The unions questioned the purchase by Continental of Texas Air Corporation's pilot training facility for $5.9 million, the purchase by Texas Air of Continental's computer services unit for $15 million, and the $1.2 million per year in management fees paid by Continental to Texas Air.

- Some of Continental's international routes were spun off as a subsidiary company of Texas Air less than two weeks before the Chapter 11 filing. As a Texas Air subsidiary, this new company would be immune to Chapter 11 restrictions.

These hearings also brought out the fact that Richard Adams, senior vice president in charge of flight operations, identified Chapter 11 as a "big stick" that could be used to gain concessions from the unions.[21]

On January 17, 1984, a bankruptcy court in Houston, Texas, ruled that Continental was entitled to protection under Chapter 11 bankruptcy laws. In so doing, the court stated that

Continental Airlines filed this proceeding only when management felt it had no acceptable alternative if it were to have a chance to keep the airline flying; the court further finds that there was no intent or motive to abuse the purpose of the Bankruptcy code.

The same court began hearings on a request filed by Continental on September 27, 1983, to reject collective bargaining agreements in conjunction with its bankruptcy filing.

Following lobbying by unions, the House passed a bill in April 1984 that would require that union contracts could not be rejected in cases similar to Continental's unless the bankruptcy court determined that without the action any financial reorganization would fail and jobs would be lost. A similar measure was under consideration in the Senate, and the unions were pressing for the measure to be retroactive. Mr. Lorenzo promptly appeared before the Senate and testified that, should Continental be subjected to these measures, the airline would be liquidated.[22] The bill did not pass in the Senate and was not enacted.

Finally, in June 1984, after nearly nine months had passed, the federal bankruptcy court ruled that Continental Airlines was justified in breaking its agreements with the Air Lines Pilots Association. The courts said that the contracts were "'burdensome' and that the carrier had made 'reasonable efforts' to get concessions from the union."

Additional maneuvers in the court system included the filing of a $250 million suit by Continental against the International Association of Machinists and Aerospace Workers, charging that the union had coerced its members to join in the strike by placing liens on the members' personal property and paychecks;[23] the filing of a similar suit for $630 million against ALPA for similar violations;[24] and the filing of claims by ALPA for more than $100 million for back pay and pension benefits for pilots.

At the same time that the unions were pleading their case in the courts, they were also trying to discredit the safety record of the new Continental Airlines to the Federal Aviation Administration (FAA) and the general public. The union ran full-page ads listing 35 reasons why Continental was unsafe. In addition, the union called to the attention of the FAA more than 90 incidents in the first six months of operation after bankruptcy. ALPA claimed that it made no organized effort to catalog and report these occurrences by Continental—that it was simply concerned with maintaining safety in the airways. In response, however, the FAA implied that it was difficult to imagine that this was not part of the vendetta against Continental, since all of the incidents that ALPA reported involved Continental Airlines.

The incidents, all of which were investigated by the FAA, included the following:

• A Continental Airlines DC-9 landed on a taxiway at Denver. Frank Lorenzo, by happenstance, was a passenger on the flight. The airport was covered with several inches of snow, and the taxiway was lighted. Minutes earlier, a private aircraft had landed on the same taxiway.

- A "hard landing" occurred at LaGuardia Airport resulting in a wrinkled fuselage that went unnoticed for several days. The landing was determined to have resulted from adverse weather conditions. The flight crew was composed of former ALPA members.

- A Continental pilot operated an aircraft one day after his proficiency check period had expired, in violation of FAA rules. Both the pilot and Continental were fined.

In addition to those incidents reported by ALPA, the FAA was investigating harassment of Continental flights involving radio frequency blockages and overt actions by other aircraft that affected Continental flights. For example:

- On its final approach to Kansas City, Mo., a Continental flight experienced a jamming of its radio frequency that blocked communication with the tower.

- A Continental flight was the second to land in Tampa, Fla., when the lead aircraft suddenly reduced speed. The lead aircraft was asked by the air traffic controllers to clear the runway as quickly as possible after landing to allow the Continental flight to land. Instead, the airplane stopped on the runway, and an anonymous radio call identified the Continental pilots as "scabs."

Meanwhile, Continental's creditors had concerns of their own, which they actively pursued in court. In October 1983, these creditors, owed a total $650 million in long-term debt, attempted to bring healthier TAC and its affiliated companies into the bankruptcy proceedings. This was done to improve their potential for recovery. Creditors claimed that close financial ties existed between Continental Airlines, its parent company TAC, and TAC affiliates. In arguments that were similar to those made by the employees' groups, the creditors tried to show that the parent company, TAC, coordinated several questionable transactions before Continental's filing for Chapter 11 protection. These transactions included the offering of 2.5 million shares of common stock of New York Air on September 15, 1983, and the previously mentioned spinoff of Continental Airlines' international routes on September 13, 1983.

These actions, Continental's creditors contended, were representative of several transactions that exhibited a commingling of financial assets and activities among Continental, TAC, and other TAC subsidiaries. Therefore, the argument went, TAC activities should also be brought within the jurisdiction of the bankruptcy court.[25] The argument was not accepted by the court, and TAC remained relatively free from additional Chapter 11 restrictions.

However, the court did intervene on occasion to protect the interests of Continental's creditors. For example, in November 1984 the bankruptcy court blocked an attempt by Continental to secure the release of $10 million in restricted cash.[26] In a similar creditor protection move four months later the court put tight restrictions on the number of aircraft that Continental could lease from its parent company, TAC.

THE CONTINENTAL TURNAROUND

Three days after the Chapter 11 filing, Continental was again flying passengers. Several unanswered questions remained. Would enough pilots be willing to cross the picket line? Would suppliers continue to service Continental planes? Would travel agents keep writing tickets on a bankrupt carrier? Finally, would passengers fly with a striking and bankrupt airline? The answers soon became clear.

The airline was operating at less than 50 percent of its prefiling capacity, and 65 percent of the work force had been laid off. The airline returned to operations as the new Continental and had low introductory fares of $49 or less to any of its markets. The first flight of the day on September 27, 1983, from Houston to Baton Rouge had six passengers on board. Other flights fared much better. The airport ticket counters were besieged, in part because of the absence of a reservation system. The mobs of people seeking refunds on previously purchased tickets also contributed to the chaos. Most analysts were skeptical of the airline's long-term viability. Significant, however, was the fact that Continental had returned to operations and had returned quickly. In so doing, the airline hoped to minimize the damage done to its credibility among passengers and travel agents.

Continental's Chapter 11 filing and rapid restructuring significantly affected the airline industry. In one fell swoop, the airline had slashed its labor costs below those of its major competition. Even though the unions were offering concessions to other carriers in 1983 and 1984, these amounted at best to the establishment of a two-tiered wage structure. The structure allowed the airlines to hire new employees at a greatly reduced wage rate while paying senior employees at the older and higher rates. At best, it would take a few years for the two-tiered wage structure to become competitive with that of Continental employees.

For a while, it appeared that Continental and Frank Lorenzo might have set an airline trend, as other airlines were threatening to follow suit and file for bankruptcy if the unions did not make the concessions that were being requested. Frank Borman of Eastern used this threat in an attempt to obtain a 20 percent wage concession in early 1984, as did TWA (10 percent concession) and Western and Republic Airlines (15 percent concession).[27] Frank Lorenzo, who had pioneered record growth levels in the airline industry, seemed also to be pioneering an industry trend toward strategic bankruptcy.[28]

Continental's competitors had good reason to seek urgently to lower costs, as Continental's new low-cost structure had them more than a little worried. While its rates were slightly above the discount, "no frills" airlines such as People Express, Continental's fares were generally 20 percent below those of the other full-service airlines. During 1984 and the first half of 1985, even though his airline was still mired in bankruptcy, Lorenzo was seen as more of a competitive threat by the airline establishment than some of the more profitable upstarts since deregulation.

As an example, Richard Ferris, the chairman and chief executive of United Airlines, told a group of security analysts, when asked about the People Express Airlines incursion into the Chicago market, "I'm more worried about Continental than People Express." Mr. Ferris could justify higher fares than People Express, but Continental was also a full-service airline.[29] On another occasion, United claimed that Continental was the major reason for maintaining discount fares west of the Mississippi River. United felt that if it could succeed in taking enough of Continental's business to drop load factors into the 50 percent range (break-even was approximately 60 percent), Continental "would hemorrhage." Continental's fare reductions also put extreme pressure on Braniff Airlines as it resumed flights in March 1984 after its Chapter 11 filing.[30] Even Southwest Airlines spokesperson Sam Coats commented that "Continental has to be considered a very formidable competitor, particularly in the long haul markets."[31]

Lorenzo, however, remained sensitive to the possibility of triggering a fare war. He did not believe that competing by just cutting fares was a rational long-run strategy, since competitors could cut too. He said, "I'm surprised how many people think you can throw a hand grenade at a competitor and expect he'll stand here and enjoy it. If you don't leave him a profitable operation, you'll hit his hot button."[32]

In addition to fighting Continental's low discount fares, some airlines protested the content of Continental's directed advertising. In mid-1984, Frontier and Western contended that Continental's ads were deceptive and irresponsible. In the ads, Continental claimed that "your money goes farther" on Continental than on other airlines. It showed that while Continental would fly passengers to a certain destination for a specified fare, the same fare on Western and Frontier would take one only about half as far—to the middle of a desert or a swamp. The Civil Aeronautics Board investigated the advertising.[33] But before the board ruled, Continental dropped the campaign, saying that it had already run its course.

In February 1984, Continental further reduced its rates in 73 markets in the Midwest, Northeast, and West, matching a low discount fare being offered by American Airlines. Continental's fares were generally the same price as the competition's, were unrestricted, and were available on every seat on every flight. In some cases there were no stated expiration dates, and the lower rates were subject only to fourteen days' advance purchase.[34] It was feared that Continental's near-nationwide fare reductions would set off an industry-wide fare war. Analysts were concerned that the fare reductions would be disastrous to the industry's still shaky recovery.[35]

Despite this, during 1984 and the first half of 1985, all of the major airlines attempted to match or beat Continental's fares in various markets. In all cases, Continental matched or beat the competition's fares while being less restrictive. Bargain fares accounted for 65 percent of Continental's seats by March 1984, but its load factor was ten points higher than that of its rivals.[36]

At the beginning of 1984, Continental was operating at 53 percent of its pre-bankruptcy capacity. By year end, operations were 120 percent of the same period as measured by the available seat miles. Continental's passenger load factor averaged 62.7 percent in 1984. This was among the highest in the industry and was 5.5 percent above the 1983 level. Continental concluded the year with over 10,000 employees while achieving better operating performance than at its pre-bankruptcy level of 12,000 employees. Labor represented only 21 percent of Continental's operating expense in 1984 compared to 37 percent before Chapter 11. As a result the cost per passenger-mile dropped from 8.5 cents in September 1983 to 6.3 cents in September 1984 (see Exhibit 9).

By the second quarter of 1984, profits were realized for the first time in five years. At year end 1984, Continental reported net profit of $50.3 million on operating revenue of $1.2 billion. Long-term debt amounted to $661 million. Lorenzo declared, however, that "for our size, those [debt] are not big numbers."

The year 1984 was also significant for Continental in terms of its relationship with the nation's travel agents. Before the end of the first quarter, Continental had succeeded in regaining their confidence—confidence it had lost during the early stages of the bankruptcy proceedings. Travel agents were accounting for more than 60 percent of all ticket sales by the end of 1984.[37]

Certainly, 1984 was a remarkable year for Continental. In early 1984, industry analysts were predicting that Continental would become the largest low-cost airline in the country.[38] The company achieved several objectives, including the following:

- The domestic route system was successfully rebuilt.
- A plan to expand its international air service was initially implemented.
- The airline was repositioned for future growth in a highly competitive deregulated industry.
- The financial position and liquidity of the organization was strengthened.
- There was a return to profitability after five years.
- The confidence of travel agents was regained.

The successful trend continued into 1985. First quarter net profits for 1985 were $15.1 million on operating revenues of $363.1 million (see Exhibit 10). The company also accrued, but was not allowed to disburse, dividends on preferred stock for 1984.[39] In keeping with his commitment, Lorenzo distributed $8.3 million of the pretax profits to the profit-sharing accounts of the 10,000 employees in April 1985. This contribution represented approxi-

EXHIBIT 9   **Continental Airlines Rebuilding after Bankruptcy Filing**

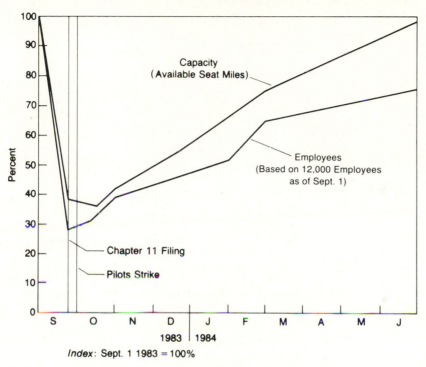

Index: Sept. 1 1983 = 100%

SOURCE: Reprinted from the March 19, 1984, issue of *Business Week* by special permission, copyright © 1984 by McGraw-Hill, Inc.

Index: Sept. 1, 1983 = 100%.

mately 5 percent of the employees' incomes, and many elected to take theirs in stock. Although the second quarter of 1985 still saw Continental operating under the restrictions of Chapter 11, it was building up its cash assets and continuing to expand its routes and modernize its fleet.

The post–Chapter 11 turnaround at Continental was astonishing even to those few observers who had given the airline any chance at all. Frank Lorenzo credited Continental's remarkably quick recovery during Chapter 11 to its winning combination of low, simple fares and full service.[40] In addition, he credited the airline's marketing philosophy of "more for less," a program that made the point that Continental offered more service for less cost than any other major carrier. Furthermore, Continental's particular hub-and-spoke system received much credit; with fewer markets, the airline sought

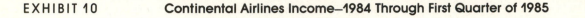

EXHIBIT 10   **Continental Airlines Income—1984 Through First Quarter of 1985**

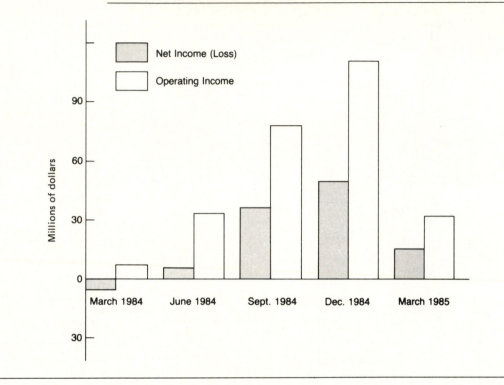

SOURCE: 1984 and first quarter 1985 Annual Reports.

to be the number one or number two carrier to all of its high-frequency destinations from its hubs in Houston and Denver.[41] Lorenzo also cited improved worker productivity. This was, to a large extent, believed to be the result of the participative management and profit-sharing plans.[42]

Despite its apparent success at being the first airline to fly itself out of bankruptcy, Continental was by no means guaranteed future success. The 1984 annual report made it clear that if union contracts were reinstated, or if claims from former employees were extensive and upheld, then management would be forced to liquidate the airline. In addition, Continental's competitive advantage was steadily getting smaller. Industry analysts predicted that the cost of air travel would be roughly the same for all airlines by the early 1990s and that the fare structure industrywide would come down. Realizing this, Frank Lorenzo admitted that "Continental's cost-advantage window is closing."[43] Furthermore, with any softening of the economy and subsequent decline in air travel, the competition could be expected to start matching Continental's discount fares.[44]

LORENZO'S "NEW" IMAGE

At the time of the Continental takeover by TI-TAC the demands for labor-cost concessions from union employees, the replacement of striking mechanics with nonunion workers, and the move of Continental's headquarters from Los Angeles to Houston had a debilitating effect on employee morale. Many Continental employees resented Lorenzo's no-nonsense style and had dubbed him "Plastic Frank." Formerly an aloof policymaker, Lorenzo undertook a turnaround in his management style and personal image. During Continental's financial crisis, Lorenzo began conducting intense brainstorming sessions about fare and flight schedules. No longer was his spartan Houston office a secluded corporate domain mostly frequented by bankers and lawyers. Instead, it was transformed into a command post with a steady stream of traffic. When traffic got too heavy, Lorenzo could slip outside for a run on the jogging trail that passed near the building.

Examples of image change began in mid-1984 when he sat in shirt sleeves inside a sultry airplane hangar handing out hundreds of stock certificates to the loyal "founding employees" of the new Continental. He held similar rituals in Denver and Los Angeles. In September 1984 he surrounded himself with 2,000 cheering Continental employees who were given free tickets to root for the Houston Astros baseball team on "Continental Airlines Night." Lorenzo also took to holding a quarterly "President's Forum" with employees to "shoot the breeze" about the company's future, and he set up employee councils to solicit their ideas on improving Continental.[45]

Some still questioned Lorenzo's tactics and viewed him with suspicion and not a little hostility. Captain Henry Duffy, president of ALPA, said, "We now know that wherever he moves we will have labor troubles."[46] Continental was called the "first national airline to break the cost barrier," and its competitors appreciated the new bargaining clout Lorenzo had given them with their unions.[47] Lorenzo was quoted as saying, "What people think is that Frank Lorenzo wanted a big airline. What we were looking for was a viable plan for the 90s. We've never been interested in size per se."[48] A graphic description of Lorenzo's determination was given by one unidentified executive for Continental as he pointed to a wall in his office and said, "You and I might run and hit that wall two or three times and give up. Frank will hit it 300 times and get through." Many analysts acknowledged that Frank Lorenzo did indeed get through the wall.[49]

TAC EXPANSION

In addition to returning rapidly to profitability, Continental also wasted no time in looking for opportunities to expand its operations. In March 1985, TAC announced the formation of a new subsidiary company, Continental

West Airlines, based in Los Angeles. Texas Air said that it was seeking federal approval to initiate service of the new six-plane carrier under a "joint marketing arrangement" with Continental Airlines. Operations of the new carrier would be initiated using six new Boeing 737 aircraft purchased by Texas Air under the direction of Sheldon Best, former executive vice president and CEO of AirCal, a Los Angeles–based carrier. Formation of the company was prompted when the bankruptcy court denied Continental permission to purchase the aircraft on its own. On June 28, 1985, TAC announced that Continental Airlines would acquire Continental West Airlines.

Continental also expanded its foreign routes in the first two years after filing for Chapter 11. Continental Airlines initiated new service to Honolulu and Guam and nonstop service from Houston to London. The service expansion in the Pacific was achieved through the use of leased DC-10 aircraft from the McDonnell-Douglas Corporation. The route expansions put another twelve aircraft into service, increasing seat capacity by 33 percent.

Likewise, fleet modernization continued even under the restrictions of Chapter 11. Using leasing arrangements from aircraft manufacturers as well as Texas Air, the parent company, Lorenzo managed to upgrade the condition of Continental's fleet, which was predominantly composed of aging Boeing 727s. In April 1984, Continental used aircraft leased from McDonnell-Douglas to facilitate its route expansions in the Pacific. In September 1984, Continental announced plans to begin flying three McDonnell MD80 aircraft.[50] In October 1984, Continental negotiated with Braniff Airlines to lease eight 727s to upgrade its fleet.[51] The only fleet modernization attempt that was partially blocked by the bankruptcy courts occurred in March 1985, when Continental tried to lease as many as 30 new aircraft from its parent, TAC. However, the court allowed Continental to sublease four Boeing 737 aircraft.[52]

TAC, "THE WHITE KNIGHT"?

In June 1985, TAC was approached by the management of TWA to play the role of "white knight" in its defense against the hostile takeover by Carl C. Icahn. Icahn had offered $18 a share for New York–based TWA. This offer was countered shortly thereafter by TAC with an offer of $23 per share in a deal signed by both firms' boards at a total value of $725 million. The merger would make TAC one of the four largest air carriers in the United States. The merger was being challenged not only by Icahn, but also by Continental's creditors and Representative Doug Bosco, a Democratic congressman from California who had introduced legislation to block the merger.[53]

TWA, one of the major airlines, faced many of the same problems that had threatened Continental. For C. E. Meyer, chairman, the board, and TWA, there was a spark of hope. The airline was not in danger of collapse and ended 1983 with more than $80 million in cash. Trans World Corp., TWA's parent company, which had spun off the airline in February 1984, had guaranteed $200 million in revolving credit. TWA's international division provided nearly one half of its $3.4 billion in revenues for 1983. Plans for 1984 were to boost capacity by over 30 percent. TWA would have an opportunity to renegotiate the mechanics' and flight attendants' contracts in 1985, and Meyer was determined to win negotiations next time.[54]

But Icahn began buying TWA stock at $10 per share and threatened a takeover. The following is a *Wall Street Journal* account of a 1985 meeting between Icahn and Meyer:

"All I'm interested in is a more efficient use of assets, and a better deal for the stockholders," said Icahn. In the half-deserted bar of the Waldorf Astoria Hotel, the talk had become ugly. Carl Icahn wanted TWA, and Meyer was resisting. "All you want is a fast buck. That's all you've ever done in any of these things [corporate raids], is go for a fast buck." Carl Icahn leaned over the table and looked directly at Meyer, the president of TWA. "Why don't you admit it, what you really care about is your job, and you're afraid I'm going to take it away from you." For the forty-nine-year-old New York financier, this sort of tense confrontation was not new. Icahn had been conducting corporate raids for several years. In the last eighteen months he had taken on J.P. Stevens & Company, Chesebrough-Ponds, Uniroyal, and Phillips Petroleum. Now it was TWA's turn. Icahn defended his role by saying his raids result in a more efficient use of assets and a better deal for stockholders. "Look at TWA. It was selling for $10, now its stockholders are getting $23. They're selling TWA only because we force them to."[55]

Starting in September 1984, Carl Icahn quietly began buying up shares of TWA, when it was selling for around $10 a share. Icahn's group made the purchases through a variety of corporations and partnerships. On April 29, 1985, the Icahn group passed the 5 percent level, which would require the public disclosure of its TWA holdings within ten days. Here, a switch in tactics occurred. In a burst of buying, an additional 16 percent of stock was added, all within the ten-day grace period. Wall Street analysts finally traced the buying of TWA stock to Icahn.[56] On May 15 TWA asked a general district court in New York City to halt the purchase of its stock by Icahn, who by this time had 23 percent of the stock. TWA lost this suit against the takeover bid in federal court.

The Icahn group relentlessly forged ahead. On May 21 the group proposed to buy all the remaining TWA stock at $18 a share. By now, the Icahn group held 33 percent of TWA's common stock. The May 28 *Wall Street Journal* reported that Frank Borman of Eastern Airlines called Mr. Meyer to broach the subject of a TWA-Eastern combination. Sources also reported that Frank Lorenzo approached TWA with a similar offer. Borman denied any Eastern interest in TWA, and Lorenzo could not be reached for comment. Meyer would say only that "no serious discussions have taken place."[57]

On May 28 the directors of TWA voted unanimously to put the airline up for sale. The board instructed its management and its financial adviser, Solomon Brothers, Inc., to pursue alternatives that would give TWA shareholders an opportunity to participate in a transaction that was superior to the Icahn proposal. "In our discussions with Mr. Icahn, all his proposals ultimately had a liquidate-the-company approach," Meyer was quoted as saying in an interview.[58]

TWA was not without friends in high places. Senators John Danforth (R) and Thomas Eagleton (D) were both from Missouri, where many jobs could be lost if TWA were to be liquidated. They introduced a bill to block the transfer of international airlines for the purpose of liquidating them. In addition, TWA hired Michael Deaver, a recent personal adviser to President Reagan, to help with lobbying in Washington. However, because of other pressing issues in Congress, many insiders believed that expecting help from Washington was little more than a pipe dream.

Many airline analysts expressed doubts that TWA could be successfully merged with another carrier because of the difficulties in merging labor forces with conflicting union contracts. As an example, they cited the Pan American acquisition of National Airlines in 1980. Pan Am became entangled in a series of labor disputes over such items as merged seniority lists. As a result, labor costs soared, especially for pensions, and the bitterness of the disputes lingered.[59] With cash in excess of $425 million and long-term debt of $1.3 billion, TWA was still not a diamond in the rough. Although TWA had revenues of $3.7 billion in 1984, profits amounted to only $30 million.[60]

As one analyst pointed out:

Airlines tend to be highly leveraged, saddled with heavy debts from the purchase of planes. Historically, they have not been that attractive from an earnings point of view. The assets of an airline are tricky to calculate. The planes are carried at book value, but it is difficult to turn these things into money.[61]

POSTSCRIPT

The following are summaries of news reports:

June 10, 1985

The *Wall Street Journal* reported, "TWA is said to be near accord with Resorts." TWA appeared to be near an agreement with Resorts International for the acquisition of TWA by the casino and hotel operator. Some TWA executives were happy over their apparent escape from Carl Icahn, who had announced that if he took over the big airline, he would fire C. E. Meyer, TWA's president and CEO. TWA's board, which had met the previous Friday, had not made an announcement. However, sources close to the company confirmed Resorts' bid for the airline's 34.5 million shares. Details of the bid could not be confirmed. TWA stock closed that Friday at $19.50, up 50 cents a share.[62]

June 14, 1985

One day after the Air Lines Pilots Association reached a tentative agreement with United Airlines, the union got another jolt. Texas Air Corp. announced that it had agreed to purchase TWA for $794 million, or about $23 per share in cash and debt securities. The deal was expected to be completed by December if approved by TWA shareholders and government regulatory agencies.[63]

June 21, 1985

Nearly 7,000 members of the Independent Federation of Flight Attendants voted overwhelmingly to strike TWA in a dispute over wage concessions. The flight attendants had been worried about a proposed acquisition of TWA by Texas Air Corp. because it viewed Texas Air and its president, Frank Lorenzo, as anti-union. Under federal laws that governed airline bargaining, the company and the union were required to wait through a 30-day "cooling-off" period before a walkout could begin. One factor that could delay the mediator's decision would be the ownership of the airline.[64]

June 27, 1985

Representative Doug Bosco (D–California), a member of the aviation subcommittee, had introduced legislation aimed at blocking the planned takeover of TWA by Texas Air Corp. Representative Bosco said

> A holding company whose largest subsidiary is using federal bankruptcy to reorganize shouldn't be able to acquire another carrier until that subsidiary completes its reorganization. It's a question of fairness. If a company is so bereft as to use U.S. laws to avoid labor contracts and creditors, it shouldn't be able to acquire another company.[65]

Bosco said that he wrote the legislation with the help of the Air Lines Pilots Association.

Depending on how quickly Rep. Bosco could get support for his bill and line up a companion bill in the Senate, the legislation might be a moot point if Continental had completed its bankruptcy reorganization before that time. Texas Air Chairman Frank Lorenzo, whom many consider the most savvy airline executive in the industry and a scrappy street fighter, had defeated several previous attempts to block his company's acquisition moves.

July 3, 1985

The TWA pilots union announced, on July 3, 1985, that they had told Carl Icahn they would be willing to take a 20 percent cut in pay if he would take over the airline. Spokespersons for the union said that the pilots felt that they would fare better under Icahn than under Texas Air Corp.'s president Frank Lorenzo, who has a reputation as a union buster.[66]

August 25, 1985

Carl C. Icahn raised his stake in Trans World Airlines to 50.3 percent, giving him control of the nation's fourth largest airline.

Sources said that attorneys for the parties involved were writing a tentative pact that would dissolve a merger agreement between TWA and Texas Air Corp., Mr. Icahn's chief rival in the bitter fight for TWA.

Together, the two steps could bring down the final curtain on the TWA takeover battle and move the New York investor closer to beginning a new role as head of an airline.

"I think we are getting close to having ourselves an airline," Mr. Icahn said over the weekend. However, he declined to comment on the talks to dissolve the merger accord, and Texas Air officials could not be reached for comment. In composite trading on the New York Stock Exchange on Friday, TWA closed at $22.375 a share, unchanged.

Many investment bankers were convinced that Mr. Icahn, long viewed on Wall Street mainly as a "greenmailer" who forces companies to buy back their stock at a premium, would soon sell all or part of TWA. He had indicated to TWA's board the previous week that he might eventually sell the airline.

Mr. Icahn's announcement Friday that he and an investor group raised their TWA stake from 47 percent to 50.3 percent was an anticlimax. On Wednesday he had said that he planned to increase his TWA stake to more than 50 percent.

TWA directors refused on Tuesday to adopt measures suggested by Texas Air to block Mr. Icahn. The board's decision was a decisive victory for Mr. Icahn, clearing the way for his group to use its big stake to defeat Texas Air's offer of $26 a share in cash and preferred stock.

Mr. Icahn was offering $24 a share in cash and preferred stock for the shares he did not already own; analysts estimated this would cost Mr. Icahn $650 million.

Sources said that attorneys were trying to put down on paper an existing verbal agreement that would end the merger pact between TWA and Texas Air. The sources said that the agreement, if adopted, was likely to assure Texas Air and Frank Lorenzo about $42 million in profit from their TWA stake.

The profit included an $18 million fee from TWA for breaking the merger agreement. It also included stock market profit from the 2.2 million TWA common shares that Texas Air already owned plus TAC's option to buy 6.4 million unissued TWA shares at $19.625 each.[67]

NOTES

1. "Continental, Texas Taking Steps to Complete Merger," *Aviation Week & Space Technology*, October 11, 1982, p. 36.

2. "Continental Reevaluates System," *Aviation Week & Space Technology*, February 1, 1982, p. 36.

3. "A Proud Bird Loses Its Wings," *Newsweek*, October 2, 1983, pp. 71–72.

4. "Continental's Crusade to Stop Frank Lorenzo," *Business Week*, May 11, 1981, pp. 110–112.

5. *Ibid.*

6. "How Texas Air Won Its Fight," *Business Week*, October 26, 1981, pp. 182–185.

7. *Ibid.*, p. 182.

8. "Continental Reevaluates System."

9. "Continental, Texas Taking Steps to Complete Merger."

10. *Ibid.*

11. "Continental Receives $40 M Investment," *Aviation Week & Space Technology*, March 31, 1983, p. 34.

12. "Continental Moving Headquarters to Houston," *Aviation Week & Space Technology*, February 21, 1983, p. 30.

13. "Is Frank Lorenzo Going Hunting?" *Business Week*, April 4, 1983, p. 30.

14. "It's Time to Regulate the Airlines," *Houston Chronicle*, September 28, 1983, p. 20, Sec. 1.

15. "Continental Says Strike," *Wall Street Journal*, August 12, 1983, p. 4.

16. "Why Airline Pilots Are Becoming Street Fighters," *Business Week*, October 31, 1983, p. 128.

17. "Turbulence in U.S. Skies," *MacLean's*, October 10, 1983, p. 39.

18. "Continental Airlines Plans to Fly Again Reaffirm Lorenzo's Bent for Long Shots," *Wall Street Journal*, September 27, 1983, p. 2.

19. "Continental Air Unions Ask Court . . . ," *Wall Street Journal*, October 12, 1983, p. 14.

20. "Why Airline Pilots Are Becoming Street Fighters," pp. 127–129.

21. "Continental Air's Bankruptcy Law Filing," *Wall Street Journal*, December 5, 1983, p. 43; "Continental Air Official Saw Chapter 11 . . . ," *Wall Street Journal*, December 14, 1983, p. 10.

22. "Lorenzo Warns Senate on Labor Contract Bill," *Aviation Week & Space Technology*, April 16, 1984, p. 36.

23. "Continental Sues IAM," *Aviation Week & Space Technology*, February 6, 1984, p. 32.

24. "FAA Probes Harassment of Continental," *Aviation Week & Space Technology*, May 7, 1984, p. 31.

25. "Continental Air Creditors Pressing . . . ," *Wall Street Journal*, October 26, 1983, p. 12.

26. "Continental Claims It's Healthier," *Wall Street Journal*, November 4, 1983, p. 4.

27. "A Struggle for Survival," *Financial World*, November 15, 1983, p. 13.

28. "Cut Rate Continental—Frank Lorenzo Vows to Keep 'Em Flying," *Barron's*, October 3, 1983, p. 53.

29. "Frontier in Talks with Texas Air," *New York Times*, April 5, 1985, p. D3.

30. "United Cuts Some Fares to Match Continental," *New York Times*, February 18, 1984, p. D1.

31. *New York Times*, September 24, 1984, p. D1.

32. "Airline's Boss Attacks Sky-High Wages," *Fortune*, January 9, 1984, pp. 66–68.

33. "Competitors Protesting Continental's New Ads," *Advertising Age*, June 11, 1984, pp. 3, 98.

34. "Continental Cuts Air Fares," *New York Times*, February 17, 1984, p. D3; "Continental Air to Reduce Fares," *New York Times*, February 1, 1985, p. D4.

35. "United Cuts Some Fares to Match Continental."

36. "The Trying Times for Continental Aren't Over Yet," *Business Week*, March 19, 1984, pp. 44–45.

37. *Ibid.*

38. "Comeback of a Trimmer Continental Airline Cuts Wages, Staff & Its Fares," *New York Times*, February 3, 1984, p. D1.

39. Continental Airlines, 1984 Annual Report.

40. "Continental Air in Black," *New York Times*, August 1, 1984, p. D3.

41. "The Trying Times for Continental Aren't Over Yet," p. 44.

42. Continental Airlines, 1984 Annual Report.

43. "The Trying Times for Continental Aren't Over Yet," p. 44.

44. "Continental Air Reports Growth," *New York Times*, May 8, 1984, p. D4.

45. "Continental Air's Lorenzo Has New Image with Aides a Year after Chapter 11 Filing," *Wall Street Journal*, September 24, 1984, p. 22.

46. "A Turnaround Artist for an Airline," *New York Times*, December 30, 1984, p. F6.

47. "Airline's Boss Attacks Sky-High Wages."

48. "A Turnaround Artist for an Airline."

49. *Ibid.*

50. "Continental Airlines," *New York Times*, September 25, 1984, p. D6.

51. "Braniff Acts to Rent Out Planes," *New York Times*, October 10, 1984, p. D4.

52. *Wall Street Journal*, March 19, 1985

53. "Legislation Filed to Block Texas Air's Takeover Bid," *Houston Chronicle*, June 29, 1985, p. 1, Sec. 3; "TWA Pilots Ask Icahn to Renew Takeover Bid," *Houston Chronicle*, July 3, 1985, p. 1. Sec. 3.

54. "TWA Gloomily Weighs Its Options," *Business Week*, April 2, 1984, pp. 37–38.

55. "Battle Tactics, Carl Icahn's Strategies in His Quest for TWA Are a Model for Raiders," *Wall Street Journal*, June 20, 1985, p. 1. Reprinted by permission of the *Wall Street Journal*, © Dow Jones & Company, Inc. 1985. All Rights Reserved Worldwide.

56. *Ibid.*

57. "Icahn Sparks Debate with Proposal for TWA," *Wall Street Journal*, May 28, 1985.

58. "TWA Put Up to Sale by Board," *New York Times,* May 29, 1985.

59. "TWA Is Said to Near Accord with Resorts," *Wall Street Journal,* June 10, 1985.

60. R. A. Dubin, "Raiders in the Sky: Will the Airline Industry Be Next?" *Business Week,* May 27, 1985, pp. 74, 79.

61. Ruth Walker, "Trans World Airlines Hopes to Shake off Icahn Takeover Turbulences," *Christian Science Monitor,* May 31, 1985, pp. 21–22.

62. "TWA Is Said to Near Accord with Resorts."

63. Michael Rogers, "News/Trends, Texas Air to Pilot TWA," *Fortune,* July 8, 1985, p. 8.

64. "Flight Attendants Union Votes to Go on Strike against TWA," *Houston Post,* June 12, 1985.

65. "Legislation Filed to Block Texas Air's Takeover of TWA."

66. Stewart Varney, "Business News Report," Cable News Network, July 3, 1985.

67. "Icahn in at TWA," *Wall Street Journal,* August 26, 1985, p. 2.

Delta Air Lines: World's Most Profitable Airline

ELIZABETH LAVIE • LARRY D. ALEXANDER

One day in mid-1982, at Hartsfield International Airport, Delta Air Lines' new midfield complex was bustling with activity. More than two dozen jets had arrived at gates within the last half-hour and all were scheduled to depart again within the next half-hour. David Garrett, Delta's president and chief executive officer, was watching the activities at the gates. The employees were not astonished to see him there. Often the president, vice presidents, and other members of senior management went over to the airport from their modest offices to chat with employees or just to watch the system. Garrett observed the smoothness of the operation that every employee at Delta had worked hard to perfect by improving customer services and easing flight connections.

Garrett walked through the complex and stopped at the spacious employee lounge. He sat down and thought back over the monumental changes that had occurred at Delta and in the aviation industry since he had become president in 1971. Throughout these dynamic and exciting changes, Delta had remained profitable. Garrett's thoughts drifted back to Delta's founder, C. E. (Collett Everman) Woolman, and the history of the company.

COMPANY HISTORY

C. E. Woolman was born in Indiana in 1889. As a child, Woolman exhibited a keen interest in aviation. He and a friend borrowed neighborhood clothesline to build and control a giant passenger kite. As he grew older, Woolman took every opportunity to be near airplanes, even traveling to France to attend aviators' meets. Despite his avid interest in airplanes, Woolman did not pursue a career in aviation because in 1908 its business potential seemed minimal. Instead, Woolman went to the University of Illinois and earned a bachelor of arts degree in agriculture in 1912. After graduation Woolman began farming in Louisiana, soon became an agricultural extension agent, and then was promoted to district supervisor of the extension service. Woolman became alarmed by the boll weevils' eating habits, which were destroying a high percentage of the cotton crop. He tried to develop ways to destroy these insects, but World War I soon interrupted his efforts.

The war, however, did change business attitudes toward aviation. Military contracts and the new U.S. postal airmail delivery rights encouraged

This case was prepared by Elizabeth Lavie, M.B.A., from Virginia Polytechnic Institute & State University in June 1982, and Larry D. Alexander, Associate Professor of Business Strategy, Virginia Polytechnic Institute & State University, Blacksburg, Virginia. This case was written as a basis for class discussion rather than to illustrate either effective or ineffective handling of an administrative situation.

many businessmen to invest in aviation. Many small airlines merged to gain the power necessary to win the rights to carry the U.S. mail. Some of these early merged firms were Transcontinental Air Transportation, United Air Lines, Aviation Corporation of America, and the North American Aviation Company. These companies later changed their respective names to World Airlines, United Airlines, American Airlines, and Eastern Air Lines. In 1920, the Huff Daland Company was formed to handle military business. Because the company achieved little success in military endeavors, company officers turned to crop dusting and formed a new division known as the Huff Daland Dusters, Inc.

Woolman was especially interested in Huff Daland Dusters because the firm represented two of his major interests: flying airplanes and killing the boll weevil. In 1925 he joined the firm as a salesman. In 1928 Woolman persuaded a group of Monroe, Louisiana, businessmen and planters to purchase the firm's American assets. The new company was chartered under the name of Delta Air Services, Inc.

Woolman was not satisfied with Delta remaining just a crop dusting outfit and began planning to make his company a more significant operation. Delta Air Services went through mergers, buy-outs, and struggles over route rights. In 1930 the company finally restructured and rechartered in Louisiana as the Delta Air Corporation.

Delta became a strong organization under Woolman's leadership with the dusting operations becoming less significant to the total operation every year. Delta survived the Depression, helped out during World War II, and profited under strict government regulation after the war.

When Woolman died in 1966, many industry watchers, officials, and employees wondered about the future of Delta. To these people, C. E. Woolman was Delta, and Delta was C. E. Woolman. But despite the appearance of one-man management, Delta did not lack for managerial talent to replace him. In fact, several inside successors were considered after his death. Woolman's personality, however, continued to influence the organization regardless of the change in management. His policies and management techniques were still used, those very principles that made the company profitable for almost four decades—profitable, that is, until 1982.

Garrett's thoughts turned back to his evening meeting with a leading industry consultant that he had hired to recommend Delta's future strategy. He had collected the following information to help the consultant appreciate the industry's adjustment to deregulation and understand Delta's present environment.

DEREGULATION: CHANGING THE INDUSTRY

The Airline Deregulation Act of 1978 ended 40 years of federal protection for the airlines. The purpose of the law was threefold: (1) to open up the industry to increased competition; (2) to maintain a high level of safety while protecting profitability; and (3) to prevent unreasonable monopoly of flight routes. Within certain limits, any airline that was ready, willing, and able could fly practically anywhere if the transportation was consistent with public convenience and necessity. All the airlines had to do was inform the Civil Aeronautics Board (CAB) that they intended to add a route and then establish the route within 60 days. Airlines could protect only one of their routes per year from competitors, and they could discontinue service to a route provided that there was still another airline covering that route. The airlines were gaining the power to adjust rates up and down, and the industry was no longer closed to new entrants. The law called for the powers of the CAB to decrease gradually, and for it to be eliminated in 1985. After 1985, the Justice Department would oversee antitrust issues, the Department of Transportation would handle subsidies, and the Federal Aviation Agency would monitor safety matters.

Deregulation may have caused more problems than it solved, especially when considering the profitability objective of deregulation. In some ways deregulation resulted in a bitter dogfight over routes, rates, and passengers that resulted in increased competition and confusion.

After deregulation, various problems arose concerning the airports themselves. The most critical problem was a shortage of landing slots and physical space for new entrants at many airports. This problem quickly became known as the slot crisis or the airport access problem. Established carriers, who had invested heavily in their airport facilities, were threatened with legal charges by various government agencies for violating the new entrants' rights to free and equal access. Agencies also warned airports about noise pollution, ground congestion, and other environmental concerns. The aviation community fought to save existing small airports and to use military bases as possible reliever airports. However, the reliever airports became crowded too.

Besides competition from the new entrants, competition from established major carriers intensified as they entered and exited markets, chasing efficiency and customers. Several airlines operating on the same route resulted in terrible fare wars. In 1978 these fare wars existed on the transcontinental routes and then moved to shorter routes. By 1981 and 1982, they had moved to Florida. During regulation, airlines could not compete on the basis of price, but rather on their levels of service. After deregulation, as soon as one airline on a route cut a fare, the others were forced to follow. The majority of the passengers were flying at discounts of up to 70 percent, and the airlines' yields suffered. In addition, these price wars started alienating the full-fare passengers, such as business travelers, who were not able to take advantage of the low fares.

Between October 24, 1978, and mid-1980, the combined total of new routes added by airlines and existing routes vacated was 1,313. The result was mass confusion for the customers because airlines were changing routes and schedules all the time. With all these changes, airlines seemed unstable rather than reliable.

Service was improved in small communities and large markets, but medium-sized cities suffered service cuts. A strong group, composed of representatives of medium-sized cities, formed and demanded some re-regulation legislation.

In-flight service also deteriorated as some airlines made in-flight service cuts to offset reduced fares. These included cutting out meals on flights, reducing contacts with cabin personnel, jamming more people on board, and adding lots of carry-on luggage. Many customers, again especially the business travelers, were dissatisfied with the poorer service.

As a result of deregulation and the economic recession, pricing became a very important tool. Many industry experts, however, claimed that management of the various airlines did not understand the complexities of pricing and that the discount fare was not always the answer, regardless of the competition. After deregulation, marketing as a whole became a more important function within organizations.

Increasing Expenses

One trend that continued from 1978 through 1981 was an alarming increase in expenses in the industry. One of the most critical expenses in the airline industry was jet fuel. The real cost of jet fuel had increased threefold since the beginning of the worldwide oil crisis in 1973. The cost of aviation fuel twenty years ago represented only 25 percent of an airline's operating cost; however, in 1980 fuel represented 55 percent of operating costs. Since 1978, the average price per gallon for jet fuel had increased as follows: $0.38 in 1978, $0.56 in 1979, $0.86 in 1980, $0.99 in February of 1981, and $1.40 in October of 1981. Because fuel represented such a large portion of expenses, many of the airlines blamed their losses or low profits on the cost of fuel.

As a result of these increasing costs, many of the major airlines began fuel conservation programs and started purchasing new fuel-efficient aircraft. Other airlines responded by owning and controlling distribution and storage facilities and forming their own energy exploration ventures. The airlines also began organizing consortiums to gain power in negotiating with the suppliers.

Computerization

The airlines themselves had already made substantial investments in computerization, and many expected to spend much more on computers in the future. Many airlines even offered other airlines and travel agents computer services and software such as maintenance control systems, reservation systems, and price management systems.

Many airlines started exploring the telecommunications revolution. Industry specialists speculated that businesses that spent a lot of money on traveling would move toward electronic conferences. This trend could damage the airlines, because 55 percent of their traffic historically came from business travelers, the very customer group that was becoming disenchanted with airline service.

Flight Equipment

In order to remain competitive, the major U.S. airlines needed to buy the most advanced and fuel-efficient aircraft or to modify their present aircraft. Generally, the majors preferred to finance these acquisitions out of internally generated funds, but, because of their recent losses, this was almost impossible for them. Paying for aircraft acquisition became a real challenge. Before deregulation the capital cost of an acquisition was about 10 percent of the total cost; this percentage increased to 25 percent by 1982. Finance departments began searching for alternative ways to fund acquisitions to update their fleets. Aircraft manufacturers started stepping up their financial assistance to airlines, but the manufacturers were beginning to have financial problems of their own.

Financing was also available from foreign export banks if the airlines were purchasing the aircraft from foreign firms. The low interest rates in other countries' banks, such as Japan, and the loans from foreign trading firms attracted many airlines. The big disadvantage of this financing method was that the airlines gambled with the exchange rate. Several new leasing opportunities for airlines also were introduced, including the Safe Harbor Lease, which was a tax benefit transfer. Industry experts, however, pointed out that there was a limit to how many planes an airline could obtain with lease financing if their equity and earnings were not high enough.

Each airline had to decide whether to buy new airplanes or to modify its existing planes. Each airline also had to evaluate its financial strength and the best type of financing for its situation.

Labor and Management Relations

Labor was one of the airlines' top two expenses. In the early 1980s, the airlines started making demands on their employees to accept concessions. The airlines needed these concessions to help keep their operating expenses down in a time when they were in trouble. Unfortunately, most of the major U.S. airlines were heavily unionized and existing contracts needed renegotiating. Airlines threatened to lay off some employees if concessions were not made. Some unions took this threat seriously and granted various concessions such as pay cuts, wage freezes, and less restrictive work rules. However, industry experts felt that in 1982 the unions would put up more resistance to any further concessions sought by management. Thus, if the recession continued, the airlines could not decrease their ticket prices unless the unions cut their wages.

The newer entrants into the airline industry were more fortunate because their employees were not unionized, resulting in lower operation costs. For example, in 1981 "captains flying DC-9-30s at New York Air were being paid $30,000 per year and were flying about 75 hours per month, while captains flying the same airplanes at the airline's parent company, Texas International, were being paid $62,000 per year for flying 55 hours per month."[1] Unionized airlines were especially careful to avoid a strike because a strike in the deregulation environment could be nearly fatal for them.

Professional Air Traffic Controllers Organization (PATCO) Strike

On August 3, 1981, PATCO went on strike. Because of their subsequent refusal to return to work, 12,500 of the air traffic controllers were fired. The initial traffic impact was disastrous—many passenger no-shows. For the first few days, the U.S. airlines lost about $34 million a day. However, once reduced schedules were established, traffic picked up. The overall traffic figures for the month of August were less than 13 percent off, which was far less than expected.

Capacity constraints were put into effect at 22 high-density airports. Many of these were key airports in the majors' hub-and-spoke route systems. This reduced capacity squelched airlines' expansion plans and was expected to last until late 1982 or early 1983. The affected airlines were able to resume 75 percent of their previous operations by rescheduling their flights to off-peak times.

The Federal Aviation Administration (FAA) then developed an $8.5 billion plan to revamp air traffic control. This plan called for the use of computers to do many of the jobs previously performed by controllers. This new plan also involved giving more responsibility to the pilots in the cockpit. If approved, the plan would force airlines to equip their aircraft with several new devices. The airlines, however, would reap one big benefit from this plan: the pilots would no longer have to follow inefficient long distance routes.

CHRONOLOGICAL OVERVIEW

1978

Despite the uncertainty involved in deregulation, 1978 was still a boom year for the U.S. airlines. In fact, 1978 was the best year ever for setting passenger traffic and financial records. Revenues for the eleven major airlines were $19.6 billion, which represented an increase of 13.8 percent over the 1977 total. The resulting profits hit an all-time industry high of $1.06 billion, which was 71.6 percent higher than 1977, and 1977 was considered a successful year.

Other important indicators of success in the airline industry were passenger boardings, traffic, revenue passenger–kilometers, load factors, and freight ton-kilometers. Passenger boardings increased 13.1 percent over 1977 to 220 million boardings, and the traffic growth rate was almost double that of 1977. Revenue passenger–kilometers were up 14.4 percent, which was double what the analysts had expected, and load factors rose from 56 percent to 61.7 percent in 1978. Load factors indicate the percentage of available seats that were occupied by paying customers on an airline's average flight. All of these indicators demonstrated that 1978 was successful for the airlines.

Most of this success was attributed to the Airline Deregulation Act, signed by President Carter on October 24, 1978, and the prevailing good economic conditions of 1978. Deregulation allowed the airlines to begin their low fare revolution, which produced a great increase in traffic. Airlines' wide-bodied jets and computerized reservation systems helped absorb and organize the large influx of passengers. The airlines soon learned that if the price was right, customers were willing to put up with indignities and inconveniences.

Two divisions of the U.S. airline industry, the charter and cargo divisions, were not as successful. Charter passenger boardings fell 22.9 percent from the 1977 level. This decrease was caused by the low fares then available on regular flights. Cargo traffic grew only 0.71 percent in 1978. This stunted growth was attributed to the emergence of cargo specialists such as Flying Tiger and Federal Express.

Despite all the airlines' success, some ominous clouds were forming by the end of 1978. The Organization of Petroleum Exporting Countries (OPEC) was monopolizing oil prices and threatening to drastically increase fuel prices, and airline labor unions were looking for higher wages to match the increase in airline profits.

1979

As expected, earnings for the U.S. major airlines spiraled downward throughout 1979 from their peak in 1978. For the ten major airlines (Pan Am and National had merged), revenues increased 15.5 percent over 1978 to $22.6 billion; however, this increase was due to fare increases of nearly 30 percent. Profits declined 75 percent from the lofty $1.06 billion of 1978 to a sad $262 million. One of the culprits in the decline in profits was a 22.6 percent increase in operating expenses caused largely by increases in the price of jet fuel. Many airlines blamed the CAB, which still had authority over fare increases despite deregulation. The airlines claimed that the CAB did not grant fare increases fast enough or high enough to offset increasing expenses.

Passenger traffic increased by 8.1 percent, but this indicated a decline in the traffic growth rate. Revenue passenger–kilometers climbed by 10.6 percent, but this also indicated a declining growth rate. Load factors increased by only 1.6 percent to 63.3 percent in 1979.

Charter traffic continued to decline in 1979 with the number of charter passengers plunging 27.4 percent. This continued decline was still attributed to low fares on the regularly scheduled flights. The cargo divisions of the major U.S. airlines reported zero growth in 1979. This figure was affected by labor strikes and the 38-day grounding of all DC-10 jets after the crash of an American Airlines DC-10. DC-10s comprised major portions of six airlines' fleets.

Individual airlines were hurt by strikes and by poor weather in the first quarter. Many of the airlines were blaming deregulation, but a stronger force was the beginning of a lengthy, severe recession. By the end of 1979, the airline industry was concerned about the outlook for 1980.

1980

Forecasts for the major U.S. airlines were particularly bleak. Revenues, expenses, and profits were expected to climb equally, and traffic growth was expected to level off in 1980.

Operating revenues in 1980 increased by 15.6 percent, almost the same percentage as the previous year. Operating expenses also increased by about the same percentage as in 1979. The industry, however, suffered combined net losses of $9.5 million. None of the forecasts came close to predicting the size of the actual loss.

Total passenger traffic decreased by 6.31 percent from 1979's level, and revenue passenger–kilometers decreased by about 5 percent. Load factors decreased by 4.1 percent, resulting in an industry average load of 59.1 percent. Charter traffic also continued to decline with the number of charter passenger boardings down by 37.8 percent.

The poor performance in 1980 was again the result of many factors; some of the factors were the same as those affecting performance in 1979, only intensified. By 1980 deregulation was affecting the major airlines. New competitors were entering the industry, and the majors were not prepared to handle the extra competition. Price wars and the decline in fares came at a time when prices should have increased to offset rocketing expenses, and the deepening recession dampened passenger traffic. As a result, the airlines were juggling routes to find the most profitable ones and furloughing employees to lessen operating costs. At the same time, they were beginning to worry about how to finance much-needed new aircraft.

1981

Substantial losses swamped the airlines in 1981. Operating revenues for the major U.S. airlines increased by the same 15 percent in 1981, amounting to revenues of $31.9 billion. Net losses increased, resulting in an industry loss of $462 million. Passenger boardings decreased 8.6 percent, and revenue passenger–kilometers decreased by 6.7 percent in 1981.

The financial situation got worse. The same factors from the previous two years acted to hurt the industry, along with a few surprises during 1981.

More new airlines entered the industry, and the ones that had entered in 1980 surprisingly survived the year. These new airlines caused problems for the established airlines through increased competition and more fare wars. The newer airlines typically had lower operating expenses than the majors and could afford to offer lower prices. For the major U.S. airlines, many labor union contracts came up for renegotiation during 1981, and operating costs continued to rise as their debts mounted. Many of the majors began to search for novel ways to finance their equipment purchases. The airlines would have preferred to purchase more fuel-efficient aircraft, which in turn would have reduced their operating expenses, but they had not generated enough revenues to do so. With high interest rates and a depressed economy, this situation seemed like a vicious cycle.

To add to the problem, in August 1981 PATCO declared a strike. Many of PATCO's members were fired as a result of their strike and the Federal Aviation Administration responded to the lack of air traffic controllers by cutting back flights and services. Airlines could no longer operate at full capacity. Industry experts believed that the airlines were pulling out of their slump before the PATCO strike, but the strike destroyed any hopes of a profitable year.

The airlines learned from their losses by striving for efficiency and co-operation from their labor and material suppliers. They mastered the complexities of pricing in a more competitive environment, and defined and capitalized on their strengths. By the end of 1981, the airlines that survived the economic downturn would be much stronger competitors than had ever existed before.

An industry summary for the years 1977–1981 appears in Exhibit 1.

EXHIBIT 1

Industry Summary (All Amounts in Millions)

	1977	1978	1979	1980	1981
Revenue	$17,200	$19,600	$22,600	$26,100	$31,900
Profit	$ 620	$ 1,060	$ 262	$ −9	$ −462
Passenger boardings	194	220	238	223	204

DELTA AIR LINES

Delta Air Lines was primarily in the business of providing scheduled air transportation for passengers, freight, and mail over a network of routes throughout the United States and abroad. Delta was one of the few major airlines that had not diversified into other businesses to improve its profits. With deregulation and the uncertainty of the economy, many airlines began searching for other revenue sources. One study indicated that 70 percent of the world's airlines provided airframe maintenance for others, 60 percent were involved in outside engine and component maintenance, many offered training and computer services to other airlines, and others were involved in totally unrelated businesses. Exhibit 2 indicates the business activities of Delta and some of its competitors.

Delta has always operated with the philosophy that running an airline requires the undivided attention of top management and the undivided resources of the organization. Furthermore, Delta was so strong financially that it could afford to weather periodic economic downturns.

Delta certainly has had financial strength through the years. Clichés and advertising taglines that were passed around in the industry, such as "Flying high at Delta," and "A wing and a cash register," indicated that Delta was doing something right for quite some time.

After being called the big little airline for years, in 1976 Delta broke into the big five of the U.S. airlines. Before 1976 the industry had only a big four, consisting of American, Eastern, TWA, and United, but Delta changed all that. For example, Delta's cumulative net earnings from 1971 through 1981 were $857 million compared with $448 million for United, the world's largest airline. For the year 1981, Delta was in the number-two spot for passenger

---

EXHIBIT 2   **Airlines' Activities and Related Businesses**

AIRLINE	RESTAURANT/ HOTEL	CATERING	TRAVEL/TOUR OPERATIONS	GROUND SUPPORT	TRAINING	COMPUTER
American	X	X	X	X	X	
Braniff	X	X	X	X	X	
Continental	X	X	X	X		
Delta						
Eastern	X	X				
National						
Pan Am	X	X	X	X	X	X
TWA	X	X	X	X	X	X
United	X	X	X	X		

SOURCE: "World Airline Ancillary Activity—1978," *Air Transport World*, June 1979, pp. 38–39.

boardings and sixth in revenue passenger–kilometers among the U.S. airlines. This was a far cry from the crop duster organization of the 1930s. Some experts and observers of this industry even predicted that by 1990 Delta will be the biggest airline in the United States.

Management

Delta was organized along functional lines. Exhibit 3 shows the eight basic divisions reporting to President Garrett in June 1981. The functional divisions were finance, marketing, flight operations, legal, corporate affairs, technical operations, personnel, and passenger service. In turn, many divisions were further subdivided into departments.

David Garrett and his senior management group always made the key decisions. The senior management group acted as a centralized unit where all members were involved in consensus decision making regardless of their departments. Each morning, they attended a short briefing to identify problems as well as opportunities. The meeting also helped educate the senior management team about the activities of other functional departments. At more lengthy weekly meetings actual decision making took place.

Although the organization was very centralized, the senior management group was always accessible to the rest of the company. Delta maintained

EXHIBIT 3   **Organization Chart (as of June 1981)**

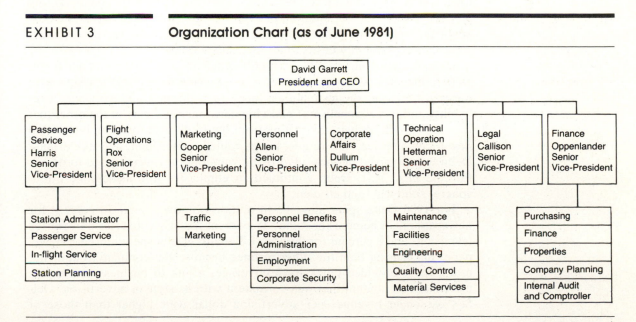

SOURCE: Delta Airlines 1981 Annual Report.

very open and often informal communication channels. Employees were encouraged to air their gripes and problems directly with senior management.

More informally, the senior vice presidents' doors usually were open to the employees in their divisions. One Delta executive declared, "You can tell from the state of my carpet that mechanics come in here all the time to talk to me—look at the grease stains on that carpet."[2] Senior management also developed the policy of making themselves visible and available to employees by walking around their divisions and stopping to talk.

The atmosphere at Delta was more like a family business, a close-knit family of 36,790 people. Members were invited to participate in management as much as possible. This family atmosphere resulted in a spirit of cooperation between labor and management.

These policies were instilled by Delta's founder, Woolman. Woolman was known as a master of personnel relations, and Delta retained this mastery despite its strong centralization.

Marketing Division

At Delta, Joe Cooper directed the marketing division, which was further subdivided into the traffic and marketing departments. Delta's marketing efforts were described as consistently innovative and aggressive since Delta's first days of operation. Starting with Woolman himself, Delta executives never minded spending money on sales promotion and media advertising as long as they were convinced that it would pay off financially. The marketing division also handled promotion, pricing, and the analysis of new route possibilities. Final route scheduling and the maintenance of the route system were the responsibility of the flight operations division.

Delta's advertising was always highly pragmatic both in content and form. Delta concentrated on reaching local as opposed to national markets with messages focusing on destinations, fares, arrival times, and its image of reliability and professionalism. Following deregulation, many of the other major airlines shifted their advertising from the traditional focus on image to a new focus on price, new routes, better routes, better food, and free drinks. Delta was involved in such advertising wars only if it was forced to do so. For the most part, Delta continued to emphasize its businesslike atmosphere, solidness, and efficiency.

For 1980 Delta spent almost $40 million on advertising: 50 percent for newspapers, 16 percent for radio, 15 percent for magazines, 11 percent for television, and 8 percent for outdoor billboards. Delta spent more for newspaper advertising than the other airlines because the company found that newspapers provided quick local coverage, a link to businessmen, and a matter-of-fact content that was consistent with its style of advertising. Delta's passenger revenues per advertising dollar were higher than those of

EXHIBIT 4

Ad Expenditures and Revenues

AIRLINE	1980 AD EXPENSE ($ THOUSANDS)	PASSENGER REVENUE PER AD
American	$50,948	$ 53.80
Braniff	16,536	55.05
Continental	16,291	49.39
Delta	36,480	79.91
Eastern	44,864	60.49
Northwest	10,974	86.38
Pan Am	23,494	36.08
Republic	6,065	136.47
TWA	38,817	51.60
United	62,776	59.64
US Air	9,930	89.65
Western	13,535	60.08

SOURCE: "U.S. Airline Advertising Analysis: 1980," *Air Transport World,* June 1981, p. 85.

some of the other majors, but were also much lower than those of some of their competitors, as shown in Exhibit 4.

Since deregulation the airlines control their prices. As a result, severe price competition developed in many markets. In 1979, Delta refused to lower both its coach fares and its economy fares, because such a reduction would have alienated its regular customers, especially its business customers. Delta viewed these price wars as misguided efforts to achieve competitive advantage, but in a 1981 policy statement Delta said: Delta will not allow any other carrier to maintain a price advantage in any market in which Delta has a meaningful amount of traffic participation.

So Delta became involved in some price wars, resulting in stagnant traffic and lost revenues. Delta established a frequent flyer program in an effort to provide some way for business and regular passengers to take advantage of the reduced fares. The frequent flyer program offered a free trip after a certain number of paid flights flown.

Since deregulation Delta has moved at a deliberate pace to strengthen and extend its route system. New routes were studied and analyzed by the route development committee, which was cochaired by Bob Oppenlander, senior vice president of finance, and Joe Cooper. The new routes or cities had to be very strong for Delta to consider them. Delta was willing to take risks on new routes, but the risks were well calculated by the route development committee.

Cooper described the expansion of Delta's system as a slow one. Since 1978, Dallas/Ft. Worth and Cincinnati were developed as new hubs, and plans were made to develop Denver as another hub. In 1981 Delta added nonstop operations in 39 markets between cities already receiving its service. In 1980 Delta added eight new cities and thirteen new nonstop routes to already serviced cities.

Passenger Service

In 1982 the passenger service division was headed by Hollis Harris. For nine of the last ten years, Delta had the best complaint record according to the CAB consumer complaint records. For 1980 Delta had only 1.4 complaints per 100,000 passengers. Pan Am had the worst record of the U.S. major airlines with a rate of 13.0 complaints per 100,000 customers.

Delta, however, consistently scored poorly (ninth or tenth) among the ten majors for on-time performance. Delta officials explained that this poor performance was due to its policy of holding departing flights until all arriving flights were in, which was done to accommodate passengers connecting to other flights. This is one of the reasons Delta's complaint record was so low.

Woolman instilled Delta with the friendly and helpful approach during his years as president. Employees were instructed to treat customers the way they would want to be treated as customers. Woolman took this policy to an extreme and even told reservation clerks to suggest a competitor's flight if it fit a customer's needs better than the Delta flight.

Delta has spent more to serve fewer passengers because the number of passengers has been decreasing. The cost of Delta's passenger service increased, which included food expense, cabin expenses, and cabin attendant salaries. In addition, Delta swallowed an extra $3 million in customer compensation when a large number of passengers were denied boarding because of overbooking in 1980. Fortunately for Delta, costs have gone up for the other major airlines as well.

In passenger service, Delta was at a competitive disadvantage when compared with other airlines. Many of the other airlines used computerized seat assignments, while Delta assigned seats by hand. On every change of plane, their customer waited at the gate to receive a seat assignment.

Technical Operations

The technical operations division was under the direction of Don Hetterman, who was responsible for the maintenance and engineering of all Delta's equipment. This division was also accountable for developing specifications for fleet purchases and for planning new facilities.

Delta's maintenance and engineering expenses were increasing by 17.4 percent each year, while the industry average increased yearly by about 15 percent. There were 6,100 employees in the division in 1982, of which only 68 were management. Only three other airlines had more employees in this division, but Delta also did more of its own maintenance and engineering work than any other major airline.

Hetterman claimed that the maintenance and engineering department was one of the many keys to Delta's success. He described his division as being self-contained. Delta did not sell its services to other airlines, and it bought as little as possible from the outside. Only 3 percent of Delta's maintenance burden went to outside suppliers. This "make rather than buy" attitude resulted in developing and producing everything from test units for aircraft to plastic decorative items for the airplanes. The next project planned to produce plastic meal trays.

Hetterman claimed that he operated a no-budget division. Forecasts were made for planning purposes, but no budgets were ever set for expenditures. Delta apparently just spent what was necessary for this department. The beauty of this method was that when justifiable expenditures were turned in, Hetterman could approve or disapprove them quickly. Also, this method eliminated the end-of-the-year rush to spend the allocated funds for that year that had not already been spent.

This division also believed that salvage means money. Delta has never thrown anything away that could be turned into a penny. Even the cardboard shipment boxes were collected and sold.

Personnel

Ron Allen headed up the personnel division. As mentioned previously, Delta treated its employees as if they were members of its family. As a result, Delta enjoyed high morale, high productivity, and low unionism. From the first day, Delta's top management recognized that Delta's employees were its greatest asset.

Delta's employees had the best job security in the industry. In fact, no permanent employee was furloughed or laid off at Delta in over 25 years, even during severe economic times. During deregulation and the recessions, other airlines laid off thousands of employees, but not Delta. Delta found something for its employees to do during reduced traffic periods. President Garrett discussed this policy:

> In the 1973 fuel crisis we had to cut back on our flying by 20 percent within sixty days. That meant we had about 200 pilots and 400 flight attendants that were surplus. But we put them to work everywhere we could—loading cargo, cleaning airplanes, selling tickets, making reservations. Sure that was a blow to the size of their paychecks, especially in the case of the pilots, but they still got paychecks and they kept their seniority and all their medical benefits.[3]

All job openings were filled from within when possible. Many firms claim to do that, but Delta actually followed that policy. Also, with the exception of various specialists, all employees started at the bottom of the ladder, even the top management team. Garrett started as a reservationist, Hetterman started as a mechanic, and Harris started as a transportation agent.

Delta established a policy that every employee will meet with a member of senior management at least once every eighteen months. The employees' immediate supervisors were usually asked to leave during part of this meeting so subordinates could voice any concerns about their bosses.

Delta's salaries were kept above the union scale. Furthermore, its employee benefit plan was known as one of the most generous in U.S. industry.

All these aspects of its personnel policies helped Delta to develop an excellent reputation. At one point in 1978, Delta's employment files were bulging with 250,000 job applications that were less than six months old.

This reputation helped develop a nonunionism philosophy at Delta. By 1982 only the pilots and the dispatchers were organized. The other employees apparently felt that they did not need a union. This fact provided Delta with a great deal of flexibility, which in turn lowered its expenses. Because Delta did not have to abide by union work rules, it assigned people temporarily to different jobs when needed. This helped Delta achieve flexibility in assignments and in scheduling. On busy days, it was not rare to find stewardesses making seat assignments or mechanics handling luggage.

Hetterman reasoned that avoiding unions and their work rules helped productivity in his division. He commented, "When we get jammed up with a lot of mechanical problems at once, I can pull people out of one part of the shop and put them in another, or I can even pull in people from other stations."[4] Union work rules in other firms forbid such action. Generally, union employees perform under very narrowly defined job responsibilities.

The nonunionism philosophy increased flexibility and decreased labor costs. It also had one other big advantage for Delta: no costly labor strikes.

Almost all training at Delta was on the job. There was no formal management training program, but Delta's personnel system helped create an environment in which knowledge and expertise were passed on from old to new employees. This informal training was monitored by managers who were required to submit a yearly plan for the upgrading of their people and for their own replacement.

Senior management at Delta was encouraged to become familiar with all aspects of the operations and not just their own. At Delta this was known as the theory of interchangeable parts. Garrett observed, "We have a group of senior officers who are almost interchangeable because lines of communication are so short you never have to worry about someone not knowing what is going on."[5] Oppenlander further added, "We do respond very quickly to fires that develop. We've all been working here together for a long time so we can work together very quickly. We're also not cluttered with a great deal of committee-type or staff-type operations around this company. People can get to us and get to us very quickly."[6]

Flight Operations

The senior vice president of the flight operations division was Frank Rox. This division was responsible for flight personnel, communications, and flight control.

As mentioned previously, the rising cost of jet fuel was a great problem to the airlines. Many of the airlines, such as American, became involved in oil exploration, and began to control fuel distribution. Delta tried changing suppliers and tried the spot market, but it resisted deeper involvement in the fuel or storage domain. Delta believed that these ventures were cost prohibitive.

Instead, Delta was taking every step possible to conserve fuel. The company began to purchase fuel-efficient equipment, to modify its current equipment, and to analyze its flight operations for possible conservations. But fuel conservation can help only so much. Antiquated flight routes that air traffic controllers required that jet pilots follow and the design of the airports also wasted a lot of fuel. Delta lobbied Congress and the FAA to try to do something about these two causes of fuel waste.

Another key to Delta's success was the interconnected schedule of short flights. Delta created a hub and spoke system where all flights either originated from or led to one of the hubs. The cities or markets that the flights flew to were known as spokes. Delta had its major hub in Atlanta and two lesser ones operating in Dallas/Ft. Worth and Cincinnati. Delta was also looking at Denver for a fourth hub.

The spoke-and-hub system worked in the following manner: Jets departed early each morning from the new terminal in Atlanta and flew along spokes of a wheel to end-point cities. At the same time, other jets flew from these end points along the spokes toward Atlanta. The inbound flights were then scheduled to land in rapid succession so that 30 or more jets would be at the terminal at the same time. The jets then roared off, one after the other, along a different spoke to another end-point city.

This method of scheduling allowed passengers traveling on Delta to go to any point on the airline's route by connecting at a hub. In fact, during the first six months of 1980, 88.3 percent of Delta's passengers on flights to Atlanta continued their journey on Delta.

Many of the other airlines tried to copy Delta's efficient hub-and-spoke system. Eastern Airlines, Delta's archrival, also established a hub in Atlanta. Because of the number of connections that occur in Atlanta, the joke has grown among southerners that, when you die, you may not know for sure whether you're going to heaven or hell, but you know for sure that you'll have to change planes in Atlanta.

Finance

The crucial finance division, including the planning subdivision, was under the direction of Bob Oppenlander. For the 34th consecutive year, Delta reported a profitable year in 1981. Delta's balance sheets, income statements, and other relevant data appear in Exhibits 5, 6, and 7. Financial information for some of Delta's competitors appears in Exhibit 8. Delta even remained

---

EXHIBIT 5   **Income Statements 1979–1981 (Dollar Amounts in Thousands Except Per Share Data)**

	1981	1980	1979
Operating revenues:			
Passenger	$3,287,511	$2,733,820	$2,213,024
Cargo	213,431	190,490	167,904
Other, net	32,384	32,650	46,918
Total operating revenues	3,533,326	2,956,960	2,427,846
Operating expenses:			
Salaries and related costs	1,306,359	1,161,487	1,014,144
Aircraft fuel	1,070,057	857,165	475,683
Aircraft maintenance materials and repairs	76,631	64,325	52,689
Rentals and landing fees	98,530	89,760	82,634
Passenger service	121,502	115,996	106,088
Agency commissions	157,710	114,304	79,183
Other cash costs	307,364	267,192	225,106
Depreciation and amortization	220,979	194,094	183,287
Total operating expenses	3,359,132	2,864,323	2,218,814
Operating income	174,194	92,637	209,032
Other expense (income):			
Interest expense	23,135	21,852	16,178
Less interest capitalized	15,539	10,790	6,717
	7,596	11,062	9,461
Gain on disposition of aircraft	(30,078)	(36,091)	(20,514)
Realized and unrealized (gain) loss on foreign currency translation, net	(6,227)	3,735	7,110
Miscellaneous income, net	(19,917)	(10,687)	(9,069)
	(48,626)	(31,981)	(13,012)
Income before income taxes	222,820	124,618	222,044
Income taxes provided	101,447	54,433	104,429
Amortization of investment tax credits	(25,101)	(22,973)	(19,129)
Net income	$ 146,474	$ 93,158	$ 136,744
Net income per common share	$7.37	$4.69	$6.88

SOURCE: Delta Air Lines 1981 Annual Report.

profitable during the difficult years when other airlines were suffering severe losses. Indeed, many industry observers felt that Delta had the best balance sheet in the industry. It was so good that banks periodically went to Delta and asked if it wanted to borrow some money.

Some of Delta's financial policies helped to maintain its health as well as

EXHIBIT 6   **Balance Sheets 1978–1981 (Dollar Amounts in Thousands)**

	1981	1980	1979	1978
ASSETS				
Current assets:				
Cash	$ 6,899	$ 38,064	$ 25,712	$ 7,347
Short-term investments			3,216	116,764
Acct. receivable	308,168	283,039	229,284	116,764
Supplies	52,648	37,836	16,275	12,892
Prepaid expense	20,808	37,836	16,275	12,892
Total current assets	388,523	369,497	284,183	325,130
Property and equipment:				
Cost less depreciation	1,734,901	1,552,829	1,419,393	1,240,552
Advance payments	149,628	90,952	78,420	71,983
Total prop./equip.	1,884,529	1,643,781	1,497,813	1,312,532
Other assets	31,275	29,261	6,329	9,018
Total assets	$2,304,327	$2,042,539	$1,788,325	$1,646,683
LIABILITIES AND STOCKHOLDER EQUITY				
Current liabilities:				
Current portion of long-term debt	$ 11,137	$ 15,225	$ 14,832	$ 9,731
Note payable	44,487	30,934	30,104	
Other	532,627	504,405	363,453	363,063
Total current liabilities	588,251	550,564	408,389	372,794
Long-term debt	198,411	147,901	125,483	167,331
Deferred credit	477,054	422,105	401,785	369,759
Stockholder equity:				
Common stock, par $3 per share				
Authorized 25,000,000:				
Outstanding 19,880,577	59,642	59,642	59,642	59,642
Additional paid-in capital	80,088	80,088	80,088	80,088
Retained earnings	900,881	782,239	712,938	597,069
Total stockholder equity	$1,040,611	$ 921,969	$ 852,668	$ 736,799
Total liabilities	$2,304,327	$2,042,539	$1,788,325	$1,646,683

SOURCE: Delta Air Lines 1981 Annual Report.

EXHIBIT 7   **Other Relevant Data**

	1981	1980	1979	1978	1977
Long-term debt	$ 198,411	$ 147,901	$ 125,483	$ 167,331	$ 237,497
Stockholder equity	$ 1,040,611	$ 921,969	$ 852,668	$ 736,799	$ 620,583
Stockholder equity per share	$52.34	$46.38	$42.89	$37.06	$31.22
Shares of common stock outstanding	19,880,577	19,880,577	19,880,577	19,880,577	19,880,577
Revenue passengers enplaned	36,743,214	39,713,904	39,360,368	33,007,670	28,811,966
Available seat miles (000)	45,428,277	43,217,372	39,326,891	35,135,046	32,614,260
Revenue passenger–miles (000)	25,192,531	26,171,197	25,518,520	20,825,722	18,042,339
Passenger load factor	55.46%	60.56%	64.07%	59.27%	55.32%
Break-even load factor	52.52%	58.51%	58.02%	52.74%	50.36%
Available ton miles (000)	6,037,476	5,748,143	5,357,995	4,743,778	4,478,038
Revenue ton–miles (000)	2,845,425	2,934,375	2,916,585	2,426,265	2,113,798
Passenger revenue per passenger mile	13.05¢	10.45¢	8.67¢	8.94¢	8.73¢
Operating expenses per available seat mile	7.39¢	6.63¢	5.57¢	5.25¢	4.84¢
Operating expenses per available ton mile	55.64¢	49.83¢	41.41¢	38.91¢	35.25¢

SOURCE: Delta Air Lines 1981 Annual Report.

EXHIBIT 8   **Financial Information on Competitors for 1981
(Dollar Amounts in Millions)**

COMPANY	SALES	PROFIT	CURRENT RATIO
American	$4,108.7	$ 16.8	1.0
Braniff	1,204.0	− 160.6	0.6
Continental	1,090.8	− 60.4	0.9
Eastern	3,727.1	− 65.9	0.9
Trans World	5,265.5	45.0	0.8
United	5,141.2	− 70.5	0.8
US Air	1,110.5	51.1	1.1

SOURCE: Corporate Scoreboard in *Business Week*, March 1, 1982, p. 53; March 15, 1982, p. 74.

its independence. Delta tried to stay away from external debt and financed its fleet acquisition with 85 to 90 percent internally generated funds. This percentage was much higher than that of the other airlines, which were only able to cover 50 to 60 percent of their debt with internally generated funds. In fact, a former chief executive at Eastern said: "When I came to work every January 2, I would say to myself, I am $15 million behind in our battle with Delta before we even start. That's how much more interest we have to pay."[7] Furthermore, when Delta turned to long-term debt for financing, the company repaid the debt as fast as banks allowed.

Delta also avoided leasing its aircraft, preferring to buy the aircraft and conservatively depreciating their values down in ten years. Although these policies were costly over the short run, they provided a hedge against the possibility that the aircraft might become obsolete more quickly than expected and enabled Delta to sell the planes while they could still command a favorable price.

Although Delta did not have a formal planning department, planning was administered by Arthur Ford, assistant vice president, long-range planning. Senior management, however, was very involved in the planning function on an ongoing basis. Planning at Delta was viewed as a line rather than staff function. Given its financial strength, Delta was one of the few airlines to stick with long-range plans even when uncontrollable events such as fuel shortages and the PATCO strike occurred. Delta looked fifteen years ahead for its fleet programs and was envied for completing its program despite all the problems in the industry.

Delta was willing to spend money on fleet modernization, giving it a competitive edge. This edge arose from the new technologies of aircraft: fuel efficiency, low noise, and lower emissions. Because Delta kept its fleet up to date technologically, it had one of the youngest fleets in the industry. In 1980 Delta bought 60 Boeing 757s valued at $3 billion. This was the largest aircraft order in history. In 1978, Delta ordered 20 Boeing 767s, which were valued at $1.5 billion. The total value of this fleet program was $4.5 billion. These new planes will burn about 40 percent less fuel per seat than the planes they replaced. However, Delta would have bought 100 more planes if it had found someone to build what it wanted. Delta developed specifications for a plane it called the "Delta III." Garrett noted that by developing the Delta III, Delta was ready for the 21st century. The Delta III would burn even less fuel than the 757s and 767s and would provide other economies as well. However, none of the aircraft manufacturers wanted the order, and it would not have made sense for Delta itself to try to manufacture the plane.

In planning for fleets in earlier years, Delta maintained a wait-and-see attitude about new technology. In the early 1980s, however, Delta was doing just the opposite. It wanted the new technology of the Delta III, so it designed the plane itself. Delta's financial position helped tremendously with its fleet programs. It could extend where other airlines could not in the days of deregulation, recession, and air traffic constraints.

Delta never backed off on a fleet improvement program because of financial limitations. Year after year, Delta stayed on course with its long-term plans regardless of external financial threats or internal problems. Oppenlander commented on this point:

> If you didn't consistently apply the financial principles, you could have generated a lot of wealth during good times and blown it. Some people have. Because we have been consistent, we are poised to attack the next growth period for the industry while the rest of the industry has laid off a lot of people and restricted its fleet improvement program because of financial limitations. We jumped off in strength after the recession in 1971 with all our people, with all their training and skills intact, and with a modern fleet. We did it again in 1975. And when the air traffic control situation returns to normal and traffic turns up again, we'll do it again. [8]

Delta's plans for the future include growth and competitiveness. Deregulation threw a monkey wrench into many of the airlines' expansion plans because of the extra competition. But deregulation also gave the airlines the freedom to enter and exit as they pleased. When deregulation was official, many of the airlines jumped right in and started expanding. Not so with Delta, which was content to expand slowly. Delta planned any move it might make very carefully, and then it made that move cautiously. Delta had intense competition on many routes and recently began to feel the pressure from Piedmont Airlines, another recently successful carrier. Delta was also at a disadvantage on many routes because it was basically a short-haul airline, and many of its competitors flew the more profitable long-haul routes.

Although the impact of the air traffic controllers' strike was very painful for many other airlines, operations at Delta were under control and Oppenlander went on vacation. Delta's reaction to the strike was to downsize, while trying to keep as much of the hub-and-spoke system intact as possible. Delta simply flew less frequently and found something else for surplus employees to do.

FICTIONALIZED CONCLUSION

Two weeks later the consultant met again with a somewhat concerned President Garrett. On his desk was a report entitled *Outlook for 1982* and a recent newspaper with the headline "Braniff Terminates Operations."

The outlook report indicated that industry leaders and experts did not anticipate any improvements in the economy or in traffic until mid-1982 at the earliest. The outlook on the entire year was not very optimistic. Estimates showed only a 3 percent expected increase in traffic.

Worse yet, Garrett had the first quarter 1982 results, shown in Exhibit 9, and Delta posted a loss, along with most of the other airlines. Although the first quarter was usually poor, Garrett was disappointed by the results. Moreover, the final results for 1981 showed that Delta's profits decreased 30 percent from the year before. Delta lost traffic in its established markets and

EXHIBIT 9

First Quarter 1982 (Dollar Amounts in Millions)

COMPANY	SALES	PROFITS
American	$ 956.9	$ −41.6
Delta	881.3	− 18.4
Eastern	908.4	− 51.4
Trans World	1,087.5	− 102.7
United	1,203.6	− 129.3
U.S. Air	279.2	10.8

SOURCE: Corporate Scoreboard in *Business Week*, May 17, 1982, p. 61.

gains were not made in new markets. The lost traffic was going to strong competitors like Piedmont, Ozark, and U.S. Air. In the past these airlines provided Delta with feed traffic, but now they had expanded their own routes with hubs and spokes that directly competed with Delta.

Also, Delta had saturated the Atlanta market, and wherever it might move, there was either some airline already there or another one was sure to follow. As one competitor's chief officer said, "Delta is just beginning to look a little more like everyone else. What's worrisome is that it can afford to bleed a little more than anyone else."[9]

Garrett paused and looked the consultant in the eye, "Well, consultant, what do you recommend we do to cope with this changing industry? What threats and major problems do you feel we need to address? I know that we've concentrated pretty much on running just an airline. I'm sure there are opportunities within this industry, and there are probably other related opportunities outside of it that we might try to exploit. What do you recommend?"

If you were hired to advise David Garrett and Delta Air Lines, how would you answer his questions?

NOTES

1. "Deregulation and Recession Realities Causing Major Shifts in Labor Relations," *Air Transport World*, December 1981, p. 45.

2. "Delta's Flying Money Machine," *Business Week*, May 9, 1977, p. 88.

3. "Delta: The World's Most Profitable Airline," *Business Week*, August 31, 1981, p. 70.

4. *Ibid.*, p. 71.

5. "Flying High at Delta Airlines," *Dun's Review*, December 1977, p. 60.

6. "Delta: The World's Most Profitable Airline," *op. cit.*, p. 72.

7. "Delta's Flying Money Machine," *op. cit.*, p. 85.

8. "Delta: The World's Most Profitable Airline," *op. cit.*, p. 72.

9. "Delta Adjusts to Flying at Less Lofty Heights," *Business Week*, January 25, 1982, p. 30.

CASE 21

Eastern Air Lines, Inc.

M. DWIGHT SHELTON • LARRY D. ALEXANDER

INTRODUCTION

In 1983, Eastern Air Lines, Inc., was the third largest airline in the United States. With 37,500 employees and an extensive route system, Eastern boasted that it continued to be America's favorite way to fly. In fact, since 1980, more people have flown on Eastern than on any other airline in the free world.

Eastern provided scheduled air transportation between the principal metropolitan areas of the northeastern and southeastern portions of the United States. Although Eastern's route system was predominantly North to South, it also serviced major cities in the West. In addition, Eastern provided air service between points in the United States and various parts of Central and South America.

Eastern operated in an oligopolistic industry. Actions taken by any one airline had to be taken in light of possible retaliation by other carriers serving the same routes. Since deregulation went into effect in 1978, significant upheaval had taken place in this industry. Surprisingly, many large, established airlines were having financial difficulties in this new setting while some new, lower cost airlines were feeling success.

Eastern Air Lines, unfortunately, was one of the major airlines that was facing difficult times. In October 1983, Eastern was on the brink of financial disaster. Despite its size and power, Eastern had recorded net losses totaling approximately $287 million since 1980 as shown in Exhibit 1. Some industry observers felt that Eastern might follow two other major U.S. airlines, Braniff International and Continental Airlines, into bankruptcy.

A key strategic issue facing Eastern in late 1983 was how to position the firm in a more competitive, deregulated industry. Did Eastern need significantly to lower its cost structure to be competitive? Could it focus on specific segments of the industry and be successful? Could it somehow differentiate itself to compete successfully against the no-frills airlines? Conversely, was the industry's future so bleak that Eastern should diversify into other industries with more promising sales and profit potential? At the same time, Eastern's day-to-day operating problems were so severe that short-term survival was becoming as important as its basic positioning in the industry.

This case was prepared by M. Dwight Shelton, M.B.A. in Management from V.P.I. in December 1983, and Larry D. Alexander, Associate Professor of Strategic Management, Department of Management, College of Business, Virginia Polytechnic Institute and State University, Blacksburg, Virginia.

EXHIBIT 1   **Eastern Net Income (Loss) (Dollar Amounts in Millions)**

YEAR/PERIOD	OPERATING INCOME (LOSS)			NET INCOME (LOSS)		
1976	$ 96.7			$ 39.1		
1977	58.1	$362.6		27.9	$191.9	
1978	96.8			67.3		
1979	111.0			57.6		
1980	1.9			(17.4)		
1981	(49.9)	(66.8)	$(123.1)	(65.9)	$(158.2)	$(287.1)
1982	(18.8)			(74.9)		
1/1/83–9/30/83	(56.3)			(128.9)		
Totals 1976–9/30/83	$ 239.5			$(95.2)		

SOURCE: Eastern Airlines, Inc., 1982 Annual Report, p. 20.

THE AIRLINE INDUSTRY

Deregulation of the Airline Industry

President Jimmy Carter targeted deregulation of the airline industry as a top legislative priority shortly after assuming office in early 1977. President Carter appointed Alfred Kahn, an economist and expert on regulations, to head the Civil Aeronautics Board (CAB). This agency had regulated commercial aviation for nearly 40 years. Under Kahn's direction, the CAB began easing airline regulatory controls in 1977. With the passage of the Airline Deregulation Act of 1978, the airline industry was rapidly transformed. Before deregulation, competition had been on the basis of service and amenities other than price. After deregulation, however, there was full-scale competition on a host of factors, including price.

Deregulation changed the CAB's powers in several ways. From October 24, 1978, to December 31, 1981, the burden of proof required to deny new route applications shifted to those opposing the applications. Then, starting on January 1, 1982, the CAB could no longer determine whether routes met the public convenience and necessity, only whether applying carriers were fit to operate on these routes. One year later on January 1, 1983, the CAB's domestic authority over fares expired. Until that time, a zone of reasonableness was to be enforced that was far more lenient than earlier price minimums that carriers could not go below. These price regulations were usually followed by all air carriers because they did not want to charge above the minimum price and lose customers. The act also eliminated the CAB's control over mergers and acquisitions, but carriers became subject to the same antitrust laws as other industries.

The Industry after Deregulation

The airline industry primarily transported passengers, cargo, and mail. During 1980 and 1981, passenger service accounted for approximately 84 percent of total air carrier revenues, cargo for 9 percent, mail for 2 percent, and other operations for the remaining 5 percent. In 1981, operating revenues were $37 billion; however, 1982 revenues declined for the first time in history.

The airline industry experienced major changes after deregulation. With artificial barriers to entry eliminated, the number and variety of airlines increased significantly. From 1976 to 1982, the increase in the number of airlines by carrier type was the following: one major carrier, eighteen national carriers, eight regional carriers, and fifteen local carriers. In return, the increasing number of airlines reduced market concentration and the market power of the ten or so major carriers.

New market entrants since deregulation were generally nonunionized, low-cost operations. They stressed high productivity and the ability of employees to perform a variety of jobs. This approach resulted in a lower cost per seat mile, the basis on which the new entrants successfully competed. Typically, they did not provide the same level of service as the older, established airlines.

Deregulation brought about significant changes to the industry. Significant route alterations occurred as airlines fought for the most profitable routes. Although the airlines differed widely in their cost structure, the number one weapon they started using was price competition. As the fortunes of individual airlines varied greatly, the overall industry had recorded major losses since 1980 and the trend was getting worse by mid-1983. Many industry analysts believed that this condition could not continue in the long term. Airlines worried that a competitive shake out might occur that might force many airlines to go under.

In May 1982, Braniff International Airlines filed for bankruptcy and ceased operations. Since then, it had continually discussed restarting operations; however, the earliest possible time would be sometime in 1984. In September 1983, Continental Airlines declared bankruptcy and then restarted operations as a significantly smaller, lower-cost carrier. By late 1983, several other major carriers were on the verge of financial disaster.

Although deregulation got its fair share of the blame for the industry's poor performance, other factors such as fare wars, excess capacity, and the economy also contributed to the losses. Regardless of the reason, it was generally conceded that the customers benefited at the expense of the airlines, which were trying to maintain their market shares. Fares increased overall by 48 percent from 1978 to 1983; however, the Civil Aeronautics Board estimated that fares under regulation would have increased by 67 percent.[1]

EASTERN'S HISTORY

1928–1972

Eastern Air Lines, Inc., began operations on May 1, 1928, as a mail transport carrier on a New York to Miami route with several intermediate stops. Passenger service started on August 18, 1930, with various stops along the East Coast. Captain Eddie Rickenbacker, a famous World War I flier, joined Eastern as general manager in 1935. During the next 28 years, he developed Eastern into one of the country's largest airlines. His overall plan was to join all viable eastern cities with the resort cities of the South. The impact of his approach was still easily seen in Eastern's route structure in the 1980s.

During 1961, Eastern launched its innovative air shuttle service between cities in the heavily traveled northeastern markets. This extremely successful service was unique because it guaranteed customers seats on a no-reservation basis. In fact, the Eastern air shuttle continued to dominate the northeastern business traveler market segment in the mid-1980s.

Eastern converted its entire fleet to jet powered aircraft during the 1960s. Also at that time, Eastern began its commitment to be the first airline to use new, improved aircraft. For example, Eastern was the first airline to place the wide-bodied Lockheed L-1011 into service in 1972.

1973–1975

In 1973, Eastern posted a staggering $51.7 million loss, the largest in its history. Although the firm had generally recorded modest profits in prior years, several factors combined to bring about Eastern's financial difficulties. First, its pilot productivity was one of the lowest in the industry. This was the result of a combination of fewer hours worked and high wages. Second, its new L-1011s were experiencing significant operating difficulties. Third, it faced significantly increased competition due to a merger between Delta and Northeast Airlines. This allowed Delta, already Eastern's biggest competitor, to enter many of Eastern's most profitable markets. Fourth, Eastern responded poorly to a sluggish economy during those years. Fifth, its management team was very large and used a disjointed management approach.

Operations improved in 1974 as Eastern's load factor, the percentage of seats occupied by paying customers, increased. Net income for 1974 was $11.5 million. However, 1975 resulted in another record loss of $88.7 million. Despite increased total traffic and revenue yield, load factors decreased as capacity increased. Eastern continued to be an overstaffed airline with excess capacity and a crushing debt load.

1976–1979

This period represented the best overall operating period in the company's history. It was a dramatic turnaround over 1975. The four years from 1976 through 1979 were the most profitable years ever for Eastern (see Exhibit 1).

Former astronaut Frank Borman, who joined Eastern as a vice president in 1970, became president and chief executive officer in December 1975. Borman was generally credited with improving the fortunes of Eastern in the late 1970s. He made and implemented several key strategic decisions that assisted Eastern's recovery. President Borman persuaded employees to accept a 1976 wage freeze. He developed an innovative five-year variable earnings program that diverted 3.5 percent of employees' earnings into corporate investment. Its fleet of aircraft was restructured to improve operating efficiency. He made Eastern shift its marketing emphasis to the business traveler. Subsidiaries that did not relate to air travel were disposed of. Significant cuts were made in top and middle management. Finally, he took action to improve Eastern's customer service image, which had long been quite poor by industry standards.

Perhaps the most significant change during the period was the new image Eastern projected under Borman. Employee loyalty increased as did customer service. Employees liked Borman and believed that he would be able to lead them into a better future. During 1978 and 1979, the period of early deregulation, Eastern's most vital operating statistics continued to increase. New operating records were set as the company followed Borman's strategy of rapid growth.

1980–1982

Although 1976–1979 represented prosperous years, 1980–1982 were filled with intense competition, labor problems, and increasing losses. Losses in 1980–1982 totaled approximately $158.2 million as shown in Exhibit 2. Although Eastern continued the strategies developed by Borman in the 1970s, external events largely beyond the company's control had a significant negative impact. While the economy faltered, costs increased significantly, especially for fuel. In fact, the increased fuel costs in 1980 and 1981 completely offset the economic gains the company had made by converting to more fuel efficient aircraft.

The airline industry suffered during 1980–1982 with operating performance indicators down for most of the airlines. As Exhibit 2 indicates, several of Eastern's key financial and operating statistics declined. Although its revenues increased by $316.7 million from 1980 to 1982, this was offset by the 4.7 percent decline in its load factor during that same period. Further-

EXHIBIT 2	Key Financial and Operating Statistics		
	1982	**1981**	**1980**
Financial results:			
Revenues (000)	$ 3,769,237	$ 3,727,093	$ 3,452,542
Yield per revenue passenger–mile	13.00¢	12.95¢	11.15¢
Net loss (000)	$ (74,927)	$ (65,877)	$ (17,358)
Per average share of common stock	$ (3.82)	$ (3.44)	$ (0.97)
Common stock and retained earnings (deficit) (000)	$ 255,274	$ 350,194	$ 435,456
Per common share outstanding	$ 9.87	$ 13.69	$ 17.21
Shares of common stock outstanding at year end	24,818,160	24,818,122	24,731,500
Operating results:			
Revenue passengers carried (000)	35,032	35,515	39,052
Revenue passenger–miles (000)	26,140,147	26,107,611	28,227,015
Available seat miles (000)	46,143,756	46,789,684	46,028,393
Passenger load factor	56.65%	55.80%	61.33%
Break-even load factor	58.76%	57.37%	62.23%
Number of employees at year-end	39,200	37,700	40,000
Average flight length	579	580	563
Jet aircraft in fleet	268	278	275

SOURCE: Eastern Air Lines, Inc., 1982 Annual Report, p. 1.

more, the actual load factor failed to meet the break-even load factor for each of the three years.

Eastern continued its strategy of rapid growth. After failing in an earlier bid to merge with National Airlines in 1979, Eastern entered into merger talks with Braniff International Airlines in 1980. Braniff's lucrative South American routes were viewed as a logical, important extension to the Eastern route system. Although the merger did not go through, Eastern still obtained the routes in 1982 for $30 million when Braniff declared bankruptcy.

1983

Eastern's financial problems continued to accelerate during 1983. The company lost $128.9 million through September 30, which almost equaled the combined losses for the previous three years. Concerns that Eastern might go bankrupt increased, and its lenders temporarily cut off additional funds to the company. Labor unrest increased significantly, and Borman lost credibility as he tried to balance contradictory goals of avoiding union strikes, appeasing lenders, and continuing cost-cutting efforts.

The U.S. economy improved as did Eastern's overall operating statistics during the first six months of 1983. However, renewed fare wars created a significant decline in the firm's revenue yield. This change resulted in a loss of approximately $84.0 million in revenues during this time period. The decline in yield was caused by the continual, intense price reductions that Eastern's competitors offered, particularly the new, low-cost airlines.

During this period, drawdowns were made on a $400 million line of credit in order to finance current operations. The increase in interest expense combined with debt repayments lowered the firm's cash reserves so much that Eastern was forced in October to cancel the payments of dividends on its preferred stock.

In September of 1983, Borman asked "all employees to accept 15 percent wage cuts, effective November 1, and other concessions . . . as a last-ditch effort to save the airline."[2] He later threatened to close Eastern permanently or have it file for protection under the bankruptcy laws if the employees did not give in to his demands.

Eastern and its unions agreed to an independent audit of the firm's financial condition and also its management strategies. Both sides agreed that the results of the audit would become the basis for joint actions to save the airline. In addition, management agreed to drop its threat of filing bankruptcy. In October 1983, management remained optimistic that its position would be vindicated by the audit and that the unions would cooperate in taking the necessary actions to enable the company to survive.

EASTERN'S FUNCTIONAL AREA STRATEGIES

Marketing/Sales

The airline industry's product (or, rather, service) was a combination of items including the seat, various in-flight services, the route network, the airline fleet, and scheduling flexibility. The actual trip itself was a highly perishable service, as an empty seat on a flight could not be stored or recovered. In addition, airline service was often described as a commodity because it was difficult to achieve product differentiation.

Eastern's response to fare wars was to match competitors' restricted fares in order to maintain its market share. Restricted fares had various day-of-travel, length-of-stay, minimum-time-booked-in-advance, and scheduling requirements that had to be satisfied. On the other hand, unrestricted fares were available to everyone without any such conditions. Because Eastern believed that unrestricted discount fares were destructive, it avoided initiating new rounds of price wars.

In general, Eastern planned to use some discounts to help increase the demand for discretionary travel but wanted to maintain higher fare levels for business travelers. Eastern tried to structure discounts so they had modest but meaningful requirements such as a seven-day advance purchase. These inducements were offered in order to try to stimulate people to fly who otherwise would not.

The company also used its frequent traveler program to generate additional travel. This program provided business customers with travel incentives, usually over a specified period of time. It was designed to stimulate business traffic while building and retaining customer loyalty among those who regularly flew on commercial airlines by providing personal discretionary travel benefits.

Eastern also developed joint promotions with other companies that usually ran for a limited time. These programs tried to encourage price-sensitive, discretionary travelers to fly by appealing to their needs for complimentary products and services. Reduced prices (sometimes even free) were offered on services and products that Eastern and the cosponsoring company were promoting. Eastern estimated that its joint promotional program with Chevrolet, which cost little, generated $70 million in revenues for Eastern. Furthermore, it was estimated that 75 percent of these travelers would not have traveled with Eastern without this program.

Coupons were used by Eastern on occasion to stimulate traffic on routes where they were handed out and on its other routes. Coupons were generally recognized as being very effective when the discount being offered was substantial. Generally, their cost was well worth it when Eastern needed to protect its market share on a route.

Eastern also utilized a mileage-based fare program. This fare structure reduced the number of fare classifications and charges on a progressive rate by travel distance. Still, the longer the trip, the lower the cost per mile. Eastern's new fare program started gaining acceptance in the industry during 1983.

One major goal of Eastern was to continue its leadership in the number of passengers boarded. This leadership was a major emphasis in Eastern's advertising campaigns. Eastern frequently used Frank Borman as the company spokesman on its television commercials. Borman's former celebrity status as an astronaut helped increase the public visibility and recognition of the airline.

The company emphasized travel agencies as the best method to distribute airline tickets. Eastern aggressively marketed its computerized reservation system, System One Direct Access (SODA), to travel agents. By early 1983, Eastern had placed its system with 1,275 travel agents, approximately 6 percent of all agencies. As the company recognized the growing use of computerized reservation systems, it also joined American Airlines as a cohost on American's SABRE reservation system. That system was used by more travel agents than any reservation system in the industry.

Flight Operations

Eastern's flight operations in the 1980s were designed to achieve several key goals. One goal was to improve its reputation as a punctual, reliable, no-nonsense airline. Eastern's customer service reputation had been very poor in years past and was still somewhat weak when Frank Borman became CEO in 1975. Under Borman, however, many industry observers felt that Eastern's service reputation was improving. Unfortunately, Eastern's strongest competitor, Delta Air Lines, had a long-standing reputation for providing excellent service.

Route consolidation and expansion were two important dimensions of Eastern's flight operations. The company's approach was to continue expansion by adding routes that logically extended its existing route system. Eastern also consolidated routes through cooperative agreements with commuter airlines. These agreements generally required Eastern to provide reservation, customer, and other marketing services to the commuter airline. In return, the commuter airline coordinated efforts to route its customers onto Eastern's flights. The company was also continuing its route expansion to Latin American markets, where competition was significantly less.

Another goal for flight operations was Eastern's desire to own a very modern fleet of airplanes. More specifically, Eastern wanted to be the first airline to try new aircraft. This was pursued through its aggressive fleet modernization program. By the end of 1983, Eastern had one of the most modern fleets in the industry.

Although the first airline to launch new aircraft faced debugging problems, Eastern felt that it received an offsetting competitive advantage in the marketplace. For example, Eastern was the first airline to use the relatively fuel- and labor-efficient European Airbus. Eastern even went to Boeing to discuss a proposed new B-757 jet in the late 1970s. Eastern wanted Boeing to develop an aircraft that would use new technology to reduce flying costs while increasing customer comfort. Not only did Boeing then build the 757, it did it to specifications that suited Eastern Air Lines.

Eastern's fleet composition clearly had changed rapidly in recent years. Exhibit 3 shows how Eastern's fleet stood at the end of 1978 and 1982, and its future deliveries. The new B-757s and A-300 Airbuses were significantly lowering Eastern's operating costs. For example, the B-757s were replacing the B-727-225s. They used less jet fuel per flight hour and carried about 25 percent more passengers, 185 versus 149. Eastern's larger, older L-1011s were deployed to longer-haul flights, such as the South American routes, which required more in-flight customer service.

Eastern believed that modern ground facilities were just as important as a modern fleet. Eastern had an ongoing program to improve its terminals. During 1982, major improvements were made at two North Carolina facilities at Charlotte and Greensboro.

Eastern had made various attempts to reduce its operational costs. East-

ern continually emphasized productivity improvements in its negotiations
with its unionized work force. In the early 1980s, it obtained a 6 percent
increase in pilot flying hours and a 20 percent reduction in their vacation
time. The fleet modernization program also helped lower operating costs.
The B-757 required only a two-pilot crew versus two pilots and a flight engineer for the aircraft that it replaced. Finally, Eastern was looking to its
employees to suggest improvements in operations and quality. During 1981,
Eastern established more than 100 quality circles throughout the company.

Finance/Accounting

Eastern's balance sheets and income statements are shown in Exhibits 4
and 5. For the year ending December 31, 1982, Eastern had total operating
revenues of $3.8 billion. Unfortunately, it had a net loss of $74.9 million

EXHIBIT 3   **Eastern Fleet Composition**

FLEET AT DECEMBER 31, 1982

| AIRCRAFT TYPE | CURRENT FLEET | | | ON ORDER | SCHEDULED DELIVERIES (RETIREMENTS) | | | ON OPTION |
	OWNED	LEASED	TOTAL		1983	1984	1985	
FOUR-ENGINE JETS								
DC-8-61*	—	5	5	—	(4)	(1)	—	—
THREE-ENGINE JETS								
L-1011†	20	11	31	—	—	—	—	—
B-727-225	38	58	96	—	—	—	—	—
B-727-100	25	—	25	—	—	—	—	—
TWO-ENGINE JETS								
A300-B2/B4	23	7	30	4	4	—	—	5
A300-600	—	—	—	—	—	—	—	21
B-757	2	—	2	25	13	6	6	24
DC-9-51	4	17	21	—	—	—	—	—
DC-9-31	37	21	58	—	—	—	—	—
Total	149	119	268	29	13	5	6	50

SOURCE: Eastern Air Lines, Inc., 1978 Annual Report, pp. 6, 8.

*These aircraft are currently grounded following their return in December 1982 from the sublessee. The prime lease
terminates in 1983 and 1984.

†Three of the owned aircraft are currently on lease to a foreign carrier.

EXHIBIT 3   **Continued**

	FLEET AT DECEMBER 31, 1978									
	CURRENT FLEET			ON ORDER	SCHEDULED DELIVERIES					ON OPTION
AIRCRAFT TYPE	OWNED	LEASED	TOTAL		1979	1980	1981	1982	BEYOND	
FOUR-ENGINE JETS										
DC-8-61*	—	5	5	—	—	—	—	—	—	—
THREE-ENGINE JETS										
L-1011†	21	11	32	—	—	—	—	—	—	13
L-1011 (seasonal)	—	2	2	—	—	—	—	—	—	—
B-727-225	32	23	55	10	10	—	—	—	—	31
B-727-100	46	—	46	—	—	—	—	—	—	—
B-727-QC	21	3	24	—	—	—	—	—	—	—
TWO-ENGINE JETS										
A310	—	—	—	—	—	—	—	—	—	25
A300-B4	3	4	7	16	4	4	4	4	—	9
B-757-225	—	—	—	21	—	—	—	—	21	24
DC-9-51	4	13	17	—	—	—	—	—	—	—
DC-9-31	33	25	58	—	—	—	—	—	—	—
DC-9-14	—	9	9	—	—	—	—	—	—	—
Subtotal jets	160	95	255	47	14	4	4	4	21	102
Electra	2	—	2	—	—	—	—	—	—	—
Total	162	95	257	47	14	4	4	4	21	102

SOURCE: Eastern Air Lines, Inc., 1978 Annual Report, pp. 6, 8.

*These aircraft are currently grounded following their return in December 1982 from the sublessee. The prime lease terminates in 1983 and 1984.

†Three of the owned aircraft are currently on lease to a foreign carrier.

for that same year. In addition, earnings per share of common stock were −$3.82.

Debt had long been used by Eastern to finance its fleet and ground facilities modernization programs. This caused the firm to be one of the most highly leveraged airlines. As of June 30, 1983, Eastern's long-term debt was approximately $2 billion. This generated approximately $111 million in net interest expense for the first half of 1983 alone.

Eastern continued to issue convertible debt and equity securities to raise funds to help finance equipment purchases. In 1980, the company issued 4.5 million shares of preferred stock, which generated $106 million in new cap-

EXHIBIT 4	Balance Sheets for 1981 and 1982 (Dollar Amounts in Thousands)

BALANCE SHEET: ASSETS

	DECEMBER 31	
	1982	1981
Current assets:		
Cash	$ 21,512	$ 14,795
Short-term investments, at cost, which approximates market	149,100	101,468
Accounts receivable, after allowance for doubtful accounts of $4,500 and $4,500	332,979	323,083
Materials and supplies, at average cost after valuation reserves of $32,368 and $36,767	180,803	184,742
Prepaid expenses and other current assets	28,407	19,509
Total current assets	712,801	643,597
Investments and advances	34,650	28,538
Property and equipment, at cost:		

	FLIGHT EQUIPMENT	OTHER PROPERTY AND EQUIPMENT	LEASED PROPERTY UNDER CAPITAL LEASES		
1982	$2,080,085	$507,379	$1,251,748	3,839,212	
1981	$1,905,837	$461,793	$1,184,176		3,551,806
Accumulated depreciation and amortization:					
1982	$ 815,872	$241,484	$ 479,842	1,537,198	
1981	$ 808,387	$221,882	$ 403,956		1,434,225
				2,302,014	2,117,581
Advance payments for new equipment				116,958	119,938
				2,418,972	2,237,519
Deferred charges, net of amortization:					
Preoperating costs				9,589	7,976
Route acquisition and development costs				26,742	1,180
Other				22,133	15,709
				58,464	24,865
				$3,224,887	$2,934,519

EXHIBIT 4   Continued

BALANCE SHEET: LIABILITIES, CAPITAL STOCK AND RETAINED EARNINGS (DEFICIT)

	DECEMBER 31	
	1982	**1981**
Current liabilities:		
Notes payable within one year	$ 82,740	$ 76,650
Current obligations—capital leases	73,560	64,291
Accounts payable and accrued liabilities	459,426	442,985
Unearned transportation revenues	232,712	159,385
Total current liabilities	848,438	743,311
Long-term debt	1,053,567	815,868
Long-term obligations on capital leases	857,330	852,055
Deferred credits and other long-term liabilities	70,727	33,753
Redeemable preferred stock:		
$2.69 cumulative preferred stock—2,000,000 shares issued and outstanding (liquidation preference $50,000)	47,722	47,611
$3.20 cumulative preferred stock—4,500,000 shares issued and outstanding (liquidation preference $97,312)	91,829	91,727
	139,551	139,338
Common stock and retained earnings (deficit):		
Common stock, par value of $1.00 per share Authorized—50,000,000 shares Issued—24,934,440 and 24,934,412 shares Reserved—21,023,054 and 21,135,982 shares	24,934	24,934
Capital in excess of par value	333,090	352,870
Earnings (deficit) retained for use in the business	(101,877)	(26,737)
	256,147	351,067
Less 116,280 and 116,290 shares held in treasury, at cost	(873)	(873)
	255,274	350,194
	$3,224,887	$2,934,519

SOURCE: Eastern Air Lines, Inc., 1982 Annual Report, pp. 12–13.

---

ital. In 1983, it issued additional preferred stock, which raised an additional $47 million. From January 1, 1982, through June 30, 1983, the company also issued $63 million in equipment trust certificates. Eastern also used various federal tax laws, such as safe harbor leases, to finance a portion of the equipment purchases. For that same eighteen-month period, this tactic provided

EXHIBIT 5	Statement of Operations and Earnings (Deficit) Retained for Use in the Business (Dollar Amounts in Thousands Except Per Share Data)

	YEAR ENDED DECEMBER 31		
	1982	1981	1980
Operating revenues:			
Passenger	$3,406,009	$3,386,731	$3,151,798
Cargo	180,022	178,193	163,472
Incidental and other revenues	183,206	162,169	137,272
Total operating revenues	3,769,237	3,727,093	3,452,542
Operating expenses:			
Salaries, wages, and benefits	1,386,257	1,347,486	1,274,211
Aircraft fuel	1,032,935	1,141,434	1,029,026
Aircraft maintenance, materials, and repairs	96,330	102,476	107,522
Rentals and landing fees	154,090	141,052	109,375
Passenger food and supplies	136,116	129,368	125,987
Commissions	220,467	195,475	158,345
Advertising and promotional	81,144	70,782	63,191
Depreciation and amortization	224,882	229,071	200,572
Other operating expenses	455,796	419,898	382,456
Total operating expenses	3,788,017	3,777,042	3,450,685
Operating profit (loss)	(18,780)	(49,949)	1,857
Nonoperating income and (expense):			
Interest income	27,784	44,839	41,118
Interest expense (net of interest capitalized in the amounts of $18,320, $12,431, and $10,276)	(178,274)	(141,234)	(109,836)
Profit on sales of equipment	32,735	36,562	17,886
Gain on sale of tax benefits	51,279	29,825	—
Other, net	10,329	14,080	2,708
Total	(56,147)	(15,928)	(48,124)
Loss before income taxes and extraordinary item	(74,927)	(65,877)	(46,267)
(Reduction in) income taxes	—	—	(4,255)
Loss before extraordinary item	(74,927)	(65,877)	(42,012)
Extraordinary item—net of a provision in lieu of income taxes of $2,498		—	—
Net loss	(74,927)	(65,877)	(17,358)
Earnings (deficit) retained for use in the business:			
Balance at beginning of year	(26,737)	56,255	78,273
Gain (loss) on distribution of treasury stock to employees	—	77	(529)

EXHIBIT 5   **Continued**

	YEAR ENDED DECEMBER 31		
	1982	**1981**	**1980**
Amortization of excess of redemption value of preferred stock over carrying value	(213)	(185)	(96)
Cash dividends—preferred stock, net of $19,780, $2,973, and zero charged to capital in excess of par value	—	(17,007)	(4,035)
Balance at end of year	$ (101,877)	$ (26,737)	$ 56,255
Earnings per common share:			
Loss before extraordinary item	$ (3.82)	$ (3.44)	$ (1.96)
Extraordinary item	—	—	0.99
Net loss	$ (3.82)	$ (3.44)	$ (0.97)
Fully diluted earnings per common share:			
Loss before extraordinary item	*	*	*
Net loss			

SOURCE: Eastern Air Lines, Inc., 1982 Annual Report, p. 14.

*Anti-dilutive

about $85 million, with another $92 million anticipated in the second half of 1983.

In light of Eastern's financial results, cash position, and status with its creditors, short-term survival was a pressing problem for Eastern in 1983. Fortunately for Eastern, a company must declare bankruptcy only when it can no longer pay its bills, not merely because its financial statements show sizable losses. Eastern's cash equivalent assets in 1983 were at roughly the same level as in the prior two years.

Eastern's survival in the long run with its current financing structure was questionable. Its high debt load brought about a high interest expense that represented an ongoing drain on its cash reserves. Eastern was drawing down on its $400 million line of credit in 1983. If this resource was exhausted, or withdrawn by lenders, securing additional financing might be a major challenge.

Human Resources/Labor Relations

A significant portion of Eastern's human resource management effort involved dealing with powerful labor unions. Approximately 22,500 of its 37,500 employees were union members. Eastern's approach in negotiations was to present openly its earnings and financial situation to the unions and all its employees. It then asked employees to share in the financial burden through salary freezes, cuts, and/or wage deferral plans. This approach had been employed continually since 1976. For Eastern, these tactics had worked well. Its success was attributed to its employees' fear of losing their jobs and the employees' loyalty to Frank Borman.

Perhaps Eastern's best-known wage tactic was its variable earnings program. This five-year program was developed in 1977 to assist the airline with its financing problems. Under the program, employees left 3.5 percent of their gross pay with the company. The money was retained for investment purposes and paid back to employees only if a 2 percent sales profit level was achieved.

During 1983, Eastern faced strike threats from two unions. Management talked tough to the unions but then settled before the strike deadline. Management settled before the contract expired because it did not believe the firm could survive a major strike, especially given its weak financial position. Still, the company obtained concessions from its pilots and nonunion employees. They accepted a securities-for-pay program in lieu of wage increases for 1983 and 1984. Nonunion employees also participated in the program on a voluntary basis.

Eastern, like most other airlines except Delta, laid off employees during economic recessions to reduce labor costs. Surprisingly, Eastern even laid off 1,600 employees after a new union contract had been signed in 1983. Management furloughed these employees three hours after a new machinists' contract was approved to counter higher labor costs.

Eastern also provided extensive training, particularly for its pilots and maintenance workers. This training emphasized how to use and maintain its new aircraft, which arrived frequently.

Management/Leadership

Eastern's management relied heavily on a strong, well-known public figure for leadership. Frank Borman's image as a "no-smoking, no-drinking, no-nonsense boss" generated significant employee loyalty.[3] Known as the Colonel, Borman was the key reason the company pursued the growth objective that he had earlier formulated. Borman's image extended beyond the corporate headquarters. For example, Eastern's ability to obtain financing for fleet modernization had been partially credited to Borman's ability to generate confidence among its creditors.

His high-growth objective was backed up by several supporting strategies to help implement it. Although many of them were discussed earlier, two additional strategies helped pursue the high-growth objective. One strategy was that Eastern might seek to merge with another airline in order to improve its market standing, equipment, and/or financial position. The other strategy was Eastern's decision to concentrate only on the airline business. In fact, restaurant and hotel subsidiaries acquired in earlier years were sold soon after Borman's appointment as CEO.

Eastern's strategy to remain a large airline was confirmed by Borman in 1983. He noted, "We're not interested in becoming seventy-five percent smaller. What we're interested in doing is lowering our unit costs so that we can be successful in very difficult economic times."[4]

Although Frank Borman was recognized as the strong leader that Eastern needed, his leadership was being questioned in the mid-1980s. Besides his loss of trust among rank-and-file unionized employees, his credibility as a manager was also on the line. In 1983, some of his key managers questioned Borman's ability to lead the firm out of its current crisis.

Responding to comments about his management and leadership abilities, Borman pointed to recent performance where Eastern's operating loss for the twelve months ending June 30, 1983, was $50.1 million as compared with rival Delta Air Lines' $207.3 million loss. This was the best performance that Eastern ever had against Delta.

However, rumors circulated in October 1983 that Borman might step down as the head of Eastern. When asked about the resignation rumors, Borman replied, "Why should I resign? I'm not going to resign. I have no intention of resigning. I don't know why everyone speculates on that. Look, this is not a management problem." He added, "I am not at all ashamed of our performance."[5]

INDUSTRY STRUCTURE

The airline industry was composed of three basic types of airlines. They were majors, nationals, and regionals, all of which existed on a continuum. Major airlines flew most domestic routes, and had annual revenues of at least $1 billion. The major carriers included Eastern, American, Delta, and United.

National airlines comprised a wide variety of carriers that had annual revenues between $75 million and $1 billion. The national airlines operated similarly to major carriers. With deregulation, they were able to enter long-haul routes that were almost exclusively served by the majors. This type of airline included Frontier, Ozark, and Southwest Airlines.

Regionals were the third type of airlines. Many of these new airlines were a direct result of the deregulation era. These airlines typically operated round-trip service between two or more points, unencumbered by the complex network of routes that full-service airlines offered. The major attraction of these carriers was their low cost. Typically, their fares were 40 to 50 percent below full-cost fares. People Express, Midway, and New York Airlines were typical regional carriers.

COMPETITOR PROFILES

American Airlines

Although American Airlines was the second largest U.S. airline, it lost $20 million during 1982. It had a reputation as a first-class, customer-oriented airline. American was led by Robert Crandall, a tough, aggressive president. Under Crandall, American had done the following: (1) strengthened existing hubs and built new ones; (2) significantly reduced its cost structure; (3) maintained personalized, full customer service; (4) abandoned unprofitable routes that were primarily in the Northeast; and (5) marketed its product aggressively.[6]

American was a recognized leader in marketing. It pioneered the successful frequent flier program. In addition, its computerized reservation system, SABRE, led the market and was placed in approximately 39 percent of all U.S. travel agencies. Being first in these areas had given American significant marketing advantages.

American was a financially stable airline in comparison with most of the major carriers. Still, its debt and cost structures were relatively high. American's fleet was much older than the average airline's and it was uncertain if sufficient capital could be raised to modernize its fleet.

In 1983, American achieved major victories in its efforts to reduce its cost structure. It obtained cost-cutting contracts with its pilots, flight attendants, and machinist unions. American's management felt that these agreements would eventually reduce its cost per seat-mile to 6.5 cents. This rate would be comparable to the costs of the low-cost airlines.

American Airlines proposed a mileage-based fare program in 1983. Its various rate classifications were reduced to four basic fares plus a business traveler classification. American simplified its new fare structure and increased revenue yield. Several other airlines, including Eastern, had similar mileage-based fare programs. Even United Airlines was able to reduce substantially the number of different fares it offered when it adopted this format.

American's success in achieving cost reductions spurred it to announce planned route expansions. It even hoped eventually to overtake United as the number-one airline.

Delta Air Lines

Delta Air Lines had consistently been the most profitable U.S. airline. Headquartered in its central hub in Atlanta, Delta's strength was in the Southeast. By 1983, however, its route structure covered almost all of the United States. From 1947 through mid-1982, Delta had never recorded a loss. From 1971 through 1980, Delta's earnings totaled $857 million, almost twice that of United Airlines, the world's largest airline.

Delta's success was attributed to a variety of factors. They included the following: (1) excellent long-range planning and a willingness to adhere to these plans during lean times; (2) excellent wages and benefits plus a no-layoff policy that kept it the least-unionized major airline; (3) high employee productivity by asking people to perform various functions during the day; (4) a highly trained management team of generalists that used consensus decision making; (5) an efficient hub-and-spoke system; and (6) a low debt level. Delta had traditionally been Eastern's biggest rival, and, since deregulation, Eastern had competed on about 80 percent of Delta's routes.

Despite its strengths, even Delta had begun to encounter the full impact of deregulation and a sluggish economy. For the fiscal year ending June 30, 1983, Delta recorded a rare loss of $87 million. This setback caused Delta to reconsider some of its strategies for the future. It moved to reduce its cost structure by freezing nonunion workers' salaries for 1983–1984 and requesting its union employees to do the same. Delta's salaries and fringe benefits costs, which were 42 percent of total expenses, had gotten too big for even it to handle. This occurred despite its high employee productivity achieved by treating employees like family and shifting them around during the day when they were needed elsewhere.

Delta was trying to give more emphasis to marketing, an area that had long been regarded as a weak part of its operations. It adopted a much more aggressive pricing strategy by trying not to be undersold in any market. In addition, Delta was making up for lost time in another area by developing and marketing its own automated reservation system. If Delta could significantly improve its marketing strategies, it could become an even stronger force to be contended with in the future.

Continental Airlines

In January 1983, Continental Airlines was the eighth largest U.S. airline. With its central hub in Houston, it serviced a large portion of the United States and some foreign countries. However, the impact of deregulation, coupled with a maturing industry, had been very tough on Continental. From 1978 through the third quarter of 1983, Continental Airlines posted losses totaling approximately $500 million.

Since his appointment as Continental's chairman in 1980, Frank Lorenzo had been striving for wage concessions and other cost cuts. He hoped to convert Continental to a low-cost carrier. In a surprise move on September 24, 1983, however, Continental filed for bankruptcy under Chapter 11. Under the protection of the courts, Continental restarted operations with only one half of its planes flying and one third of its prior work force. Returning employees received significant pay cuts and changed work rules. Pilots were forced to accept 50 percent pay cuts, a 57 percent increase in flying time, and the loss of seniority and protective work rules. Continental management stated that these changes would allow it to reduce its cost structure by 25 percent, making it competitive with other airlines.

Although Continental was not technically out of cash on September 24, company officials said that it would have ceased operations very soon without the bankruptcy action. However, some industry observers felt that the company's actions were designed to void its union contracts. Not surprisingly, Continental's unions went to court to try to reverse the bankruptcy filing. They charged that the filing was an improper use of the bankruptcy laws. However, they eventually lost out in their legal efforts; thus, Continental continued to operate with significantly lower costs.

The costs of the bankruptcy filing were high for Continental in terms of travel agent confidence, employee morale, and customer loyalty. In addition, the unions went on strike on October 1, 1983, an action that hampered Continental quite a bit.

Still, Continental survived the early restart-up period and continued to operate on a reduced scale. Lorenzo immediately stated that the new Continental would be at 80 to 90 percent of its previous flights by the spring of 1984. Its flights were operating at 67 percent capacity as of October 30, 1983 as compared to a prefiling level of less than 50 percent. Lorenzo believed that Continental was ready to compete successfully in the deregulated environment as 1983 came to a close.

Piedmont Airlines

Piedmont Airlines, which started operations as an air freight carrier after World War II, later evolved under regulation into a regional airline serving several large cities on the East Coast and in the Midwest. In addition, Piedmont served numerous smaller communities with air transportation to and from larger airports.

Under deregulation, however, Piedmont had significantly expanded and became a national carrier in the early 1980s. Piedmont used secondary markets such as Charlotte, North Carolina, and Dayton, Ohio, as hub cities. This reduced the likelihood of customers transferring to competing airlines to continue on to their destination city. In addition, it had entered new long-haul markets that were consistent with its existing route structure while eliminating some unprofitable, short commuter routes. These marketing strategies helped Piedmont achieve record earnings in 1981 of $33 million.

Piedmont had been profitable in every year since deregulation. Its total earnings during the 1978–1982 period were about $96 million. Piedmont's successful performance was also partially attributed to (1) record performances in revenue passenger–miles, the number of passengers boarded, and seating capacity; (2) a fuel-efficient fleet properly designed for its route system; and (3) high employee productivity, due in part to a high percentage of nonunion workers.

People Express

People Express was the role model of a new low-cost, no-frills airline. Started in April 1981, it began by serving New York City and surrounding cities. By the end of 1981, it was flying thirteen planes to ten outlying locations. As its strategy of providing high-frequency, low-cost service to New York had worked well, People Express expanded operations to other regions and markets. The airline had such ambitious growth plans that it expected to operate 67 jets by 1985.

People had achieved a cost per seat mile that was far below all of the major and regional airlines. People achieved this low cost by cutting a variety of operating costs and providing few of the normal customer services. For example, reservations could be made by phone but tickets were sold only on the plane. Baggage was checked for $3 per bag, and no interline baggage transfer was available. In addition, only cold meals were served, but the customer had to pay extra for them. Finally, its employees were trained to handle many different tasks, which brought about high employee productivity.

People routes covered many of the same markets serviced by Eastern. Thus, Eastern was forced to match fares with the acknowledged leading low-cost airline or lose substantial traffic. Obviously, Eastern found it difficult to compete successfully with People Express on a price basis, particularly given its higher cost structure.

In 1983, People Express operated at an annual rate of about 3.4 billion revenue passenger–miles, which was only about 12 percent of Eastern's revenue passenger–miles. However, People load factors ran about 77 percent for the same year. Thus, People had become a very serious threat to the other established airlines with competing East Coast routes.

INDUSTRY PRACTICES AND PROBLEMS

The impact of deregulation was apparent in current airline operations in various ways. However, other underlying problems existed that had a major impact on the industry. Some of these strategic problems and issues are discussed below.

Economic Conditions

The economic environment clearly had a major impact on the airline industry's performance. Unfortunately, this factor was largely beyond the control of the airlines. Although the 1974–1975 recession had a significant, negative effect on the industry, the recessionary impact increased significantly under deregulation. Exhibit 6 provides data on operating statistics during these two most recessionary periods, 1974–1975 and 1980–1982. During the later recession, airlines used various marketing tools and cost-cutting measures,

EXHIBIT 6 **Airline Traffic Data 1974–1983 (All Certificated Carriers; Scheduled Service)**

YEAR	REV. PASS. (THOUSANDS)	% CHG.	RPKS ($ MILLIONS)	% CHG.	FTKS ($ MILLIONS)	% CHG.
*						
1974	207,449	2.6	262,133	0.6	7,139	3.2
1975	205,062	(1.2)	261,961	(0.1)	6,953	(2.5)
1976	223,313	8.9	287,992	9.9	7,408	6.5
1977	240,326	7.6	310,889	8.0	7,862	6.1
1978	274,716	14.3	364,891	17.6	8,414	7.0
1979	316,863	15.3	421,595	15.5	8,626	2.5
*						
1980	296,903	(6.3)	410,604	(2.6)	8,301	(3.8)
1981	285,720	(3.8)	400,250	(2.5)	8,200	(1.2)
1982	297,149	4.0	416,260	4.0	7,790	(5.0)
1983	309,035	4.0	432,910	4.0	8,063	3.5
Total 1974–1983 increase	101,586	49.0	170,777	65.2	924	12.9

SOURCE: "1983 Forecast: A Slow Turnaround Expected," *Air Transport World*, January 1983, p. 29.
*Recessionary period

chiefly wage concessions, to reduce the negative impact of the slumping economy.

Fare Wars/Pricing Strategies

A major reason that economic conditions had such a major impact on airlines was the price elasticity of demand. The airline industry had both elastic and inelastic demand segments. The discretionary portion of air travel, such as vacationers, had often been described as "price elastic." In other words, a small change in the price of airline tickets could have a larger effect on the demand for tickets. The business traveler market segment was more price inelastic, in part because these customers were time sensitive. However, the degree of elasticity differed from one airline to another. For example, People Express, a low-cost, no-frills airline, found that its traffic was very elastic.

Airlines used various approaches to stimulate discretionary travel during weak economic times. Restricted discount fares, such as super-saver fares, were used to stimulate discretionary travel. This well-known discount fare required a seven-day advance purchase and at least one Saturday night lay-over. However, this fare discouraged business travelers from using it because they did not want to stay over Saturday night and they usually booked flights at the last minute.

Airline management teams lacked experience with pricing in a competitive environment. As a result, pricing strategies varied greatly. Industry observers often charged that airline management teams were not behaving rationally with respect to pricing. Fare wars were generally started by the use of unrestricted discount fares, which were lower than the restricted discounts. This resulted in intense competition in specific markets in which many airlines suffered losses. Once started, fare wars were perpetuated by the airlines' belief that fares must be matched in order to prevent a significant loss of market share.

Fare wars were also initiated by other factors. These included (1) financially troubled airlines pricing to generate cash flow; (2) the lower cost structure of new market entrants; and (3) excess industry capacity. Discount fares were so prevalent that, by 1983, 80 percent of all fares were discounted at an average rate of 53 percent off the stated fare.[7] Discounting became so severe that generally only the low-cost carrier made money on routes with fare wars, and even they sometimes did not cover all of their costs.

Fare wars caused significant damage because business traveler fares decreased significantly without generating much additional traffic in the business segment. This meant revenue yields declined, resulting in a corresponding decline in pre-tax profits.

Increasing Costs

Despite the carriers' desire to reduce their cost structures, cost reduction was not an easy task. Their costs were high because the airline industry was labor, energy, and capital intensive. For example, Eastern's percentages of total expenses for these three costs in 1982 were 36 percent, 27 percent, and 5 percent, respectively. See Exhibit 7, which compares Eastern's 1982 expenses with 1978. Fortunately, fuel costs, which were largely beyond the carriers' control, had stabilized in the early 1980s.

Employee Relations

The pressures to reduce costs, which included labor costs, caused considerable employee unrest and resistance. Airline employees were paid considerably more than were most other professions. Their $42,000 average salary clearly attested to that fact. After deregulation in 1978, airline employees faced major salary and benefits setbacks. The airlines felt that labor-cost reductions would help them to be more competitive.

Union leaders, especially at the more militant machinists' union, were urging strikes and national walkouts to protest these pay concessions. Union employees, however, were divided about how to respond. Although they

EXHIBIT 7   Eastern Expense and Fuel Costs Analysis

The 1982 Expense Dollar

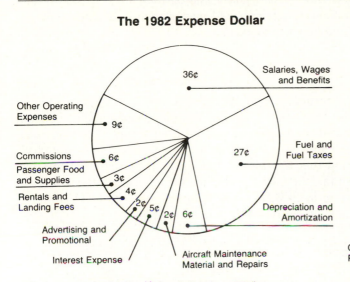

Payroll and fuel remain the major expense items.

Fuel Costs

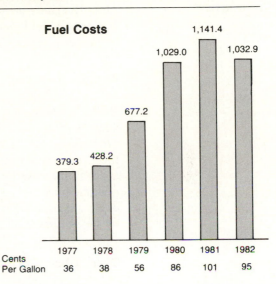

Cents Per Gallon	1977	1978	1979	1980	1981	1982
	36	38	56	86	101	95

Upward pressure on costs eased in 1982. consumption changed little in the years charted.

The 1978 Expense Dollar

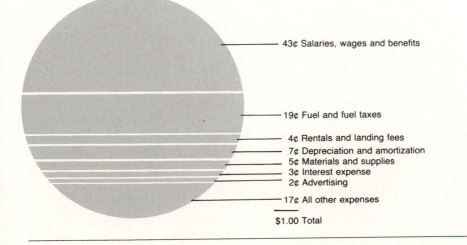

43¢ Salaries, wages and benefits

19¢ Fuel and fuel taxes

4¢ Rentals and landing fees
7¢ Depreciation and amortization
5¢ Materials and supplies
3¢ Interest expense
2¢ Advertising

17¢ All other expenses

$1.00 Total

resented the pay cuts and charged that the airlines were wasting profits on fare wars, the employees often felt that they had to go along with the carriers' demands or lose their jobs. Clearly, the bankruptcies at Braniff and Continental had significantly strengthened management's position with its employees on wage and benefit issues.

Safety

Airline unions had consistently charged that the cost-cutting procedures, such as increased pilot flying time and reduced maintenance and inspection procedures, had reduced the margin of safety for air travel to a dangerous level. FAA spokesmen and some industry analysts believed that safety had actually increased, and that the unions were making these statements for political purposes. So far, there had not been any increased pattern of accidents since deregulation in 1978, or since Reagan broke the PATCO strike by hiring almost all new air traffic controllers.

Distribution Channels

Almost all tickets were currently sold by either travel agencies (65 percent of all sales), the airlines, or through corporate in-house travel departments. This latter group acted as a branch of a travel agency for a specific organization. Although agents generally received a 10 percent commission, in-house operations often received 80 percent to 90 percent of a 3 percent commission paid to the agents. Although the airlines generally disliked the in-house operations, they had little power to curtail them. In fact, in-house operations were expected to flourish in the future, with the possible development of corporate travel subsidiaries. The airline industry feared that corporations would eventually be able to use their power to obtain commissions (discounts) in excess of those currently provided to the travel agents.

Travel agencies may face possible competition from various retailing firms in the future. In December 1982, the CAB voted to permit the sale of airline tickets by anyone starting in 1985. This might mean that such retail giants as Sears, J.C. Penney, or Kmart could begin selling airline tickets.

Computerization

Computerization had become a very important tool to the airlines, especially in the marketing area. The airlines found that it was necessary in order to utilize effectively the promotional programs currently provided by the airlines.

Computerization had been most important in the development of automated reservation systems. These systems were marketed to travel agencies as a scheduling tool, and they became a necessity with the proliferation of airline fares. A few airlines controlled most of the existing reservation systems. The market shares for these reservation systems among all travel agencies were 39 percent for American Airlines' SABRE system, 29 percent for United Airlines' APOLLO, 26 percent for Trans World Airlines' PARS I and II, 3 percent for Tymshare, Inc.'s Mars Plus, and 13 percent for other systems collectively (e.g., Eastern, Delta).[8] These systems also became an important marketing tool for the airline that developed them. All of these systems, with the exception of Delta's, had a built-in bias to favor the developing airline in the way flight data was displayed. The system also generated revenues for the developer, who charged a fee per flight segment to other airlines who were listed in the system as cohosts and received second best status. In addition, the systems also provided valuable, confidential marketing information for the host airline.

Airlines without such a computer system were at a competitive disadvantage, and many of them had complained to the government. As a result, the Justice Department was reviewing the systems for antitrust violations, and the CAB planned to remove the bias features in the system in 1984. Several airlines without such systems were suggesting divestiture of the systems by their owners to neutral companies who could compete with each other.

Possible Re-regulation

The intensity of the fare wars and the inability of some carriers to compete caused some airlines to ask for some form of re-regulation. These proposals stressed that some form of price floors be developed by the CAB to prevent destructive competition. Republic Airlines, at least three other airlines, and some U.S. Congressmen were among those advocating re-regulation. The fate of deregulation and re-regulation were dependent upon the well-being of the major carriers. If several more of them folded, re-regulation would probably gain additional support. However, it should be noted that the Reagan administration opposed any form of re-regulation.

REPOSITIONING EASTERN AFTER DEREGULATION

In order to compete successfully in a highly competitive, mature industry, Eastern needs to find a strategy to position itself in the industry that it can successfully defend. As of late 1983, Eastern had been unable to avoid the adverse impact of competition. In fact, Eastern's key routes were those that had the most highly discounted fares in the United States. Furthermore, three of its direct competitors—Delta, Piedmont, and People Express—were among the strongest airlines in the industry.

A Low-Cost Strategy

One basic alternative for Eastern would be to pursue a low-cost strategy. Eastern would have a long way to go to implement this strategy because its cost structure was still high compared with some of its major competitors. However, this strategy made a great deal of sense, especially as recent fare wars lowered operating margins. Although Eastern might have a difficult time becoming *the* low-cost major airline, failure to further reduce costs could bring about bankruptcy.

Aggressive cost-cutting efforts would be needed for Eastern to pursue a low-cost strategy. Its modern fleet of airplanes had already helped to reduce operating costs. The concessions that Borman had obtained from its employees had further reduced costs and improved employee productivity. Still, additional significant measures would be needed to really pursue this strategy.

Eastern might be able to achieve even greater cost-saving measure with its unionized and nonunionized workers. Other airlines had recently been successful. For example, in March and April of 1983, American Airlines achieved major cost-cutting contracts with its pilots', flight attendants', and machinists' unions. If American achieved its hoped-for cost reduction to 6.5¢ per seat-mile, it would become very competitive with some of the best low-cost airlines. Perhaps Eastern could be as successful as American Airlines hoped its cost-cutting efforts would be.

Another option for Eastern to use to lower its cost structure might be to declare bankruptcy, as did Continental Airlines. If a bankruptcy filing was approved, Eastern could then, perhaps quickly, reorganize the airline. It could cut down on the number of its flights, trim back its work force, lower wages and benefits, and ask for more hours worked. Although this approach may seem drastic, it could be very effective if Eastern could win any lawsuits accusing it of union busting, which would inevitably be filed by its organized employees.

A problem with this approach, however, was that it could possibly hurt both customer loyalty and employee morale. Also, many employees might feel that bankruptcy was declared just to void its union contracts. Therefore, all of these factors would have to be taken into consideration if this strategic option were to be implemented.

A Focus Strategy

Another basic alternative for Eastern would be to focus, or specialize, on satisfying specific customer segments in the industry. For example, with most airlines fighting hard for coach passengers, one overlooked customer group might be the first class traveler. The potential for Eastern's first class service could be significant. First class travel accounted for only 6.7 percent of all travel in the early 1980s, but it generated almost 10 percent of the total revenue. Furthermore, since Eastern's cost structure was high, this customer group might be a good one to focus on as it was less price conscious. Finally, expansion of first class service might also provide Eastern with a competitive advantage over its competitors during good economic times when demand for first class service grows.

Eastern might consider focusing on the business traveler or leisure traveler segments. For the business customer segment, numerous possibilities existed for expanding its frequent traveler program. In addition, innumerable joint promotions could be used with hotels, rental car agencies, restaurants, convention facilities, and others specializing in business travelers. For the leisure or discretionary traveler, lots of possibilities exist to help stimulate interest in air travel. Eastern might attract more discretionary travelers with cooperative agreements at major resorts, like its agreement with Disney World. Eastern might also emphasize joint promotions with such complimentary services as free traveler's checks, reduced prices for city tours, a free night's lodging after so many paid nights, and so on.

The company could choose to develop an all-frills air service to capture a sizable portion of that market niche. Focus on this segment would undoubtedly overlap with focus on the first class traveler segment and might produce some synergies. Air One and FirstAir were two examples of airlines that were trying to promote high-class, all-frills flights. Eastern might accomplish this by converting some of its older, wide-bodied L-1011s for all-frills, first class flights. These planes could operate efficiently on long-haul routes (e.g., New York to Miami), because Eastern possessed the necessary route structure to support such a new service.

If Eastern does pursue a focus strategy, it could choose to focus on several segments of the industry at the same time. Furthermore, it could select segments to focus on that overlapped one another. For example, all-frills flights could overlap with long-haul routes to South America and other vacation areas. Similarly, a focus on first class customers might simultaneously be pursued with business travelers.

A Differentiation Strategy

A differentiation approach involves offering a product or service that is perceived industrywide as unique. For example, Eastern had long been recognized as a technological leader. It could key in on this fact and aggressively promote it in its advertising. Along the same lines, it could also promote the safety features found in its modern, sophisticated aircraft.

Eastern could also differentiate itself with its preflight and in-flight services. In its boarding area, Eastern could have a wide-screen TV tuned to one of the cable news networks. Free copies of *USA Today* and the *Wall Street Journal* could be handed out to passengers. On the flight, they could have in-flight movies as some other airlines do on transcontinental flights. Fashion shows, in-flight telephones, television sets, and personal computers could all be gimmicks Eastern could use to differentiate itself. Low-cost airlines would have a hard time trying to match such services and keep their low-cost emphasis.

In-flight seminars on videocassettes that used headsets to gain access to tape channels could be another way to differentiate itself. Some topics for the leisure travelers might include investment strategies, tax preparation, inspirational speeches, self-improvement topics, and various do-it-yourself topics. For the business traveler, in-person talks or cassettes could be given on a variety of finance, marketing, and management topics. If Eastern did this, it might not only become the airline that business travelers use, but also the one on which they received additional business training.

Diversification

Diversification into industries outside the airline business is another possibility for Eastern. Although Frank Borman has had Eastern concentrate only on the airline business, so far its profitability in that mature industry has been very poor. The reality may be that too many firms are competing in a cut-throat fashion in a mature industry with low growth potential. As a result, perhaps Eastern needs to pursue higher profit potential opportunities elsewhere while retaining only those airline routes that make money.

Some diversification efforts might be channeled into related businesses that are complementary to Eastern's operations. Starting up or acquiring a travel/tour business is one such option that might complement its airline operations. Such a program could feed travelers to Eastern. It might also make Eastern more competitive with other major airlines that already provide such services.

Eastern could also diversify into services that its airline customers need after arriving at their destinations. Many customers, especially business travelers, need a rental car to get around. Thus, operating a rent-a-car business, even if only in selected major cities, might be a good opportunity to pursue. Similarly, Eastern could also provide limousine services to customers needing to go to hotels and business meetings. Eastern might also consider starting its own hotel chain. For example, Trans World Airlines owns Hilton International Corp., a chain of hotels, and encourages its airline customers to stay there. It might be possible for Eastern to develop a system so that when customers purchase their airline tickets, rental car and hotel reservations at Eastern facilities could also be made. These other businesses could be promoted through discounts and joint promotions.

Eastern could also start operating its own food service business. Most airlines typically bought food for their flights from outside vendors instead of preparing the food themselves. Marriott Corporation is an example of a firm that provides such food services. Thus, if Eastern decides to enter into the hotel business, operating a food service chain might be a logical extension of its operations.

EASTERN'S FUTURE DIRECTION

As Eastern prepares for the later 1980s and the coming 1990s, the basic strategy it selects will be critical. Lots of factors need to be considered in deciding how to position itself in the airline industry. Is it possible for Eastern to become a low-cost airline? Could it be successful by focusing on specific segments of the market? Are there ways for it to differentiate itself from other airlines, which would really stimulate customer loyalty? Could a combination of strategies be used creatively?

Are the future prospects for the airline industry so bleak that Eastern should consider diversifying into other businesses? Should those businesses somehow relate and be complementary to the airline industry? Should Eastern diversify into unrelated industries that look promising? These and other basic strategic options need to be addressed as Eastern tries to reposition itself for long-term profitability.

NOTES

1. "U.S. Carrier Officials Oppose Regulation in Spite of Losses," *Aviation Week and Space Technology*, June 6, 1983, p. 51.

2. Margaret Loeb, "Outlook for Eastern Air Appears Brighter Despite $34.4 Million Net Loss for Quarter," *Wall Street Journal*, October 10, 1983, p. 5.

3. Robert E. Dallos and Barry Bearak, "Eastern's Beleaguered Borman," *The Charlotte Observer*, October 9, 1983, p. 20A.

4. Margaret Loeb and Thomas E. Ricks, "Future of Eastern Airlines Hinging on Chief's Credibility with Unions," *Wall Street Journal*, September 29, 1983, p. 33.

5. *Ibid.*, p. 33.

6. "American Rediscovers Itself," *Business Week*, August 23, 1982, pp. 66–78.

7. Eugene Kozicharrow, "Carriers Attempting to Reduce Capacity," *Aviation Week and Space Technology*, March 14, 1983, pp. 188–189.

8. Cindy Skrzycki, "Airline Flight That Affects Tickets You Buy," *U.S. News & World Report*, August 22, 1983, p. 53.

INDUSTRY
BANKING

CASE 22

North Carolina National Bank Corporation Moves into Florida

KAREN L. O'QUINN · LARRY D. ALEXANDER

INTRODUCTION

North Carolina National Bank (NCNB) Corporation was the leading multi-bank holding company in the southeastern region of the United States. In 1982, it was the 26th largest bank holding company in the United States and its consolidated assets totaled $8.4 billion. The corporation was started in 1969; by the end of 1982 it had 526 offices located in North Carolina, ten other states, the United Kingdom, Australia, Brazil, Hong Kong, South Africa, and the Cayman Islands. The various banking and financial services NCNB offered included general banking, merchant banking, consumer finance, corporate finance, leasing, trust, investment management, discount brokerage services, and international banking.

In 1982, NCNB expanded its banking operations into the lucrative Florida market through the acquisition of four banks. After all four acquisitions had received Federal Reserve Board (the Fed) approval, NCNB was faced with a fundamental issue concerning these Florida banks. How should NCNB best manage these acquisitions? Should the banks be permitted to operate pretty much as they had in the past? As these banks were separately attractive enough to have been acquired by NCNB, perhaps each should be left to operate autonomously. Conversely, should the Florida acquisitions be

This case was written by Karen L. O'Quinn, Cash Management Product Manager at NCNB Corporation and M.B.A. in marketing from V.P.I. in August 1983, and Larry D. Alexander, Associate Professor of Strategic Management, Department of Management, College of Business, Virginia Polytechnic Institute and State University, Blacksburg, Virginia.

reined in and required to follow overall NCNB corporate goals, operating policy, and procedures, and become an integral part of the NCNB family? Thus, NCNB corporate management was faced with deciding which of these approaches, or a mixture, was the best way to manage its first banks located outside North Carolina.

THE BANKING INDUSTRY

The 14,500 banks operating throughout the United States are classified into one of three basic types. One type is the money center bank, such as Chase Manhattan Corporation and Manufacturers Hanover Corporation, which operates in the United States and throughout the world providing a wide variety of international lending and corporate services. A second type is the regional bank, like NCNB and Wachovia Corporation (a major competitor of NCNB in North Carolina), which are major forces in one or several states in a geographical region. Regional banks usually move into other states through acquisitions of existing financial institutions, usually not banks. The third and final type is the country bank. These are unit banks (single-branch banks) or small branch chains that offer much more limited financial services to a very small geographical area.

INDUSTRY TRENDS

Historically, banking was a conservative, highly regulated industry. Federal and state laws aimed to keep banks solvent and assure them of a steady income. However, economic and technological changes, especially since the mid-1970s, brought about major changes in the banking industry. For example, rising interest rates threatened banks by causing bank deposits to be shifted to brokerage houses and money market mutual funds, which were not limited by interest ceilings. One technological change stemmed from the rapidly expanding network of automated tellers and bank-owned computers. These networks enabled them to offer their products and services to much larger geographical regions, thus intensifying competition.

Although regional and country banks made up the vast majority of banks in the United States, this did not provide them with safety in numbers. With the increasing move toward interstate banking in recent years, the money center banks posed a significant threat. If they are permitted to enter other states in the future, their sheer size and financial strength could result in a competitive shakeout, which could cause some regional and numerous country banks to be acquired or go bankrupt. Some regional banks hoped to prepare themselves for interstate banking by first expanding their presence in a wider geographical area. NCNB hoped that its move into Florida, and perhaps other states in the future, would help turn itself into a leading money center bank when true interstate banking became legal.

Many industry observers felt that banks would no longer be able to improve their profitability by obtaining low-interest deposits and making high-interest loans. Low-interest deposits were disappearing as the U.S. Congress continued to deregulate banking by removing interest rate ceilings on deposit accounts. For example, the gradual deregulation of the banking industry resulted in the introduction of new money market deposit accounts in 1982. These new accounts paid market interest rates, were federally insured, and competed directly with money market mutual funds.

In the 1980s, an increasing number of substitute products and services competed against money center, regional, and country banks. Some 4,500 savings and loans offered many of the same services as banks. Work-related credit unions often provided low-interest loans to employees who used their jobs as collateral. Nonbanking institutions, such as Merrill Lynch, also had begun offering other close substitute products like its equity access loan, which competed with traditional loans from banks and savings and loan associations. Even Sears, Roebuck and Company was becoming accepted as a place where people could invest their money.

Banks remained divided over whether these various industry trends, taken as a whole, represented threats or opportunities. The largest banks were pushing for laws to let them compete head-on with the regional and country banks as well as other financial institutions. These banks were clearly pushing for true interstate banking. On the other hand, most smaller banks opposed interstate banking and wanted to keep the existing legal restrictions intact. Thus, many larger banks viewed these changes as opportunities whereas most smaller banks saw them as threats.

NCNB CORPORATION

History

NCNB Corporation was incorporated on July 5, 1968, as a bank holding company. Initially, this was done to acquire control of North Carolina National Bank. That bank had been originally chartered in 1933 as Security National Bank, which later merged with Depositors National Bank of Durham in 1959. The North Carolina National Bank name was adopted in 1960 with the merger of American Commercial Bank in Charlotte. From 1960 through 1967, North Carolina National Bank merged with or acquired nine additional banks in North Carolina.

North Carolina National Bank was acquired by American Security National Bank, a wholly owned subsidiary of NCNB Corporation, on November 4, 1968. American Security National Bank immediately changed its name to North Carolina National Bank. The bank then came under the control of NCNB Corporation and remained its principal subsidiary, contributing 92.6 percent of the corporation's total earnings in 1981.

NCNB Corporation formed three other subsidiaries during 1968. Amcon, Inc., was formed in November and later merged with American Commercial Agency, Inc. NCNB Properties, Inc., another wholly owned subsidiary, was also established that same month. NCNB Mortgage Corporation was established in December. Then, during mid-1969, Stephenson Finance Company, Inc., was acquired, which was later renamed Transouth Financial Corporation, an NCNB subsidiary.

NCNB Corporation pursued a number of acquisitions during the 1970s. They included, among others:

1. Factors, Inc., which provided various financial services, in 1970 for stock
2. C. Douglas Wilson and Company, a mortgage banker, in 1972 for stock
3. Trust Company of Florida in 1972 for stock
4. Blanchard and Calhoun Mortgage Company in 1974 for stock
5. MAR, Inc., which handled foreclosed properties, in 1975 for stock

NCNB's Corporate Plan for the 1980s

By the close of the 1970s, NCNB faced intense competition in North Carolina and future growth there was expected to be modest. To cope with this problem, NCNB developed an overall strategic plan to better position itself in the banking and diversified financial services industry.

In 1979, NCNB developed a three-phase strategic plan for the 1980s to support two goals. One goal was to continue as the dominant financial institution in the Southeast. The other goal was to become a significant competitor among the world's major money center banks. This corporate plan for the 1980s called for NCNB to do the following:

- Phase 1. Improve the corporation's capital position, managerial depth, and technical expertise.
- Phase 2. Expand the geographic coverage of the corporation to achieve economies of scale and offer innovative products to a broader market.
- Phase 3. Achieve profitable internal growth by managing products, pricing, and markets for increased market share.[1]

This three-phase corporate plan helped unify corporate management's strategy and that of NCNB's various strategic business units.

NCNB's corporate-level marketing, financial, human resources, and management strategies are discussed briefly in the following sections.

Marketing Strategy—
An Emphasis on Innovation

NCNB Corporation had a history of pursuing innovative products and services. During the 1970s, NCNB was the first North Carolina bank to install 24-hour automatic teller machines (ATMs). It was also the first to introduce a deposit access card called Checkmate. In addition, NCNB began to offer unique bank services to its customers with high savings balances.

More recently, in 1982, NCNB introduced several new products that may change the way NCNB and its customers do business in the future. The introduction of its money market account was the most significant step in new product development. This allowed NCNB to offer high-yielding, liquid deposit instruments to compete with the money market funds offered by nondepository institutions. That same year, NCNB joined the Plus System, a 26-bank network of automated teller operators throughout the country. This system allowed NCNB's customers to have access to most of the same services offered by NCNB's ATMs as they traveled throughout the country.

NCNB also established two new subsidiaries during 1982. A discount brokerage subsidiary was set up to handle security sales and purchases for bank customers. The second subsidiary, NCNB Futures Corporation, was created to trade in financial futures.

Domestically, NCNB did everything possible to further penetrate existing markets. It had even established an industrial development department to encourage companies, headquartered elsewhere, to open plants and offices in NCNB communities. This department had already helped Miller Brewing Company, Measurements Group, Inc., Union Carbide, and Verbatim Corporation to open facilities in cities where NCNB's banks operated.

In addition to its domestic operations, NCNB had already moved into six foreign countries. NCNB offered a wide variety of international banking services, including some of the best import/export financing programs available anywhere. NCNB wanted to penetrate further in foreign countries where it already had operations and to move into additional foreign countries throughout the 1980s.

Financial Strategy

The time period from the mid-1960s through 1981 can be divided into three distinct financial periods for NCNB. The first period was rapid growth, which continued through the early 1970s. In fact, NCNB's sales grew so fast that it was rated one of the premier bank growth stocks. The second period, from the early 1970s until 1979, focused on recovering from loan losses. These losses caused a sharp decline in NCNB's earnings, particularly in 1974. Its stock's price dropped from a high of $42 in 1973 to a low of $7 in 1974. From 1974 to 1979, NCNB concentrated on cleaning up problem loans, second-home financing, and mobile-home lending. The third period, which started in 1979, involved building capital equity.

The early 1980s brought about conflicting results for NCNB. Earnings improved slightly in the first half of 1980. Then they became somewhat depressed through mid-1981. This was caused when NCNB extended the maturity dates on many of its overseas loans in 1980. It took this action to avoid foreclosing on foreign businesses that would have been forced to default on repaying high-interest loans during a severe recessionary period. Since then, quarterly earnings have rebounded strongly due to sustained improvement in the net interest margin.

Exhibit 1 shows NCNB Corporation's consolidated balance sheet summary from 1977 through 1982. NCNB Corporation and its subsidiaries' total assets for 1982 were $8.4 billion, which excluded the Florida acquisitions. This was almost double the 1977 total of $4.8 billion. When the approximate $2.8 million assets from the Florida acquisitions were added, plus some other assets, NCNB's 1982 total assets became approximately $11.6 billion. Exhibit 2 then shows NCNB's consolidated earnings summary for the same six-year period. Net income for 1982 was $76.1 million, which represented a 274 percent increase over its 1977 total of $27.8 million.

A key part of Phase 1, improving the corporation's capital position, was accomplished in 1980 and 1981. Shareholders' equity of $240.5 million in 1977 increased by $102.9 million in 1980, but then rapidly increased by another $136.3 million to $479.7 million in 1982.

NCNB felt that it was important to accelerate the growth of equity to provide an expanded base for asset growth. Common stock issued in December 1980 provided $12 million of additional capital. Later, an exchange of shares for debentures in October of 1981 increased equity by $29 million. From 1980 through 1982, sales of shares through the dividend reinvestment program and employee stock plans brought in $12 million. Retained earnings contributed $136 million during this time and mergers brought an additional $36 million.

The company's dominant financial strategy for 1983 and beyond involved concentrating on building equity through earnings retention while maintaining its dividend policy. Thus, NCNB's catch phrase for the 1980s was asset/liability management. The goal of NCNB's asset/liability management committee was to maximize net interest margin and net interest income under prudent levels of risk.

Human Resources Strategy

NCNB strengthened its managerial depth and technical expertise, as a part of Phase 1, in an attempt to improve the quality of its 7,784 overall workforce. In addition, NCNB greatly expanded its college recruitment program starting in the late 1970s. For 1983, NCNB was planning to hire 144 college graduates, of which 40 to 50 percent would have M.B.A. degrees.

President McColl described the kind of people he wanted to work for the organization.

I put a high priority on attracting people who not only are smart and energetic, but can also relate to people, can talk to people, and can sell our company. If

EXHIBIT 1

NCNB Corporation and Subsidiaries: Consolidated Six-Year Balance Sheet Summary (Dollar Amounts in Thousands)

	1982	1981	1980	1979
ASSETS				
Cash and due from banks	$ 656,355	$ 818,957	$ 801,536	$ 815,597
Time deposits placed	895,156	965,618	953,748	678,338
Investment securities:				
Taxable	803,403	559,053	620,424	539,854
Tax-exempt	306,344	325,784	324,496	292,535
Total investment securities	1,109,747	884,837	944,920	832,389
Trading account securities	57,690	60,943	32,036	77,915
Federal funds sold and securities purchased under agreements to resell	364,405	395,687	307,437	277,363
Loans and leases—net of unearned income:				
Commercial loans	2,260,940	1,868,404	1,544,783	1,295,348
Commercial leases	150,779	110,446	80,744	60,431
Total commercial loans and leases	2,411,719	1,978,850	1,625,527	1,355,779
Consumer loans	1,181,498	1,100,794	1,000,379	933,146
Mortgage loans	267,020	236,220	266,739	272,741
Construction loans	205,736	144,379	136,734	145,543
Foreign loans and leases	581,618	507,510	269,327	147,437
Other loans	28,368	30,741	23,738	35,276
Total loans and leases—net of unearned income	4,675,959	3,998,494	3,322,444	2,889,922
Less allowance for loan and lease losses	(54,582)	(46,905)	(37,671)	(34,010)
Net loans and leases	4,621,377	3,951,589	3,284,773	2,855,912
Real estate acquired through foreclosure	17,969	22,095	26,191	31,107
Premises, equipment, and lease rights—net	135,088	104,116	98,811	95,505
Other assets	577,167	474,246	416,058	285,146
	$8,434,954	$7,678,088	$6,865,510	$5,949,272
LIABILITIES				
Demand deposits:				
Net	$ 682,383	$ 649,350	$ 744,793	$ 766,074
Float, reserves, and deposits in other financial institutions	557,932	749,140	753,261	736,217
Total demand deposits	1,240,315	1,398,490	1,498,054	1,502,291
Consumer savings and other time deposits	1,155,218	925,687	872,179	957,113
Consumer money market certificates	969,639	709,080	437,193	144,788
Certificates of deposit and other time deposits of $100,000 or more	1,007,035	897,397	738,837	709,351
Other domestic time deposits	26,737	26,268	39,901	65,623
Total domestic savings and time deposits	3,158,629	2,558,432	2,088,110	1,876,875
Foreign time deposits	1,326,152	1,346,402	1,171,550	766,243
Total savings and time deposits	4,484,781	3,904,834	3,259,660	2,643,118
Total deposits	5,725,096	5,303,324	4,757,714	4,145,409

EXHIBIT 1   Continued

	1982	1981	1980	1979
LIABILITIES				
Borrowed funds:				
Federal funds purchased and securities sold under agreements to repurchase	1,042,758	868,211	754,603	586,813
Banks	685	1,885	11,656	3,343
Commercial paper	170,713	205,200	140,976	154,927
Other notes payable	277,529	269,769	237,338	215,113
Total borrowed funds	1,491,685	1,345,065	1,144,573	960,196
Other liabilities	554,524	452,296	417,807	326,114
Capital leases	26,043	28,046	29,715	31,320
Long-term debt	157,939	147,445	172,296	184,506
Total liabilities	7,955,287	7,276,176	6,522,105	5,647,545
Shareholders' equity	479,667	401,912	343,405	301,727
	$8,434,954	$7,678,088	$6,865,510	$5,949,272

	1978	1977	ONE-YEAR INCREASE (DECREASE) 1981/82	FIVE-YEAR COMPOUND GROWTH (REDUCTION) RATE 1977/82
ASSETS				
Cash and due from banks	$ 757,909	$ 761,168	(19.9)%	(2.9)%
Time deposits placed	459,195	348,242	(7.3)	20.8
Investment securities:				
Taxable	390,346	337,192	43.7	19.0
Tax-exempt	295,537	313,147	(6.0)	(.4)
Total investment securities	685,883	650,339	25.4	11.3
Trading account securities	78,329	56,912	(5.3)	.3
Federal funds sold and securities purchased under agreements to resell	230,298	239,824	(7.9)	8.7
Loans and leases—net of unearned income:				
Commercial loans	1,249,092	1,179,889	21.0	13.9
Commercial leases	40,311	29,049	36.5	39.0
Total commercial loans and leases	1,289,403	1,208,938	21.9	14.8
Consumer loans	805,255	688,003	6.4	11.4
Mortgage loans	270,506	263,999	13.0	.2
Construction loans	133,845	130,444	42.5	9.5
Foreign loans and leases	143,515	162,983	14.6	29.0
Other loans	23,570	19,967	(7.7)	7.3
Total loans and leases—net of unearned income	2,666,094	2,474,334	16.9	13.6
Less allowance for loan and lease losses	(30,131)	(29,455)	16.4	13.1
Net loans and leases	2,635,963	2,444,879	16.9	13.6

EXHIBIT 1   Continued

	1978	1977	ONE-YEAR INCREASE (DECREASE) 1981/82	FIVE-YEAR COMPOUND GROWTH (REDUCTION) RATE 1977/82
ASSETS				
Real estate acquired through foreclosure	48,321	53,192	(18.7)	(19.5)
Premises, equipment, and lease rights—net	94,580	104,181	29.7	5.3
Other assets	181,324	145,819	22.0	31.7
	$5,171,802	$4,804,556	9.9	11.9
LIABILITIES				
Demand deposits:				
Net	$ 783,659	$ 737,113	5.1	(1.5)
Float, reserves, and deposits in other financial institutions	720,020	725,388	(25.5)	(5.1)
Total demand deposits	1,503,679	1,462,501	(11.3)	(3.2)
Consumer savings and other time deposits	966,315	929,661	24.8	4.4
Consumer money market certificates	13,357		36.7	
Certificates of deposit and other time deposits of $100,000 or more	534,921	451,721	12.2	17.4
Other domestic time deposits	78,818	72,860	1.8	(18.2)
Total domestic savings and time deposits	1,593,411	1,454,242	23.5	16.8
Foreign time deposits	584,826	483,473	(1.5)	22.4
Total savings and time deposits	2,178,237	1,937,715	14.9	18.3
Total deposits	3,681,916	3,400,216	8.0	11.0
Borrowed funds:				
Federal funds purchased and securities sold under agreements to repurchase	485,575	510,422	20.1	15.4
Banks	14,947	73,274	(63.7)	(60.7)
Commercial paper	135,563	89,315	(16.8)	13.8
Other notes payable	161,323	118,881	2.9	18.5
Total borrowed funds	797,408	791,892	10.9	13.5
Other liabilities	206,230	148,030	22.6	30.2
Capital leases	31,686	33,136	(7.1)	(4.7)
Long-term debt	189,833	190,739	7.1	(3.7)
Total liabilities	4,907,073	4,564,013	9.3	11.8
Shareholders' equity	264,729	240,543	19.3	14.8
	$5,171,802	$4,804,556	9.9	11.9

SOURCE: NCNB Corporation 1982 Annual Report, pp. 52–53.

EXHIBIT 2

NCNB Corporation and Subsidiaries: Consolidated Six-Year Earnings Summary (Dollar Amounts in Thousands Except Per Share Data)

	1982	1981	1980	1979
INCOME FROM EARNING ASSETS				
Interest and fees on loans and leases:				
Commercial loans	$ 328,092	$ 318,786	$ 220,356	$ 163,228
Commercial leases	23,859	16,942	11,769	8,362
Total	351,951	335,728	232,125	171,590
Consumer loans	192,494	167,465	138,443	124,428
Mortgage loans	30,964	24,759	27,473	27,512
Construction loans	31,832	25,606	20,426	19,369
Foreign loans and leases	85,636	82,800	38,230	18,487
Other loans	2,379	2,087	1,979	3,356
Total	695,256	638,445	458,676	364,742
Interest and dividends on investment securities:				
U.S. Treasury	58,353	29,656	31,640	30,819
Other U.S. Gov't agencies and corporations	20,607	22,499	24,190	16,668
Other	9,966	5,904	6,013	3,210
Total taxable	88,926	58,059	61,843	50,697
States and political subdivisions (exempt from federal income taxes)	17,934	17,776	17,364	14,711
Total	106,860	75,835	79,207	65,408
Interest on time deposits placed	128,406	160,228	122,175	78,936
Interest on federal funds sold and securities purchased under agreements to resell	45,642	66,067	42,872	31,181
Interest on trading account securities	6,631	7,816	3,258	7,563
Other interest income	1,280	409		
Total income from earning assets	964,075	948,800	706,188	547,830
INTEREST EXPENSE				
Savings deposits	46,973	37,956	33,303	33,880
Time deposits	280,639	243,626	160,575	110,984
Total domestic savings and time deposits	327,612	281,582	193,878	144,864
Foreign time deposits	177,524	218,215	164,710	86,659
Total savings and time deposits	505,136	499,797	358,588	231,523
Federal funds purchased and securities sold under agreements to repurchase	119,263	137,440	92,815	64,018
Commercial paper	21,419	34,762	18,780	17,634
Other notes payable	31,980	35,987	27,781	22,134
Total borrowed funds	172,662	208,189	139,376	103,786
Capital leases	2,747	3,144	2,638	2,743
Long-term debt	15,870	12,247	14,106	14,981
Total interest expense	696,415	723,377	514,708	353,033

EXHIBIT 2   Continued

	1982	1981	1980	1979
INTEREST EXPENSE				
Net interest income	287,660	225,423	191,480	194,797
Provision for loan and lease losses	30,723	21,544	22,290	17,749
Net credit income	256,937	203,879	169,190	177,048
Other operating income	88,771	81,589	84,085	56,166
Other operating expenses	243,091	208,356	182,871	160,095
Earnings				
Income before income taxes, securities losses, and extraordinary items	102,617	77,112	70,404	73,119
Income tax expense	25,615	14,268	18,897	24,478
Income before securities losses and extraordinary items	77,002	62,844	51,507	48,641
Securities losses—net	862	4,733	265	814
Extraordinary items—net		11,509	146	2,966
Net income	$ 76,140	$ 69,620	$ 51,388	$ 50,793
PER SHARE				
Income before securities losses and extraordinary items	$ 3.22	$ 2.78	$ 2.41	$ 2.30
Securities losses—net	.04	.21	.01	.04
Extraordinary items—net		.51	.01	.15
Net income	$ 3.18	$ 3.08	$ 2.41	$ 2.41
Cash dividends paid	$ .91	$ .82	$ .76	$ .62
Average shares outstanding	23,964,155	22,682,708	21,350,546	21,189,716

	1978	1977	ONE-YEAR INCREASE (DECREASE) 1981/82	FIVE-YEAR COMPOUND GROWTH (REDUCTION) RATE 1977/82
INCOME FROM EARNING ASSETS				
Interest and fees on loans and leases:				
Commercial loans	$ 122,734	$ 95,818	2.9%	27.9%
Commercial leases	5,707	4,958	40.8	36.9
Total	128,441	100,776	4.8	28.4
Consumer loans	104,011	89,632	14.9	16.5
Mortgage loans	25,030	23,036	25.1	6.1
Construction loans	14,259	10,016	24.3	26.0

EXHIBIT 2   Continued

	1978	1977	ONE-YEAR INCREASE (DECREASE) 1981/82	FIVE-YEAR COMPOUND GROWTH (REDUCTION) RATE 1977/82
INCOME FROM EARNING ASSETS				
Foreign loans and leases	13,862	12,768	3.4	46.3
Other loans	1,591	766	14.0	25.4
Total	287,194	236,994	8.9	24.0
Interest and dividends on investment securities:				
U.S. Treasury	14,123	11,122	96.8	39.3
Other U.S. Government agencies and corporations	11,541	7,100	(8.4)	23.8
Other	2,932	4,005	68.8	20.0
Total taxable	28,596	22,227	53.2	32.0
States and political subdivisions (exempt from federal income taxes)	14,188	14,908	.9	3.8
Total	42,784	37,135	40.9	23.5
Interest on time deposits placed	36,594	21,438	(19.9)	43.0
Interest on federal funds sold and securities purchased under agreements to resell	18,913	13,584	(30.9)	27.4
Interest on trading account securities	5,537	3,071	(15.2)	16.6
Other interest income			213.0	
Total income from earning assets	391,022	312,222	3.7	25.8
INTEREST EXPENSE				
Savings deposits	32,745	31,268	23.8	8.5
Time deposits	66,738	48,757	15.2	41.9
Total domestic savings and time deposits	99,483	80,025	16.3	32.6
Foreign time deposits	46,431	29,938	(18.6)	42.8
Total savings and time deposits	145,914	109,963	1.1	35.7
Federal funds purchased and securities sold under agreements to repurchase	37,478	27,389	(13.2)	34.2
Commercial paper	10,850	5,082	(38.4)	33.3
Other notes payable	14,443	11,826	(11.1)	22.0
Total borrowed funds	62,771	44,297	(17.1)	31.3
Capital leases	2,769	2,762	(12.6)	(.1)
Long-term debt	15,345	15,339	29.6	.7
Total interest expense	226,799	172,361	(3.7)	32.2

EXHIBIT 2   Continued

	1978	1977	ONE-YEAR INCREASE (DECREASE) 1981/82	FIVE-YEAR COMPOUND GROWTH (REDUCTION) RATE 1977/82
INTEREST EXPENSE				
Net interest income	164,223	139,861	27.6	15.5
Provision for loan and lease losses	15,893	14,186	42.6	16.7
Net credit income	148,330	125,675	26.0	15.4
Other operating income	49,731	42,221	8.8	16.0
Other operating expenses	140,708	130,396	16.7	13.3
Earnings				
Income before income taxes, securities losses, and extraordinary items	57,353	37,500	33.1	22.3
Income tax expense	18,670	10,486	79.5	19.6
Income before securities losses and extraordinary items	38,683	27,014	22.5	23.3
Securities losses—net	506	196	(81.8)	34.5
Extraordinary items—net	1,594	953		
Net income	$ 39,771	$ 27,771	9.4	22.4
PER SHARE				
Income before securities losses and extraordinary items	$ 1.84	$ 1.29	15.8	20.1
Securities losses—net	.02	.01	(81.0)	32.0
Extraordinary items—net	.08	.05		
Net income	$ 1.90	$ 1.33	3.2	19.0
Cash dividends paid	$ .58	$ .52	11.0	11.8
Average shares outstanding	21,075,541	21,010,160	5.6	2.7

SOURCE: NCNB Corporation 1982 Annual Report, pp. 54–55.

we get the people who have those qualities, we'll give them two important kinds of training—technical and leadership.[2]

NCNB's philosophy concerning its employees stressed that pay increases and promotions should be based on individual performance instead of automatically occurring after a set length of time. Each individual was encouraged to gain a broad range of experience and to assume responsibility for his or her own development at NCNB.

Management Strategy

Another key area of Phase 1 involved improving the corporation's managerial depth and technical expertise. NCNB emphasized a variety of in-house training and management development programs at all levels of management. In turn, this helped its employees develop a strong personal commitment to NCNB. The focus at the executive level was using strategic planning for continued success in the challenging banking environment of the future.

Members of NCNB's executive management had been with NCNB an average of fifteen years, with some having over thirty years experience in banking. In spite of their extensive experience, NCNB's top management had been described as wild and woolly innovators, unafraid to tread where the more fainthearted money men might falter.[3] This attitude helped explain NCNB's aggressive move into Florida.

Thomas Storrs, chairman and chief executive officer, explained NCNB's move into Florida this way:

> The Southeast needs a strong bank organization—one that competes with money center banks—if it is to continue to grow and prosper. We believe we are developing that organization.[4]

NCNB's president, Hugh McColl, although supporting Storrs's acquisitions, viewed NCNB's future differently. He remarked, "The major acquisition phase is over. We have achieved the size needed to be a meaningful force in interstate banking. Now our emphasis is going to be on profitability."[5] While McColl was president, he also was slated to become NCNB's next chairman when Storrs retired in August 1983.

NCNB Moves into Florida

NCNB was clearly a leading force in North Carolina. NCNB had 22.6 percent of the North Carolina consumer deposit market as of late 1982 when it ranked second. Wachovia was the state leader with a 31.1 percent market share, and First Union was third with a 20.0 percent share.[6] Because future growth prospects seemed limited in North Carolina, NCNB felt that it could be more successful by entering higher growth markets in other states. Unfortunately, all states seemed to prohibit outsiders from acquiring banks inside their states.

A top management task force was assembled at NCNB's corporate headquarters in 1980. This task force included Frank Gentry, Joe Martin from corporate affairs, Paul Polking from legal affairs, and Winston Pool, vice president of marketing. Its task was to identify potential ways that this bank holding company could grow. After various meetings, this group generated a list of some twenty to thirty possible growth alternatives. They also reviewed a separate demographic study of sixteen states that identified Florida and Texas as the two states with the highest growth rates. However, this looked discouraging as all states prohibited banks or bank holding companies from acquiring banks (or starting up new banks) in other states.

One possible alternative NCNB had identified was to set up industrial banks in other states. An industrial bank was pretty much the same as a household finance company. They operated by gathering time deposits and made consumer loans and paid interest. They were prohibited from offering checking accounts, did not have demand deposits, and were not Federal Deposit Insurance Corporation (FDIC) insured.

Paul Polking, assistant legal counsel for NCNB, was asked to research the various state laws to determine if this less desirable financial institution would be permitted. Polking later hand carried a legal opinion back to Frank Gentry that stated that he believed it would be legal for NCNB to establish an industrial bank in Florida. Attorney Polking based his opinion on the fact that NCNB had acquired the Trust Company of Florida in October 1972, three months before Florida passed a law prohibiting any banks or bank holding companies in other states from owning Florida banks. Thus, Polking believed that NCNB could be grandfathered into Florida because it already had established a presence there with its trust company.

Polking added, however, a most stunning comment. He told Gentry that by using the same grandfather clause reasoning, it looked like NCNB could also establish a commercial bank. That is, if it held up to probable legal challenges from opponents in Florida wanting to prevent outsiders from entering their lucrative market. This more attractive option of opening a bank had been disregarded earlier on by NCNB because of the general prohibition of interstate banking.

Gentry and Polking soon met with Tom Storrs, NCNB chairman of the board, to discuss the option of moving into Florida. Interestingly, some NCNB executives had even questioned over the years why NCNB was keeping Trust Company of Florida. Coincidentally, it was Storrs who squelched that idea and flatly stated that he wanted to hold on to it. Storrs was obviously pleased with the news that Polking and Gentry provided him that NCNB's earlier acquisition might prove to be the key to opening the doors to Florida.

Subsequently, NCNB top management met on several occasions to decide how to move into Florida. Some shared Polking's opinion that NCNB could legally move into that state. Other NCNB officials were more pessimistic and felt that NCNB could not legally acquire a bank there. One point was agreed upon: if NCNB did expand into Florida, it should be through acquisition rather than trying to start up a new bank itself. Despite differences over the likelihood of its success, most top management felt that NCNB should continue forward to determine if it could move into the lucrative Florida market.

NCNB finally decided that it would be best to test the Florida law by trying to acquire a small, inexpensive bank. NCNB wanted to make sure that any proposed bank acquisition would be a pure case, one that minimized several other issues that might lead to an unfavorable ruling. Thus, it established three criteria that any acquisition would have to satisfy. First, NCNB wanted any proposed acquisition to be in a county of Florida where its Trust Company of Florida or its Atlantic Discount Company of Jacksonville (a subsidiary of NCNB's TranSouth Financial Corporation) did not operate. That would help eliminate any anticompetitive issues from clouding the legal question. Second, any acquisition candidate needed to be a national, rather than a state, bank. That would prevent having additional state laws brought into consideration when the Federal Reserve ruled on the application. Third, the ownership of any potential bank would need to be tightly held. That way, it would be easier for NCNB to acquire control of the bank. If a proposed acquisition met these three criteria, NCNB's management felt that its chances for Federal Reserve approval would be greatly enhanced. Thus, a pure case would hopefully be decided on the merits of the grandfathering clause and would hopefully avoid any contaminating issues.

NCNB discreetly approached an investment banker in Florida with the various criteria that any acquisition candidates would have to satisfy. Per instructions, the investment banker kept NCNB's name confidential as it tried to identify potential acquisition candidates. The investment banker soon provided NCNB with a list of a half dozen small banks that fulfilled its three criteria.

The second bank contacted by NCNB representatives was the First National Bank of Lake City, Fla. This single-branch bank had assets of $21.6 million. NCNB offered a very high figure of $3.9 million for the bank sight unseen simply to test the law with a national bank, with closely held stock, and located in a county where no other NCNB financial institution operated.

On June 11, 1981, Chairman Tom Storrs publicly announced that NCNB would try to acquire First National Bank of Lake City. NCNB waited until after the Florida State Legislature had ended its session before making this public announcement. This prevented the legislature from introducing legislation to revise the Florida statute unless it called a special session to prevent NCNB from entering its state.

In his announcement, Storrs didn't explain how NCNB expected the Federal Reserve Bank in Richmond, Va., to approve the petition. This left many industry observers speculating about how NCNB would be able to make such an acquisition, as interstate banking was still outlawed. Storrs noted only that NCNB was proceeding on its lawyers' advice and that NCNB believed its position was sound. Storrs added, however, that the move represented an extension of NCNB's existing operations in Florida.

The Federal Reserve commented on the proposed acquisition the very next day. Floyd Boston, an enforcement official for the Federal Reserve Bank of Richmond, noted that if the Lake City acquisition was approved, it would mean that NCNB could expand further in Florida with other acquisitions. Obviously, this was exactly what NCNB management hoped to hear for a final outcome.

NCNB did not wait for a ruling by the Fed to go after other acquisitions. On Sunday, June 21, 1981, NCNB announced that it wanted to acquire Florida National Banks of Florida, Inc. It was the fourth largest bank holding company in the state with total assets of $2.5 billion. NCNB officials also noted that C. A. Cavendes Sociedad Financiera of Caracas, Venezuela, which controlled 32.5 percent of Florida National's stock, had agreed to vote for a merger. NCNB offered $210 million for this bank holding company, which owned 25 banks with 88 combined offices in the state. Stockholders of Florida National Banks would receive NCNB preferred stock worth $28.00 for each share of Florida National, which closed two days earlier at $19.68. In addition, $45 million would be put in an escrow fund to be established for Cavendes to draw income on between the time the merger agreement was signed and the time it was closed. Finally, NCNB would invest $20 million in the Cavendes-controlled South American bank. Like the earlier Lake City announcement, NCNB officials did not explain how they hoped their application to enter banking in another state would be approved by the Federal Reserve.

There was lots of discussion in the banking community over NCNB's two proposed acquisitions. Some bank analysts quickly speculated that NCNB was probably going to argue that its 1972 acquisition of the Florida Trust Company grandfathered it into Florida for future acquisitions. One industry observer even speculated that NCNB might try to argue that its Florida Trust Company already qualified as a commercial bank under Florida laws.

Later in June, NCNB formally submitted its application to the Federal Reserve to acquire the Lake City bank. Unfortunately, it had to wait quite some time for a final ruling by the Federal Reserve.

On June 27, 1981, 45-year-old NCNB Vice Chairman Hugh McColl commented on how NCNB had prepared for its move into Florida. McColl, who was talking from NCNB's temporary command post at the Holiday Inn in Jacksonville, noted:

> It was planned as sophisticatedly as you would plan an invasion. . . . We put our logistics in place, put together a team of lawyers and negotiators . . . lined up pilots and airplanes, telephones, and telexes. We had a scheme of everything that would have to be done. We built a battle plan. Everyone had assignments, and we've been carrying them out constantly. . . . We believe you must grow if you are going to survive. You either go forward or get overrun. All of us think that way.[7]

NCNB withdrew its offer to acquire the Florida National Banks of Florida on July 10, 1981. This action was not surprising, given that three days earlier Florida National Banks flatly stated that it would not consider the $210 million offer from NCNB until after the Federal Reserve or a court ruled that NCNB's efforts to move into Florida were legal. In retracting NCNB's earlier offer, Tom Storrs noted:

> It's just good business that when you make an offer and the recipient doesn't
> consider it, you withdraw it. There are a lot of other banks in Florida. We will
> continue to look at the banking structure of the state.

He further added that NCNB was willing to acquire banks as large as Barnett Banks of Florida, which was the state's second largest holding company
with $4.4 billion in assets. Storrs observed:

> Barnett is a great bank. The top management there includes some very good
> friends of mine. I certainly wouldn't rule this out.[8]

The Florida Bankers Association and two competitors of the First National Bank of Lake City urged the Federal Reserve to reject NCNB's application. The Bankers Association contended that the grandfather clause
was never intended for acquisitions by out-of-state bank holding companies.
Lloyd Boston of the Federal Reserve Board in Richmond responded to this
challenge by stating, "The board is required to consider the meaning and
applicability of state law. So the board will be looking at Florida statutes and
trying to determine if they do make it permissible for NCNB . . . to acquire
banks and/or trust companies in Florida."[9]

NCNB responded by filing a response to the Florida Bankers Association
challenge with the Federal Reserve. Its response even included a statement
from former Florida Representative Robert Hartnett, who was the main
sponsor of the legislation and chairman of the banking and finance subcommittee of the Florida House from 1968 through 1974. Hartnett said in his
statement that he was concerned with "protecting the rights and future opportunities of those non-Florida banking organizations, which already had
acquired banks or trust companies in Florida."[10]

On December 9, 1981, the Federal Reserve Board in Richmond finally
ruled in favor of NCNB's application to acquire the First National Bank of
Lake City. In making its decision, the Fed noted that NCNB would consider
reducing the bank's service charges and making credit insurance available
at lower rates. The Fed also noted that NCNB intended to offer new or
improved services and to open branches, which should provide widespread
access to all these services. Thus, the Federal Reserve felt the acquisition
was clearly in the public interest. More important, the Federal Reserve concluded:

> NCNB may, in accordance with Florida law, acquire, retain, or own all the
> assets of, or control over, any Florida bank or trust company.[11]

NCNB spokesman and attorney Paul Polking, who discovered the legal
loophole, responded as the company spokesman this time. He observed:

> We have several options. When we acquire First National Bank of Lake City,
> we have the authority to establish branches of that bank in other communities.
> We could also acquire other banks or bank holding companies in the state.[12]

Florida officials responded in different ways. Many bankers were very disappointed with the ruling. Sun Bank's Senter Fitt noted, "When NCNB is in Florida, it is here with all its assets. It is here as the largest holding company in Florida."[13] Some other bankers reacted more strongly and called for action. For example, Charles Rice, president of the Jacksonville-based Barnett Banks, publicly stated that he hoped that the NCNB ruling would spur the Florida legislature to pass reciprocal banking legislation. The legislation he envisioned would require states whose banks wanted to enter Florida to grant similar privileges to Florida banks in their home states.

Even with the Federal Reserve approval, NCNB still had to wait 30 additional days before it could acquire 82 percent of the stock for almost $4 million. This one-month delay was to give time for the Justice Department to review the decision on antitrust grounds. Since NCNB had no other operation in the county where Lake City operated, the 30-day period passed uneventfully. Finally, in early January of 1982, NCNB had moved into Florida banking through an acquisition of a bank they had never even personally visited before offering an inflated purchase price. Still, NCNB had used that small bank successfully to test the Florida statutes and get the green light to acquire larger, more important Florida banks in the future.

Although this legal loophole applied only to Florida, Florida was the best possible state for NCNB to enter in the southeastern region of the United States. Compared with North Carolina, the Florida marketplace was less developed yet substantially larger. The Florida bank deposit base ranked ninth nationwide with $43.8 billion in domestic bank deposits, whereas North Carolina finished in twenty-first place with only $19.8 billion in deposits. Florida also had twice as many corporations located in middle-sized markets. In 1982, some 4,353 such companies were identified in Florida, compared with only 2,142 in North Carolina.

Florida was an attractive market for other reasons. Its population was growing quickly, its income base was stable, the business climate was favorable, and tourists regularly visited the state. Furthermore, Florida's economy was expected to lead the nation's recovery from the recession that started in late 1980.

In the remainder of 1982, NCNB sought and received approval from the Federal Reserve to acquire three other Florida banks with combined assets of $2.8 billion. On September 3, NCNB Corporation consummated its acquisition of Gulfstream Banks, Inc., in Boca Raton. NCNB paid $91 million cash for Gulfstream, which had total assets of $787 million.

Gulfstream was a full-service national bank and a member of the FDIC. Its 21 branches were located in Broward, Palm Beach, and Dade counties. Its banks provided checking, loan, savings, and other time deposits for its individual and commercial customers. Gulfstream also had 24-hour ATMs in twelve locations, issued Visa and MasterCard credit cards, offered various trust services, offered a money market account, sold securities and funds to finance loans, purchased investment securities for its customers, and traded in foreign currencies to realize profits for its own account.

On December 31, 1982, NCNB consummated its acquisition of the Exchange Bancorporation of Tampa. Exchange operated 51 offices in eleven counties and had assets of $1.6 billion. This largest of the acquisitions was purchased for $134 million cash.

Like Gulfstream, Exchange Bancorporation also offered a wide range of banking services. It provided checking, loan, savings, and other time deposits at 44 of its branches. It also had a money market account, a direct payroll deposit system for its customers, 24-hour ATM service at 38 locations, issued name credit cards, and provided trust services. In addition, it was a dealer in governmental and municipal bonds and was an underwriter for state and municipal bonds. Finally, it had various foreign services, which included borrowing funds in overseas markets and engaging in foreign currency exchange trading to meet the needs of its customers and itself.

The fourth Florida acquisition was also finalized in December. It involved Peoples Downtown National Bank in Miami, a single-branch bank with only $9 million in assets, which was purchased for $6 million.

NCNB's earlier successful building of its equity capital position allowed the corporation to enter phase two of its plan for the 1980s, the geographical expansion of the corporation. NCNB paid $225 million alone to gain its two major Florida acquisitions, Gulfstream Banks, Inc., and Exchange Bancorporation of Tampa. These funds were obtained from a variety of sources at an after-tax cost of slightly more than 6 percent; however, it did not dilute NCNB's 1982 earnings. Exhibit 3 shows the various sources used for these Florida acquisitions that included short-term debt, long-term debt, new equity, and the use of existing corporate resources.

The Florida acquisitions combined with North Carolina gave NCNB a market that ranked sixth in size in the entire country. This tripled NCNB's potential market for deposits, retail customers, and business firms. NCNB estimated that it had gained access to over 30 percent of the total banking market of the twelve southeastern states, as compared with only 10 percent to 12 percent represented by North Carolina. Due to its size, NCNB could legally lend $100 million to a single corporate customer. This was higher than either of the leading Florida banks. Barnett could lend $88.5 million and Southeast $65 million to $70 million. Both NCNB and Wall Street were optimistic about NCNB's future after these acquisitions. Thomas Storrs, chairman, was confident that NCNB would become larger in Florida than in its home state. Salomon Brothers, a leading investment banking company, supported Storrs's optimism by recommending the purchase of NCNB's stock and raising its forecasted five-year earnings growth rate from 13 percent to 15 percent.

EXHIBIT 3

NCNB Corporation Financing Program (Dollar Amounts in Millions)

	CASH PURCHASE PRICE	NET AFTER-TAX ANNUAL INTEREST COST
1. Original issue discount debentures	$ 38.0	$ 2.2
2. 14.5% notes, due 1992	83.5	6.8
3. Special dividend, North Carolina National Bank	25.0*	1.7
4. Refund of 1981 federal income taxes	10.0	—
5. Tax benefits from sale of acquired assets with tax bases in excess of market values	21.0	—
6. Sale of parent company liquid assets	20.0	1.4
7. Utilization of uncommitted parent company equity	22.5*	1.6
	$220.0	$13.7
8. After-tax cost of funds		6.2%
9. Pre-tax cost of funds		11.5%

SOURCE: The First Boston Research Corporation, 1982.

*Prime of 13 percent used.

Consolidation of Operations

NCNB's four acquisitions offered different products and services, were of different sizes, and had varying degrees of managerial talent. They also differed in the geographical areas that they covered in Florida, along with NCNB's two existing operations, as Exhibit 4 shows. The first acquisition was no more than a one-branch country bank that had cost only a few million to purchase. Similarly, the fourth Florida acquisition, Peoples Downtown National Bank of Miami, was done basically to obtain a charter to operate in that county. Peoples had been stripped of its depositors, and its management was not going to stay on after the acquisition was finalized. Still, Peoples was acquired for a very good reason. If NCNB had tried to start up its own bank from scratch, Florida law would have required it to operate in one county for two years before being permitted to expand into other counties.

The second and third acquisitions were a different story. Gulfstream Banks, Inc., in Boca Raton, was acquired for close to $100 million and had 21 branches. Management was asked to stay on, including Gulfstream's

NCNB Corporation
Charlotte, N.C. 28255
704/374-5000

Exchange Bank & Trust Company of Florida N.A.
600 North Florida Avenue
Tampa, Fla. 33602
813/224-5151

First National Bank of Lake City
201 North Marion Street
Lake City, Fla. 32055
904/752-2524

NCNB Financial Services Inc.
P. O. Box 30533
Charlotte, N.C. 28230
704/374-5876

NCNB Leasing Corporation
Charlotte, N.C. 28255
704/374-5269

NCNB National Bank of Florida
150 East Palmetto Park Road
Boca Raton, Fla. 33432
305/393-5100

NCNB National Bank of North Carolina
Charlotte, N.C. 28255
704/374-5000

Representative Offices
Suite 1705
375 Park Avenue
New York, N.Y. 10152
212/935-8303

Suite 4060, First National Plaza
70 West Madison Street
Chicago, Ill. 60602
312/372-0742

Suite 1535, CNA Tower
255 South Orange Avenue
Orlando, Fla. 32801
305/423-0828

TranSouth Financial Corporation
518 South Irby Street
P. O. Box F471
Florence, S.C. 29501
803/662-9341

Trust Company of Florida
200 East Robinson Street
P. O. Box 2951
Orlando, Fla. 32802
305/841-6000

International:

Carolina Bank Limited
14 Austin Friars
London EC2N 2EH, England
01-628-4821

NCNB Overseas Corporation
Charlotte, N. C. 28255
704/374-5212

NCNB International Banking Corporation
44 Wall Street
P. O. Box 536
Wall Street Station
New York, N. Y. 10005
212/943-6300

NCNB (Asia) Limited
35th Floor, New World Tower
16-18 Queens Road Central
Hong Kong, B.C.C.
5-220192

NCNB Spedley Australia Ltd.
68 Pitt Street
Sydney, Australia 2001
22-33-7076

NCNB National Bank Branches
14 Austin Friars
London EC2N 2EH, England
01-588-9133

35th Floor, New World Tower
16-18 Queens Road Central
Hong Kong, B.C.C.
5-220192

Representative Offices
68 Pitt Street
G.P.O. Box 3951
Sydney, Australia 2001
22-33-7076

Edificio Olivetti
Avenida Paulista 453
Sao Paulo, Brazil
11-251-3473

16th Floor, Nedfin Place
Corner Simmonds and Kerk Streets
Johannesburg, South Africa 2001
11-834-7911

SOURCE: NCNB Corporation 1982 Annual Report, p. 59.

President Les Nell. Similarly, Exchange Bancorporation of Tampa was purchased for even more money and Don Buchanan, its CEO, stayed on as well.

NCNB wanted to improve the efficiency of its Florida operations as soon as the four acquisitions had been finalized. Clearly, NCNB wanted to do everything possible to increase its presence in Florida and to compete successfully against Barnett Banks, Flagship Banks, Inc., and Southeast Banking Corporation, its three strongest competitors in Florida.

As 1982 came to a close, a fundamental issue faced NCNB's corporate management. What should it do with these four Florida banks and how should they operate? How much autonomy should each bank be provided? Should they continue to follow the policies and procedures they had independently established before the takeover? Should NCNB require them to follow uniform procedures handed down by corporate headquarters in Charlotte, N.C.? Should their names be changed to indicate they were under the NCNB holding company? How should these four Florida banks be organized along with NCNB's other major operating units? What human resource programs might be needed to make the Florida bank employees feel a part of the friendly neighborhood bank? These and many other questions were beginning to surface as NCNB corporate management considered the best course of action to consolidate its Florida acquisitions and to start developing its new base of operation.

NOTES

1. *Meeting the Challenge of Growth* (Charlotte, N.C.: NCNB Corporation, a 1982 booklet).

2. *The Challenge of Our Future Could Be Part of Your Success* (Charlotte, N.C.: NCNB Corporation, a 1982 booklet).

3. "NCNB Defies Convention, Keeps Breaking Ground, *The Tampa Tribune*, May 29, 1982, p. A1.

4. "N.C. Bank Shines in Florida," *USA Today*, October 6, 1982.

5. *Ibid.*

6. Thomas H. Hanley, et al., *NCNB Corporation: The Sunshine Bank* (New York: Salomon Brothers Inc., February 3, 1983).

7. Dick Stilley, "NCNB Takes its Aggressive Style into Florida," *Charlotte Observer*, June 28, 1981, p. A1.

8. Dick Stilley, "NCNB Withdraws Bank Offer," *Charlotte Observer*, July 11, 1981, p. 1A.

9. Dick Stilley, "Former Legislator Supports NCNB in Florida Deal," *Charlotte Observer*, September 18, 1981, p. 8B.

10. *Ibid.*, p. 8B.

11. Dick Stilley, "Fed's Ruling Frees NCNB to Expand Florida Interests," *Charlotte Observer*, December 11, 1981, p. 7C.

12. *Ibid.*, p. 7C.

13. Dick Stilley, "NCNB Bidding for Regional Dominance," *Charlotte Observer*, December 13, 1981, p. 8C.

CASE 23

Citicorp—British National Life Assurance

JOHN M. GWIN • PER V. JENSTER • WILLIAM K. CARTER

INTRODUCTION

Ira Rimerman, group executive, consumer services group, international, Citicorp, was in his third-floor office at Citicorp's headquarters in New York City on January 16, 1986, when he received notice from the board of Citicorp that his Major Expenditure Proposal (MEP) to acquire the British National Life Assurance Company, Ltd. (BNLA) in England had been approved. For a total investment of $33.3 million, Citicorp was now in the life underwriting business.[1]

Although pleased with the board's approval, Rimerman had several issues on his mind as he thought back over the last few months when his staff analyzed and developed suggestions for a business strategy for BNLA, including key policies, tactics, and organizational changes.

CITICORP'S HISTORY

Citicorp's corporate history spanned 175 years from its inception as a small commercial bank in New York City in 1812 through its growth into one of the world's largest financial services intermediaries. A recurring historical theme seemed to be the firm's ability to identify correctly the developing trends in the marketplace and to devise appropriate strategies for taking advantage of them.

The firm first emerged as a significant bank in the latter part of the nineteenth century by responding successfully to the transition of the United States from an agricultural to an industrial economy. Since the mid-1960s, the firm had transcended the corporate treasurer and the metropolitan New Yorker as its sole funding sources and found ways to attract the more than $1.5 trillion consumer savings market in the United States.

During the 1960s and 1970s, Citicorp completed two separate but integral strategic efforts that revolutionized the company and influenced the whole financial service industry. First, in 1967, the firm formed a bank holding company, which permitted it to broaden its geographic and product bases. Second, in the early 1970s, it redefined its business from a U.S. commercial

This case was prepared by Professors John M. Gwin, Per V. Jenster, and William K. Carter of the McIntire School of Commerce, University of Virginia, for the sixth McIntire Commerce Invitational (MCI VI) held at the University of Virginia on February 11–14, 1987. We gratefully acknowledge the General Electric Foundation for its support of the MCI and of the preparation of this case. We are also grateful to Citicorp for its willing cooperation in this project.

435

bank with branches abroad to a global financial services enterprise with the United States as its home base. By 1980 the firm had further broadened its scope by defining its business as that of providing services and information to solve financial needs. Exhibits 1 and 2 provide a summary of the firm's financial profile.

CITICORP'S STRATEGY

The firm's strategic plan called for three separate kinds of world-class banks, all of which could leverage off an unrivaled global network. By the mid-1980s, the Investment Bank, also known as the Capital Markets Group, enabled the firm to fully intermediate the capital flows of the world, with over $6 billion in transactions in the swap market. The Institutional Bank was the principal supplier of financial service mechanisms to corporations and governments worldwide. Finally, the Individual Bank served the individual consumer on a worldwide basis.

Walter B. Wriston, former chairman of Citicorp/Citibank, explained the firm's strategy:

> Over time, it seemed to us, the institution without access to the consumer would slowly become an institution without adequate funding. In addition, consumer-led economic recoveries are becoming more the rule than the exception and we looked for ways to participate. For all of these reasons, you have often heard about this consumer transition and the identification of the consumer as a key to our strategy in the middle '70s. It was usually described as risky but there are also risks in doing nothing.[2]

The holding company structure was used to overcome the geographic constraints of the domestic businesses. It also allowed for a few acquisitions

---

EXHIBIT 1

Citicorp and Subsidiaries: Revenues Earned and Rates of Return Achieved

	REVENUES ($ BILLIONS)	ROA	ROE
1981	$4.0	.46%	13%
1982	5.1	.59	16
1983	5.8	.67	16
1984	6.6	.62	15
1985	8.5	.62	15

SOURCE: Citicorp's 1985 Annual Report.
ROE = (Net Income − Preferred Dividends)/Average Common Equity
ROA = Net Income/Average Total Assets

and for the creation of de novo units to build a global network that, among other things, featured a unique competitive franchise for bank cards within the Individual Bank.

Wriston also remarked:

It costs about $150 per year to service an individual through a branch system. That number plummets to $20 if we use the credit card as our primary delivery vehicle. In short, through fees and merchant discounts, the card as a stand-

EXHIBIT 2

Consolidated Balance Sheet for Citicorp and Subsidiaries (Dollar Amounts in Billions Except Per Share Data)

	1985	1984
ASSETS		
Cash, deposits with banks, and securities	$ 40	$ 31
Commercial loans	$ 58	$ 59
Consumer loans	55	43
Lease financing	3	2
Allowance for credit losses, net	1	1
	$115	$103
Premises and other assets	18	17
Total	$173	$151
LIABILITIES		
Deposits	$105	$ 90
Borrowings and other liabilities	42	39
Long-term debt	16	13
Capital notes and redeemable preferred	2	2
	$165	$144
STOCKHOLDERS' EQUITY		
Preferred stock	1	1
Common stock	1	1
Additional paid-in capital	1	1
Retained earnings	5	4
	$ 8	$ 7
Total	$173	$151

EXHIBIT 2

Continued

	1985	1984	1983
Interest revenue	$19.5	$18.2	$15.2
Less: interest expense	14.0	13.9	11.2
Provision for credit losses	1.3	.6	.5
Net	$ 4.2	$ 3.7	$ 3.5
Other revenues	3.0	2.3	1.8
	$ 7.2	$ 6.0	$ 5.3
Operating expenses	5.5	4.5	3.7
Income before income taxes	$ 1.7	$ 1.5	$ 1.6
Income taxes	.7	.6	.7
Net income	$ 1	$ .9	$ .9
Earnings per share:			
Common and equivalent	$7.12	$ 6.45	$6.48
Fully diluted	7.11	6.36	6.15

	1985	1984
ASSETS		
Cash, deposits with banks, and securities	$ 40	$ 28
Loans and lease financing, net	75	69
Premises and other assets	16	15
Total	$131	$112
LIABILITIES		
Deposits	$ 92	$ 78
Borrowings and other liabilities	29	26
Long-term debt	3	2
STOCKHOLDERS' EQUITY		
Capital stock	1	1
Additional paid-in capital	1	1
Retained earnings	5	4
Total	$131	$112

alone product is a profitable endeavor. By the 1990s, it may well become the core delivery mechanism when augmented by automatic teller machines and home banking. . . . We envision a world of 35 million Citicorp customers producing earnings of $30 per customer. . . . We had big plans for this group when it started and we can now see a time by which it will become a billion dollar business.

The 1980s also dictated a new philosophy that differed from traditional bank practice and from the media's bias for focusing on size as a measure of success. Commercial asset growth on the books of Citicorp was discouraged. In fact, management stretched its imagination to take assets off the firm's books, not to put them on. In 1983, more than $2 billion in loans generated in the United States by the Institutional Bank were sold to others by the Investment Bank. That number was expected to reach $20 billion by 1989. Wriston further explained:

> Our stockholders benefit, since we keep part of the spread while someone else keeps the assets (and the risk). But in order to make this a viable business, you must have both the asset generating capability and the distribution capability nationwide and worldwide.

The worldwide orientation was further encouraged as cross-border lending started to slow down. Citicorp predicted that individual countries would be forced to develop their own indigenous capital markets. Thus, there was an opportunity to develop a "multidomestic" strategy that would enable Citicorp to offer full financial services in 60 to 80 countries before 1990.

The Five "I"s

In the early 1980s, Citicorp added two more "I"s to the strategic thrust that had initially included development of the Investment Bank, the Individual Bank, and the Institutional Bank. The two embryonic "I"s were the Information and Insurance businesses. According to Wriston:

> We want to be in the information business simply because we are in the information business. Information about money has become almost as important as money itself. As bankers, we are familiar with the time value of money. As investors, we must think of the time value of information. The central core of any decision making process is information. The fact that you know something relevant before, or more clearly than your competitors may lead you to act sooner, to your advantage. Herein lies the problem, determining what is relevant. Hence, the packaging of information and its distribution will be critical. . . . We eventually intend to become a main competitor, as a preeminent distributor of financial data-base services worldwide. This is only possible with a truly global system, one through which information is distributed with electrons rather than the mail.[3]

The rationale for entering the insurance business was simple: insurance services accounted for fully 40 percent of all financial services in 1985. Citicorp would therefore not be a truly effective financial services enterprise without offering these products. Insurance was also a natural adjunct to the consumer business, considering the outmoded and expensive agency method of distribution that dominated the industry. Moreover, the firm was already a major factor in credit insurance. For example, one third of its second-mortgage customers bought credit life insurance.

The Banking Holding Company Act of 1956, and specifically Regulation Y, Section 4(c)-8 for the board of governors of the Federal Reserve System, prohibited banks from engaging in life insurance underwriting (with certain exceptions). Thus, the firm's insurance strategy was primarily aimed at an overseas expansion. This expansion was made possible by the Federal Reserve Board's ruling, requested by Citicorp, which enabled the firm to establish a fully competitive insurance operation in the United Kingdom. The board concluded:

> The general activity of underwriting life insurance in the United Kingdom can be considered usual in connection with banking or other financial operations in the United Kingdom.

This shift in the board's attitude enabled Citicorp to consider expansion into insurance, to identify the United Kingdom as a potential country in which to do so, and ultimately to pursue BNLA for acquisition.

Citicorp's goals for the five "I"s as of 1986 can be summarized as follows:

Institutional

- Trim work force from 20,000 to 17,000.
- Pull back from middle markets overseas.
- Push investment banking products more.
- Clean up loan portfolio and reduce write-offs.

Investment

- Build credible corporate finance group, especially in mergers and acquisitions.
- Hold on to investment banking talent.
- Wire ninety trading rooms around the globe.
- Improve coordination between London, Tokyo, and New York.

Individual

- Continue to grow fast in retail banking.
- Make all acquired S&Ls profitable.
- Push international consumer business.

Information

- Leave Quotron alone to calm customers.
- Develop new products.

Insurance

- Push for easing limits on banks.
- Grow overseas.
- Cross-sell more insurance products through customer base.[4]

The 1985 sector performance is displayed in Exhibit 3.

CITICORP'S STRUCTURE AND OBJECTIVES

The Investment Bank, the Institutional Bank, and the Individual Bank were each organized into a sector and headed by a sector executive. Activities related to insurance and information were under the auspices of group executives within the three sectors, until such time as they justified the creation of their own sectors.

Each of the three sectors was composed of several groups, divisions, and business families, headed by a group executive, with business managers reporting to him or her. The organization of the Individual Bank, which is of particular interest in this case, was somewhat different from the other Banks. As dictated in John S. Reed's (chairman of Citicorp since 1985) memorandum of March 9, 1976 (internally known as the "Memo from the Beach"), the business manager was responsible for the day-to-day operation, whereas a division executive's responsibility was strategic in nature.

This meant that a branch manager in, say Hong Kong, would report to an area manager, then a country manager, and a division manager. The policy committee to which the division manager reports includes the group executive, a vice chairman or sector executive, and then the chairman. In effect, the flat structure placed only three layers of management between the most junior branch manager and the Policy Committee (30 senior executives) of Citicorp.

In January 1986 Reed issued a set of guidelines developed by the Policy Committee, which included Citicorp's objectives for the next ten years (Exhibit 4) and its values (Exhibit 5). Exhibits 6a and b display the organizational structure of the Individual Bank and Consumer Services Group International.

The International Opportunity

In the 1985 Annual Report, the board stated:

> We recognize that, ultimately, our success will be directly attributable to our ability to offer our consumers worldwide preeminent service for each of their

EXHIBIT 3

**Sector Performance for Citicorp and Subsidiaries
(Dollar Amounts in Millions)**

	1985	1984	% CHANGE
INDIVIDUAL BANK			
Net revenue	$4,120	$3,107	33
Operating expenses	3,614	2,735	32
Other income and expense	102	(12)	n.a.
Income before taxes	608	360	69
Net income	$ 340	$ 222	53
ROA	.61%	.51%	
ROE	15.3 %	12.7 %	
INSTITUTIONAL BANK			
Net revenue	$2,168	$2,068	5
Operating expenses	1,500	1,275	18
Income before taxes	668	793	(16)
Net income	$ 392	$ 454	(14)
ROA	.54%	.64%	
ROE	13.6 %	15.9 %	
INVESTMENT BANK			
Net revenue	$1,589	$1,241	28
Operating expenses	803	587	37
Income before taxes	786	654	20
Net income	$ 425	$ 343	24
ROA	1.34%	1.33%	
ROE	33.5 %	33.2 %	
UNALLOCATED			
(Certain corporate-level items that are not allocated among sectors)			
Revenue	$ 28	$ (79)	n.a.
Operating expenses	148	116	28
Additional provision for credit losses	226	68	132
Income before taxes	(346)	(263)	(32)
Net income	(159)	(129)	(23)

EXHIBIT 4   ## Citicorp Objectives

Citicorp's objective is to continue to build the world's leading financial services organization by creating value for our stockholders, customers, staff members and the communities where we live and work. Creation of value is dependent on building an internal environment based on integrity, innovation, teamwork, and a commitment to unquestioned financial strength.

VALUE FOR THE SHAREHOLDER

- 12 percent to 18 percent compound growth in earnings per share;
- Improving return on equity to 17 percent to 18 percent (maintaining the internal hurdle at 20 percent);
- A strong balance sheet including a 10 percent capital position and a AA+ credit rating;
- Performance profile (earnings, market position, returns) improving within the top thirty companies in the world;
- Improving market position for our businesses, defined by explicit market share reporting;
- Well-diversified geographic and business earnings, assets, and liabilities.

VALUE FOR OUR CUSTOMER

Maintain and build our two customer sets, institutional and individual, through customer service excellence, professionalism, product innovation, and the energy of our response to customer needs. Regularly monitor progress through external and internal surveys.

VALUE FOR OUR STAFF

Maintain an open, challenging, rewarding, and healthy working environment characterized by excellence and fairness in dealing with our employees. Business unit management is responsible for maintaining this working environment, and will support and adhere to the People Management beliefs outlined in the attached statement. We will regularly monitor such support and adherence with specific, measurable, goals.

VALUE FOR THE COMMUNITIES IN WHICH WE OPERATE

Management of each business unit and/or geographic location is part of the community within which we operate and has an obligation:
- to contribute to community values;
- to participate in appropriate ways;
- to work to change the legal and regulatory environment to enhance our "opportunity space";
- to deal with our communities in an open, straightforward manner.

EXHIBIT 5

Citicorp: Excellence in People Management Is What We Believe

THE BASICS

While people management is a part of our business, there are certain nonnegotiable assumptions we make about how we will deal with the people who make up Citicorp. These basics must take precedence in everything we do.

- Respect for individuals
- Treating people with dignity, openness, honesty, and fairness

CITICORP VALUES

In addition to our other specific Citicorp values (Innovation, Integrity, and Service Excellence), we have a set of values related to people management. These are things we feel strongly about, and which are driven by the needs of our business.

- Meritocracy. Emphasizing excellence of performance, professionalism, and effectiveness as the determining factors for selection, retention, rewards, and advancement. Recognizing good performance wherever and whenever it occurs. Appropriately exiting consistent nonperformers.

- Independent Initiative. Promoting personal freedom to act and allowing people to succeed and to learn from failure.

- Listening. Creating an environment where we really hear what people say. Working together so that people throughout the organization have an impact.

- Development. Consciously building experience and talent of our people with the goal of professional growth. Creating a balance between developmental experiences and current contribution.

WORKING STYLE

Our working styles will vary in different business situations and environments. The following describe the ways in which we approach people management, each applied as appropriate to individual business conditions.

- Teamwork. Building effective business driven partnerships within the organization. Achieving a balance between cooperation and entrepreneurial spirit.

- Integration. Helping new people and new businesses to effectively and appropriately become part of the Citicorp culture.

relationships with us. Our view is that by pursuing service excellence across all of our efforts, we enhance our standing with our customers and thereby the likelihood that they will choose us for a growing share of their financial needs.[5]

Internationally, Citicorp expanded its presence in several markets during 1985 while maintaining returns well in excess of corporate standards. In that year, Citicorp completed significant acquisitions in Italy (Banca Centro Sud), Belgium (Banque Sud Belge), and Chile (Corporacion Financiera Atlas), as well as consumer businesses in Colombia, Guam, and India.

EXHIBIT 6a　　　　**Individual Bank**

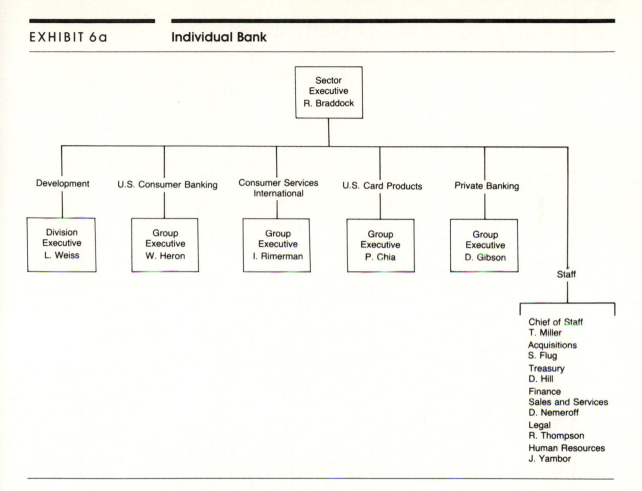

Richard S. Braddock, sector executive of the Individual Bank and director of Citicorp and Citibank, explained:

> We view our opportunities in the international marketplace as substantial, not only because our share tends to be relatively small in most places, but also because we have the opportunity to apply lessons learned from market to market and to expand attractive and proven product packages. . . .[6]

The Consumer Service Group, International (CSGI)

The Consumer Service Group, International, within the Individual Bank, was organized in separate divisions: the Asia–Pacific division had its headquarter in Tokyo; Europe–Middle East–Africa (EMEA) division, in London;

EXHIBIT 6b   Consumer Services Group—International

Group Executive
I Rimerman

- Credit — C Munoz
- Group Counsel — R Finch
- Financial Control — M Sladden
- Human Resources — J Liu

Asia/Pacific Division — A Weber
- Japan/Diners Asia — C Ludwigson
- Australia — M Cooper
- CCKK Japan — D Hardy
- Hong Kong — A Stevenson
- Japan Branches — P Chow
- South Asia — R Tahwar
- Korea — J Leung
- Asian Banking Center — A Tan
- Philippines/Guam — C Palomares
- India — J Rao
- Guam — F Asunio
- Indonesia — C Roberts
- Taiwan — T McKeon
- Malaysia — A Tan
- Singapore — D Smith
- Thailand — S Farkas

EMEA Division — P Bellows
- United Kingdom — R Selander
- France — J Roche
- Germany KKB/Austria Benelux — R Geesey
- Diners Club EMEA — W Finesell
- British National Life Insurance — P Cohen
- Greece/Turkey — D Winkler
- BSB Belgium — G Fievel
- Diners Bellux — P Haujain
- Citibank Savings — A Lee
- Samba — D Li
- Famibanque Belgium — E Bogaeris
- Diners France — Y Gaulier
- Italy — R Belliglio
- Netherlands — K Broek
- Diners Germany — P Walsh
- Span — R Angles
- Diners Greece — C Varvias
- Diners Netherlands — K DeSmet
- Diners UK — G Andrews

Diners Club International — TBA
- Marketing — E Gomez-Luengo
- Finance & Operations — R Thomas

Latin American/Canada Division — R Zeitel
- Brazil — R doValle
- Argentina — E Daniels
- Canada — H Greene
- Chile — T Sisson
- Caribbean Puerto Rico/Virgin Islands — H Luna
- Diners Mexico — E Lede
- Panama — R Cooney
- Northwest Region — A Zeller
- Upscale Business — T Mao
- Colombia — L Restrepo
- Ecuador — M Alhadeil

Payment Products Division — R Terxhorn
- International Sales — N Zaccagnino
- North America Sales — D Cox
- Distribution Services Operations — M Devine
- CTC Product Marketing — P Rogers
- CRS Product Marketing — R Stailings
- World Banknote/Treasury — A Hiller

International Systems — T Fine
- Software Systems — J Wachs
- Strategic Planning — L Heznick
- Banking Systems — R Walters
- Communications — TBA

the Western division, in Rio de Janeiro; Payment Products Division (Diners Club), in Chicago; and Systems Division, in New York. The group employed 26,000 people in 70 businesses, located in 40 countries.

John Liu, senior human resource officer, Consumer Services Group, International, summarized how Citicorp's culture was reflected by the group:

> We want to be part of the largest low-cost provider of financial service in the world. As such we don't focus only on banks such as Chase Manhattan. Rather, we look also at Sears, AMEX, and others who provide financial services. This is the stretch we hold in front of us.
>
> In order to help achieve this, we have to find new ways of doing things. Taking insurance as an example, Citicorp practices its decentralized operational mode, sometimes referred to as the "thousand flowers" approach.
>
> In insurance, to use a metaphor, we want to have a thousand flowers bloom. Over time, we'll put the flowers together in a bouquet, and if we don't like the shape of it, we'll take this or that flower away. However, today we just started our picking and that is why you'll find insurance activities in the Institutional Bank (commercial insurance), the Investment Bank (brokerage insurance activities), and with us in the Individual Bank (life underwriting, mortgage insurance). It's all emerging slowly out of our philosophy, and the BNLA acquisition is the first major life underwriting acquisition we have ever had.
>
> As part of this stretch, the corporation applies certain hurdle rates to guide this vision. We have a stated hurdle rate, internally, such as a ROE of no less than 20 percent. Additionally, we also have a ROA hurdle rate of 90 basis points. In our group, we use our own internal hurdle rate as a way of managing our businesses. One such hurdle rate which comes to mind is to target a ratio of 1.5 between consumer net revenue and delivery expenses.
>
> Within the Group, we want to more than double our earnings over the next five years. We want to do this partly through acquisitions, of which we must have done at least ten over the past three years and added more than 6,000 people. Although we still will make acquisitions, we clearly must slow down and develop these new businesses.
>
> The acquisitions have not been hostile and for the most part have been either "hospitalized" or unprofitable businesses. This has given us certain advantages, but also created challenges when it comes to integrating a new business into our organization.[7]

The unique culture and reward system of CSGI is reflected in Exhibit 7, which summarizes the results of an organizational survey of its senior managers.

The Search for an Acquisition

Liu further explained how the BNLA acquisition came about:

> About three years ago, we started a drive to get into insurance and encouraged our people in the United Kingdom, Australia, Germany, and Belgium to start to look into insurance. As you know, there are three ways you can get into a

EXHIBIT 7

Summary of Organizational Surveys Conducted by the Case Writers

		Low degree/ extent					High degree/ extent	
		1	2	3	4	5	6	7
1.	Loyalty							
2.	Promotion from within							
3.	Extent managers are free to take independent actions							
4.	Degree to which goals are venturesome							
5.	Degree of accountability for individual managers							
6.	Encouragement of risk taking							
7.	Goals used as context							
8.	Lateral communications							
9.	Clear measures to judge managerial performance							
10.	Organization successful in developing talent from within							
11.	Extent to which conflicts are discussed openly							
12.	Encouragement to innovate							
13.	Clarity of goals							
14.	Overall communication							
15.	Opportunities for individual growth and development							
16a.	Formality of planning							
16b.	Completeness of planning							
17.	Clarity of organizational roles							
18.	Performance demands							
19.	Departmental understanding of goals							
20a.	Innovativeness in decision making							
20b.	Timeliness in decision making							
21.	Fit between compensation and performance							
22.	Encouragement of constructive criticism							
23.	Downward communication							
24.	Support received to carry out job responsibilities							
25.	Clear expectations							
26.	Degree of cooperation							
27.	Degree of coordination							
28.	Extent of clear plans							

CITICORP* – – – –   BNLA* ———

* Questionnaires were completed by managers and outside observers. Items of the questionnaire are summarized and labeled because of proprietary reasons; values indicate average scores.

EXHIBIT 7   **Continued**

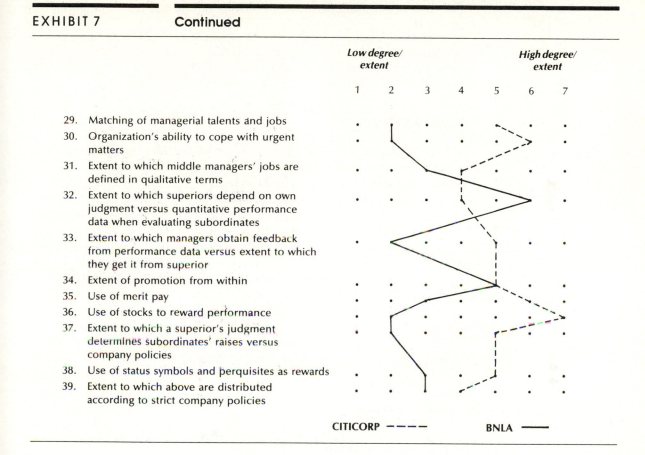

29. Matching of managerial talents and jobs
30. Organization's ability to cope with urgent matters
31. Extent to which middle managers' jobs are defined in qualitative terms
32. Extent to which superiors depend on own judgment versus quantitative performance data when evaluating subordinates
33. Extent to which managers obtain feedback from performance data versus extent to which they get it from superior
34. Extent of promotion from within
35. Use of merit pay
36. Use of stocks to reward performance
37. Extent to which a superior's judgment determines subordinates' raises versus company policies
38. Use of status symbols and perquisites as rewards
39. Extent to which above are distributed according to strict company policies

CITICORP – – – –   BNLA ———

new business: You can a) acquire, b) start a de novo unit, or c) do a joint venture.

In England, which was one of the largest and most profitable markets (relatively) for life insurance, we initially identified Excelsior Life Assurance as a possibility in early 1984.[8] As an insurance company of substantial size in the United Kingdom, the acquisition would immediately bring us into this market on a large scale. However, the more we analyzed the numbers, the more concerned we got. This was a significant investment, and we had little knowledge about life insurance. So when our joint-venture partner (a large U.S. insurance company) withdrew, we reconsidered our options.

Then Citicorp's U.K. Country Manager and the European Division Manager of the United Kingdom sponsored (identified) BNLA as a potential candidate for our move into life underwriting insurance. After the identification of the candidate, an acquisition team was put together. The team consisted of people from across our United Kingdom businesses as well as outside consultants and were all selected for their specific skills as they related to this opportunity.

One of the important issues for us is now to decide how to integrate the business—should we fully integrate, keep it at an arm's-length distance, or somewhere in between, and how should we do it. With this decision also comes the question of what type of person to put into the driver's seat.

The United Kingdom

The U.K. economy is the sixth largest in the world and is in transition, as is the U.S. economy, from an industrial to a service orientation. By 1985, the United Kingdom had the lowest level of legal and regulatory control for domestic and international financial activity of any developed country. However, U.K. regulation of life insurance underwriting, particularly with regard to reserves, was among the most stringent in the world. The government was considered politically stable, and the conservatives in power were committed to controlling inflation and government spending to provide a platform for economc growth. Even though 12 percent of the work force was unemployed, there was little social unrest.

The United Kingdom was expected to remain self-sufficient in oil for the remainder of the century. Inflation was expected to be controlled in the 5 percent to 7 percent range, and there were expected to be no major changes in either the political system or the regulatory environment. Expected growth figures for the U.K. GNP for 1986 and 1987 were 1.5 percent and 2.6 percent, respectively. Inflation was expected to be around 5.0 percent for the same two periods.

The U.K. Life Assurance Market

The U.K. life assurance market was considered large and growing. Growth in new premiums went from $1.9 British National (BN) in 1980 to $4.7 BN in 1983. During the same period, average growth of premium income rose from $7.8 BN to $13.2 BN, and total sums insured grew an average of 17 percent to $295 BN. There were 289 licensed underwriters in the United Kingdom. The relative size of the top twelve comanies is presented in Exhibit 8.

Analyses showed that life assurance in the United Kingdom was seen as both a protection instrument and a consumer investment. The policies accumulated cash value and also yielded dividends to policyholders. There were basically three types of underwriters in the marketplace: industrial, orthodox, and linked life.

The industrial companies offered small-value policies that were targeted at the lower socioeconomic groups. The premiums were collected in person usually monthly, by employed agents, who did little actual selling. The pol-

EXHIBIT 8   **Major Players in the Life Market—Premium Income**

	CLASSIFICATION	RANKING	VALUE ($ MILLION)	% OF TOTAL	% INCREASE ON 82/81	% INCREASE ON 81/80	SIZE OF LIFE FUND (END 82) $BN
Prudential	Stock	1	1656	13	12	16	9.4
Legal and General	Stock	2	775	6	15	10	6.6
Standard Life	Mutual	3	630	5	13	20	6.3
Norwich Union	Mutual	4	565	4	19	13	3.8
Hambro Life	Stock	5	464	4	20	32	2.1
Commercial Union	Stock	6	444	4	12	15	3.8
Eagle Star	Stock/Sub	7	414	3	21	28	2.2
Abbey Life	Stock/Sub	8	353	3	8	63	1.4
Sun Life	Stock	9	328	3	2	25	2.1
Scottish Amicable	Mutual	10	319	3	24	38	2.5
G.R.E.	Stock	11	318	3	14	27	2.8
Pearl	Stock	12	311	2	8	10	1.9
Subtotal			6577	53	13	21	44.9 (56%)
Others	13/48		4924	40	15	21	
Balance			823	7	5	15	36.1 (44%)
			12324	100	15	21	81.0

Note: $1.20 = £1.

icies carried high administrative overheads and were, therefore, relatively poor values for the consumer. This sector of the market was dominated by Prudential, which wrote 65 percent of the new policies issued each year. This type of insurance had a vast customer base, with over 70 million policies in existence. At the same time, this type of policy had a declining market share, and smaller companies were retrenching because of overhead efficiencies.

The orthodox life companies offered larger-value policies that catered to the more affluent customer. This type of policy was distributed through independent professionals who usually had some other relationship with the customer. These independent agents could be insurance brokers, solicitors (attorneys), accountants, banks, or estate agents. It was fairly common in the United Kingdom for all of these groups to offer insurance as a part of their service portfolio to their clients. These independent agents typically offered policies from three to six different underwriters. The firms that offered orthodox policies had traditionally not marketed them to their consumer base for fear of offending the professional intermediary. There were different classes of agents who covered specific market segments.

The linked life policy was relatively new and was introduced in the 1960s as an alternative to the orthodox life policy. It targeted the same consumer as the orthodox policy, but was sold normally by a commission-paid, self-employed sales force, much like insurance representatives in the United States. Policyholders of linked life insurance did not participate in the profits of the underwriter through dividends, but their investments were placed in several funds (similar to mutual funds) managed by the underwriter. Thus, the linked life policyholder took investment risk/return, and the underwriter provided a death guarantee. The range of products offered by the three types of underwriters is depicted in Exhibit 9.

Trends in the U.K. market indicated that the role of single premium life assurance was expanding. This type of policy was one in which a single

EXHIBIT 9   **Product Range**

	NONPROFIT/ PARTICIPATING	RELATIVE IMPORTANCE (LOW/HIGH)	INDUSTRIAL	TRADITIONAL	LINKED
PROTECTION					
Whole life	NP	L	−	√	−
	P	L	√	√	√
Term	NP	H	√	√	√
Permanent health	NP	M	−	√	−
SAVINGS					
Endowment	NP	L	−	√	−
	P	H	√	√	√
Pensions	NP	L	−	√	−
	P	H	√	√	√
Annuities	NP	M	−	√	√
Single premium bonds	P	H	−	√	√
GROUP SCHEMES					
Pension (Can include term and PH insurance)	N/A	H	−	√	√

payment was made to the underwriter at the beginning of the policy life, and no further premiums were due. Before the creation of the single premium policy, most life policy premiums were paid yearly over the life of the policy. Logically, there was no single premium industrial underwriting, given the socioeconomic status of most policyholders. The target for the single premium policies was the banked homeowner, a person who had a relationship with a bank and owned his or her home.

In addition to the expansion of the single premium policy, there had been a decline in share of the industrial policy from 13 percent of total insurance in 1980 to 6 percent in 1983. The growth sectors of the market were linked life and personal pensions (which were similar to the Individual Retirement Account in the United States).

Premium income had generally become increasingly volatile because single premium income had grown from 12 percent of total premium income in 1980 to 22 percent in 1983. Since 1968, the growth segments for premium income were linked life, personal pensions, and mortgage endowment. In 1983, the government introduced Mortgage Interest Relief at Source (MIRAS), which caused mortgage repayments on insurance-linked mortgages to appear more competitive than conventional mortgages, thus causing an increase in the mortgage endowment business. In March 1984, the British government abolished Life Assurance Premium Relief (LAPR).

In their attempt to expand their share of the market, traditional companies had begun moving into the linked life segment. Major growth was expected in pension-related policies as the most efficient (from a tax perspective) savings medium. Allied Dunbar and Guardian Royal Exchange exemplified a movement to "full financial services."

For the future, the desire of the government to increase the portability of pensions could open a major new market. At this time, personal pensions were sold only by life assurance companies (by law). The removal of this restriction was under consideration and would bring new banks into the market. There was some concern that the government policy of fiscal neutrality between savings mediums could cause further amendment to tax laws, but this was not expected in the short term.

In the future marketplace, it would be possible for banks to exploit their customer bases and sell insurance instead of being passive providers. Building Societies (very similar to U.S. savings and loan institutions, and responsible for writing most home mortgages in the United Kingdom) did not currently have legislative permission to function as insurance brokers as did the banks. It was expected that the Societies would request that power in 1986–1987, which would bring more new players to the market. There would be an increase in the pensions business to reach the large self-employed group in the United Kingdom. Exhibit 10 offers a view of the current and future importance of key segments in the U.K. market.

In summary, the U.K. life underwriting market was the seventh largest in the world and was growing. Life assurance in the United Kingdom filled a

EXHIBIT 10   Intermediaries' View of Key Market Segments

	CURRENTLY IMPORTANT	LIKELY TO INCREASE IN IMPORTANCE
Self-employed	90%	65%
People with medium incomes	82	46
Owners/directors of small companies	80	57
People with high incomes	79	53
Young couples	78	57
Middle-aged couples	72	43
Women	68	51
People with free capital	66	39
Retired couples	46	38

dual role for the consumer—protection and savings/investment. The market was led by large and well-established players, but there were major market opportunities for other well-managed companies. The market was differentiated by distribution methods, and the long-term profit stream generated by most firms led to high investor confidence and high share prices. U.K. premium income in 1982 totaled $28 billion, of which $12 billion was in life assurance underwriting. The market was predominantly U.K. owned, as were the major players, though a company did not necessarily need to be a general insurance firm to compete successfully in either market. Each market involved different legislative bases, different distribution channels, and different skills. U.K. firms were significant in world markets, particularly nonlife, where they received over 50 percent of the premium income.

The U.K. Financial Services Market

There were five major categories of financial services in the United Kingdom: transaction accounts, savings, shelter (home) financing, lending, and protection. Exhibit 11 is a chart of the major players and other entrants in these markets. The total savings market had grown from $124 billion in 1980 to $193.6 billion in 1983. The relative share figures for the major institutions in the savings market are shown in Exhibit 12. Shelter finance had grown from $62.8 billion to $108.8 billion in the same period. A synopsis of the growth and change in the unsecured loan market is shown in Exhibit 13.

Banks were leading the expansion into the related areas of mortgage financing, estate agency (trust), stockbrokerage, and life assurance underwriting. Building societies now offered checkbook access to savings and

EXHIBIT 11

Elements of the Market

	MAJOR PLAYERS	OTHER ENTRANTS
Transaction accounts	Clearing banks	—
Savings	Building societies Life assurance companies	Banks
Shelter finance	Building societies	Banks Finance houses
Lending	Banks	Finance houses In-store credit
Protection	Life assurance companies General insurance companies	—

ATM networks. Legislation intended to equalize competitive roles in the market had been passed. Technological advancements were expected at this point but were not yet in place. The market would continue to change rapidly due to continuing deregulation and increasing technological sophistication. Traditional barriers were falling, and banks were leading the way into other sectors of the economy to satisfy consumer demand. Insurance was an integral part of the market and was supported by past and present government and fiscal policy.

EXHIBIT 12

Market Movements in Savings—50 Percent of Deposits with Insurance Companies

	1980	1983
Insurance funds	45%	50%
Building societies	28	28
Banks	13	7½
National savings	7	7
Shares, etc.	7	7½
Total market	$124 B	$193.6 B

Compound growth 16 percent per annum (RPI 8.3 percent compound).
Insurance funds ($97 million at end 1983) are not accessible.
$1.20 = £1 for all years.

EXHIBIT 13

Market Movements in Unsecured Loans—Not Participating as a Principal, but Providing Cover to Repay

	1980	1983
Finance houses	34%	29%
Bank loans	29	37
Bank credit cards	18	21
In-store cards	11	9
Other	8	4
Total market	$7.1 BN	$13.2 BN

Compound growth 23 percent.
An estimated 30 percent of bank and finance house loans are covered by life/disability insurance to cover repayments.
New developments from 1982 on larger loans give bullet repayments covered by endowment insurance.
Statistics exclude "loan backs" from long-term savings under an insurance policy.

Citicorp in the United Kingdom

The Consumer Services Group (U.K.) was dominated by Citibank Savings, a mature business operating in four specific markets

Finance House:	Indirect financing for autos and home improvement
Mortgage Banking:	Consumer mortgages through association with Insurance firm partners
Retail Cards:	Private label card operation for London's High Street retailers, as well as the European Banking Centre, Traveler's Checks, and Diners Club
Consumer Banking:	Cross-selling a portfolio of products to consumers, such as personal loans, checking (transaction) accounts, mortgages, and insurance

Citibank Savings had 39 branches in the United Kingdom, 19 of which were recognized as direct branches within the consumer bank.

U.K. Life Assurance Consumers

U.K. life assurance consumers were underinsured relative to those of other developed nations. The total life coverage as a percentage of yearly average wage as compared for seven industrialized nations was

U.K.	88 percent
France	147 percent
Sweden	148 percent
Australia	178 percent
United States	183 percent
Canada	184 percent
Japan	325 percent

The product was seen by U.K. consumers as intangible and offering no present benefit. The contracts were viewed as a mass of small print and were inflexible once purchased. The purchase pattern was characterized as infrequent and having a high unit cost, and the consumer had a low knowledge base about the product. The benefits perceived were peace of mind, a response to issues of social responsibility, and investment-tax avoidance. Seventy-four percent of U.K. households had life coverage, which included 45 percent of all adults (predominantly men). A chart of U.K. consumer behavior regarding purchase by product type is presented as Exhibit 14. The major reasons for purchase were protection and house purchase. In general, no major alternatives were considered, and the decision to buy insurance coverage was a joint one in the family. The amount of coverage was generally based on affordability rather than need, and shopping among companies was minimal. Exhibit 15 characterizes the major segments of the market; required company attributes from the consumers' view are shown in Exhibit 16.

The life assurance market was not as mature as its size might indicate. Most consumers were underinsured, and over half the adult population had no coverage at all. There was a key role to be played for protection products (distinct from investment products). Linked life companies concentrated on investment policies, and the benefits to the policyholder were neither fixed

---

EXHIBIT 14   **U.K. Consumer Behavior**

KEY PRODUCT GROUPS	HOLDING	RECENT PURCHASE*	FUTURE PURCHASE†
Endowment mortgage	9%	17%	9%
Mortgage protection	16	24	16
Protection cover	35	42	19
Endowment cover	42	63	39
Total (including multipurchase)	74%	100%	57%

*Purchased in the last 12 months
†Expected purchase in the next 12 months

EXHIBIT 15   **Consumer Types**

	MEDIUM	PURCHASE	TIMING	KNOWLEDGE	MIND SET
Thinking young couple	Broker direct to company	Buys	Regular	Sophisticated	Protection
Young family man	Agent salesman	Sold	Spasmodic	Low—trusting	Protection/savings
Middle-aged man	Any	Sold	Spasmodic	Low—wants known company	Protection/savings
Self-employed	Salesman Broker	Sold	Spasmodic	Learns quickly Decision maker	Savings
Late arrivals	Direct (coupon response)	Indirectly sold	Once	Low	Protection (burial policy)

nor guaranteed by the company but were invested in a separate range of funds (at the risk/return of the consumer). In this sense, linked life firms worked very much like mutual fund companies in the United States. Their sources of income were profits from insurance underwriting, a 5 percent bid/offer differential on investments in the funds, and a ¾ percent fund management fee. The products were sold through a direct sales force, which was normally paid only by commission.

In the U.K. market, 15 percent of adults had a linked life policy (33 percent of adults with life assurance coverage). The policies were most popular in the under-55 age range, and in London and the southeast of England.

EXHIBIT 16   **Required Company Attributes—What to Look For in a Company (Excluding Industrial)**

	SPONTANEOUS	PROMPTED
Well-known	33%	60%
Good reputation	27	51
Good investment performance	23	30
Good salespeople	15	56
Long established	8	43

The History of British National Life Assurance

British National Life Assurance was a spinoff company from the British National Insurance Society. It was created in 1982 by Sir William Baltimore as a subsidiary of EXCO Corporation (a large U.S. company) when EXCO Corporation had decided to diversify into financial services. British National Insurance remained a property and casualty life underwriter, and BNLA became the life underwriting business of EXCO Corporation. The managing director of the new firm was Ernest Smith, a true English gentleman and skilled manager. The sales director was Frank Jones, a charismatic and skilled salesman with considerable experience in the insurance business.[9]

EXCO Corporation took very little interest in the performance of BNLA and allowed Smith and Jones to manage the company as they saw fit. In essence, Jones controlled sales and marketing, and Smith controlled public relations and administration.

In the interim, Sir William Baltimore retired from EXCO Corporation. He subsequently became director of insurance development (on a consulting basis) for Citicorp's Consumer Services Group International EMEA Division, headquartered in London.

The consumers' view of the Citicorp/BNLA merger was that it offered wider financial services as a result, and a bank-owned insurance company was seen positively. Negative reaction to the fact that it was American-owned could be foreseen.

In January 1986, BNLA employed 392 people, 101 at its headquarters and 250 comprising the sales force from 22 branches. Each branch had a branch manager and an administrative assistant. An organizational chart and staff analysis are provided in Exhibits 17 and 18.

There were 47,600 policyholders and $305 million in life insurance in force. However, BNLA policy lapses and salesperson turnover were twice the industry average. The commission-only sales force was the major distribution method for BNLA products, and its productivity was some 75 percent below average. The sales force was inappropriately trained, and the commission structure resulted in low pay relative to the competition.

BNLA spent considerable sums of money training a sales force that was paid poorly relative to industry averages. Jones subscribed to the philosophy that a high-quality product would essentially sell itself, and that, therefore, high commissions were unnecessary. His view was that sales goals would be achieved, in the long run, as a result of high training levels and high-quality products. This became known in the organization as "Frank's Philosophy." This philosophy also constrained promotional activities to direct selling only. The marketing department was therefore mostly engaged in arranging flashy conventions and gimmicks for the sales force.

Communication between top management and the organization was generally considered poor or nonexistent. Bad news, such as the lack of profits, the low sales force performance, and information about the negative cash

EXHIBIT 17

BNLA Organization Chart

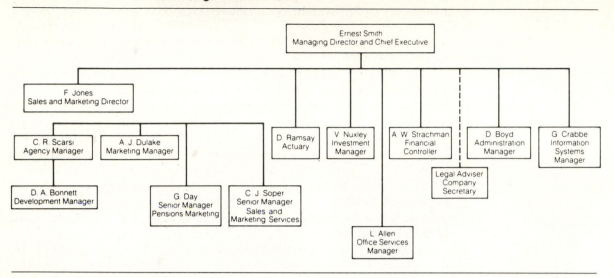

EXHIBIT 18

British National Life Staff Analysis

DEPARTMENT	JAN. 86
Actuarial	5
Administration ⎫	21
⎬ Operations	
Office services ⎭	10
Data processing	21
Finance	16
Investment	3
Personnel and training	—
Legal	1
Marketing	13
Sales	9
Credit insurance (from Nov. 86)	—
Managing director	2
Branch managers	22
Branch administrators	19
Subtotal	142
Salaried sales force	n.a.
Total	142
Sales associates	250

flows, was never passed along to the management team. Although annual budgets were compiled, their content was never shared with departments. Conversely, no formal system existed for monthly reporting on departmental activities.

Smith believed that financial reporting should be kept to a minimum, although all required disclosures were always filed on time. The financial officer had a small minicomputer at his disposal. Moreover, the firm had taken steps to automate the office environment at its headquarters by establishing a word-processing pool.

Toward the end of 1984, EXCO Corporation decided that it was not going to make a go of BNLA (or of financial services generally) and put the company up for sale. The company knew that it was on the block, and employee morale took a nosedive. This increased the sense of being rudderless in the company, as performance became even less an issue and "Frank's Philosophy" became the guiding force in the firm. A culture-reward system profile of BNLA is shown in Exhibit 7.

BNLA Product/Market Posture

At the time of the Citicorp acquisition, BNLA was a linked life firm that offered six basic products to the market:

1. Plan-for-Life: A highly flexible policy offered the consumer control over the content of his or her plan. The consumer decided what proportion of the premium to devote to savings or protection, and this could be changed as needs and circumstances warranted.

2. Plan-for-Capital: a regular savings plan with high investment content and minimum life coverage. It was ideal for someone who wanted to save dynamically for eight to ten years. The proceeds were free from basic rate income tax (the off-the-top rate in the United Kingdom), from personal capital gains tax, and, after ten years, from higher rate tax as well. This product was quite similar to the Individual Retirement Account (IRA) in its tax treatment. It differed in its small insurance cover.

3. Plan-for-Investment: a lump-sum plan to invest in the company's different funds. The capital invested was allocated a set number of units, depending on the current value of the fund. At any time, the plan had a value equivalent to the bid (sell) value of the price of units multiplied by the number of units held. This fund was similar to the mutual funds offered through brokerage houses in the United States except there were certain tax advantages not offered in U.S. mutual funds.

4. Plan-for-Retirement: a retirement annuity policy that was suitable for the self-employed and those who had no private pension scheme—unit-linked, but had outstanding tax advantages. This plan was similar to the Keogh plans in the United States, but was free of investment limits.

5. Plan-for-Executive: an individual pension plan suitable for senior members of a trading company (brokerage house) who wished to add to their retirement benefits. This was a very specialized policy and was, once again, similar to the IRA, except that both the executive and his or her employer could contribute.

6. Plan-for-Pension Preservation: a specialized plan conformed to legislation passed in 1970 that allowed the transfer of vested pension funds from a previous employer into this plan without tax penalties.

In addition to these plans, a brokerage house provided access to general insurance such as motor, house contents (homeowners), and building insurance (U.K. insurance companies are not permitted to act as insurance brokers). The BNLA product line was generally complete and well rounded and fulfilled the all-around needs of the consumer, from protection and investment to retirement planning.

BNLA—A Financial Perspective

Accounting standards in the United States required earnings on a life insurance policy to be recognized evenly over the years of premium payments. U.K. life insurance regulations, in contrast, required maintenance of prudent reserves that resulted in a new life assurance company's generating losses or very low profits during its early years. The function of the regulations was to severely restrict dividend payments and thereby protect policyholders. U.S. accounting was significantly less conservative; when the balance sheet of a U.K. life firm was recast to comply with U.S. accounting, the reported equity generally increased considerably.

Citicorp's customary financial goals and targets were designed for traditional banking businesses and did not lend themselves to evaluating an investment in a life insurance company. For that reason, Citicorp measured BNLA performance against a hurdle rate of 20 percent ROE on BNLA's recorded equity. Based on Citicorp's projections at the time of the acquisition, BNLA was expected to produce negative ROEs in 1985 and 1986 (see Exhibit 19) and to achieve the 20 percent hurdle rate for the first time in 1991. To comply with U.S. accounting, BNLA's recorded equity at the time of the acquisition was adjusted as follows (in millions; please note that all BNLA financial data have been changed for proprietary reasons).

Book values of assets	$77.1
Book amount of liabilities	66.9
Book value of equity	$10.2
Adjustments to comply with U.S. accounting:	
Write-downs of assets	−3.5
	$6.7

Reduction of reserves	+6.5	
Adjusted equity	$13.2	
Portion acquired	100%	
Purchased equity	$13.2	
Purchase price	13.7	$13.7
Goodwill	$0.5	
Additional capital infusion		19.6
Total investment[10]		$33.3

Exhibit 19 presents summary financial data on BNLA, including forecasts. For 1985, production of new life policies was 40 percent below forecast. Operating expenses were 50 percent higher than forecast and about 50 percent higher than the industry norms for a firm at this stage of development. This is fairly consistent with expense levels of previous years.

The Acquisition

During the time when Citicorp U.K. was actively seeking an insurance company to acquire, Bob Selander was the new country manager of Citicorp's U.K. business. The acquisition of an insurance company was a part of the strategic plan he inherited from his predecessor. Sir William Baltimore had previously developed a list of potential acquisitions for consideration.

The first possibility that came to light was Excelsior Life Assurance—one of the largest life assurance firms in the United Kingdom. Sir William Baltimore had been a director of Excelsior Life Assurance and knew its inner workings very well. Upon his recommendations and with the joint-venture participation of another life assurance firm, an acquisition plan was put together. Late in the process, the joint-venture partner withdrew from the deal, and Citicorp decided that Excelsior Life Assurance was too large to acquire alone. The search was reopened.

After considering several moderately sized firms, it was decided that the goodwill portion of the purchase price for a moderately sized firm would never allow such an acquisition to make Citicorp's internal hurdle rates. The search was moved to smaller firms. From a list of twelve life assurance firms, BNLA emerged as the most desirable candidate. Exhibits 20 and 21 discuss Citicorp's rationale for the acquisition. Not only was BNLA of a size that permitted the acquisition to be managed, but there was fairly little to be paid for the goodwill of the company. In short, the price was right, and the potential was there. Negotiations with EXCO Corporation and with Ernest Smith continued for some time, and finally the purchase price was agreed upon. Citicorp had its U.K. life assurance company.

In this case, the task of the students is to assume the role of Mr. Rimerman's staff and analyze and develop suggestions for a business strategy for BNLA, including key policies, tactics, and organizational changes.

EXHIBIT 19

BNLA Operating Forecast, Including Required Synergies, Restated According to U. S. Accounting Principles (Dollar Amounts in Millions)

	1985	1986	1987	1988	1989
Premiums, net	$ 19.9	$ 47.0	$74.5	$109.9	$153.1
Reinsurance	0	2.7	8.5	12.5	15.0
Investment income	3.2	8.4	12.9	19.8	30.4
Total revenues	$ 23.1	$ 58.1	$95.9	$142.2	$198.5
Benefits paid	$ 3.1	$ 4.2	$ 7.2	$ 13.3	$ 34.1
Increase in reserves	12.0	40.5	66.4	96.4	119.3
Commissions	2.9	6.7	11.6	17.2	23.4
Operating expenses	5.5	7.8	7.4	9.1	12.5
Total expenses	$ 23.5	$ 59.2	$92.6	$136.0	$189.3
Income before taxes*	$ (0.4)	$ (1.1)	$ 3.3	$ 6.2	$ 9.2
Income taxes	$ (0.4)	$ (1.1)	$ 2.5	$ 3.4	$ 4.9
Net income	0	0	0.8	2.8	4.3
ROE:					
On BNLA equity	(7%)	(5%)	7%	9%	12%
By Citicorp formulas	(30%)	(40%)	6%	11%	16%

BNLA Forecast Balance Sheets, Including Required Synergies, Restated According to U.S. Accounting Principles (Dollar Amounts in Millions, as of December 31 of Each Year)

	1985	1986	1987	1988	1989
Securities	$91	$126	$177	$257	$363
Reinsurance receivable	0	1	7	13	15
Other assets	4	8	21	38	59
Total assets	$95	$135	$205	$308	$436
Insurance reserves	$62	$103	$169	$266	$385
Other liabilities	1	1	3	6	10
Common stock	32	32	32	32	32
Retained earnings	0	(1)	1	4	10
Total	$95	$137	$205	$308	$437

BNLA Historical Balance Sheets According to U.K. Accounting Principles (Dollar Amounts in Millions, as of December 31 of Each Year; All Balances Restated at an Exchange Rate of 1 Pound Sterling = $1.4)

	1984	1983
Securities	$56	$38
Other assets	4	1
Total assets	$60	$39

EXHIBIT 19

Continued

	1984	1983
Insurance reserves	$56	$31
Other liabilities	1	5
Capital	3	3
Total	$60	$39

BNLA Historical Income Statements, According to U.K. Accounting Principles (Dollar Amounts in Millions; All Balances Restated at an Exchange Rate of 1 Pound Sterling = $1.4)

	1984	1983
Premiums, net	$ 31	$ 5
Investment income	4	3
Total revenues	$ 35	$ 8
Benefits paid	$ 3	$ 3
Increase in reserves	25	7
Commissions	1	1
Operating expenses	9	1
Total expenses	$ 38	$ 12
Income before taxes	($3)	($4)
Income taxes	0	0
Net income	($3)	($4)

SOURCE: Citicorp MEP; the data have been altered for proprietary reasons

Note: Caution should be exercised in comparing BNLA financial data with that of Citicorp, or even with that of other U.K. life assurance companies. This is because, first, there were some significant differences between traditional banking businesses and a U.K. life insurance operation, especially in rules governing the accounting recognition of earnings and in U.K. tax and regulatory requirements. Second, these differences were exaggerated in the case of a relatively new, rapidly growing U.K. life assurance company, where the reported amount of equity may have been as large as 60 percent of reported assets because of the conservatism inherent in regulatory requirements. Third, it was also difficult to make meaningful financial comparisons among different U.K. life companies. An immature firm had a financial picture bearing little resemblance to that of an older, established competitor, which may have reported equity as low as 2 percent of total assets.

*Reconciled with BNLA's stand-alone forecast, under U.K. accounting principles, as follows:

U.K. pretax income, without synergies	$(0.7)	$(3.9)	$(2.4)	$(0.6)	$ 1.5
Adjustment for U.S. accounting rules		(0.1)	(0.1)	(0.1)	(0.1)
Impact of synergies		1.1	4.0	4.9	5.6
Impact of capital infusion	0.3	1.8	1.8	2.0	2.2
Income before taxes, as reported above	$(0.4)	$(1.1)	$ 3.3	$ 6.2	$ 9.2

EXHIBIT 20

Memorandum

Memorandum

TO: Group Executive

FROM: Divisional Executive

RE: U.K. Insurance Acquisition MEP

DATE: 14th August 1985

As you know, in 1981 Citibank submitted an application to the Fed seeking permission to expand its line of insurance activities in the United Kingdom to write whole life in addition to its traditional base of credit life. This action was felt appropriate given that in the United Kingdom expanded insurance activities are considered a normal part of the banking sector with most large U.K. banks engaged in such activities through wholly owned insurance subsidiaries. Therefore for Citibank to enjoy equal footing with the competition, approval would be necessary since these activities are not otherwise permitted under Citibank's U.S. charter.

Upon receiving permission from the Fed in early '84 we were then confronted with the business decision of how best to tackle this new opportunity. A team from within Citibank Savings was formed to evaluate the market place and make a recommendation on how to proceed. In this effort they were assisted by a senior insurance consultant from the United Kingdom who had a prior relationship with Citibank. A broad range of companies were evaluated as possible acquisition candidates and several points became clear. A direct sales force (versus mass solicitation) was considered key as well as the company's ownership structure (i.e., if publicly owned how could a takeover be effected).

Considerations of size became important because additional Fed approval would be required for any takeover. A unique opportunity confronted us to acquire a major U.K. insurer, PQ Life Assurance, but the cost of such an acquisition was put at a figure several hundred million dollars higher than the desired size of investment. This acquisition, which would have been a joint venture, was approved internally at Citibank but closure with our proposed partners failed.

We then shifted our thinking back to internal de novo growth and in so doing have reevaluated several smaller acquisition candidates which had surfaced previously. Acquiring a smaller company may be regarded as accelerated de novo and we are actively pursuing the acquisition of British National Life Assurance Company at a cost of $13.7MM (goodwill of $0.5MM) with a further capital increase of $19.6MM bringing the total investment to $33.3MM. If we were to pursue the internal de novo growth route we would also require additional capital of about $19.6MM as our current capitalization of $3MM supports the credit life business only. These capital levels are prescribed by the U.K. insurance regulatory bodies in order to meet minimum solvency margins.

The following analysis compares forecasted earnings through acquisition versus internal growth. On a cumulative basis through 1990 the acquisition route produces over $17MM in incremental earnings.

EXHIBIT 20   **Continued**

It is important to note that there is a lag in profitability in an emerging life assurance business due to the slow buildup of premium income (net of commissions), which in the earlier years is not sufficient to cover the fixed costs of the distribution system. The difference in profitability between the two alternatives below is simply a reflection of this curve and that once a steady state is achieved both propositions would yield the same results.

PCE $MM	DE NOVO	ACQUISITION	B/(W)
1985	$ (0.5)	$(1.3)	$ (0.6)
1986	(1.3)	(2.9)	(1.6)
1987	(3.6)	0.4	4.0
1988	(3.5)	1.3	4.8
1989	(2.5)	2.5	5.0
1990	(1.3)	4.9	6.2
	(12.7)	4.9	17.8

This MEP assumes no tax credit against the operating losses in 1985 and 1986. In 1987, the first full year of profitability, the loss carryforward is absorbed. In any event no current U.K. taxes will likely be payable at least until 1990 and the tax expense is therefore all U.S. deferred.

Your approval of the attached MEP is recommended.

Note: All numbers in this document have been changed for proprietary reasons.

EXHIBIT 21   **Memorandum**

TO:	Office	Kensington
	Person	Divisional Executive
FROM:	Office	Hammersmith
	Person	U.K. Country Business Managers
	Subject	British National Life Acquisition
	Reference	AAA/dcb
	Date	13th August 1985

Attached is an MEP covering the proposed acquisition of 100 percent of British National Life Assurance Company Limited (BNL) for a price not to exceed U.S.$13.7MM. We have also included a $19.6MM capital injection in this MFP as

EXHIBIT 21

Continued

we anticipate this being the incremental requirement under U.K. statutory provisions prior to adequate earnings levels being achieved. Injection of this capital will also improve the company's earnings performance allowing earlier consolidation for tax purposes.

RATIONALE

Life insurance continues to be viewed as a key element to our Individual Bank strategy in the United Kingdom. Consumers view life insurance not only as protection, but also as a tax planning and investment opportunity. Fifty percent of total U.K. consumer savings are invested in insurance company managed funds. In order to meet the full financial needs of the U.K. consumer, we must offer life insurance related services. In order to do so, we filed in 1981 and received U.S. Federal Reserve Board approval in 1984 to sell and underwrite life insurance through our U.K. subsidiaries. To date these have been involved only in the credit life related areas complementary to our Citibank Savings lending activities.

We have been pursuing a full-service life insurance sales and underwriting firm to broaden our presence in the U.K. consumer market. Due to extremely high premiums, the acquisition of a large company giving us an immediate and substantial presence has been eliminated as an option. Instead, we have decided to develop our existing insurance operations and look at BNL as an opportunity to accelerate our de novo expansion. BNL gives us an existing infrastructure, including systems, investment management, and a direct sales force; a reasonably capable management team and an appropriate product line. Utilizing BNL and our existing customer base we anticipate substantial sales/revenue synergies, which could not otherwise be realized by a de novo development in less than two years.

Based on our projections, a de novo development of a direct sales insurance business involving the hiring of management, systems and product development, and branch/sales force recruitment and training would require 18 to 24 months and U.S.$3.5MM in expenses before any sales occur. Cumulative, after-tax losses through 1990 on a start-up would be U.S.$12.7MM. This compares with the BNL acquisition cumulative profits of U.S.$4.9MM through 1990.

The success of the acquisition is dependent on our providing BNL with sales prospects from our existing U.K. customer portfolio. This will enhance sales force performance by increasing new policy sales per salesperson by 50 percent in 1986 and up to 100 percent in 1990. The resultant sales per salesperson in 1990 are expected to be at the level currently achieved by mature direct sales forces in the life insurance industry.

COMPANY BACKGROUND

The origins of BNL date back to 1920, but true development started with the relaunch of the company as a direct-selling, unit linking life company in January 1983, and today it has 34M policyholders with $218MM insurance in force. 1984 premiums were $4.2MM generated through a direct sales force of 247 operating out of 22 branch offices. Its premium income in 1984 was $17.2MM single and $3.2MM regular.

EXHIBIT 21

Continued

A wholly owned subsidiary of XYZ Corporation [this company's identity is altered to protect confidentiality], the firm is now being sold as part of XYZ's efforts to refocus on its nonfinancial business activities.

FINANCIAL EXPECTATIONS

BNL presently loses approximately $3.1MM pre-tax due to start-up expenses and the higher costs in the growth phase of a life insurance company. With our purchase of BNL, the company will be able to offer insurance to the 1MM consumers with whom we have an established relationship in the United Kingdom. We expect this to nearly double sales and lead to a fifth year achievement of our corporate hurdle rates. Cumulative losses prior to breakeven in year three will amount to U.S.$4MM. Of the $1.3MM premium, goodwill is anticipated to $0.5MM after allowing for a $0.8MM adjustment to revalue policyholder liabilities. Details are contained in the attached MEP.

REGULATORY AND OTHER CONSIDERATIONS

Any agreement will be subject to U.K. and U.S. regulatory approvals where we do not anticipate any objections to the acquisition given the small size and our existing permissions.

The purchase will be subject to our audit and acceptance of:

- BNL's operating system, controls, and procedures
- a review of contracts, leases, and other documentation
- personnel, legal, and regulatory compliance
- a review of their investment portfolio
- the financial statements and tax returns (Peat Marwick will handle)
- current policyholder portfolio (we will retain an outside actuarial consultant for valuation purposes)

Additionally, we will require management continuity and will negotiate employment contracts with several key managers to ensure continuity after our acquisition.

The company's headquarters are approximately one-hour's drive from our Hammersmith offices so I envision no management complications due to location.

The company will initially be managed independently from our other Individual Bank activities focusing on the necessary adjustments to ensure Citicorp standards are met. The building of sales momentum is the next priority with further synergies to be explored at a later date. Given the apparent strength of the BNL management team, minimal personnel moves into BNL are anticipated. The existing Managing Director will report to me and I will retain the insurance expertise currently on my staff.

I recommend your approval.

Note: All numbers in this document have been changed for proprietary reasons.

NOTES

1. All financial information related to BNLA has been changed for proprietary reasons.

2. Walter Wriston, "The Citi of Tomorrow" (address to the Bank and Financial Analysts Association, New York, March 7, 1984).

3. Consistent with these plans, Citicorp acquired Quotron, a firm specializing in informational databases.

4. Citicorp and *Business Week*, December 8, 1986.

5. Citicorp's 1985 Annual Report, p. 11.

6. *Ibid.*

7. Interview with John Liu.

8. The assurance company's name has been changed to protect confidentiality.

9. All names here have been changed to protect confidentiality.

10. Investment was made in pounds sterling and was fully hedged via the forward market.

National Westminster Bank, U.S.A.

CHARLES SMITH

INTRODUCTION

When Bill Knowles, then an executive vice president at Bankers Trust, New York, was first called by a corporate headhunter in 1981 with an offer to become the chief executive officer (CEO) of National Bank of North America (NBNA), Knowles said he wasn't interested.

Two years earlier, NBNA had been acquired by National Westminster Bank Group, a London-based international financial institution with assets of more than $110 billion. NBNA was the result of more than twenty mergers and acquisitions in the 1950s and '60s, structured around MeadowBrook National Bank, a well-run bank that had built a strong presence on Long Island and expanded into New York City and Westchester. However, over a period of many years, NBNA was reputed to have become bureaucratic, depersonalized, and lacking in direction.

Knowles's initial response had no doubt been influenced by the fact that NBNA was known to be a marginal bank in the very competitive New York marketplace. His hesitation was probably reinforced by his strong roots in Bankers Trust, where he was well compensated, recognized as successful, and had a very secure career position.

However, Knowles was intrigued by NBNA's need for strategic planning and cultural redirection and understood that its new parent bank would be willing to give him a relatively free hand and the space he needed to run things as he saw fit.

Eventually he reconsidered the offer and accepted the job, later confessing that he was also excited by the challenge of a "David and Goliath" situation: NBNA was eleventh in size among New York City banks and heading for direct competition in some markets with Chase, Chemical Bank, and Citibank, the industry's giants. He had a hope, which has since become a conviction, that the bank could become a dynamic organization, a good place to work, and that it would outperform its competitors in target markets.

This case was prepared by Charles Smith of the Management Department at Hofstra University. It is based on information furnished publicly and via interview with William T. Knowles of National Westminster Bank, U.S.A. The author wishes to thank NatWest U.S.A. for their cooperation. The information presented here is for classroom discussion and is not intended to illustrate effective or ineffective handling of an administrative situation.

THE EARLY DAYS;
SYSTEMS IN PLACE
AND INITIAL
CHANGES

In his first few months at NBNA, Knowles listened and observed. For one thing, he found himself with a lot of good people and saw some changes already underway. But he also found that the bank badly needed a clear mission and a strong corporate culture. Its markets needed to be defined more clearly, and, from the customers' perspective, working with the bank needed to become simpler and more straightforward. The bank was run through a complex set of checks and balances, and most decisions were made by committees that met almost continually. A bureaucratic system allowed for little risk taking and encouraged political behavior, while control was in the hands of the auditors and staff functionaries.

NatWest U.S.A. President Bob Wallace recalled some of the early problems:

> Our good calling officers were frustrated by rules that seemed designed to guard the bank against its own customers. Endless procedural crosschecks made it difficult to put a loan on the books. The emphasis had been on control rather than on service, and line officers couldn't present the bank nor themselves in a positive manner. There were attitude problems. In one instance, a senior officer held up approval of a floor plan for the relocation of his division until he succeeded in adding three feet to his own office. Little kingdoms flourished. There was poor communication between groups, even when it was necessary for the conduct of business. Information was viewed as a source of power and wasn't shared freely.
>
> Clerical employees got no consideration at all. Several of us were shown the site of a processing operation. It was a room without windows, with inadequate lighting, and the paint was peeling off the walls. The officer in charge took pride that it had a low occupancy expense and was shocked when we told him it would have to be corrected immediately. . . .
>
> Coming in late and leaving early were not causes for reprimand and counseling. Arriving late for meetings had become the standard because they never started on time anyway. There was no sense of urgency. . . .
>
> In some areas, form was more important than substance. The best example was a system purchased to track officer calls on customers. It offered many features, including grouping customers by geographic area, sales size, and the success of the calling effort. However, the bank had only bought the module that accounted for the actual number of calls made, using information from the system for employee performance reviews. It didn't take a genius to realize that what mattered was number of calls made, rather than the results (of the calls). The system, needless to say, got an early burial. . . .
>
> All of our contacts with the calling officers convinced us that they did not have a winning mentality. They questioned the value of bringing in new business. They assumed that if we had won the business away from another bank, it had to be tainted. There were no rewards for introducing a new relationship to the bank. . . . [but there were certainly penalties if something went wrong].

Nevertheless, Knowles did find some positive elements with which to work. The new ownership held to its hands-off policy and provided support and encouragement. Also, there were talented people in the organization who knew how to get things done despite the rules and who later became valued contributors to the new culture.

Bill Knowles's first task was to describe the values and mores he felt should be operative. He prepared a detailed statement of mission and strategy he hoped would be understandable and relevant at every level in the organization. The statement identified a two-phase transition strategy, intended first to install a solid infrastructure, then to build a consistently profitable and competitive bank. In a departure from the past, the bank would concentrate on clearly defined markets rather than endeavor to be a full-service operation. The present Statement of Mission and Values is found in Exhibit 1.

The Statement of Mission and Strategy set goals for return on assets (ROA) and return on equity (ROE) at levels that would make NatWest U.S.A.'s performance comparable to its competitors, who were identified then as Irving Trust, The Bank of New York, Marine Midland, and European American Bank.

In the mission statement, Knowles emphasized the need to gain respect in the financial community, develop first-class talent, become more efficient and cost-conscious, push decision making downward, and develop group effectiveness, cooperation, and team spirit.

By identifying core businesses and setting financial goals, Knowles had set a standard by which success could be measured and established a time frame within which the goals could be reached. These goals would put NatWest at the high end of New York banks.

Some thought the new CEO appeared too optimistic. At a time when the only earnings on the bank's income statement were coming from tax credits, Knowles was calling for a benchmark ROA of .60 percent by 1987. The benchmark for ROA was reached in 1985—two years ahead of target—and surpassed in 1986. A comparison to 1981 when Knowles accepted the CEO post indicates the extent of the change—return on assets then was .22 percent[1]

With markets well defined and staff functions altered and reduced, the bank set forth strategies to achieve new objectives. The major changes focused on two areas: developing a high-quality management team and developing a customer orientation emphasizing profitability rather than growth.

Knowles felt that a complete transformation of NatWest's internal culture was crucial to building a more customer-oriented bank. In his 1981 mission statement he called for synergy, a less parochial focus on profit-center earnings, and for management to lead by example.

He communicated a sense of urgency, stressing that changes in corporate culture had to start at the top. Decision making was to be pushed down the line, and pleasing customers instead of bank examiners was underscored as paramount.

MANAGEMENT TRANSITIONS

In the 1981 statement Knowles also tackled the sensitive issue of management personnel changes—changes necessary for more effective functioning and instilling a new culture. He felt senior management needed more qualified people and recognized the need to go outside to find new managers. He recalls:

> I was very open with the staff about this. I said we were going to have to go outside because we were just too big a bank to be competitive without introducing additional talent. I said I would try to get it over with as quickly as possible, but that I needed a window of about a year to accomplish it. At the end of the year, we were able to limit outside hires to primarily specialists, tax lawyers, etc.

The following was part of his public statement, excerpted from the August 1981 Statement of Mission and Strategy:

> The single most important element that will enable us to compete more effectively in the future than we have in the past is people. We have to be uncompromising in insisting on first-class talent, because if we don't have it, or grow it, we cannot move up. Neither our name nor our ownership can compensate for less than top-flight personnel who perform in a superior way. . . .
>
> As a first step, therefore, we are identifying the 50 to 60 key jobs in the organization and determining if the incumbent either is or can operate at a superior performance level. If not, changes will be made. This does not imply a cold or heavy-handed approach to people. On the contrary, we should always conduct ourselves so as to demonstrate respect and compassion in our dealings with our staff. It does mean, however, that we will be rigorous in setting goals and measuring results and rewarding those who can do the job or making changes where results are not satisfactory. . . .
>
> Once the 50–60 key jobs are filled by people who meet high standards of performance as professionals and/or managers, they will serve as role models, and we will then attempt to build the organization by recruiting trainees and advancing people already here. We want to move away from the habit of going outside to fill our senior and even semi-senior positions. This will have to be done for a while longer, but our goal is to "grow on our own" in time.

BUILDING FROM THE TOP DOWN

The grooming of the management team became the main focus of the transition.

Knowles had the freedom to choose his principal partners: one to be the bank's chief operating officer (COO), the other to be the liaison with the NatWest parent organization. He brought in Bob Wallace as COO. Wallace had been CEO of an Oregon bank owned by a holding company. John Gale was brought in as the liaison, and the three formed a partnership, under the heading Office of the Chairman, that, according to Knowles, "is based on trust, informality and candor . . . We've developed into a team that represents the values we wanted to see projected throughout the bank."

Knowles, Wallace, and Gale meet every Monday before their individual sector meetings and also meet off site at dinner every few weeks to discuss what is going on in their respective sectors.

The Office of the Chairman saw the selection of people as the key to success. They agreed that all outside hires, as well as internal promotions, had to "buy into" the new value system, and they have held firmly to their standards.

Wallace recalled that in their internal process they found outstanding people a couple of levels down in the organization, people who had gone unrecognized before, but who were able to flourish in the changing environment.

Some jobs did have to be filled from outside, and all three members of the Office of the Chairman interviewed candidates for positions at levels of vice president and above. In each case, they looked for people with compatible values. Wallace describes the selection and promotion criteria:

> We want people who are team players who want to work in an atmosphere of openness and caring. We may have made some mistakes with the professional skills of people brought in, but never on their values. . . .
>
> At every opportunity, we promoted people who would be seen by their peers as apolitical. One of the first tasks was to pick four division heads for our United States Group. We reviewed the candidates, their qualifications, and chose the candidates who hadn't run a "campaign" for the job. This and other promotions gave a clear signal that politics were out.

DEVELOPING A CUSTOMER ORIENTATION

Selection of the management team took place simultaneously with the bank's development of competitive strategies based on customer service. Wallace was instrumental in setting the tone for this aspect of the transition:

> First, we had to get a good grip on the bank's strengths and weaknesses. We quickly concluded that the bank's senior officers should get out in the marketplace to sample our customer's attitudes and evaluate the skill level of our lending officers. While what follows may seem a litany of what was wrong with the bank, let me assure you that we were encouraged by the good things we found, including some excellent talent among our line officers.
>
> But . . . we found product deficiencies that put us at a competitive disadvantage. . . . And we were troubled by the lack of value placed on the contact with customers.
>
> For example, I once asked the head of one division to coordinate his calling with mine. He told me that would be easy, because he didn't call on customers. He viewed himself purely as an administrator, and he added that the bank knew that when he was hired. Unfortunately, while his statement was extreme, it was not inconsistent with the feelings of others. We had to show by example that customer contact was the most important job at the bank.
>
> The three members of the Office of the Chairman emphasized their desire to make calls on customers. At first, we would be taken on safe calls where the customer wouldn't embarrass the officer or the bank by telling stories of inadequate levels of service. But before long, there was less screening of the

names we called on. We are still calling on customers wherever it will do the most good in marketing the bank. More to the point, it is [now] recognized throughout the bank that you don't graduate from customer contact. It's the most important thing we do.

When we became serious about developing a customer-oriented atmosphere, changes were dramatic. It was like a dam breaking. We were literally flooded with information on why customers found us a difficult bank to deal with. On some of my early calls, I had found a key symptom of disregard for service. Officers simply did not listen to customers. Therefore, they never found out what customers wanted from the bank. Some of our officers acted as if they'd been sent in on a mission and the customers better not get in their way. Today, one of the primary thrusts of our sales training is learning to listen. In addition, we have worked hard to change how people think about customer service. We emphasized that everyone in the bank has customers to serve; the support people's customers are the line people, and the line people, in turn, have external customers. It took repeated emphasis, but I think today most people have their priorities in order.

CHANGES SLOW IN COMING

Somewhat ironically, a lack of products had forced the bank's officers to develop extraordinary skills in the only area they had available to them: lending. Several parts of the bank were successful, driven by the ability to outperform competitors and to structure difficult credit transactions. In the area of lending, NatWest could function effectively because it was one area where officers did not have to depend upon the performance of others in the organization.

In spite of an initial euphoria, changes seemed, to many, slow to come. Ed McDougal, formerly a line head and now executive vice president for human resources, recalled that his excitement when joining NatWest carried him a few months but was dampened when he saw how attempts at action and decision making were continually swamped in bureaucracy. McDougal recalls:

I found basically four types of people in the bank at that time. There were the cynics who said, "This too shall pass." There were the skeptics who said, "I'm all for it, but it will never work." Both of these groups suffered from a genuine inferiority complex about NBNA. The third group was a small corps of leaders who said, "Believe it." And finally we had a bunch of supporters who said, "Why not?" Many were young and lacked experience. But they were smart, energetic, and ambitious and had a real can-do attitude. In my opinion, we needed to convert the skeptics and develop the can-do people.

McDougal also recalled an informal talk with Knowles that kept him from becoming too discouraged. McDougal was then at a mid-manager's level, five levels down in the organization. When Knowles would drop in once in a while at NatWest's midtown headquarters, he would ask how things were going. McDougal would express his frustrations, and Knowles would encourage him and also share his own frustrations. Once he told McDougal,

"You keep pushing from the bottom, and I'll keep pushing from the top. Someday, we'll meet in the middle."

When McDougal was finally promoted to department head, he began his push. One particular frustration for him was the lack of credit approval authority at the line level. The charter for his department said that the minimum loan the department could make was $250,000, yet the largest loan anyone could approve, himself included, was $250,000. In effect, despite being solely accountable for growing a loan portfolio, McDougal or his staff could not make any loans without someone else's approval.

It was clear the time had come to stop focusing on just the problems and get on with the job at hand. As McDougal said:

> I was tired of hearing about our limited product line and our cumbersome credit approval process. The time had come to do business and to celebrate some victories. It was September [1982]. We were in our budgeting cycle, and we put together a budget for 1983 that showed a 15 percent loan growth despite a three-year history of no growth. Also in September, as a tangible demonstration of our confidence and resolve, we scheduled a party for November, to celebrate the victories we would have over the next two-and-a-half months. There were some skeptics, but we did have our victory party, and we had something to celebrate. In fact, our portfolio grew by over 25 percent in 1983 without sacrificing quality or profitability standards.
>
> My function at that time was to be a teacher of credit and marketing, and we tried to use mistakes as a springboard to learn and not an excuse to punish. I saw myself as a role model, confidence builder, cheerleader and facilitator. I learned how to use the bureaucracy to slow down the imposition of new rules, regulations, and controls and how to avoid it to get the job done.

As slow as the process was, changes were clearly happening. Success stories began to replace complaints, and the bank began to celebrate these successes openly. When a deal was completed, a senior person would make a point of saying "good job." Wallace noted that people in the bank responded immediately to the much-needed praise.

A good example that change for the better was manifesting itself was seen in the way NatWest U.S.A. handled a new problem. In an effort to build volume, the bank had accepted greater domestic risks than it should have. This, on top of an emerging international debt crisis, resulted in an overall asset quality in 1983 that was not as good as expected. Bob Wallace noted:

> The bank had good enough credit people to deal with the situation quickly. We evaluated the problem loans, devised strategies, and set out to make corrections. The plan worked, and today our asset quality is among the best of the New York banks. Best of all, it was accomplished without enormous write-offs. But solving the asset-quality problem had an additional benefit. It demonstrated clearly that we were working as a team. It showed that we were more interested in solutions than in pointing the finger. It proved that we were becoming a different bank.

Flexibility was enhanced at NatWest when the authority for lending was pushed down in the organization, allowing lending departments to make loans of up to $2 million without outside approval. McDougal noted the significance of this event and some of the critical events that followed:

No one ever believed it could happen. This was the first significant sign to the line units that the bureaucracy was in retreat. The symbolism went well beyond the actual impact. A new core of leaders had made it happen. But the biggest signpost was yet to come. The bank had waited until September 1983, until it was reasonably sure that it would show its third consecutive year of increased earnings, before taking on a name which would identify it with our parent. To celebrate the new name and our success to date, the bank held a party for the entire staff—a party complete with excellent food, music, and a fifteen-minute sound-and-slide show that actually had people cheering. This was not NBNA, it was NatWest U.S.A. There was a euphoria throughout the whole bank that lasted for weeks. Even when it finally wore away, morale was at a new, higher plateau. The bank had been permanently lifted by this one gala celebration.

Anecdotes about successes increasingly replaced jokes about failure. Stories of teamwork replaced some of the legends about the idiosyncrasies of individuals. At our victory party, we invited all branch managers to attend. Now, understand, our business customers were primarily medium-sized companies scattered over the five boroughs of New York. They used our branches to make deposits, cash checks, and bring documents. Many saw the local branch manager more often than they saw the account officer. But the branch managers were rarely thanked for their efforts. They felt that they were not appreciated. The only time they ever heard from us was when the customers felt they didn't receive the service they were entitled to. Inviting the managers to our party to thank them for their help in serving our customers seemed like a little thing at the time, but it created a bond which enhanced our ability to serve our customers.

[In addition,] my predecessor had started a tradition of quarterly profit improvement awards. We [in middle-market lending] decided to give the award to an assistant branch manager who had referred us a large piece of business. The branch people were ecstatic. It was unheard of that a branch person would receive an award from another group.

THE HUMAN RESOURCE FUNCTION

McDougal was promoted in 1984 to executive vice president and head of human resources. With the fervor of a crusader, Ed took responsibility for the staff meetings, audiovisual presentations, and gala celebrations that continue to repeat over and over again the desire for change as stated in the original mission statement. McDougal's recollection of this period indicates the importance of the human resources group and his role in the transition:

My first priority as head of human resources was to have a team. We had many people who were competent from a professional/technical point of view, but effectiveness was hampered by a lack of teamwork. It wasn't a fun place to work. I told the department heads at our first group management meeting that

I had never worked in a place for very long where I didn't have a good time, and I didn't expect to start here. That was the only threat I ever issued. From then on we met regularly to discuss all issues.

One of the first major tasks of the group management was to create a strategic plan for human resources. In effect, we needed to create a vision of our future—a vision we all shared and would work cooperatively to reach. We launched this planning process not through some technical preparation, but rather by spending three days together, off site, learning how to work together. Our next step was to create a statement of values and beliefs for the human resources group. And it was only at this point that we began the process of creating a strategic plan. That plan served as a basis for providing increasingly higher levels of service to our customers, the employees and managers of the bank.

From the bank's perspective, we went through the process in the spring of 1985 of creating a statement of values for the overall organization. This involved a series of meetings with teams composed of members of the Office of the Chairman, executive vice presidents, all senior vice presidents, and a representative group of eight people, male and female, black and white, vice president to secretary. The final result is a statement of values [see Exhibit 1] which spells out how it is appropriate to act within the bank. This statement of values was presented to all the employees of the organization during a series of eleven breakfasts, conducted in Westchester, New York, and Long Island. The presenters were all the senior and executive officers of the bank.

The final event which stands out in my mind is the bank's second victory celebration. Shortly after I became the head of human resources, Bill Knowles said we needed an occasion to have another employee party. The occasion became the launching of the bank's new quality effort. This, along with our success to date, suggested the name "Just the Beginning." In October of 1985, we held a series of "Just the Beginning" parties throughout the bank. Once again, they were a rousing success and lifted the morale of almost everyone in the organization. But there is one anecdote about the "Just the Beginning" parties which I think is a fitting story to close.

One of our division heads who managed people on off-shifts asked if we could have one of the parties other than at night, when many of her people could not attend. These were employees who often felt ignored. So we held a sit-down luncheon with music and dancing and concluded with the unveiling of a lavish dessert table. An older woman, whom I had never met before, grabbed my elbow as we walked up to the dessert table and said this reminded her of a wedding reception. Kiddingly, I said, "Well, you're really our bride today." She looked at me and said, almost with tears in her eyes, "I feel like royalty." Nothing in my entire time in the bank has ever brought home to me more how people can be made to feel special.

At a conference on organizational development in the fall of 1986 NatWest U.S.A. presented a history of its transformation process since the 1981 changeover. In closing remarks, Ed McDougal and Bob Wallace expressed their perceptions of how far the bank had come. McDougal noted:

We are a successful organization. We have done it by acting in a way that is consistent with values originally outlined in our mission statement, now codified in a statement of values. The challenges ahead of us are greater than the challenges behind. But we are prepared to meet them with a formula for success. There may still be some cynics, but most of the skeptics have been converted, and the core of believers is much larger. The younger people are still mostly here, four years older, and when they see our success to date, still say, "Why not?" I report directly to Bill [Knowles], which says something about the role human resources plays in the organization. Bill and Bob [Wallace] had both talked to me at the time of the change. They said they were looking for someone who was practical, yet sensitive. They wanted the function to have credibility within the bank and have a customer orientation. I also took it as the ultimate confirmation of a management style.

McDougal's views are consistent with Wallace's:

We now have an organization whose strengths are apparent. We have a marketing organization based on customer requirements and input from our own officers. Systems and operations areas now work in partnerships with line areas, because of the leadership provided by those who head these groups.

When something we put in place didn't work, it was changed. We were able to prove by example that there was not pride of authorship or a penalty for an innovation that didn't work. And people began to realize that there was more fun in accomplishing an objective than in trying to find out who to blame. We in the Office of the Chairman continue to walk around, to meet with customers and seek information wherever we can. People realize that there is no penalty for speaking their mind.

My own experience [illustrates] the atmosphere. . . . When Bill [Knowles] and I were looking at whether I could make a contribution, he said he was looking for a full partner. I knew he meant that, but I also know that somebody has to run the store. Well, after five years, I can honestly say that the three of us in the Office of the Chairman have a partnership. We trust, respect, and like each other and, maybe more importantly, we feel free to disagree with each other. It's worked for us, and I think it has worked for the whole bank. We are all proud to be part of a winning team.

SUMMARY: SOME CANDID OBSERVATIONS BY THE CEO

With changes apparent and financial statements that tell a story of success in many areas, there are still problems and challenges in NatWest's efforts to differentiate itself and to reach its goals. In an interview with the casewriter, Bill Knowles frankly expressed his concerns and hopes:

We're now finding that we have got to work through but also around the system to try to enrich the environment down below, to unleash the energies that are there. There are still supervisors who grew up in the old school, who use knowledge as power, who feel threatened, who will not permit their people to advance their careers by seeking positions elsewhere in the bank.

About bureaucracy:

What did disappear, fairly quickly, was the committees. There were committees for everything. All the executive vice presidents met to decide the salaries, the computer systems questions, real estate questions, loan questions. It was like the knights would consider everything, whether they had expertise or not in the particular thing.

What didn't go away, and what we had a couple of false starts on, was the clutter in the system. This was because of the mergers, sticking twenty-three banks together so quickly and the self-protective mentality that had grown up here. It was very hierarchical.

The clutter was incredibly hard to disassemble. Those vines had grown around all the pipes and wires and furniture, and it was just impossible to pull out. We established a clutter committee to monitor the process. It's like weeding a garden, you cannot do it in ten minutes. It takes a long time, and you have to pick the weeds out one at a time. We are still doing it, and we still have a six-part-form mentality in some places, where we still cannot think simply.

The people in our organization are intelligent and honest. If you catch a dishonest person you deal with that, but you don't set up a whole mechanism to protect yourself from the odd, random event.

We tried to change the whole fundamental philosophical basis of the organization, and say, "Hey, wait a minute, why in God's name do I have to sign a form [saying] that I received a report? If I received it, I received it, and if I didn't receive it, I didn't receive it."

There are still vestiges, and they stick out more now, and we can laugh at them a little.

On bringing quality to the workplace:

I gave a talk to the Long Island and New York City chapters of Young Presidents Organization. They were primarily presidents of mid-sized companies. The talk was on quality as the way that America could regain competitiveness in the world marketplace. That is more possible with companies like our bank and their companies, because there isn't so much bureaucracy. The middle-market companies of the country [there are close to 800,000 of them] could effect quality and bring back the quality that is good for our society and that we have lost so much of. . . .

I don't know that it is profound, but I am committed to quality as the only way out. Not only for this bank, but for our society as a whole. The Far Eastern economies are providing much better quality in everything, from electronics to gasoline stations. We have now put our entire staff through quality training, one- or two-day training on the techniques of quality and what is expected. . . .

We have staff parties—establish what we hope and believe in—so that if there is a bad cell at the bank, at least the people know that that is deviant, that that is not the norm. They know they are in a rotten branch, for example, and the chances are that they know somebody who is in a good branch, or who came from a good branch, and that the bank's management stands on the side of making it the way it ought to be. . . .

Everybody wants to send good news up, particularly because we have been so strong in articulating the kind of environment, the quality that we want. Anything that comes up that doesn't sound that way is considered bad news. So we have to be extremely careful to get the truth through, rather than just something that matches what we put out. . . .

It is paradoxical, it almost works against you. I think the answer is just to keep digging at it. Digging at it at the most junior levels of command, going down and talking to them. Also, we have what we call a video magazine, and once a quarter we have a tape that talks about quality successes and quality barriers.

Dealing with the isolation of the manager:

I deal with the isolation just by being informal and walking around. I have breakfast with the officers on all levels. We also have an endless series of excuses to get together for meetings and parties here. I mean, I have been to eight events here in the last three weeks with fifty or sixty officers, and it's rare if I don't know who they are. I walk around and try to see everybody in the non-branch staff at Christmas, to wish them a good holiday. I probably see 2,500 to 3,000, out of the 4,500, and the executive vice presidents do too.

You have to go breaking down isolation, and that only lasts so long, and you have to do it again. It'll just grow back, that's natural.

On basic strategy:

This has really been the story of trying to make a bank competitive by narrowing its mission, its focus, and trying to achieve superiority in the area of commodity services by working through people. Because all services are the same in the businesses we are in. It's like insurance companies. If I asked you to identify the differences among them, you can't. Nobody could name the difference between banks either. So what we've got to do is to work very hard to take a representative sample of our society, which is our employees, and somehow to work with them in delivery of "faceless" services and try to do something special.[2]

What we're doing now is having the "Executive Vice President of the Week." For a week, on a rotating basis, an executive vice president takes all the complaint calls that come into the bank, the "let me speak to the president calls." This means the EVPs are getting calls about their peers and about the organizations of other EVPs, and it saves complainers from being battered around by a dozen or so people before they get an answer.

The CEO's personal philosophy:

In our society, in the business sector of our society and, I'm sure, in other sectors as well, people are driven by the attractiveness, the appeal, of putting their stamp on something, or effecting a change that will be identified with them, putting their imprimatur on something. People go to work to do that—they don't go to work to earn a paycheck. There is a self-pride that says, "I did that, I was associated with that, I was on the team that installed this." Just so that they are a part of something that is significant. I think that's what really motivates me, but I also think it's what motivates others. And for me [it is] putting my stamp on something, not just in profit terms but in human terms as well. I have a feeling that there is a power in the ability of a staff to produce when they are committed to doing something that makes sense to them—if they can see [the mission] is productive in terms of profit and the environment is conducive to letting them put their stamp on something worthwhile.

When what you do is make it fun, make it enjoyable to be in that environment, that's part of the compensation and part of the benefits. It's more style.

Work should be fun . . . if you go out and sample six out of ten people here, they'll tell you work is tough, it's not fun, but four will tell you yes, it's fun. There is that slice. If we can make that five next year and six the next year, we're on our way.

Whether it's NatWest or some other organization, it's important to keep in mind what that organization is there for, what you are there to do. An organization left on its own will run off in different directions, because of the natural desire to experiment and grow and change. Unless that is properly channeled all the time, it will grow in a lot of directions and all those energies need to be focused on something that you and they really want. The biggest change around here is not so much what I have done, or anyone has done. The biggest turnaround here is to see what the people are doing translated into something the marketplace values—and that is profit. Can you imagine how disheartening, how debilitating it is to work very hard and to end up in a losing enterprise? That is how this organization once was—good people working hard, and it coming out all wrong.

When most people ask, "What's wrong with this place?" the answer is usually communication, teamwork. But have you ever heard of any place, any organizational system that was perfect? I think we have to work hard to keep on the track we are on now, keep at it all the time.

NOTES

1. Due to an increase in loan reserves of $295 million in 1987 (against loans to developing countries that are experiencing debt servicing problems) NatWest suffered a loss in 1987 of $212 million. Without the extraordinary item, the 1987 ROA would have been approximately .70 percent. See financial statements in Exhibit 2.

2. Exhibit 4 provides a summary of recent market research at NatWest, and gives an indication of the degree to which NatWest has been successful in differentiating itself with regard to customer service.

Appendix A

EXHIBIT 1

The NatWest Way: Our Values, Mission, and Commitment to Quality

THE STATEMENT OF VALUES

The Statement of Values provides the philosophical foundation for all we do. It is our credo, our system of fundamental beliefs.

EXHIBIT 1

Continued

As National Westminster Bank USA we share values which both support our Mission Statement and commit us to excellence in fulfilling the needs of our customers, the communities we serve, our parent organization and ourselves.

Customers

Our customers are the foundation of our business. We listen to their needs and respond in a manner which is timely, straightforward and courteous. We earn our future with them through leadership in quality and service.

Communities

The prosperity and well-being of the communities in which we live and work are fundamental to our long-term success.

Therefore, we commit to serve them by providing leadership and support which enrich the overall quality of life.

Parent

The National Westminster Bank Group has entrusted us with capital and its good name. We commit to invest these resources prudently, to earn a superior return and to work in partnership with our parent to enhance its worldwide stature.

Ourselves

We, the employees, are the strength of the Bank and the source of its character. We work together to foster an open environment where trust and caring prevail. Pride and enjoyment come from commitment, leadership by example and accomplishment. We encourage personal growth and ensure opportunity based upon performance.

We recognize our individual responsibility to uphold these values, and in turn to enhance the Bank's reputation which is rooted in integrity, achievement and quality.

THE MISSION STATEMENT

The Mission Statement is the strategic translation of the Statement of Values. It is more specific, converting the value system into goals and programs.

Mission

As the principal banking vehicle of the NatWest Group in the United States, our mission is to serve the overall marketing and operational requirements of the Group in this country. In doing so, we achieve profitable growth and an enhanced reputation.

To fulfill this mission we must continue to see ourselves not as a full-service, across-the-board competitor of the largest money-center banks in every market, but rather as a significant competitor in what we regard as our core businesses. In addition, we must continue to develop the considerable potential for synergy that exists with our parent, in international markets as well as in this country.

EXHIBIT 1	## Continued

Customers

We are in four core businesses. In each of these core markets two fundamental precepts apply: our commitment to relationship banking and the essential responsibility of our support units to provide high-quality, low-cost service.

Consumer

In this market, an area of traditional strength, we seek a stable and increasing source of core deposits that can be invested at an acceptable spread. We are relatively well-positioned for this with a sizable branch network, including offices in some key locations in New York City and substantial coverage in the desirable suburban counties surrounding it.

We will compete not by attempting to gain market share through the introduction of product breakthroughs, but by offering superior personal service, coupled with a competitive line of both deposit and consumer credit products introduced in a timely manner.

Commercial lending and deposit responsibility for companies with sales of up to $10 million is an important element of our consumer business. Commercial business adds a significant dimension to what was formerly a purely retail approach, and is aimed at enabling us to use our branch system more efficiently.

Middle Market

The Middle Market continues to be one of the natural markets for NatWest USA. By our definition, it consists of companies with annual sales ranging between $10 million and $250 million, located primarily within a 100-mile radius of New York City, as well as companies on a selective basis throughout the country wherever we can serve them effectively. We compete by meeting the credit needs of customers in a responsive and flexible manner, and by bringing specialty services—particularly Trust, Treasury, Cash Management and Trade Finance—to middle-market companies in a more effective way than do other major banks.

Corporate

Together with our parent, we have developed a rational and effective way for the Group to approach the enormous corporate market on a national basis. NatWest PLC is responsible for multinational companies and for servicing certain specialized-industry customers on behalf of London. Other than these, NatWest USA is responsible for the national market. We address this on a niche basis, both as to industry and geography, through our network of regional offices. Here again, our specialized support services—Cash Management, Trust, Treasury and Trade Finance—play a key role in our ability to compete effectively against money-center as well as regional banks.

International

While we continue to service the well-established and profitable public and quasi-public sectors, our mission in International is to increasingly concentrate on activi-

EXHIBIT 1

Continued

ties that more directly serve the offshore needs of our domestic customer base. These are principally credit and non-credit transactions that facilitate foreign trade.

Further, we will continue to build on our strengths in correspondent banking, and from that base expand selectively into private sector lending if margins are acceptable. Our areas of particular expertise are Latin America and the Far East. In Europe, we utilize the capabilities of our parent to a greater extent. Our international strategy reflects, in a complementary way, our role within the worldwide coverage of the NatWest Group.

Communities

We derive business and our profits from the communities in which we operate. Therefore, we acknowledge a responsibility to invest in those communities to keep them vigorous and attractive. This goes beyond mere compliance with the Community Reinvestment Act. It involves active participation by our staff, as well as direct financial support.

Parent

Because we have been entrusted with our parent's name, we have a responsibility to enhance its reputation in all we do, as well as to achieve a superior financial return.

We expect to achieve this year—two years ahead of schedule—the 60-basis-point return on assets (ROA) goal set forth in the original 1981 Mission Statement. Our new goal is 70 basis points by 1988. In comparing our performance, we continue to regard Bank of New York, Marine Midland and European American Bank as our peers.

Our quality effort is directly related both to achieving our new ROA goal and to enhancing the reputation of our parent.

Ourselves

The internal environment we seek, as outlined in the Statement of Values, rests on a set of strategies, policies and programs that are fundamental in our Bank:

- An uncompromising insistence on quality people.
- A pay-for-performance policy which has application Bank-wide as well as individually.
- A standard of excellence in communications.
- A lean organizational structure, free of redundant staff layers, to encourage individual initiative and decision making.
- A willingness by supervisors and managers to be judged on how well they foster the desired environment in their areas.

Quality Program

Quality represents the everyday expression of our value system. It is the means by which we carry out the strategies and goals set forth in the Mission Statement.

The Bank's commitment to quality is thoroughgoing and long-term. It is how we

EXHIBIT 1

Continued

intend to differentiate ourselves and, at the same time, achieve a cost advantage over our competitors. In addition, customers are willing to pay a premium for high-quality services.

Customers

The everyday things we do to better serve customers are obvious, but they bear repeating. These actions apply to everyone because, even where there is not direct customer contact, everything we do is related to serving customers:

- We listen to our customers to determine their needs and then attempt to fill those needs.
- We respond in a thoughtful, professional and timely manner.
- We deliver our products and services error free and in a consistent manner.
- We price our products and services fairly.
- We are always respectful and courteous.
- We do our work in essential staff areas as cost effectively as possible, because we invest our principal resources in customer-driven activities.

Communities

In all our community activities we seek to reflect the Bank's commitment to quality and excellence while helping others.

This is a dimension to our job that goes beyond day-to-day duties. It involves community service: giving generously to United Way, donating blood, taking leadership roles in significant community organizations.

We furnish substantial community support on the corporate level as well. Our contributions budget has grown each year and provides major funding for education, health care, community welfare and the arts. In addition, we have chosen to direct significant portions of our Corporate Communications budget to sponsorship of quality arts projects.

Parent

Superior quality in everything we do is the only way to meet the dual responsibility we have to our parent of enhancing its reputation and meeting our financial goals.

High-quality work is key to enhancing the NatWest name. But it is also critical to achieving our new financial goal, because we must do this by improving margins rather than by expanding assets. Quality banking involves several things:

- Wider lending and investing spreads.
- Increased fee and service-charge income, which can be expected if we deliver quality products consistently.
- Expanded demand deposits.
- Higher credit quality, resulting in lower credit costs and fewer non-performing loans and charge-offs.
- Reduced tax liability

EXHIBIT 1

Continued

An additional element that enhances our reputation as a quality institution and ensures that we achieve our goals is consistent prudence both in the extension of credit and in our asset/liability management activities.

Ourselves

The competence, dedication and hard work of our staff are the essential ingredients of our success. We need quality people. Therefore, we are very selective in hiring, and take training and promotion from within very seriously.

We closely monitor salary and benefit trends and seek to be fully competitive, increasing compensation levels in relation to those of our peers as the performance of the Bank improves. On an individual level, we reward according to contribution.

We have developed a variety of programs to improve communication: an expanded NewsBeam, staff and management bulletins, staff meetings, special surveys and the like. We constantly seek new ways to increase communication at all levels of the Bank.

We encourage leadership by example, creating an environment that is caring, trusting, fair and enjoyable.

By doing quality work, each of us contributes directly to achieving the Bank's goals. In the process, we also foster a stimulating work environment and enhance our individual well-being.

	1987	1986	1985	1984	1983
FOR THE YEAR					
Net interest income	$394,125	$371,104	$336,175	$283,699	$234,878
Provision for loan losses	349,400	57,400	51,500	44,400	31,000
Non-interest income	130,109	110,020	96,187	81,494	61,745
Operating expenses	352,574	322,638	292,978	255,276	222,808
Net income (loss)	(212,008)	67,673	54,575	40,062	25,332
AT YEAR-END					
Assets	$11,539,277	$11,080,016	$9,796,328	$8,726,726	$7,470,847
Loans	8,216,356	7,363,751	6,415,038	5,679,582	4,631,661
Deposits:					
Core	6,372,288	6,174,877	5,145,869	4,642,772	3,578,957
Other	3,166,725	2,609,434	2,764,292	2,376,446	2,167,288
Equity capital	409,036	621,044	554,443	504,534	498,067

EXHIBIT 2

Financial Statements (Dollar Amounts in Thousands): Financial Highlights (The notes accompanying these statements, found in NatWest U.S.A.'s 1987 Annual Report, are important for fair and complete interpretation of financial condition.)

Consolidated Statement of Operations

	YEAR ENDED DECEMBER 31		
	1987	1986	1985
INTEREST INCOME			
Loans	$740,775	$680,964	$665,170
Investment securities			
U.S. Treasury and federal agencies	71,683	69,622	66,339
State and municipal	52,346	55,940	29,426
Other	4,464	1,247	1,100
Trading account	1,553	6,220	4,588
Deposits with banks, federal funds sold, and securities purchased under agreements to resell	53,867	52,484	68,177
Total interest income	924,688	866,477	834,800
INTEREST EXPENSE			
Deposits (Note D)	435,424	399,530	438,027
Borrowed funds (Note E)	94,842	95,459	60,131
Long-term debt (Notes F and H)	297	384	467
Total interest expense	530,563	495,373	498,625
Net interest income	394,125	371,104	336,175
Provision for loan losses (Note B)	349,400	57,400	51,500
Net interest income after provision for loan losses	44,725	313,704	284,675
NON-INTEREST INCOME			
Service charges on deposit accounts	37,049	33,027	30,469
Letter of credit and acceptance fees	19,583	16,394	13,659
Credit card fees	14,897	14,933	14,252
Syndication and other loan related fees	13,740	5,481	2,715
Investment securities gains	4,926	7,890	8,762
Other	39,914	32,295	26,330
Total non-interest income	130,109	110,020	96,187

EXHIBIT 2   Continued

| | YEAR ENDED DECEMBER 31 | | |
	1987	1986	1985
OPERATING EXPENSES			
Salaries and benefits (Note J)	205,074	190,390	173,725
Supplies and services	48,677	43,811	40,833
Net occupancy (Notes C, H, and K)	33,839	30,618	26,659
Business development	24,472	18,386	17,154
Equipment (Notes C and K)	24,447	21,735	18,816
Other	16,065	17,698	15,791
Total operating expenses	352,574	322,638	292,978
Income (loss) before income taxes	(177,740)	101,086	87,884
Provision for income taxes (Note G)	34,268	33,413	33,309
Net income (loss)	$(212,008)	$ 67,673	$ 54,575

Consolidated Statement of Condition

| | DECEMBER 31 | |
	1987	1986
ASSETS		
Cash and due from banks (Note K)	$ 582,220	$ 677,574
Interest bearing deposits with banks	646,618	578,026
Investment securities (Notes A and K)		
U.S. Treasury and federal agencies	919,395	813,760
State and municipal	734,693	837,811
Other	155,648	25,867
Total (approximate market value of $1,787,723 and $1,724,036)	1,809,736	1,677,438
Trading account	44,560	95,791
Federal funds sold and securities purchased under agreements to resell	6,936	23,213
Loans, less unearned income of $85,348 and $60,464	8,216,356	7,363,751
Allowance for loan losses	(407,790)	(112,299)
Loans—net (Notes B and K)	7,808,566	7,251,452
Premises and equipment—net (Notes C, F, and H)	236,606	235,276
Due from customers on acceptances	249,752	365,935
Other assets	154,283	175,311
Total assets	$11,539,277	$11,080,016
LIABILITIES AND EQUITY CAPITAL		
Deposits (Note D)		
Demand	$ 2,114,470	$ 2,427,387
Retail savings and time	4,257,818	3,747,490
Other domestic time	1,335,644	983,570
Foreign office	1,831,081	1,625,864
Total	9,539,013	8,784,311

EXHIBIT 2   **Continued**

	DECEMBER 31	
	1987	**1986**
Borrowed funds (Note E)		
Federal funds purchased	*618,140*	677,957
Securities sold under agreements to repurchase	*263,220*	177,103
Other	*312,740*	313,569
Total	*1,194,100*	1,168,629
Acceptances outstanding	*252,668*	372,399
Accounts payable and accrued liabilities (Note G)	*139,733*	126,983
Long-term debt (Note F)	*4,727*	6,650
Total liabilities	*11,130,241*	10,458,972
Equity capital (Notes I and M)		
Common stock, $5 par value: Authorized 7,773,867 shares; issued and outstanding 7,675,138 shares	*38,376*	38,376
Surplus	*238,657*	238,657
Undivided profits	*132,003*	344,011
Total equity capital	*409,036*	621,044
Total liabilities and equity capital	*$11,539,277*	$11,080,016

Composition of Loan Portfolio

	DECEMBER 31				
	1987	**1986**	**1985**	**1984**	**1983**
Domestic					
Commercial, financial, and agricultural	*$5,377,938*	$4,415,500	$3,630,686	$2,749,054	$1,758,653
Real estate construction	*125,672*	110,102	164,578	168,586	131,689
Real estate mortgage and warehouse	*816,102*	967,586	691,940	715,493	718,044
Installment loans to individuals	*696,797*	587,973	541,440	446,149	362,115
Other loans to individuals	*177,576*	162,174	205,899	135,214	79,793
Lease financing	*29,581*	21,345	23,676	23,561	4,106
Other	*114,257*	96,210	39,424	96,014	31,499
Total domestic	*7,337,923*	6,360,890	5,297,643	4,334,071	3,085,899
Foreign					
Governments and official institutions	*472,009*	464,163	435,079	440,823	485,695
Banks and other financial institutions	*284,859*	348,768	368,934	438,525	508,451
Commercial and industrial	*206,477*	249,645	358,018	506,332	580,391
Other	*436*	749	1,624	811	1,090
Total foreign	*963,781*	1,063,325	1,163,655	1,386,491	1,575,627
Less unearned income	*85,348*	60,464	46,260	40,980	29,865
Total loans	*$8,216,356*	$7,363,751	$6,415,038	$5,679,582	$4,631,661

EXHIBIT 2   Continued

Maturities of Loans

		DECEMBER 31, 1987		
	TOTAL	DUE BEFORE ONE YEAR	DUE IN ONE TO FIVE YEARS	DUE AFTER FIVE YEARS
Commercial, financial, agricultural, and other	$5,492,195	$3,006,427	$1,887,733	$598,035
Real estate construction	125,672	33,931	85,797	5,944
Foreign	963,781	577,506	166,249	220,026
Total	6,581,648	3,617,864	2,139,779	824,005
Loans with interest-sensitive rates	6,131,510	3,518,861	1,870,741	741,908
Loans with fixed rates	450,138	99,003	269,038	82,097
Total	$6,581,648	$3,617,864	$2,139,779	$824,005

Excludes real estate mortgage and warehouse loans, loans to individuals, and lease financing loans.

Cross-Border Outstandings

	GOVERNMENTS AND OFFICIAL INSTITUTIONS	BANKS AND OTHER FINANCIAL INSTITUTIONS	COMMERCIAL AND INDUSTRIAL	TOTAL
December 31, 1987				
Argentina	$ 96,313	$ 23,997	$13,553	$133,863
Brazil	87,579	120,901	250	208,730
Mexico	102,608	9,303	16,858	128,769
December 31, 1986				
Argentina	$ 83,976	$ 30,350	$12,823	$127,149
Brazil	88,167	115,799	267	204,233
Mexico	93,623	9,280	18,727	121,630
December 31, 1985				
Argentina	$ 69,223	$ 40,936	$10,500	$120,659
Brazil	73,827	125,706	767	200,300
France		104,771		104,771
Mexico	96,464	4,131	20,466	121,061
South Korea	40,265	63,459	22,730	126,454

The above schedule discloses cross-border outstandings (loans, acceptances, interest bearing deposits with banks, accrued interest receivable, and other interest bearing investments) due from borrowers in each foreign country where such outstandings exceed 1.00 percent of total assets.
At December 31, 1987, 1986, and 1985, countries whose total outstandings were individually between .75 and 1.00 percent of total assets are as follows:
    1987—France and Japan, total $197.7 million.
    1986—Chile, France, South Korea, and Venezuela, totaling $362.4 million.
    1985—Canada, Chile and Venezuela, totaling $267.3 million.

EXHIBIT 2   **Continued**

Changes in Cross-Border Outstandings (Amounts in Millions)

	ARGENTINA		BRAZIL		MEXICO	
	1987	1986	1987	1986	1987	1986
Aggregate outstandings at January 1	*$127.1*	$120.7	*$204.2*	$200.3	*$121.6*	$121.1
Net change in short-term outstandings	*(2.0)*	.2	*6.7*	5.0		5.1
Changes in other outstandings:						
Additional outstandings	*7.5*	3.9	*1.8*		*8.6*	
Interest income accrued	*10.9*	8.5	*4.0*	14.9	*8.8*	11.0
Collections of: Principal	*(.2)*				*(1.1)*	(1.2)
Accrued interest	*(9.4)*	(6.2)	*(4.5)*	(15.1)	*(8.5)*	(13.4)
Other changes			*(3.5)*	(.9)	*(.6)*	(1.0)
Aggregate outstandings at December 31	*$133.9*	$127.1	*$208.7*	$204.2	*$128.8*	$121.6

THE FOLLOWING RESTRUCTURINGS OCCURRED DURING 1987 AND 1986:	ARGENTINA 1987	BRAZIL 1986	MEXICO 1986
Amount restructured	*$124.2*	$13.8	$80.7
Weighted average year of maturity			
(including any grace periods): Pre-restructuring	*1992*	1985	1998
Post-restructuring	*2004*	1993	2004
Weighted average interest rate: Pre-restructuring	*Prime + 2% on $20.0*	Prime + 1¾%	Prime + 1⅛% on $14.6
	LIBOR + 1⅛% on $104.2		LIBOR + 1⅛% on $66.1
Post-restructuring	*LIBOR + ¹³⁄₁₆%*	LIBOR + 1⅛%	LIBOR + ¹³⁄₁₆%

The above schedule discloses changes in the period and restructuring information for those countries experiencing liquidity problems with outstandings greater than 1.00 percent of total assets.

EXHIBIT 3   **A Recent Profile of NatWest U.S.A.**

In early 1988, once regulatory approvals have been obtained, First Jersey will join the National Westminster Bank Group as an affiliate of a newly formed holding company, to be named National Westminster Bancorp. The other banking subsidiary will be National Westminster Bank USA, headquartered across the Hudson River in New York City.

EXHIBIT 3

Continued

NATWEST USA: IN PERSPECTIVE

National Westminster Bank USA traces its origins to the charter of The First National Bank of Freeport, established in 1905, under which NatWest USA operates today. After a series of mergers, the bank became known as National Bank of North America (NBNA). In 1979, NBNA was acquired by the National Westminster Bank Group. In September 1983, the bank changed its name to National Westminster Bank USA, and in June 1984 dedicated National Westminster Bank Center, the 30-story corporate headquarters at 175 Water Street near Manhattan's South Street Seaport.

VALUES, MISSION, COMMITMENT TO QUALITY

From that office and others, NatWest USA's 4,600 employees supply a full range of banking services to corporate and individual customers. In doing so, they work within a framework of values and goals spelled out in a publication titled "The NatWest Way: Our Values, Mission and Commitment to Quality," which has been distributed to all employees.

   The statement outlines business goals, strategies and a commitment to excellence in responding to the needs of customers, communities, the parent organization and the bank's employees. This commitment includes a comprehensive quality improvement program, through which the bank is working to differentiate itself in the marketplace. The program makes quality the focus for each staff member and has an impact on every aspect of the bank's operations.

CUSTOMER SERVICE

Those operations include four lending areas (the Community Banking, New York City, Regional and United States groups), and five support areas (the Technology & Processing, Financial & Planning, Credit Policy & Administration, Human Resources, and Administration groups). The bank's Treasury group supports the line areas and is responsible for asset and liability management, brokerage sales and services, and trading. The bank also has Marketing and Corporate Trust divisions.

   Two subsidiaries were also formed in 1986. They are NatWest USA Credit Corporation, which offers asset-based financing to medium-sized companies, and NatWest USA Capital Corporation, a small business investment corporation (SBIC).

   NatWest USA serves its retail customers through a 135-branch network and a network of automated teller machines, called Teller Beam, in New York City, Westchester County and Long Island. Teller Beam is part of the NYCE (New York Cash Exchange) network of automated teller machines and the nationwide CIRRUS network. NatWest USA is a founding member of NYCE, which was established in 1984.

   Retail customers are also served by the bank's Consumer Credit division, which offers VISA, MasterCard and Gold MasterCard, as well as a full line of consumer credit products. Individuals whose net worth is $1 million or more may also take advantage of the personalized financial services offered by the bank's Private Banking department, through offices in Manhattan and Great Neck, Long Island. This department offers opportunities for cross-selling bank products, an important aspect of doing business at NatWest USA.

EXHIBIT 3   **Continued**

NatWest USA's other specialties include lending to middle-market corporate customers in the printing, textile and apparel, diamond and jewelry, publishing and real estate industries, particularly in New York City. Nationwide, NatWest USA specializes in meeting the financial needs of the health services, media, utilities and leasing industries.

The bank also concentrates on geographic niches, lending to middle-market corporate customers in the tri-state area outside of New York City. Large corporate and middle-market customers outside the tri-state area are served by representative offices and an Edge Act Office in Miami. NatWest USA's international division serves the international needs of the bank's domestic customers.

Two major staff areas provide key support to the bank's lending groups. They are the Administration and Technology & Processing groups. Administration encompasses the Legal, Auditing, Loan Review, Consulting Services and General Services divisions.

Two separate groups, Systems and Operations, were recently combined to form Technology & Processing. This restructuring was done to open the door to new opportunities and to further enhance customer service.

COMMUNITY INVOLVEMENT

NatWest USA recognizes that the prosperity and well-being of the communities that it serves are fundamental to its long-term success. Therefore it is committed to serve them by providing leadership and support which enrich the overall quality of life.

NatWest USA encourages voluntarism, is a leading supporter of United Way and has a substantial corporate contributions program. Also, the bank has developed a far-reaching "Arts in the Community" program which, this summer, won a Presidential Citation as part of the White House Program on Private Sector Initiatives, and awards in 1985 and 1987 from Business Committee for the Arts.

Major "Arts in the Community" events have included concerts by Luciano Pavarotti and Placido Domingo, and numerous concerts in Carnegie Hall. The bank also sponsors a wide range of arts events in local communities, such as concerts by Long Island Concert Pops, American Concert Band, New Orchestra of Westchester and Brooklyn Philharmonic.

In addition to "Arts in the Community" sponsorships, other community involvement includes employee participation in walk-a-thons and other civic functions, as well as bank sponsorship of events to benefit organizations such as the American Heart Association and Special Olympics. In all, NatWest USA was involved in 107 community events in the past year.

Among the community events sponsored by the bank are several concerned with education. Through its "Outstanding Young Achiever" award program, the bank recognized and gave financial awards to outstanding seniors at 22 New York metropolitan area high schools. And, in connection with its sponsorships of PBS broadcasts, NatWest USA develops and sends teaching kits to music teachers to encourage interest in the arts among students.

During the past four quarters, as part of the NatWest USA "Speakers in Your Community" program, bank representatives have given 102 speeches on financial

EXHIBIT 3	**Continued**

topics—an average of one every three working days—to business, civic and service organizations important to the bank.

This strong commitment to the community reflects the bank's Statement of Mission, Values and Commitment to Quality, and contributes to its growth.

The National Westminster Bank Group, headquartered in London, is among the largest, most profitable financial institutions in the world, with total assets of more than $120 billion and more than 90,000 employees worldwide. Including subsidiary companies, the Group has operations in 36 countries.

EXHIBIT 4	**Market Research at NATWEST USA**

The marketing department of NATWEST USA provided research indicative of the degree to which the firm has been able to achieve its goal of differentiation via quality programs and other strategic and cultural changes. Representatives noted that the true test for NatWest USA is the degree to which any organizational changes translated into changing perceptions by customers, i.e., whether customers feel that they are receiving more valuable products and information, and whether they feel confident about the bank and positive about the treatment received from it. It was observed that the types of changes that NatWest USA is seeking are very long term, and the full effects of programs implemented will have to be evaluated over a number of years. Nevertheless, studies conducted thus far provide glimpses of the effects of NatWest USA's efforts and of areas where further improvement is necessary.

The sheer amount of market research at NatWest USA is impressive—in the past two years alone, several major research studies have been carried out, conducted both by internal researchers and outside agencies. Each of the studies utilized sophisticated experimental designs with control groups, standard statistical sampling and data collection via interview, and survey and customer "shopping" techniques (in which researchers acted as customers and "bought" products and services).

The following describes and summarizes the conclusions of three major studies.

THE MIDDLE-MARKET STUDY

The Middle Market Study, concluded in March 1986, examined the financial behavior, needs, and attitudes of middle-market companies operating nationwide, and also examined NatWest USA's competitive position within the tri-state region of New York, New Jersey, and Connecticut. This study, along with the Commercial Banking Study (described below), provided current market research on the bulk of NatWest USA's business community markets. The "middle market" study covered firms with sales of $50–250 million and the "commercial market" study covered firms with $5–50 million.

The Middle-Market Study indicated that the middle market is dominated by manufacturing (50 percent) and wholesale trade (27 percent) businesses. The manufacturing industry was described as a "huge, attractive market, but also the most com-

EXHIBIT 4   **Continued**

petitive market segment." The wholesale trade industry, while less competitive for banking services, also uses fewer banks and fewer services. Yet the companies in the wholesale trade have the greatest demand for borrowing, both in terms of the percentage of firms in the industry that borrow as well as the amounts that they seek. The retail trade and the manufacturing industry also have heavy concentrations of borrowers.

The intense competition in the middle market is evidenced by the fact that most companies use four banks and are, on the average, actively solicited by four new banks as well. The research concluded that the intense competition "underscores the importance of staying actively involved in customer relationships, of having targeted calling programs, and of making effective calls on companies." It was observed that customers are becoming increasingly involved in their bank relationships and that this trend will continue. More companies want to know exactly where they stand with their banks and want the details of their agreements in writing. The trend is reflected in the three areas of changes in recent years that middle market customers consistently reported:

1. More calls are being made by banker's representatives.
2. More is being asked of the banks.
3. A greater participation of a company's treasury staff is present in initiating and maintaining a relationship with a bank.

With regard to bank selection issues, the study indicated that the vide president of finance was the officer most often responsible for selection of a bank as a service provider. The key selection criteria was described as "the company's overall relationship with the bank," an overall relationship seen as more important than specifics such as long terms and conditions. The specific terms do take on greater importance with certain issues, such as with respect to data processing services, leveraged buyout/acquisition loans, foreign exchange, and trade services. For firms dealing internationally, the study indicated that the key criteria for selection of a bank for international services is the presence of an existing domestic relationship and a bank's international service capabilities.

The study also indicated that the financial strength of the bank is a very important concern of the middle-market companies. Utilizing annual reports, accounting and financial officers of the middle-market companies evaluate the financial condition of the banks they use and the banks that solicit them.

Useful findings resulted when researchers asked the customers what types of things affected their view of the "importance" of a bank to their business and what factors improved the relationships of the companies with their banks. Banks were found to increase in importance to middle-market companies to the degree they were willing to lend, provide account officer service, and have competitive loan pricing. The bank's relationship with the company was found to improve with the introduction of new ideas and new services, the interest of the servicing bank in company information, the improvement of quality, and frequency of the bank's visits. Conversely, failures in these same areas, in terms of not keeping up to date with new ideas and possible services to offer, not calling often enough and not understanding

EXHIBIT 4	**Continued**

the company's decision-making processes detracted from the company's relationship. The most serious mistake, from the point of view of the customers, was the bank's not being thoroughly familiar with the company being serviced.

The Middle-Market Study concluded that, in the tri-state region, NatWest is an important competitor, with 12 percent market concentration and positioned similarly to Marine Midland, Bank of New York, and Irving Trust.

Most of its customers consider NatWest USA to be a principal bank (i.e., one of the banks they use most for domestic banking services) and one-third use NatWest USA as their overall lead bank. NatWest USA's customers and prospects are most heavily penetrated by the other four major banks.

With regard to customer calling, the study indicated that 78 percent of NatWest USA's prospects were called on more frequently by at least one or more competitors than they were called upon by NatWest USA. However, NatWest USA's customer calls were found to be highly effective in gaining new business, and more effective overall when compared to the competition.

In light of this information, the researchers concluded that NatWest USA should segment the middle market and made recommendations on reallocating the bank's resources to the most desirable segments.

THE COMMERCIAL BANKING STUDY

The Commercial Banking Study was concluded in August 1986 and examined similar issues as did the Middle-Market Study, but with respect to companies with annual sales of between $5 million and $50 million.

The Commercial Banking Study focused on the nine-county New York area where NatWest USA's principal commercial market is located (Bronx, Kings, Nassau, New York, Queens, Richmond, Rockland, Suffolk, and Westchester). This study indicated that NatWest USA is a major competitor in the commercial banking market. The bank is tied with Chase Manhattan in terms of market share, in fourth position behind Chemical Bank, Manufacturers Hanover, and Citibank.

Interviews with the commercial market customers indicated that NatWest USA's account officers and top management are doing an excellent job in terms of visiting and serving the commercial market customers. A high proportion of customers are called on regularly and interactions are perceived as highly effective.

NatWest USA is viewed as a credit provider to the commercial banking market, having a higher proportion of borrowing customers than most of the competition and a credit policy that is viewed more favorably than most of its competition. NatWest USA's noncredit services are also viewed favorably by the overall market, but ratings varied significantly among different sales size segments. NatWest USA's strongest noncredit service is in the area of cash management.

While the Banker's Trust acquisition clearly positioned NatWest USA as a major competitor, the Commercial Market Study emphasized that, in order to maintain the bank's market position, prospect calling efforts should be improved.

THE BRANCH SHOPPING STUDY

The Branch Shopping Study, concluded in January 1987, was undertaken to determine how the customers were treated and how customers perceived a NatWest USA

EXHIBIT 4   **Continued**

branch when they came in to open an account or inquire about the bank's services. The study placed emphasis on perceptions of bank employees' behavior and knowledge and attitudes when approached by customers under varying circumstances. The study also compared appearance of the branches and the presence and quality of sales efforts between NatWest USA and their competitive counterparts across different regions.

The Branch Shopping Study differed from the usual types of research wherein an interviewer obtains opinions from respondents. In this study, a researcher approached the NatWest USA branch representative as a "shopper" and recorded opinions and experiences resulting from the contact. The "shopper" came into a branch either to open a checking account or to cash a check and inquire about high-interest-bearing checking accounts.

In the case where a checking account was opened, shoppers were instructed not to specify the type of checking account they wanted to open, in an effort to see if branch representatives mentioned or discussed and explained the types of accounts available, explained about service charges and types of checks available, and counseled shoppers about appropriate accounts for them.

In the case where the customers came in to cash a check, they proceeded to the teller lines. They were instructed not to endorse the check prior to seeing the teller. They took note of any inappropriate behavior displayed by the tellers as well as the procedures followed by them. After the check was cashed, shoppers asked if the bank offered high-interest checking accounts. This procedure was designed to measure the ability of the tellers to service customers and provide information about products and services offered by the institution.

Approximately two hundred account-opening and check-cashing transactions were evaluated, two-thirds of which were with NatWest USA branches and the remaining third with the branches of competitors. The study was completed over a two-month period in late 1986.

The focus of data analysis was on overall "quality of service" measured in terms of the sales skills of tellers and representatives (defined as knowledge of service, ability to listen, ability to communicate, responsiveness to inquiry, credibility, and salesmanship), interpersonal skills (courtesy, friendliness, attitude, and establishment of rapport) and personal attributes (professional appearance, organization, promptness, business-like manner, and efficiency). An overall measure of satisfaction with the total shopping experience was included in the measure of quality.

The Branch Shopping Study's main conclusions were as follows (see Exhibit 5):

1. Overall, NatWest USA branch personnel are performing equal to, and, at times, better than the personnel of competitors in terms of quality of service they are providing. The study found that 66 percent of the shoppers were either extremely or very satisfied with NatWest USA, while only 59 percent were satisfied with competitor branch personnel.

2. The level of quality equal to competitors was found for both types of transactions studied. NatWest USA representatives scored at least as high as competitors on courtesy and friendliness and higher on attitude and the initial establishment of rapport. The perceptions of these interpersonal skills varied significantly across the NatWest USA operating regions and by the type of transaction studied.

EXHIBIT 4   **Continued**

3. In terms of the ratings of personal attributes of tellers and branch representatives, NatWest USA was rated equal to or higher than their competitors in terms of efficiency, professional appearance, promptness, organization, and business-like attitudes. Professional appearance and organizational skills rated highest for NatWest USA representatives in comparison to the competition.

4. The Branch Shopping Study compared certain measures to a similar study conducted in 1983. NatWest USA has apparently improved in the areas of product knowledge and sales-related skills, but not in customer relations skills. Another comparison to the 1983 study indicated an interesting dynamic taking place with regard to pressures upon bank personnel at peak times. Differences in the quality of service were noted in the current study between busy and non-busy hours, while the 1983 study had not perceived such differences. Interestingly, the differences noted in the present study were not in the direction that might be expected. Service at NatWest USA branches was found to be slightly better during the busy hours, and the study speculated that greater efficiency may arise at the peak times out of necessity.

5. Concerning branch environments, the study indicated that the interior and exterior environments for both NatWest USA and its competition are in excellent condition. The average waiting time in NatWest USA branches was found to be lower than the average for other banks.

EXHIBIT 5   **NatWest USA Branch Shopping Study: Satisfaction with Service Provided by Personnel—Overall by Total Bank**

		COMPETITION		
	NATWEST USA	TOTAL	COMMERCIAL	THRIFT
(Base: Total transactions)	(259)	(128)	(104)	(24)
Extremely satisfied	23%	21%	23%	12%†
Very satisfied	43	38	34	58
Neither satisfied nor dissatisfied	28	30	34	13
Not too satisfied	5	10	8	17
Not at all satisfied	1	—	—	—
No response	—	1	1	—

* = significantly higher
† = significantly lower

EXHIBIT 5

Continued

Satisfaction with Service Provided by Personnel—Overall by Transaction

	OPENING A CHECKING ACCOUNT		CASHING A CHECK AND HIGH-INTEREST-BEARING ACCOUNT INQUIRY	
	NATWEST USA	COMP.	NATWEST USA	COMP.
(Base: Total transactions)	(130)	(64)	(129)	(64)
Extremely satisfied	25%	27%	22%	16%
Very satisfied	46	33	40	44
Neither satisfied nor dissatisfied	22	25	33	34
Not too satisfied	5	14	5	6
Not at all satisfied	1	—	—	—
No response	1	1	—	—

Ratings of Branch Representatives on Interpersonal Skills (Percentage of Shoppers Rating "Extremely Satisfied") by Total Bank

		COMPETITION		
	NATWEST USA	TOTAL	COMMERCIAL	THRIFT
(Base: Total transactions)	(259)	(128)	(104)	(24)
Courtesy	46%	47%	48%	43%
Friendliness	41	42	43	41
Attitude	36	31	31	31
Establishing rapport	28	26	27	24

Ratings of Branch Representatives on Interpersonal Skills (Percentage of Shoppers Rating "Extremely Satisfied") by Transaction

	OPENING A CHECKING ACCOUNT		CASHING A CHECK AND HIGH-INTEREST-BEARING ACCOUNT INQUIRY	
	NATWEST USA	COMP.	NATWEST USA	COMP.
(Base: Total transactions)	(130)	(64)	(129)	(64)
Courtesy	53%	51%	39%	42%
Friendliness	45	44	35	41
Attitude	44	31	29	31
Establishing rapport	35	32	22	20

EXHIBIT 5

Continued

Ratings of Branch Representatives on Personal Attributes (Percentage of Shoppers Rating "Extremely Satisfied") by Total Bank

	NATWEST USA	COMPETITION		
		TOTAL	COMMERCIAL	THRIFT
(Base: Total transactions)	(259)	(128)	(104)	(24)
Efficiency	42%	38%	39%	33%
Professional appearance	40*	32	32	34
Promptness	37	37	40	28
Organization	32*	24	24	25
Business-like	31	26	25	29

Branch Environment: Total Transaction Time

	NATWEST USA	COMPETITION		
		TOTAL	COMMERCIAL	THRIFT
(Base: Total transactions)	(259)	(128)	(104)	(24)
Less than 10 minutes	26%	30%	32%	17%
10–19 minutes	42*	27	27	29
20–29 minutes	24	29	31	21
30–39 minutes	6	9	9	8
40 or more minutes	2	5	1	25
Average waiting time (in minutes)	15.1	17.1	15.4	24.3

* = significantly higher
† = significantly lower

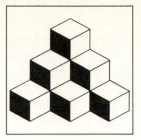

STRATEGIC ISSUES
SMALL BUSINESS

Fourwinds Marina

W. HARVEY HEGARTY • HARRY KELSEY, JR.

Jack Keltner had just completed his first day as general manager of the Four-winds Marina. It was mid-August and though the Marina slip rentals ran until October 30, business took a dramatic downturn after Labor Day. It would be unwise to change any of the current operations in the next three weeks, but he would have to move swiftly to implement some of the changes he had been considering, and at the same time would have the better part of a year to develop and implement some short-range and long-range plans that were sorely needed if the Marina were to survive.

The day before, Jack had been called in by Sandy Taggart, president of the Taggart Corporation, owners of the Fourwinds Marina and the Inn of the Fourwinds. Leon McLaughlin had just submitted his resignation as general manager of the marina. McLaughlin and Taggart had disagreed on some compensation McLaughlin felt was due him. Part of the disagreement concerned McLaughlin's wife, who had been hired to work in the parts department but had spent little time there due to an illness.

McLaughlin had been the fifth manager in as many years that the marina had been in operation. He had had fifteen years of marine experience before being hired to manage the marina. His experience, however, consisted of selling and servicing boats and motors in Evansville, Indiana, not in marina management. He took pride in running a "tight ship" and felt that the marina had an excellent chance of turning around after some hard times. It was fairly easy to keep the marina staffed because the resort atmosphere was so attractive, and his goal was to have the majority of the staff on a full-time basis year round. Even though the marina was closed from November until April there was a considerable amount of repair work on boats needed during those months. McLaughlin was told when hired that he had a blank check to get the marina shaped up. This open policy, however, was later rescinded. He and his wife had a mobile home near the marina but maintained a permanent residence in Evansville. For the most part he put in six full days a week but had an aversion to working on Sunday. McLaughlin was an effective organizer but weak in the area of employee and customer relations.

Keltner had no experience in marina management but was considered a hard worker willing to take on tremendous challenges. He had joined the Taggart Corporation after four years as a CPA for Ernst and Ernst, an accounting firm. Functioning as controller of the Taggart Corporation, he found that there was a tremendous volume of work demanded, necessitating late hours at the office and a briefcase full of work to take home with him most evenings. At this point, Keltner lived in a small community near the marina but still had to commute frequently to the home office of the Taggart Corporation in Indianapolis, an hour-and-a-half drive from Lake Monroe. He had indicated that he hoped to move the offices to Lake Monroe, site of the Marina and Inn, as soon as possible. Handling the accounting for the Marina, the Inn, and other Taggart Corporation interests could be done effectively at the Marina. The Inn and the Marina composed 90 percent of the corporation.

Much of the explanation for the heavy work load lay in the fact that there had been virtually no accounting system when he first joined Taggart. He had, however, set up six profit centers for the Marina and generated monthly accounting reports.

The other principal investors involved in the Taggart Corporation besides Sandy (A. L. Taggart III) were William Brennan, president of one of the state's largest commercial and industrial real estate firms, and Richard DeMars, president of Guepel-DeMars, Inc., the firm that designed both the Marina and the Inn.

Sandy Taggart was a well-known Indianapolis businessman who was chairman of the board of Colonial Baking Company. This organization was one of the larger bakeries serving the Indianapolis metropolitan area and surrounding counties. He did his undergraduate work at Princeton and completed Harvard's A.M.P. program in 1967. He was an easygoing man and appeared not to let problems upset him easily. He maintained his office at the Taggart Corporation in Indianapolis but tried to get to the Marina at least once every week. He kept in daily contact with Leon McLaughlin and continued to do the same with Keltner. He enjoyed being a part of the daily decision making and problem solving that goes on at the Marina and felt that he needed to be aware of all decisions due to its weak financial position. Taggart felt current problems stemmed from a lack of knowledge of the Marina business and lack of experienced general managers when it began operation some six years ago. He also admitted that their lack of expertise in maintaining accurate cost data and controlling their costs hurt them but felt Keltner has already gone a long way in correcting this problem.

Keltner had been intimately involved in the operation and felt that at a minimum the following changes needed to be made over the next twelve months:

1. Add 80 slips on E, F, and G docks and put in underwater supports on these docks to deter breakage from storms. Cost: $250,000–300,000. Annual profits if all slips are rented: $75,000 + .

2. Add a second person to assist the present secretary-receptionist-book-keeper. This will actually be a savings if the Indianapolis office is closed. Savings: $300 + /month.

3. Reorganize the parts department and put in a new inventory system. Cost: $3,000. Savings: $2,500–$3,000/year.

4. Keep the boat and motor inventory low. Boat inventory as of mid-August is approximately $125,000. It has been over $300,000.

5. Reduce the work force through attrition if a vacated job can be assumed by someone remaining on the staff.

6. Use E, F, and G for winter storage with the improved and more extensive bubbling system. Profits to be generated are difficult to estimate.

7. Light and heat the storage buildings so repair work can be done at night and in the winter. Cost: $12,000, which he estimates probably would be paid for from the profits in two winters.

Each of these changes would add to the effectiveness and profitability of the marina operation and that was his prime concern. The operation of the Inn was under the control of another general manager and the Inn operated as a separate corporate entity. Keltner was responsible only for the accounting procedures of the Inn.

As he reviewed the structure, background, and development of the Inn and the Marina he realized the problems that faced him in his new role as general manager—and at the same time controller of Taggart Corporation. Managing the Marina was a full-time seven-day-a-week job, particularly during the season. The questions uppermost in his mind were: (1) What would be the full plan he would present to Taggart for the effective, efficient and profitable operation of the Marina? and (2) How would it be funded? The financial statements presented a fairly glum picture, but he had the available back-up data to analyze for income per square foot on most of the operations, payroll data, and so on, as well as the knowledge he had gleaned working with the past general managers and observing the operation of the marina. Exhibit 1 presents an organizational chart for Fourwinds Marina. Exhibits 2 and 3 contain relevant financial data for Fourwinds Marina.

EXHIBIT 1 **Organization Chart for Fourwinds Marina**

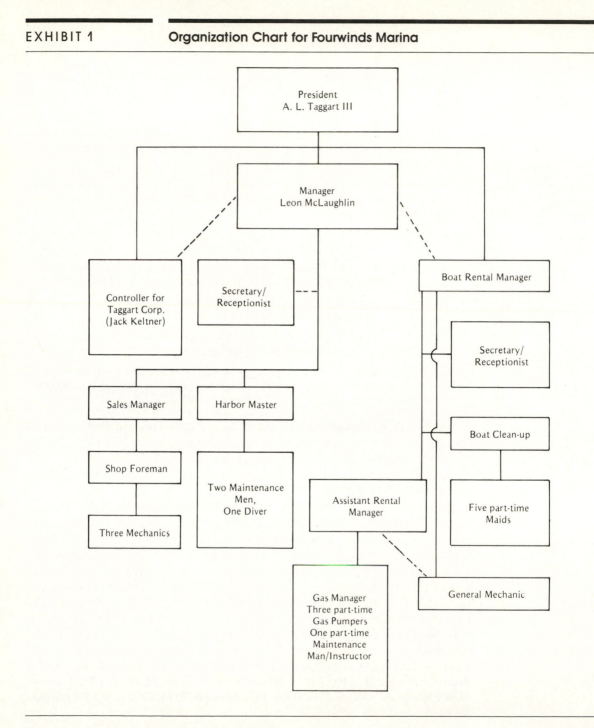

EXHIBIT 2 Profit–Loss Statement (Fiscal Year Ending March 31, 1974)

REVENUE			OPERATING EXPENSES		
Sale of new boats	$774,352		Wages and salaries	$228,154	
Sale of used boats	179,645		Taxes	23,725	
Sale of rental boats	17,051		Building rent	58,116	
			Equipment rent	8,975	
Total sales		$971,048	Utilities	18,716	
Other income:			Insurance	25,000	
Service and repair	$128,687		Interest on loans	209,310	
Gasoline and oil	81,329		Advertising	30,150	
Ship store	91,214		Legal expense	19,450	
Slip rental	174,808		Bad debt expense	8,731	
Winter storage	32,177		Miscellaneous	39,994	
Boat rental	99,895				
			Total operating expenses		670,321
Other income		$ 608,110			
			Total costs		$1,650,380
Total income		$1,579,158			
			Operating loss		$ 71,222
			Depreciation		122,340
EXPENSES					
			Total loss*		$ 193,562
Fixed costs:					
Cost of boats	$798,123				
Cost of repair equipment	56,698				
Ship store costs	64,405				
Cost of gasoline	51,882				
Boat rental costs	8,951				
Total fixed costs		$980,059			

*This represents the total operating loss of the Fourwinds Marina in the fiscal year ending March 31, 1974. Fourwinds sold a subsidiary in 1973 (boat sales firm in Indianapolis) on which they wrote off a loss of $275,580.

BACKGROUND DATA ON FOURWINDS MARINA

The Setting

The Fourwinds Marina and the Inn of the Fourwinds are located on Lake Monroe, a manmade reservoir over 10,000 acres in size nestled in the hills of southern Indiana. Both facilities are owned and operated by the Taggart Corporation but are operated as totally distinct and separate facilities. They cooperate in promoting business for each other.

The Inn occupies some 71,000 square feet on 30 acres of land. It is designed to blend into the beautifully wooded landscape and is constructed of rustic and natural building materials. It is designed to appeal to a broad segment of the population, with double rooms priced from $21 to $33. The Inn

EXHIBIT 3   **Balance Sheet (March 31, 1974)**

ASSETS				LIABILITIES	
Current assets:				Current liabilities:	
Cash	$ 31,858			Accounts payable	$ 89,433
Accounts receivable	70,632			Intercompany payables	467,091
New boats	199,029			Accrued salary expense	8,905
Used boats	60,747			Accrued interest expense	20,383
Parts	53,295			Accrued tax expense	43,719
Ship store	2,741			Accrued lease expense	36,190
Gas/oil	2,626			Prepaid dock rental	178,466
				Boat deposits	4,288
Total current assets	$ 420,928			Current bank notes	177,600
				Mortgage (current)	982,900
Fixed assets:		Less depr.		Note payable to floor plan	225,550
Buoys and docks	$ 984,265	$ 315,450		Note on rental houseboats	71,625
Permanent bldgs.	201,975	17,882		Notes to stockholders	515,150
Office furniture	3,260	704		Dealer reserve liability	13,925
Houseboats	139,135	15,631		Total current liabilities	$2,835,225
Work boats	40,805	7,987			
Equipment	72,420	38,742		Long-term note on houseboats	117,675
	$1,441,860	$ 396,396		Common stock—1,000 shares at par value $1/share	1,000
Net fixed assets	$1,045,464				
				Retained earnings deficit	(990,105)
Other assets:				Loss during year ending March 31, 1974*	(469,142)
Prepaid expense	$ 2,940				
Deferred interest expense	25,321				
				Total liabilities	$1,494,653
	$ 28,261				
Total assets	$1,494,653				

*Loss during year ending March 31, 1974 is composed of an operating loss of $71,222 plus depreciation of $122,340, and a write-off loss of a sold subsidiary of $275,580.

has a total of 150 sleeping rooms (singles, doubles, and suites) and has meeting rooms to appeal to the convention and sales meetings clientele. The largest meeting room will seat 300 for dining and 350 for conferences. Recreation facilities include an indoor-outdoor swimming pool, tennis courts, sauna, whirlpool bath, and a recreation room with pool tables and other games. Added facilities include two dining rooms and a cocktail lounge. The Inn is open year round, with heavy seasonal business in the summer months.

It is the first lodge of its nature built on state property with private funds. By virtue of the size of its food-service facilities (in excess of $100,000 per annum), it qualifies under Indiana state law for a license to serve alcoholic beverages on Sunday.

A brief description of the Pointe is also in order as its development promises a substantial boost to the Marina's business. The Pointe, located three miles from the Marina, consists of 384 acres on the lake. It is a luxury condominium development designed to meet the housing needs of primary and secondary home buyers. Currently 70 units are under construction. Twenty of these have been sold, and the down payment has been received on 80 more. These condominiums range from $25,000 to $90,000, with an average of $60,000. Approval has been secured for the construction of 1,900 living units over a seven-year period. The development has a completed eighteen-hole golf course. Swimming pools and tennis courts are now under construction. The Pointe is a multimillion dollar development by Indun Realty, Inc., Lake Monroe Corporation, and Reywood, Inc. Indun Realty is a wholly owned subsidiary of Indiana National Corp., parent firm of Indiana National Bank, the state's largest fiduciary institution.

The Fourwinds Marina occupies four acres of land and is one of the most extensive and complete marinas of its type in the United States. It consists of the boat docks, a salesroom for boats and marine equipment, an indoor boat storage facility, and marine repair shop.

There are seven docks projecting from a main connecting dock that runs parallel to the shoreline. The seven parallel docks extend from 330 to 600 feet into the lake at a right angle to the connecting dock. The center dock houses a large building containing a grocery store, snack bar, restrooms, and a section of docks used as mooring for rental boats.

At the end of the dock is an office for boat rental, five gasoline pumps, and pumping facilities for removing waste from the houseboats and larger cruisers.

The three docks to the right of the center dock (facing the lake) are docks A, B, and C and are designed for mooring smaller boats—run-abouts, fishing boats, and so on. A bait shop is on A dock. A, B, and C slips are not always fully rented. The three docks to the left are the prime slips (E, F, G) and are designed for berthing houseboats, large cruisers, etc.[1] There are a total of 460 rentable slips priced from $205 to $775 for uncovered slips and $295 to $1,125 for covered slips per season (April 1–October 30). Seventy-five percent of all the slips are under roof and are in the more desirable location; hence they are rented first. Electric service is provided to all slips, and the slips on E and F docks have water and trash removal provided at no extra cost. To the left of the prime slips are 162 buoys, renting for $150 per season. This rental includes shuttle boat service to and from the moored craft. Buoys are not considered to be a very profitable segment. The buoys shift and break loose occasionally, requiring constant attention. Time is required to retrieve boats that break loose at night or during storms.

Lake Monroe, the largest lake in Indiana, is a 10,700-acre reservoir developed by the U.S. Army Corps of Engineers in conjunction with and under the jurisdiction of the Indiana Department of Natural Resources. With the surrounding public lands (accounting for some 80 percent of the 150-mile shoreline) the total acreage is 26,000. It is a multipurpose project designed to provide flood control, recreation, water supply, and flow augmentation benefits to the people of Indiana.

The reservoir is located in the southwestern quadrant of the state, about nine miles or a 15-minute drive southwest of Bloomington, Indiana, home of Indiana University, and a 90-minute drive from Indianapolis. The Indianapolis metropolitan area has a population of over one million with some $3.5 billion dollars to spend annually. It is considered a desirable site for future expansion by many of the nation's top industrial leaders, as reported in a recent *Fortune* magazine survey. The city is the crossroads of the national interstate highway system, with more interstate highways converging here than in any other section of the United States. Its recently enlarged airport can accommodate any of the jet aircraft currently in operation and is served by most of the major airlines. The per capita effective buying income is $4,264 as contrasted with $3,779 for the United States as a whole, with almost half of all households falling in the annual income bracket of $10,000 and above. Although approximately 75 percent of the customers of the marina come from the Indianapolis area, it is estimated that there is a total potential audience of some 2.9 million inhabitants within a 100-mile radius of Bloomington.

The 34 acres of land on which the Fourwinds complex is located is leased to the corporation by the state of Indiana. In 1968 a prospectus was distributed by the Indiana Department of Natural Resources asking for bids on a motel and marina on the selected site. Of the eight to ten bids submitted, only one other bidder qualified. The proposal submitted by the Taggart Corporation was accepted primarily based on the economic strength of the individuals in the group as well as the actual content of the bid.

The prospectus specified a minimum rental for the land of $10,000. Taggart Corporation offered in its bid a guarantee of $2,000 against the first $100,000 in marina sales and income and 4 percent of all income over that amount. For the Inn, it guaranteed $8,000 against the first $400,000 of income plus 4 percent of all room sales and 2 percent of all food and beverage sales over that amount.

An initial lease of 37 years was granted to Taggart with two options of 30 years each. At the termination of the contract, all physical property reverts to the state of Indiana and personal property to Taggart. The entire dock structure is floating and is considered under the personal property category.

Prior to tendering a bid, the corporation visited similar facilities at Lake of the Ozarks, Lake Hamilton in Hot Springs, and the Kentucky Lakes operations. It received a considerable amount of information from the Kentucky Lakes management.

Construction of the initial phase of the marina began in May 1969 and the first 100 slips were opened in August under a speeded up construction schedule. The Inn had its formal opening in November 1972.

Sources of Income

Note: The Indiana Department of Natural Resources exercises total control over the rates that can be charged on slip rental as well as room rates at the Inn.

SLIP RENTAL   Reservations for slips must be made by November 15 of each year or the slip is subject to sale on a first-come basis. Ordinarily all slips are rented for the year. Rental period runs from April 1 to October 30. Rental varies from $205 to $1,125 depending on the size of slip and whether or not it is covered.

BUOY RENTAL   One hundred and sixty-two buoys are rented for the same April 1–October 30 season at a rate of $150. Shuttle boat service for transporting boat owners to and from their craft moored at the buoy area is operative 24 hours a day. It is not a scheduled service but operates as the demand occurs. This requires the primary use of a runabout and driver. The charge for the service is included in the buoy rental fee for the season. As long as the buoy field is in existence the shuttle service must operate on a 24-hour basis in season.

BOAT STORAGE—WINTER   It is more expensive to remove a boat from the water than to allow it to remain moored at the dock all winter. The prime rate for storage is based on the charge for storage in the covered area of the main inside storage building. This area is not heated or lighted, so repair work cannot be done in this building. An investment of about $12,000 would afford lighting and spot heating to overcome this drawback. When boats are stored, they are not queued according to those needing repair and those not needing service. As a result, time is lost in rearranging boats to get to those on which work must be performed. The storage facility is not utilized in the summer months. The addition of lights in the facility would allow display of used boats for sale that are currently stored out of doors. Rates for storage charges are

- 100 percent base rate—inside storage
- 70 percent of base rate—bubbled area of docks covered
- 60 percent of base rate—bubbled area of docks open
- 50 percent of base rate—open storage areas out of water

Storage rate is computed by the size of the boat. A six-foot-wide boat has a rate of $7. This is multiplied by the boat length to determine the total rate. So a 20-foot-long boat 7 feet wide would cost $140. Last winter the storage facility was filled. One hundred boats were stored with the average size somewhat larger than the 7 × 20 example given above. This rate does not include charges for removing the boat (approximately $75) from the water and moving it to either inside or outside storage areas. There has been, in the past, vandalism on the boats stored in the more remote areas of the uncovered, out of water storage. The marina claims no responsibility for loss, theft, or damage.

BOAT AND MOTOR RENTAL Available equipment is up to date and well maintained and consists of

- 15 houseboats—rental Monday to Friday $300; Friday to Monday $300
- 10 pontoon boats—hourly rental $20 for 3 hours; $35 for 6 hours
- 6 runabouts for skiing—$15–$20 per hour
- 12 fishing boats—$12 for 6 hours; $18 for 12 hours

Maximum hourly rental is thirteen hours per day during the week and fifteen hours per day on Saturday and Sunday (the rental rate does not include gasoline).

It is not uncommon to have all fifteen houseboats out all week long during the height of the season. (Season height is from Memorial Day weekend to Labor Day weekend.) Pontoons are about 50 percent rented during the week. Utilization of runabouts is 50 percent and fishing boats approximately 40 percent. The man who operates the boat and motor rental for the marina has a one-third interest in all of the boat rental equipment. The marina holds the balance. Funds for the purchase of the equipment were contributed on the same one-third to two-thirds ratio. Net profits after payment of expenses, maintenance, depreciation, and so on are split between the two owners according to the same ratio. The area utilized by the rental area could be converted to slips in the $500 range as a possible alternative use for the dock space. Rental income after expenses, but before interest and depreciation, was slightly less than $20,000 last season.

SMALL-BOAT REPAIR SHOP A small-boat repair shop is located between C and D docks. It is well equipped with mechanical equipment and a small hoist for removing small boats from the water for repair at the docks. This facility is currently standing idle. One qualified mechanic could operate it.

GROCERY STORE The grocery store is subleased and is effectively operated. Prices are those expected at a small grocery catering to a predominantly tourist clientele. Income from the leased operation is approximately $500 per month.

SNACK BAR The snack bar is operated by the Inn of the Fourwinds and returns a 5 percent commission to the marina on food sales. Currently it is felt that the manager of the snack bar is not doing a reliable job in operating the unit. The snack bar is sometimes closed for no apparent reason. Food offered for sale includes hot sandwiches, pizza, snack food, soft drinks, milk, and coffee. Prices are high and general quality is rated as good.

GASOLINE SALES   Five pumps are located around the perimeter of the end of the center dock. They are manned thirteen hours per day, from 7:00 A.M. to 8:00 P.M., seven days a week. The pumps for the removal of waste from the houseboats and other large craft are located in this area. It takes an average of five minutes to pump out the waste and there is no charge. These gasoline pumps are the only ones available on the lake that permit access to the pump from the water.

BOAT AND BOAT ACCESSORY SALESROOM   A glass-enclosed showroom occupying approximately 1,500 square feet of floor space is located at the main entrance to the marina property. Major boat lines Trojan Yacht, Kingscraft, Burnscraft, Harris Flote Bote, and Signa, as well as Evenrude motors, are offered for sale. In addition, quality lines of marine accessories are available. The salesroom building also houses the executive offices of the marina and the repair and maintenance shops. Attached to the building is the indoor storage area for winter-housing a limited number of boats. Last year total boat sales were approximately $971,048. The boat inventory has since been reduced from last year's $300,000, removing some lines while concentrating on others that offered higher profit on sales.

Fourwinds Marina is the only operation in the state that stocks the very large boats. They are also the only facility in Indiana with large slips to accommodate these boats. With E, F, and G filled and a waiting list to get in, selling the larger, more profitable boats has become nearly impossible.

MARINA DOCKING AREA FACTS

Dock Construction

The entire section is of modular floating construction. Built in smaller sections that can be bolted together, the construction is of steel frameworks with poured concrete surfaces for walking upon and styrofoam panels in the side for buoyancy. In the event of damage to a section, a side can be replaced easily, eliminating repair of the entire segment of dock. Electrical conduits and water pipes are inside the actual dock units. The major damage to the styrofoam dock segments comes from ducks chewing out pieces of the foam to make nests and from gasoline spillage that eats the styrofoam. An antigas coating is available. Damage from boats to the dock is minimal. The docks require constant attention. A maze of cables underneath the sections must be kept at the proper tension or the dock will buckle and break up. Three people are involved in dock maintenance. If properly maintained the docks will have twenty to thirty more years of use. Original cost of the entire dock and buoy system was $984,265.

Winter Storage

Winter storage can be a problem at a marina that is located in an area where a freeze-over of the water occurs. It is better for the boat if it can remain in the water. Water affords better and more even support to the hull. By leaving the craft in the water possible damage from hoists used to lift boats and move them to dry storage is avoided. These factors, however, are not common knowledge to the boat owner and require an educational program.

A rule of the marina prohibits any employee from driving any of the customers' boats. Maintaining a duplicate set of keys for each boat and the cost of the insurance to cover the employee are the prime reasons for this ruling. This means, however, that all boats must be towed, with possibility of damage to the boats during towing.

Bubbling Process

To protect boats left in the water during the winter season, Fourwinds Marina has installed a bubbling system. The system, simple in concept, consists of hoses that are weighted and dropped to the bottom of the lake around the individual docks and along a perimeter line surrounding the entire dock area. Fractional horsepower motors operate compressors that pump air into the submerged hose. The air escaping through tiny holes in the hose forces warmer water at the bottom of the lake up to the top, preventing freezing of the surface or melting ice that might have frozen before the compressors were started. The lines inside the dock areas protect the boats from being damaged by ice formations while the perimeter line prevents major damage to the entire dock area from a pressure ridge that might build up and be jammed against the dock and boats in high wind.

NOTES

1. E, F, and G are the most profitable slips and are fully rented. There is a waiting list to get into these slips.

King, Lyons, Musak, and Company*

D. L. BATES

COMPANY DEVELOPMENT

King, Lyons, Musak, and Company (KLM) was formed 24 years ago by three partners, Leo King, Bill Lyons, and Jim Musak, who had left a Big Eight accounting firm. The partners felt that a market existed for a local accounting firm that would cater to the needs of larger and stronger local companies. The firm was not interested in the financial-statement accounts of small local companies. KLM secured new clients through referrals as a result of doing a fine job for its present clients. It built a good reputation in its original office by being sensitive to the needs of non-national, strong, local firms. KLM was able to keep its clients' accounting costs at a reasonable level. It was able to help them design systems that provided all relevant operating information but at the same time were fairly inexpensive and easily understood. KLM also recruited business through the activities of its partners in the local community. The firm was successful in its original location at Dallas, Texas, and in nine years it grew to include eleven partners and a staff of 51. At that time the partners decided to expand, as many of their clients had multiple facilities. It was decided that two additional offices should be opened, each under the direction of one of the original partners. Three years later, five more partners were added to the firm. The expansion offices proved to be quite profitable, and their supervision was given to new managers so that the two original partners could return to Dallas.

This change in personnel occurred because the majority partner, Leo King, had become somewhat concerned about maintaining the quality of the firm's audits, as well as about the direction the firm was taking. King said, "We want to remain one firm, not three loosely associated entities with the same name. To preserve this, we need a strong central management to provide planning and control. We need the planning in order to determine what directions the firm will take in the future as well as the kind of controls needed to ensure that we do not lose sight of our target market."

Fifteen years after the founding of KLM, additional offices were opened in Kansas City and Los Angeles. Six years later a Phoenix office was added, and one year later an Omaha office was opened. The firm now had 33 partners and a total staff of 312.

The growth of KLM's offices and staff is shown in Exhibit 1. Information about each office is contained in Exhibit 2.

KLM's present organizational design is shown in Exhibit 3. Leo King is the majority and managing partner. The executive committee consists of all

---

*This case was prepared by D. L. Bates, Professor of Management, California State University. Reprinted with permission.

EXHIBIT 1

King and Associates Five-Year Statistical Summary

STAFF	PREVIOUS YEARS				
	20TH	19TH	14TH	11TH	9TH
Number of partners	3	5	11	18	23
Number of staff	21	51	106	185	225
Audit	16	37	84	160	188
Tax	5	14	22	25	37
Number of offices	1	1	3	4	5

STAFF	PREVIOUS YEARS				
	4TH	3RD	2ND	1ST	LAST
Number of partners	25	26	29	31	33
Number of staff	238	246	284	294	312
Audit	196	199	230	235	253
Tax	42	47	54	59	59
Number of offices	5	6	7	7	7

senior partners, and their various staff positions are as shown. All staff positions and committees are occupied by partners. The organization of each branch office is illustrated in Exhibit 4. A partner—usually a senior partner—is in charge of each office, and junior partners are in charge of auditing and personnel practices at each office.

EXHIBIT 2

Previous Years' Local Office Operation

LOCATION	OPENING DATE	NO. OF PARTNERS	NO. OF STAFF	GROSS REVENUE	OPERATING EXPENSES*
Dallas (head office)	24 years ago	7	86	$1,921,914	$223,614
Houston	13 years ago	5	41	1,081,276	93,125
Kansas City	9 years ago	4	33	816,734	62,175
Phoenix	4 years ago	3	31	834,662	53,128
Oklahoma City	13 years ago	6	43	1,198,806	126,340
Los Angeles	9 years ago	5	60	1,128,288	96,321
Omaha	1 year ago	3	18	470,120	30,297
Totals		33	312	$7,451,800	$685,000

*Does not include partners' salaries.

EXHIBIT 3   **Organizational Chart**

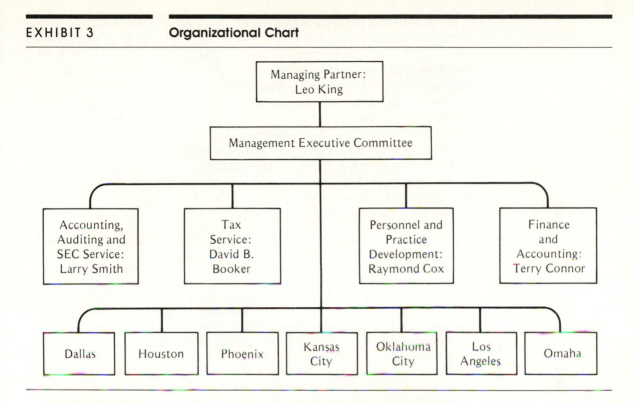

EXHIBIT 4   **Branch Office Organization**

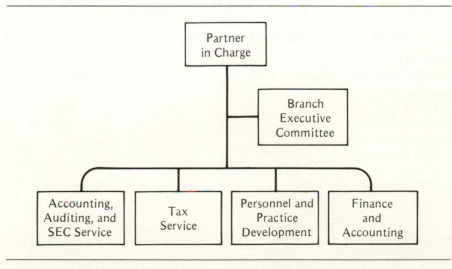

If well-trained partners are available, they are placed in charge of the remaining functions at each office. The partners in charge of each branch office are the critical elements. They must keep the quality of client relationships high, provide for the training of the staff, and ensure that all technical work adheres to company standards.

The management's executive committee meets quarterly, and an annual meeting held in October is attended by all partners. The partners in local offices meet regularly to discuss any problems that may arise and to evaluate periodically their offices' progress and personnel.

The three original partners are quite satisfied with the firm's past performance. However, lately, discussion has centered around what direction the firm should take in the future.

Leo King states his position this way:

Why get off a winning horse? We've been successful at opening new branches or existing practices in the past; hence, we have the expertise. There are any number of potential cities we should consider. There are Portland, Seattle, and San Francisco on the West Coast; Minneapolis, St. Louis, Chicago, Cleveland, Cincinnati, Memphis, and Indianapolis in the Midwest; New Orleans, Atlanta, and Miami, to name but a few, in the South. And, of course, there's the whole eastern seaboard that hasn't been touched. If Bill and Jim don't want the risk of opening new offices, let's buy out some existing small practices. After all, the Los Angeles and Phoenix offices were buy-out operations, and Bill and Jim certainly cannot complain about the Los Angeles office. Perhaps we need to be more restrictive in our selection of firms to purchase. I've had data collected on two firms in each of two cities that I think deserve additional consideration, that is, if Bill and Jim don't want to risk starting from scratch. [See Exhibit 5.]

EXHIBIT 5   **Firms to Consider for Purchase**

LOCATION	MINNEAPOLIS (A)	MINNEAPOLIS (B)	NEW ORLEANS (A)	NEW ORLEANS (B)
Office staff	1	1	1	1
Number of clients	440	560	840	633
Number of partners	2	3	3	6
Number of staff	6	11	7	12
Gross revenue	130,000	230,000	90,000	330,000
Net profits (before partner compensation)	43,000	77,000	(5,000)	150,000
Reason for selling	Both partners retire in one year	Partners desire to join larger firm	No reason given	Two retiring; remainder want opportunities associated with larger firm

Bill Lyons thinks that a redefinition of the target market may be in order:

The greatest future potential for our firm is in tax preparation for upper-middle and high-income individuals. With the computerized tax services available today, this market now becomes economical to tap. True, the average billing may only be about $200, but our cost will run only about $100. With the increasing complexity of tax laws, and the increasing family-income levels, this market will continue to have a tremendous future growth. We don't need to open new offices, and we can use our established reputation to gain a foothold in this market. Perhaps beefing up the existing tax service staff is all that will be needed.

As for Leo's contention that new offices are the only way to go, I say, look at our latest additions. How about Omaha? It's struggling along with Kansas City. Sure, both places are earning a profit—we're pleased with that—but the growth has not occurred as planned. As for buying out existing practices, we tried that at Phoenix, and it hasn't proven any better. If we look at the performance of these three offices, it seems to me that competition in our market is increasing either from the Big Eight or other firms like ourselves, or from both. It seems to me that the potential in cities cited by Leo doesn't exist anymore.

Jim Musak believes that the firm should hold down its number of branch offices for the present but expand the services offered to client firms. Specifically, he recommends adding a management advisory service (MAS) division. Jim says:

Look, we're in the client firm; we have access to information from the audit that indicates present or potential problem areas. We now point these areas out to the client in the course of the audit. If the client firm secures the consulting service from a consulting firm, the consulting firm's people must become familiar with the information we already possess, so it's costing the client firm more for the advice. We could provide the advice just as easily and at a substantial savings in costs.

Of course, new staff would be needed but not to the extent that Leo and Bill think. Our audit staffs are roughly specialized by industry now. They already possess a great deal of problem-solving skills, and many would welcome the opportunity to move to a MAS position. It will give them greater variety in their positions. If the idea of beginning from scratch scares them, let's buy out an existing firm. I already have one in mind and have done some preliminary work.

A copy of Musak's preliminary report is in Appendix A at the end of this case.

All three partners agree that the firm cannot just stop where it is. There are too many young, ambitious people in the pipeline who were recruited on the basis of joining a growth firm. If the firm stagnates, aggressive new personnel will be hard to find and existing personnel may not remain with KLM.

WHAT CPA FIRMS DO

In general, the professional service of a CPA firm is divided functionally into three principal areas: auditing, taxes, and management advisory services (MAS). The auditing function is viewed as pivotal.

Auditing

A primary function of the public accounting profession is to render independent and expert opinions on the fairness of presentation of a corporation's annual report. For example, the CPA firm makes an examination of the objective evidence underlying the data reported. This examination is called an *audit*.

Taxation

The area of taxation includes the preparation of income tax returns and the necessary accounting information for this purpose as well as advising clients on tax matters and helping them in taxation planning.

MAS

In public accounting some firms provide advice and consultation on management services similar to the kind of advice and consultation provided by management consultants.

DEVELOPMENT OF THE CPA INDUSTRY

The accounting profession in this country can be traced back to about 1880 when English and Scottish investors began to put their money into American securities. The investors who bought heavily into American breweries sent their own auditing firms to the United States to check on the health of their investments. Two members of the Big Eight, Price Waterhouse and Peat, Marwick & Mitchell, were originally British firms that got their start in the United States in this way. Today, of course, they are entirely American-owned but have working relationships with the British partnerships.

By World War I the ownership of public securities had become fairly widespread, and there was a growing awareness of the need for more uniformity in financial reporting. In 1917, with the help of the accounting profession, the Federal Reserve Board produced a memorandum (subsequently published in booklet form) entitled "Approved Methods for the Preparation of Balance Sheet Statements." This booklet was the first major step toward systematized financial reporting. It made business leaders aware of the need to employ accountants who understood what was required in making reports.

During the 1920s the New York Stock Exchange also boosted the accountants' business by waging a continuous campaign to persuade corporations to provide more financial information. In 1933, after the crash of 1929, the Exchange, with advice from the American Institute of Certified Public Accountants, initiated a whole new series of standards for the treatment of unrealized profit, capital surplus, earned surplus, and other corporate financial items. These standards were incorporated into the accounting principles approved by the American Institute of Certified Public Accountants. That same year the Exchange also began requiring of all listed corporations an audit certificate by an independent CPA. Both of these developments enhanced the prestige and acceptance of the independent accountant.

The profusion of taxes and tax complications have also accelerated the growth of the profession. Many Americans had their first contacts with accountants in the period just after 1913, the year when the first income tax law was passed. The income tax laws are wryly referred to as the "accountant's full-employment act."

This tax practice is still growing. The staff in tax departments of CPA firms often number in excess of 250 specialists. Their clients today include not only corporations and wealthy individuals but an increasing number of upper-middle-income citizens who find it necessary or convenient to pay $150 or $250 to have their taxes handled by a specialist. No one knows just how many such people there are, but estimates have placed the total market for individuals at about 1.5 million—roughly the same as the number of individuals whose annual taxable income is over $25,000.

In the post–World War II years the rise of the accountant has been accelerated by three rather special phenomena: a vast wave of corporate mergers; the need for better accounting about the financial affairs of labor unions, pension and welfare funds, foundations, and other institutions; and the push of the big auditing firms into a vast, sprawling area called "general management services."

During the 1950s the number of mergers involving manufacturing companies, for example, rose from about 300 to above 500 a year. The market for noncorporate accounting services expanded continuously. The 1959 disclosure law required labor unions to file financial statements with the Department of Labor but did not require these statements to be audited unless the secretary requested an audit. Over 50,000 unions were affected.

The MAS business burgeoned in the accounting profession during the 1960s. In effect, the auditors were going into competition with the management consultants. The independent auditor who was requested to examine a corporation's financial records often became aware of the full range of problems facing the company. Moreover, many auditors were experts in some fields; for example, an auditor who had spent twenty years auditing department stores might know more about merchandising than some of his or her clients—and it was probably inevitable that such auditors, observing the surge of business to professional management-consultant firms, would feel a desire to sell their own expertise too.

The MAS division of each of the Big Eight firms is included among the top twenty management-consulting groups in the United States. For example, Ernst & Ernst; Peat, Marwick & Mitchell; and Price Waterhouse all have staffs of 350 in their MAS divisions. The rate of expansion in management services is 15 percent per annum, which is higher than the growth of non-CPA firms that do consulting. Projections foresee the maintenance of this growth rate through 1980.

Those who staff the management-consulting departments come increasingly from disciplines other than accounting. Many of these specialists do not possess a CPA certificate, yet they play a significant role in the forward thrust of the profession. CPA firms will undertake such nonaccounting assignments as labor negotiations, personnel selection, new product planning, and factory design.

THE INDUSTRY IN GENERAL

Dominating the large CPA firms are the Big Eight firms. Information on them appears in Exhibit 6. What sets the Big Eight apart from most other auditing firms is not only their size and influence but also the fact that they are national and international in the scope of their operations. The bulk of public accounting in the United States is done by some thirty thousand small local firms. In between these firms and the giants are a number of well-known seminational firms, whose senior partners are also influential in the

---

EXHIBIT 6   **Summary of Big Eight CPA Firms**

FIRM	NO. OF U.S. OFFICES	NO. OF U.S. PARTNERS AND PRINCIPALS	ESTIMATED U.S. NET BILLINGS (DOLLAR AMOUNTS IN MILLIONS)			
			AUDITING	TAX	MANAGEMENT SERVICES	TOTAL
Arthur Anderson & Co.	41	650	$55	$17.5	$17.5	$190,000
Ernst & Ernst	108	390	60	20	20	180,000
Haskins & Sells	75	400	70	20	10	155,000
Coopers & Lybrand	70	450	78	17	5	135,000
Peat, Marwick & Mitchell	106	660	65	20	15	225,000
Price Waterhouse & Co.	54	250	70	18	12	180,000
Touche Ross & Co.	60	450	58	25	17	110,000
Arthur Young & Co.	60	370	66	17	17	100,000

SOURCE: *Business Week*, April 1972, p. 54.

profession. These include Seidman & Seidman, Scovell Wellington, S. D. Leidesdorf, Main & Co., Horwath & Horwath, and Alexander Grant. Like the Big Eight, many of these firms are headquartered in New York. However, they characteristically have only a few branch offices, and their gross revenues run below $10 million. It is this group with which KLM must compete. A breakdown of the CPA industry is shown in Exhibit 7.

The problem of bigness aggravates the accounting profession as much as it does any other industry. Virtually any member of the Big Eight or of the seminational accounting firms will say that the backbone of the profession is the small, local, independent accounting firm. Such firms still are the training ground for the great majority of independent accountants. These firms have the bulk of personal tax business, and most of whatever auditing is done for the more than 4 million small business enterprises in the United States. These local firms, however, have never been able to compete effectively with national and seminational firms for the business of big clients—for example, those that pay over $15,000 a year in fees. The medium-sized firm—its mainstay client—outgrows the seminational CPA firm. It often happens that a local company separates from a local auditor when the company makes its first public offering of stock. At such a time the underwriters are likely to insist that the prospectus bear the name of a national auditing firm.

CPA firms, in common with most professional organizations, are partnerships. The management of the partnership is vested in a committee of senior partners, which in certain firms is referred to as the *board of directors*. The chief executive officer is usually referred to as the *chairman* or *managing partner*.

The executive or senior partner of any CPA firm views the organization as a whole, studies the reasons underlying the loss of clientele, introduces legitimate publicity, encourages staff members to meet at regular intervals, projects the expansion of the firm, attends meetings of the firm, maintains

---

EXHIBIT 7   **Employment of AICPA Membership**

SIZE	FOURTEEN YEARS AGO		FOUR YEARS AGO	
	NO. OF PRACTICE UNITS	PERCENT OF AICPA MEMBERSHIP	NO. OF PRACTICE UNITS	PERCENT OF AICPA MEMBERSHIP
Largest 25 firms	25	24.6%	25	38.6%
Firms with:				
Ten or more AICPA members	148	6.7	258	7.5
Two to nine AICPA members	3,455	39.2	5,104	33.6
One AICPA member	7,787	29.5	9,588	20.3

contacts with clients, surveys weak points in operations of the firm, and stresses independence relative to its clients. The executive partner rises through the ranks, his or her length of service varying with the firm's policy and the retirement set for his or her predecessor. Most staff members retire at 60 or 65 years of age. In some firms financial arrangements become progressively less attractive after age 65 while mandatory retirement is set at age 70.

The chain of command ranges downward from partner to manager to senior to junior (or staff) accountant. Typical progression between ranks is: junior to senior, two to three years; senior to manager, two to three years; and manager to partner, four to six years. Heavy emphasis is placed on training, performance evaluation, and career planning at all levels. In recruiting, CPA firms tend to look for young, ambitious, and aggressive members. A major firm will expect an applicant to the firm to have maintained at least a B-grade average in his or her higher education.

KLM

Developing talented personnel is one of the most important criteria for a firm that markets professional services. Selecting the best college graduates is one way of maintaining the high standards required. For firms recruiting college graduates, the starting salaries are by no means the fundamental issue. New accounting graduates do not base their choice primarily on what their entry-level position pays, although pay may be a deterrent if it is too far out of line with what they might make in other fields. KLM has been successful in its recruiting efforts because it has emphasized the firm's rapid growth, which provides rapid advancement.

KLM, however, does subscribe to an "up-or-out" policy. The time limitations are shown in Exhibit 8. Although KLM's time for advancement is moderate compared to the one used by the Big Eight, its reason is easily

EXHIBIT 8

Promotion Time Schedule

POSITION MOVEMENT	YEARS EMPLOYED BEFORE MOVING TO NEXT POSITION	
	KLM	BIG EIGHT
Junior to Senior	1–3	1–2
Senior to Manager	2–5	2–3
Manager to Partner	4–9	4–7

justifiable. KLM does not allocate the funds or time for training that are required to meet the accelerated schedule of a Big Eight firm.

Under KLM's normal selection procedures, a new graduate is expected to become a CPA at about age 26. Movement from the rank of junior to senior accountant is virtually automatic if the CPA has been obtained. Promotion to manager is also not very difficult, however. It is the pool of managers that receives the most attention. The strength of the firm is largely determined by its managers because of the operational responsibilities they are delegated in conducting audits and supervising departments. They must be technical experts, but in addition they must be supervisors. It is from the managerial pool that partners are selected, and the managers have until they are about 34 years of age to prove that they are of partnership caliber.

During tenure in the managerial position, each manager is encouraged by KLM to join and become active in civic and public organizations; KLM defrays all expenses associated with such activities. KLM also encourages its managers to become members of social clubs, both for relaxation and to broaden their base of acquaintanceship with people of their own age who will become the directors and executives of the major commercial and industrial firms in the area.

If KLM does not wish to retain an individual as a partner, it feels that it has an obligation to assist the person in finding a desirable executive position in industry or government. This not only preserves the morale of the pool of managers but it is also a good way to develop and maintain client relationships. Obviously, managers are in training for partnership positions, and just as obviously, all managers will not be promoted.

KLM's starting salaries for the past year averaged $11,580. The average salary for each class of employees is as follows: managers, $24,000; seniors, $16,800; juniors, $14,680; and office and supporting staff, $9,000.

Partners are compensated by a salary plus profit sharing. The salary is a reflection of the time devoted to the company, variations in productivity, and differences in services performed. The profit sharing is based on capital proportions. For the past year the average compensation received by partners was $62,400. The average age of the partners was 40, and all but two had been promoted through the ranks of KLM. The two exceptions were specialists in tax services.

The company has two retirement plans: one for partners and the other for staff. Retirement for partners commences at age 65 and provides for fifteen annual payments starting at the end of the first full year of retirement. The yearly benefit payable out of distributed profits is an amount equal to the annual average of the total salary and profit share earned by the retiring partner in the ten years preceding the year of retirement. These payments will continue for fifteen years or upon the partner's death, whichever occurs first. In addition, the retiring partner is repaid any capital or credits. No one at KLM has retired so far.

For members of the professional and office staff, similar retirement rules apply, except that salaries are the only consideration. However, there are ten annual payments that occur, which are not terminated at the death of the beneficiary.

CLIENT RELATIONSHIPS

For a particular engagement the client relationships are handled at either the partner's or manager's level, and the junior partner is responsible for the technical aspects whereas the senior partner's responsibility is principally supervisory. The majority of the senior partner's time is devoted to what KLM calls "diplomacy" effort, that is, persuading a client that office furniture cannot be written off in two years. The remainder of the time should be devoted to making recommendations on some phases of the client's business and attempts to pursue new business.

The pursuit of new business, for a CPA firm, is hampered by several kinds of restrictions contained in the code of professional ethics. Not only is advertising unethical but any competitive bidding is also frowned upon. In addition, contacting a prospective client without the knowledge of his or her incumbent auditing firm is discouraged. Open competition for a new account is permissible only when a potential client has never had an auditing firm and decides to seek the services of one; then it is permissible to make a direct approach.

The most common source of new clients is a recommendation from a satisfied client. The recommendation of a satisfied client is more convincing than anything that can be said about the company's skills. Referrals by present clients are the result of good, sound work that has been previously performed.

Another common mode of developing new clients is the cultivation of good relationships and friendships with executives, bankers, attorneys, and other individuals or professionals who are or will be in a position to recommend the use of KLM's services. In addition, maintaining good public relations through planned activities that demonstrate KLM's possession of knowledge is also important. This is accomplished through memberships in important business associations and as a result of the willingness of employees of KLM to deliver major speeches before professional and nonprofessional groups. Given the fact that local client firms often outgrow local accounting firms as they go public, the maintenance of an inflow of new clients is essential to KLM.

FEE DETERMINATION

An accounting firm's revenues are derived from renting out the services of its professional staff. Its professional staff is the production capacity of the firm, and an idle professional staff member is viewed with the same dismay

EXHIBIT 9

KLM Fee Schedule

RANK	AVERAGE HOURLY RATE
Junior	$22 to $25
Senior	$27 to $32
Manager	$35 to $42
Partner	$52 to $60

a manufacturing firm might view an idle plant. Generally, KLM feels that its professional staff is properly utilized if 75 percent of the staff's time is billed to customers. At this rate the professional staff would generate revenues about twice their salaries, which lowers their direct and indirect costs and also gives an acceptable profit. The rate of each class of professional staff is computed on the basis of an annual chargeable time standard of 200 seven-hour days. Although the actual performance time billed occasionally exceeds 1,400 hours, KLM feels that this is a realistic yardstick to use. The previous year's fee schedule is shown in Exhibit 9.

In establishing its fees, KLM must first estimate the length of time it takes its people to become familiar with the client firm. Obviously, for existing clients this estimate is very low. However, for new clients a variety of factors have to be considered, such as sales volume, number of operations the client firm performs, and the number of branches or divisions. In general, KLM's work load is heaviest in the first year, and occasionally KLM expects to lose money on a very large account—even with normal fees. However, KLM expects to recover this loss in the second year when the work load drops by 25 percent. In the third year the account should be highly profitable.

One-time engagements are not billed at KLM's regular rates but at a premium rate. KLM does not reduce rates for work done in the so-called slack season, as some of its competitors do.

KLM utilizes a separate billing procedure. One statement is utilized for the regular audit services. Separate statements cover special services, such as budgeting, tax planning, revenue agent's examination, or other special services. Final billing for a client is the responsibility of the partner in charge of the engagement, and the billing may be adjusted according to the factors listed in Exhibit 10.

KLM's comparative income statements and balance sheets are shown in Exhibits 11 and 12 respectively.

EXHIBIT 10

Factors Influencing Final Bill to Client

1. Amount of time devoted to the engagement
2. Expense, including overhead and unusual expenses caused by the engagement
3. Skill and experience of the staff members who undertake the work
4. Technical importance of the work and amount of responsibility assumed by KLM
5. Value to the client of the service rendered
6. Difficulty of the engagement
7. Established client versus new or casual client
8. Size and character of the community
9. Inconvenience to the accounting firm
10. Ability of the client to pay
11. Acceptability of the fee to the client
12. Customary fees within the community

EXHIBIT 11

King, Lyons, Musak, and Company Comparative Income Statements for Years Ending July 31

	FIFTH PREVIOUS YEAR	FOURTH PREVIOUS YEAR	THIRD PREVIOUS YEAR	SECOND PREVIOUS YEAR	LAST YEAR
Income: professional fees	$5,342,225	$5,712,000	$6,300,030	$6,510,050	$7,451,800
Distribution of income:					
Personnel salaries:					
Partners	960,000	1,092,000	1,222,400	1,340,000	1,486,000
Managers	790,653	856,803	923,804	940,197	1,080,000
Professional staff	1,762,934	1,884,962	2,232,011	2,082,471	2,464,000
Office support	320,533	342,720	372,003	378,603	423,108
Total salaries	3,834,120	4,176,485	4,750,218	4,741,271	5,453,018
Operating expenses:					
Office operating costs	201,002	228,480	228,000	225,311	231,013
Training and research	148,732	171,360	198,401	189,302	211,544
Insurance	114,367	115,312	118,921	119,210	141,036
Interest	40,130	45,680	41,054	42,076	40,518
Other	613,227	623,145	589,700	621,410	685,000
Total operating expenses	1,117,458	1,183,977	1,176,806	1,197,309	1,309,121
Retained earnings (for profit sharing and expansion)	390,647	351,538	373,736	571,470	689,571
Billings by line of business percent					
Audit	84%	83%	79%	78%	78%
Tax	16	17	21	22	22

EXHIBIT 12	King, Lyons, Musak, and Company Comparative Balance Sheets for Years Ending July 31		

	THIRD PREVIOUS YEAR	SECOND PREVIOUS YEAR	LAST YEAR
ASSETS			
Current assets			
Cash in bank and on hand	531,741	545,000	788,850
Notes receivable	10,575	11,515	16,312
Accounts receivable—current	612,015	642,016	851,354
Accounts receivable—over 90 days	24,510	16,519	52,103
Unbilled receivables	411,436	403,210	581,216
Unbilled expenses	41,250	36,721	41,106
Total	1,631,527	1,654,981	2,330,941
Less estimated doubtful accounts	(15,671)	(26,000)	(31,241)
Total	1,615,865	1,628,981	2,299,700
Partners' and employees' accounts	21,000	32,145	48,312
Deposits and prepaids	5,000	8,000	7,200
Total current assets	1,641,856	1,669,126	2,355,212
Fixed assets			
Leasehold improvements	78,990	78,990	78,990
Furniture, equipment, and auto	531,075	621,048	729,059
Library	21,010	21,010	23,010
Less accumulated depreciation and amortization	(245,932)	(336,722)	(423,100)
Total fixed assets	385,143	384,326	407,959
Total assets	2,026,999	2,053,452	2,763,171
LIABILITIES AND CAPITAL			
Current liabilities			
Notes and loans payable	27,000	29,000	31,000
Accounts payable	38,574	32,716	39,815
Unearned income	98,327	80,535	96,542
Employee withholdings	12,389	14,572	15,180
Accrued expenses	13,545	16,210	15,321
Total current liabilities	189,835	173,033	197,858
Long-term debt*	312,000	325,000	392,000
Total liabilities	501,835	498,033	589,858
Capital			
Capital accounts	1,525,164	1,555,419	2,173,313
Total liabilities and capital	2,026,999	2,053,452	2,763,171

*$300,000 notes payable to six partners in June 1979 (ten-year-term loans).

APPENDIX A

Preliminary Report on Jackson and Associates

BACKGROUND

Jackson and Associates has a well-established position in the growing, changing profession of management consulting. It is considerably larger than a great majority of its competitors but still much smaller than the leading firms. Jackson and Associates is 25 years old and a member of the Association of Consulting Management Engineers. The firm has a total staff of 33, including 12 nonprofessionals and 21 professionals who operate from 4 offices. Twenty of the professional staff have formal engineering training and a minimum of 5 years' industrial experience in a staff capacity.

Jackson and Associates has no formal training program. The firm relies on personal development through an informal process. The informal process consists of securing the counsel of more experienced professionals working on the same assignment, the use of unassigned time for personal study, and an active participation in professional organizations.

Recruiting and training is a never-ending task for Jackson and Associates. The kind of people the firm employs and the consulting process make its professional staff attractive recruits to its clients. Job offers of twice staff members' present salary are common, and Jackson and Associates has not tried to match every offer a member of its professional staff receives. Instead, it has encouraged its staff to evaluate the freedom, opportunity, and challenge of consulting as compared with the monotonous and political environment of a company.

Jackson and Associates pays a new member of its professional staff about what he or she was earning in the previous position. Raises occur as the staff member's time becomes billable to clients. Average salaries for Jackson and Associates' professional staff are shown in Exhibit 13.

EXHIBIT 13

**Levels, Number, and Average Annual Salary
of Jackson and Associates**

POSITION	NUMBER OF PERSONNEL	AVERAGE ANNUAL SALARY
Partners	3	$25,000
Principals	5	16,000
Consultants	13	12,000

In addition to salary, all regular employees of Jackson and Associates receive a bonus, which depends upon the profitability of the firm during the past year. The distribution is contingent upon two factors: (1) the amount of new client billing attracted and (2) the gross profit earned. The former receives the greatest weight in determining an individual staff member's bonus, and the latter is computed by subtracting the staff member's salary from billings to clients. The bonuses for the professional staff typically average 20 percent of their salaries.

KEY PERSONNEL

The key figures in the management of the firm are Art Bailey and Don Gordon. However, Pat Connors, at age 51, is still active as a holdover from the founding partners. Connors's specialty is the transportation industry, specifically truck transportation, in which the firm has an excellent reputation. Connors is a 35-percent-ownership partner and appears to be the most influential of the three. In his specialty he has an intimate knowledge of the state of the art and many acquaintanceships with executives in the trucking industry. As a result, the firm has an excellent reputation and is often called upon to deal with many other aspects of the industry than might otherwise be expected. Connors is not too pleased with the merger idea because he is afraid that he will not be accorded the full rights of a partner if it goes through, as he does not wish to be downgraded to the level of a manager. He has expressed concern at becoming a second-class citizen in a CPA firm since he does not have a CPA certificate.

Bailey and Gordon both have engineering training and industrial experience. Bailey was an industrial engineer for Mead Johnson for six years prior to joining Jackson and Associates. Bailey, at 31 years of age and a 33 percent partner, has expressed a great deal of enthusiasm for the offer and is openly pushing for acceptance.

Gordon is 42 years old and has over ten years' experience as a production specialist. He has had mixed reactions to the offer and wishes to take more time to assess the advantages and disadvantages of the proposed merger.

ORGANIZATION

Three levels are provided for within the professional staff: partner (both senior and junior), principal, and consultant. Each engagement is placed under the personal supervision of a partner with primary supervisory duties falling to a principal. The partner performs mostly client-relationship work. A staff is then assembled that possesses the requisite expertise to carry out a particular engagement.

A principal may serve as a supervisor in one assignment and as a consultant in another assignment. It is also not uncommon to find professionals in one office working under the supervision of a principal from another office.

EXHIBIT 14

Jackson and Associates Office Locations and Personnel Assignments

	PROFESSIONAL	NONPROFESSIONAL
St. Louis*	10	6
New Orleans	4	2
Chicago	3	2
Indianapolis	2	1
Cincinnati	2	1

*Home base

Jackson and Associates have offices and personnel assigned in five cities, as shown in Exhibit 14.

CLIENTS, SERVICES, AND FINANCIAL PERFORMANCE

Most of the clients Jackson and Associates serve are trucking or manufacturing concerns normally located in the Midwest and occasionally in the South, except for its transportation clients, which ask Jackson and Associates to work anywhere in the country.

Most of Jackson and Associates' work has been in the general area of production, output standards, production control, inventory control, layout work, quality control, and incentives for mechanics in the transportation industry. In addition, routing, scheduling, and the economic analysis of markets in the transportation industry are common engagements.

After some ups and downs during the Korean crisis, the volume of work obtained by Jackson and Associates stabilized at about a 10 percent growth rate until the past five years, when total billings appear to have leveled out at around $580,000 annually with an average increase of about 2 percent annually.

Past financial performance is shown in Exhibit 15. The desired normal year's distribution should be as follows: operating profits to be allocated 50 percent for bonuses (20 percent of salaries for the professional staff and 10 percent for the nonprofessional staff) and 50 percent of profits to the owners. As shown in Exhibit 15, the last time this occurred was four years ago.

The reasons for the decline in operating profit are as follows: (1) clients are either not involved in as many production changes as previously, or the urgency for change has dissipated; (2) client firms have developed internally the expertise that was previously acquired from Jackson and Associates; (3) the competition from small firms has increased; and (4) competition from CPA firms has increased.

EXHIBIT 15	Jackson and Associates Comparative Income Statements August 30			
	LAST YEAR	**SECOND PREVIOUS YEAR**	**THIRD PREVIOUS YEAR**	**FOURTH PREVIOUS YEAR**
Gross billings	$588,000	$580,000	$579,000	$580,000
Expenses:				
Professional salaries	305,500	300,000	290,000	270,000
Nonprofessional salaries	73,200	70,800	68,500	60,000
Rent	77,500	68,300	62,100	45,000
Public relations	35,000	20,000	20,000	20,000
Other expenses	40,600	36,000	31,000	18,000
Operating profit	56,200	84,900	108,600	167,000
Bonuses	56,200	84,900	64,850	60,000
Income for owners	-0-	-0-	43,750	107,000

An analysis of how the average professional staff member spent his or her time during the past year is shown in Exhibit 16. As this exhibit indicates, the staff could work about 10 percent more time on client business. Although engagements cannot be fitted neatly one after another, the public relations and training time could be allocated to obtain the necessary flexibility. About four years ago, most members of the firm had at least 200 days a year billed to client firms, and the ratio of supervisors to consultants was about one half the present ratio.

EXHIBIT 16	Analysis of Staff Member's Time	
	Total workdays (52 × 5)	260 days
	Vacations, holidays, etc.	40 days
	Workdays available	220 days
	Training	20 days
	Public relations	25 days
	Available for billing	175 days
	Actually billed	150 days
	Slack time	25 days

TENTATIVE MERGER PROPOSAL TERMS

It is hoped that all employees would continue with KLM. The partners would be paid $150,000 for their investment in Jackson and Associates and would be given a five-year employment contract with a guaranteed minimum salary of $30,000 annually. As the business developed, the former partners would presumably receive additional salary and bonuses. If for any reason they left the employ of KLM, they would agree not to set up a competing consulting business for five years after their resignation.

Inner-City Paint Corporation

DONALD F. KURATKO • NORMAN J. GIERLASINSKI

HISTORY

Stanley Walsh began Inner-City Paint Corporation in a rented, run-down warehouse on the fringe of Chicago's downtown business area. The company is still located at the original 1976 site.

Inner-City is a small company that manufactures wall paint. It does not compete with giants such as Glidden and DuPont. There are small paint manufacturers in Chicago that supply the immediate area. The proliferation of paint manufacturers is due to the fact that the weight of the product (52.5 pounds per five-gallon container) makes the costs of shipping great distances prohibitive. Inner-City's chief product is flat white wall paint sold in five-gallon plastic pails. It also produces colors on request in 55-gallon containers.

The primary market of Inner-City is the small- to medium-sized decorating company. Pricing must be competitive, and until recently, Inner-City had shown steady growth in this market. The slowdown in the housing market combined with a slowdown in the overall economy caused financial difficulty for Inner-City Paint Corporation. Inner-City's reputation had been built on fast service, frequently supplying paint to contractors within 24 hours. Speedy delivery to customers became difficult when Inner-City was required to pay cash on delivery (COD) for its raw materials.

Inner-City had been operating without management controls or financial controls. It had grown from a very small, two-person company with sales of $60,000 annually in 1976 to sales of $1,800,000 and 38 employees in 1981. Stanley Walsh realized that tighter controls within his organization would be necessary if the company was to survive.

EQUIPMENT

Five mixers are used in the manufacturing process. Three large mixers can produce a maximum of 400 gallons per batch per mixer. The two smaller mixers can produce a maximum of 100 gallons per batch per mixer.

Two lift trucks are used for moving raw materials. The materials are packed in 100-pound bags. The lift trucks also move finished goods, which are stacked on pallets.

This case was prepared by Dr. Donald F. Kuratko, from the College of Business, Ball State University, and Dr. Norman J. Gierlasinski from the School of Business, Central Washington University. It was presented at the 1984 Workshop of the Midwest Society for Case Research. It also appears in *Annual Advances in Business Cases, 1984*, pp. 243-251, edited by Charles Douds. Reprinted by permission.

A small testing lab ensures the quality of materials received and the consistent quality of the finished product. The equipment in the lab is sufficient to handle the current volume of product manufactured.

Transportation equipment consists of two 24-foot delivery trucks and two vans. This small fleet is more than sufficient because many customers pick up their orders to save delivery costs.

FACILITIES

Inner-City performs all operations from one building consisting of 16,400 square feet. The majority of the space is devoted to manufacturing and storage, with only 850 square feet assigned as office space. The building is 45 years old and in disrepair. It is being leased in three-year increments. The current monthly rent on this lease is $2,700. The rent is low in consideration of the poor condition of the building and its undesirable location in a run-down neighborhood (south side of Chicago). All of these conditions are suitable to Inner-City because of the dusty, dirty nature of the manufacturing process and the small contribution of the rent to overhead costs.

PRODUCT

Flat white paint is made with pigment (titanium dioxide and silicates), vehicle (resin), and water. The water makes up 72 percent of the contents of the product. To produce a color, the necessary pigment is added to the flat white paint. The pigment used to produce the color has been previously tested in the lab to ensure consistent quality of texture. Essentially, the process is mixing powders with water, then tapping off into 5- or 55-gallon containers. Color overruns are tapped off into 2-gallon containers.

Inventory records are not kept. The warehouse manager keeps a mental count of what is in stock. He documents (on a lined yellow pad) what has been shipped for the day and to whom. That list is given to the billing clerk at the end of each day.

The cost of materials to produce flat white paint is $2.40 per gallon. Colors are approximately 40 percent to 50 percent higher. Five-gallon covered plastic pails cost Inner-City $1.72 each. Fifty-five-gallon drums (with lids) are $8.35 each.

Selling price varies with the quantity purchased. To the average customer, flat white sells at $27.45 for five gallons and $182.75 for 55 gallons. Colors vary in selling price, owing to the variety in pigment cost and quantity ordered. Customers purchase on credit and usually pay their invoices in 30 to 60 days. Inner-City telephones the customer after 60 days of nonpayment to inquire when payment will be made.

MANAGEMENT

The president and majority stockholder is Stanley Walsh. He began his career as a house painter and advanced to become a painter for a large decorating company. Mr. Walsh primarily painted walls in large commercial buildings and hospitals. Eventually, he came to believe that he could produce a paint that was less expensive and of higher quality than what was being used. A keen desire to open his own business resulted in the creation of Inner-City Paint Corporation.

Mr. Walsh manages the corporation today in much the same way that he did when the business began. He personally must open *all* the mail, approve *all* payments, and inspect *all* customer billings before they are mailed. He has been unable to detach himself from any detail of the operation and cannot properly delegate authority. As the company has grown, the time element alone has aggravated the situation. Frequently, these tasks are performed days after transactions occur and mail is received.

The office is managed by Mrs. Walsh (Mr. Walsh's mother). Two part-time clerks assist her, and all records are processed manually.

The plant is managed by a man in his twenties whom Mr. Walsh hired from one of his customers. Mr. Walsh became acquainted with him when the man would pick up paint from Inner-City for his previous employer. Prior to the eight months he has been employed by Mr. Walsh as plant manager, his only other experience has been that of painter.

EMPLOYEES

Thirty-five employees (twenty workers are part-time) work in various phases of the manufacturing process. The employees are nonunion, and most are unskilled laborers. They take turns making paint and driving the delivery trucks.

Stanley Walsh does all of the sales work and public relations work. He spends approximately one half of every day making sales calls and answering complaints about defective paint. He is the only salesman. Other salesmen had been employed in the past, but Mr. Walsh felt that they "could not be trusted."

CUSTOMER PERCEPTION

Customers view Inner-City as a company that provides fast service and negotiates on price and payment out of desperation. Mr. Walsh is seen as a disorganized man who may not be able to keep Inner-City afloat much longer. Paint contractors are reluctant to give Inner-City large orders out of fear that the paint may not be ready on a continual, reliable basis. Larger orders usually go to larger companies that have demonstrated their reliability and solvency.

EXHIBIT 1

Balance Sheet for the Year Ended June 30, 1982

CURRENT ASSETS

Cash	$ 1,535	
Accounts receivable (net of allowance for bad debts of $63,400)	242,320	
Inventory	18,660	
Total current assets		$262,515
Machinery and transportation equipment	47,550	
Less accumulated depreciation	15,500	
Net fixed assets		32,050
Total assets		$294,565

CURRENT LIABILITIES

Accounts payable	$217,820	
Salaries payable	22,480	
Notes payable	6,220	
Taxes payable	38,510	
Total current liabilities		$285,030
Long-term notes payable		15,000

OWNERS' EQUITY

Common stock, no par, 1,824 shares outstanding		12,400
Deficit		(17,865)
Total liabilities and owners' equity		$294,565

EXHIBIT 2

Income Statement for the Year Ended June 30, 1982

Sales		$1,784,080
Cost of goods sold		1,428,730
Gross margin		$ 355,350
Selling expenses	$ 72,460	
Administrative expenses	67,280	
President's salary	132,000	
Office manager's salary	66,000	
Total expenses		337,740
Net income		$ 17,610

Rumors abound that Inner-City is in difficult financial straits, that it is unable to pay suppliers, and that it owes a considerable sum for payment on back taxes. All of the above contribute to a serious lack of confidence in the corporation by customers.

FINANCIAL STRUCTURE

Exhibits 1 and 2 are the most current financial statements of Inner-City Paint Corporation. They have been prepared by the company's accounting service. No audit has been performed as Mr. Walsh did not want to incur the expense it would have required.

FUTURE

Stanley Walsh wishes to improve the financial situation and reputation of Inner-City Paint Corporation. He is considering the purchase of a computer to organize the business and reduce needless paperwork. He has read about consultants who are able quickly to spot problems in businesses, but he will not spend more than $300 on such a consultant.

The solution that Mr. Walsh favors most is one that requires him to borrow money from the bank, which he will then use to pay his current bills. He feels that as soon as business conditions improve, he will be able to pay back the loans. He believes that the problems Inner-City is experiencing are due to the overall poor economy and are only temporary.

CASE 28

The Artisan's Haven

NEIL H. SNYDER • BROOKE GARRETT

THE DECISION TO GO INTO BUSINESS

John and Katie Owen were confronted with a serious problem in 1973. John was fired from his job with a large chemical company in Trenton, New Jersey, after 33 years. The OPEC oil embargo had caused a recession in the U.S. economy, and the nation was bracing itself for anticipated high inflation. After working for one company for so long and giving the firm his best years, John was upset over his dismissal. He had not made a big mistake or done anything wrong. He simply was one of the older employees whom the company wanted to replace with younger, more energetic people. The recession gave the firm the opportunity it needed to make wholesale changes in personnel.

Finding a job during a recession is not easy, and for a 55-year-old man whose experience is limited to one industry, it is almost impossible. John felt helpless. He did not know what to do, and his frustration turned into anger as he realized for the first time in his working life that he was just a pawn in a great game of corporate chess. After several weeks of fear, anxiety, and doubt, John reached a major turning point in his life. He knew that he never wanted to work for anyone or any firm again.

The decision not to work for others was a major one, but John still did not know what to do. Should he retire? If he did, it would not be a comfortable retirement. Should he start his own business? If so, what kind of business should it be? He knew that he did not want to be involved with chemicals. Even before he was fired, John had begun to have reservations about producing dangerous chemicals and dumping harmful wastes into rivers. But his pay was good, and he did not have the time or the inclination to think about these questions very seriously. It was more important to John to pay his bills, to take nice vacations, and, in general, to have fun.

Although John likes to take credit for the idea, Katie is the one who suggested that he consider opening a store to sell arts and crafts. John's hobby for many years had been making gold jewelry, and he had become a very good goldsmith. Katie was an amateur interior designer, and she also enjoyed doing cross-stitch and making dried floral arrangements. Starting a business to sell something they enjoyed making and knew something about seemed like a very good idea. In addition, John and Katie could work together in this kind of business, and Katie had always wanted to spend more time with John.

In 1974 they opened their first store in Trenton, New Jersey, and it was very successful. Their location was excellent, and their merchandise was high quality. Everything they did seemed to work, and by 1980 the Owens owned six stores in New Jersey and Pennsylvania.

In 1980, John and Katie were both 62 years old, and they were more secure financially than they had ever been. When John lost his job with the chemical company, his net worth had been about $150,000, and almost all of it was tied up in his house and furnishings. His income at the time was comfortable, but not great. Now his net worth was in excess of $1 million, and John and Katie could do many of the things they had always dreamed of doing. One thing they had dreamed of doing was retiring to a nice southern town and enjoying life.

At age 62, John and Katie decided to sell their stores in New Jersey and Pennsylvania and move to Athens, Georgia. A couple with whom they were very close had moved to Athens several years before, and John and Katie had visited them several times. They liked the town, they liked the University of Georgia, they liked the people, and they liked the climate. The move seemed like the right thing to do.

MOVING TO ATHENS, GEORGIA

John and Katie settled into their new way of life in Athens very quickly. They joined a local church that consumed a fair amount of their time. Katie got actively involved in the Christian Women's Club. John joined the Lions Club and was able to contribute a great deal of time to many of its projects.

However, one thing was missing. While they were in business, John and Katie had enjoyed making decisions and watching the bottom line of their income statement change to reflect the quality of their judgment. None of their activities in Athens provided the same sense of excitement and satisfaction as owning and operating a business. After a year, John asked Katie about opening a business in Athens, and Katie agreed.

STARTING OVER AGAIN

In the fall of 1981, the Owens opened The Artisan's Haven in downtown Athens directly across the street from the University of Georgia, and the community responded enthusiastically. The store sold handmade gold and silver jewelry, pottery, dried floral arrangements, woodcrafts, and various other handmade objects. Upon entering the store, customers were overwhelmed by the quality of the merchandise. It looked like it could have come out of a magazine like *Country Living* or *Southern Living*. All of the merchandise was made with great care and attention to detail.

Part of the immediate success of the new store was due to the popularity of arts and crafts at the time. But the Owens themselves were the main attraction. John and Katie seemed to be relaxed about life, and the rapport they developed with their customers was nothing short of amazing. They offered classes to teach their customers how to make many of the items sold in the store. Katie became an interior decorator whose advice was sought by many prominent and influential people in the community. John organized the artists and crafts people in the northeast Georgia area into a guild. As a result of their work, the Owens developed a large, wealthy customer base and an excellent supply of high-quality goods to sell.

DEMOGRAPHICS OF ATHENS

The population of Athens and Clarke County, the county surrounding Athens, is approximately 83,000 people. Twenty-one percent of the residents are professionals, and almost a third of them are students at the University of Georgia. A recent study of household incomes in Athens revealed the following:

HOUSEHOLD INCOME*	NUMBER OF HOUSEHOLDS
Greater than $50,000	4719
$35,000–$49,999	6426
$25,000–$34,999	7691

COMPETITION

The Artisan's Haven has no direct competition in Athens. Traditionally, few residents in the community have shown much interest in high-quality goods and services. Cultural events such as plays and musical shows are occasional attractions. Until very recently, the best restaurants in town were steak houses that catered primarily to students, fast-food chains, and small, locally owned operations. Big events in Athens that set it apart from other communities in the area are University of Georgia football games and fraternity and sorority parties.

However, things in Athens are changing, and the wealthier residents in the community are beginning to pay attention to their quality of life. The only stores selling products that compete with The Artisan's Haven include jewelry stores, department store chains, and a few lower-end specialty shops. These stores are not considered direct competitors because the quality of their merchandise is inferior to that sold in The Artisan's Haven. The store's closest direct competitors are in Atlanta, the state's capital, about 70 miles away, and many of Athens' wealthier residents go there routinely to shop.

---

*An average household in Athens is composed of 2.5 people.

MANAGEMENT AND PERSONNEL

John and Katie own and operate their store. In addition, they make many of the products they sell. The Owens have been very fortunate to get to know two retired upper-middle-income women who are looking for opportunities to stay busy doing things they enjoy. These two women work part-time for the Owens for nominal wages. Besides being excellent employees, they are visited by their friends in the store, and many of those friends have become regular customers.

The Owens' most recent important employee is Rachel Thompson. She is 57 years old. They first met her when she was a customer in the store. After they got to know her, they discovered that Rachel's hobby was interior decorating and that most of what she bought was for friends' homes. She was not paid for any of this work. When she was approached by the Owens, Rachel was more than delighted to accept their offer of employment. Rachel's primary responsibility is to work with Katie on interior decorating jobs and to wait on customers in the store. She works about twenty hours a week.

Madeline Murray lives next door to the Owens. She is 53 years old and a very skillful craftswoman who developed her talent by doing needlework for her home and for the homes of her children, relatives, and many friends. The Owens first bought needlework from her by the piece because it was impossible for Katie to do all of the cross-stitching and wait on customers all day. After it became obvious to the Owens that Madeline enjoyed working with and being around them and that they enjoyed her, they invited her to join them at the store. Her job was to do needlework for sale in the store and to work with customers who wanted custom-designed needlework made for their homes. Madeline also works about twenty hours a week.

Rachel and Madeline are like part of the family. Customers frequenting The Artisan's Haven sense the warmth and friendliness of everyone in the store, and they tell John and Katie regularly how enjoyable it is to shop there.

MARKETING

When the Owens first opened the store in Athens, their marketing efforts targeted local residents, tourists, and students. They used radio and newspaper advertising primarily. After several months of operation, they surveyed their customers to evaluate the effectiveness of their promotion effort. Not surprisingly, they learned that word-of-mouth and the Owens themselves were by far the most effective forms of advertising. Additionally, they learned that students were not attracted to their store in large numbers because of the prices of the goods sold and because they were not furnishing homes in which they intended to live for lengthy periods. Tourists did not flock to the store either because Athens is not known as a tourist attraction.

The Owens decided early that The Artisan's Haven did not need extensive print or broadcast media support. However, they did continue to run an occasional radio spot or ad in the local newspaper.

ORGANIZATION

The Owens incorporated The Artisan's Haven in the beginning because they wanted to limit their liability. They were not certain about their options in this area, so they contacted an attorney who helped them make a choice about how to incorporate. They learned that there are major differences between a Subchapter C corporation and a Subchapter S corporation. Both offer several important features such as continuity of life, centralization of management, limited liability, and easy transferability of interest. The S corporation is usually preferred by small business owners because it is treated like a partnership for tax purposes.

Although the Owens could have incorporated The Artisan's Haven as an S corporation, they chose the C corporation. The C corporation allowed the Owens to deduct certain fringe benefits, like medical and health insurance, and to shelter earnings for later use. Because of their age, these were important issues to the Owens.

The major disadvantage of a C corporation is double taxation. The Owens were not as concerned about this issue as the others because they were able to pay themselves attractive salaries that were tax-deductible expenditures.

FINANCE

Exhibits 1, 2, and 3 contain pertinent financial information for The Artisan's Haven. The income statement shown in Exhibit 1 indicates that the largest expenses for the Owens are wages, travel, and rent. The 1981 data is a little misleading because the store was in operation for only half the year. Travel is a major budget item because the Owens travel a great deal to visit craftspeople and art shows. Advertising in 1981 was a large expense item because the Owens were establishing their name and reputation.

A MAJOR DECISION

In July 1987, John Owens suffered a massive heart attack and was told by his doctors to restrict his activities significantly. Before the heart attack, John and Katie had discussed the possibility of selling the business. Now Katie was certain that she wanted to sell it.

Four months before the heart attack, a local entrepreneur named Don Lassiter, who was in the business of buying and selling businesses, had approached the Owens about buying The Artisan's Haven for his wife. They had told him no. At the time, the Owens were in no hurry to sell, but John's physical condition had caused Katie to become very anxious. She was

EXHIBIT 1   **Consolidated Income Statements for the Period Ending January 31, 1986**

	1981	1982	1983	1984	1985	1986
Sales	16,610	55,673	78,736	105,928	123,683	153,186
Cost of sales	8,305	27,837	35,968	43,441	60,201	75,806
Gross profit	8,305	27,836	42,768	62,487	63,482	77,380
Expenses:						
Rent	3,900	7,800	7,800	7,800	7,800	7,800
Wages to officers	10,000	11,000	15,500	20,000	25,000	50,000
Other salaries	0	0	0	4,526	9,688	10,803
Utilities	434	612	712	862	1,002	1,165
Advertising	35,000	2,000	2,000	2,000	2,000	2,000
Travel	391	774	933	1,171	1,394	1,654
Supplies	649	835	971	1,175	1,366	1,589
Insurance	145	560	560	560	560	560
Depreciation	168	535	535	535	535	535
Interest	0	278	278	278	409	409
Total expenses	50,687	24,394	29,289	38,907	49,754	76,515
Profit before tax	(42,382)	3,442	13,479	23,580	13,728	865
Tax	0	0	0	0	5,805	423
Net income	(42,382)	3,442	13,479	23,580	7,923	442

EXHIBIT 2   **Consolidated Balance Sheets as of January 31, 1986**

ASSETS	1981	1982	1983	1984	1985	1986
Cash	0	68	5,823	16,532	22,018	20,996
Inventory	18,000	26,262	30,651	35,398	40,782	62,168
Prepaid expenses	2,089	1,973	1,862	2,239	2,355	2,451
Total current assets	20,089	28,303	38,336	54,169	65,155	85,615
Long term assets:						
Equipment	4,675	4,675	4,675	5,752	5,752	7,860
Furniture	3,897	3,897	3,897	3,897	3,897	4,623
Less accumulated depreciation	168	703	1,238	1,773	2,308	2,843
Total P, P & E	8,404	7,869	7,334	7,876	7,341	9,640
Total assets	28,493	36,172	45,670	62,045	72,496	95,255

EXHIBIT 2	Continued						
ASSETS		**1981**	**1982**	**1983**	**1984**	**1985**	**1986**
LIABILITIES AND STOCKHOLDERS' EQUITY							
Current maturities		278	278	278	278	278	597
Accounts payable		2,122	7,899	10,211	14,447	17,901	21,870
Accrued expenses		1,093	1,240	1,829	1,942	2,068	2,189
Total current liabilities		3,493	9,417	12,318	16,667	20,247	24,656
Long-term debt		47,382	45,695	38,813	27,259	26,207	34,115
Total liabilities		50,875	55,112	51,131	43,926	46,454	58,771
Stockholders' equity:							
Common stock		20,000	20,000	20,000	20,000	20,000	30,000
Retained earnings		(42,382)	(38,940)	(25,461)	(1,881)	6,042	6,484
Total equity		(22,382)	(18,940)	(5,461)	18,119	26,042	36,484
Total liabilities and equity		28,493	36,172	45,670	62,045	72,496	95,255

EXHIBIT 3	Sales by Quarter		
YEAR	**QUARTER**	**SALES BY QUARTER**	**TOTAL SALES**
1981	3	3,246	16,610
	4	13,364	
1982	1	3,080	55,673
	2	10,397	
	3	4,512	
	4	37,684	
1983	1	5,511	78,736
	2	17,321	
	3	8,663	
	4	47,241	
1984	1	9,533	105,928
	2	25,422	
	3	10,595	
	4	60,378	
1985	1	10,021	123,683
	2	32,033	
	3	14,841	
	4	66,788	
1986	1	12,195	153,186
	2	44,906	
	3	17,961	
	4	78,124	

concerned that John would want to keep the business and literally work himself to death. She was also worried that she could not take the pressure of running the business and taking care of John. Katie wanted to sell the business, and the sooner the better. When she raised the issue with John, he agreed.

Once they decided to sell The Artisan's Haven, John and Katie had to determine how much the business was worth and if Don Lassiter still wanted to buy it. There were other issues to be considered, too. For example, Mr. Lassiter might not be the only potential buyer. How would they contact other people who might be interested in their business?

Although they had gone through the process of selling a business several years before, neither John nor Katie knew much about the intricacies of calculating the value of a firm. They had relied heavily on their accountant, who was a close friend, to help them in that deal. The Owens were very knowledgeable about arts and crafts and people, but not finance.

The more they thought about it, the more they realized that a multitude of decisions had to be made. John told Katie that any buyer would require them to sign an agreement not to compete. Neither of them objected to that stipulation. Also, there was a question about how much time John and Katie were willing to work with the new owner, and in what capacity, after the business was sold. Both of them were uncertain about how to approach this question, and this was not the kind of question they could rely on a financial advisor to answer.

How many more questions would they need to answer? John and Katie did not know.

Carmike Cinemas, Inc.*

MARILYN L. TAYLOR

Mike Patrick, president of Carmike Cinemas, Inc., put the September 1986 month-end reports in his drawer. He glanced at the pile of notes he had written as he went through the reports. He would ask his secretary to distribute them to various company managers. For the most part, the notes asked for the reasons behind specific expenditures in September or gave directions regarding expense reduction.

In half an hour Mike planned to join his father, Carl Patrick, chairman of Carmike. The father and son team had purchased Carmike, then named Martin Theatres, in 1982. At the time of the purchase Martin was the seventh largest U.S. theater chain and had been a subsidiary of Fuqua Industries, Inc., for over twelve years. Fuqua was a large diversified company. The equity in Carmike was held entirely by Carmike, Inc., a private Georgia company owned by the Patrick family and a New York investment company.

Mike knew his father would spend some time on the issue of taking the company public. There were a number of issues to be considered before making the decision. Jay Jordan and others at the investment company wanted to withdraw all or a major part of their investment. His own family would likely be able to reduce their investment in Carmike by offering some of their stock in a secondary issue. However, the Patrick family owned 51 percent of Carmike's stock, and Mike felt strongly that he wanted to be clearly in charge of the company. Mike wondered how the broader investment community would view the various strategic and operational moves undertaken at Carmike over the previous four years. He thought briefly of the acquisition of the video movie chain. An infusion of cash and reduction of debt would position Carmike to take advantage of other potential acquisitions on a timely basis. Mike also realized that resiliency was important as the company faced numerous challenges, including difficult industry conditions and continuing capital requirements. However, going public entailed some costs including scrutiny by shareholders, public disclosure of company moves, and the costs of required reports and public relations with shareholders, the investment community, and the general public.

Whether to go public was a dilemma. He began to jot some notes under the heading, "Pros and Cons of Going Public in Fall 1986."

This case was presented to North American Case Research Association in November, 1988 and was selected as the recipient of the 1989 Curtis E. Tate, Jr. Outstanding Case Award sponsored by Irwin Corp. and North American Case Research Assn.

HISTORY OF THE COMPANY

Carmike Cinemas was originally founded as the Martin Theatres circuit in 1912. C. L. Patrick, the company's chairman of the board, joined Martin Theatres in 1945 and became the general manager and director in 1948. Fuqua Industries, Inc., purchased the Martin family business holdings including Martin Theatres in 1969. Mr. Patrick served as president of Fuqua from 1970 to 1978 and as vice chairman of the board of directors of Fuqua from 1978 to 1982.

During the thirteen years that Martin was a part of Fuqua the subsidiary had been a cash generator for its parent company. Fuqua sold a number of the Martin properties. In 1981 Fuqua completed the sale of three television stations that had come with the original purchase. Only the theater circuit remained.

Mike felt strongly that the executives at Martin had largely kept the theater chain in a holding pattern during its time as a Fuqua subsidiary. The treasurer, for example, had been promoted because he was ". . . sort of in the right place at the right time . . . when the previous treasurer, a brilliant man . . ." had a stroke in 1969. Further, Mike explained that when Carl Patrick moved to Atlanta in 1970 as president of the parent company, Fuqua, Ron Baldwin, the next Martin president, was ". . . good in real estate but very poor in accounting. . . ."

The purchase price for Martin Theatres was $25 million. Financing arrangements for purchasing Martin Theatres were very favorable; the total investment by the Patrick family was less than $250,000. However, the purchase of the theaters was highly leveraged. Early efforts were directed toward improving the company's cash flow in order to reduce the debt. At the same time the company had significant capital improvement requirements. To make the venture viable, the Patricks undertook a number of changes in operations that are described in the ensuing sections of this case. Success was by no means assured, as Mike Patrick explained:

> When we bought Martin, Martin was going downhill. It looked bad. And I want you to know that it looked pretty bad for us for awhile. I mean it really did. For a while there we were asking ourselves, "Why are we in this mess?" Not only were we leveraged 100 percent, but we realized that we had to spend somewhere in the neighborhood of 25 million more dollars to renew the company.

At the time of Carmike's acquisition of Martin Theatres, the circuit had 265 screens (excluding 26 drive-in theater screens) located in 128 theaters. Carmike had acquired or constructed an additional 215 screens and closed or disposed of 44 screens since 1982.

MIKE PATRICK'S BACKGROUND

Mike Patrick had worked in Martin Theatres first as a high school student in Columbus, Georgia, later in Atlanta as a student at Georgia State University, and still later back in Columbus as he finished his studies in economics at Columbus College. He explained these periods in his life and how he became acquainted with the company:

> Movie theaters was the only business in which I wanted really to work—it's a fun business. If you are in construction, no one cares about your business. But if you tell someone that you are in the theater business, then everybody has seen a movie. Everyone has something they want to talk about. So it's an entertaining industry. Plus when I got into it, I was in the night end of it. I wasn't into administrative. So I got captured, as I called it. If you have never worked at night, then you don't understand. I really went to work at 8 A.M. and got off at 10 A.M. and then went back at 2 P.M. and got off at 11 P.M. at night. So your whole group of friends is a total flip-flop. You have nighttime friends. Before you know it, you are trapped into this life. All your friends work at night. So your job becomes a little important to you because that's where you spend all your time. Working in a theater . . . is a lot of fun. It really is, especially when you are nineteen and you get to handle the cash. A theater is a cash business.
>
> My father was president of Martin. In 1970 he became president of Fuqua and moved to Atlanta. My father wanted to sell the house in Columbus and my mother did not want to. I was very homesick for Columbus. . . . So I said, "I will go to Columbus College and I will live in the house." I moved back here in the summer of 1970 and worked in the accounting department because I wanted to understand the reports, why I filled out all these forms, and where they went. I learned then that the treasurer of the accounting department did not understand the paper flow at all.

The Patrick family and a limited number of investors acquired Martin Theatres in April 1982 in a leveraged buyout for $20 million in cash and a 10 percent note in the principal amount of $5 million. Mike Patrick became president of Carmike Cinemas as the new company was called. He explained the advantage of working so long in the company:

> I had done every job in the company except that of Marion Jones, our attorney. But my brother is an attorney, so I have someone in the family to talk to if I have a question. No one can put one over on me . . . I've fired them too, and I want to tell you something—I do my own firing . . . and firing a man who is incompetent when he doesn't know it is hard. He breaks down because he thinks he's good. When I first became president there was a member of my family who had to go. The other management noticed that.

POST-BUYOUT: STREAMLINING THE ORGANIZATION

In considering the purchase of Martin, Mike Patrick had described the firm to his father as "fat." Mike described what he did after purchasing the firm:

> It appeared that each layer of management got rid of their responsibilities to the next echelon down. For example, I could not figure out what the president did . . . I kept looking at senior management trying to figure out what they did. I sort of took an approach like zero budgeting. Instead of saying my budget was $40,000 last year and I need 10 percent more this year, I required that each

individual justify everything he did. For example, there is now only one person in our financial department. The young man in there makes less than the guy that had the job as vice president of finance three years ago and the current guy does not have a subordinate. The advertising department went from a senior vice president level to a clerk. You are talking about the difference between an $80,000 and a $19,000 salary.

When we got hold of the company, we let go the president, the financial vice president, and the senior vice president. At the same time the film procurement people retired because they were over 65. So I have streamlined the organization tremendously. When we got Martin, Martin had 2,100 employees. Since then we bought a circuit called Video out in Oklahoma. They had 900 employees. Today I have 1,600 employees. Let me double check than number. As of October 31, I had 1,687 and the year before I had 1,607. So I actually have 80 more employees than I had last year. But when I got the company, it had 2,100 and the other company had 900.

Of the employees, approximately 65 percent were paid minimum wage. Another 9 percent were paid sub-minimum wage. About 8 percent of the employees were in a managerial capacity, and the company was totally nonunion. Employee relationships were generally good. Initially, however, there were difficulties. Mike Patrick recalled the initial time period:

Management was not well disciplined when we came into Martin. I had to almost totally clean house: I eliminated all of top management but it took about six months to get second-level management to where it felt secure and at the same time develop a more aggressive attitude. I call it a predator attitude. But that first year we had some great hits, such as *E.T.* We did so well that first year breaking all previous records so that the management team, even though it was new, became really confident, maybe too confident. Today they don't believe we can lose. Here's a list of the directors and key employees. [See Exhibit 1.]

The company also implemented improved technology in order to trim the number of employees. Mike Patrick explained what happened in one city when he wanted to replace the projectionists with totally automated projection booths. He consulted with the company attorney regarding action the projectionists could take in retaliation:

I called our attorney in and I asked him, "What is the worst that could happen?" The attorney said, "You might have to reinstate the projectionists and pay them the back pay." I said, "You mean there is no million dollar fine?" He replied, "No, you just got to worry about reinstatement and back pay." He went on to say, "Well, why are you going to get rid of the projectionists?" I said, "There is automated projectionist equipment for showing movies that will work very similar to an eight-track tape player. If we convert the theaters, we won't need projectionists." And he said, "Well, you can do it."

However, the city had a code which said to be a projectionist you must take a test from the city electrical board to be certified. That law was put in about 1913 because back in the old days, they didn't have light bulbs. A projector

EXHIBIT 1	**Backgrounds of Directors, Officers, and Key Employees**

C. L. Patrick (61), who has served as chairman of the board of directors of the company since April 1982, joined the company in 1945, became its general manager in 1948, and served as president of the company from 1969 to 1970. He served as president of Fuqua from 1970 to 1978, and as vice chairman of the board of directors of Fuqua from 1978 to 1982. Mr. Patrick is a director of Columbus Bank and Trust Company and Burnham Service Corporation.

Michael W. Patrick (36) has served as president of the company since October 1981 and as a director of the company since April 1982. He joined the company in 1970 and served in a number of operational and film booking and buying capacities prior to becoming president.

Carl L. Patrick, Jr. (39) has served as a director of the company since April 1982. He was the director of taxes for the Atlanta, Georgia, office of Arthur Young and Co. from October 1984 to September 1986 and is currently self-employed. Previously, he was a certified public accountant with Arthur Andersen and Co. from 1976 to October 1984.

John W. Jordan, II (38) has been a director of the company since April 1982. He is a co-founder and managing partner of The Jordan Company, which was founded in 1982, and a managing partner of Jordan/Zalaznick Capital Company. From 1973 until 1982, he was vice president at Carl Marks and Company, a New York investment banking company. Mr. Jordan is a director of Bench Craft, Inc., and Leucadia National Corporation, as well as the companies in which The Jordan Company holds investments. Mr. Jordan is a director and executive officer of a privately held company which in November 1985 filed for protection under Chapter 11 of the Federal Bankruptcy Code.

Carl E. Sanders (60) has been a director of the company since April 1982. He is engaged in the private practice of law as chief partner of Troutman, Sanders, Lockerman and Ashmore, an Atlanta, Georgia, law firm. Mr. Sanders is a director and chairman of the board of First Georgia Bank, and a director of First Railroad and Banking Company of Georgia, Fuqua Industries, Inc., Advanced Telecommunications, Inc., and Healthdyne, Inc., and a former governor of Georgia.

David W. Zalaznick (32) has served as a director of the company since April 1982. He is a co-founder and general partner of The Jordan Company, and a managing partner of Jordan/Zalaznick Capital Company. From 1978 to 1980, he worked as an investment banker with Merrill Lynch White Weld Capital Markets Group, and from 1980 until the formation of The Jordan Company in 1982, Mr. Zalaznick was a vice president of Carl Marks and Company, a New York investment banking company. Mr. Zalaznick is a director of Bench Craft, Inc., as well as the companies in which The Jordan Company holds investments. He is a director and executive officer of a privately held company which in November 1985 filed for protection under Chapter 11 of the Federal Bankruptcy Code.

John O. Barwick, III (36) joined the company as controller in July 1977 and was elected treasurer in August 1981. In August 1982 he became vice president, finance of the company. Prior to joining the company, Mr. Barwick was an accountant with the accounting firm of Ernst and Whinney from 1973 to 1977.

Anthony J. Rhead (45) joined the company in June 1981 as manager of the film office in Charlotte, North Carolina. Since July 1983, Mr. Rhead has been vice pres-

EXHIBIT 1   **Continued**

ident, film of the company. Prior to joining the company he worked as a film booker for Plitt Theatres from 1973 to 1981.

Lloyd E. Reddish (58) has been employed by the company since 1948. He served as a district manager from 1971 to 1982 and as eastern division manager from 1982 to 1984, when he was elected to his present position as vice president-general manager.

Marion Nelson Jones (39) joined the company as its general counsel in December 1984 and was elected secretary of the company in March 1985. Prior to joining the company, Mr. Jones was a partner in the law firm of Evert and Jones in Columbus, Georgia, from 1979 to 1984.

---

then used two carbon arcs and it was a safety issue back then because film was made out of something that burned. That was before my time that film burned like that. Often they had fires in the lamp house. Now we have Zenith bulbs. The projectionists hadn't gone and gotten their certification from the electrical board for years. But the rule was on the books. So I figured the only problem we had was the city. As soon as we fired projectionists, they went to the council. They complained that the managers were doing the projectionist job without certification from the electrical board. The police raided my theater. I sued the City of Nashville. . . . In the meantime we sent an engineer up from Columbus and started teaching all our managers how to pass the electrical board test. As they began to pass the board, the rule became a moot question.

Martin had already leased and installed all the needed equipment except an automatic lens turn. The cost of $15,000 per projector was not justified when it took only a few seconds to change the lens. The new equipment eliminated the position of projectionist. The theater managers took over the job of changing the lens. Mike explained how he was able to get the theater managers to cooperate:

I told our managers that once the automated projectionist booth was in operation and the job of projectionist eliminated I would give them a raise consisting of 40 percent of whatever the projectionists had made. So all of a sudden the manager went from being against the program of converting to automated projectionist booths to where I got a flood of letters from managers saying, "I passed the projectionist test. I'm now certified by the electrical board. Fire my projectionist."

Improving Theater Profitability

At the time they purchased the Martin Theatre circuit, the Patricks were well aware that some of the theaters were losing money and that much of Martin's facilities were quickly being outmoded. A 1981 consulting report on Martin underscored that during the 1970s Martin had not aggressively moved to multiplexing. In addition, one of the previous presidents had put a number of theaters into "B locations" where, according to Mike Patrick, there were "great leases . . . but the theaters were off the beaten track." Mike explained his approach for handling the situation:

> I looked at all the markets we were in, the big markets where the money was to be made, and I said, "Here's what we will do. First, let's take the losers and make them profitable. At the time the losing theaters were a $1.2 million deficit on the bottom line. So I decided to experiment . . . Phoenix City is a perfect example. I took the admission price from $3.75 to $.99. Everybody said I was a fool. The first year it made $70,000, which I thought was a great increase over the $26,000 it had been making. The next year what happened was the people in Phoenix City are poor, very poor blue collar workers, but the theater is as nice as anything I have over here (in Columbus). So as word of mouth got going that theater kept getting better, and better. Now it almost sells out every Friday, Saturday, and Sunday. And I still charge $.99. That theater will make over $200 thousand this year.

As Mike put it, the conversion to "dollar theaters" was ". . . a new concept. No one else is doing that." By 1986, Carmike had twenty "99¢ theaters." The company also offered a discount in admission prices on Tuesdays and discount ticket plans to groups. Two facilities called "Flick 'n' Foam" had restaurants and bar services in the theater.

In addition Mike Patrick continued to consider potential acquisitions.

> I'm looking at a circuit of theaters in a major metropolitan area. Now the owner hasn't told me that it is for sale yet. He wants me to make him an offer and I won't do it. I want him to make me the first offer. He has no new facilities. All his theaters are twins except one and that's a triple. He's getting killed. A large chain is coming against him with a twelve-plex. He's located all around the metro area and he's getting killed. He had that town for years and now he's almost knocked out of it. His circuit is going to be worthless. I've been up there. There are no 99¢ or dollar theaters anywhere. His locations are good for that. You see, for a 99¢ theater, the location must not be a deterrent. It cannot be downtown, because downtown cannot support a night life so that's a deterrent.

Facility Upgrading

When the Patricks purchased Martin Theatres in 1982, its facilities were quickly becoming outmoded. As Mike put it, "We were basically noncompetitive . . . we were just getting hit left and right in our big markets . . . the biggest thing we had was a twin and we had competitors dropping four- and six-plexes on us." One reason for Martin's earlier reluctance to convert to multiscreen theaters was the tendency to put emphasis on the number of theaters rather than screens. In addition, management of the theater company had managed the circuit for its cash flow although not required by the parent to do so. Patrick explained, ". . . Ron [Baldwin] really never understood working for a $2 billion company. He still managed the firm as though it were privately owned."

Mike Patrick explained the difficulties in the early '80s:

> Oh, we were just outclassed everywhere you went. Ron Baldwin told me that Columbus Square was doomed. I made it an eight-plex. With our nice theater, the Peachtree, I added one screen but I didn't have any more room. But I took the theater no one liked and made it an eight-plex. It is also one of the most profitable theaters we have today.

New theaters, either replacements or additions, were undertaken usually through build, sale, and leaseback arrangements. Carl Patrick explained that in 1985 the theaters were about 75 percent leased and about 25 percent company owned.

By 1986 the company had become the fifth largest motion picture exhibitor in the United States and the leading exhibitor in the southern United States in terms of number of theaters and screens operated. The company operated 156 theaters with an aggregate of 436 screens located in 94 cities in eleven southern states with a total seating capacity of 125,758. (See Exhibit 2.)

All but 22 theaters were multiscreen. Approximately 95 percent of the company's screens were located in multiscreen theaters, with over 62 percent of the company's screens located in theaters having three or more screens. The company had an average of 2.79 screens per theater. The company's strategy was designed to maximize utilization of theater facilities and enhance operating efficiencies. In the fiscal year ending March 1986, aggregate attendance at the company's theaters was approximately 15.3 million people.

The company owned the theater and land for 37 of its 156 theaters. The company owned 30 other theaters that were built on leased land. Another 78 theaters were leased. In addition, Carmike shared an ownership or leasehold interest in eleven of its theaters with various unrelated third parties.

The following table describes the scope of the company's theater operations at the indicated dates:

Date	Theaters	Screens
March 1982	128	265
March 1983	126	283
March 1984	158	375
March 1985	160	407
March 1986	156	415

EXHIBIT 2		Number of Screens per Theater, 1986						
	1 SCRNS.	2 SCRNS.	3 SCRNS.	4 SCRNS.	5 SCRNS.	6–8 SCRNS.	TOTAL SCRNS.	PERCENT OF TOTAL SCREENS
STATE								
Alabama	1	16	9	12	0	15	53	12.2
Florida	1	0	3	0	0	0	4	0.9
Georgia	3	12	15	4	10	16	60	13.8
Kentucky	0	2	0	4	5	6	17	3.9
New Mexico	0	2	0	0	0	0	2	0.4
North Carolina	0	28	9	4	0	0	41	9.4
Oklahoma	9	24	3	12	10	18	76	17.4
South Carolina	0	10	6	0	0	0	16	3.7
Tennessee	6	24	12	32	0	18	92	21.1
Texas	2	16	3	28	0	18	67	15.4
Virginia	0	8	0	0	0	0	4	1.8
	22	142	60	96	25	91	436	100.00
Percent of total screens	5.0	32.6	13.8	22.0	5.7	20.9	100.0	

The company currently operates 156 theaters with an aggregate of 436 screens in 94 cities in 11 Southern states, with a total seating capacity of 125,758.

Carmike's screens were located principally in smaller communities, typically with populations of 40,000 to 100,000, where the company was the sole or leading exhibitor. The company was the sole operator of motion picture theaters in 55 percent of the cities in which it operated, including Montgomery, Alabama; Albany, Georgia; and Longview, Texas. The company's screens constituted a majority of the screens operated in another 22 percent of such cities, including Nashville and Chattanooga, in Tennessee, and Columbus, Georgia.

Carmike gave close attention to cost control in construction as Mike Patrick explained:

> Under Fuqua, Martin usually owned the theater. In some instances the land was also owned; in others the company had a ground lease. Since theaters were basically the same from one site to another, the cost of construction of the building was fairly standardized once the site, or pad, was ready.

Mike Patrick built his first theater in 1982 at a cost of $26 per square foot. At the time the usual price in the industry was $31 per square foot. He explained that even his insurance company had questioned him when he turned in his replacement cost estimate. In order to reduce his costs Mike Patrick had examined every element of cost. Initially the Patricks worked with the E & W architectural firm as Martin Theatres had done for years. Mike Patrick explained that their costs were so favorable that other theater companies began to use E & W. Eventually, E & W costs went up. In 1985 Mike employed a firm of recent University of Alabama graduates to be the architects of a new theater in Georgia.

Costs were also carefully controlled when a shopping-center firm built a theater Carmike would lease. The lease specified that if construction costs would exceed a certain amount, Carmike had the option of building the theater. Without that specification there was, as Mike Patrick explained, no incentive for the development firm to contain costs. Carmike's lease payment was based on a return on investment to the development firm. On a recent theater the estimated costs had come in at $39 per square foot versus the $31 per square foot that the lease specified. Mike Patrick convinced the development company to use one of his experienced contractors in order to reduce the $39 per square foot cost.

Zone Strategy

The orientation under Martin management in the 1970s had been a system-wide operations approach. Mike Patrick's approach to theater location and number of screens was zone by zone and theater by theater.

Mike explained that the basic strategic unit in a theater chain was a geographic area called a zone. A small town would usually be one zone. Larger cities usually had two or more zones. Considering competitive activity in a zone was critical. Mike explained what happened over a period of two years in one major metropolitan area:

> This city has a river which divides it in two. There is only one main bridge and so there are automatically two zones. There is also a third zone which is isolated somewhat. When we first bought Martin there were seven theaters and fourteen screens.
>
> Let me tell you what happened in that Zone A. A strong competitor came in and built a six-plex against me in a shopping center. I leased land, built a six-plex theater, and did a sale leaseback. I built the six-plex here right off one of the two shopping centers. I leased the equipment and I leased the building. I actually have no investment. Last year that theater made $79,000. Think about the return you have with no investment!
>
> I took the single theater in the shopping center and put a wall down the middle of it. That cost me $30,000. I added an auditorium to a triple. Both of these theaters are near the competitor's six-plex. Now it's six—four here and

two here. So that is six against his six. So now I have twelve screens in Zone A. That's about the number of screens the population in Zone A can support. So no one else can come in. My competitor has no advantage over me in negotiations with Warner Brothers and Paramount. In fact, I have an advantage over him. He's only here in one location and I am in three.

In the other zone I took a twin and added three auditoriums. Then I took a triple theater and made it a dollar house, $.99 discount. . . . It was way off the beaten track, way off. So I had eight screens against the competitor theaters. There was an opposition single screen, but he closed. We now have twenty screens in those two zones.

If you are playing *Rocky,* you can sell three prints to this town. If you choose your theaters carefully as to where you show it, you can make a lot more money. That's something the previous president [of Martin] never understood.

EXPANSION

In May 1983 Carmike acquired the outstanding stock of Video Independent Theatres, Inc. The purchase price included $1.1 million cash and $2.7 million in a note. The note was at 11 percent payable in three equal installments. Mike talked about the acquisition:

During the 1970s Martin had not been aggressive. In our industry if you are not on the attack you are being attacked. Then you are subject to what the industry does. We believe in making things happen.

Video was owned by a company which had bought Video for its cable rights. In the mid-1970s the management was killed in an air crash. I went up and talked to the guy in charge of Video. He told me the parent company wasn't interested in theaters.

The circuit had a lot of singles and a lot of profitable drive-ins. We borrowed $1 million as a down payment and the parent accepted a note for the remainder due in three equal yearly installments.

We immediately looked at all the drive-ins and sold two drive-ins for about $1.5 million. So immediately we paid back the down payment. We planned to use the cash flow to meet the installment payments and the depreciation to rebuild the circuit. Today Video is completely paid for.

In some of the towns we went into a tremendous aggressive buying program for film which was very successful. In another we bought out an independent who was building a five-plex. In others we converted twins into four-plexes. We closed singles and in some instances overbuilt with four-, five-, or six-plexes. Our revenue per screen as a result is low.

In one town we went in with a new six-plex which cost $620,000. We had used basic cement-block construction and furnished the facility beautifully. An independent had put in a four-plex, about the same size facility, which had cost $1.1 million. A large circuit also had a twin. I attacked with a six-plex during a time when the state economy was down. In addition, there were a lot of bad pictures. The two companies really beat each other up during the period bidding up what pictures were available. The independent went under. We'll pick up that theater from the bank. The circuit was bought by a larger company which wants to concentrate on large cities. They've offered us their twin.

Control Systems

The company also put considerable emphasis on budgeting and cost control. As Mike Patrick explained, "I was brought up on theater P & Ls." The systems he set in place for Carmike theaters were straightforward. Every theater had what Mike called, ". . . a PL . . . I call them a Profit or Loss Statement." Results came across Patrick's desk monthly and results for the theaters were printed out in descending order of amount of profit generated for that month. No overhead was charged to the theaters. As Mike explained, ". . . if you can charge something to an overhead [account], then no one cares, no one is responsible . . ." Rather, each administrative department had a monthly statement. Mike Patrick explained his approach:

> I used something like zero budgeting on every department. For example, here's the Martin Building. It cost me $18,700 for the month. The report for the Martin Building even has every person's name. . . . What they made last year, what they made this year, what they made current month, every expense they have. . . . For example I know what my dad's office cost me each month and mine also.
>
> Everyone must answer, be responsible, for everything they spend. They can't come to me and say, "Well, we've done it every year this way." Since 1982 we have become more efficient and more efficient each year.

Every department head received a recap each week. Mike noted that in a recent weekly report he had a charge for $2,000 for new theater passes reading Carmike instead of Martin. Charges for business lunches appeared on the statement of the person who signed the bill. Mike checked the reports and required explanations for anything out of line. Theater expenses also received close scrutiny as he explained:

> Then I go a step beyond that. All district managers have a pet peeve. They all want their facilities to look brand new. You can write them letters, you can swear, you can cuss. It makes no difference. They are in that theater and that's the only thing they see. It's their world. They want new carpet every week. They want a new ticket machine every week . . . the government says you have to capitalize those expenditures [but] I hate to capitalize on expenses. The government says if the air conditioning breaks, you capitalize it. Bull. I wrote the check for $18,000. The money is gone.
>
> So now I give every district manager a repair report. It shows anything charged to repairs. Yes, I could probably accomplish the same thing with a cash flow statement, but they wouldn't understand it.

Managing the Theaters

The company did not have a nepotism policy. Indeed, Mike Patrick encouraged the hiring of family. Especially in smaller towns where there might be several family members in visible positions, hiring family was seen as a deterrent to theft. As Mike Patrick explained:

> I will let them hire family for two reasons: One, they don't want to quit me. They're married to me as much as they are the family. Second, you get people who just would not steal. They have more to lose than just the job. None of the family will steal from me because it would have a direct bearing on the father, the uncle, the whole family. I am in a lot of little towns and in a small town a son is either going to work on a farm, a grocery store, a filling station, or a theater, cause there is no industry there. The cleanest job in town is the theater manager. Also, in a small town we allow the manager to look like he owns the theater. Cause I don't go in and act like "Here's the boss," and all that.
>
> Theater managers are paid straight salary. Under Fuqua ownership the manager's salary was linked to theater performance. But, changes in company operations led to the change. Theater managers don't make the theater profit; the movie does. Theater managers used to select the movies. But now they don't have anything to do with selection. I am the only theater chain in the United States in which the booking and buying for the circuit is done by computer from right here on my desk. This computer is hooked to Atlanta and Dallas, which are my two booking offices.

Mike Patrick had hired both booking managers after the retirements of the previous incumbents. He explained how one came to work for Carmike:

> Let me tell you how I got Tony Rhead. Tony Rhead was the biggest S.O.B. I went against. He was the booker in a small city and that circuit was the best in town. He used to give me fits. And I used to spend more time trying to figure out how to get prints away from him than anybody else. So what did I do? I hired him. He made $19,000 a year working for a competitor and he makes $65,000 working for me. That's a lot of difference.

The planning system for booking films was set up so that past, current, and future bookings could be called up by theater, zone, or film. In addition, competitors' bookings were also available. The system allowed interaction between home office and the two booking offices, one in Atlanta and the other in Dallas.

The Outlook in 1986

As the 1985 fiscal year came to a close, Carmike, along with much of the industry, faced disappointing year-end results. Part of the problem was attributed to the number of executive turnovers in the movie production companies. Mike explained:

> A number of production executives changed jobs within a 90-day period. That meant that production stopped. Production is like developing a shopping center. It takes eighteen months from the time you decide to do it to the time it opens. This year is off because there were no pictures out there. I believe that it will get better. . . . *Rocky IV* has just come out so we will end the year on an up beat.

The industry faced a number of challenges that affected Carmike. Lack of films was a negative factor. However, the increase in ancillary markets for films, such as video purchase and rental, was viewed as a positive factor as Mike explained:

> By 1979–80 the ancillary market became very big. I understand the ancillary market is now about $3 billion and our side is $4 billion . . . [but] I talked to a man in Home Box Office when he first started. He told me that they could not figure a way to sell a movie on its first run at all. If it was a bad movie, he couldn't give it away. If it was a good movie, he had all the attendance watching it he needed. He told me, "Mike, I want you to do better every year. The more blockbusters you get the more demand I have. If you get, *Who Shot Mary* and it dies in your theater, no one will watch it on Home Box Office." The theater is where you go to preview a movie. That establishes the value. So I realized then that CBS will pay more for a big movie than they will a lousy one, so anything that comes through the tube is no problem with me. I love it because [the revenues] help create more new movies.

An increase in films might be offset by the unabated increase in the number of screens. However, unlike others, the Patricks did not predict the demise of the movie theater. Mike especially felt that the difficult times offered opportunities to those who were prepared:

> There is more opportunity in bad times than in good times. The reason is that no one wants to sell when business is good and if they do the multiples are too high. So you want to buy when business is bad [and] . . . you got to plan for those times.
>
> I have to know where my capital is. I run this company through this set of reports. This is every financial thing you want to know about Carmike theaters—construction coming up, everything we are going to spend, source of cash, where it's going to go, everything. One of the critical things we are thinking about is how to expand. I know that if industry business goes bad, within 90 days three or four more circuits are going to come up for sale. I must be in a position to buy them and I must have the knowledge to do it with. I will not bet the store on any deal.
>
> I am trying to buy a theater circuit right now [priced] at $16 million. At $16 million I am paying a premium for that circuit, a big premium because it loses money every year, but I am going to fire its management. I could buy it as part of Martin [but] if Martin would buy it then Martin would be liable for the

money, so I don't want to do that. So what's my alternative? . . . I will take $2 million or $3 million out of Carmike or have Carmike borrow $13 million and purchase the theater circuit. Then we expect that the cash flow from the purchased circuit will pay back the $13 million.

Mike Patrick was always looking for new opportunities. One of those opportunities was outside the theater industry, as he explained:

Our new office building is 100 percent financed with an Industrial Revenue twenty-year bond issue. In case the theater business goes bad, I want to own an asset that is not a theater.

Sharpco, Inc. (1988)

ARTHUR SHARPLIN

In 1972 James Sharplin and two brothers decided to open a welding and steel fabrication shop in Monroe, Louisiana. The Sharplins formed a corporation, Sharpco, Inc., bought a parcel of land at the eastern edge of Monroe, and built a small shop building. Most of the initial equity investment was in the form of welding machines, tools, and other items contributed by the three owners. James worked full-time at Sharpco while his brothers pursued other interests. The company was profitable from the first year. Sales grew steadily and the shop was expanded several times during the 1970s. In the early 1980s, James exchanged his interest in some commercial property the Sharplins owned for his brothers' shares of Sharpco stock.

Sharpco is engaged in four distinct business areas—all related to heavy equipment, especially crawler tractors (often called "bulldozers" or "Caterpillars"). First, the company makes and sells a number of welded steel items for heavy equipment. Second, Sharpco markets new and used crawler tractor parts. Third, James and his workers provide repair service for heavy equipment owners. Finally, Sharpco does high-strength repair welding for heavy equipment. Each of these business areas will be discussed later.

In January 1985 the business was moved to a new 30,000-square-foot facility in what had become a rapidly expanding commercial and industrial area along Interstate Highway 20. Among the more than twenty firms on Highway I-20 near Sharpco are heavy equipment dealers representing Deere and Company (makers of John Deere equipment), Case Power and Equipment Company, and Fiat-Allis, Inc. (successor to Allis Chalmers, Inc.). Dealers for the other two major brands of heavy construction equipment, International Harvester and Caterpillar, are located about three miles away. Exhibit 1 shows the location of the new Sharpco plant. Exhibit 2 provides geographic and demographic data relevant to Sharpco's main trade area.

PERSONNEL AND ORGANIZATION

In recent years the work force at Sharpco has varied from as many as 30 down to its 1985 level of 11. As a general rule, Sharpco keeps a cadre of experienced workers and fills in with temporary welders and mechanics during busy periods. The company has no formal organization chart. However, Exhibit 3 was drawn by James Sharplin to represent the organization as it existed in 1985.

The lines of authority at Sharpco are not rigidly followed. James routinely bypasses each of his direct subordinates and deals directly with workers. "The managers all work as a team," says James. "Any one of us can make

This case was prepared by Dr. Arthur Sharplin, Distinguished Professor of Management, McNeese University, Lake Charles, La. Reprinted with permission.

EXHIBIT 1 **Sharpco's Location**

Monroe, Louisiana, and Surrounding Region

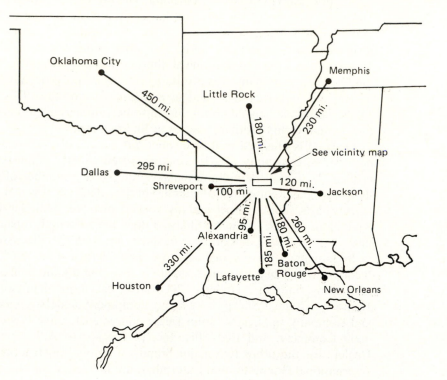

Sharpco Vicinity

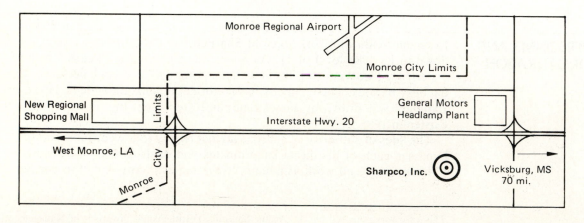

EXHIBIT 2		**Geographic and Demographic Data**			
	MONROE	**OUACHITA PARISH (COUNTY)**	**NORTHEAST LOUISIANA (16 PARISHES)**	**LOUISIANA (ENTIRE STATE)**	**UNITED STATES**
Population, July 1982 (thousands)	57	141	434	4,373	230,000
Per capita income, 1981	$6,973	$7,486	$ 5,897	$ 8,113	$ 8,917
Change in population 1980–82 (percent change for entire period)	−0.9	1.2	1.4	4.0	2.8
Change in *real* per capita income, 1979–81 (percent change for entire period)	−5.1	−3.1	−2.9	1.0	−0.4
Value of agricultural production, 1982 (millions)	n/a	$ 14	$ 48	$ 1,407	$ 158,700
Personal income, 1982 (millions)	n/a	$1,380	$16,010	$44,000	$2,578,600
Work force employed in manufacturing, 1982 (percent)	n/a	18.1	14.9	14.6	20.0
Work force employed in construction, 1982 (percent)	n/a	8.6	5.7	9.6	5.8
Work force employed in farming, 1982 (percent)	n/a	1.2	6.6	3.2	2.0
Approximate land area, 1982 (thousands of acres)	n/a	401	6,519	28,494	2,264,960
Proportion of land area in farms, 1982 (percent)	n/a	23.4	40.7	31.3	46.0

a major or minor decision—or write a $10,000 check." Everyone in the organization is expected to pitch in wherever there is a need for extra help and to accept direction from whomever knows most about the particular job being done. James Sharplin comments on each of the key employees:

Jerry is 30 years old. He is my mother's grandnephew. Jerry is dedicated to Sharpco. He has a great deal of ability to get the job done. He is a good welder and the best mechanic we have. The men respect him and that helps make him a good manager. Customers like him; they ask for him. They know they can depend on what he says. During the move, when we were all running just to keep up, Jerry sold two excavator buckets. He worked right through a weekend, even though he had the flu, to get the buckets built. He has a good memory, too. He can usually tell a customer if we have a part without even checking the computer. Jerry's main recreation is hunting. I try to make sure he has some time off during hunting season. When I decided to furnish him a company pickup, I made sure it was something he has always wanted but never felt that he could afford—a four-wheel-drive "mud hog."

EXHIBIT 3

Organization Chart

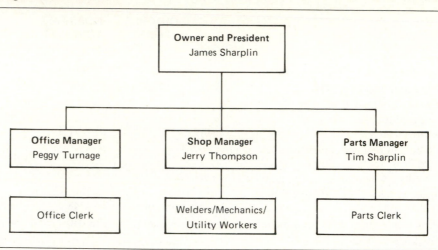

Peggy is in her forties. She has taken a number of college courses. Although Peggy does not have a degree, she knows much more than most college graduates. She is as dedicated as any employee I have. She is the most cost-conscious person in the whole organization, including me. After just a year of working with computers she knows more about them than the computer "expert" who sold us the machine. Somehow Peggy and the computer were an instant match. Peggy is a highly religious lady. I think this accounts in some degree for her diligence, and I know I can trust her with anything I have. There has never been the slightest need for me to check up on her. Everyone here respects her and her presence helps keep foul language and rowdy behavior at a minimum. Peggy is usually miles ahead of me with any information I need—like sales statistics. She put the used parts on the computer without any guidance. And the information was in a form she knew I could use. If things move too fast she just works nights and Saturdays. She does all the advertising better than any ad agency could. She comes up with the ideas, does the copy, and just runs it by me for approval. Peggy is a perfectionist.

Tim is 25 years old. He is my nephew. Tim is strictly work, family, church, and school. He attends Northeast Louisiana University part-time studying business. Tim has a good number of outside obligations, including school. But whenever I need him he is here. He asked me if he should let his school wait while we get over the move and get things back on an even keel. I told him that he might take one course instead of two, only if he thought it best, but I felt he should continue his education without a break. He works hard—wants to do things right. He grew up on a farm, where he often had neither the time nor the equipment to do quality work. Tim is learning fast. In the long term I think he will be one of our most important people. In fact, he is now. He had to come almost from ground zero—learning welding, learning crawler tractors, learning fabrication. He has done remarkably well in the two years since he came to work here.

There is no formal performance appraisal at Sharpco and no written compensation policy. Sharpco furnishes medical insurance for James, Jerry, and Tim (Peggy is covered under her husband's policy). The company also pays about half the cost of insurance for each worker. The managers are paid on a salary basis. Hourly paid workers make from $6 to $9 an hour, about average for the area. Every year, James says, he ranks the employees in order of what he considers to be their contribution to the company. Then he adjusts any inequitable pay. Practically all hiring and firing is done by James personally, although Jerry Thompson has authority to terminate any of his workers.

OPERATIONS

Exhibit 4 shows a typical crawler tractor with the main relevant parts labeled. Practically all of Sharpco's mechanical repair work and most of the parts sales are related to tractor undercarriages, final drives, and steering clutches. The undercarriage is that part of the tractor nearest the ground, including the heavy steel tracks, along with rollers, sprockets, and structural members designed to pull the tracks and keep them in alignment. The final drive is a large closed gearbox that transmits power to the track. In Exhibit 4 the final drive is hidden from view behind the sprocket. The steering clutches are located above the final drives. They allow either the left or right final drive to be disengaged so that the brake can be applied on the respective side, causing the tractor to turn.

The tracks and related components cannot be insulated from the sand, dirt, and gravel in which a tractor usually operates. Consequently, all of the moving surfaces wear away steadily, especially those that are in contact with one another. The track chain is similar to a large bicycle chain. As the track is pulled by the sprocket around the idler and rollers, the pins wear mainly on just one side. Each pin fits into a bushing that also wears in the direction of the stress. A typical undercarriage will require major repair after 3,000 hours of use and overhaul after 1,500 additional hours. Major repair consists of removing the tracks and turning each pin and the respective bushing half around so that the least worn surfaces are in contact. To do this, a portable hydraulic press is used to press out one of the pins. This may require 200 tons of force. Then the tracks, weighing as much as 3,000 pounds each, are moved to the track press where the remaining pins are pressed out, along with the respective bushings. All parts are then inspected and the tracks reassembled with the pins and bushings in their new positions. While the track is off, all undercarriage components are inspected for cracks, leaking oil seals, excessive wear, and other defects. Of course, any needed repairs are made before the tractor is reassembled.

EXHIBIT 4   **A Typical Crawler Tractor**

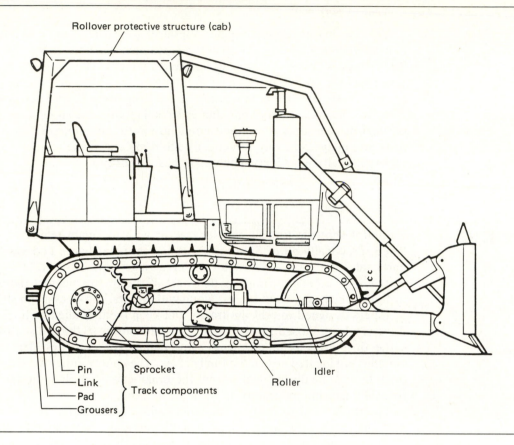

Rollover protective structure (cab)

Pin
Link
Pad
Grousers

Sprocket

Track components

Roller

Idler

When major overhaul is due, pins and bushings are replaced, idlers and rollers exchanged or reconditioned, and new sprockets are installed. With about every second major overhaul, worn grousers have to be cut off and new ones welded onto the track pads. The entire track chain may also have to be replaced. Less frequently, final drives and steering clutches require repair.

Among the items Sharpco manufactures are rollover protective structures (cabs) such as that shown on the tractor in Exhibit 4. Many of Sharpco's customers are involved in land clearing. The tractors they use must have heavy steel screens welded or bolted around the cabs to protect the operator from tree limbs. Sharpco makes and installs those screens as well. The cabs and screens are made from ordinary steel. However, most of the items the company makes involve the use of high-strength steel, about three times as

EXHIBIT 5   **Items Sharpco Makes Using High-Strength Steel**

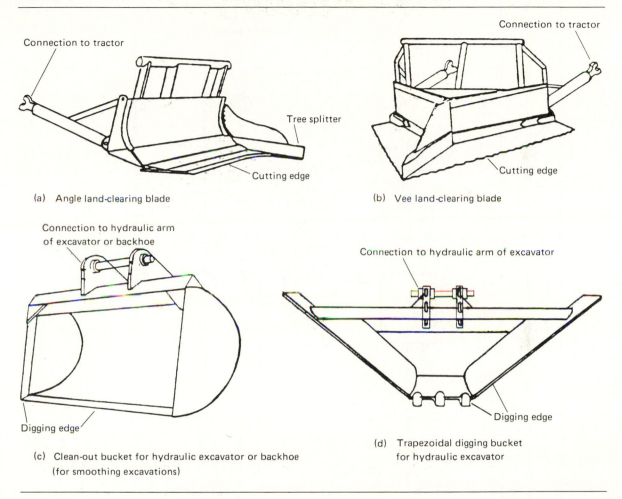

(a)   Angle land-clearing blade

(b)   Vee land-clearing blade

(c)   Clean-out bucket for hydraulic excavator or backhoe
      (for smoothing excavations)

(d)   Trapezoidal digging bucket
      for hydraulic excavator

strong and hard as ordinary steel (and more than twice as costly). Several of these items are shown in Exhibit 5.

The special steel is used for cutting edges and strength members on the blades and buckets. This steel is purchased from major steel distributors and stocked in eight-foot by twenty-foot sheets, ranging in thickness from three-eighths of an inch to two inches. A portable acetylene cutting torch that runs on a small track is used to cut the steel to shape. Pieces that are to become cutting or digging edges are clamped in a vertical position and the edge beveled at a steep angle using the same kind of automatic torch. Curved pieces of mild steel (used for noncritical parts of digging buckets) and the steel pins

EXHIBIT 6   Sharpco Plant Layout

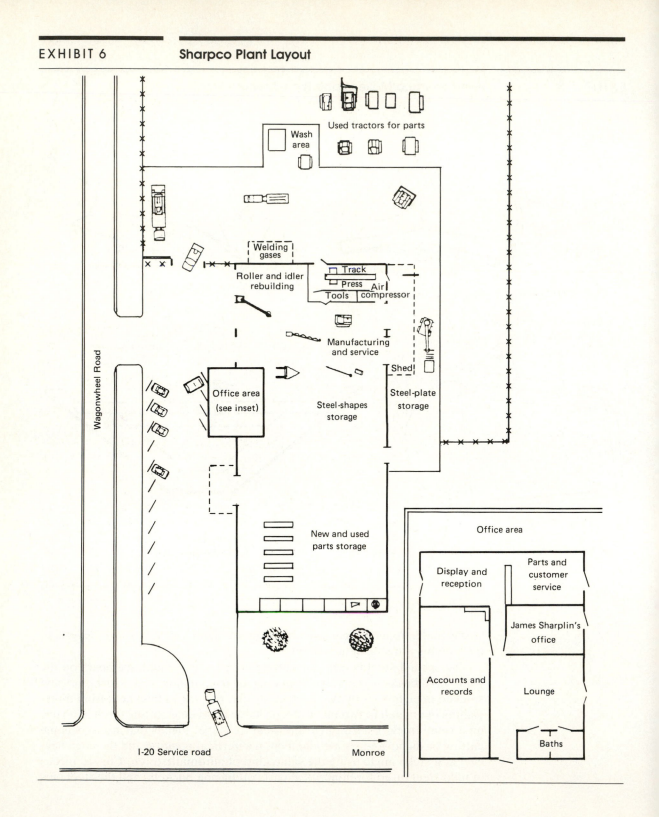

and bushings used to attach the buckets to hydraulic excavators and back-hoes are furnished by a local machine shop.

After the parts of a digging bucket or land-clearing blade are cut and shaped they are welded together just enough to hold them. Then they are carefully inspected prior to final welding. To ensure against failure, Sharpco workers weld all critical points manually, allowing components to cool between layers of weld material. This process requires special high-strength electrodes (welding rods). Less critical welds can be made with semi-automatic machines, which are much faster and easier to operate than manual ones and which use large rolls of wire instead of individual welding electrodes.

Sharpco digging buckets range in size from small standard buckets weighing only 300 pounds to trapezoidal buckets weighing over a ton and measuring seventeen feet across. A trapezoidal bucket is designed to dig a complete drainage canal as the hydraulic excavator or backhoe to which it is attached slowly drives along the intended canal path, scooping out as much as three feet of new ditch with each stroke and laying the dirt aside. Sharpco land-clearing blades and rakes weigh up to eight tons. The largest Sharpco vee-blade has two serrated cutting edges, each twenty feet long. Pushed by the largest production model tractor made by Caterpillar or Fiat-Allis, one of these blades clears a swath sixteen feet wide through timber up to thirty inches in diameter.

Blades and buckets require replacement of cutting edges and other wearing surfaces after extended use. Each item is designed so that the worn parts can be cut loose and new ones installed through a procedure similar to the original manufacture.

All of the items Sharpco reconditions or manufactures are painted at the Sharpco plant. Rollers and small parts are simply dipped into a paint vat. Larger items are spray painted. In addition, practically all of the equipment that comes in to be repaired is covered with dirt and mud. Cleaning is accomplished in the wash area using a special high pressure washer. Construction machinery and components to be repaired are usually brought to the Sharpco plant on customers' trucks, although Sharpco does keep several trucks of varying sizes to make pickups and deliveries when necessary. The layout of the new Sharpco facility is shown in Exhibit 6.

MARKETING

Sharpco's customers include contractors, large farmers, and other heavy equipment owners, as well as equipment dealers who purchase Sharpco products and services for resale. Several equipment dealers employ Sharpco to repair tracks and recondition rollers and idlers for them.

Sharpco subscribes to a computerized used-parts dealer network whereby subscribers exchange price and availability information on needed parts.

As a result, the company ships an increasing number of parts, especially used ones, to dealers around the country.

Although the customer list totals more than 1,000, 100 contractors accounted for two-thirds of Sharpco's 1984 cash flow. For example, one land-clearing contractor, with just four tractors, was billed $86,000 during 1984. Eighty percent of Sharpco's 1984 sales were to customers within a 100-mile radius of Monroe. "That is changing rapidly, though," said Peggy Turnage. "We are getting inquiries from all over the country because of the dealer network." For the months of August, September, and October 1984, 90 equipment owners, mostly contractors, were billed $342,742 out of Sharpco's total sales of $416,557. Shown this list of customers, James Sharplin identified 57 of them as having been regular customers for at least three years.

Sharpco's overall pricing policy, as expressed by James Sharplin, is "whatever the traffic will bear." For new tractor parts, he says, this is normally about 80 or 85 percent of dealer retail price. For used parts, it ranges from 25 to 60 percent of retail, depending upon whether the part in question is a frequently needed one or one that seldom fails. Sharpco prices its digging buckets at or above dealer list prices. According to James Sharplin, this is justified because the Sharpco buckets have a significantly lower failure rate than those equipment dealers furnish. When repair jobs are priced in advance, parts and labor are usually combined. Sharpco tries to stay just below usual original equipment dealer prices on such work. This often results in the loss of jobs to smaller independent service shops, which often price well below what major tractor dealers charge. About one-third of Sharpco's repair work is done on a time and materials basis. Under this kind of billing procedure, customers usually bargain on major components to be installed. But minor items (such as bolts, steel plate for welding reinforcement, and replacement track pads or links) are priced at 90 percent suggested retail, while labor is billed at standard billing rates—currently $26 per hour (local new tractor dealers charge an average of $28 per hour).

Prices are also used to keep Sharpco concentrated in its main businesses. When a customer insists that the company repair a transmission or engine, for example, the price for that work is intentionally elevated. Price changes are also used to control the overall level of work activity. When spurts in demand occur, hourly rates and markups on materials are increased, both for time and materials work and for work that is priced in advance. When demand slackens, workers are laid off until the crew is down to the ten- or twelve-person cadre of experienced workers. Only then are prices and markups sacrificed to sustain sales volume.

The primary means of promotion is direct mail. Currently the mailings are sent to all customers once a month. James has made plans, however, to program the company's computer to segment the mailing list along several dimensions and to mail more personalized advertisements to different customer groups. Sharpco also spends about $700 a month on telephone yellow pages advertising. This provides for one-fourth page under "Contractors Equipment and Supplies," one-fourth page under "Welding," and a business-card-type advertisement briefly listing Sharpco's businesses under "Tractor Equipment & Parts." About once a quarter Sharpco inserts a series of three two-page advertisements in consecutive issues of *The Contractor's Hotline,* a national weekly newspaper offering heavy equipment and parts for sale to about 5,000 equipment owners and dealers. These advertisements cost about $1,400 for each three-week sequence. James, Jerry Thompson, and Tim Sharplin make infrequent sales calls within about 50 miles of Monroe.

FINANCE AND ACCOUNTING

Summaries of Sharpco's recent financial statements are provided in Exhibit 7. The short-term borrowings shown on the 1984 balance sheet are represented by 180-day notes held by a small bank in Delhi, Louisiana, the Sharplin family's hometown. These notes are secured by mortgages on Sharpco's inventories and the Sharpco plant. As they mature, accrued interest is paid and principal refinanced as needed. James has signed continuing guarantee agreements with regard to all present and future Sharpco debt at the bank.

The bank has agreed to convert the short-term debt to a single five-year loan with fifteen-year amortization and interest established annually at the bank's prime rate, normally about 1½ percent above New York prime. In addition to the five-year loan, the bank has agreed that it will provide Sharpco a $150,000 credit line for any needed additional working capital.

The long-term debt on the 1984 balance sheet includes a $200,000 purchase-money obligation on the new Sharpco plant and the land on which it sits. The purchase-money mortgage is subordinated to the bank debt mentioned above. Sharpco's old plant with related long-term debt attached was given in part payment to the developer who built the new plant. By prior agreement with the developer, James Sharplin designed the office area and mechanical features (piping and electrical systems, cranes, etc.) of the new plant and constructed them using Sharpco workers and several subcontractors. This effort was financed with short-term bank borrowing. Upon completion, the new Sharpco facility was appraised at $760,000.

In early 1984 Peggy Turnage computerized the company's accounting records. The computer in use is a Dynabyte featuring twenty megabytes of hard-disk storage, a sixteen-bit microprocessor, and three interactive terminals. The two extra terminals are located in James Sharplin's office and on the customer-service counter. The new-parts inventory of about 1,500 items is carried on a first-in, first-out basis. When a used tractor is purchased for parts the cost of the tractor, plus all labor required to disassemble it, is added to used-parts inventory. When a used part is sold, the entire selling price of the part is subtracted from the inventory line item representing the tractor from which it came. A subsidiary file is kept for each tractor, indicating which parts have been sold. So anyone inquiring at one of the terminals can easily determine which used parts are available for sale. James Sharplin has been advised that the accounting procedure he is following significantly understates the used-parts inventory. Despite a recommendation from the company's CPA, he has not authorized changing the procedure.

Sharpco's steel inventory is taken at the end of each year and priced at current costs. The steel consists of plates (rectangular flat pieces four or more feet in both width and length) and shapes (long, straight pieces of various cross-sectional configurations, e.g., rounds, angles, beams, and channels). No plate or shape is included in inventory if any part of it has been used. In addition, a large quantity of steel, all entirely usable but of slow-selling shapes and sizes, is not counted because it has been declared "obsolete." As a result of these practices, the steel inventory is shown on company books at perhaps one-half its current market value. In addition, Sharpco owns many land-clearing blades, digging buckets, and tractor parts that were "traded in" or abandoned by customers but for which no actual credit was given. Many of these items were later restored to usable condition during slack periods. Total value of these, as estimated by James Sharplin, is $15,000.

A job record is prepared for each customer order requiring shop work. One copy is kept in the office and another in a rack in the shop. Each worker is responsible for entering time worked on respective jobs. Parts and other materials issued to jobs are recorded on the office copies of job records. When a job is finished the shop copy of the job record is brought to the office and an invoice is completed.

Several years ago Peggy Turnage compared the time applied to customer jobs to the total time for which employees were paid. She found that fully one-third of employee time was unaccounted for. After telling of that experience, she said, "As soon as I can get the right computer program, I will set up a control system to charge every hour for which we pay employees to a customer job or to cleanup and maintenance."

INTERVIEW WITH JAMES SHARPLIN

The following are excerpts from an interview conducted in February 1985.

Q James, what do you think is your most important business area?

A Well, I'd say used tractor parts are going to be our biggest money maker in the long run. When you can buy a D7E [a mid-size Caterpillar tractor] for $10,000, sell $25,000 worth of parts off it and still have two-thirds of it left, that's got to be a good situation. More and more people are looking at saving that 10 or 15 percent, or whatever it is. They don't really care if the part is used or not as long as it is not hurt. The major tractor dealers have done a really good job, but their prices have just continued to climb. We're able to offer the customer a good part at 50 or 60 percent off dealer list. Customers are looking for that. They also know they can depend on us to install the parts we sell and to stand behind them. There is no question, also, that we are better at providing parts and undercarriage service for the whole list of crawler tractors—John Deeres, Caterpillars, Cases—than the average dealer is for just one brand of tractor.

Q What do you think are the major attributes that you or Sharpco has that will allow you to be successful—just in a general way?

A We know a great deal more about any undercarriage than dealers do. Of course, dealers have to know the whole tractor and we limit our mechanic work to the undercarriage. The various undercarriages are quite similar, of course, and we've just had a world of experience in that particular area. Also, there's not a better high-quality welding shop, especially for construction equipment, in North Louisiana. We know that business. We're good at it.

Q What do you think about your crew right now, James? How does it stack up?

A On the whole, they're the best group of workers for this type of business in the Monroe area. We have to pick and choose the jobs that we put individual workers on, but we put them on the jobs they're best at doing. Gene Lowe, for instance, is probably the best layout man and general welder that we've got. We use him just for that. But look at Jerry Hodges, who is our fastest welder. We'll let him weld the project out after Gene has cut out the pieces and tacked them together. Charlie LaBorde is real good with customers. So we like to send him out on field jobs, where he'll be in direct contact with the customer. Rodney Gee is another excellent man. He's a kind of handyman. He takes care of our tractor-trailer rig like it was his own. He's a good welder and a good mechanic. He just generally has a great attitude about anything Sharpco wants him to do.

Q What about the production things you do, the track press, for example, and the roller and idler shop?

A We run our track press operation quite differently from the way dealers do. We arranged the track press in a room by itself with all the necessary equipment—the turntable, all the tooling. We have it where one man can run the whole operation. It's a two-man job at most dealers. We've kept real good account of the number of hours it takes to do a job and we've steadily improved on that. The track-press operator we have now, Juan Hernandez, has run the press for six years. He's by far the best I've ever seen. About a year ago, Juan hurt his back and Jerry Thompson and I filled in for him until he recovered enough to work again. He had major surgery. For at least a month or a month and a half after he came back we wouldn't let him lift anything. Just having him here during that time was a great help because he knew so much about how to set up the machine. We rebuild idlers by building up [with an automatic welder] the wear surfaces and replacing the seals— and they are as good as new. We do not weld on the rollers, though, like some dealers do. To get "new" quality, we replace the worn outer shells of rollers and reuse the shafts, bushings, and collars if they are not hurt. This costs more, and we lose some sales when customers just look at price. But I can't think of a single failure on one of our re-shelled rollers.

Q Why is the crew so small right now?

A I prefer to keep it small and work just a bit of overtime in order to keep a good steady crew over a long period of time. Besides that, it's so much easier to manage ten people compared to twenty people. I know all these people. I know their problems. I know what makes them tick. I know what will motivate them. When I had twenty or thirty people, I couldn't say that.

Q What are your long-term plans now for Sharpco?

A Just to continue doing what we're good at and to keep our eyes open for any area where we can do a good job and make money: Grow if it will; but the big thing is to stay profitable and get it to where we can take just a little more time off.

Q Do you mean where *you* can take a little more time off?

A No. I mean the key people—Peggy, Jerry, Tim—and myself, of course.

Q What problems concern you most?

A Well, the problem is always the same: How to keep expenses down and jack up revenue. I do not ignore human costs but I have to focus mainly on dollars. There seems to be a conspiracy out there to keep us from making money. Besides, if we are profitable enough, I can handle most of the other problems that crop up. One thing I'm going to do, as soon as we get over the move, is to spend most of my time for two or three months with the computer and the accounting system, just getting on top of the numbers. I want to know where the sales and profits are coming from—geographically, of course; but also, what kinds of customers; what parts and services. I want to know where the costs are, too. We already know a lot of that. I just need to study it and set up the reporting system a little better. I also want to figure out the best ways to promote sales of parts, especially used ones, and digging buckets. The farm economy is down and land clearing is about dead. But there is always some construction work going on and people are tending to fix their old equipment rather than buy new stuff. We are broadening our market area, too.

Q James, how do you feel about your customers? Just tell me what your feelings are.

A Quite often, in dealing with them in the past from the place we had built over the years and which was at best just adequate for the job, I felt a little inferior. From the instant we moved into our new place I have felt better. For one thing, I'm not apologetic about a price, not timid at all about giving a man a price quick. I offered no apology yesterday when Charles Brooks said, "You're killing me." I sense a new attitude on the part of customers. They seem to be more favorable towards us.

Q The question I was asking had more to do with whether you develop any kind of personal relationship with your customers.

A Absolutely, with every one that I possibly can. Any way we can get interaction, joking or talking about common interests, we do. These things help me to remember the customer, of course. But it also gives us something to talk about and ask about the next time we see them. We've developed relationships with people that go back to when we first went in business. Take the Costello brothers. We're able to deal with them and do a great deal of business. Certainly, we give them prices, but I think the work—most of it anyway—would be ours regardless of the price. We know not to get ridiculous and they trust that we won't. Other customers, like Tom Fussel, have just become real close friends over the years. Tom came by here last week and said, "I'm gonna send you a picture of Sharpco when you first went in business. You had three blades in your only building. You didn't even have a door in the back. The shop was so small those three blades completely filled it." He said, "From there to here, you've come a long way—and during that time all the dealers seem to have gone downhill." And he just looked at me and said, "I wonder why that is?"

EXHIBIT 7	Financial Summaries: Sharpco, Inc., Balance Sheets			
	1981	**1982**	**1983**	**1984**
ASSETS				
Current assets				
Cash	$ 49,420	$ 8,760	$ 10,205	$ 8,108
Accounts receivable	58,791	56,887	148,531	114,320
Reserve for bad debts	(9,974)	(19,702)	(22,311)	(20,659)
Notes receivable, stockholder	49,427	61,604	79,221	87,637
Inventory	177,322	95,308	144,499	315,108
Total current assets	$324,986	$202,857	$360,145	$504,514
Fixed assets				
Building and improvements	120,766	120,766	188,668	294,491
Machinery and equipment	141,897	141,897	113,444	113,444
Office furniture and equipment	15,856	15,856	13,464	27,943
Vehicles	54,431	62,556	104,021	95,896
Total	332,950	341,075	419,597	531,774
Less accumulated depreciation	163,271	197,074	194,408	138,219
Net depreciated assets	169,679	144,001	225,189	393,555
Land	34,010	47,770	55,530	95,000
Total fixed assets	$203,689	$191,771	$280,719	$488,555
Other assets				
Utility deposits	500	500	950	1,180
Total assets	$529,175	$395,128	$641,814	$994,249

EXHIBIT 7 | **Continued**

	1981	1982	1983	1984
LIABILITIES AND STOCKHOLDERS' EQUITY				
Current liabilities				
Accounts payable	$ 28,458	$ 5,839	$ 48,487	$ 23,124
Accrued expenses	19,819	12,587	13,860	12,602
Withheld and accrued taxes	6,171	5,391	1,467	1,252
Accrued payroll	—	—	—	1,163
Accrued income taxes (overpayment)	11,636	(4,533)	(318)	6,430
Notes payable	171,600	81,281	185,872	268,505
Deposit from customers	9,000	—	—	—
Total current liabilities	$246,684	$100,565	$249,368	$313,076
Long-term liabilities				
Notes payable	21,293	8,094	59,390	259,009
Stockholders' equity				
Common stock	33,582	33,582	33,582	33,582
Less treasury stock	(11,316)	(11,316)	(11,316)	(11,316)
Retained earnings	238,932	264,203	310,790	399,898
Total stockholders' equity	$261,198	$286,469	$333,056	$422,164
Total liabilities and stockholders' equity	$529,175	$395,128	$641,814	$994,249

Sharpco, Inc., Income Statements

	1981	1982	1983	1984
REVENUE				
Welding shop	$278,101	$ 297,547	$ 219,137	$ 268,366
Undercarriage shop	289,344	568,378	642,610	577,298
Direct parts sales	145,304	144,971	197,098	312,915
Steel	82,115	53,460	42,188	44,924
Miscellaneous	10,819	9,048	8,194	17,447
Total revenue	$805,683	$1,073,404	$1,109,227	$1,220,950
DIRECT COSTS				
Materials	327,829	565,993	559,097	570,100
Labor	80,117	100,499	112,259	118,684
Subcontractors	5,548	11,339	16,846	13,756
Freight	5,813	5,422	6,757	8,007
Other direct costs	238	77	50	560
Total direct costs	$419,545	$ 683,330	$ 695,009	$ 711,107
Gross profit	386,138	390,074	414,218	509,843
Indirect costs	318,779	359,336	361,599	408,125
Profit before taxes	67,359	30,738	52,619	101,718
Income taxes	11,636	5,467	6,032	12,610
Net profit	$ 55,723	$ 25,271	$ 46,587	$ 89,108

EXHIBIT 7 | **Continued**

Sharpco, Inc. Inventories, December 31, 1984

Steel	34,685
New parts	162,995
Used parts	100,152
Supplies	548
Finished goods	12,120
Work in process	4,608
Total	315,108

Sharpco, Inc. Sales by Month (Unadjusted)

	1981	1982	1983	1984
Jan.	55,974	73,463	60,666	51,492
Feb.	67,743	91,547	82,996	74,689
Mar.	78,002	111,144	69,295	41,780
Apr.	73,360	79,510	52,365	70,196
May	85,944	126,957	45,374	151,595
Jun.	32,936	77,153	94,390	142,620
Jul.	65,898	108,988	137,806	142,505
Aug.	69,470	138,695	138,878	116,862
Sep.	66,891	95,743	87,621	183,710
Oct.	77,054	83,119	149,283	115,987
Nov.	76,967	56,725	105,716	49,168
Dec.	51,325	24,812	76,682	64,228

Cunningham's Bookstore, Inc.

NEIL H. SNYDER • RICHARD F. DEMONG • JOHN H. LINDGREN, JR. •
DAVID M. MALONEY

John Jacobson, owner of Cunningham's Bookstore, Inc., must come to grips with an unpleasant reality. A branch store that he opened in 1984, one of his three bookstores, is not doing well, and a decision must be made soon about the store's future. It was to be his model store, and his customers responded very favorably to his basic concept. In an era when many bookstore owners are adopting the mass marketing approaches used by Kroger, K-mart, Walmart, and others, John wanted to develop a bookstore with a contemporary flair that focused on quality and service.

Service is a word people use a great deal these days, but it is not found in most businesses. Bookstores are no different. Once, most bookstores were owned and operated by book lovers who cared a great deal about learning, and they understood the value of books in the learning process. Additionally, they tended to be very community-minded individuals who took pleasure in knowing that they were playing a part in helping preserve our culture and heritage. The notion of service was not foreign to them. Today, however, when book buyers go into bookstores that are run like supermarkets or discount stores, it is unlikely that anyone in the store will go out of his or her way to help them, and, besides, employees in these stores know very little about the books they sell.

That's what made John's idea so interesting. He hired people who loved books as much as he did, and he taught them to share their love of books with the stores' customers. He explained to his employees that knowing about authors and their histories was important, and that a critical part of their jobs was to communicate to customers that they were enthusiastic about reading and that they were anxious to help satisfy their needs.

John stresses service above all else in all of his stores. He believes that Cunningham's Bookstore not only sells a product, but it also offers a service to its customers. He defines the service he delivers as experienced salespeople, knowledge about frequent customers, and the ability to aid customers in finding the books they need.

At times when a store is not busy John and his employees will discuss books in addition to carrying out their normal duties. These discussions

© 1989. This case was prepared by Neil H. Snyder, Richard F. DeMong, John H. Lindgren, Jr., and David M. Maloney of the McIntire School of Commerce, University of Virginia. It is designed to be used in classroom discussions and as a case for discussion in management training programs. The characters in the case are not real. They were developed to assist the authors in highlighting critical issues in bookstore management. The use of this case in whole or in part without the written permission of the authors is prohibited.

The authors thank the American Booksellers Association and the McIntire School of Commerce Center for Entrepreneurial Studies for their generous support in the development of this case.

often result in decisions to stock certain books that the employees and John believe their customers will want to read. It is not unusual for John's customers to become involved in these conversations as well. John is convinced that this approach enables Cunningham's Bookstore to stay on top of its customers' desires.

Although not everyone is interested in this approach, real book lovers are, and that was the niche John wanted to find with his concept. One problem with this approach is that its market is small. John must decide if his concept is flawed, and if it is not, he must identify ways to increase the profitability of his business.

BACKGROUND	### John Jacobson

John is 42 years old with a wife, Sue Ellen (age 40), a son, John, Jr. (age 15), and a daughter, Caroline (age 12). Looking back over the years, John concludes that he has come a long way since his early days. He was the son of a dirt farmer and was raised in a village of about 300 people that is located 25 miles from Richmond, Virginia. As a boy, he was a good student who enjoyed reading, and he developed a strong work ethic by doing farm chores. Although he worked hard on the farm, he decided at a very young age that being a farmer was not his goal.

When he was eighteen years old, John enrolled at the University of Richmond and embarked upon what he thought would be a rewarding career: medical research. He majored in biology but took enough courses in English to satisfy the university's requirements for a double major.

In his sophomore year John took a part-time job at Cunningham's Bookstore working in the afternoon and evening two days a week and on weekends. At first he did not enjoy the job because he believed his knowledge about books was inadequate. John even suggested to Mr. Cunningham that he wanted to quit, but Mr. Cunningham talked him out of it. After several weeks of on-the-job training, John's attitude changed, and he developed a sense of confidence in his knowledge and in his ability to deal effectively with book lovers.

By the time John was ready to graduate from college, his goals had changed, and he had become very fond of the bookstore business. It was different from anything he had done before, and his love of reading had grown stronger each year as he realized how many good books there were to read. Furthermore, John enjoyed spending time with fellow book lovers. In short, John had found his element, and he was excited when Mr. Cunningham asked him to continue working at the bookstore after graduation.

However, John could not justify in his own mind staying indefinitely with Cunningham's Bookstore as an employee. He was a college graduate; he had already worked in the business for three years; and he believed that he should become a partner with Mr. Cunningham. In addition, John thought that he should work toward owning the business outright when Mr. Cunningham was ready to retire. Mr. Cunningham liked the idea, and a deal was struck.

John became a stockholder in the business (legally he was a stockholder, but in practice he was a partner), and it was agreed that he would eventually take it over. In December 1986, the buyout agreement was completed, and John became the stores' sole stockholder (in practice, he was a sole proprietor). The essence of the transaction was that all of Mr. Cunningham's stock interest (45 shares) was redeemed by the corporation, which currently holds that stock in its treasury. As a result of the redemption, John became the sole owner of the entity's stock (15 shares). The terms of the corporation's purchase of the stock from Mr. Cunningham included the transfer of a $30,000 promissory note (which is expected to be paid off by 1997) and cash for the balance of $178,625. The cash that the corporation needed to make this payment to Mr. Cunningham was borrowed from John in the form of a demand note. The three stores operate as a single corporation. John, who is the corporation's president, has elected to be taxed as an S corporation for federal income-tax purposes.

John's Goals

When asked about his goals for Cunningham's Bookstore, John said, "My primary goal is to keep the three stores viable and operating." His rationale is simple. He wants to be a contributor to his community, and he believes that he can accomplish his objectives by operating his stores and by emphasizing the values he cherishes: honesty, integrity, quality, and service.

When one talks to John, it becomes apparent very quickly that he really loves owning a bookstore, but that he does not enjoy the details of running a business. The things that John finds unattractive about running his stores include paperwork, dealing with the stores' finances, the long hours (John works ten to twelve hours a day, six or seven days a week), the low financial return on his time investment, the large amount of time it takes to implement his ideas, and dealing with personnel problems.

One could say that John has a love/hate relationship with the bookstore business. He enjoys it more than anything he has ever done, but there are days when he wonders why he is in it. John takes a salary of about $30,000 a year, and he reinvests the rest in the business. When John considers how much he earns for the amount of time he works and how much more he could be making if he worked for someone else, he becomes frustrated. About a year ago, John was offered a good job that would have paid him more and would have relieved him of the responsibility of running the business, but he turned it down. He said, "I've been my own boss for so long, I'm just not sure I could work for anyone."

Richmond, Virginia

Richmond, the capital of Virginia, is located in the center of the state. Its economy is strong with a diverse group of industrial firms, universities, state government activities, hospitals, etc., that buffer its citizens from the effects of economic reversals. Until ten years ago, Richmond was a sleepy community. Virginia is a blue-blood state, and Richmonders were commonly known as the bluest of the blue bloods. They did not like change, and they did not take kindly to outsiders who tried to impose it on them.

But in the early 1980s things started to change, and Richmond took off economically. What was once a close-knit, self-centered community became a prosperous, developing metropolis with a population of about one million people. Outsiders moved to Richmond in large numbers, and the business people who catered to them were more interested in doing business than in maintaining the status quo. Young, urban professionals (Yuppies) were especially attracted to Richmond, and they brought with them the convenience-oriented, mass-marketing psychology that has been in vogue for many years.

The Bookstore

Cunningham's Bookstore is well known and respected by residents of Richmond who have lived in the city for more than ten years. The stores have a reputation for offering high quality, personal service, and a wide range of attractive conveniences including free gift-wrapping, charge accounts, and free delivery to local hospitals. Other deliveries are made for a rate equal to that charged by a carrier such as UPS.

In fact, Cunningham's was once regarded as the premier bookstore in the city. However, competition from national bookstore chains, discount stores of all types, and more aggressive independents, along with changes in the city of Richmond and its citizens, have led to the perception among many book buyers that bigger stores are better stores. Thus, Cunningham's stature in the community has diminished during the last decade.

John Jacobson is responsible for the day-to-day management of the business. To assist him in running its three locations, he has a general manager, two store managers, and 25 full-time and part-time employees. While the compensation of the stores' employees is adequate, it is not extravagant by any means. Furthermore, the employee fringe benefits are somewhat limited. For example:

- There is no retirement program through the store for John or for any of the employees;
- There is a key-man life insurance policy on John's life in the amount of $250,000;

- A limited group medical insurance plan is available to employees who regularly work more than 30 hours per week; and
- Books may be purchased by employees at a 25 percent discount.

Receiving is done at the central location, which has approximately 2,400 square feet of selling space and 1,800 square feet of storage and office space. The two satellite locations each have about 1,700 square feet of selling space.

All of the fixed assets, such as shelving, display cases, and cash registers, are owned by the store. None of the assets are leased, either from John or independent third parties, except for the store locations themselves. John has agreed to noncancelable operating leases whereby he may rent the facilities as follows:

LOCATION	LEASE EXPIRATION
Boulevard	9-30-89
Chesterfield	5-1-89
Westend	12-31-91

John does most of the buying for all three locations, although other employees get involved in buying on occasion. Books are received at the main store and then delivered to the satellite locations.

The central location for Cunningham's Bookstore is on The Boulevard, an older section of town near Virginia Commonwealth University. Cunningham's has been in business at that location since it was founded. The Boulevard store caters primarily to nearby residents and V.C.U. students, faculty, and staff. Cunningham's second store is located in an affluent section of Richmond known as the Westend area. It has been in business at that location for more than fifteen years. The Westend store caters to a stable population of very wealthy individuals who are among Richmond's best-known blue bloods.

Cunningham's third store, which was opened in 1984, is having difficulty. It is located in a strip shopping center in Chesterfield County, a rapidly growing and prosperous part of the Richmond metropolitan area that is popular among the Yuppie group. There are several problems with the Chesterfield store. First, the strip center in which it is located is designed poorly. Its one anchor store, Kroger, is located at the entrance of the center, and Cunningham's Bookstore and the other stores in the center are located behind the grocery store. Thus, shoppers who come to the center to buy groceries can complete their shopping without having to walk by, or even see in some cases, many other stores in the center.

Second, in 1985 the center's developers added several stores, one of which was a bookstore with more than two times the floor space of Cunningham's store. The fact that the shopping center now has two bookstores is bad enough, but to make matters worse, the new bookstore is only about

50 yards from Cunningham's. Although both stores are located behind the Kroger store, the competitor's store has a much larger front and a large sign. Thus, it is much easier to see from the grocery store. John complained to the center developer when he learned that they were planning to put another bookstore in the center, but his concerns fell on deaf ears. There was no clause in his lease that would prohibit it, and that was all that seemed to matter to them.

Third, in 1984 when Cunningham's opened the Chesterfield store, they entered the hottest area in town in the hottest shopping center in the area. But the area has grown a great deal since then, and today there are numerous shopping centers and a large mall under construction within a three-mile radius of the Chesterfield store. Small stores in the center are moving out rapidly. About 10 percent of the tenants in the center have closed already, and Cunningham's lease is up for renewal in May 1989. John must decide whether he wants to continue investing his time and money in the Chesterfield location.

John's manager at the Chesterfield store is Wesley Carter. Wesley was responsible for persuading Mr. Cunningham and John to explore moving into the strip shopping center in the first place, and he has been resistant to the idea of closing the store. Each time John suggests that closing the Chesterfield store may be his only option, Wesley tells him that the store should stay put and not give up in the face of competition. Wesley, however, has little understanding or appreciation for John's overall business and the problems he is experiencing.

Wesley is a 36-year-old veteran of the Vietnam War who has a macho image of himself. He is intelligent and he loves reading. He sometimes wears on people because of his abrasive manner, but he is extremely effective and affable with the people he likes. Some of John's customers comment on occasion that Wesley's interpersonal style is crude. John likes Wesley nonetheless, even though John admits that he visits the Chesterfield store less frequently than he should, primarily because he does not want to deal with Wesley. In addition, John feels frustrated because he has been unable to improve the situation in the Chesterfield store. Thus, he devotes most of his time and attention to the other two stores, and Wesley feels neglected.

| **FINANCIAL CONTROL AND REPORTING** | See Exhibits 1 through 7, which show financial data for Cunningham's Bookstore, Inc. |

See Exhibits 1 through 7, which show financial data for Cunningham's Bookstore, Inc.

While the financial accounting and control system has evolved over many years as the stores have grown, it continues to be a fairly simple system. The accrual accounting system is manually based and is maintained by the store's full-time bookkeeper, who graduated from a local commercial business school (not a college) many years ago. She is intimately familiar with

EXHIBIT 1   Income Statement for Period Ending December 31, 1988

	BOULEVARD	PERCENT OF SALES	CHESTERFIELD	PERCENT OF SALES	WESTEND	PERCENT OF SALES	TOTAL	PERCENT OF SALES	BUDGETED	VARIANCE	PERCENT VARIANCE
SALES	$823,943	100.0	$260,486	100.0	$492,222	100.0	$1,576,651	100.0	$1,745,347	($168,696)	−0.10
Cost of goods sold (COGS)											
Purchases and freight-in	568,058	68.9	180,845	69.4	308,717	62.7	1,057,620	67.1			
Inventory (increase) decrease	(10,969)	−1.3	(15,112)	−5.8	6,628	1.3	(19,453)	−1.2			
Total COGS	557,089	67.6	165,733	63.6	315,345	64.1	1,038,167	65.8	1,117,022	(78,855)	−0.07
Gross profit	266,855	32.4	94,753	36.4	176,877	35.9	538,484	34.2	628,325	(89,841)	−0.14
OPERATING EXPENSES											
Direct store											
Fixed costs											
Salaries	72,129	8.8	45,669	17.5	74,802	15.2	192,600	12.2	193,749	(1,149)	−0.01
Depreciation	545	0.1	142	0.1	405	0.1	1,092	0.1	1,092	0	0.00
Dues	949	0.1	1,975	0.8	520	0.1	3,444	0.2	2,094	1,351	0.64
Insurance	11,539	1.4	0	0.0	0		11,539	0.7	11,170	369	0.03
Miscellaneous	1,673	0.2	363	0.1	619	0.1	2,655	0.2	3,841	(1,186)	−0.31
Taxes and licenses	17,876	2.2	0		520	0.1	18,396	1.2	20,420	(2,024)	−0.10
Rent	6,747	0.8	25,980	10.0	30,054	6.1	62,781	4.0	61,446	1,335	0.02
Utilities	10,128	1.2	5,987	2.3	6,845	1.4	22,960	1.5	15,257	7,702	0.50
Repairs and maint.	4,722	0.6	4,260	1.6	3,646	0.7	12,628	0.8	7,680	4,948	0.64
Variable costs											
Advertising	747	0.1	899	0.3	0	0.0	1,646	0.1	9,076	(7,430)	−0.82
Postage	1,470	0.2	277	0.1	1,053	0.2	2,800	0.2	3,614	(814)	−0.23
Supplies	184	0.0	402	0.2	629	0.1	1,215	0.1	1,919	(704)	−0.37
Total direct store expenses	128,709	15.6	85,954	33.0	119,093	24.2	333,756	21.2	331,358	2,398	0.01

GENERAL AND ADMINISTRATIVE

	Amount	%	Amount	%	Amount	%	Amount	%	Amount	%
Fixed cost										
Salaries—officer	10,000	1.2	10,000	3.8	30,000	2.0	68,749	1.9	(38,749)	−0.56
Salaries—other	46,507	5.6	46,507	17.9	139,521	9.4	77,500	8.8	62,021	0.80
Amortization	1,396	0.2	1,396	0.5	4,188	0.3	4,187	0.3	0	0.00
Automobile	978	0.1	978	0.4	2,934	0.2	2,618	0.2	317	0.12
Credit bureau	58	0.0	58	0.0	174	0.0	176	0.0	(2)	−0.01
Dues	540	0.1	540	0.2	1,620	0.1	872	0.1	748	0.86
Insurance	4,247	0.5	4,247	1.6	12,741	0.9	6,223	0.8	6,517	1.05
Legal and accounting	1,667	0.2	1,667	0.6	5,001	0.3	6,223	0.3	(1,223)	−0.20
Miscellaneous	76	0.0	76	0.0	228	0.0	176	0.0	51	0.29
Office expense/supplies	4,639	0.6	4,639	1.8	13,917	0.9	17,802	0.9	(3,884)	−0.22
Repairs and maintenance	535	0.1	535	0.2	1,605	0.1	1,919	0.1	(316)	−0.16
Taxes and licenses	3,449	0.4	3,449	1.3	10,347	0.7	11,869	0.7	(1,522)	−0.13
Variable costs										
Advertising	16,033	1.9	16,033	6.2	48,099	3.3	35,605	3.1	12,493	0.35
Postage	5,138	0.6	5,138	2.0	15,414	1.0	11,520	1.0	3,893	0.34
Travel/entertainment	877	0.1	877	0.3	2,631	0.2	3,142	0.2	(511)	−0.16
Total general/administrative costs	96,140	11.7	96,140	36.9	288,420	19.5	244,395	18.3	44,019	0.18
Total operating expense	224,849	27.3	215,233	69.9	622,176	43.7	575,753	39.5	46,417	0.08
Operating income (loss)	42,005	5.1	(38,356)	−33.5	(83,692)	−7.8	52,572	−5.3	(136,258)	−2.59
Interest expense	(14,641)	−1.8	(8,728)	−1.8	(28,155)	−1.8	(28,155)	−1.8	0	0.00
Other income (expense)—net	(14,991)	−1.8	(8,937)	−1.9	(28,829)	−1.8	(28,829)	−1.8	0	0.00
Income (loss) before provision for income taxes	12,373	1.5	(97,028)	−37.2	(140,676)	−11.4	(4,412)	−8.9	(136,258)	30.88
Provision (credit) for income taxes	0		0		0		0		0	
Net income (loss)	12,373	1.5	(97,028)	−37.2	(140,676)	−11.4	(4,412)	−8.9	(136,258)	30.88

EXHIBIT 2   **Balance Sheets at December 31, 1988**

	BOULEVARD	CHESTERFIELD	WESTEND	TOTAL
CURRENT ASSETS				
Cash	$ 9,245	$ 300	$ 300	$ 9,845
Accounts receivable				
Trade	17,271	5,646	10,296	33,213
Other	39,561	12,934	23,585	76,080
Inventory—lower of cost or market (FIFO)	187,257	111,749	120,630	419,636
Total current assets	253,334	130,629	154,811	538,774
Property and equipment—at cost				
Leasehold improvements	8,610	320	3,974	12,904
Furniture and equipment	21,922	24,090	20,422	66,434
Automobiles	14,338	0	0	14,338
Less: Accumulated depreciation	41,944	16,938	22,989	81,871
Net property and equipment	2,926	7,472	1,407	11,805
Other assets				
Deposits	0	0	36	36
Loan costs, net of accumulated amort.	716	0	0	716
Total assets	256,976	138,101	156,254	551,331
LIABILITIES AND STOCKHOLDERS' EQUITY				
Current liabilities				
Notes payable—bank	8,458	2,765	5,042	16,265
Current portion of long-term debt	11,580	3,786	6,904	22,270
Accounts payable	82,615	118,372	138,372	339,359
Accrued taxes	11,444	3,741	6,822	22,007
Total current liabilities	114,097	128,664	157,140	399,901
Long-term debt, less current portion	129,259	42,258	77,058	248,575
Long-term leases, commitments, and contingencies				
Total liabilities	243,356	170,922	234,198	648,476
Stockholders' equity				
Common stock—no par value, 150 shares authorized: 60 shares issued and outstanding at stated value	7,229	0	0	7,229
Additional paid-in capital	49,500	0	0	49,500
Retained earnings	65,376	2,645	(13,271)	54,750
Less treasury stock, at cost	108,485	35,466	64,674	208,625
Total equity	13,620	(32,821)	(77,946)	(97,146)
Total liabilities and stockholders' equity	256,976	138,101	156,254	551,331

EXHIBIT 3 Income Statement for Period Ending December 31, 1987

	BOULEVARD	PERCENT OF SALES	CHESTERFIELD	PERCENT OF SALES	WESTEND	PERCENT OF SALES	TOTAL	PERCENT OF SALES
SALES	$933,128	100.0	$290,496	100.0	$603,184	100.0	$1,826,808	100.0
Cost of goods sold								
Purchases and freight-in	632,694	67.8	234,442	80.7	398,398	66.0	1,265,534	69.3
Inventory (increase) decrease	(49,958)	−5.4	(29,815)	−10.3	(18,358)	−3.0	(98,131)	−5.4
Total COGS	582,736	62.4	204,627	70.4	380,040	63.0	1,167,402	63.9
Gross profit	350,392	37.6	85,869	29.6	223,145	37.0	659,406	36.1
OPERATING EXPENSES								
Direct store								
Fixed costs								
Salaries	70,769	7.6	44,384	15.3	73,692	12.2	188,845	10.3
Depreciation	726	0.1	189	0.1	540	0.1	1,455	0.1
Dues	2,112	0.2	1,942	0.7	543	0.1	4,597	0.3
Insurance	10,138	1.1	0	0.0	0	0.0	10,138	0.6
Miscellaneous	3,969	0.4	276	0.1	348	0.1	4,593	0.3
Taxes and licenses	19,015	2.0	0	0.0	694	0.1	19,709	1.1
Rent	5,904	0.6	27,918	9.6	26,395	4.4	60,217	3.3
Utilities	11,235	1.2	6,136	2.1	7,610	1.3	24,981	1.4
Repairs and maint.	2,440	0.3	4,890	1.7	3,653	0.6	10,983	0.6
Variable costs								
Advertising	2,310	0.2	3,651	1.3	45	0.0	6,005	0.3
Postage	8,681	0.9	244	0.1	998	0.2	9,922	0.5
Supplies	839	0.1	437	0.2	917	0.2	2,192	0.1
Total direct store expenses	138,137	14.8	90,067	31.0	115,433	19.1	343,637	18.8

EXHIBIT 3 Continued

GENERAL AND ADMINISTRATIVE

	Amount	%	Amount	%	Amount	%	Amount	%
Fixed costs								
Salaries—officer	10,000	1.1	10,000	3.4	10,000	1.7	30,000	1.6
Salaries—other	36,815	3.9	36,815	12.7	36,815	6.1	110,445	6.0
Amortization	191	0.0	191	0.1	191	0.0	573	0.0
Automobile	1,166	0.1	1,166	0.4	1,166	0.2	3,498	0.2
Credit bureau	51	0.0	51	0.0	51	0.0	153	0.0
Dues	139	0.0	139	0.0	139	0.0	417	0.0
Insurance	4,868	0.5	4,868	1.7	4,868	0.8	14,604	0.8
Legal and accounting	5,322	0.6	5,322	1.8	5,322	0.9	15,966	0.9
Miscellaneous	0	0.0	0	0.0	0	0.0	0	0.0
Office expense/supplies	3,949	0.4	3,949	1.4	3,949	0.7	11,847	0.6
Repairs and maintenance	548	0.1	548	0.2	548	0.1	1,644	0.1
Taxes and licenses	4,599	0.5	4,599	1.6	4,599	0.8	13,797	0.8
Variable costs								
Advertising	17,724	1.9	17,724	6.1	17,724	2.9	53,172	2.9
Postage	616	0.1	616	0.2	616	0.1	1,848	0.1
Travel/entertainment	1,259	0.1	1,259	0.4	1,259	0.2	3,777	0.2
Total general/administrative costs	87,247	9.3	87,247	30.0	87,247	14.5	261,741	14.3
Total operating expense	225,384	24.2	177,314	61.0	202,680	33.6	605,378	33.1
Operating income (loss)	125,008	13.4	(91,445)	−31.5	20,465	3.4	54,028	3.0
Interest expense	(12,331)	−1.3	(3,868)	−1.3	(7,979)	−1.3	(24,178)	−1.3
Other income (expense)—net	(9,928)	−1.1	(3,118)	−1.1	(6,431)	−1.1	(19,487)	−1.1
Income (loss) before provision for income taxes	102,739	11.0	(98,431)	−33.9	6,055	1.0	10,363	0.6
Provision (credit) for income taxes	0		0		0		0	
Net income (loss)	102,739	11.0	(98,431)	−33.9	6,055	1.0	10,363	0.6

EXHIBIT 4	**Balance Sheet at December 31, 1987**			
	BOULEVARD	**CHESTERFIELD**	**WESTEND**	**TOTAL**
CURRENT ASSETS				
Cash	$ 18,638	$ 300	$ 300	$ 19,238
Accounts receivable				
Trade	32,000	10,039	20,706	62,745
Other	33,432	10,488	21,632	65,552
Inventory—lower of cost or market (FIFO)	198,226	126,861	114,002	439,090
Total current assets	282,296	147,689	156,640	586,625
Property and equipment—at cost				
Leasehold improvements	8,610	320	3,974	12,904
Furniture and equipment	21,922	24,090	20,422	66,434
Automobiles	14,338	0	0	14,338
Less: Accumulated depreciation	41,399	16,796	22,584	80,779
Net property and equipment	3,471	7,614	1,812	12,897
Other assets				
Deposits	0	0	36	3
Loan costs, net of accumulated amort.	1,289	0	0	1,289
Total assets	287,056	155,303	158,488	600,847
LIABILITIES AND STOCKHOLDERS' EQUITY				
Current liabilities				
Notes payable—bank	9,524	2,988	6,163	18,675
Current portion of long-term debt	11,358	3,563	7,349	22,270
Accounts payable	119,847	37,599	77,548	234,994
Accrued taxes	13,631	4,276	8,820	26,727
Total current liabilities	154,360	48,426	99,880	302,666
Long-term debt, less current portion	129,874	40,745	84,036	254,655
Long-term leases, commitments and contingencies				
Total liabilities	284,234	89,171	183,916	556,321
Stockholders' equity				
Common stock—no par value, 150 shares authorized: 60 shares issued and outstanding at stated value	7,229	0	0	7,229
Additional paid-in capital	49,500	0	0	49,500
Retained earnings	53,002	99,672	42,748	195,422
Less treasury stock, at cost	106,909	33,540	69,176	209,625
Total equity	2,822	66,132	(25,428)	43,526
Total liabilities and stockholders' equity	287,056	155,303	158,488	600,847

EXHIBIT 5

Income Statement for Period Ending December 31, 1989—Projected

Sales	$1,889,775
Cost of goods sold	1,209,455
Gross profit	680,319

OPERATING EXPENSES

Direct store	
Fixed costs	
Salaries	205,888
Depreciation	9,540
Dues	2,267
Insurance	12,094
Miscellaneous	4,157
Taxes and licenses	22,111
Rent	65,747
Utilities	27,590
Repairs and maintenance	8,314
Variable costs	0
Advertising	9,643
Postage	6,992
Supplies	2,077
Total direct store expenses	376,420
General and administrative	
Fixed costs	
Salaries—officer	71,317
Salaries—other	80,395
Amortization	4,187
Automobile	2,742
Credit Bureau	183
Dues	914
Insurance	6,413
Legal and accounting	6,413
Miscellaneous	183
Office expense/supplies	18,645
Repairs and maintenance	2,010
Taxes and licenses	12,430
Variable costs	0
Advertising	37,290
Postage	12,064
Travel/entertainment	3,290
Total general/administrative costs	258,475
Total operating expense	634,896
Operating income (loss)	45,423
Interest expense	(6,347)
Other income (expense)—net	(3,589)
Net income (loss)	35,487

EXHIBIT 6

Departmental Sales and Ending Inventory Analysis

	YEAR ENDED 12/31/87				YEAR ENDED 12/31/88			
	BOULEVARD	CHESTERFIELD	WESTEND	TOTAL	BOULEVARD	CHESTERFIELD	WESTEND	TOTAL
Department 1X	$ 84,694	$ 34,318	$108,009	$ 227,021	$ 85,425	$ 31,366	$ 87,447	$ 204,239
Department 2X	433,142	137,804	340,452	911,398	346,860	117,939	246,983	711,782
Department 3X	125,765	5,486	18,769	150,020	111,305	6,070	17,316	134,690
Department 5X	289,526	112,888	135,954	538,368	280,353	105,111	140,476	525,940
Total	933,128	290,496	603,184	1,826,808	823,943	260,486	492,222	1,576,651

ANALYSIS OF ENDING INVENTORIES

	BOULEVARD	CHESTERFIELD	WESTEND	TOTAL	BOULEVARD	CHESTERFIELD	WESTEND	TOTAL
Department 1X	13,849	28,788	25,869	68,506	12,031	8,128	28,401	48,560
Department 2X	69,942	43,719	39,288	152,949	66,118	37,420	40,247	143,786
Department 3X	8,665	904	812	10,381	10,261	911	589	11,761
Department 4X	105,770	53,451	48,033	207,253	98,846	65,290	51,393	215,529
Total	198,226	126,861	114,002	439,090	187,257	111,749	120,630	419,636

EXHIBIT 7

Ratio Analysis

	YEAR ENDED 12/31/87	YEAR ENDED 12/31/88
PROFITABILITY RATIOS		
Gross profit margin gross profit/sales	36%	34%
Net profit margin net profit after taxes/sales	1%	−9
Return on equity net profit/owner's equity	23%	n/a
Return on assets net profit/total assets	2%	−25%
Turnover ratio sales/total assets	3.04	2.85
LIQUIDITY RATIOS		
Current ratio current assets/current liabilities	1.94	1.34
Quick ratio C.A.—inventories/current liabilities	0.49	0.30
Inventory turnover COGS/avg. inventory	2.88	2.47

EXHIBIT 7

Continued

	YEAR ENDED 12/31/87	YEAR ENDED 12/31/88
LEVERAGE RATIOS		
Debt to equity total debt/total equity	12.8	−6.7
Debt-to-assets total debt/total assets	0.93	1.18

the system and is probably the only one on the staff who is fully aware of all of the system's ins and outs.

In addition to her daily duties of posting revenues and expenses to the appropriate ledgers, preparing and depositing cash receipts, and making cash disbursements, she prepares a monthly tabulation of the sales revenues, direct store expenses, and general and administrative expenses. John then compares these summaries to similar reports of the previous year for the same month and year to date. In addition, he compares the data with industry-wide statistics (what little that is available). At the end of each year, while the financial records are not subject to an audit or a review, the stores' public accountants compile the financial data into formalized income statements and balance sheets.

John does not use a formal budgeting procedure that could serve as the basis for the development of the stores' financial plan. Instead, he does things the way Mr. Cunningham taught him. Because there is no formal budgeting procedure, there can normally be no comparison of revenues and expenses to expected amounts at the end of a particular period.

The budget numbers for 1988 and the projected income statement for 1989 that are presented as a part of Exhibits 1 and 5 are derived from projections made by the bookstore's independent public accountant prior to the time when John purchased the business. These budgets were based on projections that were made in order to determine a reasonable sales price for the company at the time of the purchase.

Inventory records are also manually maintained. The stores' inventory/department categories that are detailed in Exhibits 1 through 6 are as follows:

Department 1X: Nonbook items such as stationery, calendars, etc.

Department 2X: Hardback books and audio cassettes

Department 3X: Textbooks, workbooks, and newspapers

Department 5X: Paperbacks

John has found that over the years the utilization of selling floor space by department at each store has approximated the following:

Department 1X: 25 percent

Department 2X: 36 percent

Department 3X: 3 percent

> Note: While this percentage is true for most of the year at the Boulevard store, because it is located close to the V.C.U. campus, its textbook inventory swells at the beginning of each of the two academic semesters (i.e., August/September, and January).

Department 5X: 36 percent

John has instructed his bookkeeper to retain accounting and legal records (e.g., cancelled checks, cash receipts journals, general ledgers) for whatever periods of time the law requires. But at a minimum, all such records are kept for three years. John tends to see the financial records as reporting instruments instead of planning tools. He does not use balance sheet information, partly because he does not see it as important and partly because he does not understand it. John focuses most of his attention on the bottom line of the income statement. That figure he does understand.

Working Capital Management

John would like to maintain a balance in his one checking account that is large enough to meet his spending needs for an entire month, so that he is not dependent on his cash receipts in any given month to pay his bills. In essence, John would like to keep a cash reserve on hand as a cushion that is equal to one month's bills. Unfortunately, he is rarely able to keep that much cash on hand, so he pays his bills with the cash flow of the three stores.

John maintains all his commercial accounts at the Boulevard store. However, the other two stores have many retail customers with well-established credit accounts. All retail customer accounts are maintained at the First Bank of Richmond's bank card center. The bank card center does all of the billings.

A customer can open a credit account with any of Cunningham's three stores by filling out a simple application form that asks for standard information about the applicant's income, net worth, other credit accounts, and job history. The bookkeeper then does a credit check with the Richmond Credit Bureau. If the credit check is favorable, the bookkeeper establishes the account. If there is a problem, John decides whether to establish the account.

John is proud of the fact that he is often the first retailer to extend credit to many young customers who do not have any credit cards or other accounts. Credit customers are charged 1½ percent interest per month for balances that are more than 30 days past due. John writes off balances that are not paid within 120 days as bad debts.

The accounts receivables of Cunningham's Bookstore reached a peak in December of 1987, because John was the primary promoter of a local photographer's book, *Richmond: The First and Last Capital of the Confederacy*. This book sold for $185 per copy, and it was unveiled at the Westend store with a party and much fanfare on November 30, 1987. Many of John's regular customers bought the book on credit, as did 25 first-time customers. The mark-up on this book was lower than usual, but selling it was seen as a great promotion for the store. Thus, the stores' financial records for the year show much higher sales volume than usual with little change in the bottom line.

John orders books based on his knowledge of his customers' tastes, his knowledge of particular authors, and intuition. Fortunately, one of his major wholesale suppliers is located near Richmond. Therefore, if John needs to obtain a book for a customer quickly, he is able to obtain it in only two or three days. He tries to review the selections in his inventory on a weekly basis, but he reviews it on a semi-monthly basis at the very least.

Each month, John pays as many suppliers as he can. First, he pays the most important publishers and the nonbook suppliers. Next, he pays publishers who were not paid the previous month and others to whom he owes money on the basis of how much he buys from them. The more he buys from a particular supplier, the sooner he pays them.

John does not like to skip a payment to a publisher more than once. He always pays his nonbook suppliers promptly because he has learned through experience that gift and stationery suppliers will cut off deliveries if he falls behind in his payments. In contrast, the publishers will carry him beyond the 30-day terms if he makes a payment to them every other month or if he makes a partial payment. John has found that most publishers will carry him for at least 90 days.

John is reluctant to borrow money from a bank because he believes that his stores already have too much long-term debt. Additionally, he is concerned about his current earnings and cash flow and the effect the interest payments on bank debt would have on the stores' financial condition. However, he has found that his suppliers are more than willing to give him extensions in his payments that are better for the store than bank loans. John is unable to commit any additional personal funds to Cunningham's Bookstore at this time, and he does not want another owner in his business.

MARKETING AT CUNNINGHAM'S BOOKSTORE

Cunningham's present marketing consists predominantly of advertisements in local newspapers. These advertisements have generally focused on bestsellers that the store is presently stocking and on books that have been reduced in price. The advertising people at the newspaper help John with layout and design, and the advertisements usually run from Friday to Sunday in the lifestyle section of the paper. Newspaper advertising accounts for 85 percent of the company's advertising expenditures. The remaining portion of advertising expenditures is spent on in-store signage that is produced by a local printer.

Cunningham's advertising expenditures have declined recently. They reached a high of $59,176 in 1987 and a low of $49,744 in 1988. In addition, John plans to reduce his advertising expenditures to $46,933 for 1989.

Most small bookstores in the area follow a very similar advertising strategy. John's competition at the Chesterfield store recently experimented with the use of fliers and brochures. They delivered them door-to-door in the neighborhood surrounding the Chesterfield center. While John had no way of measuring the effectiveness of this type of promotion, he believed that it was effective because many of his regular customers mentioned it when they were in the Chesterfield store.

John has always been reluctant to cut prices to get people to shop in his store. His reasoning was that customers interested only in price would buy paperbacks from a drugstore, a grocery store, or anyplace convenient to them. Pricing issues are not handled well by the industry either. Most publishers print the price right on the book, so it is difficult to increase prices. However, John has reduced his prices on occasion to attract attention to certain books.

Recently, while reading a book about excellence in business, John saw a reference to a method of segmenting markets called VALS. VALS was developed by the Stanford Research Institute and was a system for classifying consumers into nine distinct groups based on VAlues and LifeStyles.

Exhibit 8 summarizes the VALS system and describes each of the classifications. While John did not believe he could afford to conduct a thorough study of his market using this approach, he recognized the potential it had for his stores if he could implement it on a small scale. John gave a copy of Exhibit 8 to his general manager and asked him to read the book on excellence in business. In addition, John indicated that he would like to have his general manager think about how Cunningham's Bookstore might use some of the ideas in VALS to market the bookstore.

THE FUTURE

John must make several major decisions about the future of Cunningham's Bookstore. The first order of business is to decide what to do with the Chesterfield store. Wesley Carter wants to keep the store open, but John has doubts about it. There is not much time to make a decision because of the lease expiration date.

There are also broader issues that need to be addressed. For example, John is beginning to ask himself what he wants to do with the rest of his life, and what role Cunningham's Bookstore will play in it. These are especially

---

EXHIBIT 8   **The VALS System**

PERCENTAGE OF POPULATION (AGE 18 AND OVER)	CONSUMER TYPE	VALUES AND LIFESTYLES	DEMOGRAPHICS	BUYING PATTERNS
NEED-DRIVEN CONSUMERS				
4	Survivors	Needs are survival and security Lack confidence Little life satisfaction	Poverty-level income Little education Older Median age = 65	Price dominant Focused on basics Buy for immediate needs
7	Sustainers	Least satisfied with financial status Angry, rebellious	Low income Low education Much unemployment Live in country as well as cities Median age = 30	Price important Want warranty Cautious buyers
OUTER-DIRECTED CONSUMERS				
38	Belongers	Conforming, conventional Unexperimental Traditional, formal Nostalgic	Low to middle income High school graduates, older Median age = 57	For family, home Middle and lower mass markets
10	Emulators	Ambitious, show-off Status conscious Upwardly mobile Macho, competitive	Good to excellent income Youngish Highly urban Traditionally male, but changing	Conspicuous consumption "in" terms Imitative Popular fashion
20	Achievers	Achievement, success, fame Materialism Leadership, efficiency Comfort	Excellent incomes Leaders in business, politics, etc. Good education Suburban and city living Median age = 42	Buys to give evidence of success Top of the line Luxury and gift markets "New and improved" products

important questions now that John's children are growing up. In addition, he is wondering what the future will be like for small independent bookstores in a world dominated by large bookstore chains. He is even beginning to wonder if he will ever be able to earn enough money to retire in comfort if he continues in the bookstore business. No matter what he decides to do, the next several months are critical for John and for Cunningham's Bookstore.

EXHIBIT 8	Continued			

PERCENTAGE OF POPULATION (AGE 18 AND OVER)	CONSUMER TYPE	VALUES AND LIFESTYLES	DEMOGRAPHICS	BUYING PATTERNS
INNER-DIRECTED CONSUMERS				
3	I-Am-Me	Fiercely individualistic Dramatic, impulsive Experimental Volatile	Young Many single Student or starting job Affluent backgrounds	Display one's taste Experimental fads Clique buying
5	Experiential	Drive to experience directly Active, participative Person-centered Artistic	Bimodal incomes Median age = 26 Many young families Good education	Will try anything once Vigorous, outdoor sports Action-oriented products
11	Societally conscious	Societal responsibility Simple living Smallness of scale Inner growth	Moderate to high incomes Excellent education Diverse ages and places of residence	Conservation emphasis Simplicity Frugality Environmental concerns
2	Integrated	Psychological maturity Sense of fittingness Tolerant, self-actualizing World perspective	Good to excellent incomes Age varies Excellent education Diverse jobs and residential patterns	Varied self-expression Esthetically oriented Ecologically aware One-of-a-kind items

Other questions that John must ask include:

• What effect would closing the Chesterfield store have on his overall profit picture and cash flow?

• How can he increase his sales?

• What should he do with Wesley if he closes the Chesterfield store?

Walsh Petroleum

GEORGE OVERSTREET, JR. • STEWART MALONE • BERNARD MORIN

John Walsh sighed as he looked again at the financial statements his accountant had delivered that morning (see Exhibits 1 and 2). When John's father died two years ago, his accountant had advised against selling the business. "It's a good business, John," he said, "and I think you could do a lot to improve it."

While Walsh Petroleum, Inc., had increased profits in 1985, John still considered them unacceptably low. Company sales had declined for the third straight year, and, while John realized that other oil distributors faced the same problems, he had to wonder what type of future he could expect if he stayed with the family business. Now 31 years old and just married, maybe he should consider selling the business and starting another career before he got too old.

COMPANY HISTORY

Walsh Petroleum was founded in 1957 by John's mother and father as commission agents in the oil business. By 1976 the senior Walsh had converted the company to a conventional oil distributorship. Both the family and the company were well respected in the local community, and the company grew steadily. The 1970s and early 1980s were a period of relative prosperity for Walsh Petroleum. Dollar sales in 1982 were four times higher than sales in 1977 (although most of this increase was a result of increased unit sales prices). Nonetheless, profits were at their highest level in 1982. A year later, sales gallonage started a decline that had continued unabated. In 1984, John's father died, leaving John's mother and John to manage the firm.

COMPANY OPERATIONS

Walsh Petroleum distributed oil products throughout a seven-county area of the southeastern United States. The marketing area was semi-rural but contained two county seats with populations of 15,000 and 25,000. The area's proximity to a growing major city was expected to result in higher-than-average population growth over the next ten years, but in no way was the area likely to become a suburb of the city. The firm represented a major branded oil company and carried a full line of petroleum products. There were three basic classes of customers for Walsh:

RESELLER ACCOUNTS Walsh served as a distributor of oil products to ten reseller locations, most of which were local gas stations. Gaining new reseller customers depended more on financial considerations than marketing

---

Prepared by Professors George Overstreet, Jr., Stewart Malone, and Bernard Morin, McIntire School of Commerce, The University of Virginia. Reprinted with permission.

EXHIBIT 1   Walsh Petroleum's Income Statements, 1981–85

	1981	1982	1983	1984	1985
GALLONS					
Premium	386,144	687,087	584,076	617,420	593,777
Unleaded	1,193,356	1,236,757	830,002	898,065	841,184
Regular	1,930,719	2,656,736	1,660,004	1,290,969	1,039,110
Lube	24,847	17,793	18,184	16,660	15,725
Heating oil	491,583	409,267	327,845	373,609	335,054
Diesel	375,478	373,704	338,249	348,420	327,098
Kerosene	79,769	96,215	99,733	138,555	125,182
Other products	1,810	414	713	5,301	10,682
Total	4,483,886	5,477,973	3,858,806	3,688,999	3,287,812
SALES					
Premium	$ 322,225	$ 533,091	$ 551,540	$ 517,510	$ 533,998
Unleaded	1,195,855	1,493,304	1,020,024	1,019,856	881,903
Regular	2,385,763	2,967,718	1,633,912	1,187,458	854,324
Lube	84,438	64,681	66,005	60,491	58,988
Heating oil	533,368	478,842	368,468	411,344	364,539
Diesel	397,663	410,090	332,637	345,317	310,858
Kerosene	92,252	119,845	117,952	162,359	147,066
Other products	53,960	10,757	48,261	140,259	177,768
Net sales	5,065,524	6,078,328	4,138,829	3,844,594	3,329,444
Cost of sales:					
Beginning inventory	77,420	84,927	84,804	136,862	131,592
Purchases—net of discounts	4,725,693	5,691,682	3,885,577	3,528,264	2,942,582
	4,803,113	5,776,609	3,970,381	3,665,126	3,074,174
Ending inventory	84,927	84,804	136,862	131,592	149,007
Cost of sales	4,718,186	5,691,805	3,833,519	3,533,534	2,925,167
Gross profit	347,338	386,523	305,310	311,060	404,277
Selling, general, and administrative expenses					
Licenses and nonincome taxes	22,447	22,462	18,472	22,604	8,917
Vehicle expense	23,362	41,510	36,837	43,950	32,583
Officers' salaries	68,248	63,370	53,970	52,952	50,780
Other salaries and wages	78,763	92,138	121,160	135,692	140,623
Other expenses	132,880	135,589	136,903	127,892	150,957
Depreciation	46,524	68,676	72,842	73,404	69,441
Interest on borrowing needs	6,457	7,410	11,232	11,999	9,299
Operating income (loss)	(31,343)	(44,632)	(146,106)	(157,433)	(58,323)
Earnings on marketable securities	4,456	2,853	3,009	2,943	3,739
Other income (for hauling)	83,587	112,425	103,109	144,878	85,038
Earnings before taxes	56,700	70,646	(39,988)	(9,612)	30,454
Provision for federal income taxes	6,590	11,870	(15,294)	(2,229)	2,485
Net income	$ 50,110	$ 58,776	$ (24,694)	$ (7,383)	$ 27,969

Note: Inventory is recorded on a LIFO basis.

EXHIBIT 2   **Walsh Petroleum's Balance Sheets, 1981–85**

	1981	1982	1983	1984	1985
ASSETS					
Current assets					
Cash	$ 36,305	$ 7,704	$ 38,510	$ 55,652	$ 14,003
Marketable securities	0	0	0	0	0
Accounts receivable	262,047	254,809	190,673	143,802	155,839
Inventories	84,927	84,804	136,862	131,592	149,007
Refundable taxes	3,964	0	27,194	2,665	200
Prepaid expenses	5,756	7,121	13,698	8,625	9,609
Notes receivable	0	0	0	0	9,368
Other assets	0	0	0	0	116,607
Total current assets	392,999	354,438	406,937	342,336	454,633
Property, plant, and equipment					
Land	25,201	28,134	25,489	34,893	30,544
Equipment	154,029	140,493	163,011	130,797	144,965
Vehicles	51,930	60,678	42,367	37,032	24,604
Furniture and fixtures	5,544	3,730	3,449	4,102	3,425
Total	236,704	233,035	234,316	206,824	203,538
Long-term investments	677	1,202	1,202	1,202	1,202
Cash surrender value—officers' life insurance	30,970	35,117	690	3,116	0
Loan fees—net	370	277	195	0	0
Total other assets	32,017	36,596	2,087	4,318	1,202
Total assets	$661,720	$624,069	$643,340	$553,478	$659,373
LIABILITIES AND STOCKHOLDERS' EQUITY					
Current liabilities					
Accounts payable	$264,812	$155,012	$157,254	$ 80,624	$ 98,505
Notes payable	0	0	50,000	30,000	0
Current portion of long-term debt	18,163	18,315	18,204	17,900	50,675
Income taxes payable	334	4,506	0	235	2,485
Accrued expenses	42,834	45,944	55,125	44,424	40,724
Other current liabilities	0	0	522	846	0
Total current liabilities	326,143	223,777	281,105	174,029	192,389
Long-term debt	19,849	10,305	0	0	0
Other long-term	14,572	30,054	26,992	51,592	0
Total liabilities	360,564	264,136	308,097	225,621	192,389
Owners' equity	301,157	359,933	335,240	327,856	466,984
Total liabilities and owners' equity	$661,721	$624,069	$643,337	$553,477	$659,373

Note: Walsh has limited underground tank liability due to placing tanks in reseller's name and having installed double-walled tanks at the bulk plant over the past five years.

techniques, because gasoline and oil products were generally considered commodities and most distributors offered similar types of services. When a new gas station was about to be constructed (an event that had been occurring with decreasing frequency over the past twenty years), the operator would contact several distributors such as Walsh. The distributor would formulate a proposal based on expected sales gallonage. In return for an exclusive long-term contract to supply the location with gasoline and oil products, the distributor provided the station with fuel storage tanks, pumps, remote consoles, and a canopy. Walsh's profit margin per gallon declined as the reseller's volume climbed based on a sliding scale. If up to 50,000 gallons a month were delivered, he received 4.5 cents over delivered cost (including freight). If 50,000 to 65,000 gallons a month were delivered he received 4.0 cents per gallon. For 65,000 to 75,000 gallons, he received 3.65 cents, and for over 75,000 gallons he received 3.5 cents per gallon. Over the course of the contract, the station operator could switch suppliers if he or she was willing to make a settlement on the equipment provided by the original distributor.

John had recently audited the profitability of his reseller accounts and found that many of the accounts yielded over a 20 percent after-tax internal rate of return. New reseller contracts also tended to be very lucrative, but there were relatively few high-gallonage locations left in Walsh's trading area, and only two or three new reseller accounts were out for bid each year. The capital requirements for such investments had grown over the years and ranged from $60,000 to $100,000. Exhibit 3 presents sales trends at the ten contract locations.

In addition to the ten contract locations, Walsh operated a reseller location on which it had constructed a convenience store (C-store). This diversification move was initiated by Mr. Walsh, Sr., in 1983. The C-store facility was located on three acres with 300 feet of road frontage on a four-lane U.S. highway. The property had been appraised at $356,000 and included not only the convenience store but also the bulk storage facilities (144,000 gallons). Mrs. Walsh owned the site and leased it to Walsh Petroleum at $4,000 per month ($2,500 for the bulk storage plant and $1,500 for the C-store). The property had a $100,000 note payable over five years at 9 percent.

HOME HEATING OIL   Active accounts numbered 624, of which 325 were classified as automatic (with refills scheduled by the distributor). While the home heating oil business was relatively profitable, it was also highly seasonal, and, thus, efficient utilization of equipment and personnel was viewed as a problem. Some other distributors had taken on equipment sales and service, as well as related businesses such as air conditioning, in order to balance the seasonality of fuel oil sales. John had concluded that heating oil sales would have to double in order to justify the equipment investment and personnel training for an in-house sales/service department.

EXHIBIT 3   Walsh Unit Sales Trends, 1984–87

		AVERAGE GALLONAGE PER MONTH (000S)		
UNIT	TYPE	1984	1985	1986 (EST.)
1	4,000-square-foot rural grocery, owner change in 1984	6.0	10.5	10.8
2	Village two-bay, financial problems, cash only, pool hall	11.7	16.8	14.3
3	5,000-square-foot rural grocery in low-growth area	—	—	8.2
4	C-store in growing rural area	—	6.7	18.1
5	Two-bay station with marina service, new C-store competition	20.3	17.9	20.7
6	Rehab two-bay on front of bulk plant property, owned by mother and leased to corporation, good location on four-lane with crossover access, growth area	28.4	35.3	37.5
7	Three-bay station in low-growth rural area, father and son	9.9	9.9	10.1
8	1,500-square-foot rural grocery with new owner, business recovery	14.0	9.1	11.6
9	3,000-square-foot rural C-store with interceptor location, sell on consignment with Walsh controlling price, considering canopy to be leased by Walsh from owner	17.6	18.8	20.0
10	3,000-square-foot rural C-store with interceptor location	21.9	22.4	22.7

COMMERCIAL/AGRICULTURAL ACCOUNTS Approximately 120 businesses and/or farms maintained their own tanks and pumps for which Walsh supplied oil products. While these accounts had generally shown some loyalty to their petroleum supplier, there was no contractual relationship that would prevent them from changing suppliers.

Within Walsh Petroleum's trading area, there were three other gasoline and oil distributors. Competitive pressures were moderate for existing gasoline reseller and home heating oil accounts, but John had recently noticed an increased level of competition for the one or two new reseller locations constructed each year. None of the four distributors possessed a large competitive advantage over the others. Each competitor had about the same level of sales, and all possessed a similar amount of financial resources. Since gasoline and oil products have a significant freight-cost-to-value ratio, distributors of these products generally had a trading radius of approximately 75 miles around their terminal or distribution point. While the local competitors did not really worry John, some of the distributors that served the nearby metropolitan area were significantly larger than Walsh, and a move by one of these larger competitors into Walsh's trading area could well upset the competitive equilibrium that had evolved over the years.

FAMILY AND MANAGEMENT	Mrs. Walsh assumed the chairmanship of the company following the death of her husband, and she held 52 percent of the voting stock of the corporation (the remaining 48 percent being held equally by John and his two younger brothers). Having worked with her husband for several years, she was very knowledgeable about the firm's operations. While she held the title of chairman, Mrs. Walsh's duties consisted of supervising the convenience store adjacent to the distributorship and maintaining relationships with the fuel oil customers. A prominent citizen of the local community, Mrs. Walsh also served on the town council.

John Walsh had been employed as a geologist with an energy consulting firm in Denver before 1982. When he was visiting at home one weekend, he mentioned to his father that he was concerned his career would be hurt by the recent recession in the oil drilling business. Later that weekend, while having coffee together in the local doughnut shop, John, Sr., said, "John, our business here is changing rapidly, too. If you have any interest in joining the family business, you better make up your mind soon, because I may just sell the business rather than put up with all the changes that are occurring."

John returned to Denver, but after several months he decided the opportunity at Walsh Petroleum might offer a better future than his current job. John returned home in late 1982 and began to learn the business from his father. Not only did John assume many of the administrative duties, but he also managed the marketing relationships with the major accounts.

John's two younger brothers were not active in the management of the business at the time, although each held 16 percent of the corporate stock. Richard was 26 years old and was employed in another city. Daniel was a sophomore in college.

Aside from John and his mother, Walsh Petroleum employed three clerks and four driver/maintenance workers. The three clerks handled much of the administrative paperwork for both the oil distributorship and convenience store. Convenience stores have a multitude of vendors, all of which expect payment within ten days. Managing the payables took a great deal of time, and Walsh's bookkeeping clerk had complained that she couldn't keep up with the work load. All the accounting was done manually, and John planned to install a computer system in the near future.

In addition, the convenience store employed two full-time and three part-time workers. Salaries and benefits for these workers corresponded to industry averages, and all employees were nonunionized. During the first quarter of 1986, John purchased a new tractor/trailer for $60,000 (9,000-gallon capacity). In addition, Walsh had three older "bobtail" trucks for short deliveries (2,000-gallon capacity) and two used service delivery vans.

THE OIL DISTRIBUTION INDUSTRY

Few industries have experienced the volatility and changes connected with the oil business in the past fifteen years. In 1973 the OPEC oil embargo resulted in a 119 percent increase in the price of crude oil during a twelve-month period. While demand fell slightly from 1973 to 1981, prices were expected to continue climbing. Spurred by higher prices, oil exploration and refinery construction continued to increase. In 1981 President Reagan decontrolled gasoline and crude oil prices. The acquisition price of crude oil began to drop, and demand also fell as the world economy entered a recession.

The changes that occurred upstream in the oil production industry had a large impact on the independent petroleum market:

1. Between 1974 and 1985, American auto manufacturers doubled the miles per gallon of new cars, from 13.2 to 26.4.

2. During the same period, gasoline consumption of passenger cars declined from approximately 75 billion gallons to 65 billion.

3. The number of service stations (defined as outlets with 50 percent or more dollar volume from the sale of petroleum products) fell from 226,459 in 1972 to 121,000 in 1985.

In addition to these changes, oil distributors also faced declining margins, increased real estate costs, and a proliferation of environmental regulations.

News for distributors had not been all bad. The past two years had seen firmer gross profit margins and increased gallonage pumped. Although the market had not recovered to the volume levels of the late 1970s and early 1980s, gasoline gallonage used by motorists increased 1.5 percent in 1983, 1.5 percent in 1984, and 3.4 percent in 1985.[1] A significant portion of the increased demand had to be attributed to the oversupply of world crude and, hence, to lower prices during each of the last three years (down 3.3 percent for 1983, 1.6 percent for 1984, and 1.6 percent for 1985).

Independent petroleum marketers are entrepreneurs involved in the sale and distribution of refined petroleum and ancillary products. While the exact number of the companies was unknown, one trade association report estimated their number between 11,000 and 12,000 in 1985.[2] The trade association membership is broken down in terms of size in Exhibit 4.

Independent petroleum marketers have responded to the pressures in their industry in one of two ways: diversification or consolidation (mergers and acquisition). Exhibit 5 shows how many oil distributors were engaged in various types of diversified activities.

Aside from diversifying into other areas, the number of acquisitions had increased in the past few years, spurred by industry decontrol. Independent marketers, particularly larger ones with the capital available to make acquisitions, had acquired other distributors to take advantage of economies of scale in storage, distribution, and other areas such as billing and general administrative services. A 1984 study found that 56 of 135 marketers had

EXHIBIT 4

Percentage of Marketers by Size Distribution

MILLIONS OF GALLONS SOLD	1984	1982
Less than 1.0	13.8%	18.0%
1.0–2.49	23.8	26.3
2.5–4.99	21.9	20.8
5.0–7.49	12.2	9.7
7.5–9.99	6.6	6.7
10.0–14.99	9.3	7.1
15.0–19.99	3.8	2.8
20.0–24.99	2.2	1.8
25.0–29.99	1.7	1.4
30.0–39.99	1.8	1.5
40.0–49.99	1.1	1.2
50.00 and above	1.8	2.7
Average volume	7.80	7.12
Median volume	3.91	3.18

SOURCE: *1985 Petroleum Marketing Databook* (Alexandria, Va.: Petroleum Marketing Education Foundation, 1985), p. 12.

purchased one or more marketing companies within the last five years, and 24 of the 56 had purchased more than one.[3] Most of the acquisition activity occurred among marketers with assets greater than $1 million. Of the 90 firms in this category in the sample, 46 had acquired one or more businesses during the period.

As a result of increasing profit pressure, a number of operating changes had occurred on the distribution level.[4] First, the total number of distributor-owned transportation vehicles had declined dramatically from 106,868 in 1982 to 96,972 in 1984. Second, distributors had decreased the amount of their storage facilities from a 2.5-billion-gallon capacity in 1982 to 1.7 billion in 1984. Finally, credit terms to distributors had tightened. In 1982, net 30-day payment terms were reported by 21 percent of trade association members, while in 1984 this percentage had dropped to 8.2 percent. These changes and others had led gasoline and oil distributors to redefine the term *good customer*. Whereas in the 1960s and 1970s, distributors were willing to inventory product and deliver relatively small amounts of gasoline on small bobtail trucks, the new market realities made these practices less attractive. Instead of inventorying product, successful distributors would now send a large transport truck (9,000-gallon capacity) to the terminal, or distribution

EXHIBIT 5

Types of Diversified Activities Engaged in by Oil Distributors

TYPES OF DIVERSIFIED ACTIVITIES	NUMBER OF DISTRIBUTORS
Auto repair/maintenance center	7,081
Auto/truck/trailer rentals	638
Beverage-only stores	228
Car washes	2,961
Convenience stores	14,235
Fast-food operations	1,002
Heating/air-conditioning service	3,189
Kerosene heater sales	1,275
Lube centers	1,549
Plumbing service	501
Tires/tires, battery, and accessory stores	3,507
Truck stops	1,734
Truck stops	1,734
Towing service	911
Coal sales	164
Other	1,000

SOURCE: *1985 Petroleum Marketing Databook* (Alexandria, Va.: Petroleum Marketing Education Foundation, 1985), p. 15.

point, and transport the gasoline directly to one service station. Since it was inefficient to have the large truck tied up making multiple deliveries, customer emphasis was on the volume gas station with tank capacity large enough to handle one large delivery. The "mom-and-pop" gasoline retailer was now considered undesirable. John Walsh stated, "In 1980 we considered a good account one that pumped 20,000 to 25,000 gallons per month, while in 1986 we consider a good account to be in the range of 40,000 to 50,000 gallons per month."

In addition to the deregulation of gasoline and crude oil prices in 1981, another regulatory development that affected oil distributors was the issuance of Environmental Protection Agency (EPA) regulations regarding leakage of gasoline from underground steel storage tanks. According to one authority, as many as 30 percent of steel tanks currently in the ground might be leaking.[5] Since both past and present owners of property with underground tanks could be held legally liable for leakage pollution, many companies were completely removing older tanks (more than ten to fifteen years old) at a cost of approximately $1,000 for a 1,000- to 3,000-gallon tank. The cost of removing and then reinstalling a similar size tank was approximately

$6,000. If there was a minor leak, clean-up costs would be approximately $5,000 extra. Liability insurance for tank leakage had become exceedingly expensive and difficult to obtain, especially for older, single-wall steel tanks.

The Current Situation

From his study of trade journals and attendance at industry conferences, John Walsh concluded basic industry trends portended a bleak future for Walsh Petroleum unless the company's strategy was changed substantially. It seemed apparent to John that his company had to do something different or get out of the business. Being relatively young, John was confident he could start a career elsewhere, but he enjoyed living in his hometown of Lancaster and liked the idea of being his own boss. Furthermore, his mother was currently receiving an annual salary of $50,000 in addition to rent she received on the C-store. If they sold the company, would the proceeds generate sufficient income to replace his mother's current income?

If they decided not to sell the business, John wondered how the business could be changed. He had received an offer to purchase a competitor, Valley Oil, only weeks before.

THE VALLEY OIL ALTERNATIVE

In many respects, it seemed as though Valley Oil faced the same problems as Walsh. The two companies sold basically the same product lines, although Valley's percentage of heating fuel sales was higher than Walsh's. This aspect of Valley was attractive to John because heating fuel commanded higher margins than gasoline (25 cents per gallon versus 8 to 10 cents per gallon), and customers were a little less sensitive to price than gasoline resellers. Overall, though, Valley's unit sales were declining and unit profit margins were being squeezed. Many of Valley's contract resellers were low-volume accounts and had experienced declining sales volumes. Furthermore, their underground tanks were old.

The owner of Valley had died recently, and Valley's current 55-year-old CEO wanted to get out of the business. Valley's CEO had sent along a copy of the company's recent financial statements—see Exhibits 6 and 7. Valley's CEO said that, while the company wasn't for sale on the open market yet, he believed an $800,000 offer would buy the company.

John thought that acquiring Valley Oil could offer some unique advantages—adventages that many other potential acquirers could not realize. First, many of the selling and administrative expenses that Valley incurred could be performed by Walsh's personnel. A potential buyer from outside the industry would probably have substantially higher operating costs than John would have.

Rather than beginning his analysis with what employees he would be able to eliminate from Valley's payroll, John decided to examine how many

EXHIBIT 6

Valley Oil Company's Income Statements, 1981–85

	1981	1982	1983	1984	1985
GALLONS					
Premium	NA	NA	NA	NA	382,869
Unleaded	NA	NA	NA	NA	1,152,730
Regular	3,956,353	3,316,151	4,004,842	3,101,595	1,418,560
Lube	NA	NA	NA	NA	NA
Heating oil	978,113	1,004,000	1,057,131	1,137,072	1,267,011
Diesel	NA	NA	NA	NA	NA
Kerosene	286,870	286,430	262,802	310,066	315,739
Other products	NA	NA	NA	NA	NA
Total	5,221,336	4,606,581	5,324,775	4,548,733	4,536,909
SALES					
Premium	NA	NA	NA	NA	$ 298,068
Unleaded	NA	NA	NA	NA	1,038,871
Regular	NA	NA	NA	$2,831,323	1,222,758
Lube	NA	NA	NA	95,781	100,922
Heating oil	NA	NA	NA	942,600	871,031
Diesel	NA	NA	NA	NA	295,955
Kerosene	NA	NA	NA	364,573	359,583
Other products	NA	NA	NA	NA	92,493
Net sales	$4,734,881	$4,332,049	$4,657,833	4,234,277	$4,279,681
Cost of sales:					
Beginning inventory	211,832	210,000	192,449	153,639	160,344
Purchases net of discounts	4,292,934	3,873,798	4,138,784	3,752,969	3,714,003
	4,504,766	4,083,798	4,331,233	3,906,608	3,874,347
Ending inventory	210,000	192,449	153,639	160,344	153,135
Cost of sales	4,294,766	3,891,349	4,177,594	3,746,264	3,721,212
Gross profit	440,115	440,700	480,239	488,013	558,469
Selling, general, and administrative expenses					
Licenses and nonincome taxes	23,584	24,450	25,943	25,810	22,252
Vehicle expense	100,471	61,397	85,365	74,066	81,748
Officers' salaries	45,500	49,414	48,700	51,000	53,100
Other salaries and wages	155,843	142,087	154,104	148,434	162,161
Other expenses	145,081	168,015	168,076	186,921	224,159
Depreciation	44,428	38,032	36,920	54,639	61,015
Interest on borrowing needs	10,025	3,496	5,272	7,144	11,203
Operating income (loss)	(84,817)	(46,191)	(44,141)	(60,001)	(57,169)
Earnings on marketable securities	8,746	14,493	5,134	6,426	8,103
Other income (for hauling)	72,552	74,672	90,703	96,501	95,066
Earnings before taxes	(3,519)	42,974	51,696	42,926	46,000
Provision for federal income taxes	(1,983)	4,942	10,776	707	9,049
Net income	$ (1,536)	$ 38,032	$ 40,920	$ 42,219	$ 36,951

Note: From 1981 to 1984, gallonage data are available only as aggregate gasoline sales—these are entered as regular. Likewise, during the entire five-year period, heating oil and diesel are combined under heating oil. During the same time period, dollar values are often unavailable.

EXHIBIT 7   **Valley Oil Company's Balance Sheets, 1981–85**

	1981	1982	1983	1984	1985
ASSETS					
Cash	$ 64,468	$ 31,922	$ 24,076	$ 10,000	$ 26,558
Accounts receivable	656,187	579,313	471,803	470,120	421,308
Inventories	210,000	192,449	153,639	160,344	153,135
Refundable taxes	33,054	0	0	9,920	3,888
Prepaid expenses	2,636	1,535	1,526	1,766	25,883
Notes receivable	1,804	40,277	14,481	59,342	5,099
Total current assets	968,149	845,496	665,525	711,492	635,871
Property, plant, and equipment					
Land	79,942	79,942	79,942	79,942	79,942
Buildings	0	0	0	0	0
Equipment	207,463	216,139	208,116	207,873	227,444
Vehicles	247,339	274,634	253,153	279,634	255,355
Furniture and fixtures	5,032	21,588	22,393	24,388	30,464
Total	539,776	592,303	563,604	591,837	593,205
Less accumulated depreciation	392,800	430,332	427,310	392,465	422,781
Net property, plant, and equipment	146,976	161,971	136,294	199,372	170,424
Other assets					
Long-term investments	0	0	0	0	0
Deposits and licenses	0	0	0	0	0
Cash surrender value—officers' life insurance	0	0	0	0	0
Loan fees—net	0	0	0	0	0
Advances to affiliated companies	0	0	0	0	0
Total other assets	0	0	0	0	0
Total assets	$1,115,125	$1,007,467	$801,819	$910,864	$806,295
LIABILITIES AND STOCKHOLDERS' EQUITY					
Current liabilities					
Accounts payable	$ 670,524	$ 474,892	$272,434	$295,092	$196,670
Notes payable	0	45,000	0	50,000	0
Income taxes payable	0	4,942	5,832	0	6,899
Total current liabilities	670,524	524,834	278,266	345,092	203,569
Long-term debt	0	0	0	0	0
Total liabilities	670,524	524,834	278,266	345,092	203,569
Owners' equity	444,601	482,633	523,553	565,772	602,726
Total liabilities and owners' equity	$1,115,125	$1,007,467	$801,819	$910,864	$806,295

people he would have to add to Walsh Petroleum to serve Valley's customers. He figured that initially he would need at least two additional clerks to handle the scheduling and the billing for Valley accounts. Two additional full-time drivers would be needed for deliveries and two seasonal drivers for fuel oil. Salaries for clerks and drivers were estimated at $9,000 and $18,000 a year, respectively, and fringe benefits would probably add about 35 percent. John thought he could get someone to manage the new business at $30,000 (benefits included). John also felt that if he could get his computerized account system running within a year for approximately $40,000 he might be able to eventually eliminate one of the clerks. John was also pleased with the thought that the Valley acquisition would allow him to spread the significant upfront investment in hardware and software over a greater number of accounts, and by adding a delivery scheduling module to the computer system, he should be able to schedule his deliveries more efficiently. In addition, John's accountant recommended that he use a conservative tax rate of 30 percent in his analysis of Valley. Exhibit 8 shows the gallonages at Valley Oil's eighteen locations. Exhibit 9 shows the age and capacity of the underground tanks at various Valley Oil locations.

Even with the operating savings John might be able to utilize, Valley would probably be an attractive acquisition to some of the large distributors in the nearby city. Compared to the fierce competition in that city, John's trading area would probably look very attractive to them. While John's knowledge of the local market gave him an advantage, the larger city-based distributors could achieve many of the operating cost savings John was contemplating. By purchasing Valley, John believed his gross profit margin would improve due to a reduced level of competition.

The more John thought about the possibility of combining Walsh and Valley, the more likely it seemed he wouldn't need most of Valley's physical assets to service the accounts he would be acquiring. John had scheduled a lunch with Valley's CEO to discuss the possible acquisition. John's hopes of acquiring Valley's customers only were quickly dashed. Valley's CEO stated that if he was getting out of the business, he was going to sell the whole business as a unit, not hold a "rummage sale." Moreover, he seemed firm about the price of $800,000. The rise in Valley's gross profit margin in 1985 had continued through the first half of 1986 because of the unprecedented drop in oil prices and "sticky" retail prices. However, John knew Valley's CEO would want to sell the business this year before long-term capital gains rates expired.

A big issue in John's mind was how to finance the acquisition. Neither he nor his mother had enough liquid funds outside the business to acquire Valley. Valley's owners indicated they might be willing to hold a note, but they would require certain covenants regarding Walsh Petroleum's financial condition in order to protect their position. Also, personal guarantees from John, his mother, and his brother would be required. John decided to try to

EXHIBIT 8   **Gallons Pumped at Valley Oil's 18 Station Locations, 1985**

STATIONS*	1985 GALLONAGES
1	346,279
2	160,316
3	128,620
4	111,702
5	105,036
6	116,286
7	37,894
8	19,746
9	121,440
10†	244,802
11	304,772
12	189,422
13	196,152
14	148,226
15	47,118
16	130,472
17	100,106
18	220,440
Total	2,728,829

*Reseller locations with contracts ranging from two to five years.
†Wholly owned by Valley Oil with appraised value of $100,000 (good potential, four-lane interceptor, C-store location).

get Valley's owners to finance 75 percent of the acquisition price over ten years. While he would have to pay a premium over the prime rate, in his opinion it might still be a good investment.

To help him in his decision about the Valley Oil acquisition, John employed an independent consultant to Valley Oil. Excerpts from the consultant's report are shown in Exhibit 10. John was somewhat skeptical about the consultant's conclusions, however, because the consultant did not have experience in the petroleum business.

THE C-STORE ALTERNATIVE

One of the relative bright spots in Walsh Petroleum's operation had been the C-store. C-stores originated as a convenient alternative to the traditional grocery store, and the premise that consumers would pay higher than

EXHIBIT 9

Characteristics of Underground Tanks at Valley Oil Sites

SITES*	CAPACITY	AGE	TYPE	PRODUCT
1	4,000 gallons	12 years	Steel	Gasoline
	4,000	12	Steel	Gasoline
	3,000	25	Steel	Gasoline
	4,000	25	Steel	Gasoline
	3,000	25	Steel	Gasoline
2	2,000	7	Steel	Gasoline
	2,000	7	Steel	Gasoline
	1,000	2	Steel	Gasoline
3	1,000	8	Steel	Gasoline
	1,000	8	Steel	Gasoline
4	1,000	10	Steel	Gasoline
	1,000	10	Steel	Gasoline
	1,000	10	Steel	Gasoline
5	2,000	20	Steel	Gasoline
	1,000	20	Steel	Gasoline
	1,000	20	Steel	Gasoline
6	1,000	12	Steel	Gasoline
	1,000	10	Steel	Diesel
	1,000	10	Steel	Diesel
7	1,000	15	Steel	Gasoline
	1,000	15	Steel	Gasoline
	2,000	10	Steel	Gasoline
	1,000	1	Steel	Gasoline
	1,000	1	Steel	Gasoline
8	1,000	25	Steel	Gasoline
	2,000	3	Steel	Gasoline
	2,000	3	Steel	Gasoline
	2,000	3	Steel	Gasoline
9	2,000	10	Steel	Gasoline
	4,000	11	Steel	Gasoline
	3,000	11	Steel	Gasoline
	3,000	11	Steel	Gasoline
	1,000	11	Steel	Gasoline
10	1,000	12	Steel	Gasoline
	1,000	5	Steel	Gasoline
11	1,000	15	Steel	Diesel
	1,000	15	Steel	Gasoline
12	10,000	15	Steel	Gasoline
	4,000	15	Steel	Gasoline
	4,000	15	Steel	Gasoline
	1,000	15	Steel	Kerosene
13	1,000	12	Steel	Gasoline
	1,000	12	Steel	Gasoline
	1,000	12	Steel	Gasoline
14	2,000	14	Steel	Gasoline
	1,000	14	Steel	Gasoline

EXHIBIT 9   **Continued**

SITES*	CAPACITY	AGE	TYPE	PRODUCT
15	1,000	12	Steel	Gasoline
	1,000	12	Steel	Diesel
	2,000	12	Steel	Fuel Oil
16	10,000	10	Steel	Gasoline
	2,000	10	Steel	Gasoline
17	2,000	10	Steel	Gasoline
18	1,000	5	Steel	Gasoline
	1,000	5	Steel	Gasoline
19	1,000	9	Steel	Gasoline
	1,000	9	Steel	Gasoline
	1,000	9	Steel	Gasoline
20	10,000	35	Steel	Diesel
21	20,000	15	Steel	Fuel oil
	20,000	15	Steel	Fuel oil
	20,000	15	Steel	Fuel oil
	20,000	15	Steel	Fuel oil
	20,000	15	Steel	Gasoline
	20,000	15	Steel	Gasoline
	20,000	15	Steel	Gasoline
	20,000	15	Steel	Gasoline
	10,000	15	Steel	Gasoline
	6,266	35	Steel	Kerosene
	6,266	35	Steel	Kerosene
	5,631	35	Steel	Kerosene
	6,266	35	Steel	Kerosene
	6,266	35	Steel	Kerosene
	6,266	35	Steel	Kerosene
	6,769	35	Steel	Kerosene
22	4,000	10	Steel	Gasoline
	4,000	10	Steel	Gasoline
	3,000	10	Steel	Gasoline
	3,000	25	Steel	Gasoline
	3,000	25	Steel	Gasoline
23	1,000	20	Steel	Gasoline
	1,000	20	Steel	Gasoline
24	2,000	7	Steel	Gasoline
	1,000	7	Steel	Gasoline
	1,000	7	Steel	Gasoline
	1,000	7	Steel	Kerosene
25	2,000	11	Steel	Gasoline
	2,000	11	Steel	Gasoline

*Sites include reseller locations, large individual users, and bulk plant (number 21).

EXHIBIT 10

Excerpts from Consultant's Report on the Value of Valley Oil Company

INCOME-BASED VALUE

In any discounted, income-based valuation, two factors must be determined: the discount rate and the earnings base. Theoretically, the discount rate can be assumed to be the rate of return an investor could earn on a portfolio of similar risk assets. As a starting point, one can consider that for the week of August 1, the Standard and Poor's zero-bond utility average yielded 9.03 percent. This range of 9 percent is consistent with performance over recent months and actually is low for the past decade. Working from this starting point, one can logically assume that there would have to be some risk premium; therefore, a minimum capitalization rate would be 10 percent. As an earnings base, one can use a weighted average of the last five years. This both eliminates any unusual blip in the last year and takes into account the overall trend.

YEAR	WEIGHT FACTOR	INCOME	W × I
1981	1	$(1,536)	$ (1,536)
1982	2	38,032	76,064
1983	3	40,920	122,760
1984	4	42,219	168,876
1985	5	36,951	184,755
	15		$550,919

Weighted average earnings = $36,728

When this average earnings figure is capitalized at 10 percent, an income-based valuation of $367,280 emerges. Using a more reasonable discount rate of 12 percent yields a value of $306,067.

ADJUSTED ASSET VALUE

Another step that must be taken in any valuation is an assessment of the asset value of the company. If the market-related asset value is higher than the income-based value, then the business has negative operating value and is worth more liquidated.

When this step is taken with Valley, the analysis is fairly simple. All of the current assets can be liquidated at their book value except for accounts receivables. These must be carried across to market less a 10% bad debt adjustment. This brings the value of total current assets to $620,557.

Adjustments for the fixed assets are a bit more complex. First, the land/buildings account must be adjusted to $100,000 market value. Equipment, with the exception of tanks, is valued at about $20,000 (79 pumps @ $250). The vehicles have an appraised market value of $156,500. The market value for furniture and fixtures is $7,050, giving a total market value to long-term assets of $283,550. The next step to be followed is to deduct any liabilities. These are deducted at book value of $203,569.

The final step in the adjusted asset valuation is to consider any hidden assets or liabilities. These can take several forms.

EXHIBIT 10	**Continued**

- Undervalued real estate which would actually bring much more than its book value.
- Exclusive distribution contracts or other market-related, hidden assets.
- Contingent liabilities such as pending lawsuits or potential lawsuits from sources such as leaking underground tanks.

The first of these is ruled out by the fact that Valley owns only one piece of real estate, which was recently appraised and is included in the valuation at its appraised value of $100,000. Neither does the second factor enter into the value—Valley has no unique market-related advantages.

The question of contingent liabilities is important; the possibility that one or more of the approximately 90 tanks could develop or already possess a leak is far from remote. According to Steffen Plenn, author of *Underground Tankage: The Liability of Leaks,* as many as 30 percent of the steel tanks currently in the ground may be leaking. What's worse, that number is expected to rise. The volatile nature of this problem is most clearly seen in its propensity to wind up in court. Plenn explains that these leaks, when discovered, are disasters of a magnitude that will not avoid court.* The most serious implication, however, is that the liability has historically extended to all owners of the tanks, both past and present, vis-à-vis the concept of joint and several liability. Thus, in the process of any rationally executed liquidation, the seller would have to remove each of the older tanks. In the case of Valley, this cost would amount to approximately $90,000. Deducting this contingent tank liability (cost of removal) from the previously computed values yields a liquidation value of $610,538.

CONCLUSION

This now presents us with two different values for consideration:

1. The income-based value of $367,280.
2. The adjusted asset liquidation basis of $610,538.

Realizing that

- The liquidation value exceeds the income-based value;
- There is a trend toward decreasing blue sky premiums;
- Good will is usually paid for growing or unusually profitable gallons, of which Valley has none;
- There is a significant contingent liability attached to the tanks, all of which cannot be eliminated by tank removal (due to potential for previous leaks); and
- Valley is a declining firm in a mature industry.

We recommend use of the adjusted asset liquidation value of $610,538 as our best estimate of market value.

---

*Steffen W. Plenn, *Underground Tankage: The Liability of Leaks* (Alexandria, Va.: Petroleum Marketing Education Foundation, 1986), pp. 9–12.

grocery store prices in exchange for convenience proved correct. Since customers typically bought only a few items, checkout lines were very short. C-stores carried a relatively limited product line of items generally regarded as necessities. Milk, bread, snack foods, cigarettes, beer, and soft drinks made up a substantial percentage of C-store sales. Although a majority of C-stores carried a very similar product mix, opportunities did exist for C-store operators to differentiate themselves. A number of operators offered video rentals, hot food service (hot dogs, pizza, and so on), and other amenities. Geographic location was also a critical success factor. Customers selected a C-store based on its proximity to their home or their daily route of travel.

Many motor fuel operators had taken the traditional gas station, closed the maintenance bays, and remodeled them into small convenience stores (800 to 1,200 square feet) with gasoline pumps out front. Likewise, convenience store operators, such as Southland (7-Eleven), added self-service gas pumps. According to the National Association of Convenience Stores, gasoline margins averaged 7.3 percent, while nongasoline margins averaged 32.2 percent.[6]

In early 1982 the Walshes had commissioned a marketing consultant group to conduct a feasibility study of a C-store location adjacent to the fuel oil distributorship. The location had approximately 300 feet of frontage on a major highway, and the traffic count looked as though it would make the operation feasible. Mr. Walsh, Sr., had remodeled an existing two-bay station, and within two years the unit was meeting and then exceeding the marketing consultants' projections.

Walsh Petroleum currently owned an unoccupied two-bay service station on a corner lot with good access from all directions and a stable traffic flow in a growing, nearby community. In the past the Walshes had leased the property to a number of service station operators. None of them had made a success of the operation, and it was John's opinion that the day of the traditional two-bay station was past its prime. Customers wanted either the pricing and convenience of a self-service station or a super-premium station that provided clearly superior maintenance and service. The turnover of operators was consuming much of Walsh's time, and the station was often empty.

John believed it might be possible to demolish the station and erect a C-store with self-serve gasoline pumps on the site. To investigate this possibility, John commissioned the same market research firm that had provided the feasibility study for the original C-store to analyze the new location. This firm had developed a forecasting model that would generate fairly accurate sales estimates for both gasoline and in-store sales for a C-store. Among the many variables included in the model were highway traffic flow, store size and layout, distance to the nearest existing C-store, as well as a variety of demographic data on the area. John's corner lot had a traffic count of 14,000 vehicles per day on the main road and 4,000 vehicles a day on the side street. The resulting sales forecast for gasoline was 915,000 gallons a year, reached by the end of year two, and first-year sales of 410,000 gallons. Kerosene sales were forecast at 7,500 gallons in year one and 10,000 gallons per annum thereafter. Inside sales items totaled $213,000 (year one), $428,000 (year two), maturing at $530,000 in year three. Expected margins were 50 cents a gallon for kerosene, 8 cents a gallon for gasoline, and 32 percent for inside sales.

John also retained an architectural firm as a design consultant. Exhibit 11 shows the costs that had been estimated under John's close supervision. Another option John had was to build a C-store using his major oil supplier's generic C-store design plan. The generic design included a smaller C-store (40 by 50 feet) under a 90-by-40-feet canopy with pumps on either side of the store (35 feet from pump to entrance). The advantage to this design was that the major oil company would refund Walsh 2 cents per gallon on all gallons sold (up to 150,000 gallons per month) for 36 months and provide a

---

EXHIBIT 11

C-store Estimated Costs

Appraised value of lot	$100,000
Building (~ $60 for 2,400 square feet of C-store)	144,400
Market research	1,000
Equipment costs	
Gas equipment	150,000
Food equipment	60,000
Canopy	17,500
Capitalized site plan (consultant)	20,000
Inventory	
Food	40,000
Fuel	14,500
Net operating capital	20,000
Total	$567,400
Salvage value	
Gas equipment	$13,500
Food equipment	6,000
Canopy	1,750
Capitalized site plan	0
Asset lives	
Gas equipment	5 years
Food equipment	7 years
Canopy	10 years
Site plan and building	31.5 years
Depreciation method	
Gas, food, and canopy equipment	Double declining balance
Site plan and building	Straight line

detailed site plan without charge. John felt he would lose some inside sales with the oil supplier's fatter margins and he wouldn't get to build his own C-store identity and goodwill. The overall cost would be approximately the same for the two options, and John was uncertain which choice was best from a marketing point of view.

Based on those of his other store, John estimated the operating expenses per annum for the new store as follows: salaries and benefits for a 126-hour week at $80,000, utilities at $14,000, property taxes at $2,000, and other miscellaneous expenses at $20,000.

While the research pertaining to the original C-store had been highly accurate, John wondered how reliable the model could be in forecasting future sales for the proposed C-store. Because even the major highways were relatively undeveloped in his rural market, there were desirable road frontage locations near his site. A one-acre site directly across the street could be used for a C-store location. While he had considered buying the property as a defensive move, he felt he really couldn't afford to buy it at $150,000.

John felt that the threat of new C-store competitors was very real. Even though a half-million-dollar investment for a C-store was a substantial investment to John, this sum might look like a bargain to the major C-store chains that had been paying up to $1 million for prime suburban locations. Surely, John reasoned, a competing C-store within a mile or two of his location would hurt the validity of his financial projections. The design consultant had added a drive-in window at a cost of approximately $25,000 to differentiate the store and build customer loyalty. John felt a drive-in window would add 15 percent annually to projected inside sales.

At a recent petroleum distributors conference, John discussed his C-store plans with several fellow distributors. Most felt that the generic C-store designs offered by the major oil companies were too small to provide the maximum level of in-store sales, particularly in a rural market. They questioned the wisdom of the drive-in window, suggesting a car-wash operation instead.

While John believed the C-store alternative had potential, he also was aware that the move had its risks. Nationally, the number of C-stores had increased rapidly. At the end of 1981 there were 38,000 C-stores, and only 16,416 of these sold gasoline. Just four years later, the C-store population had reached 61,000, with 33,500 selling gasoline.[7]

There was general agreement in the industry that the danger of C-store saturation was greatest in suburban areas, but substantial opportunities remained in both urban and rural markets. One rural operator who competed successfully in towns with as few as 1,000 residents said, "For the rest of the industry, the mark-up on gas is 6 to 8 cents a gallon, while we get 8 to 10 cents. Often we are the only gas station in town."[8] While gas margins would be higher in rural areas, C-stores often increased margins on other products as well. Fast foods and video rentals were extremely profitable in the absence of strong competitors. Pizza, for example, carried a 70 percent profit margin. One C-store/pizza vendor said the pizza concept probably wouldn't work in cities where people could go to a Pizza Hut, "but out in the rural areas, there's no place else to get a good pizza."[9]

Until recently, most of the competitors in the C-store industry were convenience store chains, such as Southland, and locations operated by independent oil distributors. There were increasing indications that the big oil refiners were entering the industry in force. Eight refiner/supplier oil companies, such as Texaco, Mobil, and Exxon, were ranked in the top 50 C-store operators. Many industry observers expected that the entry of the big-oil-owned C-stores would touch off a price war in the industry, particularly in the in-store segment. The rationale behind this expectation was that oil companies would lower in-store merchandise mark-ups in order to increase pump gallonage. However, the major oil companies had tended to concentrate on the urban areas, leaving the rural markets to the distributors.

THE FUTURE OF WALSH OIL

During one of the recent executive education programs John had attended, a few sessions had been devoted to evaluating investment opportunities. He knew he should try to determine an appropriate hurdle rate to use. There were some discussions at these sessions about calculating a cost of capital, but that seemed too academic and complicated. Instead, he went to the library and looked up various interest rates and decided to add a couple of percentage points to them. He figured a small company like his would have to pay somewhere between 2 and 5 percent over the going rate. The interest rates as of August 1986 are listed in Exhibit 12.

As he reviewed his notes from the training sessions, John found that real estate investments were evaluated differently from other types of investments. Rather than using the total acquisition price as a measure of investment, real estate investments were analyzed on the basis of equity cash investment to determine the payback. One of John's friends in the real estate business told him that, rather than using the purchase price of the acquisition as a measure of its cost, he should use the down payment, or the immediate

EXHIBIT 12

Selected Interest Rates, August 1986

Prime rate charged by banks	7.75%
U.S. Treasury bonds—10 years	7.17%
Corporate bonds—AAA seasoned	8.72%
Home mortgages—FHLBB	10.26%

cash investment, as the cost measure and calculate a levered rate of return on investment.

John scheduled an initial meeting with his banker to see what type of financing he might be able to obtain. While the banker expressed interest in the C-store, he didn't believe the bank would be willing to lend funds for the acquisition of Valley Oil. "John, it's just too risky for us," he said. "Valley's assets just aren't liquid enough to qualify as high-quality collateral. With those old tanks and trucks, we would never get our money out. Now the C-store is something I could sell to the loan committee. It's my guess that we could finance 80 percent of the land and building at 11.5 percent for fifteen years.[10] In addition, we could finance 80 percent of the equipment including the site plan over seven years at a 9.75 percent fixed rate."

The banker paused, as if unsure how to proceed. "You know, John, what I'm about to bring up is somewhat sensitive," he said, "so just tell me to stop if I'm out of line. I've watched you work like a dog over the past year to turn your business around, but at some point you have to start thinking about yourself. You can work like hell for 30 years and still only be a minority stockholder. If your mother and two brothers wanted to sell out at some point in the future, all your efforts, not to mention your career, are down the drain.

"Here's an alternative you might just think about," said the banker. "Walsh Petroleum owns the C-store site you are talking about developing. Why don't you buy the land personally and construct the C-store on it? We here at the bank would lend you the money, although we would probably have to have Walsh Petroleum guarantee the loan. You could then lease the C-store back to Walsh Petroleum and start building up some personal equity for yourself through the real estate investment."

As John Walsh pondered his alternatives, one thing seemed certain to him—he would have to act soon. Many of his friends he met at the trade association meetings seemed to be complacent about the pressure on their industry, but as John glanced at the financial statements again, he knew that a few more years like these past two would threaten not only his family's financial security, but his own as well. After all, he was really the only member of the family whose income was directly related to the future of Walsh Petroleum. He remembered the discussion of these issues at a recent dinner with his mother and brothers.

"John, I agree with the idea of expanding the business, and I think it would have pleased your dad," said Mrs. Walsh, "but you have to remember that Walsh Petroleum is really all I have. If we take on too much debt and get into trouble, I don't know what I'll do in my old age."

"I see your point, Mom," said John, "but the fact is that I'm the only one in the family who is devoting the rest of my life to running the business. You already own C-store One, and Richard and Daniel either don't want to be in the business or aren't sure yet. I don't want to sound selfish, but my interest in the business is only 16 percent. I don't want to wake up when I'm 50 and find that I've spent my whole life running this business for the rest of the family and have relatively little to show for it."

Richard puffed on his pipe and said, "John, I'm not sure the C-store alternative is a good idea for the family business. Sure, it's a good deal for you personally, but the rest of us have to guarantee your loan at the bank. I think Walsh Petroleum should give serious consideration to the Valley Oil deal."

"And why do you think that Valley is better than the C-store?" asked John.

"The main reason," Richard replied, "is that Walsh Petroleum is primarily a gasoline distributor. The original C-store was a great idea of Dad's, but the oil business is this family's cash cow. This is an opportunity to take out a competitor. We all agree there aren't a whole lot of new people going into this business, but if a big gasoline distributor in the region buys Valley, then Walsh Petroleum has got some major problems on its hands. The increased competition could certainly lower our gross margin 1 to 2 cents a gallon, and we all know that there are two large distributors that are interested in Valley."

"But, Richard, can't you see that we're in a declining industry?" said John. "If you looked at those financials I sent you, it should be obvious that our gallonage has been declining for several years."

"What do you think, Daniel?" asked Mrs. Walsh. "After all, it's as much your business as it is John's or Richard's."

"I think that John and Richard both have good points," said Daniel. "While John is the only one of us three in the business now, I may want to join the company when I finish school, and I really don't care to be a clerk in a convenience store. And while John certainly has a right to try to accumulate some wealth, I don't know that using the family business's credit rating to guarantee his personal investments is really fair to the rest of us. After all, John is at least getting a decent salary, and Richard and I don't even receive any dividends."

"Wait a second, Dan," said John, somewhat resentfully. "I'm not riding a gravy train here. My $30,000 salary at Walsh is no higher than what my market worth is, and especially the way things are going, my upside potential is much lower than I could get working for someone else. Even more importantly, the family couldn't find anyone else to do this job for any less than what I'm getting."

The family discussion had ended without resolving anything, but John was certain the business would be worth substantially less if he was unable to turn the operation around. Aside from the purely financial considerations, John knew that the major oil companies were now evaluating their distributors on sales levels and sales growth. A distributor in an attractive market who wasn't showing the appropriate level of sales or sales growth might soon find itself without a supply contract.

Further, while John was eager to stop the decline in the company's financial performance, he also felt strongly that the business plan he developed now should lay the foundation for the business growth for the next five to ten years. The questions in his mind were, "How do we do it, and is it worth the trouble?"

NOTES

1. *1986 State of the Convenience Store Industry* (Alexandria, Va.: National Association of Convenience Stores, Inc.), p. 7.

2. *1985 Petroleum Marketing Databook* (Alexandria, Va.: Petroleum Marketing Education Foundation, 1985), p. 12.

3. *1984 Petroleum Marketing Databook* (Alexandria, Va.: Petroleum Marketing Education Foundation, 1984), p. 19.

4. *1985 Petroleum Marketing Databook* (Alexandria, Va.: Petroleum Marketing Education Foundation, 1985), pp. 15–16.

5. Steffen W. Plenn, *Underground Tankage: The Liability of Leaks* (Alexandria, Va.: Petroleum Marketing Education Foundation, 1986). pp. 9–12.

6. "Why the C-store Image Race Could Lead to a Shakeout," *National Petroleum News,* September 1987, p. 40.

7. *Ibid.,* p. 41.

8. "Rural versus Urban: A Site Selection Dilemma," *Convenience Store News,* July 13–August 2, 1987, p. 54.

9. *Ibid.*

10. It should be noted that the bank is refinancing land that Walsh currently owns.

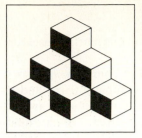

STRATEGIC ISSUES

ETHICS

A.H. Robins and the Dalkon Shield

NEIL H. SNYDER • ELIZABETH BOGDAN • TRACY COX • JOAN LESORAVAGE • BETH GHAPHERY • MARISA HAUSMAN • LARRY ROSENBERGER

Founded in 1866, A.H. Robins is a diversified multinational company with base operations in Richmond, Virginia. Robins is primarily a manufacturer and marketer of two types of pharmaceuticals: those marketed directly to the consumer and those dispensed solely through the medical profession (commonly known as *ethical pharmaceuticals).* However, Robins is more than a pharmaceutical company. Pet-care products, health and beauty aids, and perfumes are among the many products manufactured by the company under brand names that include Robitussin cough syrup, Sergeant's pet-care products, Chap Stick lip balm, and Caron perfumes.

In 1866, Albert Hartley Robins opened a tiny apothecary shop for the purpose of providing to the medical profession research-formulated, clinically proven, and ethically promoted pharmaceuticals. Over a century later, the Robins philosophy remains unchanged. After three generations of operation, Robins is still led by members of the Robins family. Currently, the company has almost 6,000 full-time employees. Making employees feel like family has long been recognized as important to the overall success of the company. The ability to "converse as decision makers and to be treated as first-class" causes Robins's employees to take great pride in their company and to demonstrate a very high degree of loyalty to the firm. As an example of this concern for the views of employees, one Robins salesman said "that his advice often carries greater weight than that of the firm's market research department."[1]

This sense of family extends beyond work, too. The company sponsors activities that include a company softball team and company trips, and it offers employees little things that tend to make a big difference, such as free coffee and birthday holidays. Clairborne Robins believes that "his greatest assets are the people that work for him."[2] According to the *Richmond Times-Dispatch*, "When a person is employed by A.H. Robins, it's almost for life. Only on rare occasions do people not reach retirement with this company."[3]

THE INTRAUTERINE DEVICE ENVIRONMENT

The market for birth control devices in the 1970s was very volatile. Before the inception of intrauterine devices (IUDs), several other artificial methods of birth control were available to consumers. Included in this group were the diaphragm, the condom, and the birth control pill. Each of these methods offered women significantly better birth control protection than afforded by natural measures. However, the diaphragm and the condom lacked what women seemed to want most from birth control devices—spontaneity. Thus, the pill was viewed by consumers as the ultimate form of contraception. Unquestioned because it solved the perennial problem of birth control, the pill enjoyed wide use. The pill was convenient and safe, and it offered exceptional birth control protection.

The discovery of the pill's harmful side effects caused many women to lose confidence in oral contraceptives. The realization of problems such as an increased risk of heart disease, dramatic mood swings, and excessive weight gain gave rise to a national concern over the safety of the pill. This concern was the focus of the Gaylord Nelson hearings of the early 1970s. These hearings publicly exposed the harmful side effects of oral contraceptives. "It is estimated . . . that within six months of the Gaylord Nelson hearings . . . up to one million women went off the birth control pills."[4]

As the pill was no longer viewed as the ultimate answer to birth control, women returned to traditional methods of contraception. However, they refused to sacrifice convenience and almost foolproof protection. What could have been better than a device—not a drug with potentially harmful side effects—that offered the same protection as the pill at a comparable price with more convenience? The stage was set for the introduction of the IUD. Previously, IUDs had been used only on a small scale in various Planned Parenthood clinics. It was not until the harmful side effects of the pill were made public that IUDs were viewed as commercially viable.[5]

An IUD is a "small, flexible piece of sterile plastic which is inserted into the uterus by the physician to prevent pregnancies."[6] The minute the device is inserted it is effective. "Once an IUD has been inserted, it entails no further costs, no daily protective procedures. It works only inside the uterus—without effects on your body, blood, or brain; it doesn't cause you to gain weight, have headaches, or mood changes. And it provides the user with a most satisfying method of contraception."[7]

Because of the simplicity of the device, manufacturing costs are low and profits can be high. When volume is sufficient, an IUD can be manufactured, sterilized, and packaged for 35 to 40 cents, and it can be sold for $3.00 to $3.50.[8] Due to the size and profit potential of the birth control market, the manufacturers of IUDs were well positioned to reap a bountiful harvest, but competition was tough. The secret to success was timing, and the winners would be the first in the market. Firms competing in the market realized that "unlike most consumer products, new drugs and delivery devices must first gain acceptance among a small group of specialists. If the specialists accept this their patients will too."[9] Therefore, the marketing effort was directed at physicians, knowing that they would refer the device to their patients.

THE DALKON SHIELD

Dr. Hugh Davis, an assistant professor of medicine at Johns Hopkins University and an expert in birth control, was instrumental in developing the Dalkon Shield. Dr. Davis conducted research on patients using the Shield, and he reported a pregnancy rate of 1.1 percent (comparable with the pill). The competitive advantage the Dalkon Shield had over other IUDs was the "larger surface area designed for maximum coverage and maximum contraceptive effect."[10] The potential of the Dalkon Shield was great, and drawing from its already established reputation and distribution channels in the pharmaceutical industry, this version of the IUD seemed to be a logical addition to Robins's product offerings.

On June 12, 1970, A.H. Robins paid $750,000, a royalty of 10 percent of future net sales, plus consulting fees to acquire the Dalkon Shield. At the time of purchase, Robins had no expertise in the area of birth control. Although it did hire consultants, Robins had neither an obstetrician nor a gynecologist on its staff.[11] The company assigned assembly of the Shield to its corporate division that manufactures Chap Stick lip balm. Before buying the product, however, Robins's medical director, Frederick A. Clark, Jr., reviewed statistical tests performed by Dr. Davis on the Shield.[12] These tests showed that in 832 insertions, 26 women became pregnant. Dr. Davis's tests, however, were done on the original Shield, not the one ultimately sold by Robins. The major difference between the original Shield and the one sold by Robins was the addition of a multifilament tail.[13]

When Robins went to the market, the company was excited about its product. "Possibly no other IUD has received the benefit of such ecstatic claims by its developer, its manufacturer, and the admiring multitude."[14] Robins used promotional methods that were designed especially for acceptance of the Shield within the medical profession. Foremost among these promotions was a text written by Dr. Davis, *Intrauterine Devices for Contraception—The IUD*. The appendix of his book lists complications reported with the use of ten major IUDs. The Shield was presented in a very good light with only a 5.4 percent complication rate. The complication rate of the competition ranged from 16.9 percent to 55.7 percent.

DIFFICULTIES EMERGE

A.H. Robins began selling the Dalkon Shield on January 1, 1971. On June 22, 1971, when a doctor reported that his Shield-wearing daughter suffered a septic spontaneous abortion (miscarriage caused by infection), the company was particularly concerned about the safety aspects of the Shield. The main concern was the Shield's unique multifilament tail, which has since been accused of actually drawing infection from the vagina into the normally sterile uterus.[15] Ironically, the product that was thought to be the ultimate form of birth control turned sour (36 alleged deaths and 13,000 alleged injuries), and it had a devastating effect on A.H. Robins.

DIFFICULTIES WITH RESEARCH[16]

Although the text written by Dr. Davis had been accepted by the medical profession as a major textbook on IUDs, the problems with IUDs raised many concerns, and the text was referred to as a "thinly disguised promotion of the Shield." Examination revealed that Robins possessed data from five formal studies based on the experience of about 4,000 Shield users. Three of these five studies were performed by people with financial interests in the Shield. The foremost of these studies was done by Dr. Davis. He claimed a pregnancy rate of 1.1 percent, an expulsion rate of 2.3 percent, a medical removal rate of 2.0 percent, and a total complication rate of 5.4 percent. However, another study conducted over an eighteen-month period that was dated October 25, 1972, showed a 4.3 percent pregnancy rate.

In an interview broadcast on the television show "60 Minutes," Paul Rheingold, a New York attorney who had represented 40 Dalkon Shield users, said that "this IUD got on the market with no animal tests, and with whatever minimal clinical . . . or testing on human subjects . . . the company wanted to do, which turned out to be practically nothing."[17]

FINANCIAL IMPLICATIONS

Approximately 4.5 million Dalkon Shields were sold by Robins, producing an estimated profit of $500,000.[18] "The product generated total revenues to the company of $13.7 million in 4.5 years. But during the first six months of 1985, Robins paid out $61.2 million in Dalkon-related expenses."[19] By June 30, 1985, Robins and Aetna Life and Casualty Company (Robins's insurance company) had paid $378.3 million to settle 9,230 Dalkon Shield cases. This exhausted all but $50 million of Robins's product liability insurance. Legal fees and other costs related to the Shield have totaled $107.3 million. Robins's portion of the total Dalkon claims has been $198.1 million. Robins announced an anticipated minimum cost to handle future Dalkon expenses of $685 million excluding punitive damages.

Exhibits 1 through 11 present financial information on the company contained in its 1984 Annual Report. Appendix A contains necessary notes to the exhibits.

BANKRUPTCY

On August 21, 1985, A.H. Robins filed for bankruptcy under Chapter 11 of the Federal Bankruptcy Code. "When it filed its request for reorganization on August 21, Robins listed $2.26 in assets for each $1.00 in debts and talked publicly about the strengths of the company when items related to the Dalkon Shield birth control device were excluded."[20]

Robins noted that it had a profit of $35.3 million from net sales of $331.1 million in the first six months of 1985. What the sales and profits did not show was the extent to which Robins was having to dip into its retained earnings to pay Dalkon-related bills. "Dalkon payments had taken away only 1.7 cents from each $1.00 in Robins sales from 1974 through 1983, but then jumped to 12.3 cents in 1984. And when it jumped to 18.5 cents in the

EXHIBIT 1

Net Sales (Dollar Amounts in Millions)

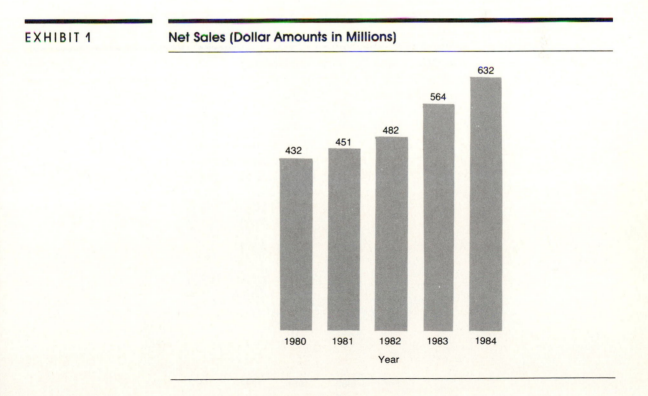

EXHIBIT 2

Net Earnings or Loss (Dollar Amounts in Millions)

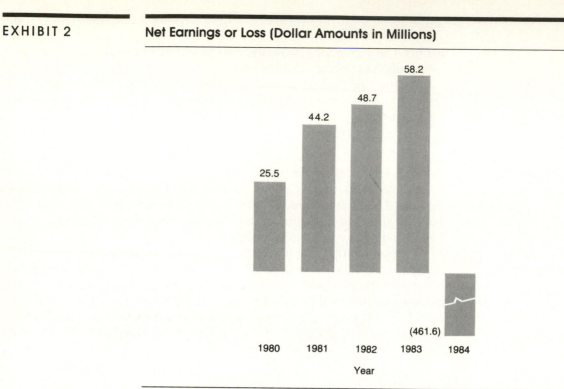

EXHIBIT 3

Earnings or Loss Per Share (in Dollars)

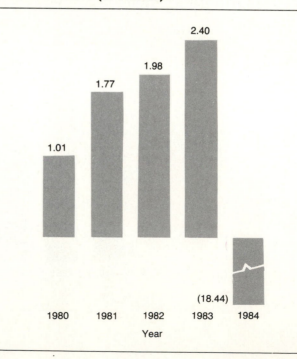

EXHIBIT 4

Dividends Per Share (in Dollars)

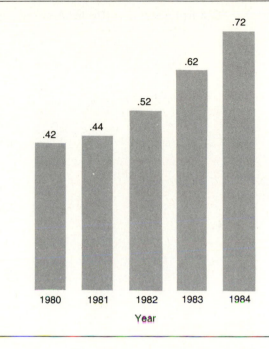

EXHIBIT 5

**Worldwide Research and Development Expenditures
(Dollar Amounts in Millions)**

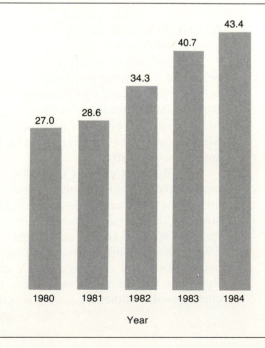

EXHIBIT 6   **Capital Additions (Dollar Amounts in Millions)**

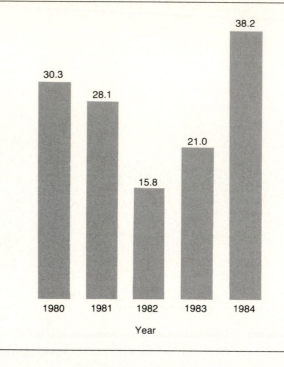

Year

first six months of this year [1985] there wasn't enough left from sales to meet other expenses."[21]

"The petition in bankruptcy court stops the flow of Dalkon payments. A perceived advantage for Robins in seeking the Chapter 11 route is that the company's reorganization plan would likely stretch out Dalkon payments so that a cash flow problem wouldn't recur."[22] "The action was taken [in bankruptcy court] in an effort to ensure the economic vitality of the company, which is, of course, critical to our ability to pay legitimate claims to present and future plaintiffs."[23]

A.H. Robins's petition in bankruptcy court has been at the center of a heated debate. Those in support of the company have argued that "A.H. Robins's move into bankruptcy court could ensure that there is money for all who are suing the company instead of letting 'the first wolves who tear at the carcass' get it all."[24] On the other hand, Aaron M. Levine, a lawyer for women filing against Robins, believes that "this is a company that's saying, 'we'll pay our suppliers and we'll pay for TV ads and we'll pay for the syrup for the Robitussin and we'll pay our workers, but as far as this one particular group of creditors—the women we have maimed—we won't pay."[25]

EXHIBIT 7

A.H. Robins Company, Incorporated and Subsidiaries: Consolidated Statements of Operations (Dollar Amounts in Thousands Except Per Share Data)

	YEAR ENDED DECEMBER 31		
	1984	**1983***	**1982***
Net sales	$631,891	$563,510	$482,324
Cost of sales	237,508	220,628	195,008
Marketing, administrative, and general	222,939	196,495	168,963
Research and development	43,352	40,686	34,279
Total operating costs and expenses	503,799	457,809	398,250
Operating earnings	128,092	105,701	84,074
Interest income	7,560	8,350	8,085
Interest expense	(3,240)	(5,441)	(10,308)
Litigation settlement income	1,205	2,256	3,135
Reserve for Dalkon Shield claims	(615,000)		
Litigation expenses and settlements	(77,950)	(18,745)	(7,091)
Other, net	(13,190)	(144)	(3,740)
Earnings (loss) before income taxes	(572,523)	91,977	74,155
Provision for income taxes (benefits)	(110,910)	33,756	25,462
Net earnings (loss)	$(461,613)	$ 58,221	$ 48,693
Earnings (loss) per common share	$(18.44)	$2.40	$1.98
Average number of shares outstanding	25,037	24,295	24,552

*Reclassified to conform to 1984 presentation.
The Notes to Consolidated Financial Statements (Appendix A to this case) are an integral part of these statements.

Levine pointed to Robins's own estimates that it has $466 million in assets and only $216.5 million owed to creditors. "Certainly this is far from the usual type of debtor who files a bankruptcy court petition." According to Levine's motion, Robins's petition was instituted not to benefit a corporation in distress, as the laws are intended, "but to enable the petitioner to escape the jurisdiction of another court when the day of reckoning for their alleged acts of misconduct was at hand."[26] The National Woman's Health Network, for instance, said at a news conference that the company is financially healthy but is trying to duck its responsibility to women who have filed lawsuits. On the other hand, Roscoe E. Puckett, Jr., a spokesman for Robins, contends that "the best hope for all concerned is for A.H. Robins to remain financially healthy. To do that, we had to stop the financial

EXHIBIT 8

A.H. Robins Company, Incorporated and Subsidiaries: Selected Financial Data (Dollar Amounts in Thousands Except Per Share and Ratio Data)

	1984	1983	1982	1981	1980†
OPERATIONS					
Net sales	$631,891	$563,510	$482,324	$450,854	$432,328
Cost of sales	237,508	220,628	195,008	190,759	187,496
Marketing, administrative, and general	222,939	196,495	168,963	157,852	160,477
Research and development	43,352	40,686	34,279	28,572	27,033
Total operating costs and expenses	503,799	457,809	398,250	377,183	375,006
Operating earnings	128,092	105,701	84,074	73,671	57,322
Interest income	7,560	8,350	8,085	8,437	5,614
Interest expense	(3,240)	(5,441)	(10,308)	(3,564)	(4,741)
Litigation settlement income	1,205	2,256	3,135	3,379	3,590
Reserve for Dalkon Shield claims	(615,000)				
Litigation expenses and settlements	(77,950)	(18,745)	(7,091)	(3,318)	(4,616)
Provision for losses on disposition of businesses					(9,129)
Other, net	(13,190)	(144)	(3,740)	(4,997)	(4,112)
Earnings (loss) before income taxes	(572,523)	91,977	74,155	73,608	43,928
Provision for income taxes (benefits)	(110,910)	33,756	25,462	29,380	18,458
Net earnings (loss)	$(461,613)	$ 58,221	$ 48,693	$ 44,228	$ 25,470
PER SHARE DATA					
Earnings (loss) per share	$(18.44)	$2.40	$1.98	$1.77	$1.01
Dividends per share	0.72	0.62	0.52	0.44	0.42
Stockholders' equity (deficit) per share	(5.23)	14.69	13.29	12.52	11.16
Weighted average number of shares outstanding	25,037	24,295	24,552	25,015	25,314
BALANCE SHEET DATA					
Cash and cash equivalents	$ 91,627	$133,381	$ 79,986	$ 89,024	$ 49,705
Working capital	122,344	229,525	200,810	177,259	146,258
Current ratio	1.7:1	3.2:1	4.0:1	3.1:1	3.0:1
Property, plant, and equipment, net	$135,685	$107,651	$ 98,079	$ 96,457	$ 80,511
Depreciation and amortization	16,310	10,253	10,384	10,096	10,950
Total assets	648,129	509,663	439,983	443,942	390,570
Long-term obligations, exclusive of Dalkon Shield reserve	25,330	48,322	51,040	48,232	35,346
Stockholders' equity (deficit)	(127,851)	355,837	321,085	310,201	280,394

EXHIBIT 8   Continued

1979*†	1978*†	1977*†	1976*†	1975*†	1974*†
$386,425	$357,070	$306,713	$284,925	$241,060	$210,713
157,895	146,636	122,374	108,519	89,304	71,233
139,782	131,195	114,490	101,568	85,378	77,128
20,522	18,951	16,107	12,729	10,690	9,568
318,199	296,782	252,971	222,816	185,372	157,929
68,226	60,288	53,742	62,109	55,688	52,784
5,767	3,469	2,033	2,355	1,726	2,465
(4,194)	(3,469)	(2,106)	(1,719)	(1,189)	(1,134)
28,934					
(6,005)	(9,560)	(3,331)	(1,146)	(5,065)	
(13,539)	901	(2,675)	(2,710)	(2,518)	(1,209)
79,189	51,629	47,663	58,889	48,642	52,906
34,443	21,713	20,862	27,534	23,095	25,989
$ 44,746	$ 29,916	$ 26,801	$ 31,355	$ 25,547	$ 26,917
$1.71	$1.15	$1.03	$1.20	$0.98	$1.03
0.40	0.34	0.32	0.30	0.27	0.26
10.52	9.20	8.39	7.69	6.79	6.04
26,107	26,127	26,127	26,127	26,127	26,126
$ 69,381	$ 72,058	$ 43,611	$ 50,769	$ 41,763	$ 29,228
153,411	156,632	128,838	126,904	100,387	89,459
2.9:1	3.7:1	3.5:1	4.1:1	3.5:1	4.5:1
$ 59,994	$ 55,350	$ 49,751	$ 39,066	$ 34,640	$ 30,418
8,806	8,427	6,837	6,076	5,007	4,322
379,597	326,073	287,045	262,668	223,544	190,263
26,518	27,809	16,718	20,412	6,740	5,620
272,673	240,275	219,242	200,802	177,275	157,695

Amounts for 1983 and prior years have been reclassified to conform to 1984 presentation.
See Note 12 of Notes to Consolidated Financial Statements (Appendix A to this case) for information on litigation.
*Results were computed on a FIFO basis.
†Results preceded adoption of Statement of Financial Accounting Standards No. 52, which revised the method of translating foreign currency.

EXHIBIT 9

A.H. Robins Company, Incorporated and Subsidiaries: Consolidated Balance Sheets (Dollar Amounts in Thousands)

	DECEMBER 31		
	1984	1983	1982
ASSETS			
Current assets			
Cash	$ 1,792	$ 1,534	$ 5,792
Certificates of deposit and time deposits	13,426	57,700	14,349
Marketable securities	76,409	74,147	59,845
Accounts and notes receivable—net of allowance for doubtful accounts of $2,613 (1983—$2,560, 1982—$2,473)	111,313	112,260	107,790
Inventories	84,611	82,714	72,219
Prepaid expenses	5,643	6,674	5,136
Deferred tax benefits	15,800		3,537
Total current assets	308,994	335,029	268,668
Property, plant, and equipment			
Land	6,313	6,552	6,940
Buildings and leasehold improvements	106,165	89,374	75,933
Machinery and equipment	90,260	70,169	68,453
	202,738	166,095	151,326
Less accumulated depreciation	67,053	58,444	53,247
	135,685	107,651	98,079
Intangible and other assets			
Intangibles—net of accumulated amortization	82,502	50,201	53,140
Note receivable, less current maturity			8,044
Deferred tax benefits	106,700		
Other assets	14,248	16,782	12,052
	203,450	66,983	73,236
	$648,129	$509,663	$439,983

hemorrhaging that threatened to destroy the company to the detriment of everyone, including the legitimate Dalkon Shield claimants."[27]

"Other factors include our desire to ensure that all persons to whom the company has an obligation are treated fairly, to preserve the assets of the company and maintain its current operations."[28]

To supplement Dalkon expenses and to alleviate the tight cash flow position that Robins has experienced recently, it requested a $35 million credit

EXHIBIT 9   **Continued**

	DECEMBER 31		
	1984	**1983**	**1982**
LIABILITIES AND STOCKHOLDERS' EQUITY (DEFICIT)			
Current liabilities			
Notes payable	$ 16,129	$ 7,116	$ 5,419
Long-term debt payable within one year	21,600	3,225	1,325
Current portion of reserve for Dalkon Shield claims	51,000		
Accounts payable	23,855	23,989	20,807
Income taxes payable	11,850	28,589	12,269
Accrued liabilities:			
Dalkon Shield costs	22,653	11,094	2,134
Other	39,563	31,491	25,904
Total current liabilities	186,650	105,504	67,858
Long-term debt	11,400	33,000	36,225
Reserve for Dalkon Shield claims, less current portion	564,000		
Other liabilities	13,930	12,270	14,022
Deferred income taxes		3,052	793
Stockholders' equity (deficit)			
Preferred stock, $1 par—authorized 10,000,000 shares, none issued			
Common stock, $1 par—authorized 40,000,000 shares	26,234	26,213	26,151
Additional paid-in capital	11,310	1,682	966
Retained earnings (deficit)	(104,477)	375,072	331,848
Cumulative translation adjustments	(35,776)	(25,725)	(16,475)
	(102,709)	377,242	342,490
Less common stock in treasury, at cost—1,793,347 shares (1983— 1,996,650 shares, 1982—1,996,650 shares)	25,142	21,405	21,405
	(127,851)	355,837	321,085
	$ 648,129	$509,663	$439,983

The Notes to Consolidated Financial Statements (Appendix A to this case) are an integral part of these statements.

limit "to meet $25 million of cash needs of its U.S. operations, $2 million in letters of credit for foreign suppliers, and $8 million of credit for its foreign units."[29] This credit limit was the subject of heated debate among the Internal Revenue Service, the attorneys for more than 10,000 women who have filed suit against Robins, and various Robins creditors. "The IRS contends that Robins owes about $61 million in corporate income taxes from as far back as 1978. Arguing on behalf of the agency, Assistant U.S. Attorney

EXHIBIT 10

A.H. Robins Company, Incorporated and Subsidiaries: Consolidated Statements of Stockholders' Equity (Deficit) (Dollar Amounts in Thousands Except Per Share Data)

	COMMON STOCK ($1 PAR VALUE)	ADDITIONAL PAID-IN CAPITAL	RETAINED EARNINGS (DEFICIT)	CUMULATIVE TRANSLATION ADJUSTMENTS	TREASURY STOCK (AT COST)	TOTAL
Balance—January 1, 1982	$26,127	$700	$295,851	$ 84	$(12,561)	$310,201
Net earnings			48,693			48,693
Cash dividends—$0.52 per share			(12,696)			(12,696)
Translation adjustment for 1982				(16,559)		(16,559)
Purchase of treasury stock—644,000 shares					(8,844)	(8,844)
Issued for stock options—24,550 shares	24	266				290
Balance—December 31, 1982	26,151	966	331,848	(16,475)	(21,405)	321,085
Net earnings			58,221			58,221
Cash dividends—$0.62 per share			(14,997)			(14,997)
Translation adjustment for 1983				(9,250)		(9,250)
Issued for stock options—61,900 shares	62	716				778
Balance—December 31, 1983	26,213	1,682	375,072	(25,725)	(21,405)	355,837
Net loss			(461,613)			(461,613)
Cash dividends—$0.72 per share			(17,936)			(17,936)
Translation adjustment for 1984				(10,051)		(10,051)
Purchase of treasury stock—1,040,404 shares					(17,070)	(17,070)

EXHIBIT 10	Continued					
	COMMON STOCK ($1 PAR VALUE)	**ADDITIONAL PAID-IN CAPITAL**	**RETAINED EARNINGS (DEFICIT)**	**CUMULATIVE TRANSLATION ADJUSTMENTS**	**TREASURY STOCK (AT COST)**	**TOTAL**
Issued for stock options—20,300 shares	21	201				222
Shares reissued with acquisition— 1,243,707 shares		9,427			13,333	22,760
Balance— December 31, 1984	$26,234	$11,310	$(104,477)	$(35,776)	$(25,142)	$(127,851)

The Notes to Consolidated Financial Statements (Appendix A to this case) are an integral part of these statements.

EXHIBIT 11	A.H. Robins Company, Incorporated and Subsidiaries: Consolidated Statements of Changes in Financial Position (Dollar Amounts in Thousands)

	YEAR ENDED DECEMBER 31		
	1984	**1983***	**1982***
Cash provided by operations:			
Net earnings (loss)	$(461,613)	$58,221	$48,693
Noncash expenses			
Depreciation and amortization	16,310	10,253	10,384
Deferred tax benefit, reserve for Dalkon Shield claims	(125,933)		
Reserve for Dalkon Shield claims	615,000		
Other, net	6,140	2,477	3,201
	49,904	70,951	62,278
Operating requirements, (increase) decrease:			
Accounts and notes receivable	1,686	(7,212)	(18,172)
Inventories	125	(10,424)	(4,647)
Accounts payable, income taxes payable, and accrued liabilities	(147)	36,279	(13,936)
Other, net	2,955	4,910	5,477
	4,619	23,553	(31,278)

EXHIBIT 11   Continued

| | YEAR ENDED DECEMBER 31 | | |
	1984	1983*	1982*
Investments			
Capital additions	(38,155)	(20,955)	(15,815)
Acquisitions	(51,809)	(5,700)	(2,035)
	(89,964)	(26,655)	(17,850)
Cash flow from operations	(35,441)	67,849	13,150
Cash provided by (utilized in) financial activities			
Notes payable and long-term debt	5,933	543	(648)
Purchase of treasury shares	(17,070)		(8,844)
Issuance of treasury shares for acquisition	22,760		
	11,623	543	(9,492)
Less cash dividends paid	17,936	14,997	12,696
Net increase (decrease) in cash and cash equivalents	$ (41,754)	$53,395	$ (9,038)

*Reclassified to conform to 1984 presentation.
The Notes to Consolidated Financial Statements (Appendix A to this case) are an integral part of these statements.

S. David Schiller told the judge that Robins had failed to prove that it needs the entire $35 million of credit or that it couldn't get the loans elsewhere under more favorable terms."[30] The credit line requested by Robins was ultimately approved by a federal court judge. "Under the agreement, Robins will receive $23 million from Manufacturers Hanover Trust Co., New York, and $12 million from Bank of Virginia. The arrangement, which was opposed vigorously by the Internal Revenue Service and others with claims pending against Robins, assigns the two banks priority for payments among all Robins creditors. . . .

"In approving the credit agreement, Judge Robert R. Merhige, Jr., acknowledged that some of the terms 'could be questioned.' But he said he felt compelled to 'give way to the business judgment' of the company's managers. He also expressed concern that denying the request might harm the company's prospects for obtaining credit."[31]

THE FUTURE   "In October [1984], the company filed in Federal District Court in Richmond a motion seeking a class action to resolve all punitive damage claims arising from Dalkon Shield litigation. The goal is a single trial for the purpose of determining if A.H. Robins should, in fact, be liable for punitive damages and, if so, the amount of those damages in respect to all present and future Dalkon Shield claimants. It is our view that this is the only fair means of settling this issue. In addition to the class action, the court has been requested to establish a voluntary opt-in proceeding to dispose of claims for compensatory damages on a facilitated basis. Such a proceeding would allow those plaintiffs who so desire to advance their claims with a minimum of delay and expense.

"Additionally, the company initiated an advertising campaign for the purpose of persuading women using the Shield to have them removed at the company's expense." As of the publication date of the company's 1984 Annual Report, "More than 18,250 inquiries [had] been received, . . . the company [had] paid for 777 examinations and 4,437 removals."[32]

APPENDIX A

NOTES TO CONSOLIDATED FINANCIAL STATEMENTS

1. SIGNIFICANT ACCOUNTING POLICIES

Consolidation

The consolidated financial statements include the accounts of A.H. Robins Company, Incorporated and all majority-owned subsidiaries. Accounts of subsidiaries outside the U.S. and Canada are included on the basis of a fiscal year beginning December 1 (or date of acquisition) and ending November 30. All significant intercompany accounts and transactions have been eliminated.

Inventories

Inventories are valued at the lower of cost or market. The cost for substantially all domestic inventories is determined on the last-in, first-out (LIFO) method while cost for foreign inventories is based on the first-in, first-out (FIFO) method.

Property, Plant, and Equipment

Property, plant, and equipment are recorded at cost and are depreciated over their estimated useful lives. Depreciation for all companies is computed on the straight-line method for assets acquired after 1979. Depreciation on assets acquired in 1979 and prior years is computed on the declining balance method for domestic companies and on the straight-line method for foreign companies.

Intangible Assets

Excess of cost over net assets of subsidiaries acquired after October 31, 1970 is being amortized over a period of 40 years or less. Excess cost of $17,357,000 relating to companies acquired prior to that date is not being amortized. Expenditures for development of patents are charged to expense as incurred. Patents purchased and trademarks are being amortized over their determinable lives.

Income Taxes

The company provides for deferred income taxes on items of income or expense reported for tax purposes in different years than for financial purposes. The investment tax credit is included in earnings in the year the credit arises as a reduction of any provision for income taxes.

The company files a consolidated federal income tax return with its domestic subsidiaries. Income taxes, if any, are provided for on earnings of foreign subsidiaries remitted or to be remitted. No provision is made for income taxes on undistributed earnings of foreign subsidiaries reinvested in the companies.

Retirement Plans

The company and certain of its subsidiaries have retirement plans for their employees. Costs of the plans are funded when accrued except for the plans of certain foreign subsidiaries. Unfunded prior service costs are provided for over periods not exceeding 40 years. Certain medical and life insurance benefits are provided for qualifying retired employees. The annual costs for these programs are not material and are expensed when paid.

Earnings (Loss) per Share

Earnings (loss) per share are based on the weighted average number of common shares and common share equivalents outstanding during each year.

2. ACQUISITIONS AND DIVESTITURES

On January 5, 1984, the company acquired all of the outstanding stock of Quinton Instrument Company, Inc., for which the company issued 1,243,707 shares of its common stock valued for accounting purposes at $18.30 per share and paid $20.1 million in cash. The total acquisition cost was $42.9 million, which consisted of the assigned value of the above-mentioned shares, the cash paid, and acquisition expenses. The company accounted for the acquisition as a purchase and accordingly has included Quinton's results of operations in its financial statements beginning January 5, 1984. On an unaudited pro forma basis, assuming the acquisition had occurred on January 1, 1983, the company's net sales, net earnings, and earnings per share would have been $587,328,000, $56,992,000, and $2.23, respectively. The pro forma amounts reflect estimated adjustments for goodwill amortization, depreciation, and interest expense. Goodwill of $27,118,000 is being amortized on a straight-line basis over a period of forty years.

On April 2, 1984, the company acquired substantially all of the assets associated with radio stations WRQK-FM and WPET-AM in Greensboro, North Carolina. The acquisition price was $7.6 million.

In December 1984, the company acquired all of the outstanding stock of Lode B. V., an established ergometer manufacturer located in the Netherlands. Lode B. V., an addition to the company's Medical Instruments Division, has been accounted for by the purchase method and did not result in a significant impact on 1984 financial results.

In March 1983, the company acquired substantially all of the assets of Scientific Protein Laboratories, a company primarily engaged in the manufacture of animal-derived pharmaceutical products.

Also in March 1983, the company sold its Quencher cosmetics line at an after-tax gain of $801,000.

In November 1982, the company acquired the assets of U.S. Clinical Products, Incorporated, located in Richardson, Texas. U.S. Clinical Products engages primarily in the manufacturing and marketing of tamper-resistant seals used in hospitals on intravenous containers after the manufacturer's closure has been removed.

3. FOREIGN OPERATIONS

At December 31, 1984, undistributed earnings of foreign subsidiaries totaled approximately $70,981,000 including amounts accumulated at dates of acquisition. Of this amount, $14,600,000 might be subject to net additional federal income taxes if distributed currently. No provision has been made for income taxes on these undistributed earnings.

Foreign currency exchange losses included in earnings amounted to $1,187,000 in 1984 (1983—$938,000, 1982—$2,436,000). Net foreign assets included in the consolidated financial statements at December 31, 1984 were $75,098,000 (1983—$93,011,000, 1982—$101,271,000).

4. INVENTORIES (DOLLAR AMOUNTS IN THOUSANDS)

	1984	1983	1982
Finished products	**$41,814**	$43,462	$38,467
Work in process	**18,425**	16,186	8,221
Raw materials and supplies	**24,372**	23,066	25,531
	$84,611	$82,714	$72,219

Substantially all domestic inventories were valued on the last-in, first-out (LIFO) method while most foreign inventories were valued on the first-in, first-out (FIFO) method. Approximately 68 percent of inventories was valued under LIFO in 1984 (1983—70 percent, 1982—65 percent) and the remainder under FIFO. Current cost (FIFO method) of inventories exceeded the LIFO values by $3,281,000 in 1984; $4,424,000 in 1983; and $3,546,000 in 1982.

5. LONG-TERM DEBT

Long-term debt, net of amounts payable within one year, is summarized as follows (dollar amounts in thousands):

	1984	1983	1982
8¾ percent promissory note due annually to 1988 ..		$19,700	$21,025
Bonds, interest rate 55 percent of prime, due annually from 1984 to 1991	**11,400**	13,300	15,200
	$11,400	$33,000	$36,225

Annual maturities of long-term debt for the next five years are:

1985—$21,600,000

1986—$1,900,000

1987—$1,900,000

1988—$1,900,000

1989—$1,900,000

The 8¾ percent promissory note was redeemed at par subsequent to year end and therefore has been reclassified as long-term debt payable within one year.

Interest incurred during 1984 of $2,500,000 was capitalized and included in property, plant, and equipment. No interest was capitalized in 1983 or 1982.

| | 6. LINES OF CREDIT | At December 31, 1984, unused lines of credit which do not support commercial paper or similar borrowing arrangements and may be withdrawn at the banks' option amounted to $12 million with domestic banks. Aggregate compensating balances were not material. |

6. LINES OF CREDIT

At December 31, 1984, unused lines of credit which do not support commercial paper or similar borrowing arrangements and may be withdrawn at the banks' option amounted to $12 million with domestic banks. Aggregate compensating balances were not material.

7. STOCK OPTIONS

The company has stock option plans for officers and certain key employees. The qualified stock option plan of 1973 as amended in 1982 was terminated on January 31, 1983 except as to outstanding options. A new incentive stock option plan was approved by the stockholders on April 26, 1983 under which 1,000,000 shares of common stock were made available for the granting of options. The plans are administered by a committee, subject to certain limitations expressly set forth in the plan, with authority to select participants, determine the number of shares to be allotted to a participant, set the option price, and fix the term of each option.

Transactions of the qualified and nonstatutory stock option plans are summarized below:

	SHARES AVAILABLE FOR OPTION	OPTIONS OUTSTANDING	
		SHARES	PRICE PER SHARE
Balance—Dec. 31, 1981	1,355,300	241,350	$10.19 to $11.38
Exercised		(24,550)	10.19 to 11.38
Canceled and expired	4,150	(4,150)	10.19
Balance—Dec. 31, 1982	1,359,450	212,650	10.19 to 11.38
Terminated—1973 Plan	(602,450)		
Exercised		(61,900)	10.19 to 11.38
1983 Plan	1,000,000		
Balance—Dec. 31, 1983	1,757,000	150,750	10.19 to 11.38
Granted	(488,500)	488,500	13.69
Exercised		(20,300)	10.19 to 13.69
Canceled and expired	13,700	(13,700)	11.38
Balance—Dec. 31, 1984	1,282,000	605,250	10.19 to 13.69

The options are exercisable at any time until their expiration dates, which are in 1986 (136,550 shares) and 1994 (468,700 shares).

8. PROVISION FOR INCOME TAXES

The provision for income taxes includes (dollar amounts in thousands):

	1984	1983	1982
Currently payable:			
Domestic	$ (4,061)	$13,563	$ 1,572
State	1,580	2,745	3,639
Foreign	9,234	10,947	11,859
	$ 6,753	$27,255	$17,070
Deferred:			
Domestic	$(110,009)	$ 5,917	$ 8,238
State	(8,648)	270	292
Foreign	994	314	(138)
	$(117,663)	$ 6,501	$ 8,392
Total provision	$(110,910)	$33,756	$25,462
Earnings (loss) before income taxes consist of:			
Domestic	$(590,925)	$71,613	$52,974
Foreign	18,402	20,364	21,181
	$(572,523)	$91,977	$74,155

Note 12 in the Notes to Consolidated Financial Statements discusses a minimum reserve established by the company in 1984 for pending and future claims related to the Dalkon Shield. These claims are deductible for tax purposes as incurred by the company. It is the company's belief that the currently recognized claims will be fully deductible against its future taxable income. However, generally accepted accounting principles limit the recognition of future tax benefits to those amounts assured beyond any reasonable doubt. Accordingly, the company has recognized for financial statement purposes only those benefits arising from the carryback of product liability expenses against income tax expenses previously recognized by the company. At December 31, 1984, the company had, for financial statement purposes only, unrecognized loss carryforward deductions in the amount of $138,132,000 and unrecognized foreign and investment tax credits carryforward of $86,939,000.

Should the realization of product liability claims produce a taxable loss in a future period, the company is permitted under provisions of the U.S. Internal Revenue Code to carry such loss back as a deduction against previous taxable income for a period up to ten years. Such loss may also be used to reduce future taxable income for a period up to fifteen years.

In 1984, the company realized net tax benefits of $65,206,000, primarily in the form of investment tax credit and depreciation, from its investment in tax benefit leases under the "safe harbor" leasing provisions enacted in 1981 and 1982. These benefits reduced the 1984 provision for domestic taxes currently payable and increased the provision for deferred taxes. As current tax benefits are realized, the company has reduced its purchase cost of the leases and established a deferred tax liability for the leases' future taxable income. Interest income is accrued on the unrecovered purchase cost. The excess of the purchase cost and accrued interest over the cumulative tax savings expected is amortized on an interest method during the years temporary excess tax savings are produced. The interest accrued and investment amortized during the lease terms have no material effect on earnings. At December 31, 1984, the balance of unrecovered investment and accrued interest was $1,071,000.

Deferred income taxes result from tax leases and from income and expense items reported for financial accounting and tax purposes in different periods. The source of these differences and the tax effect of each is shown below (dollar amounts in thousands):

	1984	1983	1982
Reserve for Dalkon Shield claims	$(125,933)		
Discounted portion of installment note receivable	574	$1,106	$1,520
Tax depreciation in excess of books	2,134	1,480	1,096
Other	356	988	585
Tax benefit from tax leases	$ 5,206	2,927	5,191
	$(117,663)	$6,501	$8,392

Reconciliation of the effective tax rate and the federal statutory rate is as follows:

	PERCENT OF PRETAX INCOME (LOSS)		
	1984	1983	1982
Statutory federal tax rate	(46.0)%	46.0%	46.0%
Product liability claims in excess of amounts carried back	15.2		
Foreign, investment and other tax credits not recognized after loss carryback	11.1		
Federal tax on foreign earnings	1.4	(1.1)	(3.1)
State taxes on income, net of federal tax benefit ...	(1.3)	2.8	3.6
Investment and other tax credits		(2.1)	(2.8)
Foreign earnings taxed at higher (lower) effective tax rate	0.1		0.3
Puerto Rican earnings exempt from tax	(1.1)	(6.7)	(9.0)
Tax exempt interest	(0.1)	(0.3)	(1.2)
All other, net	1.3	(1.9)	0.5
	(19.4)%	36.7%	34.3%

A wholly owned subsidiary in Puerto Rico operates under partial income tax exemptions granted for periods through 1999. The estimated tax saving from the Puerto Rican operation was $6,200,000 in 1984 (1983—$6,200,000, 1982—$6,700,000). Puerto Rican withholding taxes are provided on those earnings expected to be repatriated prior to expiration of the exemptions.

During 1983, the Internal Revenue Service completed its examination of the company's tax returns for the years 1978 through 1980 and proposed a deficiency of income taxes of approximately $6,400,000. The company is contesting the proposed deficiency which arises from a proposed reallocation of income from the company's Puerto Rico subsidiary. It is likely that a similar deficiency will be proposed for the years 1981 and 1982.

Management believes that any additional income taxes that may result from the proposed deficiency, and from the probable proposed deficiency related to the same issues for the years 1981 and 1982, should not have a materially adverse effect on the consolidated financial position of the company.

9. BUSINESS SEGMENT INFORMATION

Information about operations in different business segments and in various geographic areas of the world is . . . incorporated herein by reference.

10. RETIREMENT PLAN

The company and certain of its subsidiaries have retirement plans covering substantially all of their employees. The total retirement expense for 1984 was $6,908,000 (1983—$6,246,000, 1984—$5,435,000). The actuarial present value of accumulated plan benefits, assuming a weighted average rate of return of 8 percent in 1984 (1983—8 percent, 1982—6.5 percent), and plan net assets available for benefits of domestic defined benefit plans as of January 1, 1984, 1983, and 1982 are as follows (dollar amounts in thousands):

	1984	1983	1982
Actuarial present value of accumulated plan benefits:			
Vested	**$40,895**	$35,601	$30,925
Nonvested	**3,472**	3,250	4,351
	$44,367	$38,851	$35,276
Net assets available for benefits	**$55,621**	$47,287	$36,017

Assets available for benefits and the actuarial present value of accumulated benefits have not been determined for several minor foreign pension plans which are not required to report such information to government agencies.

Other liabilities include $6,635,000 of accrued pensions and severance benefits in foreign subsidiaries (1983—$7,063,000, 1982—$7,100,000).

11. COMMITMENTS

Rentals of space, vehicles, and office and data processing equipment under operating leases amounted to $6,718,000 in 1984 (1983—$6,428,000, 1982—$5,843,000).

Minimum future rental commitments under all noncancelable operating leases at December 31, 1984 with remaining terms of more than one year are as follows (dollar amounts in thousands):

1985	$2,515
1986	1,804
1987	1,634
1988	1,265
1989	822
Later years	1,853
Total minimum future rentals	$9,893

The company has agreed to repurchase, at the option of the shareholder until such time as the securities are registered, the shares of the company issued to the former Quinton Instrument Company, Inc., shareholders. Upon tender of the shares, the company will repurchase them at the current market price. At December 31, 1984, there were 1,017,103 shares subject to this agreement.

As of December 31, 1984, the company had outstanding commitments of $8 million for the construction of plant, office, and research and development facilities.

12. LITIGATION

Dalkon Shield—In June 1970, the company acquired the rights to the Dalkon Shield, an intrauterine contraceptive device. Approximately 2.8 million devices were sold in the United States through June 1974. Approximately 1.7 million of the devices were sold abroad.

Numerous cases and claims alleging injuries claimed to be associated with use of the device have been filed against the company in the United States ("Claims"). Only a few claims have been filed in foreign jurisdictions. The alleged injuries fall under the following general groups: perforation of the uterus or cervix, infection of the female reproductive system, pregnancy, ectopic pregnancy, spontaneous abortion which may be accompanied by sepsis, death, sterility, fetal abnormality and premature delivery, painful insertion and removal, and miscellaneous injuries. In addition to compensatory damages, most cases also seek punitive damages.

As of December 31, 1984, there were approximately 3,800 Claims pending against the company in federal and state courts in the United States. The company expects that a substantial number of new Claims will be filed against the company in the future.

Through December 31, 1984, the company had disposed of approximately 8,300 Claims. In disposing of these Claims, the company and its insurer have paid out approximately $314.6 million. Prior to 1981, substantially all disposition costs (including legal expenses, but excluding punitive damages) were charged to applicable products liability insurance carried by the company. The company incurred costs in excess of insurance in the following amounts: 1981—$3.3 million; 1982—$7.1 million; 1983—$18.7 million; and 1984—$78.0 million (exclusive of the reserve described below).

Of the Claims disposed of prior to December 31, 1984, 50 were tried to conclusion. Of that number, 27 resulted in verdicts for compensatory damages in favor of plaintiffs and 23 in verdicts in favor of the company. Seven of the plaintiff verdicts (involving compensatory awards aggregating approximately $5 million) and one verdict in favor of the company are the subject of pending appeals. Eight of the plaintiff verdicts also included awards of punitive damages in an aggregate amount of $17,227,000. Six of these punitive awards aggregating $8,827,000 have been paid; two are the subject of appeals. Punitive damage awards are not covered by insurance and are payable by the company.

The company is unable to assess its potential exposure to additional punitive damage awards. It has recently filed a motion in the United States District Court for the Eastern District of Virginia seeking certification of a class of present and prospective claimants in both federal and state courts for the purpose of determining and finally resolving in a single proceeding whether the company should be liable for punitive damages by reason of the Dalkon Shield and, if so, the aggregate amount of additional punitive damages that should be awarded.

The company had product liability insurance covering compensatory awards with respect to the Dalkon Shield for pertinent periods prior to March 1978. In October 1984, the company settled its suit, commenced in 1979, against its insurer concerning coverage of Dalkon Shield liability. From existing coverage and some additional coverage resulting from the settlement of this suit the company had at December 31, 1984, approximately $70 million of insurance coverage that it expects to be able to use.

In anticipation of the conclusion of the insurance coverage suit, the company commissioned a study, the purpose of which was to provide management of the company with data to establish a loss reserve for the future costs in compensatory damages and legal expenses of the disposition of pending and future claims. The study estimated the amount of this future disposition cost based on the following: (1) an estimate of total injuries based on an epidemiological analysis of published literature regarding the Dalkon Shield and other IUDs; (2) a statistical analysis of all Claims filed during the period 1981 through 1983 which constitute 51 percent of all Claims filed since the inception of the litigation through December 31, 1983; and (3) a statistical analysis of disposition timing and costs of all Claims filed during the period January 1, 1979 through December 31, 1983 and disposed of prior to October 1, 1984. The information on Claims filed and disposition timing and costs was extracted from a database which contains information on Claims filed through December 31, 1983. The study utilized information from the periods discussed above, which was believed to be more representative of future experience, rather than the entire litigation period which would have produced a materially higher estimate of disposition cost.

Based on the study's estimate of disposition cost and a review of 1984 fourth-quarter settlement cost data, management established a reserve, net of insurance, of $615 million against 1984 earnings in the accompanying consolidated financial statements. Management believes this represents a reasonable estimate of a minimum reserve for compensatory damages and legal expenses for pending and future Claims. The reserve does not provide for any punitive damages or damages from Dalkon Shield litigation abroad since there is no substantive basis to quantify such exposures. In taking into account 1984 fourth-quarter settlement cost data, management excluded the cost of a single group settlement which management believes is reasonable to assume is not representative of the expected future disposition of Claims. If the excluded settlement cost had been factored as an increasing trend into projected future cost of disposition of Claims, the reserve would have been increased by a material amount.

Based on the study's projected schedule of disposition of pending and future Claims, the payout of the reserve will take place over many years. The Company has reduced its 1984 provision for income taxes by $125.9 million, representing the expected minimum tax benefit to be realized by loss carrybacks to 1983 and prior years, plus reductions in deferred taxes expected to turn around in the tax loss carryforward period. The net effect of the reserve, less estimated tax benefits, is $489.1 million or $19.53 per share.

Continuing uncertainties associated with the litigation preclude a determination of the ultimate cost of the Dalkon Shield litigation to the company. There has been a significant increase in the number of new Claims filed per month and additional pressure on and a resulting increase in some settlement values which, if continued, would result in a greater Claim disposition cost than the amount estimated by the study. Whether this represents a long-term trend or is, as management believes is reasonable to assume, the temporary result of publicity associated with several Dalkon Shield-related events in

1984 and 1985 causing a temporary acceleration in the rate of filing of Claims with a subsequent leveling to those shown in the study, will only be determined by future experience.

In addition to these uncertainties, there are other factors which could affect, either favorably or unfavorably, the ultimate outcome of the Dalkon Shield litigation and the resulting financial impact on the company. Among them are:

- The Dalkon Shield removal campaign initiated on October 29, 1984
- The types of injuries alleged in future Claims
- The effect of the passage of time, including the effect of statutes of limitations
- The level of litigation activity relating to devices sold abroad
- The method of disposition of Claims
- The class action intended to resolve the question of punitive damages.

Accordingly, the reserve may not necessarily be the amount of the loss ultimately experienced by the company. It is not likely, however, that the ultimate loss will be less than the amount reserved. Further, the exposure of the company for additional compensatory and punitive damages awards over and above this reserve, although not presently determinable, may be significant and further materially adversely affect the future consolidated financial condition and results of operations of the company.

Other—In December 1982, the United States District Court for the Southern District of New York determined that the suit filed in 1977 by Kalman and Anita Ross, stockholders of the company, should be certified as a class action for damages on behalf of persons who purchased the company's common stock during the period March 8, 1971, through June 28, 1974. In addition to the company, certain of its present and former officers and directors are defendants. This suit alleges dissemination of false and misleading information and failure to disclose other information concerning the Dalkon Shield. After completion of discovery, an agreement was reached under which the company will pay $6.9 million in settlement of this class action. This agreement is subject to final judicial approval. The action against the individual defendants will be dismissed, subject to final judicial approval. A provision for this settlement has been recorded in 1984 and included in Other, Net.

In March 1980, Zoecon Corporation filed a civil action against the company and Miller-Morton Company, a subsidiary since merged into the company, alleging unfair competition (a claim since abandoned) and patent infringement in connection with the marketing of the Sergeant's Sentry V flea and tick collar. The company counterclaimed alleging patent invalidity on the part of Zoecon Corporation. The case has now been disposed of by way of a settlement having no material financial impact on the company.

NOTES

1. *Product Management*, October 1972.
2. A.H. Robins's *75th Anniversary Book*.
3. *Richmond Times-Dispatch*, June 23, 1985.
4. Committee on Government Operations, House of Representatives, June 13, 1973; Dr. Thomsen testimony.
5. *Ibid.*
6. SAF-T-COIL pamphlet.
7. *Ibid.*
8. Thomsen testimony, *op. cit.*
9. *Ibid.*
10. *Ibid.*
11. *Richmond Times-Dispatch, op. cit.*
12. *Ibid.*
13. *Ibid.*
14. Thomsen testimony, *op. cit.*
15. *Richmond Times-Dispatch, op. cit.*
16. Most of the information in this section is taken from Dr. Thomsen's testimony before the Committee on Government Operations, House of Representatives, May 30–31, 1973; June 1, 12–13, 1973.
17. "60 Minutes," CBS Television Network, Sunday, August 5, 1984.
18. *Richmond Times-Dispatch*, August 25, 1985. Reprinted with permission.
19. *Richmond Times-Dispatch*, August 22, 1985. Reprinted with permission.
20. *Richmond Times-Dispatch*, September 1, 1985. Reprinted with permission.
21. *Ibid.*
22. *Richmond Times-Dispatch*, August 24, 1985. Reprinted with permission.
23. *Richmond Times-Dispatch*, September 1, 1985. Reprinted with permission.
24. *Richmond Times-Dispatch*, August 25, 1985. Reprinted with permission.
25. *Richmond Times-Dispatch*, August 24, 1985. Reprinted with permission.
26. *Ibid.*
27. *Ibid.*
28. *Richmond Times-Dispatch*, August 22, 1985. Reprinted with permission.
29. *Wall Street Journal*, October 2, 1985.
30. *Wall Street Journal*, October 10, 1985.
31. *Wall Street Journal*, October 2, 1985.
32. A.H. Robins's 1984 Annual Report.

Union Carbide of India, Limited: The Bhopal Gas Incident

ARTHUR SHARPLIN

December 2, 1984, began as a typical day in the central Indian city of Bhopal. Shoppers moved about the open-air market. Here and there a customer haggled with a merchant. Beasts of burden, donkeys and oxen, pulled carts or carried ungainly bundles through the partly paved streets. Children played in the dirt. In the shadow of a Union Carbide pesticide plant, tens of thousands of India's poorest citizens milled about the shanty town they called home. A few miles away, wealthy Indians lived in opulence rivaling that of the first-class districts of London or Paris. Inside the plant, several hundred Indian workers and managers went about their duties, maintaining and operating the systems that produced the mildly toxic pesticide Sevin. Most of the plant was shut down for maintenance and it was operating at far below capacity.

At about 11:00 P.M., one of the operators noticed that the pressure in a methyl isocyanate (MIC) storage tank read 10 pounds per square inch (psi)—four times the normal. The operator was not concerned, thinking that the tank may have been pressurized with nitrogen by the previous shift. Around midnight several of the workers noticed that their eyes had begun to water and sting, a signal experience had taught them indicated an MIC leak. The leak, a small but continuous drip, was soon spotted. The operators were still not alarmed because minor leaks at the plant were quite common. It was time for tea and most of the crew retired to the company canteen, resolving to correct the problem afterward.

By the time the workers returned it was too late. The MIC tank pressure gauge was pegged. The leak had grown much larger and the entire area of the MIC tanks was enveloped in the choking fumes. The workers tried spraying water on the leak to break down the MIC. They sounded the alarm siren and summoned the fire brigade. As the futility of their efforts became apparent, many of the workers panicked and ran upwind—some scaling the chain-link and barbed-wire fence in their frantic race for survival.

By 1:00 A.M., only a supervisor remained in the area. He stayed upwind, donning his oxygen breathing apparatus every few minutes to check the various gauges and sensors. By that time the pressure in the MIC tank had forced open a relief valve and the untreated MIC vapor could be seen escaping from an atmospheric vent line 120 feet in the air.

The research assistance of Aseem Shukla is gratefully acknowledged. Reprinted with permission of Dr. Arthur Sharplin, Distinguished Professor of Management, McNeese University, Lake Charles, La.

The cloud of deadly white gas was carried by a southeasterly wind toward the Jai Prakash Nagar shanties. The cold temperature of the December night caused the MIC to settle toward the ground (in the daytime, or in the summer, convection currents probably would have raised and diluted the MIC).

As the gaseous tentacles reached into the huts there was panic and confusion. Many of the weak and elderly died where they lay. Some who made it into the streets were blinded. "It was like breathing fire," one survivor said. As word of the gas leak spread, many of Bhopal's affluent were able to flee in their cars. But most of the poor were left behind. When the gas reached the railroad station, supervisors who were not immediately disabled sent out word along the tracks and incoming trains were diverted. This cut off a possible means of escape but may have saved hundreds of lives. Because the whole station was quickly enveloped in gas, arriving trains would have been death traps for passengers and crews.

Of Bhopal's total population of about 1 million, an estimated one-half million fled that night, most on foot. The surrounding towns were woefully unprepared to accept the gasping and dying mass of people. Thousands waited outside hospitals for medical care. There was no certainty about how to treat the gas victims and general purpose medical necessities were in hopelessly short supply. Inside the hospitals and out, screams and sobs filled the air. Food supplies were quickly exhausted. People were even afraid to drink the water, not knowing if it was contaminated.

During the second day, relief measures were better organized. Several hundred doctors and nurses from nearby hospitals were summoned to help medical personnel in Bhopal. Just disposing of the dead was a major problem. Mass cremation was necessary. Islamic victims, whose faith requires burial rather than cremation, were piled several deep in hurriedly dug graves. Bloated carcasses of cattle and dogs littered the city. There was fear of a cholera epidemic. Bhopal's mayor said, "I can say that I have seen chemical warfare. Everything so quiet. Goats, cats, whole families—father, mother, children—all lying silent and still. And every structure totally intact. I hope never again to see it."

By the third day, the city had begun to move toward stability, if not normalcy. The Union Carbide plant had been closed and locked. A decision was made to consume the 30 tons of MIC that remained by using it to make pesticide. Most of the 2,000 dead bodies had been disposed of, however inappropriately. The more than 100,000 injured were being treated as rapidly as the limited medical facilities would allow, although many simply sat in silence, blinded and maimed by an enemy they had never known well enough to fear. For them, doctors predict an increased risk of sterility, kidney and liver infections, tuberculosis, vision problems, and brain damage. The potential for birth defects and other long-term effects is not clear. However, months after the incident newspapers reported a high incidence of stillbirths and congenital deformities among the population that had been affected by the gas.

COMPANY BACKGROUND

The Ever-Ready Company, Ltd. (of Great Britain), began manufacturing flashlight batteries in Calcutta in 1926. The division was incorporated as the Ever-Ready Company (India), Ltd., in 1934 and became a subsidiary of Union Carbide Corporation of New York. The name of the Indian company was changed to National Carbide Company (India), Ltd., in 1949 and to Union Carbide (India), Ltd. (UCIL) in 1959. The 1926 capacity of 40 million dry cell batteries per year was expanded to 767 million by the 1960s. In 1959, a factory was set up in India to manufacture the flashlights themselves.

By the 1980s, UCIL was involved in five product areas: batteries, carbon and metals, plastics, marine products, and agricultural chemicals. Exhibit 1 provides production statistics for UCIL products. The company eventually operated fourteen plants at eight locations, including the headquarters operation in Calcutta. Union Carbide's petrochemical complex, established in Bombay in 1966, was India's first.

In 1971, UCIL began its marine products operation with two shrimping

---

EXHIBIT 1   **Production Statistics**

CLASS OF GOODS	1983 CAPACITY	PRODUCTION LEVELS					
		1983	1982	1981	1980	1979	1978
Batteries (millions of pieces)	792	510.4	512.2	411.3	458.8	460.3	430.3
Flashlight cases (millions of pieces)	7.5	6.7	6.7	7.4	6.9	6.4	5.7
Arc carbons (millions of pieces)	9.0	7.5	7.0	7.0	6.7	6.2	6.1
Industrial carbon electrodes and shapes (millions of pieces)	2.5	0.5	0.5	0.5	0.3	0.5	0.2
Photo-engravers' plates/strips for printing (tonnes*)	1,200	412.0	478.0	431.0	399.0	469.0	506.0
Stellite castings, head facings and tube rods (tonnes)	150	17.5	12.7	16.4	14.5	15.8	18.2
Electrolytic manganese dioxide (tonnes)	4,500	3,335	3,085	3,000	2,803	2,605	2,700
Chemicals (tonnes)	13,600	7,349	6,331	6,865	7,550	8,511	8,069
Polyethylene (tonnes)	20,000	18,144	17,290	19,928	19,198	16,324	12,059
MIC-based pesticides (tonnes)	5,000	1,647	2,308	2,704	1,542	1,496	367
Marine products (tonnes)	5,500	424	649	642	601	648	731

SOURCE: The Stock Exchange Foundation, Bombay, India, *The Stock Exchange Official Directory,* Vol. XVII/29, July 18, 1983.

*One tonne = 1,000 kilograms = 2,214 pounds. One British long ton = 2,240 pounds. One U.S. ton = 2,000 pounds.

ships. The business is completely export oriented and employs fifteen deep-sea trawlers. Processing facilities are located off the east and west coasts of India. The trawlers now harvest deep-sea lobsters in addition to shrimp.

In 1979, UCIL initiated a letter of intent to manufacture dry-cell batteries in Nepal. A 77.5 percent-owned subsidiary was set up in Nepal in 1982 and construction of a rupees (Rs.) 18 million plant was begun.

The agricultural products division of UCIL was started in 1966 with just one office in Bombay. Agreement was reached with the Indian government in 1969 to set up a pesticide plant at Bhopal. Land was rented to UCIL for about $40 per acre per year. The initial investment was small, only $1 million, and the process was simple. Concentrated Sevin powder was imported from the United States, diluted with nontoxic powder, packaged, and sold. Under the technology transfer provisions of its agreement with UCIL, Union Carbide Corporation (USA) was obligated to share its more advanced technologies with UCIL. Eventually the investment at Bhopal grew to exceed $25 million and the constituents of Sevin were made there. Another Union Carbide insecticide, Temik, was made in small quantities at Bhopal.

UCIL's assets grew from Rs. 558 million in 1974 to Rs. 1,234 million in 1983 (the conversion rate stayed near 9 rupees to the dollar during this period, moving to about 12.50 as the dollar strengthened worldwide during 1984 and 1985). The *Economic Times* of India ranks UCIL number 21 in terms of sales among Indian companies. Union Carbide Corporation (USA) owns 50.9 percent of UCIL's stock and Indian citizens and companies own the remainder. When Indira Gandhi was voted out of office in 1977, the Janata (People's) Party strengthened the Foreign Exchange Regulation Act (FERA) (see Exhibit 2). As a result, IBM and Coca-Cola pulled out of India. IBM's business in India was taken over by ICIM (International Computer Indian Manufacturers), a domestic firm. Another similar firm performs the maintenance services for the existing IBM computers.

Since 1967 the chairman of the board of UCIL has been an Indian and foreign membership on the eleven-member board of directors has been limited to four. One expert on Indian industry affairs said, "Though the foreigners on the board are down to four from six in previous years, they continue to hold sway over the affairs of the company." Major capital expenditures by UCIL were required to be approved by Union Carbide Corporation. Also, the Bhopal plant submitted monthly reports to U.S. corporate headquarters detailing operations and safety procedures. And inspections of the plant were carried out from time to time by Union Carbide technical specialists.

OPERATIONS AT BHOPAL

On the surface, the UCIL insecticide factory is a typical process plant. A wide diversity of storage tanks, hoppers, and reactors are connected by pipes. There are many pumps and valves and several tall vent lines and

EXHIBIT 2   **The Foreign Exchange Regulation Act**

The Act was originally enacted as a temporary measure in 1947 and made permanent in 1957. It was revised and redrafted in 1973. It covers various aspects of foreign exchange transactions, including money changing, buying or selling foreign exchange in India or abroad, having an account in a bank outside India, and remitting money abroad.

The purpose of the Act is to restrict outflow of foreign exchange and to conserve hard currency holdings in India. One requirement of the Act is that any company in which the nonresident interest is more than 40 percent "shall not carry on in India or establish in India any branch or office without the special permission of the Reserve Bank of India." But the Reserve Bank of India has authority to exempt a company from the provisions of the Act. The 40 percent requirement was changed to 49 percent by Rajiv Gandhi's government.

High technology companies are frequently exempted from the equity ownership provisions of the Act. Other companies that have operated in India for many years are sometimes exempted if they agree not to expand their Indian operations.

Policies in India regarding nationalization of foreign-owned companies have varied. Several major oil companies have been nationalized. For example, Indian Oil Corporation, Bharat Petroleum, and Hindustan Petroleum used to be, respectively, Burmah Shell, Mobil, and Stanvae (Standard Vacuum Oil Company, an Esso unit). More typically, a multinational company is asked to reduce its holdings to 49 percent or less by offering shares to the Indian public and Indian financial institutions. Multinationals that have diluted equity to meet the 49 percent requirement include CIBA-GEIGY, Parke-Davis, Bayer (aspirin), Lever Brothers (which operates as Hindustan Lever in India), Lipton, and Brooke-Bond.

---

ducts. Ponds and pits are used for waste treatment and several railway spur lines run through the plant. Exhibit 3 is a diagram of the factory and Exhibit 4 is a schematic of the MIC process. The plant was designed and supplied by Union Carbide Corporation, which sent engineers to India to supervise construction.

Sevin is made through a controlled chemical reaction involving alpha-naphthol and MIC. Alpha-naphthol is a brownish granular material and MIC is a highly reactive liquid that boils and becomes a gas at usual daytime temperatures. When plans were first made to begin production of alpha-naphthol at Bhopal in 1971, a pilot plant was set up to manufacture the product. Because the pilot plant was successful, a full-sized alpha-naphthol plant (in fact, the world's largest) was constructed and placed in operation in 1977.

In the meantime, work had begun on the ill-fated MIC plant. But even before the MIC plant was completed in 1979, problems began to crop up with the alpha-naphthol plant, resulting in a shutdown for modifications in 1978. In February 1980, the MIC plant was placed into service. The alpha-naphthol plant continued in various stages of shutdown and partial operation

EXHIBIT 3   **Union Carbide (India), Ltd.: Pesticide Plant at Bhopal**

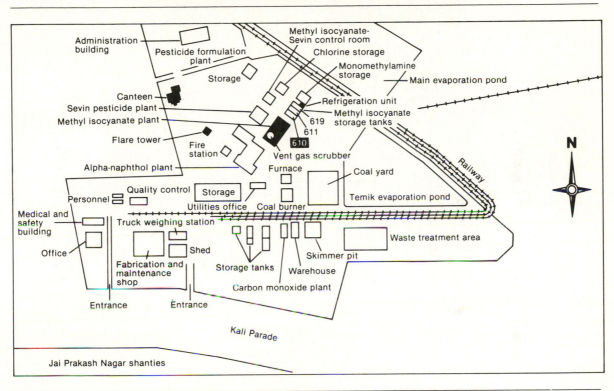

Notes: MIC Tank 610 is tank that leaked.
Major discharge occurred above vent gas scrubber 120 feet high.
Wind was variable, three to seven miles per hour in a southeasterly direction when leak occurred.

through 1984. Mr. V. P. Gokhale, managing director of UCIL, called the alpha-naphthol plant a "very large mistake." But he said the company was forced to build it to keep its operating license from the Indian government. The Bhopal factory was designed to produce 5,000 tons per year of Sevin, but it never operated near capacity. UCIL has generally been the third-largest producer of pesticides in India, sometimes slipping to number four.

FINANCE   Exhibits 5, 6, 7, and 8 provide financial facts and figures for UCIL. As mentioned earlier, Union Carbide Corporation (USA) holds 50.9 percent of UCIL's common shares. The remainder are publicly traded on major Indian stock exchanges. Most of these shares are held by about 24,000 individuals.

EXHIBIT 4   **The MIC Manufacturing Process**

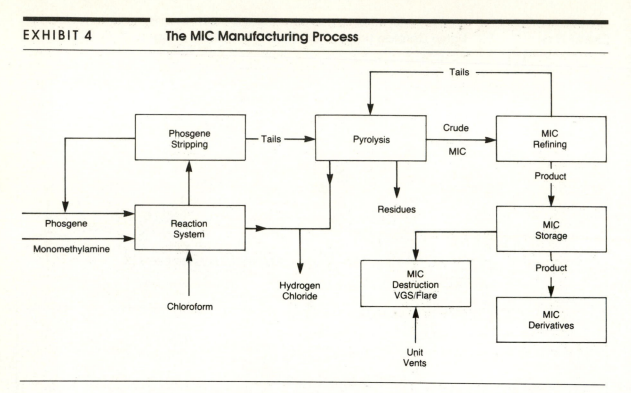

However, several institutional investors own substantial blocks. The Indian government does not directly own any UCIL stock, although the Life Insurance Corporation of India, the country's largest insurer and owner of many UCIL shares, is owned by the Indian government. During the months before the Bhopal disaster, UCIL's common shares hovered around Rs. 30 but dropped to a low of Rs. 15.8 on December 11, recovering only slightly in succeeding weeks.

In 1975, the United States Export-Import Bank in cooperation with First National Citibank of New York agreed to grant loans of $2.5 million to buy equipment for the MIC project. Also, the Industrial Credit and Investment Corporation of India (ICICI) authorized a Rs. 21.5 million loan, part of which was drawn in 1980. Finally, long-term loans were provided by several Indian financial institutions and insurance companies. Some of these loans were guaranteed by the State Bank of India.

Profits of several million dollars from the Bhopal facility were originally predicted for 1984. Several factors kept these expectations from being realized. First, an economic recession made farmers more cost conscious and

EXHIBIT 5 — **Summary of Income Statements (Rupee Amounts in Thousands Except Per Share Data)**

	1983	1982	1981	1980	1979
Net sales	2,100,682	2,075,282	1,854,214	1,615,926	1,449,664
Cost of goods sold	1,733,999	1,720,303	1,518,538	1,307,042	1,190,242
Operating expenses	138,509	136,834	115,550	103,318	83,501
Profit from operations	228,174	218,145	220,126	205,566	175,921
Other income	24,684	27,426	26,955	23,528	13,685
Profit from operations plus other income	252,858	245,571	247,081	229,094	189,606
Interest expense	57,529	57,082	30,950	31,468	19,871
Depreciation expense	47,579	41,614	40,913	36,524	32,016
Earnings before taxes	147,750	146,875	175,218	161,102	137,719
Provisions for taxes	54,520	50,200	80,300	80,000	73,000
Net earnings	93,230	96,675	94,918	81,102	64,719
Earnings per share	2.86	2.95	2.91	2.49	2.98
Earnings as percent of price	11.31	11.73	10.96	10.20	11.46
Cash dividends per share	1.50	1.50	1.50	1.40	1.60

Average conversion rate for 1978–82, $1 = Rs. 9.00; for 1985, $1 = Rs. 12.50.
Note: The conversion rate was fairly stable from 1978 to 1982 at about $1 = Rs 9.00. From 1983 to 1985 the rupee weakened steadily. In mid-1985, the conversion rate was about $1 = Rs. 12.50. Within the country, inflation from 1978 to 1984 proceeded at rates of about 2 percentage points below the corresponding U.S. rates.

caused them to search for less expensive alternatives to Sevin. Second, a large number of small-scale producers were able to undersell the company, partly because they were exempt from excise and sales taxes. Seventeen of these firms bought MIC from UCIL and used it to make products virtually identical to Sevin and Temik. Finally, a new generation of low-cost pesticides was becoming available. With sales collapsing, the Bhopal plant became a money loser in 1981. By late 1984, the profit estimate for that year had been adjusted downward to a $4 million *loss* based on 1,000 tons of output, one-fifth of capacity.

To forestall what may have seemed inevitable economic failure, extensive cost-cutting efforts were carried out. The staff at the MIC plant was cut from twelve operators on a shift to six. The maintenance team was reduced in size. In several instances, faulty safety devices remained unrepaired for weeks. Because a refrigeration unit designed to keep the methyl isocyanate cool continued to malfunction, it was shut down. Though instrumentation technology advanced at Union Carbide's other pesticide plants, the innovations were only partly adopted at Bhopal.

EXHIBIT 6

Summary of Balance Sheets December 25, Respective Years (Rupee Amounts in Thousands)

	1983*	1982	1981	1980	1979
ASSETS					
Current assets:					
Cash	58,234	52,285	52,173	56,589	53,026
Receivables	410,000	375,672	244,158	169,015	121,718
Inventories	369,172	327,317	368,606	311,612	292,935
Other current assets	6,000	6,088	9,230	9,277	11,237
Total current assets	843,406	761,362	674,167	546,493	478,916
Net fixed assets	465,806	449,546	393,516	405,890	401,422
Miscellaneous assets	21	21	21	57	57
Intangible assets	3,000	3,000	3,000	3,000	3,000
Total assets	1,312,233	1,213,929	1,070,704	955,440	883,395
LIABILITIES AND OWNERS' EQUITY					
Current Liabilities:					
Accounts payable and accruals	590,667	530,641	390,990	341,956	320,942
Provision for taxes	51,839	57,739	63,266	60,216	49,000
Total current debt	642,506	588,380	454,256	402,172	369,942
Long-term liabilities:					
Debentures	30,000	29,340	54,823	31,315	20,300
Long-term loans	20,000	20,836	34,049	40,420	46,306
Total long-term debt	50,000	50,176	88,872	71,735	66,606
Stockholders' equity:					
Common stock	325,830	325,830	325,830	325,830	217,220
Retained earnings and surplus	293,897	249,543	201,746	155,703	229,627
Total owners' equity	619,727	575,373	527,576	481,533	446,847
Total liabilities and owners' equity		1,213,929	1,070,704	955,440	883,395

*Due to an apparent change in accounting procedure, some 1983 amounts could not be determined from available reports and have been estimated.

PERSONNEL

Until 1982, a cadre of U.S. managers and technicians worked at the Bhopal plant. The Americans were licensed by the Indian government only for fixed periods. While in India they were expected to train Indian replacements. From 1982 onward, no U.S. citizen worked at Bhopal. Whereas major decisions such as approval of the annual budget were cleared with Union Car-

EXHIBIT 7   **Summary of Common Stock Issues**

	PAID-UP COMMON STOCK			
YEAR	NUMBER OF SHARES	PAID-UP PER SHARE (RS.)	TOTAL AMOUNT (RS.)	REMARKS
1959–1960	2,800,000	10	28,000,000	800,000 right shares issued premium Rs. 2.50 per share in the proportion 2:5.
1964	3,640,000	10	36,400,000	840,000 right shares issued at a premium of Rs. 4 per share in the proportion 3:10.
1965	4,095,000	10	40,950,000	455,000 bonus shares issued in the proportion 1:8.
1968	8,190,000	10	81,900,000	2,047,500 right shares issued at par in proportion 1:2. 2,047,500 bonus shares issued in the proportion 1:2.
1970	12,285,000	10	122,850,000	4,095,000 bonus shares issued in the proportion 1:2.
1974	18,427,500	10	184,275,000	6,142,500 bonus shares issued in the proportion 1:2.
1978	21,722,000	10	217,220,000	3,294,500 shares issued at a premium of Rs. 6 per share to resident Indian shareholders, the company's employees, and financial institutions.
1980	32,583,000	10	325,830,000	10,861,000 bonus shares issued in the proportion 1:2.

bide (USA), day-to-day details such as staffing and maintenance were left to the Indian officials.

In general, the engineers at the Bhopal plant were among India's elite. Most new engineers were recruited from the prestigious Indian Institutes of Technology and paid wages comparable with the best offered in Indian

EXHIBIT 8   **Financial Charts**

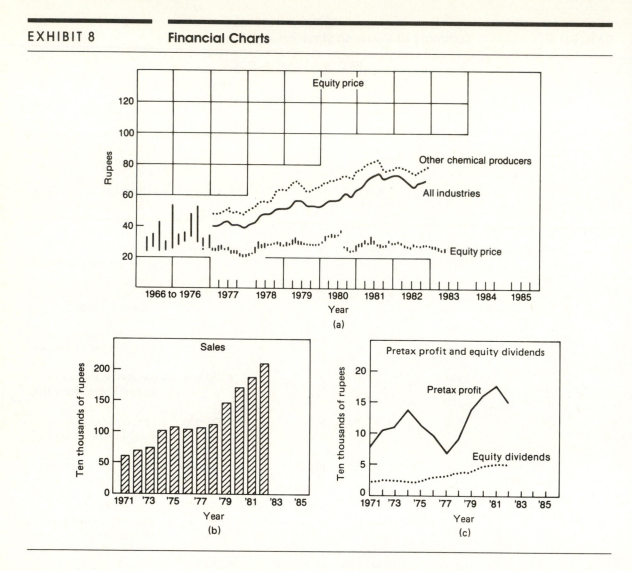

industry. Successful applicants for engineering jobs with UCIL were provided two years of training before being certified for unsupervised duty.

Until the late seventies, only first-class science graduates or persons with diplomas in engineering were employed as operators at Bhopal. New hires were given six months of theoretical instruction followed by on-the-job training. As cost-cutting efforts proceeded in the eighties, standards were lowered significantly. Some operators with only a high school diploma were employed, and training was much less rigorous than before. In addition, the number of operators on a shift was reduced by about half and many supervisory positions were eliminated.

The Indian managers developed strong ties with the local political establishment. A former police chief became the plant's security contractor and a local political party boss got the job as company lawyer. *Newsweek* reports that a luxurious guest house was maintained and lavish parties thrown there for local dignitaries.

In general, wages at the Bhopal plant were well above those available in domestic firms. A janitor, for example, earned Rs. 1,000 per month compared with less than Rs. 500 elsewhere. Still, as prospects continued downward after 1981, several senior managers and the best among the plant's junior executives began to abandon ship. The total work force at the plant dropped from a high of about 1,500 to 950. This reduction was accomplished through voluntary departures rather than layoffs. An Indian familiar with operations at Bhopal said, "The really competent and well-trained employees, especially managers and supervisors, got sick of the falling standards and indifferent management and many of them quit despite high salaries at UCIL. Replacements were made on an ad hoc basis. Even guys from the consumer products division, who only knew how to make batteries, were drafted to run the pesticide plant."

MARKETING

The population of India is over 700 million people, whereas its land area is only about one-third that of the United States. Three-fourths of India's people depend on agriculture for a livelihood. Fewer than one-third are literate. Modern communications and transportation facilities connect the major cities, but the hundreds of villages are largely untouched by twentieth-century technology. English tends to be at least a second language for most Indian professionals but not for ordinary Indians. There are sixteen officially recognized languages in the country. The national language is Hindi, which is dominant in five of India's 22 states. The working classes speak hundreds of dialects, one group often unintelligible to another who lives just miles away.

India's farmers offer at best a challenging target market. They generally eke out a living from small tracts of land. Most have little more than subsistence incomes and are reluctant to invest what they have in such modern innovations as pesticides. They are generally ignorant of the right methods of application and, given their linguistic diversity and technological isolation, are quite hard to educate. To advertise its products, UCIL has used billboards and wall posters as well as newspaper and radio ads.

Radio is the most widely used advertising medium in India. The state-owned radio system includes broadcasts in local languages. Companies can buy advertising time on the stations but it is costly to produce commercials in so many dialects. Much of the state-sponsored programming, especially in rural areas, is devoted to promoting agriculture and instructing farmers about new techniques. Often the narrators mention products such as Sevin and Temik by name.

Movies provide another popular promotional tool. Most small towns have one or more cinema houses, and rural people often travel to town to watch the shows. Advertisements appear before and after main features and are usually produced in regional languages (though not in local dialects).

Until recently, television was available only in the cities. During 1984, a government program spread television relay stations at the rate of more than one each day, with the result that 80 percent of the population was within the range of a television transmitter by the end of the year. Still, few rural citizens had access to television receivers.

Pesticide sales are highly dependent on agricultural activity from year to year. In years of drought, such as 1980 and 1982, UCIL's pesticide sales have suffered severe setbacks. In 1981, abundant rains helped spur pesticide sales.

EXHIBIT 9   **Map of India**

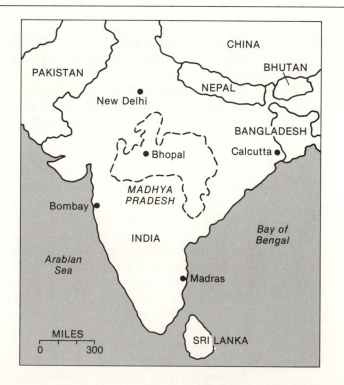

Exhibit 9 is a map of India. India has a very extensive network of railways. The total track mileage in India is second only to the USSR. The road and highway system crisscrosses the areas in between railway lines. The railway system was especially significant to UCIL's pesticide operation because Bhopal lies near the junction of the main east-west and north-south tracks in India. Bhopal is also just south of the vast Indo-Gangetic plain, the richest farming area in India. An Indian familiar with the agricultural economy remarked, "Overall, physical distribution of pesticides is not too monumental a task. Getting farmers to use them and teaching them how are the real problems."

The marketing division for agricultural products was headquartered in Hyderabad. Under the headquarters were eight branch offices scattered all over the country. Sales were through a network of distributors, wholesalers, and retailers. Sales representatives from the branch offices booked orders from the distributors and wholesalers. Retailers got their requirements from wholesalers, who, in turn, were supplied by distributors. The distributors got their stocks from the branch offices. The branch office "godowns" (warehouses) were supplied directly from the Bhopal plant. The retailers' margin was 15 percent. Wholesalers and distributors each received about 5 percent. Most of the retailers were family or individually owned, although some of UCIL's pesticides were sold through government agricultural sales offices.

EVENTS OF 1985

In early 1985, the government of India canceled the operating license of the Bhopal plant, clearing the way for the plant's dismantlement. The likelihood that this would happen provoked a Bhopal political leader to remark, "We've lost two thousand lives, now must we lose two thousand jobs?"

Manslaughter and other charges were filed against UCIL executives. Union Carbide Corporation Chairman Warren Anderson had been briefly detained by Indian officials when he went to India shortly after the incident. Still, both companies continued for months to enjoy good relations with the Indian government. This may have been true in part because many leading Indian citizens and institutions have a financial interest in UCIL. And, except for the Bhopal incident, Union Carbide had an excellent safety record in India.

Warren Anderson said, "The name of the game is not to nail me to the wall but to provide for the victims of the disaster." He said he expected to be mainly concerned with the incident for the rest of his working life. In keeping with these ideas, Union Carbide Corporation helped provide funding for a hospital to treat the Bhopal victims. The company also contributed at least $2 million to a victim-relief fund and offered to build a new plant, one that would use nontoxic inputs, on the Bhopal site.

Within months after the incident, Union Carbide (USA) faced lawsuits in amounts far exceeding the company's net worth. That company's stock dropped from its mid-50s trading range to the low 30s. A dozen or more U.S. attorneys signed up thousands of Bhopal victims and relatives of victims and filed suits in the United States purporting to represent them. The attorney general of India was authorized to sue Union Carbide in a U.S. court. He stated that compensation had to be in accordance with U.S. standards. A Minneapolis law firm that specializes in product liability cases was retained to represent India.

By March 1985, the streets of Bhopal were bustling again. There were cars, cattle, and crowds of people. But everywhere there were reminders of the disaster. Many wore dark glasses and covered their faces with shrouds to protect their injured eyes from the sunlight or to keep others from seeing their blindness. At the city's main police station, women and children continued to seek help. Vegetables shriveled by the poison gas were putting forth green shoots here and there. Occasionally, someone still fell sick from eating fish contaminated by MIC.

In the modernistic masonry-and-glass headquarters in Danbury, Connecticut, Union Carbide officials looked out on the beautiful Connecticut countryside and wondered how best to manage the company's public affairs and how to grapple with the needs in India. Half a world away, in spatial as well as philosophical distance, the poor of Jai Prakash Nagar, now poorer than ever, peered out from their shanties on dusty streets and pondered quite different questions: From where would tomorrow's food come? How long would the pain inside and the dimming of vision last? And, just as importantly, what source of wealth would replace the pesticide plant? And how long would it be before its effects were felt?

In late June 1985, a lawsuit consolidating about 100 claims was filed in the United States by famed attorney F. Lee Bailey and his associates. The Indian government continued to press its lawsuit and to engage in out-of-court negotiations with Union Carbide. As the lawsuits in the United States moved forward, the legal issues involved became clearer: (1) Should the cases be tried in U.S. courts or in Indian courts? Both legal systems are based on English common law, but punitive damages are almost unheard of in Indian courts and compensatory damage awards are much lower than in the United States. (2) Should settlements be based on U.S. standards simply because Union Carbide, the 51 percent parent of UCIL, is a U.S. company, or on the much lower standards in India? (3) Who is responsible for the incident—Union Carbide, the Indian managers at Bhopal, the mostly Indian board of directors of UCIL, or the Indian government? (4) Which victims should be represented by the Indian government and which by the U.S. attorneys who went to India after the incident and signed up clients? (5) Did Union Carbide fail to properly warn the Indian managers at UCIL of the dangers posed by MIC? (6) Did Union Carbide fail to ensure that appropriate safety equipment was installed at the Bhopal facility?

Negotiations between Union Carbide and Asoke K. Sen, the Indian law minister, seemed to have broken down in June 1985. Union Carbide had made a $230 million offer, with payment to be spread over twenty years. Mr. Sen said the offer was worth only $100 million in current terms and continued, "Union Carbide's offer is based on a total lack of appreciation of the magnitude of the problem, so is hardly worth consideration." He said that doctors have treated 200,000 Indians injured by the gas leak and that the government must build 15,000 housing units and a 100-bed hospital to care for the most seriously ill.

On the other hand, a Union Carbide spokesperson said that $100 million could "pay the heirs of each dead person 100 years' annual income . . . and the seriously injured 20 years' annual income," with funds left over. The U.S. district judge under whom the Indian court cases were consolidated requested that Union Carbide pay $5 million in emergency aid, but that was rejected by the Indian officials. Mr. Sen said that India has already spent several times more than that on relief and that $5 million would not serve a critical need.

As Union Carbide (USA) struggled to recover from the disaster and restore its favorable public image, four events thrust the company back to the forefront of national and international news coverage. In June 1985, hundreds of people were poisoned by California watermelons grown on soil to which the Union Carbide pesticide Temik had been improperly applied. In August a leak of the chemical intermediate aldecarb oxime at the company's Institute, West Virginia, plant, the only U.S. facility to make MIC, sent 135 people to hospitals. A few days later another accidental discharge of chemicals at a Union Carbide plant just miles from the Institute facility caused a public health scare. Finally, a group of investors headed by corporate takeover specialist Carl Icahn increased their holdings of Union Carbide stock and were rumored to be seeking control of the corporation. Even though West Virginia Governor Arch Moore publicly criticized Union Carbide's handling of the aldecarb oxime leak and CEO Warren Anderson admitted that the company had waited too long to warn residents, Union Carbide stock moved above $50.00 a share for the first time since the Bhopal incident.

BIBLIOGRAPHY

"Bhopal." *Chemical and Engineering News*, February 11, 1985, pp. 3, 14–65.

"The Bhopal Disaster" (and other related articles). *The New York Times*, January 28, 30, 31, February 3, 1985.

"Carbide's Anderson Explains Post-Bhopal Strategy." *Chemical and Engineering News*, January 21, 1985, pp. 9–15.

"City of Death" (and other related articles). *India Today*, December 31, 1984, pp. 4–25.

"Gassed." *The Week*, December 16, 1984, pp. 15–27.

"India's Night of Death" (and other related articles). *Time*, December 17, 1984, pp. 22–31.

"It Was Like Breathing Fire . . ." *Newsweek*, December 17, 1984, pp. 26–32.

The Stock Exchange Foundation, Bombay, India. *The Stock Exchange Official Directory*, Vol. XVII/29, July 18, 1983.

"Union Carbide Fights for Its Life." *Business Week*, December 24, 1984, pp. 52–57.

"Whose Life Is It Anyway?" (and other related articles). *The Illustrated Weekly of India*, December 30, 1984, pp. 6–17.

A number of articles from *The New York Times, Wall Street Journal, India Abroad,* and the Indian newspapers *The Indian Express, The Financial Express, The Times of India, The Economic Times*, and *The Hindustan Times*.

Manville Corporation (1989)

ARTHUR SHARPLIN

Perhaps no other mineral is so woven into the fabric of American life as is asbestos. Impervious to heat and fibrous—it is the only mineral that can be woven into cloth—asbestos is spun into fireproof clothing and theater curtains, as well as into such household items as noncombustible drapes, rugs, pot holders, and ironing board covers. Mixed into slurry, asbestos is sprayed onto girders and walls to provide new buildings with fireproof insulation. It is used in floor tiles, roofing felts, and in most plasterboards and wallboards. Asbestos is also an ingredient of plaster and stucco and of many paints and putties. This "mineral of a thousand uses"—an obsolete nickname: the present count stands at around 3,000 uses—is probably present in some form or other in every home, school, office building, and factory in this country. Used in brake linings and clutch facings, in mufflers and gaskets, in sealants and caulking, and extensively used in ships, asbestos is also a component of every modern vehicle, including spaceships.[1]

The above was written by columnist Bruce Porter in 1973, just as the dangers of breathing asbestos dust were becoming widely recognized by those outside the asbestos industry. From about the turn of the century, Johns-Manville Corporation (renamed Manville Corporation in 1981) was the world's leading asbestos company, involved in the mining and sale of the raw fibers as well as development, manufacture, and marketing of intermediate and finished asbestos products. Personal injuries to Manville employees caused by exposure to asbestos resulted in lawsuits against the company beginning in the 1920s. Thousands of lawsuits would later be filed by insulation workers and others who installed or were otherwise exposed to Manville asbestos.

Beginning in about 1970, Manville tried to diversify out of the asbestos business. But loss of asbestos profits, a construction industry recession, and a crush of asbestos lawsuits propelled Manville toward economic disaster as the 1980s began. Late on the evening of August 25, 1982, the Manville board of directors, after a briefing on bankruptcy reorganization and upon the recommendation of three senior outside directors who had been studying the issue, voted to file a petition for protection from creditors under Chapter 11 of the U.S. Bankruptcy Code. The petition was filed the next day. It would be more than four years before a plan to emerge from court protection would be offered for approval by creditors and stockholders. Even then, opposition by stockholders' representatives and the need to settle major constitutional issues raised by the plan would stand in the way of payments to asbestos victims and other creditors.

This case was prepared by Arthur Sharplin, Distinguished Professor of Management, McNeese University, Lake Charles, La. Reprinted with permission.

COMPANY BACKGROUND

Until the seventies, Manville was successful according to the usual standards. The company had seen consistent growth in sales and profits. Dividends had been paid every year except the war years of 1915–1916 and the depths of the Depression, 1933–1934. The company was one of the "Dow Jones Industrial Thirty" for many years.

In the decades before 1970, Manville's sales had grown somewhat slower than the U.S. gross national product. But the company had benefited from relatively low fixed costs, due to a largely depleted and depreciated capital base and the total absence of long-term debt in the capital structure. With low operating and financial leverage, the firm had been able to adapt to sales downturns in 1957, 1960, 1967, and 1970 and still earn profits in each of those years. By 1970, Manville had over $400 million in book value net worth garnered almost entirely from the mining, manufacture, and sale of asbestos products, for which it held a dominant market position.

During the 1960s, several of the senior officials who had been with the company since the 1930s died or retired. Compared with the 1966 board of directors, the 1970 board had a majority of new members. In 1970, departing from a tradition of promoting from within, the company installed an outsider, psychologist Richard Goodwin, as president. Goodwin had worked as a management consultant to Manville for a time before his appointment as president. He immediately set about changing Manville's image. Corporate headquarters were moved from Manville's old Madison Avenue brick building to Denver. The company purchased a 10,000-acre ranch outside Denver as site for its luxurious world headquarters, the first phase of which was to cost $60 million.

Goodwin led the company through more than twenty small acquisitions—in lighting systems, golf carts, irrigation sprinklers, and other products. In the process, Manville's long-term debt went from zero to $196 million and fixed costs increased severalfold. A short, steep recession in 1975 cut Manville's profits in half, back to 1970 levels. U.S. asbestos sales had begun a rapid decline, which was to accelerate and total more than 50 percent in just five years. During the same period the company was suffering reverses in its fight against asbestos tort lawsuits.

In what *Fortune* magazine called "The Shootout at the J. M. Corral," Goodwin was removed in September 1976, and John A. McKinney, Manville's legal/public affairs chief—who had joined the company before 1950—took over as chief executive. McKinney divested many of the Goodwin acquisitions and turned his attention to what he called "aggressive defense" of the asbestos lawsuits and the search for a "substantial acquisition." He also made plans for a $200 million expansion in the company's fiberglass operations. In his 1977 "President's Review," McKinney wrote, "[W]e do not expect asbestos fiber to dominate J-M earnings to the extent it has in the past." (In 1976, asbestos fiber alone—not including manufactured asbestos products—provided about half of Manville's operating profit, though it constituted only about one eighth of sales.)

Ideal Basic Industries, a major producer of potash and portland cement, spurned a Manville buyout initiative in 1978. (The chief executive of Ideal Basic Industries, John A. Love, was a Manville director.) Then Manville began a takeover battle (with Texas Eastern Corporation) for Olinkraft Corporation, a wood-products company concentrated in paperboard and paper. Olinkraft's main assets were about 600,000 acres of prime southern timberland and several paper mills.

Manville won the battle and closed the deal in the last half of 1978. The purchase price was $595 million, half paid in cash. The other half was represented by a new issue of 8.3 percent preferred stock with a requirement for repurchase by the company beginning in 1987. The total price was 2.24 times Olinkraft's book value and over twice its recent market value. While the Olinkraft merger was being negotiated, Manville common stock declined in value to $22.00, a total drop of over $225 million. Olinkraft's shares rose to approximately the purchase price of $65 a share. In conformity with purchase method accounting, Olinkraft's assets were placed on Manville's books at the purchase price, creating over $300 million in new net worth.

THE 1980s

Manville's sales and common stock earnings reached peaks of $2.92 billion and $144 million (expressed in constant 1981 dollars), respectively, in 1978. But both fell steadily afterward, to $1.64 billion and a $101 million *loss* in 1982.

In 1981, management reorganized the company, separating the asbestos operations into incorporated divisions. Also, the executives created special termination agreements, providing for large severance settlements after any change in control of the company. The company also reaffirmed its commitment to indemnify its executives and directors against the asbestos lawsuits.

Although Manville was able to defer the asbestos health costs (payments totaled only $12 million in 1981) and extract more than $100 million in cash flows from the Olinkraft assets, the situation in early 1982 was worsening. Company debt had been downgraded. Coopers and Lybrand, the company's accounting firm, had qualified its opinion on Manville's financial reports. Manville's insurance carriers had stopped paying asbestos settlements and providing defense against the asbestos lawsuits. At the same time, the number and size of the asbestos health judgments were skyrocketing (although the large awards were all stayed by appeals). Many suits named Manville officials in their personal capacities. And after 1980, several juries awarded punitive damages, over $1 million per claimant in some cases, in addition to compensatory damages.

The five highest-paid executives of Manville in 1982 had all been with the company since at least 1952. The 1982 board of directors had the same membership as the 1976 board and was mostly unchanged since the 1960s. One of the five long-tenured executives left just before the Chapter 11 filing and others left afterward, generally with severance pay and pensions. For example, on August 1, 1986, John A. McKinney retired with $1.3 million in severance pay and retirement pay exceeding $300,000 per year. His salary increased from $408,750 to $638,005 per year while Manville was in Chapter 11.

Financial summaries are shown in Exhibits 1, 2, and 3 (1978 until August 26, 1986) and Exhibits 4, 5, and 6 (after August 26, 1986). Exhibit 7 shows how Manville Corporation's common share price varied from 1978 through mid-1986.

THE ASBESTOS TORT LAWSUITS

Beginning in the 1920s a steadily increasing number of lawsuits were filed on behalf of Manville employees who had fallen ill or died from breathing asbestos dust (made up of microscopic fibers released as the product is mined or otherwise handled—or through normal deterioration as asbestos-containing buildings and machines vibrate and as asbestos tiles, roof cover-

EXHIBIT 1   **Manville Corporation Income Statements before August 26, 1982 (Dollar Amounts in Millions)***

	1982–6 MOS.	1981	1980	1979	1978
Revenue	$949	$2,186	$2,267	$2,276	$1,649
Cost of sales	784	1,731	1,771	1,747	1,190
Selling, G & A exp.†	143	271	263	239	193
R & D and eng. exp.	16	34	35	31	33
Operating income	6	151	197	259	232
Other income, net	1	35	26	21	28
Interest expense	35	73	65	62	22
Income before taxes	(28)	112	157	218	238
Income taxes	2	53	77	103	116
Net income	(25)	60	81	115	122
Div. on preferred stock	12	25	25	24	0
Net income for common stock	$ (37)	$ 35	$ 55	$ 91	$ 122

*Totals may not check due to rounding.
†Includes asbestos health costs of $12 million for 1981.

EXHIBIT 2

Manville Corporation Statement of Revenues and Income from Operations by Business Segment Before August 26, 1982 (Dollar Amounts in Millions)*

	1981	1980	1979	1978	1977	1976
REVENUES						
Fiberglass products	$ 625	$ 610	$ 573	$ 514	$ 407	$ 358
Forest products	555	508	497	0	0	0
Nonfiberglass insulation	258	279	268	231	195	159
Roofing products	209	250	273	254	204	171
Pipe products and systems	199	220	305	303	274	218
Asbestos fiber	138	159	168	157	161	155
Industrial and special products	320	341	309	291	301	309
Corporate revenues, net	12	9	11	20	12	(22)
Intersegment sales	(95)	(84)	(106)	(94)	(74)	(56)
Total	$2,221	$2,292	$2,297	$1,677	$1,480	$1,291
INCOME FROM OPERATIONS						
Fiberglass products	$ 90	$ 91	$ 96	$ 107	$ 82	$ 60
Forest products	39	37	50	0	0	0
Nonfiberglass insulation	20	27	27	35	28	18
Roofing products	(17)	9	14	23	14	8
Pipe products and systems	0	(5)	18	26	24	(3)
Asbestos fiber	37	35	56	55	60	60
Industrial and special products	50	55	43	36	25	19
Corporate expense, net	(23)	(38)	(23)	(23)	(24)	(49)
Eliminations and adjustments	3	11	(2)	1	3	2
Total	$ 198	$ 223	$ 280	$ 260	$ 212	$ 116

*Totals may not check, due to rounding.

ings, brake linings, water pipes, and so forth, are eroded or abraded). By 1982 there was litigation pending against the company on behalf of over 16,000 persons, who generally claimed that their injuries (mostly asbestosis—see the box on page 679) had resulted from Manville's failure to warn users of asbestos coupled with active suppression and manipulation of research and publicity about asbestos dangers. An average of 425 cases was being filed each month in the first half of 1982 and the company's projections

EXHIBIT 3

**Manville Corporation Balance Sheets
(Dollar Amounts in Millions)***

	JUNE 30	DECEMBER 31			
	1982	1981	1980	1979	1978
ASSETS					
Current assets					
Cash	$ 10	$ 14	$ 20	$ 19	$ 28
Marketable securities	17	12	12	10	38
Accounts and notes receivable	348	327	350	362	328
Inventories	182	211	217	229	219
Prepaid expenses	19	19	20	31	32
Total current assets	$ 576	$ 583	$ 619	$ 650	$ 645
Property, plant, and equipment					
Land and land improvements		119	118	114	99
Buildings		363	357	352	321
Machinery and equipment		1,202	1,204	1,161	1,043
Less accum. depreciation and depletion		(525)	(484)	(430)	(374)
Net property, plant, and equipment		$1,160	$1,195	$1,197	$1,088
Timber and timberland, net		406	407	368	372
Net fixed assets	$1,523	$1,566	$1,602	$1,565	$1,460
Other assets	148	149	117	110	113
	$2,247	$2,298	$2,338	$2,324	$2,217
LIABILITIES					
Short-term debt	$	$ 29	$ 22	$ 32	$ 23
Accounts payable	191	120	126	143	114
Employee compensation and benefits		77	80	54	45
Income taxes		30	22	51	84
Other liabilities	149	58	61	50	63
Total current liabilities	$ 340	$ 316	$ 310	$ 329	$ 329
Long-term debt	499	508	519	532	543
Other noncurrent liabilities	93	86	75	73	60
Deferred income taxes	186	185	211	195	150
Total liabilities	$1,116	$1,095	$1,116	$1,129	$1,083
STOCKHOLDERS' EQUITY					
Preferred	$ 301	$ 301	$ 301	$ 299	$ 299
Common	60	59	58	208	197
Capital in excess of par	178	174	164	0	0
Retained earnings	642	695	705	692	643
Cum. currency transl. adj.	(47)	(22)	0	0	0
Less: cost of treasury stock	(3)	(3)	(4)	(4)	(6)
Total stockholders' equity	$1,131	$1,203	$1,222	$1,196	$1,134
	$2,247	$2,298	$2,338	$2,324	$2,217

*Totals may not check, due to rounding.

EXHIBIT 4

**Manville Corporation Income Statements after August 26, 1982
(Dollar Amounts in Millions)***

	1985	1984	1983	1982
Revenue	1,942	1,873	1,791	1,806
Cost of sales	1,473	1,400	1,370	1,391
Selling, G&A expenses	246	238	224	222
R&D and engineering expenses	35	36	35	29
Operating income	188	200	161	163
Gain on disp. of assets	151	0	(3)	110
Asbestos health costs	52	26	20	16
Interest expense	23	21	26	52
Chapter 11 costs	9	17	18	2
Income from cont. oper. before taxes	(47)	135	100	(56)
Income taxes	(2)	58	40	32
Net income from continued operations	(45)	77	60	(88)
Net income from discontinued operations	0	0	7	(10)
Net income	$ (45)	$ 77	$ 67	$ (98)

*Totals may not check, due to rounding.

EXHIBIT 5

**Manville Corporation Statement of Revenues and Income from
Operations by Business Segment after August 26, 1982
(Dollar Amounts in Millions)***

	1985	1984	1983	1982
REVENUES				
Fiberglass products	$ 803	$ 781	$ 718	$ 609
Forest products	459	451	415	436
Specialty products	674	645	683	829
Corporate revenues, net	43	38	36	15
Intersegment sales	(37)	(42)	(61)	(82)
Total	$1,942	$1,873	$1,791	$1,806
INCOME FROM OPERATIONS				
Fiberglass products	$ 106	$ 115	$ 97	$ 75
Forest products	43	63	52	48
Specialty products	33	28	19	51
Corporate expense, net	(1)	(6)	(6)	(18)
Eliminations and adjustments	7	0	0	7
	$ 188	$ 200	$ 161	$ 164

*Totals may not check, due to rounding.

EXHIBIT 6

Manville Corporation Balance Sheets
(Dollar Amounts in Millions)*

| | DECEMBER 31 | | | |
	1985	1984	1983	1982
ASSETS				
Current assets				
Cash	$ 7	$ 9	$ 19	$ 12
Marketable securities, at cost	314	276	240	206
Accounts and notes receivable	314	285	277	311
Inventories	153	164	141	152
Prepaid expenses	29	17	22	17
Total current assets	817	752	700	696
Property, plant, and equipment				
Land and land improvements	95	96	97	108
Buildings	299	308	303	332
Machinery and equipment	1,160	1,121	1,056	1,090
Less accum. depr. and depl.	(538)	(513)	(472)	(547)
Net prop., plant, and equip.	1,017	1,013	984	983
Timber and timberland, net	385	392	395	402
Net fixed assets	1,402	1,505	1,379	1,385
Other assets	174	182	174	154
	$2,393	$2,339	$2,253	$2,236
LIABILITIES AND STOCKHOLDERS' EQUITY				
Short-term debt	$ 26	$ 20	$ 94	$ 12
Accounts payable	84	102	65	86
Accrued employee comp. and benefits	94	81	14	63
Accrued income taxes	12	18	10	32
Other accrued liabilities	69	35	26	29
Total current liabilities	286	256	209	221
Long-term debt	92	84	713	736
Liab. subj. to Chap. 11 proceedings	578	574	4	12
Other noncurrent liabilities	115	67	61	60
Deferred income taxes	144	162	136	140
Total liabilities	1,214	1,142	1,122	1,170
Preferred stock	$ 301	$ 301	$ 301	$ 301
Common stock	60	60	60	60
Capital in excess of par	178	178	178	178
Retained earnings	667	713	635	568
Cum. curr. transl. adj.	(26)	(53)	(41)	(39)
Cost of treasury stock	(2)	(2)	(2)	(2)
Total stockholders' equity	878	896	831	765
	$2,393	$2,339	$2,253	$2,236

*Totals may not check, due to rounding.

EXHIBIT 7

Manville Corporation Monthly Common Stock Trading Range, 1976–1986

were for over 32,000 new cases by the year 2001. Appendix A provides a chronology of selected events related to the asbestos lawsuits.

Asbestos Diseases

Ingested asbestos causes mechanical injury to moving tissue, especially the lungs. The microscopic fibers are impervious to bodily fluids and oxygen and are almost impossible to filter out of air. The constant motion of the lungs causes tissue to be penetrated and cut by the fibers. This leads to progressive and irreversible scarring, thickening, and calcification of the lungs and their linings, a condition called *asbestosis*. A rare and always fatal cancer, mesothelioma, is strongly connected with asbestos exposure as are increased incidence and severity of many other respiratory ailments. The first outward symptoms of asbestos disease typically appear ten to thirty years after exposure begins. But early damage is easily detectable by X rays, and some cancers and respiratory deficiencies show up in a small percentage of exposed persons after only a year or two.

THE BANKRUPTCY REORGANIZATION

As mentioned earlier, Manville Corporation and its twenty main subsidiaries filed petitions for reorganization under Chapter 11 of the U.S. Bankruptcy Code on August 26, 1982. (Appendix B provides a description of bankruptcy reorganization.) The company later cited management's desire to obtain prompt and equitable payment of all allowed claims and to create and preserve values to the extent possible for the equityholders as reasons for the filings.

Manville's two Canadian divisions, which owned the world's largest asbestos mine and some asbestos manufacturing facilities, emerged from reorganization in 1983, and Manville sold the common stock of those divisions to a group headed by the divisions' managers. Under the sale agreement, Manville continued to share the profits of these divisions. Also, the forest products division emerged from reorganization in 1984, paying all its creditors essentially the full value of their claims. That division remained a subsidiary of Manville Corporation.

Various equityholders and their representatives tried to force management to conduct annual or special meetings of shareholders. The apparent objective was to reconstitute the board of directors to obtain stronger representation of equity interests. However, the bankruptcy judge refused to order any such meeting and finally disbanded the equity committee.

While operating under Chapter 11, Manville filed and pressed a lawsuit for $5 billion in damages against its insurers. The company claimed the insurers had irreparably harmed it by failing to defend and pay the asbestos claims. (Manville's insurance companies had argued among themselves about who should pay each claim, the one who provided coverage when exposure occurred or the one who provided coverage when the claimant's asbestos disease became apparent—often twenty or more years after exposure.) Out-of-court settlements in the case totaled over $700 million. Practically all the settlements were contingent upon final court orders (orders which have survived all possible appeals) prohibiting future asbestos claims against the insurers and against Manville and its executives.

On May 23, 1986, Manville submitted its "Second Amended and Restated Plan of Reorganization," for the remaining divisions. The plan provided for substantially full payment of unsecured commercial creditor claims, although some of this payment was to be deferred for up to four years—with interest. Most secured claims were to be simply paid up to date and reinstated.

The plan contemplated the establishment of two trusts, one to compensate asbestos health claimants (the Trust, or AH Trust) and one to pay property damage claims (the Property Damage Trust, or PD Trust). The property damage claims, totaling over $80 billion, arose due to the need to clean up asbestos in buildings nationwide.

The AH Trust was to own about 80 percent of Manville's common stock and have a right, starting four years after consummation, to 20 percent of company profits if needed to pay asbestos health claims. Other AH Trust assets were to include $615 million of the insurance proceeds, $55 million in cash, certain receivables totaling about $150 million, and two unsecured Manville Corporation bonds providing for payment of $75 million a year for

24 years commencing in the fourth year after consummation. Upon satisfactory proof of claim, asbestos victims would be offered a cash settlement by the Trust.

The plan is described in greater detail in Appendix C.

The plan had the support of each of the claimant committees except the one representing equity holders. In a personal letter to the casewriter, prominent asbestos plaintiff attorney Ronald Motley wrote:

> After four years of discussions, negotiations and consultations with our committees and investment consultants, the overwhelming majority of the AH (asbestos health) Committee, including the representative of the Asbestos Victims of America (the bankruptcy judge had appointed the head of that organization, James Vermuelen, to the AH Committee), voted in favor of the Plan of Reorganization which was largely shaped by Leon Silverman (a New York attorney appointed to represent future asbestos victims), in consultation with myself, Stan Levy (another plaintiff attorney), and our counsel, Elihu Inselbuch. While there are, of course, shortfalls with this Plan of Reorganization, nevertheless we believe it is in the best interest of the vast majority of claimants, both present and future.

Ballots were mailed to unsecured creditors (including asbestos claimants) and equityholders in September 1986. A national multimedia advertising campaign during October and November that year urged asbestos victims to vote for the Manville plan. All classes of claimants except common shareholders voted to accept the plan and confirmation hearings were held in December that year. Judge Burton Lifland, the bankruptcy judge in charge of the case, wrote in his decision confirming the Manville plan:

> [M]anville has established by convincing evidence, that the plan is fair and equitable in accordance with the requirements of Section 1129(b). The Debtor is insolvent and no value remains for common equity. No class of interests junior to common equity shall receive property of the estate. Distribution under the Plan to classes senior to common equity is exceeded by the aggregate value of the claims of those classes.

In January 1987, Manville CEO Thomas Stephens wrote, "There are a lot of us in this case who didn't cause this problem. As professionals, however, we were brought in to solve it." (Stephens was an executive with Olinkraft when Manville acquired it in 1978 and took over as CEO of Manville when John A. McKinney retired in 1986.) Stephens continued, "Personally, I am proud that we have found a solution to a very, very complex legal, social, and financial problem. It's a solution that came about through the process of compromise—everyone gave and everyone took in the process."

Some claimed Manville's "solution" was inadequate, however. Among the complaints: Unsecured commercial creditors would be paid in full, with interest, by about the time the first payment on the AH Trust bonds is due; Manville executives had voted themselves and other employees large raises and improved benefits while the company operated under Chapter 11; AH

Trust assets would be used to defend Manville, its present and former executives, and its insurers against asbestos claims and for reimbursing other asbestos companies for Manville's share of asbestos health judgments they paid while Manville was protected by Chapter 11; present and future asbestos victims would lose all rights to sue Manville or its insurers; no interest would be paid on amounts due the AH Trust; after five years of delay, during which several thousand asbestos claimants died, consummation of the plan would be further delayed while appeals wound their way to the U.S. Supreme Court; most payments to the AH Trust would be dependent upon Manville's profitability, which had been minimal after 1981. Finally, liquidation of the company could have provided an estimated $2.0 billion in 1982, although the plan *promises* much less in present value some five years later.

Three appeals of Judge Lifland's confirmation order were filed by certain asbestos claimants, creditors, and stockholders. Consummation, or the placing of the plan into effect, was to occur if and after all the appeals could be overcome, optimistically expected in late 1987. In the meantime, Judge Lifland approved limited funding of the AH Trust and the PD Trust so that trustees could meet and prepare to administer the trusts.

APPENDIX A

SELECTED EVENTS CONCERNING ASBESTOS AND HEALTH

1898: Manville founder and inventor of uses for asbestos, Henry Ward Johns, dies of "dust phthisis pneumonitis," later known as asbestosis.

1929: Manville defends early lawsuits for asbestos deaths. The company claims employees assumed the risks of employment, knew or should have known the dangers, and were contributorily negligent. Legal documents in these cases bear signatures of senior Manville officials who would remain with the company until the 1960s.

1930: Dr. A. J. Lanza of Metropolitan Life Insurance Company (Manville's insurer) begins a four-year study on the "Effects of Inhalation of Asbestos Dust upon the Lungs of Asbestos Workers."

1933: Based on interim results of his study, Dr. Lanza suggests Manville engage an outside consultant to do dust counts at company plants. A decision is made to train an insider to do this rather than bring in someone from outside the company.

1934: Asbestosis considered for classification as a disease for workmen's compensation purposes. Manville's chief attorney writes to the company in 1930:

> In particular we have urged that asbestosis should not at the present time be included in the list of compensation diseases, for the reason that it is only within a comparatively recent time that asbestosis has been recognized by the medical and scientific professions as a disease—in fact one of our principal defenses in actions against the company on the common law theory of negligence has been that the scientific and medical knowledge has been insufficient until a very recent period to place on the owners of plants or factories the burden or duty of taking special precautions against the possible onset of the disease in their employees.

After reviewing a draft of Dr. Lanza's report (above), Manville Vice President and Corporate Secretary Vandiver Brown writes Dr. Lanza requesting changes. His letter states, "All we ask is that all of the favorable aspects of the survey be included and that none of the unfavorable be unintentionally pictured in darker terms than the circumstances justify. I feel confident that we can depend upon you and Dr. McConnel to give us this 'break' . . ."

1935: Brown writes another industry executive, Sumner Simpson, "I quite agree that our interests are best served by having asbestosis receive the minimum of publicity." He is commenting on Simpson's response to a letter by Anne Rossiter (editor of the industry journal *Asbestos*) in which she has written, "You may recall that we have written you on several occasions concerning the publishing of information, or discussion of, asbestosis . . . Always you have requested that for obvious reasons, we publish nothing, and, naturally your wishes have been respected."

1936: Messrs. Brown and Simpson convince nine other asbestos companies to provide a total of $417.00 per month for the industry's own three-year study of the effects of asbestos dust on guinea pigs and rabbits by Dr. LeRoy U. Gardner. Simpson writes Gardner, "[W]e could determine from time to time after the findings were made, whether we wish any publication or not." In a separate letter, Brown states, "[T]he manuscript of your study will be submitted to us for approval prior to publication." Gardner will tell the companies of "significant changes in guinea pigs' lungs within a period of one year" and "fibrosis" produced by long fibers and "chronic inflammation" caused by short fibers. He will make several requests for additional funding but will die in 1946 without reporting final results.

1940: Lawsuits have increased in number through the 1930s, but Manville continues successfully to defend or settle them, using the same defenses as in the 1920s but adding a statute-of-limitations defense, made possible by the long latency period of asbestos diseases. The companies continue to be able to prevent significant publicity about asbestos and health. The war will bring spiralling sales and profits, as thousands of tons of asbestos is used in building war machines, mainly ships—resulting in exposure of tens of thousands of shipyard workers and seamen, thousands of whom will die of asbestos diseases decades later.

1947: A study by the Industrial Hygiene Foundation of America finds that from 3 to 20 percent of asbestos plant workers already have asbestosis and a Manville plant employing 300 is producing "5 or 6 cases annually that the physician believes show early changes due to asbestos."

1950: Dr. Kenneth W. Smith, Manville chief physician, has given superiors his report showing that of 708 Manville workers he studied only four were free of asbestos disease. Concerning the more serious cases he wrote, "The fibrosis of this disease is irreversible and permanent so that eventually compensation will be paid to each of these men but as long as the man is not disabled it is felt that he should not be told of his condition so that he can live and work in peace and the company can benefit from his many years of experience."

1952: John A. McKinney, Fred L. Pundsack, Chester E. Shepperly, Monroe Harris, and Chester J. Sulewski, who will be Manville's top five officers as it prepares to seek bankruptcy court protection in 1982, have all joined the company in various capacities.

1953: Dr. Smith tries to convince senior Manville managers to authorize caution labeling for asbestos. In a 1976 deposition he will characterize their responses: "We recognize the potential hazard that you mentioned, the suggested use of a caution label. We will discuss it among ourselves and make a decision." Asked why he was overruled, Smith will say, "[A]pplication of a caution label identifying a product as hazardous would cut out sales."

1956: The board of governors of the Asbestos Textile Institute (made up of Manville and other asbestos companies) meet to discuss the increasing publicity about asbestos and cancer and agree that "[E]very effort should be made to disassociate this relationship until such a time that there is sufficient and authoritative information to substantiate such to be a fact."

1957: The Asbestos Textile Institute rejects a proposal by the Industrial Health Foundation that asbestos companies fund a study on asbestos and cancer. Institute minutes report, "There is a feeling among certain members that such an investigation would stir up a hornet's nest and put the whole industry under suspicion."

1959: An increasing number of articles connecting asbestos with various diseases have appeared in scholarly medical journals over the last few years.

1963: Dr. I. J. Selikoff of Mt. Sinai Medical Center in New York reads a report of his study of asbestos workers before the American Medical Association meeting. Like the earlier research, the Selikoff study implicates asbestos ingestion as the causal factor in many thousands of deaths and injuries. Selikoff will soon estimate that at least 100,000 more Americans will die of asbestos diseases this century. The study and the articles, news stories, and academic papers that follow will focus public attention on the asbestos and health issue. An estimated 100 articles on asbestos-related diseases will appear in 1964 alone.

1964: For the first time, Manville agrees to place caution labels on asbestos products. The labels say, "Inhalation of asbestos in excessive quantities over long periods of time may be harmful," and suggest that users avoid breathing the dust and wear masks if "adequate ventilation control is not possible." The consistent position of Manville managers regarding their failure to warn users earlier will be restated in 1986:

> During the periods of alleged injurious exposure, medical and scientific authorities, government officials and companies supplying products containing asbestos fiber believed that the dust levels for asbestos recommended by the United States Public Health Service did not constitute a hazard to the health of workers handling asbestos-containing insulation products. *Accordingly, the company has maintained that there was no basis for product warnings or special hazard controls until the 1964 publication of results of scientific studies linking pulmonary disease in asbestos insulation workers with asbestos exposure.* [emphasis added]

1970: The senior managers and directors from the 1930s have retired, most within the last few years. Compared with the 1966 board of directors, the 1970 board has a majority of new members. The five managers who joined the company in the late 1940s and early 1950s and who will lead Manville into Chapter 11 reorganization are in senior positions now—McKinney and Pundsack, for example, are vice presidents. However, outsider Richard Goodwin is installed as president.

1973: Manville and other asbestos companies lose their last appeal in the case of Clarence Borel, who died of mesothelioma and asbestosis before the decision. In reviewing the case, the U.S. Court of Appeals writes what some consider a scorching indictment of Manville and the other defendants. The court concludes:

> By the mid-1930s the hazard of asbestos as a pneumoconiotic dust was universally accepted . . . Indeed the evidence tended to establish that the defendants gave no instructions or warnings at all . . . The unpalatable facts are that in the twenties and thirties the hazards of working with asbestos were recognized . . . [N]one of the so-called "cautions" [which appeared only after Borel's exposure] intimated the gravity of the risk: the danger of a fatal illness caused by asbestosis and mesothelioma or other cancers . . . The admonition that a worker should "avoid breathing the dust" is black humor: there was no way for insulation workers to avoid breathing asbestos dust.

1976: Psychologist Richard Goodwin is asked to resign as president and lawyer/public affairs specialist John A. McKinney takes over. McKinney will shortly be elevated to chairman of the board and Fred Pundsack will become president. Asbestos use is dropping rapidly and Goodwin has increased long-term debt from zero to $196 million buying companies in other fields. But asbestos is still so profitable that the fiber alone—not including manufactured asbestos products—produces 51 percent of Manville's operating profits while constituting only about 12 percent of sales.

1977: A mass of papers from asbestos company files, variously called the "Sumner Simpson Papers" and the "Raybestos-Manhattan Correspondence," is accidentally discovered by plaintiff attorneys and presented in a New Jersey asbestos lawsuit. The papers include the letters from the 1930s mentioned earlier. In admitting the new evidence in another trial, a South Carolina judge will soon write:

> The Raybestos-Manhattan correspondence reveals written evidence that Raybestos-Manhattan and Johns-Manville exercised editorial prerogative over the publication of the first study of the asbestos industry which they sponsored in 1935. It further reflects a conscious effort by the industry to downplay, or arguably suppress, the dissemination of information to employees and the public for fear of the promotion of lawsuits.

1978: The stream of asbestos lawsuits has become a flood. Armed with the Raybestos-Manhattan correspondence, asbestos victims are seeking huge amounts, often including punitive damages. The Manville executives choose not to mention the lawsuits in the 1977 Annual Report, but the Securities and Exchange Commission report on Form 10K reveals that there are now 623 asbestos lawsuits for amounts totaling at least $2.79 billion. This year alone, the number of suits will double. Many court decisions are going against Manville, although the company is able to delay paying in most cases by appealing decisions, requesting new trials, and other legal tactics.

1979: Asbestos use declines another 35 percent this year alone. This is compounded by a recession in construction, which will last through 1982. Manville's sales and earnings, buoyed by the Olinkraft acquisition to $2.92 billion and $144 million, respectively, start a steady decline that will lead to sales of only $1.64 billion in 1982 and a $55 million annual-rate loss for the first half of that year (these figures are in constant 1981 dollars).

1981: No significant changes in senior managers or directors have occurred since 1976. The directors decide to reorganize the company, segregating the asbestos-related elements into separately incorporated divisions. Special termination agreements, commonly called *golden parachutes,* are approved for all the top executives. Actual asbestos health costs have never been a significant expense and this year total only $12 million, less than 0.5 percent of sales. But Manville is now losing many cases—and, shown the Raybestos-Manhattan correspondence and other new evidence, juries frequently award hundreds of thousands of dollars in punitive damages. Manville's insurers are refusing to pay, or even to provide defense against, the asbestos lawsuits. Many of the recent lawsuits name the directors and officers personally—but the recently restated corporate bylaws promise that the company will indemnify them.

1982: Manville continues to forestall payments to asbestos claimants—through repeated appeals and other legal tactics. But the company's operations are increasingly unprofitable and major losses are reported for both the first and second quarters. The asbestos judgments increase in number and magnitude. A consulting firm hired by Manville reports that 40,000 additional lawsuits will cost the company $1.9 billion by the year 2001. Upon the recommendation of McKinney and three outside directors, the board of directors approves the Chapter 11 filing on the evening of August 25 and the necessary papers are filed in the U.S. Bankruptcy Court for the Southern District of New York the next day. All the asbestos lawsuits and all efforts to collect previously won judgments are stopped. Within a few days the company is awash in cash, as accounts receivables flow in and $615 million in debt is stayed. An estimated 2,000 of the 16,500 present asbestos claimants will die during the years Manville is negotiating its reorganization plan, and with few exceptions none of the 16,500 will be paid. In support of Manville's decision to reorganize under bankruptcy law, First Boston Corporation and Morgan Stanley and Company prepare secret reports estimating the "going concern value" of the company's assets at slightly above their $1.8 billion liquidation value.

APPENDIX B

HOW CHAPTER 11 WORKS

Chapter 11 of the U.S. Bankruptcy Code is based upon the assumption that a business is worth more as a going concern than in liquidation. If this is true, stockholders and creditors may get more out of a troubled company by allowing it to continue operating than by shutting it down. Additional benefits of keeping the company operating are that employees keep their jobs and the community keeps the tax base and economic and social activity related to the firm.

To assure maintenance of the company's value and equitable distribution of claims on that value, a U.S. bankruptcy judge assumes oversight of any firm that desires to reorganize under Chapter 11. Insolvency is not a prerequisite, although some Chapter 11 filings are contested on the basis that they are not made in good faith. A committee of unsecured creditors and another made up of stockholders is appointed to assist management and the court in arriving at an equitable plan. Other committees or advocates may be established to represent interests that diverge from those of shareholders and unsecured creditors.

Company executives have 120 days to prepare a formal reorganization plan and submit it to creditor and stockholder groups for approval. Another 60 days is allowed to get the plan approved. If either of these periods expires any party at interest in the case can offer a reorganization plan for approval. Apparently to avoid such a confusing prospect, both periods are routinely extended in most jurisdictions.

If all impaired classes of claimants approve a plan, the court may confirm it and place it into effect. *Impaired* claimants are those whose legal, equitable, or contractual rights are modified by the plan, except by curing defaults and reinstating maturity or providing for cash payment. The plan may also be confirmed if the judge holds that it treats nonapproving impaired classes equally with respect to other classes of equal rank and that allowed claims of nonapproving classes will be fully satisfied under the plan before more junior classes receive any distribution at all.

While the plan is being negotiated, approved, confirmed, and consummated, all prefiling claims are stayed. Executory contracts may be unilaterally canceled by the debtor and mortgaged assets may be abandoned to mortgagees. Management operates the company in the ordinary course of business and is generally protected against direct control or removal by stockholders. Major assets, including whole divisions, may be divested with court approval.

Ideally, the plan will provide that the value of the going concern that emerges from reorganization will be allocated first to the administrative costs of the proceeding and then to the claimant classes in order of their absolute priority in liquidation. This suggests that prefiling claims on the debtor estate will be satisfied in this sequence: (1) secured debt (up to the value of respective collateral as of the filing date), (2) unsecured debt, and (3) equity claims in order of preference (preferred, then common). However, plans commonly depart from this fair and equitable standard in order to elicit the support of junior claimant classes. Also, the value claimants receive may be in the form of cash, securities, or other real or personal property.

Provision is made to pay postfiling claims as they come due. To ensure that the reorganized firm is viable, prefiling claims not provided for in the plan are discharged.

APPENDIX C

SELECTED PROVISIONS OF THE MANVILLE PLAN

Class 1 claims (unpaid administrative expenses totaling about $26 million—most administrative costs were paid as accrued) will be paid in full upon consummation.

Class 2 claims (secured debts) will be reinstated, with interest, and $13.4 million in arrearages will be paid in cash. Some secured claims have been kept up to date, with court approval, during the Chapter 11 proceedings.

Class 3 claims (over $80 billion in property damage claims—due to the need to remove asbestos from existing buildings—most of which were filed after 1982) will be paid as they are liquidated from the PD Trust (set up to pay the property damage claims). The PD Trust will be initially funded with $125 million in cash and any insurance proceeds in excess of the $615 million committed to fund the trust for asbestos health claims (the Trust). Any future funding for the PD Trust will come from the excess of that needed by the Trust to pay asbestos health claims.

Class 4 claims (existing asbestos health claims, totaling over $30.5 billion, and claims for contribution and indemnity by Manville's asbestos company codefendants) will be paid from the Trust as they are liquidated and approved by the Claims Resolution Facility, to be controlled by a panel of trustees approved by the bankruptcy court (none of the initial trustees has been affiliated with Manville Corporation). The Trust will also be responsible for defending asbestos lawsuits brought against it, Manville, past and present Manville executives and directors, and certain insurance companies. Future asbestos health claims are not classified, but they will also be paid from the Trust as liquidated. The Trust will be funded with the following assets:

1. All rights under Settlement Agreements Manville has or will execute with its insurers by the Consummation Date (thirty days after an order of the bankruptcy court confirming the plan becomes final and unappealable). Manville reported the face value of these agreements to be $505 million as of May 23, 1986. Payment of the agreed amount by the Settling Insurers is contingent upon several conditions, among them approval of the agreements by the bankruptcy court (none had been approved when Manville filed its plan) and a final and unappealable court order barring future asbestos claims against the insurers.

2. $150 million in cash and accounts receivable.

3. A $50 million unsecured Manville Corporation note, promising payment with interest in two equal installments in the third and fourth years after the Consummation Date.

4. A Manville Corporation unsecured bond requiring payments of $75 million a year, without interest, from the fourth through the twenty-fifth year after the Consummation Date, subject to deferral after the thirteenth year if the Trust is adequately funded in accordance with specified standards.

5. A Manville Corporation unsecured bond requiring payment of $75 million in each of the twenty-sixth and twenty-seventh years after the Consummation Date, subject to deferral if the Trust is adequately funded in accordance with specified standards.

6. Certain interest on amounts set aside to fund the Trust if consummation occurs later than July 1987.

7. If needed by the Trust in accordance with specified standards and starting in the fifth year after consummation, up to 20 percent of Manville's profits and 20 percent of proceeds from the federal government. (Manville claims government should pay part of the asbestos costs mainly because many of the claims resulted from work on navy ships.)

8. One-half of Manville's common stock at consummation. For four years after consummation the Trust must vote this stock for management's nominees for directorships unless Manville allows certain events to occur that might prejudice the Trust. With certain exceptions, this stock cannot be transferred by the Trust for five years after consummation. The company has the right of first refusal on any sale of common stock by the Trust, which would result in the buyer holding more than 15 percent of Manville's outstanding common stock.

9. New convertible preferred stock, which would give the Trust 80 percent of the firm's common equity if converted on the Consummation Date (convertibility is restricted).

Class 5 claims (about $20 million in miscellaneous claims on behalf of employees, users of defective roofing and siding products, and so forth) will be paid in full as liquidated, requiring payment of about $1 million in cash upon consummation.

Class 6 claims (unsecured claims not to exceed $472.5 million and not included in other classes) will be paid as follows:

1. Paid in cash if under $10,000—or if holder is willing to reduce claim to $10,000;

2. Paid pro rata share of $247.5 million less amounts paid in compliance with (1) above;

3. Issued Class 6 Note for remaining principal amount of claim. Class 6 Notes will be four-and-one-half-year, unsecured obligations of Manville Corporation drawing 12 percent interest and requiring biannual payments after consummation of at least $33.75 million each. They may be redeemed by Manville at any time and may be accelerated under certain conditions;

4. Paid cash for certain interest and investment income that will accrue if consummation does not occur by July 1, 1987;

5. Issued Class 6 Interest Debentures, Series B Preference Stock, common stock, and common stock warrants for interest accrued from August 26, 1982 (the date of Manville's Chapter 11 petition) to the Consummation Date.

Class 7 claimants (preferred-stock holders) will receive for each preferred share a share of new Series B Preference Stock, which will pay cumulative dividends of $2.70 per share beginning six years after consummation (if certain conditions are met) and about 1.94 shares of common stock.

Class 8 claimants (common-stock holders) will receive their pro rata share of 8.3 percent of common shares outstanding at consummation, subject to further dilution down to about 3 percent.

Class 9 claimants (certain purchasers of Manville common stock who have sued the company and certain of its officers and directors in federal court) will receive payment to the extent of certain insurance proceeds.

Among the conditions precedent to consummation of the plan are final and unappealable court orders establishing the following:

1. Any future asbestos health claims against Manville, the Settling Insurers, or the Canadian subsidiaries that were divested in 1983 are prohibited.

2. Allowed Class 6 claims (unsecured claims not elsewhere classified) will never exceed $472.5 million.

3. No punitive damages will be allowed for Class 3 or Class 4 claims (asbestos property damage and asbestos health claims) except for previously issued final judgments respecting liquidated asbestos health claims.

4. All transfers of property to the trusts by Manville are legal, valid and effective transfers, vest good title to such property free and clear of all encumbrances, debts, obligations, liabilities and claims other than asbestos claims as contemplated by the plan, are not fraudulent, and do not except as contemplated by the plan, subject the Trusts to any liability.

5. Certain agreements with the Settling Insurers are approved.

After consummation of the plan Manville's fifteen-person board of directors will consist of eight preconsummation directors and seven new directors. Two of the new directors will be chosen from persons suggested by representatives of the asbestos health claimants, three from a list of candidates approved by Manville and representatives of the asbestos health claimants, one from a list approved by Manville and the Unsecured Creditors Committee, and another selected by the board of directors in consultation with claimant committees.

The eight preconsummation directors include six outside directors. The years they joined the Manville board are as follows: three in 1969, one in 1972, one in 1976, and the last in 1982. The outside director who joined in 1982 did so when his firm was hired as Manville's Chapter 11 law firm. The two inside directors are Manville's senior inside lawyer, G. Earl Parker, and the president, W. Thomas Stephens. The chairman of the board will be George C. Dillon, who has been a director of Manville since 1969.

The new directors include the chief executive of a regional discount-store chain, the chief financial officer of a national department-store chain, a professor of finance, a management consultant, a lawyer, and a financial consultant.

NOTES

1. Bruce Porter, *Sunday Review of the Society,* 1973.

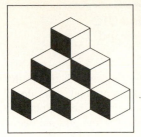

STRATEGIC ISSUES
MERGERS, ACQUISITIONS, AND LEVERAGED BUYOUTS

CASE 36

The Thermometer Corporation of America: Division of Figgie International, Inc.

PER V. JENSTER • HENRY ODELL • KEN BURGER

It was late November 1982 when Harry Figgie, Jr., chairman of Figgie International, and Joe Skadra, group vice president and treasurer, were meeting in the company's new headquarters complex in Richmond, Virginia. Figgie International (FI) was a diversified company that had 40 different businesses ranging from fire engines to clothing. Included in these businesses was the manufacture of thermometers, which was conducted under the name Thermometer Corporation of America (TCA). The TCA plant was located in Springfield, Ohio, a city of 86,000 in the west-central part of the state.

FI recently received a proposal from Ohio Thermometer Co. (OTC) dated November 17, 1982, and entitled "An Analysis of a Merger and Future Between TCA and OTC" (Exhibit 1). The proposal was presented by Charles L. Wappner and Jerome P. Bennett, president and vice president, respectively (and co-owners), of OTC. OTC was a competitor in the thermometer

---

This case was prepared as a basis for class discussion rather than to illustrate either effective or ineffective handling of an administrative situation.

This case was used in the fourth McIntire Case Competition (MCI IV) held at the University of Virginia on February 9–11, 1985. We gratefully acknowledge the General Electric Foundation for support of the MCI and the writing of this case.

EXHIBIT 1

An Analysis of a Merger and Future Between TCA and OTC Presented to Harry E. Figgie, Jr. by Jerome P. Bennett and Charles L. Wappner November 17, 1982

We at Ohio Thermometer are of the opinion that our company's growth is tied to the economy. When times are good, sales are good and when times are bad, sales drop. The reason is our product base. Ohio Thermometer is very weak in the inexpensive category, kitchen, or cooking category and almost nonexistent in the gift and decorator field. Without these three areas it is impossible for us to replace another thermometer company. We don't have the necessary capital to tool for all of these areas, hence our need for TCA's products. We feel, as competitors of TCA, that they have the same problems in the housewares field, only more severe. They have been unable to come up with a dial that is competitive with Ohio's; consequently they have no ammunition to replace any other company. Companies such as TCA are being replaced by Springfield or Taylor. Ohio Thermometer is, however, not being replaced mainly because everybody has to have our dials. We can't see TCA making much movement in the housewares industry because of the above problems. We feel TCA is also tied to the economy in this particular area.

In other areas of thermometry Ohio Thermometer has the advertising thermometer business locked up. This is an area that's up and expanding and profitable. TCA is in the auto field and scientific area, which are areas that we don't get into, so we really don't know how they are doing in those areas. They also have a gourmet thermometer line that we feel has tremendous potential, but they lack the customer base that we have. If they had our customer base, those items could perform miracles. In addition to the mentioned areas, Ohio has the Detroit automobile business under control, in our pocket, and we are the dominant people in the poultry industry.

Put the two companies together and you wind up with the most balanced thermometer company in the country. Together the companies would be the answer to many of our customers' problems. Most purchasing agents at this time want to cut down the list of vendors. In the thermometer field, if you talk to them, they say they must carry Taylor because of their name, and they must have Ohio because of their dials. Most have Springfield and they usually have a fourth vendor, which is either Chaney, Cooper, or TCA, but very, very seldom do they ever have a fifth vendor, so they take their pick among one of the three, either Chaney, Cooper, or TCA. With a combined company, TCA and Ohio, we certainly would be in a position to eliminate the fourth vendor and very possibly eliminate the third vendor. I am not too sure that, at certain areas, that you couldn't really take a good shot at Taylor. We know Chaney's and Cooper's customers and we know their weaknesses and we know their strengths. I think a combined company would have a field day or a Marianna's turkey shoot in the foreseeable future.

Looking at both sides, if Ohio could buy TCA, and I might add we have tried to do this in 1978, at this point it would probably stretch our finances. We feel that our borrowing would be somewhere close to $1 million. This would cover our current borrowing, allow $0.5 million to be paid to Figgie International, with the rest going toward working capital. We would have to have some other type of financing for the remainder of the purchase price of TCA, and pay these off over a number of years. Could we get this financing? Questionable.

If Figgie International takes over Ohio these problems are eliminated and with Kiefer running a lean operation, we see immediate profits and probably large profits.

I, personally, feel that by taking the best sales reps from Ohio and the best sales reps from TCA and combining them, figures don't lie, we would have one of the strongest sales operations in the thermometer field. I feel that because of our contacts and our personal relationships with all of our customers, that we would keep

EXHIBIT 1   **Continued**

all of them and be able to expand the entire base thermometer business. In addition, we sell to almost all of TCA's housewares accounts, so I can't see where we would lose any of that business. Quite frankly, with the two companies, the housewares end of the business would be a bonanza to the customers, at the same time solving their problems of too many vendors.

Our four or five year sales forecast would be in the $10 million plus range. Even if the economy didn't bounce back, we could still project many inroads in the thermometer business and even if the economy stays as it is today, we would project a 10 percent to 15 percent to 20 percent sales increase per year. Again, with these sales and with the idea of running a lean company, there would be enough profit to go into the thermometer business with new items in-depth. We look at weather stations that Taylor sells in the $300 to $400 range and it makes our mouths water. We sell to the same accounts that they sell to, only we can't compete with them, as we don't have the product.

Lastly, whether together or separately, both TCA and Ohio are going to have to get into the electronics area. Obviously TCA would have the jump on us, because they could use other Figgie operations. However, individually, we doubt that they would have the necessary profits to make the expenditures to do this.

A HAPPY MARRIAGE!

Intangibles that Ohio has to sell:

1. Dial thermometer business
   Making TCA the major factor in the dial thermometer business with $2.8 million in existing business; this is the heart of the thermometer business today.

2. Advertising thermometer business
   This would make TCA the major and dominant supplier in the advertising and point of sale thermometer business with $0.5 million of existing business. Ohio now supplies almost all of the major corporations with their advertising thermometer needs, controlling an estimated 95 percent of this business.

3. Industrial and special products
   This would make TCA the dominant company in the automobile thermometer business and the major supplier of thermometers and instruments to the poultry industry, both in the United States and Canada.

4. Customer base
   Ohio now has a very broad base of customers because all major accounts carry Ohio dials. The list of Ohio's customers is attached. This would automatically expose all TCA products to the major discounters, distributors, department and variety stores, hardware chains, drug chains, food chains, and catalog and catalog showrooms.

5. Ohio expertise in thermometer business
   Ohio Thermometer is about to start its fiftieth year in the thermometer business. Over the years we have consistently ranked number one or two with Taylor Instrument in accuracy and quality, according to past published consumer reports.

6. Sales operation
   In looking over our customer base, it should be obvious that Ohio has the dominant sales rep organization between the two companies. In addition, Bennett and Reeder know the buyers on a first-name basis at the major accounts such as K-Mart, Sears, Penney's, etc. We feel this will automatically prevent the loss of customers and would actually increase the thermometer base. Almost all accounts that Ohio now sells are TCA's accounts, which would add to protecting our business.

business and was also located in Springfield, Ohio. Figgie and Skadra arranged this meeting to discuss the November 17 proposal. Their conversation began as follows:

FIGGIE As you know, I met with Charlie Wappner and Jerry Bennett on November 17th at their request. At that meeting they presented a proposal, which calls for Figgie [International] to purchase OTC.

SKADRA As I recall, they [OTC] tried to acquire TCA from us back in 1978.

FIGGIE Yes, but at that time we felt that the growth potential for TCA was too good to consider divesting. I have kept in touch with Charlie and Jerry since then, so their proposal wasn't a complete surprise.

SKADRA How did the meeting go?

FIGGIE The atmosphere was very friendly. I pointed out, as best I could, that while we regard ourselves as a good parent company to work with, several changes would have to be made if we assimilated OTC. I'm sure from the comments they made that they understand this and would be willing to work with us.

SKADRA Living and working in the same community, they must know Bill Kieffer [TCA president].

FIGGIE They know him and apparently have considerable respect for him and for his abilities as a manager, as do we. In the proposal they specifically refer to his [Kieffer's] "running a lean operation." This tells me that if a merger of TCA and OTC were to take place, they would be willing to accept Kieffer as their leader.

SKADRA In terms of return on investment, TCA has been one of our top businesses—until recently.

FIGGIE True enough, but we haven't been able to get the sales growth we had hoped. Bill Kieffer has asked me for help in acquiring businesses that would help us expand the thermometer business and help him in getting that growth.

SKADRA I remember looking at a couple that just couldn't be justified.

FIGGIE Despite the recent decline in sales at TCA I still think it has potential, and I don't want to consider selling it. We have a proven manager in Bill and a good operation. But we're not fully utilizing the managerial capabilities of Bill and his team.

SKADRA The proposal indicates several possible synergies that might be realized by combining the two operations. We'll certainly have to identify those before negotiating.

FIGGIE Yes, and I also keep thinking about that idle manufacturing plant we have in Springfield, which is now being used for storage.

SKADRA As I recall, that plant has 65,000 square feet on one floor.

FIGGIE Charlie said that their present plant has 100,000 square feet on one floor. Apparently it's not being fully used now. Charlie and Jerry own it personally.

EXHIBIT 2

Proposed Terms of Sale of Assets of Ohio Thermometer to Figgie International

	NET SOUND VALUE
Lloyd-Thomas Appraised Values May 31, 1982:	
Machinery	$ 555,985
Furniture and fixtures	135,361
Office furniture and fixtures	39,921
Office machines	19,808
Industrial power trucks	10,758
Dies*	213,473
Tools and trucks*	4,000
	979,306
Inventories complete at cost September 30,1982 values	513,740
Total value	$1,493,046

Acceptable terms: $1,493,000 cash at closing or at your option: $500,000 cash at closing and balance in acceptable securities or notes.

a) Jerry Bennett and Charles Wappner would agree to stay for at least two years.

b) We would agree to lease our 100,000 sq. ft. factory and office building to Figgie International for two years at $5,000 per month on a net net basis.

c) Our NCR 8271 computer system is leased from U.S. Leasing. There are 30 months remaining at a rental of $1,672 per month. We would agree to transfer this lease to Figgie International if desired.

*Owners' valuation

SKADRA From a quick look at the figures, their asking price of $1.5 million (Exhibit 2) seems very high. I'd like to take a closer look at the whole situation, especially the financial aspect.

FIGGIE I agree. Let's analyze the offer from a strategic and financial standpoint, looking at all the angles.

SKADRA Since both TCA and OTC have had declining sales and profits in the last couple of years, I think we should pay special attention to costs.

BACKGROUND

In late 1963, Harry E. Figgie, Jr., acquired the controlling interest in Automatic Sprinkler Corporation of America, a family-owned firm with sales of $22 million. Figgie recalled:

> On January 2, 1964, I drove ninety miles to Youngstown, Ohio, to take over a company I'd never seen. Their top officer said to me, "You've got to be the dumbest man alive." I said, "I'm the second dumbest. You sold it!"

Since then Figgie and his executive team had expanded the corporation to a multidivisional firm with sales of $770 million in 1981. This growth came about through an aggressive acquisition phase to obtain what Figgie referred to as a "critical mass" of $300 million in annual sales. To do this, he applied a management concept of a lean organization with a small, highly mobile corporate staff. According to Harry Figgie:

> In those days, it was not uncommon for the team to look over as many as fifty companies a month. In one rush of buying (in 1976), they closed five deals in just twenty-five days.

This phase ended in 1970, after Figgie had acquired more than 50 new divisions. Among these acquisitions was Mid-Con, Inc., a minor conglomerate consisting of several smaller companies in the Ohio Valley, one of which was the Thermometer Corporation of America. Most of the other small firms obtained in this particular acquisition had been divested since then.

During the next ten years the company grew from $356 million in sales to $770 million through internal growth. Harry Figgie recalled:

> Such growth was not without problems as we chewed up working capital and sent our debt-to-equity ratio up to 1.36 to 1 [1979].

In 1981, the company changed its name to Figgie International, Inc. (FI), and prepared itself for a new period of aggressive growth. As the recession hit the company in 1982 and overall sales dropped about 8 percent, cost reduction became Harry Figgie's number one priority in 1982 (see Exhibit 3 for balance sheet and income statement data).

Figgie International, Inc.

In a recent interview in *The Craftsman,* an internal publication of FI, Harry Figgie discussed his ambitious plan of growth for the future. The plan entailed a new phase of acquisitions that would build on the company's present business groups. Figgie's goals for the future included:

- Further reduce the company's debt-to-equity ratio
- Top $1 billion in sales and start building toward $2 billion through an aggressive acquisition program
- Continue to emphasize internal consolidation, bringing the minimum divisional size up to $25 million in sales
- Pursue high technology and bring robotics and CAE/CAD/CAM into the workplace by adapting new techniques and strategies
- Remain faithful to the company's commitment of producing quality products at competitive prices

EXHIBIT 3	**Figgie International, Inc. Balance Sheet and Income Statement Data**

INCOME DATA (DOLLAR AMOUNTS IN MILLIONS)

YEAR ENDED DEC. 31	REVS.	OPER. INC.	% OPER. INC. OF REVS.	CAP. EXP.	DEPR.	INT. EXP.	NET BEF. TAXES	EFF. TAX RATE	NET INC.	% NET INC. OF REVS.
1982*	708	51.0	7.2%	31.9	14.9	21.4	38.6	32.4%	26.1	3.7%
1981†	770	72.3	9.4	28.1	14.5	22.2	48.1	46.6	25.7	3.3
1980‡	760	65.2	8.6	22.4	13.8	23.6	40.3	48.8	20.6	2.7
1979	691	62.0	9.0	24.0	16.1	21.3	33.8	48.0	17.6	2.5
1978	628	52.4	8.3	29.1	12.9	16.8	30.4	49.0	15.5	2.5
1977	568	40.5	7.1	34.4	9.7	12.5	21.8	47.1	11.5	2.0
1976	518	41.4	8.0	12.7	8.1	9.5	25.7	48.7	13.1	2.5
1975	480	40.2	8.4	13.5	7.7	9.9	23.7	48.2	12.2	2.5
1974	476	41.4	8.6	14.8	6.6	13.3	22.9	48.6	11.2	2.4

BALANCE SHEET DATA (DOLLAR AMOUNTS IN MILLIONS)

DEC. 31	CURRENT ASSETS CASH	ASSETS	LIAB.	RATIO	TOTAL ASSETS	RET. ON ASSETS	LONG-TERM DEBT	COMMON EQUITY	TOTAL CAP.	% LT DEBT OF CAP.	RET. ON EQUITY
1982*	15.6	268	111	2.4	465	5.5%	122	164	343	35.7%	15.9%
1981	6.8	298	131	2.3	475	5.4	127	146	335	37.8	17.6
1980	10.6	318	141	2.3	485	4.3	140	128	335	41.7	15.7
1979	7.0	316	143	2.2	478	3.8	145	111	326	44.5	15.2
1978	9.8	285	111	2.6	436	3.8	154	98	315	48.7	14.7
1977	9.2	256	108	2.4	376	3.5	117	90	260	45.0	11.5
1976	8.8	217	63	3.4	312	4.3	110	88	244	45.0	13.8
1975	15.2	213	63	3.4	300	4.0	112	79	232	48.2	13.9
1974	14.8	228	80	2.9	309	3.8	113	72	224	50.6	14.1

*Estimated
†Reflects acquisitions
‡Reflects accounting change

HARRY E. FIGGIE, JR., AND HIS MANAGEMENT PHILOSOPHY   Most people would probably say that Harry Figgie was well prepared when he took over the small, troubled Automatic Sprinkler Corp. in 1964. After earning his B.S. in metallurgical engineering at Case Institute of Technology, Harry Figgie earned an M.B.A. at Harvard Business School, a J.D. at Cleveland Marshall Law School, and an M.S. in industrial engineering at Case. Later, as a partner with Booz, Allen & Hamilton, a management consulting firm, Harry Figgie was exposed to a wide range of business situations in smaller and medium-sized firms. The experience he gained in management consulting, as well as in his capacity as chairman and chief operating officer of Figgie International, had made him known as one of the foremost cost-reduction authorities in the world. In his book, *The Cost Reduction and Profit Improvement Handbook,* he stresses the importance of a lean organization.

> The first point to remember about the concept of cost reduction is that it can be used interchangeably with the term "profit improvement." If profit improvement is the glass of water half full, then cost reduction is the glass half empty. . . . [p. 1]
>
> As will be demonstrated, a 10 percent reduction in costs can increase profits by 25 percent to 50 percent, or more if the savings can be preserved. . . . [p. 3]

Harry Figgie's management concept also placed responsibility for profit-making decisions at the basic profit-center level, the division president. Accordingly, each president had "entrepreneurial" control of his division's profit and growth performance. He reported to a group vice president, who, in turn, reported directly to Figgie. One subdivision president commented:

> I have full responsibility for my division but will receive help from corporate headquarters if I ask. And you'd better ask before the trouble arrives; they [corporate headquarters] don't like surprises. . . . Figgie International is our banker and adviser.

ORGANIZATION Figgie International was divided into five groups: consumer, fire protection/safety, machinery, technical, and service. The contribution by group is shown in Exhibit 4.

The consumer group included Rawlings sporting goods (baseballs, baseball gloves, basketballs, footballs, golf clubs, and related equipment),

EXHIBIT 4

Figgie International's Five Groups

BUSINESS GROUP (1982)*	SALES	PROFITS
Consumer	18%	8%
Fire protection/safety	43	41
Machinery and products	19	−6
Technical	19	21
Services	1	36

*Sales to the U.S. Government accounted for an estimated 21 percent of the total in 1982.

Adirondack baseball bats, Fred Perry sportswear (tennis clothing and other sportswear), home fire alarms, vacuum cleaners, and thermometers (TCA).

The fire protection/safety group consisted of custom-made fire engines, sprinkler systems, chemical fire extinguishers, aerial-type water delivery systems for fire-fighting apparatus, protective breathing equipment, and security systems and equipment.

The machinery and products group encompassed capping, sorting, and sealing machinery, high-speed automatic bottling equipment, road-building and maintenance equipment, hydraulic pumps, vibrating road rollers, material-handling systems, battery-powered vehicles, and mortar and concrete mixers.

The technical products group consisted primarily of aircraft and missile components, aircraft display instruments and armament control systems, telemetry and electronic instrumentation systems, and electronic access control and monitoring systems.

The service group included sales financing, computer software, real estate, and natural resources investments.

MANAGEMENT SYSTEMS   Cash was managed centrally at Figgie International, and divisions submitted all receivable collections to headquarters. Conversely, cash for payables was sent to divisions upon request. Corporate capital and headquarters expenses were paid for in two ways: payment for debt service (assets less current liabilities at FI's cost of capital rate [Beta = 1.10]), and incremental costs of working capital, which were charged at slightly over prime for changes in working capital calculated on a monthly basis.

The capital budgeting procedure ran parallel to the allocation of working capital. Here, a division manager could make discretionary decisions up to $1,000, and a group vice president up to $5,000. All other capital investments had to be encompassed in the budget or submitted for Harry Figgie's approval.

Planning was also an integral part of the management process. In line with the management philosophy of keeping things simple, divisional presidents presented with their group officer the annual business plan between October 1 and November 30 to Harry Figgie and the corporate staff. The plan included a detailed budget for the coming year and a summary for the following four years. As one corporate officer noted: "Three things can happen to a plan at the annual meeting, and two are not good." Operational performance (actual) and a rolling five-month forecast were reported by divisions on a monthly basis.

The reward system was a central part of the management system at Figgie International and was highly integrated with the planning and budgeting process. The division presidents receive bonuses based on their achievement of pretax return on sales (50 percent) and pretax return on assets (50 percent).

THERMOMETER CORPORATION OF AMERICA (TCA)

The operations of TCA were in a 35,000-square-foot, two-story plant in the southern part of the city of Springfield. The office consisted of 2,500 square feet on the second floor. A wide variety of thermometer products was manufactured, including scientific and houseware products. The main manufacturing processes included:

1. The blowing of glass tubes to modify them by adding bulbs, or joining tubes of different diameters. Standard lathes had been customized so that the glass tubes could be heated and rotated as the blowing took place.

2. Etching of glass tubes as needed to provide the degree markings for the scientific and other special-use thermometers. The tubes were coated with wax and a special machine formed slits through which acid could reach the glass surface.

3. Calibration of the thermometer required the right combination of tube bore and bulb size, amount of liquid enclosed (mercury or alcohol-based), and degree marking (etched on the glass or printed on an enclosure in the tube or on a mounting). The operators worked with controlled temperature baths and made the adjustments.

Since the operations did not lend themselves to automation, the machines required full-time operators to load each piece and perform the operations. Considerable manual skills were required, especially in the glass-blowing. Most operations required the glass to be in a heated, semimolten state so that the machines could process it. Heating attachments, some of which have been designed by TCA, maintained the processing temperature.

Many of the machines were "dedicated" for a particular operation and were not changed. As a result such machines, remaining idle for much of the time, were typically older machines but were deemed to be as effective as newer models. The plant was operating at 40 percent of capacity. About 50 percent of the total cost of sales was raw materials and purchased parts.

There were 31 hourly paid employees in the plant, most of whom were women. They belonged to the United Auto Workers union. The average hourly wage rate was $4.39 plus $1.48 in fringe benefits. There had been one brief strike in recent years. The relationship between management and workers seemed good; many of the employees had been with TCA for many years, and turnover was low.

Salaried workers are shown in the organization chart (Exhibit 5). A manual accounting system was used, which Mr. Kieffer considered adequate for generating needed information for his operating purposes and for the required reports to FI headquarters. He indicated that he would want to study the situation very carefully and find just the right hardware before shifting to computerization.

Financial information is shown in Exhibits 6, 7, 8, and 9.

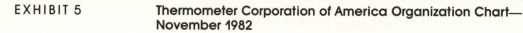

EXHIBIT 5   **Thermometer Corporation of America Organization Chart—
November 1982**

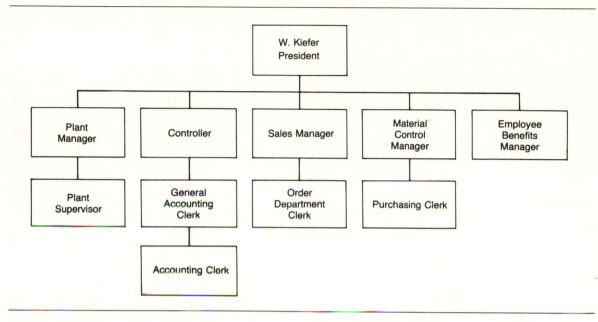

OHIO THERMOMETER COMPANY (OTC)

OTC was located in a one-story, 100,000-square-foot building in Springfield. The plant was about five miles from the TCA plant. The current operations (equipment and storage) used 60 percent of the floor space. The primary product was dial thermometers of 12″ and 18″ diameters. The primary parts were the coated-steel dial face (which was printed with the thermometer readings and other desired backgrounds), the aluminum outer band, brass bushings and shaft, temperature indicator, clear acrylic plastic dial cover (lens), and the bimetallic coil (which moved the indicator as the temperature varied). OTC used more durable materials than competitors did. The total material purchases, including raw materials and purchased parts, such as coils and indicators, were about 50 percent of the total cost of sales.

The plant operations were divided into three areas. One area contained the punch presses, which cut out the dial faces and the outer bands from sheet metal. A second area held the printing line with various printing presses and a drying oven connected by a circular conveyor belt. The third area was where the assembly took place. The punch presses were the only metalworking equipment used and were standard models.

EXHIBIT 6

Thermometer Corporation of America Comparative Balance Sheets at December 31, 1981, 1980, and 1979

	1981	1980	1979
ASSETS			
Current assets:			
Cash	$ (27,000)	$ —	$ —
Accounts receivable (net)	162,000	211,000	193,000
Inventory	869,000	642,000	638,000
Prepaid expenses	6,000	2,000	1,000
Total current assets	$1,010,000	$ 855,000	$ 832,000
Property and equipment			
Land	9,000	9,000	9,000
Machinery and equipment	1,192,000	1,176,000	1,164,000
Total	$1,201,000	$1,185,000	$1,173,000
Less accumulated depreciation	1,088,000	1,072,000	1,046,000
Total property and equipment	$ 113,000	$ 113,000	$ 127,000
Other assets			
Patents	36,000	42,000	47,000
Other assets	1,000	1,000	1,000
Total other assets	$ 37,000	$ 43,000	$ 48,000
Total assets	$1,160,000	$1,011,000	$1,007,000
LIABILITIES AND STOCKHOLDERS' EQUITY			
Current liabilities:			
Accounts payable	$ 10,000	$ 78,000	$ 23,000
Unpaid withheld taxes	33,000	30,000	25,000
Accrued expenses	225,000	186,000	165,000
Total current liabilities	$ 358,000	$ 294,000	$ 213,000
Long-term debt	0	0	0
Total liabilities	$ 358,000	$ 294,000	$ 213,000
Stockholders' equity:			
Original investment	$ 151,000	$ 151,000	$ 151,000
Retained earnings	1,121,000	1,015,000	93,000
Intracompany current	(470,000)	(449,000)	550,000
Total stockholders' equity	$ 802,000	$ 717,000	$ 794,000
Total liabilities and stockholders' equity	$1,160,000	$1,011,000	$1,007,000

EXHIBIT 7

Thermometer Corporation of America Comparative Income Statements for the Years ended December 31, 1981, 1980, and 1979

	1981	1980	1979
Net sales	$1,677,000	$1,730,000	$1,762,000
Cost of sales	1,096,000	1,193,000	1,220,000
Gross profit	581,000	537,000	542,000
Operating expenses:			
Selling	134,000	123,000	124,000
Administrative	172,000	153,000	160,000
Debt service	72,000	80,000	78,000
Other	7,000	(3,000)	8,000
Total operating expenses	385,000	353,000	370,000
Income (loss) from operations	196,000	184,000	172,000
Provision for income taxes	90,000	85,000	79,000
Net income (loss)	$ 106,000	$ 99,000	$ 93,000

There were 70 hourly paid shop employees who belonged to the International Association of Machinists union. The average wage rate was $4.92 per hour. Fringe benefits were $1.60 per hour. The work in the plant was not highly skilled. As shown in Exhibit 10, the plant had five supervisors.

OTC had an art department, which generated a wide variety of advertising for printing on the dial face. The equipment provided photographic and silk-screening capabilities.

Exhibit 10 shows 23 salaried employees, including the three officers, Charlie Wappner (president), Jerry Bennett (vice president, sales), and V. Bennett (secretary). V. Bennett was Wappner's sister and Bennett's wife and filled the position of secretary on a part-time basis at a salary of $3,000 annually. Aside from these corporate officers the average annual salaries were as follows:

1. Managers and engineers—$25,000

2. Supervisors, technicians, and artists—$18,000

3. Clerks, computer operators, and secretaries—$14,000

Fringe benefits were about 35 percent of salaries.

The NCR 8271 computer (leased) was used for accounting, inventory, and production control. It had far larger capabilities than were needed for the operation.

EXHIBIT 8   **Thermometer Corporation of America Schedule of Cost of Goods Sold for the Year Ended December 31, 1981**

	1981
Materials	$ 467,992
Direct labor	211,066
Manufacturing expenses:	
Indirect labor	$ 60,497
Supervision	59,760
Vacation and holiday	39,996
Payroll taxes	42,439
Industrial welfare	550
Employee insurance	43,534
Supplies	32,110
Maintenance and repairs	10,269
Truck	5,896
Freight	41,816
Utilities	49,161
Depreciation	12,352
Insurance	39,450
Taxes	—
Scrap	17,584
Travel	221
Rentals	17,018
Miscellaneous	—
	$ 472,653
Burden (absorbed)	(363,601)
Burden from inventory	307,593
Total cost of goods manufactured	$ 416,645
Decrease in finished goods inventory	—
Cost of goods sold	$1,095,703

Financial information is shown in Exhibits 11, 12, 13, and 14.

Wappner stated that since July 1, 1982, several steps had been taken to increase profits. A 6 percent price increase was in effect. Improvements had been made in plant operations. Some overhead items, such as retirement benefits, had been reduced. As a result of these changes, Wappner was projecting income from operations for the fiscal year ending June 30, 1983, at $130,000.

EXHIBIT 9

Thermometer Corporation of America Schedule of Selling and Administrative Expenses for the Year Ended December 31, 1981

	1981
Selling expenses:	
Salaries	$9,586
Commissions	61,295
Travel	715
Advertising	31,172
Samples	2,917
Telephone	4,037
Show expense	20,460
Payroll taxes	899
Depreciation	2,439
Supplies	131
Miscellaneous	—
	$133,651
Administrative expenses:	
Salaries	$110,433
Payroll taxes	9,301
Pension	11,000
Travel	4,278
Office supplies	3,892
Telephone	2,422
Legal and professional	2,800
Depreciation	1,595
Dues and subscriptions	3,572
Insurance	1,274
Bank charges	4,106
Contributions	914
Data processing	4,238
Rent—autos	3,643
Amortization patents	5,700
Bad debt expense	3,000
Miscellaneous	386
	$172,554

The Thermometer Industry

MARKET STRUCTURE In the early '80s, the thermometer industry was composed of two major segments: the consumer market and the industrial market. The ratio of industrial to consumer sales for the total thermometer market was approximately 20 percent to 80 percent. TCA maintained an interest

EXHIBIT 10   Ohio Thermometer Organization Chart—November 1982

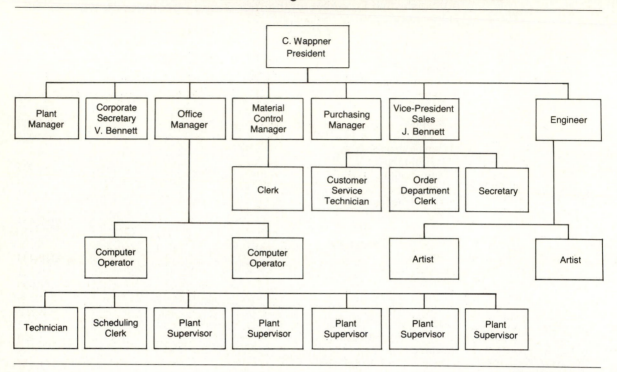

in both segments with about the same split as the total industry. OTC, however, was predominantly focused in the consumer segment, especially the weather components of that market, which comprised over 80 percent of their total thermometer sales.

Marketing information for the industrial sector was generally not available on a per-company basis or by type of thermometer instrument. This situation was due to the fact that the production of thermometers in most companies was but a small part of a huge product line of all types of recorders, gauges, and instruments. As a result, it was virtually impossible to isolate meaningful information on the industrial market.

Therefore, the majority of information was on competitive activities within the consumer market. The product lines in this market included weather, houseware/decorator, cooking, and a miscellaneous line that included medical, automobile, and other small uses of thermometers as shown in Exhibit 15. The total market for thermometers (consumer and industrial) was estimated at $100 million in 1982.

EXHIBIT 11

**The Ohio Thermometer Company Comparative Balance Sheets
at June 30, 1982, 1981, 1980, 1979, and 1978**

	1982	1981	1980	1979	1978
ASSETS					
Current assets:					
Cash	$ 7,939	$ 4,934	$ 4,330	$ —	$ —
Federal income tax refundable	—	55,216	90,546	—	—
Accounts receivable (net)	247,057	282,055	339,342	559,238	481,374
Inventory	626,796	708,409	853,579	903,762	795,181
Prepaid expenses	24,513	20,808	19,737	45,392	23,552
Total current assets	$ 906,305	$1,071,422	$1,307,534	$1,508,892	$1,300,607
Property and equipment:					
Land	51,851	51,851	51,851	51,851	51,851
Building	308,418	308,418	308,418	308,418	308,418
Machinery and equipment	380,362	356,235	353,300	320,180	281,792
Trucks	9,518	9,518	9,518	9,518	9,518
Furniture	97,717	87,570	86,480	85,320	83,790
Total	$ 847,866	$ 813,592	$ 809,567	$ 775,287	$ 735,369
Less accumulated depreciation	691,896	663,478	635,337	610,816	577,634
Total property and equipment	$ 155,970	$ 150,114	$ 174,230	$ 164,471	$ 157,735
Other assets:					
Cash value life insurance	21,860	21,679	109,958	135,833	135,833
Advances to employees	1,544	12,912	10,635	—	—
Deposits on leased equipment	1,202	2,220	2,220	5,256	5,410
Total other assets	$ 24,406	$ 36,811	$ 122,813	$ 141,089	$ 141,243
Total assets	$1,086,881	$1,258,347	$1,604,577	$1,814,452	$1,599,585
LIABILITIES AND STOCKHOLDERS' EQUITY					
Current liabilities:					
Notes payable	$ 300,000	$ 175,000	$ 185,000	$ 175,000	$ 85,000
Current maturities on long-term debt	9,993	10,290	8,728	5,753	5,255
Accounts payable	418,671	519,981	418,566	506,937	450,094
Accrued expenses	73,390	67,136	83,414	106,679	132,510
Total current liabilities	$ 802,054	$ 722,407	$ 695,708	$ 794,369	$ 672,859
Long-term debt	20,473	53,374	159,173	187,464	196,197
Total liabilities	$ 822,527	$ 825,781	$ 854,881	$ 981,833	$ 869,056
Stockholders' equity					
Common stock	250,000	250,000	250,000	250,000	250,000
Retained earnings	111,634	279,846	596,976	679,399	577,809
Less: treasury stock	97,280	97,280	97,280	97,280	97,280
Total stockholders' equity	$ 264,354	$ 432,566	$ 749,696	$ 832,619	$ 730,529
Total liabilities and stockholders' equity	$1,086,881	$1,258,347	$1,604,577	$1,814,452	$1,599,585

EXHIBIT 12   **The Ohio Thermometer Company Comparative Income Statements for the Years Ended June 30, 1982, 1981, 1980, 1979, and 1978**

	1982	1981	1980	1979	1978
Net sales	$3,654,311	$3,649,931	$4,286,345	$4,735,234	$4,367,128
Cost of sales	2,788,718	2,882,232	3,337,012	3,538,663	3,248,270
Gross profit	865,593	767,699	949,333	1,196,571	1,118,858
Operating expenses:					
Selling	513,136	593,627	654,647	615,489	525,870
Administrative	441,451	472,730	435,530	422,065	334,121
Interest	63,317	56,546	40,668	30,706	18,461
Bad debts	15,206	15,241	—	—	—
Other	—	—	(4,976)	(4,474)	41,950
Total operating expenses	1,033,110	1,138,144	1,125,869	1,063,786	920,402
Income (loss) from operations	(167,517)	(370,445)	(176,536)	132,785	198,456
Provision for income taxes	—	—	—	30,000	78,000
Tax benefit of net oper. loss carrybacks	—	54,010	70,546	—	—
Net income (loss) before special items	(167,517)	(316,435)	(105,990)	102,785	120,456
Insurance proceeds on deceased officer	—	—	23,762	—	—
Net income (loss)	$ (167,517)	$ (316,435)	$ (82,228)	$ 102,785	$ 120,456

MARKET CONDITIONS   The sale of consumer thermometer lines generally fluctuated with the economy. Several items within the decorator line, for example, were positioned as gift items, and sales corresponded to the general consumer buying mood, especially during holidays.

Products within all categories ranged from low-price, mainly discount items to high-quality, high-price specialty items. Most of the seven major competitors within the consumer market had at least one strong product that acted as the anchor for the rest of their lines.

Distribution of consumer thermometer products was generally accomplished through retailers, including department/variety, hardware, discount, drug, grocery, and showroom and catalog stores. Retail outlets that commonly carry thermometer products are shown at Exhibit 16. Because of shelf-space limitations and high costs of dealing with multiple vendors, most retail outlets preferred to do business with vendors who represent manufacturers that produce a wide variety of thermometers. Historically, most re-

EXHIBIT 13

The Ohio Thermometer Company Schedules of Cost of Goods Sold for the Years Ended June 30, 1982, and 1981

	1982	1981
Materials	$1,423,055	$1,462,728
Direct labor	$ 513,231	$ 555,098
Manufacturing expenses:		
Indirect labor	$ 63,303	$ 59,041
Production office	3,157	4,034
Engineers	41,780	41,984
Supervision	120,874	112,258
Vacation and holiday	88,482	91,659
Retirement	29,372	33,198
Payroll taxes	81,298	87,391
Industrial welfare	210	2,527
Employees' insurance	109,956	94,604
Supplies	104,784	106,549
Maintenance and repairs	66,883	69,858
Truck	2,645	2,780
Freight	16,465	17,090
Utilities	58,373	50,676
Depreciation—building	9,850	9,850
Depreciation—other	14,918	11,312
Insurance	5,125	7,234
Taxes	5,616	5,788
Dues and subscriptions	420	1,148
Travel	222	267
Rent	490	442
Miscellaneous	2,236	2,187
	$ 826,459	$ 811,877
Total cost of goods manufactured	$2,762,745	$2,829,703
Decrease in finished goods inventory	25,973	52,529
Cost of goods sold	$2,788,718	$2,882,232

tailers limited the number to three or, at most, four separate vendors. Most would welcome the opportunity to reduce that number if a manufacturer could expand to include thermometers from more of the standard lines.

COMPETITIVE SITUATION   The largest share of the thermometer market was held by *Taylor* with 30 percent. Not only did this company have a balanced array of products that spanned all of the consumer lines, it was also strongly

EXHIBIT 14

The Ohio Thermometer Company Schedules of Selling and Administrative Expenses for the Years Ended June 30, 1982, and 1981

	1982	1981
Selling expenses:		
Salaries	$135,936	$157,883
Commissions	159,211	202,616
Travel	18,088	23,873
Advertising	20,662	15,219
Prospect	10	32
Samples	3,657	6,392
Freight	167,595	179,743
Telephone	5,818	4,780
Dues and subscriptions	2,159	3,089
	$513,136	$593,627
Administrative expenses:		
Executive salaries	$ 99,611	$ 88,299
Office salaries	124,401	126,898
Payroll taxes	36,584	24,862
Executive pension	28,293	60,638
Director fees	3,300	2,400
Travel	9,139	4,625
Postage	5,872	6,132
Office supplies	30,610	50,332
Telephone	8,109	7,194
Legal and professional	19,077	19,133
Depreciation	3,649	6,980
Dues and subscriptions	2,056	2,354
Insurance	17,007	14,468
Life insurance on officers	10,398	8,564
Contributions	3,520	753
Taxes	15,458	21,961
Rent—computer	20,064	20,064
Rent—autos	4,303	7,073
	$441,451	$472,730

positioned in the industrial market. Its industrial line included all types of sensing, recording, and control devices.

Taylor had used its expertise in the industrial sector to develop specialized, high-quality products that competed at the high end of the consumer market. Decorator units included top-of-the-line thermometers and hydrometers as well as recording devices for amateur meteorologists. Taylor had

EXHIBIT 15 **Examples of Products Included in Each of the Product Lines**

Weather
    12″ and 18″ dials—plain and decorated
    Window units
    Remote reading units
    Wall weather units
    Patio units

Houseware—decorator
    Gift lines
    Clock component
    Oven-refrigerator units

Cooking
    Meat units
    Candy units
    Thermo spoon/fork units
    Cheese/yogurt units

Miscellaneous
    Mercury units
    Car units
    Dairy and poultry units
    Laboratory/hobby units

positioned most of its products as specialty items or heterogeneous shopping-good items.

Springfield held the second-largest share of the market with 15 percent. This company concentrated on the price-sensitive consumer. It emphasized high volume, limited product lines, low raw material costs, and large production runs to hold down production costs. Springfield had strong positions in the weather, cooking, and decorator components of the consumer market.

Airguide had a narrow product line with 6 percent market share. Its initial entry into the consumer market was through its compass line. Since then, the company had diversified into consumer weather thermometers. Airguide actively pursued international markets and currently imported many of its products.

Cooper maintained fourth position in the consumer market with 5 percent. This company had products in the weather segment; however, its main strength was its line of bimetal cooking thermometers. Patents on manufacturing processes provide a competitive edge in terms of best quality combined with the lowest production costs in the industry for these types of thermometers.

EXHIBIT 16   **Examples of Retail Outlets by Type**

Discounters

Kmart	Wilson's
Woolworth	Frank's Nursery
Target	Hill's
G. C. Murphy	Western Auto
Shopko	Rink's
Fedco	Meijer-Thrifty Acres

Department and Variety

Sears	Hoffritz
Montgomery Ward	Mercantile
J.C. Penney	Allied
Alden's	Ben Franklin
Hammacher-Schlemmer	Neiman-Marcus

Hardware

American
Ace
Cotter-True Value
Geo. Worthington—
Security
HWI
S & T
Bostwick-Braun—Pro
Clark-Siviter
S. B. Hubbard
Stratton-Baldwin
Woodward-Wight
Farwell, Ozmun, Kirk
Our Own Hardware
Coast to Coast
United
Central

Drug Stores

Walgreen
Super X
Skaggs
Eckerd
Rexall
Cunningham
Skillern
Osco
Fays
K & B
Affiliated
Long's
Zahn
Kerr
McKesson
Thrifty
Payless

Foods

Certified
Kroger's
T.G. & Y.
Lucky (Ch)
Von's
Publix
Safeway
National Tea
Gemco
Albertson's
Western Grocers
National Grocers
Lucky (L.A.)
Super Valu

Distributors

Dutch Peddler
Washington
Peyton's
Mid States
Invento-H & S
Benny's
Manor Sales
Edwin Jay
Comer-Hanby
Superior Merchandise
Ely
Ideal School Supply
Orchard Supply
Mid States Distributing

Catalog and Show Rooms

E. F. MacDonald	Brookstone
Top Value	Bolinds
Premium Corporation	Harriet Carter
L. L. Bean	Miles Kimball
Century	Eastern Mountain Sports
Southern States	Orvis Stitchery
Edward Don	Edmund Scientific
Joan Cook	Gander Mountain
Sportsman's Guide	Gokey's
Johnny Appleseed	Taylor Gifts

Advertising and Premium

General Motors	Jack Daniels
Ford	Standard Oil
Coca-Cola	Firestone
Pepsi	Calverts
Seagrams	Dupont
National Distributors	Cargill
Seven Up	Goodrich
Dr. Pepper	RCA
E. H. Lilley	Fram
Monroe	Homelite
R. C. Cola	Chrysler
Coors	Briggs and Stratton
Anderson Anco	Bolens
Bendix	Stihl

OTC occupied fifth position by virtue of its strength in round-dial thermometers with 3.5 percent. Springfield had captured the low end of this segment. OTC produced higher quality products and had an established reputation as the most reliable name in this segment of the market. In addition, OTC had captured the market dealing in promotional and scenic display thermometers (12″ and 18″ round-dial types). Its Achilles' heel was the lack of competitive products across all parts of the consumer market. Over 80 percent of OTC's total thermometer sales were concentrated in its dial thermometers. It did manufacture thermometers for miscellaneous uses such as automobiles, but these areas were considered to be rather limited in terms of growth potential. OTC had, however, compensated for its lack of a wide product selection by developing one of the best vendor representative groups in the consumer thermometer industry. This network of vendor representatives provided excellent breadth and depth of reach into all retail markets.

TCA struggled in sixth place in the total consumer market with 1.5 percent. Most of its revenues (80 percent) originated from weather and cooking thermometers. In addition, TCA maintained a small presence in the industrial market (15 percent of revenues) as well as the housewares and miscellaneous markets.

Although TCA had managed to maintain product lines that crossed all consumer markets, it had failed to dominate in any of these markets. Consequently, it was experiencing low market share across the board and had no flagship product that could ultimately provide a dominant level of consumer awareness and interest in its products. TCA also appeared to have somewhat weak representation in the marketplace due to its inability to develop a strong, comprehensive vendor network.

Chaney was seventh among the top competitors with 1 percent and was really focused in only two areas. Its major strength was based on strong candy and meat thermometer products. The company did offer weather instruments, but none of its weather products were well known.

Exhibit 17 summarizes the relative positions of each of the seven top competitors in the consumer market and indicates which segments are served by their products.

DISTRIBUTION CHANNELS   Most of the companies had comparable channel configurations. For example, all of the seven competing manufacturers used vendor systems in which manufacturers' reps contacted all types of retail outlets.

Taylor, Springfield, and OTC had the strongest network of reps. Since most retail outlets preferred to do business with only those companies that carried broad, well-established product lines, it was difficult for the other companies to break into the retail marketplace. Thus, TCA used a combination of manufacturers' reps and its own sales reps to maintain a stronger presence in the marketplace. Normally its sales force reps concentrated on key accounts based on geographical location and size.

EXHIBIT 17		Relative Market Position and Breadth of Product Lines			
COMPANY	PERCENT OF TOTAL THERMOMETER MARKET	SEGMENTS OF CONSUMER SECTOR			
		WEATHER	HOUSEWARE AND DECORATOR	COOKING	MISC.
Taylor	30.0	Y	Y	Y	Y
Springfield	15.0	Y	Y	Y	N
Airguide	6.0	Y	N	N	Y
Cooper	5.0	Y	Y	Y	N
OTC	3.5	Y	N	Y	Y
TCA	1.5	Y	Y	Y	Y
Chaney	1.0	Y	N	Y	N

CONCLUDING DIALOGUE

The conversation between Figgie and Skadra continued:

FIGGIE Jerry Bennett told me that he thought the addition of TCA products for his present OTC manufacturers' reps would immediately increase the rate of sales by $500,000 annually. He also thinks that within five years the combined companies would have a sales potential of $10 million.

SKADRA Very optimistic! He sounds like a salesman.

FIGGIE I had a chance later to talk with Bill Kieffer. He has concerns about working with the OTC plant personnel. He thinks they are used to doing things in their own way and may be difficult to change. And he thinks that their processes can be made more efficient.

SKADRA Do you think we can assimilate Charlie and Jerry into TCA without losing their interest and effort?

FIGGIE We'll have to do some thinking about that.

SKADRA By agreeing to cut their salaries by a combined total of $72,000 per year and by agreeing to work for two years they are demonstrating support for the continuing operation.

FIGGIE Charlie and Jerry have apparently taken title to the building in their own names and would like to rent the building to us as part of a merger.

SKADRA With FI's vacant plant, we may have an alternative to renting from them.

FIGGIE Springfield is a small town; we have little chance of leasing the idle plant. How much do you estimate we would have to spend for improvements to make the plant usable for manufacturing?

SKADRA About $100,000.

FIGGIE The possible loss carry-forward does not justify assuming the risk of potential liabilities that would accompany the purchase of the stock of OTC Corporation.

There are several factors to consider here, Joe. Will you and your staff take a good look at the November 17th offer and prepare a complete counterproposal with supporting justification? Also I'd like to have a strategy for conducting the negotiations.

Exhibit 18 provides economic indexes for review and consideration.

EXHIBIT 18   **Economic Indexes**

TITLE	UNIT OF MEASURE	FOURTH QUARTER 1982	OCTOBER 1982	EST. OF NOVEMBER 1982	EST. OF DECEMBER 1982	AVERAGE		
						1980	1981	1982 (EST.)
Twelve leading indicators	1967 = 100	131.4	130.6	130.8	132.8	131.2	133.3	128.4
Four coincident indicators	do.	128.3	128.5	128.3	128.2	140.3	141.3	132.2
Six lagging indicators	do.	165.1	168.4	165.0	161.9	176.8	187.7	177.4
Total unemployed	Thousands	11,839	11,576	11,906	12,036	7,448	8,080	10,678
Unemployment rate, total	Percent	10.7	10.5	10.7	10.8	7.1	7.9	9.7
New private housing units started, total	A.r., thous.	1,253	1,126	1,404	1,229	1,292	1,087	1,061
Change in business inventories, 1972 dollars	do.	(17.7)				(2.9)	8.2	(8.5)
Change in money supply	Percent	1.29	1.72	1.41	0.74	0.52	0.52	0.69
Federal funds rate	Percent	9.29	9.71	9.20	8.95	13.36	16.38	12.26
Treasury bill rate	do.	7.93	7.75	8.04	8.01	11.61	14.08	10.72
Bank notes on short-term business loans	do.	11.26				15.17	19.56	14.69
Average prime rate charged by banks	do.	11.96	12.52	11.85	11.50	15.27	18.87	14.86
Consumer prices (CPI), all items	1967 = 100	293.4	294.1	293.6	292.4	246.8	272.4	289.1
Producer price index (PPI), all commodities	do.	300.3	299.9	300.4	300.6	268.8	293.4	299.3

EXHIBIT 18   **Continued**

TITLE	UNIT OF MEASURE	AVERAGE			1982 (EST.)	FIRST QUARTER 1982	SECOND QUARTER 1982	THIRD QUARTER 1982	FOURTH QUARTER 1982 (EST.)
		1979	1980	1981					
GNP in 1972 dollars	A.r., thous.	1,483.0	1,474.0	1,502.6	1,475.5	1,470.7	1,478.4	1,481.1	1,471.7
GNP in current dollars	do.	2,413.0	2,633.1	2,937.7	3,057.5	2,995.5	3,045.2	3,088.2	3,101.3
Personal saving rate	Percent	5.2	5.8	6.4	6.5	6.6	6.7	6.9	5.8

GENICOM Corporation

PER V. JENSTER • JOHN M. GWIN • DAVID B. CROLL

Curtis W. Powell, president of GENICOM, faced the morning of June 18, 1985, with uncertainty. His upcoming meeting with the labor union at the firm's Waynesboro, Virginia, facility was one that raised some disturbing questions about the company's future, and even its past.

Prior to that day's meeting, GENICOM had proposed wage and benefit reductions, which resulted in increasing confrontation with union representatives. Mr. Powell pondered what strategic alternatives the company should pursue if the union did not accept the proposed reductions. And even if the union did make the concessions needed, what strategy should GENICOM follow in the competitive computer printer market over the next three to five years?

BACKGROUND

GENICOM was founded in June 1983, as a result of a leveraged buyout of General Electric's (GE's) Data Communication Products business department in Waynesboro, a relatively self-contained entity that produced computer printers and relay components. The department operated as one of GE's strategic business units.

GE came to Waynesboro, a small town in central Virginia, in 1954 as part of a major decentralization effort that also included the establishment of facilities in nearby Lynchburg and Salem, Virginia. Between 1954 and 1974, the Waynesboro plant produced a wide variety of highly sophisticated electromechanical devices such as process controls, numerical controls, and aircraft controls, many of which are now produced by other GE divisions.

Products once manufactured in the Waynesboro facility account for several hundred million dollars in annual sales revenues for GE. As a result, the Waynesboro factory has a long-standing reputation for its skill in electromechanical design and engineering and for its ability to solve difficult design tasks in its highly vertically integrated facilities.

The first electromechanical printer was created by GE in Waynesboro as a result of the firm's own dissatisfaction with the performance of the Teletype 33 printers. The new GE printer was three times faster than the Teletype 33 and gained quick popularity. In 1969, a send–receive printer was introduced with such success that it evolved into one of GE's fastest-growing product lines. Other products were added using the same technology, and by 1977 the business in Waynesboro had attained annual revenues of $100 million.

Copyright © 1986. This case was used in the fifth McIntire Commerce Invitational (MCI V) held at the University of Virginia on February 13–15, 1986. We gratefully acknowledge the General Electric Foundation for support of the MCI and the writing of this case. Reprinted with permission.

In 1980, GE changed corporate leadership. The new GE chairman, John F. Welch, initiated a major review of the corporation's businesses to determine which ones were critical to GE's future strategies. Businesses with products that did not rank number one or number two in their served industries or did not have the technological leadership to become first or second required special review. The Waynesboro products did not rank number one or number two in their served industry, nor were they critical to GE's long-term strategies, and in 1981 the department's strategic planning process investigated the possibility of divestiture as an alternative course of action.

During 1981, the then-current general manager resigned and Curtis Powell, the financial manager and long-term GE employee, was appointed the new general manager.[1]

During the same time frame the printer business's line of reporting was dismantled; the general manager, the division manager, and his superior, the group vice president, left GE, and the executive vice president and sector executive retired. As a result, there were no administrative levels between the Waynesboro facility and a newly appointed sector executive. Powell received the dual task of (1) positioning the business for divestiture and (2) making it viable if no acceptable buyers could be found. To accomplish these two objectives, Powell implemented programs to improve the competitiveness of the department's printer products and productivity programs to reduce the cost of operations. To support aggressive new product design efforts, funding of research and development activities were increased by $1 million per year. The first product, the new 3000 series printer, was introduced in the latter part of 1981. By 1982, the 3000 series product had received an excellent reception in the marketplace. Variable costs had been reduced by 28 percent, primarily as a result of the relocation of 300 jobs from Waynesboro to the department's Mexican facility, fixed costs had been reduced by 25 percent, and net assets in the business had been reduced by $14 million. Despite the successful introduction of the new printer product and rapidly increasing orders, GE was still interested in divesting the business.

After several months of meetings with potential acquirers, GE had not received an acceptable offer. During the fourth quarter of 1982, Powell and a group of plant managers offered to purchase the Waynesboro-based business from GE.

The Buyout of GENICOM

During early 1983, GE agreed to sell the business as a leveraged buyout, but required a substantial cash payment. In order to complete the transaction, the management team was joined by two New York–based venture capital firms that provided the financial resources needed to purchase the business.

The price agreed upon for the business was net depreciated value plus $8 million. (Note that the business had been in Waynesboro since 1954 and the net depreciated value was significantly less than the appraised value.) The purchase price amounted to less than six months' sales revenue.

The assets purchased included every printer ever designed by the Waynesboro facility, all customers and contracts, all patents and cross-licenses, tools, and buildings, as well as the Relay business. The purchase agreement was signed October 23, 1983, at which time GE received approximately 75 percent of the purchase price in cash and subordinated notes for the balance. The purchase amount was financed through sale of shares to the venture capital firms and to local management (approximately 45 of the top managers received stock or stock options). Twelve million dollars were borrowed against fixed assets in the business, and a revolving credit line was secured against equipment leases, receivables, and selected inventory. Given the assessed value of the firm, GENICOM had not exceeded 65 percent of its borrowing capacity.

The GENICOM Corporation

By 1983, GENICOM was one of the larger independent computer printer companies that manufactured teleprinters (i.e., keyboard send–receive units), dot-matrix printers, and line printers. These printers were primarily industrial grade, and thus were not widely used for personal computer output. They served a wide variety of data processing and telecommunication needs, with printing speeds ranging from 60 characters per second (cps) in the teleprinter version to 400 lines per minute (lpm) in their line printer series. GENICOM was also the industry leader in crystal relays sold to defense, space, and other industries where there was a need for highly reliable electrical switches.

GENICOM was also a multinational company with production facilities in Waynesboro (1,300 employees) and Mexico (700 employees). Approximately 20 percent of the 1984 sales revenue of $140 million was derived from international customers, primarily original equipment manufacturers (OEMs). GENICOM was in the process of establishing its own sales affiliates in the United Kingdom, France, Germany, and Sweden in order to further serve its foreign customers.

Prior to the change in ownership, GENICOM's management negotiated a comprehensive benefits package that was essentially the same as GE's. Furthermore, a new agreement with the union was settled, and customers and suppliers were briefed. All but fifteen current employees were offered positions with GENICOM at the same salary and similar benefits as provided by GE, and all accepted.

According to Powell, "Everything considered, the buyout went extremely well. 1984 was an excellent year, a very successful year for GENICOM. We are still trying to change the culture we inherited from GE, where people feel they have unlimited resources, to a small company climate, a climate in which costs must be contained. Some of our people in Waynesboro believe that the success we had in 1984 will continue forever. They don't realize that in our industry product life cycles are short and even if your products are doing well today, you need to prepare for tomorrow. This transition from GE to GENICOM has been difficult.

"When we were a part of GE all employees were paid GE wages and salaries. Other firms in our industry and other firms in Waynesboro paid considerably less than GE rates." As part of the two largest employers in Waynesboro, GENICOM's actions when dealing with its employees became public very soon. "We have a very quality-conscious work force in Waynesboro and quality has always been extremely important to us. But in our competitive market quality is not enough, we must be cost competitive also."

Management and Structure

GENICOM's management inherited an organizational structure and an information system that reflected GE's standards and procedures. Consequently, GENICOM was probably the most vertically integrated printer company in the world (largely encouraged by GE's capital budgeting and performance evaluation system), making almost everything in house from tools to printer ribbons to sales brochures. This high degree of vertical integration enabled GENICOM to respond quickly to specific requests for redesign of products to suit individual customer needs.

The firm's information system was also aligned with GE's reporting system, which led one outside observer to conclude that he "had never seen an organization with such a sophisticated information system which used it so little." As an illustration, Exhibit 1 shows GENICOM's MIS budget vis-à-vis industry averages. Exhibit 2 compares GENICOM's data processing department with a similar organization in the industry. According to Coopers and Lybrand, a consulting firm retained by GENICOM, the cost problem, highlighted in these two exhibits, could also be found in other areas: finance, materials, shop operations, manufacturing engineering, quality control, marketing, product engineering, and relays.

The management team of GENICOM (April 1985) consists of the following members:

- Curtis W. Powell, president and chief executive officer: Powell graduated from Lynchburg College, Lynchburg, Virginia, in 1961 with a B.A. in business administration and economics. Prior to the purchase of the

EXHIBIT 1   **Comparisons with Industry Averages**

	MANUFACTURING (ELECTRONICS, ELECTRICAL)			GENICOM		
	($ THOUSANDS)*	PERCENT OF REVENUE	PERCENT OF MIS BUDGET	($ THOUSANDS)	PERCENT OF REVENUE	PERCENT OF MIS BUDGET
Total revenue	$75,590	100	N/A	$165,000	100	N/A
MIS operating budget	723	1.01	100	2,567.4†	1.56	100
Personnel	308	.43	42.5	1,271.0	.77	49.5
Hardware	208	.29	28.4	400.6‡	.24	15.6
System software	21	.03	3.1	27.5	.02	1.1
Application software	36	.05	4.9	76.5	.05	3.0
Supplies	57	.08	7.8	110.3	.07	4.2
Outside services	36	.05	7.8	559.0	.34	21.8
Communications	21	.03	3.3	19.8	.01	0.8
Other	36	.05	5.0	102.7§	.06	4.0

SOURCES: Infosystems 25th and 26th annual salary surveys, June 1983 and June 1984.

Survey of 642 firms conducted for Datamation, and published March 15, 1985, shows that firms averaging $200 million in revenue employ an average of 20.1 people in data processing (equivalent to IS&S at GENICOM without office services). This provides an index of average revenue of $9,950,200 per data processing employee.

*Represents average amounts reported in source survey.

†GENICOM's IS&S actual expenses January to May 1985 have been annualized and have been modified to (1) remove office services expenses and (2) to add estimated hardware depreciation expense and estimated occupancy expense in order to correlate to survey figures.

‡This category includes equipment rental, maintenance, and depreciation expense. Depreciation expense is drawn from GENICOM's fixed asset register and includes annual depreciation (book) for all assets acquired through December, 1984.

§This category includes occupancy expense estimated at 4 percent of total MIS expense budget.

Waynesboro business by GENICOM, Powell had served 22 years in various General Electric assignments, the last two as department general manager of the Waynesboro business.

- John V. Harker, executive vice president: Harker was responsible for the sales and marketing functions, including product planning, market and new business development, marketing administration, customer service, domestic sales and international operations. He formerly held positions as senior vice president for marketing and corporate development at Dataproducts, vice president of Booz, Allen, and Hamilton, Inc., a management consulting firm, and with IBM in various marketing capacities. Upon joining GENICOM, he initiated the hiring of six new marketing and sales executives from the computer peripherals industry.

EXHIBIT 2   **Personnel Information Comparison for a Data Processing Department with Some Similarities to GENICOM**

	GENICOM	OTHER FIRM
Hardware	5 H-P 3000s	4 H-P 3000s
Number of data centers	1 current 1 planned	2
Annual revenues of organization	$165 million (1985 budget)	$550 million (1985 budget)
Type of business	Manufacturing	Manufacturing
Number of employees in MIS	34 (Includes staff at one data center)	44 (Includes staff at both data centers)
Salary expense	$1,051,300	$1,075,200 (1984 + 5%)
Processing characteristics	In-house plus heavy use of remote computing service	In-house plus heavy use of remote computing service
Company revenues per MIS employee	$4,852,900	$12.5 million

- Robert C. Bowen, vice president and chief financial officer: Bowen has served in various financial capacities with GE since 1964, and with GENICOM's predecessor for the past ten years.
- W. Douglas Drumheller, vice president of manufacturing: Drumheller joined GE's manufacturing management program in 1970 and was appointed vice president at GENICOM in 1983.
- Dennie J. Shadrick, vice president of engineering: Shadrick recently joined GENICOM after seventeen years with Texas Instruments, where he served in a variety of engineering and management positions in the terminal and printer business unit.
- Charles A. Ford, vice president of relay operations: Ford has had a long career with GE and GENICOM serving in the areas of manufacturing, engineering, and general management.
- Robert B. Chapman, treasurer: Chapman has been with GENICOM since 1984, after holding positions with Centronics Data Computer Corporation, Honeywell, Inc., and the Datapoint Corporation, where he was assistant treasurer.

According to Curtis Powell, "Part of our GE heritage was a strong engineering and manufacturing orientation and this is a valuable asset. However, as a new and independent company, we needed to establish a marketing presence, we needed a new and aggressive approach to our marketing and sales activities. One of our first action items was to recruit the best marketing and sales executives we could locate. GENICOM's strategy for developing marketing strengths has been to bring experienced and capable people from other firms in the computer peripherals industry."

Financial Statements

The 1984 financial statements are included in Exhibits 3–6, and footnotes are included in Appendix A. Due to the time period constraints associated with any financial statements, GENICOM's balance sheet for December 30, 1984, did not include the subsequent private placement of stock that took place on January 3, 1985. GENICOM sold 353,000 shares of its unissued common stock for $5 per share. If these shares had been issued at December 30, 1984, unaudited pro forma stockholders' equity would have been $16,993,000.

The two period comparisons used in the financial statements for December 30, 1984, and January 1, 1984, are not true comparisons as the time periods covered are not equal. The first column for the year ending December 30, 1984, represents a twelve-month period, but the second column for the year ending January 1, 1984, represents only a two-month-and-ten-day period.

The remaining statements and ten footnotes in Appendix A are complete and self-explanatory. The strong financial orientation of the management is evident in the statement presentation.

Cost Accounting

A major cost accounting issue was that GENICOM's product costs were well above those of its competitors. GENICOM's willingness to customize its products to meet its customers' individual needs allowed it to charge a premium price. The costs that seemed disproportionately high were salary and hourly wages. GENICOM's salary and wage structures were established over many years while it was a part of GE. General Electric traditionally provided its employees with both a generous base salary and a generous fringe package. As wages and benefits were negotiated with the union on an overall corporate basis, the printer department had avoided serious conflicts with the union.

Consultants from Coopers and Lybrand were hired by GENICOM to evaluate the firm's cost structure. Although the study was not completed, preliminary research had focused on this labor cost problem. The preliminary findings suggested that most areas of the firm seemed overstaffed and salary and wage levels exceeded both industry norms and local community standards (see Exhibits 1 and 2).

An interesting point was that GENICOM's wage and salary differential over other local companies was so great that it proved detrimental to some

EXHIBIT 3   **GENICOM Corporation and Subsidiaries: Consolidated Balance Sheet (Dollar Amounts in Thousands)**

	DECEMBER 30, 1984	JANUARY 1, 1984
ASSETS		
Current assets:		
Cash	$ 451	$ 3,023
Accounts receivable, less allowance for doubtful accounts of $958 and $483	21,224	22,459
Inventories (Note 3)	26,917	24,343
Prepaid expenses and other assets	1,368	356
Total current assets	49,960	50,181
Property, plant, and equipment (Note 3)	27,821	27,314
Other assets	239	180
	$78,020	$77,675
LIABILITIES AND CAPITAL		
Current liabilities:		
Current portion of long-term debt	1,600	11,841
Accounts payable and accrued expenses (Note 3)	16,104	15,682
Deferred income	1,519	1,359
Income taxes (Note 8)	5,579	
Total current liabilities	24,802	28,882
Long-term debt, less current portion (Note 4)	36,400	44,500
Deferred income taxes	1,590	504
Redeemable preferred stock, $1 par value; 32,000 shares issued and outstanding at January 1, 1984; stated at liquidation value of $100 per share		3,200
Stockholders' equity (Note 11):		
Common stock, $.01 par value; 20,000,000 shares authorized; shares outstanding: December 30, 1984—10,995,500 and January 1, 1984—8,575,000	110	86
Additional paid-in capital	9,297	772
Retained earnings (deficit)	5,821	(269)
	15,228	589
	$78,020	$77,675

Note: See Appendix A for notes.

EXHIBIT 4

GENICOM Corporation and Subsidiaries: Consolidated Statement of Income (Dollars Amounts in Thousands, Except Per Share Data)

	YEAR ENDED DECEMBER 30, 1984	OCTOBER 21, 1983 TO JANUARY 1, 1984
Net sales	$136,661	$26,752
Cost of goods sold	90,647	20,403
Gross profit	46,014	6,349
Expenses:		
Selling, general, and administration	22,442	3,965
Engineering, research, and product development	4,795	890
Interest	6,900	1,386
	34,137	6,241
Income before income taxes	11,877	108
Income tax expense (Note 8)	5,787	377
Net income (loss)	$ 6,090	$ (269)
Net income (loss) per common share and common share equivalent:		
Primary	$.61	$(.03)
Fully diluted	$.59	$(.03)
Weighted average number of common shares and common share equivalents:		
Primary	9,967	8,753
Fully diluted	10,292	8,892

Note: See Appendix A for notes.

laid-off employees. Other companies in the region had reported that they were hesitant to hire a laid-off GENICOM employee knowing that as soon as an opening existed the employee would be lost back to GENICOM.

Union Negotiations

Negotiations with Local 124 of the United Electrical Radio and Machine Workers (UE) of America started on April 23, 1985. Management's primary goal was to reduce the average costs of an applied direct labor hour by four dollars. Included in the employee benefit package were vacation (five weeks maximum), holidays (ten days), comprehensive medical benefits, life insur-

EXHIBIT 5

GENICOM Corporation and Subsidiaries: Consolidated Statement of Changes in Capital Accounts (Dollar Amounts in Thousands) for the Year Ended December 30, 1984, and the Period from October 21, 1983 (Commencement of Operations) to January 1, 1984

	REDEEMABLE PREFERRED STOCK	COMMON STOCK	ADDITIONAL PAID-IN CAPITAL	RETAINED EARNINGS
Issued in connection with acquisition:				
32,000 shares of redeemable preferred stock	$ 3,200			
8,000,000 shares of common stock		$ 80	$ 721	
Issuance of 525,000 shares of common stock		5	47	
Exercise of stock options		1	4	
Net loss				$ (269)
Balance, January 1, 1984	3,200	86	772	(269)
Issuance of 1,297,000 shares of common stock		13	5,288	
Redemption of preferred stock	(3,200)	6	3,194	
Exercise of stock options		5	43	
Net income				6,090
Balance, December 30, 1984	—	$110	$9,297	$ 5,821

Note: See Appendix A for notes.

EXHIBIT 6

GENICOM Corporation and Subsidiaries: Consolidated Statement of Changes in Financial Position (Dollar Amounts in Thousands)

	YEAR ENDED DECEMBER 30, 1984	OCTOBER 21, 1983 TO JANUARY 1, 1984
Sources of working capital:		
From operations:		
Net income (loss)	$ 6,090	$ (269)
Charges to income not affecting working capital:		
Depreciation	4,664	630
Amortization	49	
Deferred income taxes	1,086	504
Working capital from operations	11,889	865

EXHIBIT 6   **Continued**

	YEAR ENDED DECEMBER 30, 1984	OCTOBER 21, 1983 TO JANUARY 1, 1984
Issued or assumed in connection with acquisition:		
Redeemable preferred stock		3,200
Common stock		801
Long-term debt		57,841
Proceeds from issuance of common stock	8,501	52
Exercise of options	48	5
Other, net	357	(189)
Total sources	$20,795	$62,575
Applications of working capital:		
Additions to property, plant, and equipment	5,636	918
Noncurrent assets purchased in acquisition		27,017
Reduction of long-term debt	8,100	13,341
Redemption of preferred stock	3,200	
Total applications	$16,936	$41,276
Analysis of working capital components:		
Increase (decrease) in current assets:		
Cash	(2,572)	3,023
Accounts receivable	(1,235)	22,459
Inventories	2,574	24,343
Prepaid expenses and other assets	1,012	356
Totals	(221)	50,181
Increase (decrease) in current liabilities:		
Current portion of long-term debt	(10,241)	11,841
Accounts payable and accrued expenses	422	15,682
Deferred income	160	1,359
Income taxes	5,579	
Totals	(4,080)	28,882
Increase in working capital	3,859	21,299
Working capital, beginning of period	21,299	
Working capital, end of period	$25,158	$21,299

Note: See Appendix A for notes.

ance, temporary disability, overtime premium, pension, breaks, night-shift bonus, paid sick days/personal time, and job structures that included seventeen pay grades. Appendix B provides a picture of the negotiations as the confrontation grew.

Earlier in April, a different local of UE in a nearby Virginia town had been involved in an almost identical situation. A former department of Westinghouse, which had been sold to outside interests, was confronted with wage and benefit structures originally negotiated at the national level and attempted to win major financial concessions from its work force in order to become cost competitive in its market. The local refused to accept any cutbacks in its package and, after several months of negotiation, went on strike. Two days later the company announced it would begin hiring permanent replacements for the striking workers on the following Monday and placed help-wanted ads in the local newspapers. On Sunday afternoon, in a close vote, the union members voted to end the strike and accept management's proposals.

THE PRINTER INDUSTRY

The demand for printer hardware is derived from the demand for computing machinery. As the demand for computing capability shifted from mainframe computers to minicomputers to microcomputers, so did the demand for printing capacity shift from output capability to output quality. Similarly, the attributes of printers that determined their success in the marketplace changed from reliability and performance when dealing with mainframe applications to price and capability when dealing with microcomputer applications. At the same time, as business applications of microcomputers moved into networking situations, where several microcomputers are linked to a central data base and a single printer, the demands placed on the printer hardware changed from the demands of a stand-alone microcomputer.

In addition to the changes that took place in the printer industry as a result of changes in the computer industry, there was change in the competitive structure of the marketplace. The presence of the Japanese manufacturers had altered the competitive nature of the industry. As had been the strategy in other industries, Japanese manufacturers entered the market at the bottom of the price structure. Because of lower labor rates and efficient production capability, the Japanese products forced extreme price pressure into the market. Once established, the Japanese manufacturers then began to trade up through product improvement and brand extension. As a result, the Japanese printer manufacturers became a formidable force in the marketplace, particularly in the microprinter (for personal computer use) segment. This set of competitors was a force all U.S. manufacturers of printers must have accounted for in the formulation of new product introductions and pricing strategies. Several U.S. manufacturers had licensed off-shore

(Mexican, Korean, Taiwanese, and Japanese) manufacturers to produce price-competitive products under the U.S. manufacturer brand names as a means of competing with the Japanese manufacturers.

THE MARKET

The total market for printers of all types was predicted to be $10.44 billion in 1986. The breakdown of sales by printer type is shown in Exhibit 7. The market was segmented by impact (printers that use a printhead that actually strikes the paper) and nonimpact (printers that do not strike the paper but apply ink in some other fashion). Within the impact market, printers were also segmented by dot matrix (printers that use dots to form the characters printed) and fully formed (printers that print an entire character at once, such as a daisy-wheel printer). This market was further segmented according to whether a printer was a serial printer (one that prints character by character in a serial fashion) or a line printer (one that prints an entire line at a time—in general, line printers are called high speed and print faster than serial printers, but often at a lower quality); finally, the impact market segment was subdivided according to speed of printing. The nonimpact segment was divided further according to printer technology (electrostatic, ink jet, laser), and by speed (in characters per second). Certain nonimpact printers were also segmented as page printers (those that print a complete page at a time). All nonimpact printers were considered to have fully formed characters. A schematic representation of the complete market for printers is shown in Exhibit 8.

Besides print quality, different classes of printers had advantages and disadvantages for end users. Fully formed character printers, whether daisy wheel or band line, offered no graphics capability as they were limited to alphanumeric characters. These printers also were very noisy while printing unless special quietized enclosures were used to surround them. Additionally, daisy-wheel printers, which were found almost exclusively in offices for word processing applications, were extremely slow.

The primary drawback to dot-matrix printers was perceived print quality, although several technological developments had improved their performance. These printers, however, supplied excellent adaptability to applications needs—graphics, spreadsheets, data and word processing, for instance—and prices had been dropping very rapidly in this market segment.

Nonimpact printers offered much of the best aspects of performance—quiet operation, flexible application, and outstanding print quality—but drawbacks included high prices, inability to print multiple copies simultaneously (i.e., continuous multipart forms printing), higher cost of operation because of their utilization of consumable supplies such as toner, and some perception on the part of users that nonimpact printers, like the copiers their technology was derived from, were less reliable.

EXHIBIT 7

The U.S. Printer Market

	1983				1986			
	NUMBER OF UNITS	PERCENT SHARE	$ VALUE	PERCENT SHARE	NUMBER OF UNITS	PERCENT SHARE	$ VALUE	PERCENT SHARE
Serial daisy wheel	712,000	25	1.37 billion	25	2,000,000	24	2.4 billion	23
Serial dot matrix	1,857,000	66	2.28 billion	41	4,600,000	54	4.14 billion	40
Serial nonimpact*	132,000	5	162 million	3	1,600,000	19	990 million	9
Nonimpact page printers†	5,200	0	222 million	4	150,000	2	1 billion	10
Fully formed line printers	86,000	3	1.13 billion	21	100,000	1	1.4 billion	13
Dot matrix line printers	31,000	1	318 million	6	55,000	0	510 million	5
Total	2,823,000		5,482 billion		8,505,000		10.44 billion	

SOURCE: Datek Information Services, Inc.

*Inkjet and thermal transfer printers
†Laser and similar printers

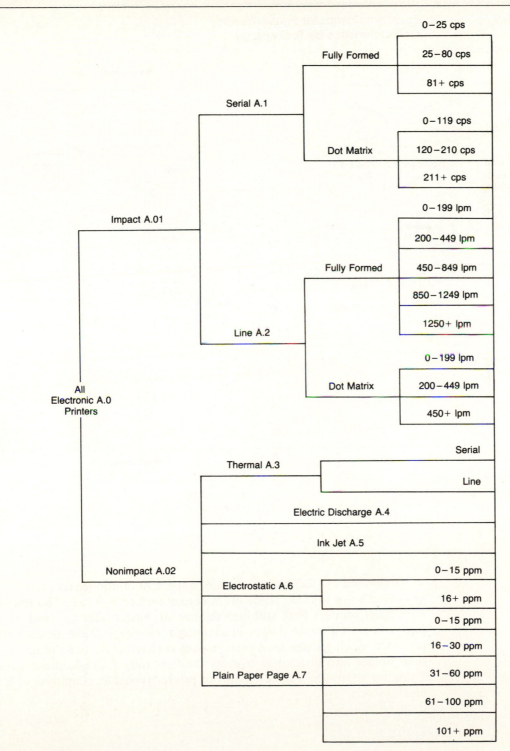

EXHIBIT 9 **Personal Computer Printer Trends:
Characteristics by Technology**

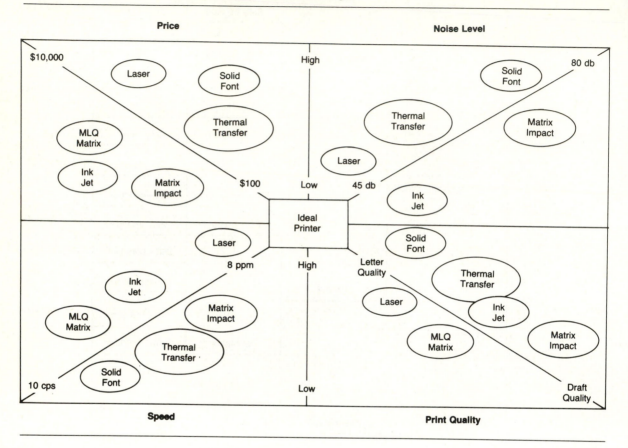

As advances in technology decreased the cost of nonimpact printers, the growth of sales in these segments was expected to increase. The prices of nonimpact printers were still high relative to impact offerings, and the impact printers still enjoyed a speed advantage. However, the nonimpact printers were much quieter than their impact counterparts, and the quality of their output was at least as high as the best fully formed impact output. Exhibit 9 shows the characteristics of printer types, as compared with the ideal printer.

GENICOM PRODUCT LINE

By April 1985, GENICOM primarily produced dot-matrix impact printers, though $6 million of revenue in 1984 was derived from a 300 lpm fully formed–character line printer. The company produced line and serial printers that could print from 60 cps in an office environment to 600 lpm in a high-speed line printer used for volume production. Most of the GENICOM product line also offered letter-quality printing at slower speeds, so the machines were flexible, depending on the user's needs. GENICOM offered branded printers as peripheral devices, and produced OEM printers for several major customers. GENICOM's products generally were more expensive than those of their major competitors but had higher performance capabilities and greater durability. GENICOM sales by product for 1984 are shown in Exhibit 10.

GENICOM Competitors

GENICOM had several major competitors in each of the market segments it served. Its two major U.S. competitors were Centronics and Dataproducts, both competing essentially head-on with GENICOM in almost every

---

EXHIBIT 10

GENICOM 1984 Sales

	($ THOUSANDS)		UNITS
Printers:			
340/510	5980		1749
200	8564		4016
2030	6131	}	
		}	9623
2120	5011	}	
3000	30924		20495
3014/3024	3879		5036
4000	—		—
Other	399		—
Subtotal		60888	31296
Parts		16962	
Ribbons		7846	
Lease		18140	
Service		9380	
Printer business total		113216	
Relays		23426	
Company total		136642	

market segment. There were other, smaller competitors for special applications and certain of GENICOM's market segments. Exhibit 11 offers market share estimates for major competitors in each major segment.

End User

The end user for GENICOM products was faced with a complex decision process in the choice of a printer. The current products operated faster, printed more legibly, and cost less than those of a few years ago. However, there were more machines to choose from, so the choice needed to be carefully made.

EXHIBIT 11	Market Share (Units) U.S. Serial Impact Printer Market—1984			
COUNTRY OF MANUFACTURE	**MANUFACTURER**	**PERCENT SHARE**	**FULLY FORMED**	**DOT MATRIX**
Japan	Epson	20.1		X
	C. Itoh (TEC)	13.9	X	X
	Okidata	11.4		X
	Star	3.2		X
	NEC	2.4	X	X
	Brother	2.0	X	X
	Ricoh	2.0	X	
	Toshiba	1.1		X
	Canon	0.9		X
	Juki	0.9	X	
	Fujitsu	0.6	X	X
	Subtotal	58.5		
United States	Xerox	3.2	X	
	IBM	3.0	X	
	Texas Instruments	2.2		X
	DEC	2.2		X
	Teletype	2.0		X
	Qume	2.0	X	
	Centronics	1.6		X
	GENICOM	1.1		X
	Anadex	0.6		X
	Datasouth	0.4		X
	Dataproducts	1.6	X	X
	Subtotal	19.9		
Europe	Mannesmann	0.9		X
	Facit	0.5	X	X
	Philips	0.3		X
	Hermes	0.2		X
	Subtotal	1.9		
Other		19.7		

EXHIBIT 11	Continued

COUNTRY OF MANUFACTURE	MANUFACTURER	PERCENT SHARE		PAGE	FULLY FORMED	DOT MATRIX
Japan	Canon	17.3		X		X
	Okidata	17.0			X	X
	Star	12.8			X	
	Sharp	8.5			X	X
	Brother	4.5			X	
	Subtotal		60.1			
United States	IBM	8.0		X	X	X
	Hewlett-Packard	4.5			X	X
	Xerox	3.6		X	X	X
	Texas Instruments	2.5			X	
	Subtotal		18.6			
Europe	Siemens	3.5		X		X
	Honeywell	1.0		X		
	Subtotal		4.5			
Other			16.8			

COUNTRY OF MANUFACTURE	MANUFACTURER	PERCENT SHARE			FULLY FORMED	DOT MATRIX
United States	Dataproducts	31.0			X	
	IBM	23.0			X	X
	Teletype	8.0			X	
	Centronics	7.0			X	
	Hewlett-Packard	6.0				X
	Printronix	6.0			X	X
	GENICOM	1.5			X	
	Subtotal		82.5			
Japan	NEC	4.1			X	
	Fujitsu	1.6			X	
	Hitachi	0.7			X	X
	Subtotal		6.4			
Europe	Mannesmann	2.1			X	
Other		8.0				

GENICOM MARKETING STRATEGY

GENICOM's general marketing strategy had been one of improving current products and expanding product lines rather than developing entirely new products or diversifying into new technologies. The strategy could have been characterized as evolutionary rather than revolutionary. GENICOM's main distinctive competencies in the market had been flexibility in production and the quality of its products. It had traditionally been on the upper end of price points for similar products and had sought to gain market share by stressing the advantages its machines offered relative to the competition. Each of GENICOM's products offered some distinct advantage—speed, print quality, quietness, or flexibility—which was thought to offset price disadvantages.

GENICOM had an important presence in the OEM market, offering those customers a wide variety of choices regarding specifications for products. The GENICOM presence in the branded printer market was not so strong, though efforts were underway to increase the importance of that market.

The product positioning of the GENICOM line had been for the professional user. Both for data processing and for word processing, the strength of GENICOM's product line had been in the commercial rather than the personal segments. The current product line was more durable, had more capability, and was more expensive than the bulk of the personal printer market. The GENICOM products could be compared to IBM office type-

---

EXHIBIT 12 **Domestic Multitier Distribution Channels**

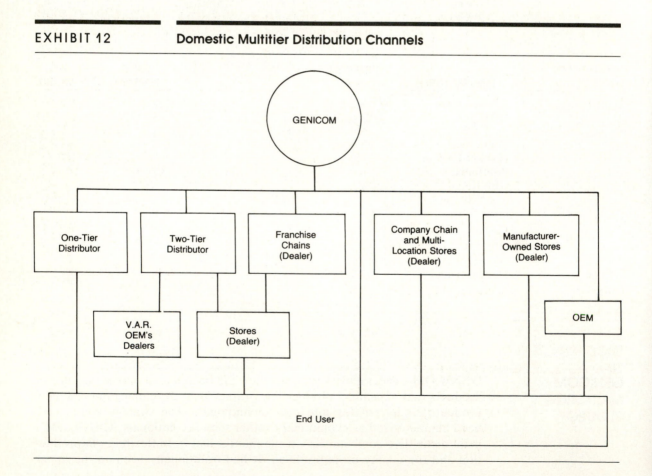

writers; they were generally considered overengineered for the home market. GENICOM was giving some consideration to the personal printer market to compete with Epson, Okidata, Toshiba, and others. It recognized that among other factors a new product line, rather than modification of an existing product, would be necessary to compete in this highly price-competitive market.

Distribution

In early 1985, GENICOM products were distributed through a distributor network that focused on industrial users and on wholesale/retail distributors who serviced end-user needs. Consideration was given to entering retail distributorship relations with large companies or with independently owned and franchised chains.

The GENICOM distribution system was not vertically integrated at that time. Although GENICOM had been contemplating expanding the distributor network slightly to effect better geographic coverage of markets, other plans suggested that it develop recognition of authorized dealers through the current distributor network. A schematic representation of the GENICOM distribution system is presented in Exhibit 12.

Although prices and margins for dot-matrix impact printers had been dropping as market pressures grew, the future could be said to be nothing but certain. Curtis Powell considered the union negotiations a critical turning point in the firm's history.

APPENDIX A

GENICOM CORPORATION AND SUBSIDIARIES—NOTES TO CONSOLIDATED FINANCIAL STATEMENTS

**1.
INCORPORATION
AND ACQUISITION**

GENICOM Corporation (the Company) was incorporated on June 1, 1983, and had no activity other than organizational matters until October 21, 1983, when it acquired substantially all of the net assets of the Data Communication Products Business Department and all of the outstanding common stock of Datacom de Mexico, S.A. de C.V., both wholly owned by General Electric Company (GE), a related party. These entities together functioned as a single business unit and were acquired in a purchase transaction for consideration totaling $62.1 million. The consideration was financed by (a) borrowing $41.0 million under a revolving credit and term loan agreement; (b) issuing $16.8 million in subordinated notes to GE; (c) assuming $340,000 of liabilities; and (d) selling $800,000 of common stock and $3.2 million of redeemable preferred stock.

The consideration was allocated to working capital ($35.1 million) and property, plant, and equipment and other assets ($27.0 million). The allocation of the purchase price to assets acquired and liabilities assumed is subject to adjustment resulting from refinements in the application of purchase method accounting.

If the acquisition is assumed to have been made as of January 1, 1983, unaudited pro forma consolidated net sales, net loss, and net loss per share (computed by adjusting historical operations for acquisition financing and purchase method accounting) would approximate the following for the year ended January 1, 1984 (dollar amounts in millions, except per-share amounts): net sales = $113.5; net loss = $3.4; net loss per common share and common share equivalent: primary = $0.42 and fully diluted = $0.42.

---

2. SUMMARY OF SIGNIFICANT ACCOUNTING POLICIES

The Company, one of the largest independent computer printer companies, is a manufacturer and leading supplier of teleprinters, serial dot-matrix printers, and line printers serving a wide variety of data processing and telecommunication markets. Additionally, the Company is a recognized leader in the manufacture and supply of high-quality, crystal/can relays, which are used in the aerospace and defense industries.

- Principles of consolidation: The consolidated financial statements include the accounts of the Company and its wholly owned subsidiaries. All significant intercompany accounts and transactions have been eliminated.

- Fiscal year: The Company's fiscal year ends on the Sunday nearest December 31. Accordingly, the Company is reporting on the period October 21, 1983 (commencement of operations) to January 1, 1984, and for the 52-week period ended December 30, 1984.

- Inventories: Inventories are stated at the lower of cost or market. Cost is determined on a first-in, first-out basis.

- Property, plant, and equipment: Property, plant, and equipment are stated at cost. Depreciation is computed using the straight-line method for financial reporting purposes based on estimates of useful lives at their acquisition date (generally fifteen to twenty-five years for buildings and three to eight years for machinery and equipment). Significant improvements and the cost of tooling are capitalized, while repairs and maintenance costs are charged to operations.

- Income taxes: Timing differences exist in the computation of income for financial and tax reporting purposes, which give rise to deferred taxes. The principal reason for these differences is the use of alternative methods for computing depreciation. The Company accounts for investment tax credits as a reduction of current taxes in the year realized.

- Research and development: Research and development costs are charged to operations as incurred. The costs were $3,367,000 for the year ended December 30, 1984, and $475,000 for the period October 21, 1983, to January 1, 1984.

- Foreign currency translation: Through its subsidiary, Datacom de Mexico, S.A. de C.V., the Company operates in a country considered to have a highly inflationary economy. As such, translation adjustments, which are not material, are included in results of operations. The consolidated financial statements of the Company include foreign assets and liabilities of $2,643,000 and $526,000 at December 30, 1984, and $1,291,000 and $96,000 at January 1, 1984.

- Employee benefit plans: Substantially all of the Company's employees are eligible to participate under the Company's employee benefit plans described in Note 5. These plans are contributory and each employee must elect to participate and make contributions to the plans. Employee contributions vest immediately.

- Net income per common share and common share equivalent: Primary net income (loss) per share was computed by dividing net income (loss) by the weighted average number of common shares and common share equivalents outstanding during the period. Common share equivalents include the weighted average number of shares issuable upon the assumed exercise of outstanding stock options and warrants after assuming the applicable proceeds from such exercise were used to acquire treasury shares at the average market price during the period.

Fully diluted net income (loss) per share was based upon the further assumption that the applicable proceeds from the exercise of the outstanding stock options and warrants were used to acquire treasury shares at the market price at the end of the period if higher than the average market price during the period.

3. SUPPLEMENTAL BALANCE SHEET INFORMATION

Inventories consist of:

	(DOLLAR AMOUNTS IN THOUSANDS)	
	DECEMBER 30, 1984	JANUARY 1, 1984
Raw materials	$10,110	$ 9,897
Work in process	9,781	9,708
Finished goods	7,026	4,738
	$26,917	$24,343

Property, plant, and equipment consist of:

| | (DOLLAR AMOUNTS IN THOUSANDS) | |
	DECEMBER 30, 1984	JANUARY 1, 1984
Land	$ 709	$ 709
Buildings	5,383	5,268
Machinery and equipment	25,628	21,760
Construction in progress	1,291	207
	33,011	27,944
Less accumulated depreciation	5,190	630
	$27,821	$27,314

Accounts payable and accrued expenses consist of:

| | (DOLLAR AMOUNTS IN THOUSANDS) | |
	DECEMBER 30, 1984	JANUARY 1, 1984
Trade accounts payable	$ 6,297	$ 7,881
Accrued liabilities:		
Compensated absences	2,801	2,532
Payroll and related liabilities	1,589	808
Interest	1,337	1,426
Employee benefits	1,830	332
Other	2,250	2,703
	$16,104	$15,682

4. LONG-TERM DEBT

Long-term debt consists of:

| | (DOLLAR AMOUNTS IN THOUSANDS) | |
	DECEMBER 30, 1984	JANUARY 1, 1984
Revolving credit notes	$21,000	$27,500
Term loan	12,000	12,000
Subordinated notes payable to GE	5,000	16,841
	38,000	56,341
Less current portion	1,600	11,841
	$36,400	$44,500

On October 21, 1983, the Company entered into a financing agreement with several banks that provides the Company with $31 million of revolving credit and a $12 million term loan.

The revolving credit and term loan bear interest at the prime rate (10.75 percent at December 30, 1984) plus 1.5 percent, payable quarterly. In addition, a commitment fee of one-half of 1 percent is payable quarterly on the average daily unused portion of the revolving credit borrowing base. The Company is also required to maintain compensating balances of at least 5 percent of the total outstanding revolving credit and term loan. Withdrawal of the compensating balances is not legally restricted and any deficiency in maintaining such balances is subject to a fee based upon an average borrowing rate on amounts outstanding under this agreement.

The initial revolving loan base of $31 million decreases by $1.55 million beginning on October 1, 1986, and continues to decrease by $1.55 million each quarter thereafter and expires on October 1, 1991.

The term loan is payable in quarterly installments of $600,000 beginning October 1, 1985.

All borrowings by the Company under the agreement are collateralized by liens on all of the Company's assets. The agreement requires the Company to meet certain financial ratios related to indebtedness, net worth, and current assets and current liabilities. The agreement also limits additional borrowing, purchase of property and equipment, the sale or disposition of certain assets, and restricts the payment of dividends to 50 percent of retained earnings. Under the most restrictive covenant, $2.9 million of retained earnings was available for payment of dividends at December 30, 1984.

In connection with the acquisition, at October 21, 1983, the Company issued subordinated notes to GE in the amount of $16.8 million. These notes bear interest at the prime rate, payable quarterly. During 1984 in accordance with the terms, the Company paid $11.8 million of the notes. The remaining $5 million is payable as follows: October 21, 1985—$1 million; October 21, 1986—$2 million; and October 21, 1987—$2 million.

Maturities of long-term debt for the five fiscal years subsequent to December 30, 1984, are (in millions): 1985—$1.6; 1986—$4.4; 1987—$4.4; 1988—$6.4; and 1989—$8.6.

---

5. EMPLOYEE BENEFIT PLANS

Effective January 1, 1984, the Company established a defined benefit pension plan for hourly employees. Employees must elect to participate and the plan is contributory. Employee contributions are 3 percent of compensation in excess of $12,000 per year. The Company makes contributions to the plan and records as pension expense an amount that is actuarially determined to be sufficient to provide benefits provided for under the plan, including amortization of unfunded liabilities over a maximum of 30 years. For the year ended December 30, 1984, pension expense was $408,000. Details of accumulated plan benefits and net plan assets as of the initial valuation date (January 1, 1984) are as follows:

Actuarial present value of accumulated plan benefits are:

Vested	$ 74,777
Nonvested	28,067
	$102,844
Market value of assets	$ 49,969
Rate of return assumed	7.5%

Certain hourly employees have the additional benefit of receiving Unemployment Supplemental Income if their employment is terminated due to reductions in the Company's work force.

Substantially all salaried employees are eligible to participate in the Company's deferred compensation and savings plan. The plan provides for contributions to be made by employees through salary reductions. The Company makes certain matching contributions that are allocated to the participants and vest as called for by the plan. For the year ended December 30, 1984, the Company's expense under this plan was $1,002,000.

6. WARRANTS AND REDEEMABLE PREFERRED STOCK

In connection with the acquisition the Company issued to GE stock purchase warrants to acquire 2,500,000 shares of the Company's common stock at a price of $0.50 per share. The warrants are currently exercisable and expire October 21, 1988.

On December 20, 1984, the Company redeemed all of the outstanding redeemable preferred stock ($3.2 million) by issuing 640,000 shares of common stock. Holders of the redeemable preferred stock waived payment of the cumulative preferred stock dividends for all periods the stock was outstanding.

7. RESTRICTED STOCK PURCHASE AND INCENTIVE STOCK OPTION PLANS

Under the Company's restricted stock purchase plan, the Company may offer to sell up to 975,000 shares of common stock to employees of the Company at a price per share equal to 100 percent of the fair market value as determined by the Board of Directors on the date of offer. Purchased shares vest to the employees as provided for under the agreement and, in certain cases, is dependent upon the attainment of annual financial objectives. Shares issued under the plan that are not vested at an employee's termination are subject to repurchase by the Company at the lower of original issue price or their then fair market value.

EXHIBIT 13   **Activity of GE's Stock Plan**

	YEAR ENDED DECEMBER 30, 1984		OCTOBER 21, 1983 TO JANUARY 1, 1984	
	NUMBER OF SHARES	MARKET VALUE	NUMBER OF SHARES	MARKET VALUE
Unvested shares outstanding, beginning of period	525,000	$ 52,500		
Shares issued	250,000	95,000	525,000	$52,500
Shares vested	(175,000)	(17,500)		
Unvested shares outstanding, end of period	600,000	$130,000	525,000	$52,500

	YEAR ENDED DECEMBER 30, 1984			OCTOBER 21, 1983 TO JANUARY 1, 1984		
	NUMBER OF SHARES	OPTION PRICE		NUMBER OF SHARES	OPTION PRICE	
		PER SHARE	TOTAL		PER SHARE	TOTAL
Outstanding, beginning of period	780,000	$0.10	$78,000			
Granted	82,500	$0.20–$1.00	46,500	830,000	$0.10	$83,000
Exercised	483,500	$0.10	48,350	50,000	$0.10	5,000
Canceled	65,000	$0.10–$.20	7,250			
Outstanding, end of period	314,000		$68,900	780,000		$78,000
Options, exercisable, end of period	5,000	$0.10	$ 500			
Options available for future grants	177,500					

At December 30, 1984, 200,000 shares of common stock are reserved for future grants under this plan. Exhibit 13 summarizes the activity of the plan during the respective fiscal periods (fair market value as determined at date of purchase).

Effective October 21, 1983, the Company adopted an incentive stock option plan whereby 1,300,000 shares of unissued common stock were reserved for future issuance. The plan was amended on October 20, 1984, to reduce the number of shares available under the plan from 1,300,000 to 1,025,000. Stock option activity for the respective fiscal periods is as follows:

The plan provides for the exercise of the outstanding options at 20 percent per year beginning five years from date of grant. The Company accelerated the exercising provisions of 475,000 options granted, and these options were exercised prior to December 30, 1984. Of these shares issued, 425,000 shares are restricted and subject to certain vesting provisions related to annual financial objectives. Additionally, under the plan, other options granted also become exercisable at earlier dates if these same financial objectives are attained. During the year ended December 30, 1984, such objectives were attained and 45,000 shares of those restricted above accrued to the benefit of the holders and 63,500 options became exercisable, of which 58,500 were exercised and shares of common stock issued. The Company must continue to attain certain financial objectives annually in order to continue to have accelerated exercise dates (with respect to options) and continue to vest (with respect to restricted shares). In the event of employee termination prior to full vesting in these shares, the Company may purchase such shares at the lower of fair market value at date of termination or the original option price.

8. INCOME TAXES

Income tax expense consists of:

	(DOLLAR AMOUNTS IN THOUSANDS)	
	YEAR ENDED DECEMBER 30, 1984	OCTOBER 21, 1983 TO JANUARY 1, 1984
Current:		
Federal	$ 4,788	
State	936	
Foreign	(72)	
	5,652	—
Deferred:		
Federal	73	$302
State	1	75
Foreign	61	
	135	377
	$ 5,787	$377

Total tax expense amounted to an effective rate of 48.7 percent for the year ended December 30, 1984, and 44.9 percent for the period October 21, 1983, to January 1, 1984. Income tax expense was different from that computed at the statutory U.S. federal income tax rate of 46 percent for the following reasons:

	(DOLLAR AMOUNTS IN THOUSANDS)	
	YEAR ENDED DECEMBER 30, 1984	OCTOBER 21, 1983 TO JANUARY 1, 1984
Tax expense at statutory rate	$ 5,463	$ 50
Increases (decreases) related to:		
Investment tax credits	(249)	(56)
State income tax, net of federal income tax benefit	515	40
Purchase method accounting for inventories	103	370
DISC income	(70)	
Other, net	25	(27)
Actual tax expense	$ 5,787	$ 377

Deferred income tax expense results from timing differences in the recognition of revenue and expense for tax and financial statement purposes. The sources of these differences and the tax effect of each are as follows:

	(DOLLAR AMOUNTS IN THOUSANDS)	
	YEAR ENDED DECEMBER 30, 1984	OCTOBER 21, 1983 TO JANUARY 1, 1984
Depreciation	$ 728	$ 497
Inventory valuation	(668)	
Other, net	75	(120)
	$ 135	$ 377

9. LEASING ARRANGEMENTS

As lessee the Company leases certain manufacturing and warehousing property. Rent expense included in the consolidated statement of income amounted to $740,000 for the year ended December 30, 1984, and $120,000 for the period October 21, 1983, to January 1, 1984.

Annual future minimum lease commitments for operating leases as of December 30, 1984, are immaterial.

As lessor the Company has rental plans for the leasing of printers. Operating lease terms vary, generally from 1 to 60 months. Rental income for the year ended December 30, 1984, and for the period October 21, 1983, to January 1, 1984, was $18,139,000 and $3,807,000, respectively. Minimum future rental revenues on noncancelable operating leases with terms of one year or longer at December 30, 1984, are (in thousands): 1985—$2,900; 1986—$500; 1987—$400; and 1988—$300.

At December 30, 1984, and January 1, 1984, the cost of equipment leased was (in thousands) $4,087 and $4,040, which is included in property, plant, and equipment, net of accumulated depreciation of $1,072 and $131, respectively.

10. RELATED-PARTY TRANSACTIONS

The Company at present utilizes GE for various services, such as repair services for customers and data processing, under contracts expiring generally in 1985. The Company also purchases various raw materials from GE. The cost of these materials and services for the year ended December 30, 1984, and the period October 21, 1983, to January 1, 1984, totaled $8.4 million and $1.1 million, respectively.

Sales to GE were $12.4 million for the year ended December 30, 1984, and $3.3 million for the period October 21, 1983, to January 1, 1984. In addition, sales to GE affiliates, who serve as distributors to third-party customers in certain markets, and sales of parts for maintenance services to customers amounted to $14.4 million for the year ended December 30, 1984, and $1.7 million for the period October 21, 1983, to January 1, 1984. Accounts receivable from GE were $4.6 million at December 30, 1984, and $5.2 million at January 1, 1984; accounts payable to GE were $0.8 million at December 30, 1984, and $0.9 million at January 1, 1984.

APPENDIX B

LABOR NEGOTIATIONS BETWEEN GENICOM AND THE LOCAL 124 UNION

LOCAL 124 MEMO OF APRIL 25, 1985

The United Effort

NEGOTIATIONS REPORT   On Tuesday afternoon the negotiating committee met with Relations and a lawyer to start contract talks. Right away, without putting any paperwork on the table, this lawyer wanted us to tell him ways management can cut *four dollars an hour* off the cost of labor. According to him, the cost per hour, including wages and benefits, is fourteen dollars an hour and this is "significantly higher" than other workers are making in Waynesboro and must drop to ten dollars total of wages and benefits. He was even so helpful as to offer selections, like a smorgasbord, if you will, of items from which *we* could decide where to make the cuts.

For our consideration he laid out: rate cuts, night shift differential pay, vacation time cuts and other paid time off, give up bump rights, retraining, premium pay for some overtime, call in pay, medical benefits, and the list goes on. All he wants *us* to do is decide where to cut to come up with a four-dollar price cut. He pointed out that the wages in the lower job rates are much too high and will have to be cut to make us more comparable with other wage earners in Waynesboro.

Based on the claim that GENICOM needs for us to cough up four dollars worth of wages and benefits, we naturally figured the company was going broke so we asked a question about the financial condition of the business. The reply was contrary to what you might suspect based on them wanting cost cuts. It turns out that the company is *making* money but wants to make *more* money and in order to do that they want to get into our pocket.

Just as we figured, when the word got out in the plant, you became furious to think that the company would be so greedy as to come after the wages and benefits you have worked years for and some of you even walked a picket line for a hundred and two days in 1969 to get. There is a growing demand from the union membership to hold work stoppages to protest these unrealistic demands by management and it appears the time will come for that kind of action! The next meeting with management is scheduled for May 6th and Boris "Red" Block will be here for that meeting. We will have a full membership meeting the next day, Tuesday, May 7th, to let you know what is going on and how negotiations are progressing. At that time we will be *led by the membership* about what action you want to take.

After we listened to what management had to say about their thoughts we laid out our proposals and informed them that the list was only a partial list of what we think is needed in a new contract. Some of what we are looking at includes strong job security language, improvement in pensions and downward adjustments in our contributions to the pension plan, a better severance pay clause, insurance coverage to be nothing less than we now have, improvements in S&A benefits, cost of living clause, contract language improvements, and a general wage increase. And, as we pointed out, there are other things we are looking at which we will lay on the table later. What happens in negotiations and what we are able to do is directly dependent on you and how much support you are willing to give.

It's your Local and "The Members Run This Union!"

LOCAL 124 MEMO OF MAY 10, 1985　**The United Effort**

THE MEMBERS DECIDE　At the end of the second session of negotiations management still insists on demanding a $4.00-an-hour wage and benefit concession from you. They set the record straight so there would be no mistake in anyone's mind we were told "we are taking it." We asked time and time again what they would do with the $4.00 if they can take it and we were told rather matter-of-factly, "we are going to put it in our pockets." It's not that GENICOM didn't make a profit last year, it's just plain and simple they just want to add an additional $3200.00 an hour to their pockets (300 employees × $4.00 per hr. = $3200.00 an hour) at your expense.

At a full house special membership meeting, 1st and 2nd shift, the committee was instructed to take a secret ballot strike vote. We normally keep the meetings to one hour but due to the number of members who wanted to speak, the meeting lasted well over the normal length of time and then a vote was taken, which was in favor of a strike action. As we have said before, this local doesn't have a history of strike action but the workers at GENICOM feel they have no choice but to fight on the issues of wages and working conditions in this plant. Management sometime ago decided to cut the rate of the mold machine operators from R13 to R9 and it seems this only whetted their appetite to want to take even more. We filed a grievance and processed it through the required steps of the grievance procedure and we will be taking action on that grievance at the proper time of which you will be notified.

We don't need to tell you how important it is for everyone to support the strike action. The issue is over a rate cut on one job but remember, the bigger issue is now management is saying they are going to cut $4.00 off of everyone in wages and benefits. Whether they can get away with it or not depends on you and everyone in the plant. The stakes are high and it's up to you to decide. Do you just fork over the $4.00 in wages and benefits or do you join your fellow workers and fight?

SHOP STEWARD ELECTION   There will be a meeting today, five minutes before the end of lunch break, to nominate and elect a shop steward.

GENICOM MEMO OF MAY 31, 1985

To All Employees:

In response to the excessive amount of publicity in the local press concerning GENICOM's negotiations with the UE Local 124, the following advertisement will appear in tomorrow's Waynesboro *News-Virginian* and Sunday's *Staunton News Leader*. We felt you, as GENICOM employees, should be the first to have this information.

What's Really Happening at GENICOM

GENICOM and its negotiations with Local 124 have been the subject of much discussion in our community and among GENICOM employees in recent weeks. All the information to this point has come from the Union.

Since so much is at stake for GENICOM, its employees, and our community, we believe management should do its best to assure that the people who may be affected understand what is happening—and why.

GENICOM is a Waynesboro company that is dedicated to remaining a Waynesboro company. That dedication is reflected in GENICOM's proposals to UE Local 124 to establish a wage and benefit program that will allow GENICOM to meet competition while providing GENICOM workers with wages and benefits in line with community standards.

As part of the negotiations process, GENICOM provided wage survey data to Local 124 on both GENICOM's national competition and its Waynesboro neighbors. Reflecting that data, GENICOM's proposal includes job rates from $6.50 to $12.00 per hour, three weeks paid vacation, eight holidays, medical and dental insurance at a cost of $4.00 per week to employees, a defined benefit pension plan with limited contributions by employees, as well as company-paid life and disability programs.

Starting in 1954, and for nearly 30 years, General Electric Company conducted manufacturing operations at the current GENICOM facility in Waynesboro. Under General Electric, wages were negotiated on a national basis. As a result, Waynesboro wage and salary costs reached levels that are out of line with the electronics industry and with the Waynesboro community. GENICOM Corporation was formed to operate the business purchased from G.E. GENICOM is now managed by people who are committed to establishing and maintaining a successful and profitable business—because it is our only business. In the 19 months since GENICOM acquired its business, it has been operated on a profitable basis. This was particularly true in 1984, when the market for computers and related equipment was robust. The business is less profitable now that its market has become much softer and competition for sales of electronic products such as GENICOM's has become very intense. GENICOM management is determined and committed to reducing costs and competing.

These cost reductions can be accomplished either by moving operations to GENICOM's existing lower-cost locations or by lowering costs in Waynesboro. GENICOM has decided to stay in Waynesboro. The wage and benefit concessions requested will make Waynesboro a competitive manufacturing location—a manufacturing location with a future. These concessions will not be easy or insignificant for GENICOM workers to accept, but they are not unreasonable. Competitive wages will make operations in Waynesboro much more economically attractive for GENICOM and increase GENICOM's incentive to maintain and expand those operations, thus offering more job security to Waynesboro workers and greater stability to the Waynesboro community.

C.W. Powell
President and Chief Executive Officer
GENICOM Corporation

LOCAL 124 MEMO OF JUNE 4, 1985

The United Effort

GENICOM SHOULD TELL IT LIKE IT IS, INSTEAD OF WANTING TO POCKET 6½ MILLION DOLLARS OF ITS EMPLOYEES AND THE COMMUNITY   That's what GENICOM wants in concessions from the hourly workers. GENICOM said that's not all. They are going to get a like amount from the lower paid salary workers and supervisors.

Not once have they said they are going to cut top paid GENICOM employees such as Mr. Powell.

GENICOM says they are dedicated to remaining in Waynesboro. If that is so, why have they moved over 600 jobs to Mexico, and continue to move jobs out of Waynesboro? They say they need concessions from their employees to do this. But they refuse to put in writing to the Union that these concessions will keep jobs in Waynesboro.

Instead the Company tells us they want to "put the money in their pockets." They go on to say they will use some of this money to buy other plants in other states. This will not bring jobs to Waynesboro. The Company is going to run the plants where they buy them. Not once has the Company said they would bring jobs back from Mexico with the $4 per hour concessions that they want.

THE TRUTH IS!   The Company proposal to the Union means two less paid holidays per year; it means that most employees would lose 2 weeks paid vacation per year. All employees would take pay cuts. Some GENICOM families would take cuts of $12,000 per year. As for the pensions and the insurance, the proposal is to leave it as it is now. The Company proposal would take away all of the night shift bonus, the few sick days workers have now, and would do away with rest breaks.

If the Company really means that they will bring more jobs to Waynesboro, they should be willing to put it in writing.

If the Company really means to have greater stability for the Community they should reinvest the extra profits in the GENICOM Waynesboro plant. Not take the money and buy plants in other states.

GENICOM would like the Community to believe that GE negotiated the last Union contract. *THAT IS NOT SO. GENICOM NEGOTIATED THE LAST CONTRACT.* Mr. Stoner of GENICOM Management was part of the last negotiations and he is part of these negotiations. Mr. Stoner plays a big part in negotiations.

The Company admits in their paid ad that they made money with the last Union Contract. They could make money with the new contract that has no cuts.

It's time for GENICOM to put in writing to its employees that the Company will keep jobs in Waynesboro. GENICOM is making a profit. They should let the employees keep what they have. There should be NO CUTS.

Workers should keep their 6½ Million Dollars. This would keep the money in the Community. Not take it to other States and Mexico.

If GENICOM takes this money and "puts it in their pockets." Merchants will lose, taxes for other people in the Community will go up and everyone in the Community will lose.

Only top management like Mr. Powell will gain when they line their pockets with our money at Community expense.

GENICOM MEMO OF JUNE 13, 1985

This letter was mailed to all hourly employees on 6/14/85. This copy is for your information.

To: Our GENICOM Employees and Their Families

I would like to take this opportunity to express my appreciation for the patience being displayed by the majority of our employees during a very difficult time in which we are negotiating a new labor agreement.

GENICOM and its Management team remain dedicated to the resolution of differences with UE Local 124 and the adoption of a new collective bargaining agreement through the negotiation process. Nevertheless, in reflecting on Local 124's recent newsletter concerning strike preparations, we feel compelled to offer our thoughts on some questions and other appropriate subjects that should be addressed by the Union's lawyer at Sunday's meeting.

QUESTION Is the Company required to pay wages to strikers during an economic strike?

ANSWER No, the Company is not required to pay wages to economic strikers.

QUESTION Is the Company required to pay the premiums to continue health insurance, life insurance, and other benefits for strikers during an economic strike?

ANSWER No, the Company is not required to continue payments for benefits to economic strikers.

QUESTION Are economic strikers eligible for Virginia unemployment benefits during an economic strike?

ANSWER No, state law disqualifies employees involved in a "labor dispute."

QUESTION Is it possible for the UE to guarantee that GENICOM will change its proposals because of strike action?

ANSWER No, negotiations are a give-and-take process that may remain unchanged in the face of employee strikes or Company lockouts.

QUESTION If there is no agreement for a new contract by June 23rd, is the Company required to keep the current contract in effect?

ANSWER No, at that time the Company may unilaterally implement its final proposal.

QUESTION Can economic strikers be permanently replaced by new workers if the Company decides to continue operations without them?

ANSWER Yes, federal law allows a company to continue operations with new employees. The law also does not require the Company to discharge these employees to allow returning strikers to resume their jobs. Replaced strikers who indicate they wish to return to work on the Company's terms may fill open positions if any exist or be placed on a hiring list ahead of nonemployees.

Once again let me say we, as GENICOM's Management team, remain dedicated to reaching agreement with UE Local 124 *without* any strike action. However, we are also dedicated to continue the growth of a viable business in Waynesboro. In order to accomplish this, we *must* reduce our cost structure to a level that will allow GENICOM to meet our competition.

Currently, the demand for our printers is poor due to a downturn in the computer market and foreign competition. This market situation, and GENICOM's decision to maintain Waynesboro as our primary production location, demand the changes we have proposed to the UE.

We have furnished wage data on Waynesboro and our national competition to the Union negotiating committee establishing that our proposals are competitive with both Waynesboro and national rates.

Under one proposal, wages would run between $6.00 per hour and $11.50 per hour and benefits would remain at current levels or slightly better. In recognition of the economic impact that such concessions may have, we have offered alternative proposals such as eliminating sick days, night shift differential and afternoon breaks. These reductions would increase the wage proposal to between $6.50 and $12.00 per hour. All other benefits would remain the same or slightly better.

We hope that our employees, their families and their collective bargaining representatives will consider all these factors before taking any action that could be injurious to both the Employees and the Company.

Sincerely,

Curtis W. Powell
President/Chief Executive Officer

Levi Strauss and Company: Taking an Industry Giant Private

NEIL H. SNYDER • LLOYD L. BYARS

Levi Strauss and Company, founded in 1850, is the world's largest brand name apparel manufacturer. It designs, manufactures, and markets a diversified line of apparel for men, women, and children including jeans, slacks, shirts, jackets, skirts, and hats. Most of the company's products are marketed under the Levi's trademark and are sold in the United States and in numerous foreign countries throughout North and South America, Europe, Asia, and Australia.

BACKGROUND

Levi Strauss, a Bavarian immigrant who was lured to the West during the gold rush in search of prosperity, did not strike it rich in gold, but instead found his fortune in blue jeans. He sold his first pair of jeans in 1853 to a San Francisco gold digger who wanted a sturdy pair of pants that would hold up in the mines. In time, his jeans became so popular that young Strauss set up a shop in San Francisco. Today the headquarters of Levi Strauss and Company stands near the same location as young Strauss's original shop.

It was not until the 1930s that Levi's jeans reached the eastern market. Although attempts were made to promote jeans for resort wear, the basic clientele continued to be limited. World War II, however, created a sharp increase in demand, and jeans were sold only to individuals engaged in defense work. It also marked a turning point for Levi Strauss. The company had been largely a wholesale operation prior to World War II, but after it began concentrating on manufacturing and direct sales. Before the war, the company's annual sales were around $8 million, but by 1961 sales reached $51 million, mainly because of aggressive product diversification.

In 1981 the company was the largest manufacturer of jeans in the world, controlling about one-third of the jeans market. Additionally, it was the largest firm in the apparel industry with products in virtually every product line and with sales and profits by far the greatest in the industry. According to the company chairman of the board, Peter H. Haas, "We'd like to outfit people from the cradle to the grave."

Levi's success resulted in part from its skill in sensing emerging new markets and responding quickly, and in part from its strong management and

The authors would like to thank Debie Alford, Karen Davis, Allison Gillum, Jim Tucker, and Jeff Walker for their work on an earlier version of this case and Earlinda Elder for her work on this case.

exceptional brand name acceptance. In addition, the company identified market opportunities through segmentation. In recent years this has aided in its diversification strategy. As a result, the company's growth and success has been strong despite the extreme competitiveness and cyclical nature of the apparel industry. See Exhibits 1, 2, 3, 4, 5, and 6.

OPERATIONS

In November 1984, the company reorganized certain domestic operations. The company's three major operating entities are now identified as the Jeans Company, Levi Strauss International, and Battery Street Enterprises. The company's corporate staff performs financial, legal, and administrative functions.

EXHIBIT 1

Consolidated Statements of Income of Levi Strauss and Co. and Subsidiaries (Dollar Amounts in Thousands Except Per Share Data)

	YEAR ENDED NOVEMBER 25, 1984	YEAR ENDED NOVEMBER 27, 1983	YEAR ENDED NOVEMBER 28, 1982
Net sales	$ 2,513,536	$ 2,731,273	$ 2,572,172
Cost of goods sold	1,652,476	1,648,502	1,635,539
Gross profit	861,060	1,082,771	936,633
Marketing, general, and administrative expenses	674,322	710,442	665,660
Operating income	186,738	372,319	270,973
Interest expense	28,763	39,793	42,766
Other (income) expense, net	46,612	(44,287)	(21,614)
	111,363	376,823	249,831
Income before taxes	111,363	376,823	249,831
Provision for taxes on income	69,976	182,300	113,256
Net income	41,387	194,523	116,575
Net income per share	1.07	4.61	3.05
Average common and common equivalent shares outstanding	38,517,526	42,206,980	41,553,553

EXHIBIT 2

Consolidated Balance Sheet for Levi Strauss and Co. and Subsidiaries (Dollar Amounts in Thousands Except Per Share Data)

	YEAR ENDED NOVEMBER 25, 1984	YEAR ENDED NOVEMBER 27, 1983
ASSETS		
Current assets:		
Cash	$ 37,452	$ 16,967
Temporary investment of cash	225,937	449,351
Trade receivables (less allowance for doubtful accounts) 1984 = $8,676; 1983 = $9,682	334,798	425,464
INVENTORIES		
Raw materials and work-in-process	170,510	183,734
Finished goods	217,150	180,427
Other current assets	51,731	70,995
	1,042,579	1,427,443
Total current assets	1,042,579	1,427,443
Property, plant, and equipment (less accumulated depreciation: 1984 = $208,217; 1983 = $182,573)	330,455	347,150
Other assets	48,068	57,282
	$1,421,103	$ 831,875
LIABILITIES AND STOCKHOLDERS' EQUITY		
Current liabilities:		
Current maturities of long-term debt	$ 9,354	$ 32,440
Short-term borrowing	21,077	58,429
Accounts payable	83,361	128,658
Accrued liabilities	123,023	96,496
Compensation and payroll taxes	72,923	74,508
Pension and profit sharing	4,257	26,397
Taxes based on income	40,235	73,724
Dividend payable	17,070	19,375
	371,305	504,017
Total current liabilities	371,305	504,017
Long-term debt—less current maturities	199,017	225,045
Deferred taxes and other items	43,339	44,094

EXHIBIT 2	**Continued**		

STOCKHOLDERS' EQUITY

Common stock = $1 par value:		
Authorized 100,000,000 shares		
Issued 43,998,808 shares	43,999	43,999
Additional paid-in capital	63,266	63,063
Retained earnings	1,066,068	1,093,417
Translation adjustment	(81,051)	(56,993)
Employee stock ownership plan		
shares	(38,638)	(36,499)

PURCHASED WITH DEBT

Treasury stock at cost: 1984—		
7,091,288 shares; 1983—		
3,108,120 shares	(246,203)	(53,278)
Total stockholders' equity	807,441	1,053,709
	$1,421,102	$1,831,875

The Jeans Company

The Jeans Company, the company's largest operating unit in terms of sales and profits, is the leading manufacturer of jeans in the United States. It consists of marketing units, each with specialized sales personnel. In addition to basic jeans for men and women, this entity markets a broad line of westernwear and knit and woven shirts. It is also one of the world's largest brand name manufacturers of children's clothing, including basic and fashion jeans, slacks, shirts, knit and woven tops, jackets, blouses, vests, and active wear. In 1984 approximately 21 percent of the Jeans Company's apparel production was provided by independent contractors.

The Jeans Company serves the domestic jeans market, which consists primarily of young men and women aged fourteen to thirty years old. Due to demographic changes in the 1980s, this market is forecasted to decrease as a percentage of the population.

Levi Strauss International

Levi Strauss International is structured along geographic lines and primarily consists of the European, Canadian, Asian/Pacific, and Latin American divisions. These divisions are generally divided into countries, each consid-

EXHIBIT 3   **Consolidated Statement of Changes in Financial Position of Levi Strauss and Co. and Subsidiaries (Dollar Amounts in Thousands Except Per Share Data)**

	YEAR ENDING NOVEMBER 25, 1984	YEAR ENDING NOVEMBER 27, 1983	YEAR ENDING NOVEMBER 28, 1982
WORKING CAPITAL INCREASED BY:			
Operations:			
Net income	$ 41,387	$ 194,523	$ 126,575
Add items not requiring working capital:			
Depreciation and amortization	47,832	44,524	43,219
Other net	6,492	6,837	7,957
Working capital provided by operations	95,711	245,884	177,751
Increases in long-term debt	5,083	125,542	31,116
Payment of debt by ESOP	—	10,419	—
Common stock issued to employees	6,970	12,384	6,067
Reductions in long-term deposits	9,611	42	1,453
	117,375	394,271	216,387
WORKING CAPITAL REDUCED BY:			
Purchase of treasury stock	199,693	—	—
Additions to property, plant, and equipment	41,398	50,937	54,171
Cash dividends declared	68,736	73,111	68,292
Reductions in long-term debt	30,391	61,562	18,472
Effect of exchange rate changes on working capital items	20,175	10,814	30,705
Purchase of shares by ESOP with company-guaranteed debt	2,139	46,918	—
Other, net	1,986	(2,653)	6,863
	364,517	240,684	178,503
Increased (decrease) in working capital	$(247,142)	$153,582	$ 37,884
INCREASE (DECREASE) IN WORKING CAPITAL, REPRESENTED BY CHANGE IN:			
Cash and temporary investments of cash	$(202,924)	$ 113,056	$ 179,571
Trade receivables, net	(85,666)	31,301	(50,387)
Inventories	(77,006)	68,633	(117,184)
Other current assets	(19,263)	6,844	1,111
Current maturities of long-term debt and short-term borrowings	60,433	(20,511)	(28,176)
Accounts payable and accrued liabilities	18,770	(25,289)	14,987
Other current liabilities	58,519	(20,452)	(18,390)
Increase (decrease) in working capital	$(247,142)	$ 153,582	$ 37,884

EXHIBIT 4

Financial Highlights of Levi Strauss and Co. and Subsidiaries (Dollar Amounts in Thousands Except Per Share Data)

	1984	1983	(DECREASE) INCREASE
Net sales	$2,513,536	$2,731,273	(8.0)%
Net income	41,387	194,523	(78.7)
Dividends declared	68,736	73,111	(6.0)
Stockholders' equity	807,441	1,053,709	(23.4)
Working capital	671,274	918,416	(26.9)
Property, plant, and equipment—net	330,455	347,150	(4.8)
Average common and common equivalent			
Shares outstanding	38,517,526	42,206,980	(8.7)
Per share:			
Net income	1.07	4.61	(76.8)
Dividends declared	1.85	1.75	5.7

EXHIBIT 5

Comparative Sales Data (Dollar Amounts in Millions)

	1984	1983	INCREASE DOLLARS	DECREASE UNITS
The Jeans Company	$1,432.6	$1,497.5	(4.3)	(4.2)
Battery Street Enterprises	485.1	529.2	(8.3)	(7.4)
Levi Strauss International				
European operations	321.7	416.4	(22.7)	(15.8)
Latin American operations	87.2	94.1	(7.4)	(14.3)
Canada division	93.3	95.4	(2.2)	—
Asia/Pacific division	89.0	94.8	(6.0)	(5.2)
Total Levi Strauss	591.2	700.7	(15.6)	(13.2)
International	4.6	3.9	18.1	12.2
Other operations				
Consolidated	2,513.5	2,731.3	(8.0)	(6.7)

EXHIBIT 6

Financial Summary of Levi Strauss and Co. and Subsidiaries (Dollar Amounts in Millions Except Per Share Data)

	1984	1983
Net sales	$2,513.5	$2,731.3
Gross profit	861.1	1,082.8
Interest expense	28.8	32.8
Income before taxes	111.4	376.8
Provision for taxes on income	70.0	182.3
Net income	41.4	194.5
Earnings retained in the business	(27.3)	121.4
Cash retained in the business	27.0	172.8
Income before taxes as percent of sales	4.4%	13.89
Net income as percent of sales	1.6	7.1
Net income as percent of beginning stockholders' equity	3.9	20.1
Current assets	1,042.6	1,427.4
Current liabilities	371.3	509.0
Working capital	671.3	918.4
Ratio of current assets to current liabilities	3.8/1	2.8/1
Total assets	1,421.1	1,831.9
Long-term debt—less current maturities	199.0	225.0
Stockholders' equity	807.4	1,053.7
Capital expenditures	41.4	50.9
Depreciation expense	42.6	40.0
Property, plant, and equipment, net	330.5	347.2
Number of employees	37,000	44,000

PER SHARE DATA

	1984	1983
Net income	$1.07	$4.61
Dividends declared	1.85	1.75
Book value (of shares outstanding at year's end)	21.88	25.15
Market price range	43 1/6–23	56–32 2/8
Average common and common equivalent shares outstanding	38,517,516	42,206,980

ered a separate market. Each country within the European division is responsible for sales, distribution, and finance activities. The headquarters, located in Europe, coordinates international merchandising and production activities. With few exceptions, Canada and each country in Latin America and the Asia/Pacific region is staffed with its own merchandising, production, sales, and finance personnel.

Levi Strauss International is substantially independent of the Jeans Company and Battery Street Enterprises in terms of manufacturing and distribution. Sales are derived primarily from basic lines of jeans, shirts, and jackets although women's fit jeans, youthwear, menswear, and related tops are also marketed in most areas. In 1984, approximately 28 percent of Levi Strauss International's apparel production was provided by independent contractors.

Battery Street Enterprises

Battery Street Enterprises consists primarily of Koret of North America, Menswear, and Battery Street Sportswear divisions. In addition, Battery Street Enterprises includes several smaller operations. The manufacturing and distribution activities of Battery Street Enterprises are substantially independent of the Jeans Company and Levi Strauss International. In 1984, approximately 43 percent of Battery Street Enterprises' production was provided by independent contractors.

The Koret of North America division manufactures and markets coordinates and related separates for women including skirts, pants, jackets, blouses, and other tops in misses, petite, and larger sizes in the United States and Canada. The Menswear division manufactures and markets men's casual and dress slacks, sport coats and vests, including the Levi's Action garments. The Battery Street division markets lines of casual sportswear under the Levi's brand name, including pants, skirts, tops, and jackets. Size ranges are misses, large, petite, and tall.

Other business units within Battery Street Enterprises provide a variety of apparel lines. The Resistol division produces western and fashion hats. The Oxxford division produces fine men's and women's clothing under the Oxxford trademark. The David Hunter division produces fine men's jackets, blazers, and slacks. The Perry Ellis America division markets a collection of men's and women's casual clothes designed by fashion designer Perry Ellis. The fashion Portfolio division markets a collection of fashionable men's casual apparel under the Tourage SSE and CMA trademarks. The Frank Shorter Running Gear division manufactures and markets athletic competition apparel.

EXECUTIVE OFFICERS OF THE COMPANY

Listed below are the executive officers of the company as of November 26, 1984.

NAME	OFFICE AND POSITION	AGE
*†‡Peter E. Haas	Chairman of the Board	65
*†‡Robert D. Haas	President and Chief Executive Officer	42
*†‡Walter A. Haas	Chairman of the Executive Committee	68
Leo P. Isotalo	Senior Vice President and President of Battery Street Enterprises	48
David K. Lelewer	Senior Vice President, Human Resources	44
*Karl F. Slacik	Senior Vice President of Finance and Chief Financial Officer	55
Lee Smith	Senior Vice President and President of Levi Strauss Intl.	42
*Peter Thigpen	Senior Vice President and President of Jeans Company	45
*†Thomas W. Tusher	Executive Vice President and Chief Operating Officer	43

*Member of the board of directors.
†Member of the executive committee.
‡Walter A. Haas, Jr., is the father of Robert D. Haas and the brother of Peter E. Haas.

BACKGROUND OF EXECUTIVE OFFICERS

- *Peter H. Haas* joined the company in 1945. He was appointed president in 1970 and chief executive officer in 1976. He assumed his present position as chairman of the board in 1981. He has served as a director since 1948.

- *Robert D. Haas* joined the company in 1973. He was elected senior vice president, corporate planning and policy in 1978 and was appointed president of the new business group in January 1980. He became president of the operating groups in December 1980. He was named executive vice president and chief operating officer in 1981 before assuming his current position as president and chief executive officer in 1984. He has served as a director since 1980. He is the son of the great-grandnephew of Levi Strauss.

- *Walter A. Haas, Jr.*, joined the company in 1939 and served as its president from 1958 to 1970 and as its chief executive officer from 1958 to 1976. He was chairman of the board from 1970 to 1981 and has been chairman of the executive committee since 1976. He has served as a director since 1943. He is the great-grandnephew of Levi Strauss.

- *Leo P. Isotalo* joined the company in 1975. In 1978 he became vice president and general manager of the continental European division and in 1980 was named its president. In 1982, he became a vice president of the company and executive vice president of Group II, Levi Strauss International. His current position, which he assumed in 1984, is senior vice president and president of Battery Street Enterprises.

- *David K. Lelewer* joined the company in 1980 as director of special projects and assistant to the chief executive officer. In June 1981, he became director of personnel, Levi Strauss USA, and in November 1981 was elected a vice president of the company and director of personnel. He became director of human resources in 1984. Prior to joining the company, he was vice president and manager of employee relations at Wells Fargo Bank.

- *Karl F. Slacik* joined the company in 1978 as vice president, financial operations and was appointed to the additional position of treasurer in 1979. He became vice president, finance in January 1980 and retained the title of treasurer until he assumed his present position as senior vice president finance and chief financial officer in May 1980. He has served as a director since 1982.

- *Lee Smith* joined the company in 1966. From 1978 to 1980 he served as division president, Levi Strauss International. In 1981, he was named a vice president of the company and executive vice president of Levi Strauss International in 1984.

- *Peter Thigpen* joined the company in 1967. In 1980 he was appointed executive vice president of Group I, Levi Strauss International and became president of Group I, Levi Strauss USA in 1981. He became president of Levi Strauss USA and was elected a senior vice president of the company in 1982. He assumed his present position as president of the Jeans Company in 1984. He has served as a director since 1983.

- *Thomas W. Tusher* joined the company in 1969. In 1976, he served as executive vice president of the International Group and was elected a vice president of the company. In 1977, he was elected a senior vice president of the company. From 1980 he held the position of president of Levi Strauss International before he assumed his present position as executive vice president and chief operating officer in 1984. He has served as a director since 1979.

COMPETITION IN THE APPAREL INDUSTRY

The apparel industry is characterized by ease of entry and is therefore highly competitive. In its traditional market for jeans in the United States, the company has a large market share. Competition in this market includes a large number of domestic and foreign concerns that manufacture and sell jeans and other lines of apparel. Outside of the jeans market, competition includes numerous manufacturers ranging from small to large companies. Neither the company nor any of its competitors has a large share of these highly diverse and shifting consumer apparel markets.

Outside of the United States, the company typically has a smaller share of the jeans market, but is generally either the major or one of the major brands in each country where it has an established market. There are numerous domestic and multinational competitors in most of the company's principal markets.

According to Standard and Poor's, the U.S. apparel market has been saturated by both foreign and domestic producers. Imports of apparel have been growing gradually since the 1950s. In recent years imports have captured a large portion of the domestic market, and imports have continued to increase. Thus, domestic producers have found that it is becoming increasingly difficult to pass along to their customers the increased costs of raw materials, labor, and energy. In response to this trend, domestic manufacturers are turning to mechanization, adoption of a global view of the business, diversification into other products that are more import resistant, and a reliance on brand name marketing and product exclusivity to counteract pressures on price.

TRADEMARKS

The company has registered the Levi's trademark, one of its most valuable assets, in over 150 countries. The company owns other trademarks that it utilizes in marketing its jeans and other products. Of these other trademarks, the most important in terms of product sales are the Pocket "Tab" device, 501, the Two-Horse brand, and Arcute Design. The company also markets products under other trademarks, including Koret, Resistol, Oxxford, Tourage SSE, CMA, and David Hunter. The company vigorously defends its trademarks against infringement and, when necessary, initiates litigation to protect such trademarks.

ADVERTISING

In the United States, the company relies on advertising on radio and television and in national publications. It also participates in local cooperative advertising programs under which the company shares with retailers the cost of advertising Levi's products.

The company has similar advertising programs internationally, which are modified as required by market conditions and applicable local laws.

In 1984 Levi Strauss and Company boosted its advertising expenditure by more than 20 percent to $150 million.

MARKETING

The marketing orientation of Levi Strauss has undergone significant change since the company's inception in the 1850s. Originally, Levi's jeans were worn almost exclusively by gold miners who considered them to be essential equipment because they were both rugged and durable. However, in the 1950s jeans became a trend. Thus, Levi Strauss and Company adjusted their marketing orientation to take advantage of this trend. Currently, Levi's products are oriented toward the more fashion-conscious consumer. At this time Levi's is moving toward a market for men, women, and children. This is evident in that, for the first time, Levi Strauss and Company has formed an alliance with a well-known designer, Perry Ellis, to initiate a line of sportswear.

BRAND AWARENESS

While Levi Strauss and Company is the leading producer in the apparel industry, much of its success can be attributed to the marketing strengths developed over many years of producing and selling jeans. The most important and competitive advantage the company has, and its most important marketing strength as well, is wide consumer acceptance of the Levi's brand. The company sells high-quality products at reasonable prices, and this is recognized throughout the world.

DISTRIBUTION

The Jeans Company sells primarily to department stores, specialty stores for men, women, and children, pants-only stores, and two national retail stores, Sears, Roebuck and Company and J.C. Penney Company. At the end of 1984, retail accounts were serviced by approximately 400 sales representatives.

Levi Strauss International sells directly to retailers in its established markets, although elsewhere in the world it has other distribution arrangements. Battery Street Enterprises sells principally to department stores and men's and women's specialty stores. The Menswear and Battery Street Sportswear divisions also sell to Sears, Roebuck and Company and J.C. Penney Company. At the end of 1984, retail accounts were serviced by approximately 300 sales representatives.

No single customer accounts for more than 10 percent of the company's net sales.

RESEARCH AND DEVELOPMENT

Research is considered one of the company's most important competitive advantages. Its product research and development department is responsible for the company's progress in new fabrics and garments and its goal is to improve functional performance. Additionally, an equipment research and development center is maintained by the company so that it can remain a leader in automated and semiautomated production equipment. Further, corporate marketing research has an on-line computerized data bank to monitor major fashion directions, general apparel pricing, retail point-of-sale trends, the company image, and consumer attitudes toward products currently offered. Research also pretests the effectiveness of proposed advertisements and receptivity of the marketplace to new products.

PERSONNEL

The company employs approximately 37,000 people, a majority of whom are production workers. A significant number of the production workers are employees in plants where the company has collective bargaining agreements with recognized labor unions. The company considers its relationship with its employees to be generally satisfactory.

Production Facilities

Levi Strauss and Company has numerous plants and distribution centers located in North America and throughout Asia, Latin America, and Europe. In response to the downturn in the market for jean apparel, Levi Strauss began a painful revamping of its production operation in 1984. In recent years the company closed 23 of its 128 factories.

MARKETING PROBLEMS

Despite its numerous marketing strengths and its position in the apparel industry, Levi Strauss and Company is having its share of problems. First, the company has been battered by a downturn in the market for jeans apparel. Levi Strauss International has been plagued by the drop in demand for jeans abroad and a strong dollar. Second, its pricing policy is subject to Federal Trade Commission (FTC) regulations. Specifically, the FTC does not permit manufacturers to force retailers to maintain prices. In recent years, this has cost the company millions of dollars for out-of-court settlements of cases in which it was accused of price maintenance. As a result the company is susceptible to price wars. Retailers will drastically cut the price of Levi's products to attract customers to their stores from their competitors' stores. This may pose a threat to the quality image of a branded product.

Outlook for the Domestic Apparel Market

The future of the domestic apparel industry looks good for various product lines such as designer fashions, active wear, sportswear, womenswear, jeans, and western styles. The purchase of clothing has remained remarkably stable through 1980 according to the MRCA Information Services. The present emphasis is on designer fashions and leisure fashions.

Many firms that survived increased competition did so primarily because of diversification into various other segments of the apparel market. By broadening their scope and focusing on different markets, firms find it easier to avoid the potentially serious negative effects resulting from rapid style changes that characterize the industry.

Outlook for the International Market

As the U.S. apparel market has become more saturated, growth-oriented apparel producers in the United States have directed their attention toward the market potential overseas. U.S. clothing makers are increasingly being forced into overseas production because of higher domestic labor costs and competition from other big importers, all resulting in imports of about 20 percent or $11.5 billion of their brand name products.

FUTURE

Levi Strauss and Company directors have proposed a $1.45 billion buyout to take the company private. The Strauss family currently controls about 40 percent of the company's 36.9 million common shares outstanding. The family wants to take Levi Strauss and Company private so that management can broaden a corporate reorganization now underway without having to answer to shareholders, Wall Street analysts, or the media. The company intends to sharpen the focus of its jean business domestically and internationally and review the performances of its eleven fashion apparel units. The tender offer for all outstanding Levi shares started August 2, 1985. The buyout is virtually guaranteed. The family group will then own between 80 percent and 92 percent of the company.

The family has arranged $2.1 billion in financing for the proposed buyout. San Francisco–based Wells Fargo and Company has agreed to lead a bank syndicate that will lend the group $1.7 billion, the remainder coming from other "major money centers." About $1.45 billion will be used to finance the leveraged buyout and $250 million will be used for working capital. However, paying off the debt used to finance the $2 billion leveraged buyout will pose a heavy burden. Net interest expense is estimated at $182.6 million in 1986, $174.2 million in 1987, $166 million in 1988, and $157.5 million in 1989.

The company expects operating earnings to be up 136 percent in 1985. The company projects net income will shoot up to $82 million in 1986 aided by "other income" of $64 million. Net income is projected to drop 18 percent in 1987, and increase by 20.4 percent in 1988 and 21.7 percent in 1989 as interest expense declines and operating income rises.

Levi's anticipates sales growth of 2.6 percent in 1986, 5.5 percent in 1987, and 5.6 percent in 1988 and 1989. After the strong operating income recovery in 1985, Levi's expects an additional 20 percent gain in 1986 to $322.7 million. For the next three years the company projects more modest gains of 6.4 percent in 1987, 5.7 percent in 1988, and 7.4 percent in 1989.

Battery Street Enterprises is expected to show the strongest sales gains of the three divisions. Battery Street Enterprises, which includes Levi's nonjean designer operations such as Perry Ellis, is expected to gain 11.5 percent, to bring 1985 sales to $540.9 million.

The Jeans Company is expected to gain 4.1 percent in sales in 1986 and grow steadily at 4 percent annually for the following three years.

Sales for the International Division are expected to drop 2.4 percent in 1986, but the company expects them to grow after that: 5.4 percent in 1987, 7.2 percent in 1988, and 7 percent in 1989.

The assumptions used to formulate the projections include a decline in corporate expenses to 1.8 percent of sales in 1989, from 2.1 percent in 1985, and capital expenditures to range between $43.2 million and $48.6 million over the five-year period.

If the projections are correct, Levi's debt-to-equity ratio will go from 8 to 1 in 1985 to 2.4 to 1 in 1989 and the book value of each common share will increase from $23.69 to $54.77. Total long-term debt will shrink from $1.5 billion in 1985 to $1.24 billion in 1989.

REFERENCES

Daily News Record, August 22, 1985
New York Times, July 2, 1985
Wall Street Journal, January 18, 1985
Wall Street Journal, April 5, 1985

Wall Street Journal, July 16, 1985
Wall Street Journal, July 29, 1985
Women's Wear Daily, July 12, 1985